17-8-79 Supra 31.60

POLICY AND POLICE

THE ENFORCEMENT OF THE REFORMATION
IN THE AGE OF THOMAS CROMWELL

POLICY AND POLICE

THE ENFORCEMENT OF
THE REFORMATION IN THE AGE OF
THOMAS CROMWELL

G. R. ELTON

CAMBRIDGE
AT THE UNIVERSITY PRESS
1972

Published by the Syndics of the Cambridge University Press
Bentley House, 200 Euston Road, London NW1 2DB
American Branch: 32 East 57th Street, New York, N.Y.10022

© Cambridge University Press 1972

Library of Congress Catalogue Card Number: 79–172831

ISBN: 0 521 08383 4

Printed in Great Britain
at the University Printing House, Cambridge
(Brooke Crutchley, University Printer)

CONTENTS

PREFACE

This book has been a long time in the making. Virtually all the research and about a third of the writing were done in 1964. At that point I agreed to offer a Special Subject in the Historical Tripos, and for the next five years a selection of the relevant documents were annually discussed round seminar tables in Clare College and the History Faculty Building in Cambridge. I am deeply grateful to the undergraduates who in the course of those labours contributed substantially to our understanding of the evidence and the analysis of the problems; they have shared in the production of this book. Then, just as I was about to resume writing, I received the honour of an invitation to deliver the Ford Lectures on English History in the University of Oxford. The book was finished in May 1971, and the lectures, delivered in the Hilary Term of 1972, represented a condensed version of it. I wish to record my gratitude to the senior University for the honour done to me and for enabling me to try out the substance of my findings on a very friendly audience.

The theme of the book has been in my mind for even longer. Ever since I started work on the age of the early Reformation I have wanted to study the manner in which the changes of that time impinged on the nation. In particular, I have wished to answer the question whether the regime of Thomas Cromwell practised a 'reign of terror', but beyond that I have also thought that the investigation might do something to reveal the realities of government. Critics of my earlier writings have several times pointed out that it is not enough to discover the structure of government and how it was supposed to work: they have wanted to know how the thing operated in practice. So have I, and in this book I hope to have offered some sort of answer to that difficult and ramifying question.

The limits of the study were set by the master that rules all historians, the evidence available, with some minor assistance from myself. Thanks to the confiscation of Thomas Cromwell's papers, the years of his ascendancy are very much better documented than any other period before 1558; in particular, the questions touching enforcement of decisions, relations between the government and the parts of the realm, or the making of policy receive illumination from Cromwell's correspondence which is lacking for the years after his fall. Since we are thus exceptionally (not, of course, perfectly) informed about the inwardness of events, this book confines itself to the years 1532–1540. Furthermore, because it was my intention to investigate the ordinary processes of government, I have omitted from the study the highly special case of the northern rebellions (1536–1537) and the case, special for different reasons, of the dependencies of Ireland and Calais. Traitors from the north and from Calais are included in the final count, but the discussion of methods and behaviour concentrates on what may be called the normal setting of government action.

Despite these limitations, this has become a very long book. I am uneasily aware of the barriers to enjoyment set by so many stories of often petty events, too many of them, moreover, devoid of that satisfaction which knowledge of the final outcome would bring. But I could see no way of avoiding a method which must at times seem painfully anecdotal if I was to present anything like the truth of events. I have before this been told that a few examples prove nothing one way or another, and I agree that this is so. The only remedy, however, is to produce many examples. If the task of government and the methods of enforcement are to become plain – if the reality of ruling and being ruled is to be understood – it is necessary to put before the reader a large accumulation of the sort of things that went on. I have told the story from the records, and generally speaking from the point of view, of government, though I have endeavoured to remember that all the people involved were human beings. Very possibly additional details, especially about the outcome of conflicts and denunciations, may be discovered in more local materials, especially in the unprinted records of Church courts. Like all historical writing, this book constitutes a stage in the acquisition of knowledge, and it will serve its author's purpose best if it becomes the cause of further study in others.

Clare College, Cambridge   G.R.E.

ABBREVIATIONS

APC	*Acts of the Privy Council of England*, ed. J. R. Dasent (1890–1907)
BM	British Museum
Burnet	Gilbert Burnet, *History of the Reformation of the Church of England*, ed. N. Pocock, 7 vols. (1865)
CUL	Cambridge University Library
Dodds	M. H. and R. Dodds, *The Pilgrimage of Grace, 1536–37, and the Exeter Conspiracy, 1538*, 2 vols. (1915)
Ellis	Henry Ellis, ed., *Original Letters illustrative of English History*, 3 series, 11 vols. (1824–46)
Fac. Off. Reg.	*Faculty Office Registers 1534–1549*, ed. D. S. Chambers (1966)
Foxe	John Foxe, *Acts and Monuments*, ed. G. Townsend and S. R. Cattley, 8 vols. (1837–41)
Gee and Hardy	*Documents illustrative of English Church History*, ed. H. Gee and W. J. Hardy (1896)
Hall	Edward Hall, *The Union of the Two Noble and Illustre Families of Lancaster and York*, ed. H. Ellis (1809)
Harpsfield	Nicholas Harpsfield, *The Life and Death of Sir Thomas More, Knight*, ed. E. V. Hitchcock and R. W. Chambers, E.E.T.S. orig. ser. 186 (1932)
Knowles	M. D. Knowles, *The Religious Orders in England*, 3 vols. (1950–9)
Le Neve	John Le Neve, *Fasti Ecclesiae Anglicanae*, new ed., 12 vols. (1962–7)
LP	*Letters and Papers, Foreign and Domestic, of the Reign of Henry VIII*, ed. J. S. Brewer, J. Gairdner, R. H. Brodie, 36 vols. (1862–1932)
Merriman	Roger B. Merriman, *Life and Letters of Thomas Cromwell*, 2 vols. (1902)
Pocock	Nicholas Pocock, ed., *Records of the Reformation: the Divorce 1527–1533*, 2 vols. (1870)
PPC	*Proceedings and Ordinances of the Privy Council of England 1368–1542*, ed. N. H. Nicolas, 7 vols. (1834–7)

Rogers   Elizabeth F. Rogers, ed., *The Correspondence of Sir Thomas More* (1947)

Roper   William Roper, *The Life of Sir Thomas More*, in *Two Early Tudor Lives*, ed. R. S. Sylvester and D. P. Harding (1962)

SR   *The Statutes of the Realm*, 11 vols. (1810–28)

STC   *A Short-Title Catalogue of Books printed in England, Scotland and Ireland, and of English Books printed abroad 1475–1640*, ed. A. W. Pollard and G. R. Redgrave (1926)

StP   *State Papers of Henry VIII*, 11 vols. (1830–52)

TRHS   *Transactions of the Royal Historical Society*

TRP   *Tudor Royal Proclamations*, ed. Paul L. Hughes and James F. Larkin, 3 vols. (1964–9)

Wright   Thomas Wright, ed., *Three Chapters of Letters relating to the Suppression of the Monasteries*, Camden Old Series 26 (1843)

Wriothesley   Charles Wriothesley, *A Chronicle of England during the Reigns of the Tudors*, ed. W. D. Hamilton, 2 vols.; Camden New Series, 11 and 20 (1875–7)

Manuscripts cited without location are from the Public Record Office, London; the following classes have been used:

C 82   Warrants for the Great Seal, Series II

E 36   Exchequer, Treasury of Receipt, Miscellaneous Books

E 135   Exch., King's Remembrancer, Ecclesiastical Documents

E 163   Exch., King's Remembrancer, Miscellanea of the Exchequer

KB 9   King's Bench, Ancient Indictments

KB 27   King's Bench, *Coram Rege* Rolls

KB 29   King's Bench, Controlment Rolls

SP 1   State Papers, Henry VIII

SP 2   the same, folio volumes

SP 6   Theological Tracts

St Ch 2   Star Chamber Proceedings, Henry VIII

NOTE. I have nearly always gone behind the Calendar to complete texts. Where these have been printed, the edition is cited; where MSS have been used, the *LP* reference is added for the convenience of readers. Throughout I have modernised and standardised the spelling and punctuation of quotations, even where these are taken from printed books or editions. Neither the idiosyncrasies of writing clerks, nor those of modern editors, seemed to call urgently for preservation, and on this occasion the exact form of the record never conveys anything that would justify burdening the reader with what only too readily appears as pedantry or quaintness. An earlier version of Chapter 6 appeared in the *Historical Journal*, xi (1968), 211–36, and I am grateful to the Editor for permission to use it here.

THE END OF DOMESTIC PEACE

IN THE FOUR YEARS between the rejection of Queen Catherine of Aragon and the execution of Queen Anne Boleyn, between the Act against Appeals to Rome (1533) and the Act Extinguishing the Pope's Authority in England (1536), many fundamental and instinctive aspects of life in England underwent some very drastic changes. The nation's age-old allegiance to the universal Church governed by the pope of Rome, an adherence in no way weakened by various kinds of partial independence,[1] was declared to be contrary to the laws of God, Scripture and nature; the King was to be accepted as the spiritual head of his realm; and upheavals in politics were soon followed by innovations in religion and ceremonies which cut deeply into the customs of the people. New laws of vast import appeared in quantity; obedience to them was demanded in uncompromising terms; and the demands were backed with formidable penalties to which some of the most eminent men in the realm fell victim. Whether one calls these events a revolution or believes that at most they consolidated changes already well apparent, may be a matter in dispute, though one of the few issues on which Thomas More and Thomas Cromwell did not disagree touched their recognition of a revolution when they saw one. What, in any case, cannot be doubted is that official policy treated these events as constituting a great change, producing an order very different from what had gone before, however much that new dispensation was represented as the restoration of a good old order long since abated by the usurpations of Rome. Yet it is a fact that on the whole the changes went off with surprising ease. By the time that Thomas Cromwell, architect of most of what was planned and done, died on the scaffold in July 1540, the realm had accepted the new situation and was, for the moment, obedient as instructed.

[1] See, e.g., the attitude displayed by Sir John Fortescue, a reasonably typical representative of conventional political thinking in the fifteenth century. He saw no difficulty in holding both to the pope's high station and supremacy, and to the claims of English law to rule in certain limited spheres. G. L. Mosse, 'Sir John Fortescue and the problem of papal power,' *Mediaevalia et Humanistica*, vii (1952), 89–94.

How was it done? The usual explanations, it seems to me, skate rather readily over this question or beg it altogether. The commonest answer is still that there was really no problem: the government of Henry VIII found itself so well supported by opinion and temper in the country that it could pursue its formidable policies without fear of resistance or rebellion. There was, said Pollard, general harmony between King and Parliament, a harmony based on 'a fundamental similarity of interests', and beyond the Parliament, the King ('the typical embodiment' of his age) commanded the general allegiance of his nation in which occasional opposition was hampered by Englishmen's habitual reluctance 'to turn out one government until they see at least the possibility of another'.[1] Using rather less vapoury language, Fisher came to essentially the same conclusion.[2] This simple view is best summed up in Mackie's entry in his table of contents – 'a revolution easily made' – a phrase which in the text receives such dubious enlargement as that 'revolution was in the air', there was 'an alliance with the most effective part of his people', 'there is no evidence that the cruel hangings and burnings produced...popular resentment'.[3] It depends how much evidence one requires: that quite a few people expressed themselves forcibly about these doings is readily shown. The major examples of opposition – More and Fisher, the northern risings – are treated by this view as aberrations, as unexpected whirlpools in a generally placid stream, or even as minor signs of grace in a nation otherwise given to mindless obedience and materialist satisfaction.

Now it will not be denied that there lurks behind some of those empty phrases a modest measure of truth. The early Reformation certainly benefited from commanding a substantial quantity of support in various parts of realm and nation. There is no need to stress once more that many influential people disliked clerical pretentions, coveted ecclesiastical wealth, had their doubts about traditional religion and the state of the Church, and welcomed attacks on a foreign power like the pope's. The explanations derived from Pollard – recognising the revolution but supposing that for various reasons it was easily accomplished – are certainly to be preferred to those that eliminate the whole problem by

[1] A. F. Pollard, *Henry VIII* (1905), 262 ff., 313 ff., 431.
[2] H. A. L. Fisher, *The History of England from the Accession of Henry VII to the Death of Henry VIII, 1485–1547* (1906), 482.
[3] J. D. Mackie, *The Earlier Tudors, 1485–1558* (1952), xiv, 335, 363.

supposing that there was no revolution at all, but only just another stage in familiar policies widely known and practised. The implication then is that the government could readily do as it would because no one was really surprised by what happened.[1] Dr Harriss can thus tell us that by the time it happened the break with Rome was no longer 'a task of any great political difficulty or danger', and, conversely, that 'unless the inexorable development towards a national church in the later middle ages is appreciated, the facility of the eventual breach with Rome will appear unintelligible'. But whether the breach was facile, whether there was neither danger nor difficulty, are surely questions which cannot be solved by mere assumption. One may regret that Thomas Cromwell, or even Henry VIII, lacked the advice of the modern scholar: they would have worried and laboured less. Of course, they did their best to pretend that they were breaking no tradition and instituting no innovation, but it would certainly surprise them to hear that this device of propaganda born out of physical weakness should still prove so effective 400 years later. Faced with the evidence of opposition, subversion and even rebellion, they supposed that they had a political task of some magnitude on their hands. Faced with that same evidence, modern historians, content with conventional explanations, fall back on their second arm: such opposition as showed itself was destroyed by a violent, ruthless and illegal reign of terror. This is an opinion best summed up in the words of the historian who finally consolidated the picture of Cromwell as the hateful wielder of lawless force. Searching out all offenders and opponents, so Merriman explained, Cromwell relentlessly killed them off; punishments were always severe, and although 'there are almost no records of the penalties inflicted...there is reason to believe that comparatively slight misdemeanours were not seldom rewarded with death'.[2]

The nation was ready for the changes – or did not really notice that there were any because all that happened merely fulfilled earlier 'trends' – and any signs of resistance were stamped out by violence. even though the evidence for that violence is not as a rule to be found. It is difficult to rest content with such answers. Henry VIII's own govern-

---

[1] For this 'medievalist' interpretation, which denies that anything new happened in the years 1530–40, see e.g. G. L. Harriss, 'Medieval Government and Statecraft,' *Past & Present* 25 (1963), 8 ff., and my remarks in reply, ibid. 29 (1964), 32 ff. For the quotations see vol. 25, pp. 9, 17.

[2] Merriman, i. 116 ff.; quotation on p. 118.

ment presided over what at any rate appeared to be a major political upheaval which they were determined to get established and accepted; and
if they thought at all responsibly, they were bound to take into account
the possibility of serious opposition. If ever they had supposed that no
problem of enforcement did exist, reports from all over the realm
would soon have created doubts, and the northern risings of 1536–1537
would surely have disabused them. As the rest of this book will demonstrate, the policy of the 1530's encountered sufficient, if often sporadic,
opposition: many men disliked what was going on, and said so, and a
number tried to take positive action. Therefore, there *was* a problem.
How was the country to be persuaded of the justice of the King's doings,
how was it to be kept in obedience through rapid changes in the course
of events, and how was resistance to be suppressed? Could mere force
do it, and was there a reign of terror? How did means answer to ends?

Henry VIII's England was not an easy country to govern. On the
contrary, breaches of the peace were distinctly commonplace and could
arise from the most trivial of causes. At Cambridge, a University proctor led the student mob which attacked a townsman's house, and undergraduates, on riot bent, hid weapons under their long gowns.[1] A tithe
dispute could be complicated by the behaviour of a young priest who
playfully shot arrows at the parishioners after dark.[2] One random story
will suffice to demonstrate what is perhaps familiar enough.[3] At some
date unknown in the reign of Henry VIII, one John Smith, accompanied
by two women, visited Roger Hilton's tavern in St Bride's parish,
London. While he was waiting to be served, a crowd led by William
Kyng came in and called for a pint of wine, which was brought to them.
Smith took offence at this jumping of the queue, 'rose out of his seat
and came to the said William Kyng, saying, Thou whoreson, why takest
thou away my wine?' Kyng protested that the wine was his, whereupon Smith 'of cruel malice took the said pot of wine and smote the
foresaid William on the head'; he also drew his dagger. Bloodshed was
averted by the intervention of Kyng's friends and the providential entry
of the ward beadle who told Smith to keep the peace and Kyng to go
home. Kyng did leave, but he drifted back to a pub called the Standard
where he met two friends; while they were talking, one of them,
pointing across the street, said, 'Yonder goeth he that struck thee in the

[1] G. R. Elton, 'Cambridge Riots,' *Star Chamber Stories* (1958), 52 ff.
[2] 'Tithe and Trouble,' ibid. 174 ff.   [3] St Ch 2/26/154.

tavern'. He was mistaken; the passer-by was one Mr Oystreche of Clifford's Inn. Thus misled, Kyng stopped Oystreche and challenged him, but Oystreche naturally enough replied, 'I know thee not nor yet I smote not at thee'. So Kyng hit him, and Oystreche fled to a house for safety whose inhabitants intervened. Kyng now realised that he had made a mistake and apologised. But Oystreche went back to Clifford's Inn where he told everybody of the assault. Thereupon a company issued from the Inn, led by the principal, to call on Kyng's master and make complaint. The master promised to punish Kyng if the story turned out to be true, and the young lawyers departed after agreeing to sort the business out next day. But not everybody was satisfied: within half an hour, between 10 and 11 o'clock at night, two young gentlemen of Clifford's Inn armed themselves and went to lie in wait 'in an alley going down to a common draught beside Fleet Bridge'. There they attacked John Penyngton, a bowyer, who was making his way home and thinking no harm. His cries for help brought others out and saved him from being killed. His two attackers were arrested and taken to the constable who decided to put them in ward, but before he could do so, the parish clerk of St Dunstan's, who had witnessed the arrest, ran to Clifford's Inn and raised the alarm. The Inn roused itself for its own: the principal and fourteen or fifteen others, 'in harness, with bills, halberts, swords long and short', sallied forth once more and crossed the Fleet Bridge to invade the neighbouring parish. They engaged the constable's party and caused some injuries, but a counterforce was raised which drove them back. The situation, however, was so violent that, for fear of a rescue, the constables dared not arrest anyone and let even the original rioters go home harmless. Apparently peace then returned to Fleet Street.

A silly quarrel over a pot of wine rapidly escalated into a proper battle in the streets of London: events like these must be considered typical enough. Men had weapons about them and were readily enough moved to use them. Arguments quickly became quarrels, and there were always daggers handy to draw blood. The records are full of such violence because too many men (and women) believed in taking the law into their own hands. This was the rough, superstitious, excitable and volatile society which the King's government had to rule and on which they attempted to impose new beliefs about the pope, the worship of saints, means of salvation, the use of superstitious ceremonies and such like matters that touched all men closely. It would have unsettled a more stable society to hear of those strange goings-on among the great, not to mention having the old ways of easy piety and readily bought roads to eternal bliss called in doubt. The proclamation of the royal supremacy, the noisy disputes of conservatives and innovators, and the religious changes which followed from 1536 onwards in fact provoked a great deal of unrest, all of it potentially dangerous when so few means existed for keeping good order in the scattered towns and villages of England. If the government had ever inclined to rest in false hopes nourished by the absence of trouble in its immediate neighbourhood, there were men ready to alert it to the less satisfactory state of the country at large. As early as 1534, Latimer wrote to question the efficiency of the commissioners administering the oath of succession and to cast doubts on that universal acquiescence beloved by historians. 'If you might make progress throughout England,' he told Cromwell, 'you should find how acts declares hearts.'[1] Two years later, Andrew Borde, an ex-Carthusian who for once rejoiced in his liberation, travelled the whole realm to Glasgow, an experience he found to be ominous: 'as I went through England, I met and was in company with many rural fellows, Englishmen, that love not our gracious King.'[2] Henry's famous awareness of the nation's feelings seems to have had its gaps.

A good deal, in fact, depended on the King's 'charismatic' standing, on his ability to preserve his unchallenged kingliness, but however popular Henry VIII was with some, opinion about him cannot be called unanimous. Of course, Cromwell was an even more obvious target, but talk about him, though often suggestive of serious disaffection, no doubt troubled Henry less. Sayings were reported to Cromwell about himself which it seems to have given the informers pleasure to relate. His humble origin stirred Thomas Molton to the outburst that 'there is one of the King's Council, one of so low in birth that the world shall never be quiet and rest for so long as he doth continue'.[3] Thomas Toone, parson of Woodford in Essex, reflected bitterly on the fact that the realm was ruled by councillors that included an ostler, now archbishop of Canterbury, and that shearman Cromwell (from Ipswich – a curious confusion with Wolsey).[4] The comminations accumulated over the

---

[1] Hugh Latimer, *Works*, ed. G. E. Corrie (1844–5), ii. 367.
[2] Ellis, iii. II. 304.
[3] SP 1/162, fo. 157 (*LP* xv. 1029 [49]).   [4] SP 1/116, fo. 7 (*LP* xii. I. 407).

years. Cromwell and Audley, in the opinion of William Barton, a priest and Richard Smith, a surgeon, were 'the greatest thieves and traitors living within this realm, and trusted once to see your heads leap from your bodies'.[1] Sir Ralph Ellercar, in the aftermath of the Pilgrimage of Grace which he had opposed, also spoke of treason among councillors 'which he would prove if the King's grace would hear him'.[2] About the same time, 'seditious and slanderous' flysheets were circulating in the Isle of Ely against Cromwell and other councillors, and they were having an effect amongst the common people; characteristically, the disseminators included men who in the past had benefited from Cromwell's favour.[3] A local official in Buckinghamshire longed to thrust his dagger into the lord privy seal's heart.[4] In Wakefield, the vicar's chaplain apparently taught the boys slanderous songs against Cromwell; he denied having written an offending ditty but not apparently singing one (though not the one of which a copy was sent to the victim of the lampoon).[5]

People hoped that this traitor would soon be exposed at court, and stories about the King pummelling him in his displeasure, or of the marquess of Exeter trying to kill him with a dagger (the crafty villain wore a cuirass) were retold with relish.[6] One Robert ap Reynolds, at Calais, claimed to have sold Cromwell some stuff of the late duke of Buckingham's for which Cromwell still owed forty-seven angels; he thought that now that Cromwell had been promoted (1532) he stood a chance of getting his money and uttered obscure threats turning on what would happen if he revealed all.[7] A Herefordshire man, it was alleged, railed against him, called him a harlot and recalled the old saying 'that when two dogs strive for a bone, the third dog cometh and fetcheth the bone away'; but he denied the first and claimed that in the second he had the King in mind who took the benefits of the quarrels between the northern men and the Scots.[8] John Woodward, a learned doctor of law in Staffordshire, bored his friends by frequently mourning

---

[1] SP 1/162, fo. 127 (*LP* xv. 1029 [21]).
[2] SP 1/120, fo. 255 (*LP* xii. I. 1320). [3] SP 1/113, fo. 36 (*LP* xi. 1375).
[4] SP 1/129, fo. 73 (*LP* xiii. I. 306). [5] SP 1/132, fo. 163 (*LP* xiii. I. 1054).
[6] *StP* ii. 551–4, the remarks of Sir William Paulet's brother George, a government commissioner in Ireland who accused Cromwell of wasting the King's money and doing everything for bribes. SP 1/121, fo. 67 (*LP* xii. II. 51): John Howell, a Somerset butcher, ascribed the arrest of the marquess to a personal quarrel with Cromwell and vowed to raise a band to rescue him.
[7] SP 1/69, fo. 213 (*LP* v. 896). [8] SP 1/112, fo. 257 (*LP* xi. 1328).

the fact that 'we never had good world since the Lord Cromwell and his master [Wolsey] did rule. . . He trusted that he should have as short an end as his said master had'.[1] In the opinion of John Tutton, of Mere near Glastonbury, Cromwell was 'a stark heretic, and so were all his withholders [those who held with him]'; he talked darkly of wicked men around the King who were deceiving his majesty and should come to a bad end.[2]

Cromwell gives the impression of being little troubled by these frequent indications of his personal unpopularity, nor does he ever seem to have done much about them. When the abbot of Peterborough was accused of making such personal attacks, the minister reassured the much troubled man by return of post and declared himself fully satisfied by his explanations.[3] Early in his days of power he sent one James Kelly to the Gatehouse to cool his heels, and temper, because he had (so Kelly said) misunderstood some angry words: Kelly had not, of course, threatened 'to pluck your mastership out of your bed', but said that Cromwell's agent Swift could as readily get Kelly some outstanding payment as he had pulled him (Kelly) out of bed.[4] However, wrapped up in this obscurity there appears to hide some actual face-to-face physical threat. George Gower, who earlier still had, as he admitted, showered abuse on Cromwell for some misapprehension, got into no trouble; but it is true that by now he was supplying evidence of Lord Chancellor More's dubious dealings against suspected heretics.[5] In general, the evidence suggests that Cromwell cared little for hard words when they rained on his broad back, an attitude considered more sensible in the twentieth century than the sixteenth when such lack of pride was taken to be further proof of a low-born and cur-like disposition. But signs that the King might not be so popular, either, were another matter. Not only did Henry possess all the pride necessary for deeply resenting insulting remarks from his inferiors, but, more important, talk against the King could hide action against the King's policy.

Thus, for instance, certain conversations in Over (Cambs.) combined too many of the lines that loose talk could follow. The information produced an investigation, though no known outcome.[6] The man in

---

[1] SP 1/115, fo. 6 (*LP* xii. I. 193). [2] SP 1/116, fos. 185–7 (*LP* xii. I. 567).

[3] SP 1/241, fos. 289, 294 (*LP Add.* 1299, 1305). The denunciation in SP 1/242, fo. 94 (*LP Add.* 1363), dated 18 Oct. 1538 by *LP*, belongs to the previous year and is the reason for the abbot's apprehension. [4] SP 1/239, fo. 111 (*LP Add.* 963).

[5] SP 1/70, fo. 183–4 (*LP* v. 1176). [6] SP 1/128, fo. 110 (*LP* xiii. I. 95).

trouble was one John Raven who talked at large from the closing months of 1536 onwards, though it was a year before anyone, apparently, thought to do anything about him. He had, it seems, reflected on the evanescence of worldly glory:

Was not my lord cardinal a great man and ruled all the realm as he would? What became of him? Is he not gone? Also Sir Thomas More, high chancellor of England: did not he in like wise rule all the whole realm? What became of him? Is he not gone? And now my lord privy seal ruleth all, and we shall once see the day that he shall have as great a fall as any of them had.

Thus he not only doubted the King's rule but hinted at his instability and dangerousness. However, he denied speaking anything except the last sentence, in reply, he claimed, to his own accuser who had been responsible for saying the rest. Actually, he admitted the only dangerous words – those which forecast and possibly provoked trouble, for the rest was history. But he also admitted, with unusual veracity or rashness, that in July 1536 he had said that 'the King was a fool and my lord privy seal another..., selfwilled men and would have their purpose'. This went beyond disrespect to Cromwell; it would not do so to speak of God's deputy on earth.

It must be stressed that, however much the King formed 'the typical embodiment' of his age, a good many people held and voiced less than respectful opinions of him. Some of the talk about Henry underlined the danger, a danger to which the government were bound to be sensitive, that the upheavals of the day would reflect back upon his popularity and undermine his personal hold upon his people. Henry's sex-life, real or imagined, offered the obvious subject for dubious talk. People believed him to be dissolute, and some may have had the sneaking admiration for his supposed prowess which constitutes the ordinary reaction of the present day. However, it would be seriously to misunderstand Henry's own time to suppose that stories of adultery and fornication were, in that censoriously puritanical age, told with real affection: kings were supposed to be great and good and set an example. It would certainly be to misunderstand Henry himself to suppose that he regarded such talk as anything but offensive to his royal dignity; he was neither loose nor prurient and observed the conventions faithfully. His embarrassment is plain in the extraordinary scene recalled by Sir

George Throckmorton in 1537.[1] Sir George, a burgess in Parliament who had spoken against the Act of Appeals and had therefore been called up for an interview, told Henry to his face that if he married Anne he would be worse troubled in conscience than by his worry over the impediment to his first marriage, 'for that it is thought yet have meddled both with the mother and with the sister'. To this Henry, surprisingly, could only mutter, 'never with the mother', but Cromwell, standing by, interjected sharply, 'nor never with the sister neither, and therefore put this out of your mind'. Unfortunately, this was just the sort of thing that ordinary, decent Englishmen would find it difficult to put out of their ordinary, dirty minds. James Macok, of Long Buckby (Northants.), lamenting the turning of abbeys into granges ('long of men of law'), added for good measure that the King had 'the foul gout or the wild gout' (one of the many terms for syphilis) and would not reign beyond a year or two.[2] John Gurle, master of Manton College (Rutland), ascribed Henry's notorious difficulties in siring children to the fact that he 'did occupy with so many whores and harlots'.[3] The parson of Freshwater in the Isle of Wight, hearing a wandering pedlar tell of Queen Anne's execution, rejoiced to think that the King, busy putting down abbeys and pulling down 'the right of Holy Church', had been made a cuckold in his own house.[4] The King's private life was a bit too near the bone for such remarks to be harmless.

The most extraordinary story to turn upon the King's alleged habits centred round William Webbe, keeper of the Westminster sanctuary and gaoler in the Palace there.[5] In September 1537, one Henry Atkinson explained to Cromwell how he had come to land in Webbe's gaol.[6] Maurice Bull, a sanctuary man, had spread a tale about a man who rode along 'with a fair maid behind him' and met a king by the way who complimented the man upon his choice, took the girl, 'and had his pleasure of her'. The man thus treated thereafter called the anonymous king an adulterer – and what would it be worth to report this to the real King? Atkinson claimed to have said many loyal things and to have told Bull to inform the Council. The result was that Webbe (the person

---

[1] SP 1/125, fo. 253 (*LP* xii. II. 952), a deposition taken four and a half years after the event.
[2] SP 1/127, fo. 149 (*LP* xii. II. 1269).   [3] SP 1/114, fo. 169 (*LP* xii. I. 126).
[4] *LP* xiii. I. 493.
[5] In 1532 Webbe was described as keeper of the Convict House in the Palace (KB 27/ 1083, Rex, rot. 5); by 1538 he had also become head of the sanctuary (KB 9/541/85–6).
[6] SP 1/124, fo. 205 (*LP* xii. II. 672).

intended) descended upon the sanctuary men, breathing fire and threats of murder; he put them in irons and vowed 'to hang them and as many as has spoken in this matter'. Atkinson was moved to remark, 'Well, Webbe [will] win his spurs now', for which Webbe threw him in gaol as well. This story could not be ignored, and Cromwell ordered an investigation by the abbot of Westminster (owner of the franchise) and Sir Anthony Denny, a gentleman of the Privy Chamber.[1] They heard five witnesses from whose depositions it appears that the story was going round the Westminster sanctuary, and also that the inmates had decided to get Webbe. The witnesses all gave different versions of what the King was supposed to have said about Webbe's pillion rider – from 'Webbe, thou hast a pretty wench behind thee' to 'Webbe, thou art never without a fair and pretty piece of flesh'. They involved Richard Sharp of Westminster, and one Kendall of Launceston in Cornwall,[2] by alleging that these two had earlier reported the tale to the abbot. This put the abbot on the spot, and he hastened to explain himself to Denny.[3] Sharp and Kendall had indeed come to see him about ten months before, in an attempt to get him to take Sharp, dismissed for incompetence, into his service again. The abbot, who had already bestowed the office in question on Webbe, refused to change his mind, whereupon his callers went into a tirade about Webbe. Bored with them, the abbot told them to leave unless they had anything of significance to say. After more bluster, they came out with the story about Webbe, his wench and the King: only at that time the lady was 'a gentlewoman' and the King contented himself with a kiss and the promise of a damask gown to back up his compliments. Webbe had called even this mild version a lie. Clearly the story had grown in the telling, and grown significantly to benefit from the King's reputation for unbridled lust.

The commonest scurrilities about Henry arose out of his association with the Lady Anne whom Marjorie Copeland, drunk (as was apparently usual with her), called 'a strong whore' for whose sake the King had turned traitor.[4] His cuckoldry supplied an additional subject

[1] This examination of witnesses is in SP 1/125, fos. 46–8 (LP xiii. II. 764).
[2] Possibly William Kendall who in 1539 was executed for treason, having been involved with the marquess of Exeter (Ellis, i. II. 104–6).
[3] SP 1/127, fo. 249 (LP xii. II. App. 43).
[4] A case of 1535, partially misplaced in LP: SP 1/88, fo. 21; 93, fo. 42 (LP vii. 1609; viii. 844). Poor Marjorie was an old woman, often drunk and always a little out of her wits.

for jests to Barton and Smith who, as we have seen, were also in the habit of slandering Cromwell and Audley; but they further called Henry a traitor to God in presuming 'to take upon him the pope of Rome his authority' and made other offensive remarks.[1] This puts them among the many who spoke against the supremacy, a rather different matter from mere scurrility and much more serious. William Hoo, vicar of Eastbourne, tried to exempt the King from any responsibility for what was happening, but his explanation hardly made matters better: 'they that rule about the King make him great banquets and give him sweet wines and make him drunk, and then they bring him bills and he putteth his sign to them.'[2] King Henry as glutton, drunkard, lecher and cuckold was hardly an improvement on King Henry the wicked tyrant, traitor to God and his Church. This was the kind of talk which did not help to keep the people in their obedience, and it had to be taken note of. It does not, however, look as though extreme measures were tried against any of these brabblers.

All things considered, it is in fact surprising that in all the mass of information received by the government there is but one story of a plot to kill the King, and that single one so crazy and unconvincing that one must have grave doubts whether anything lay behind it at all. The information was offered in two letters, one from Thomas Woddale, a priest, and one from John Byrde of Hornchurch in Essex, both abominably spelt and redolent of minds deranged.[3] They accused Thomas Duke, the vicar of Hornchurch, John Laurence, and one Osborn of planning an assassination; other men also were brought in, as John Brewer, sent to Ireland with secret letters 'under the boss of his buckler', who on his return was not paid the £3 agreed, made a noise about it, and was murdered at Laurence's instigation (so ran the story). The essence of the information was that Osborn was to have dressed up as a beggar (with 'the liver of beast lapped about his legs in linen cloths in

---

Sir Walter Stonor felt obliged to put her in prison to await Cromwell's pleasure, but urged that she be set free because 'there is nobody to tend to her husband, which is mad'. A sad case: and the charges had malice and interest behind them. It seems certain that nothing happened to her.

[1] SP 1/162, fo. 127 (LP xv. 1029 [21]), an undated letter belonging to ca. 1536.
[2] SP 1/105, fo. 295 (LP xi. 300).
[3] SP 1/68, fos. 148–9; 104, fo. 300; 113, fo. 234 (LP v. 649; x. 1264; xi. 1495). The dates are uncertain, but LP are wrong about the first; 1536 or 1537 is most likely. Woddale's letter was addressed to 'Ryet honarobol kyeng Hare the viij', and Byrde's to 'Herry viij god saue yow' nobyll grace long to Contynu in Long lyffe'.

thin pieces'), beg about the Court, and spy his opportunity to destroy King and Council with 'wildfire balls'. Duke seems to have been one of the many priests who opposed the new order and may well have talked, as he was accused of doing, against the Dissolution, but Byrde had in fact a personal grievance, having been indicted at Duke's instance. When Byrde and his wife were examined by a body of J.P.s presided over by Sir Brian Tuke, tresaurer of the Chamber, they were silenced every time they tried to speak – tried, that is, to bring Duke's treason into the open. The letters are really rather insane, with touches of persecution mania and quite wild invention, and there is no sign that anyone bothered any further with the accused or the accusations. Whatever people might say about the King, plots to kill him seem to have been nonexistent. It is thus not suggested that Henry was positively or widely hated – after all, he had ministers to take the odium of his deeds – but hostile talk about him was serious enough in the country's unsettled state. At a time when he demanded, newly, to be taken for the realm's spiritual head, he could not afford the sort of descriptions that were common enough.

To an administration engaged in putting through disturbing innovations, nothing could be more troublesome than public expressions of resistance and especially denunciations from the pulpit, easily the most effective platform for influencing the popular mind. As we shall see, the government valued the pulpit for the use they could make of it; by the same token, they had to be wary of its usefulness to the opposition. Those who believe either that there was no widespread opposition, or that a reign of terror soon silenced all dissent, may be surprised at the vigour with which opponents continued to speak throughout the decade. On the face of it, evidence of reckless free speaking by the clergy, especially friars, attached to the old ways is very striking, especially when we remember that we are likely to know of it only when someone in the congregation got sufficiently annoyed, or conscious of the loyalty demanded of him, to make report. No doubt, some of the words reported were maliciously invented, but it must be said that in general the reports worth quoting appear to be accurate. That there was some public speaking against the early stages of the King's proceedings causes less surprise than that we hear of few such occasions while the later years produced far more. It looks as though exasperation mounted and not as though the country was getting cowed. In March 1532,

Chapuys reported the arrest of a priest who had preached against the Divorce, coupling this information with the gleeful tale of a preacher for the Divorce who had been mobbed in the diocese of Salisbury.[1] In the following year, Cromwell heard of a friar's sermon at Newark which was 'somewhat seditious and slanderous' and had perturbed the congregation; the friar admitted nearly all the words remembered, enclosed with the information but now lost.[2] In June 1534, Cranmer protested to Cromwell about William Oliver, O.P., lately appointed prior of Blackfriars, Cambridge; the man not only lacked all the necessary qualifications, being of 'very small learning, sinister behaviour, ill qualities and of suspected conversation of living', but was also notorious as one who 'most indiscreetly preached against the King's grace's great cause and most defended the authority of the bishop of Rome'. Indeed, Cranmer had previously sent Cromwell a note of one of Oliver's sermons, 'which bill, if you had remembered, I doubt not but that ye would have provided for the said friar afore this time'.[3] In fact, Cromwell maintained his negligence, and to very good purpose: Oliver was in 1535 promoted to be prior of the Dominicans at Bristol where in 1537 he is found preaching most conformably and even championing Luther's doctrines, attacking friars' cowls and habits, and invoking God's wrath on sedition.[4] Unfortunately, it appears that his conversion had left him still unpopular with his hearers, now for the opposite reason.

Some preachers were careful, though their real opinions came through. Thus Gabriel Pecock, warden of the Observants at Southampton, apprehensive of authority, yet took his opportunity when preaching at the abjuration of a heretic on Easter Sunday 1534. He used the example of St Maurice to press upon his audience the need both to stand firm in one's faith and yet to offer no resistance to one's prince, but then turned to the question of the pope's authority, still at that date, of course, not finally settled though the first Act of Succession left few loopholes:

First he lamented the diversity of preaching that is used nowadays, and the contradictions of clerks and learned men, saying he was credibly informed that divers hath preached and daily do preach that St Peter had never more

[1] LP v. 879. [2] SP 1/81, fo. 126 (LP vi. 1664).
[3] SP 1/84, fo. 178 (LP vii. 807).
[4] Victoria County History, Cambridgeshire, iii. 274–5; SP 1/119, fo. 123 (LP xiii. I. 508).

power ne authority given unto him by God than any other of the apostles, and that the pope should have no more authority, power and jurisdiction out of Rome than the bishop hath without of his diocese, nor a bishop no more than a simple priest, and so consequently the pope was no more than a simple curate: which sayings, he said, were grievous errors...They brought their books into the pulpit with them...He would show his books also for the contrary.

He then read some five or six passages proving the papal supremacy from a Latin book in his hand and translated them into English.[1] This was all sailing very close to the wind, but in his complaint about the varieties of opinion preached from the pulpit he had hit on the point most disturbing to the government. People's minds were being unsettled by all these conflicting certainties, and where their minds led their bodies, brandishing weapons, might soon follow. Pecock was investigated by Cromwell but sent home again.[2]

Dr Richard Thornton, warden of Canterbury College, Oxford, was denounced in early 1534 for regularly preaching against the King; he died peacefully in 1557.[3] Less culpable was Dr Carsley, canon of Wells, guilty on 21 February 1535 of the sort of slip familiar to any experienced public speaker. In his prayers, he mentioned 'the Lady Catherine, the Queen' and her daughter, the Princess Elizabeth. The clerk stopped him, and the poor old man of nearly eighty 'staggered a season' and denied he could possibly have spoken of Catherine. However, assured that he had done so he expressed his regret and said: 'I call God to record that I thought not of the Lady Catherine; I meant only Queen Anne, for I know no queen but her.' Though obviously he spoke the truth, his slip had occurred in the full cathedral and was likely to be noted; his bishop therefore thought it necessary to inform Cromwell.[4] Friar Benchley's preaching near Canterbury a month later was another matter: 'Masters, take heed, we have nowadays many new laws. I know we shall have a new God shortly.'[5] That particular pulpit seemed to induce a subtle deviousness in its occupants, for on the following Sunday a visiting monk from Canterbury told there a story of a king who had lost his kingdom because he kept to himself the goods of

[1] SP 2/P, fo. 159 (LP vii. 449).
[2] LP vii. 448, 450, 472–3 (April 1534); on July 16th he was writing from Southampton in good health and confident of a fair response (SP 1/85, fos. 63–4 [LP vii. 982]).
[3] SP 1/82, fo. 123 (LP vii. 101); J. Foster, Alumni Oxonienses.
[4] StP i. 427.   [5] SP 1/91, fo. 91 (LP viii. 386).

certain transgressors; the congregation buzzed with the supposition that he meant King Henry and was preaching insurrection.[1]

Kent had its problems: one Friar Arthur, grey friar of Canterbury, was denounced for preaching an extraordinary sermon at Herne, on Easter Sunday 1535 (congregations were naturally largest at Easter).[2] He delivered himself of a violent tirade against the innovators with their attacks on fasting, prayer and pilgrimages. 'I say, he that gives or offers one penny to St Thomas's shrine, it is more meritorious for the soul than he had given a noble to poor people, for one is spiritual and the other corporal.' An interesting assessment of alms to the poor being eighty times less effective for salvation than gifts to the saints. He wished the congregation to take example from those 'in my country' who go two hundred miles to 'that blessed shrine: and when they come and see the goodly jewels that there be, how they think in their hearts, I would to God and that good saint I was able to offer such a gift, and by such good thoughts thousands of souls are saved'. If Thomas had been 'a devil in hell', he was to be worshipped 'if the Church had canonised him...for you ought to believe us prelates though we preach false'. Nor did he pray for the King as supreme head, or for the Queen at all. However, perhaps he was traduced. We cannot be very sure of the truth, for Friar Arthur was in Dieppe by November that year, having been denounced, imprisoned and then let go. He claimed to be the King's loyal subject maltreated by enemies who had resented his rule of the Franciscan house at Canterbury and his attempts to stamp out popery there; now he was appealing to Cromwell for aid and favour.[3] If this was true, his flight out of the King's dominions seems unnecessary; most likely he had said enough at Herne to get into trouble with King and Council, though not so much – and what was reported was not treasonable, merely very disturbing – as to suffer more than a caution. However, even if that sermon was never preached, or not in those words, it shows the friar's enemies displaying a vigorous imagination itself suggestive of the sort of things that were being said and causing unrest.

Disobedient preachers continued to trouble Cromwell, as the case of Edward Harcocke, prior of the Blackfriars at Norwich, shows. In April 1535 he preached a sermon in which he said:[4]

[1] Ibid. [2] SP 1/91, fo. 176 (*LP* viii. 480).
[3] SP 1/99, fos. 11–12 (*LP* ix. 789).
[4] E 36/153, fo. 27 (*LP* viii. 667): deposition of Richard Hore, 5 May 1535.

Ye shall pray for our sovereign lord, King Henry, of the Church chief head, so called. Here riseth a question: may the King be head of the Church? To this grow two answers. Some say yea and some say nay. They that say nay have Scripture that teaches us Christ to be our head of the Church. [Here he cited *Ephes. 1, Ephes. 5, Coloss. 1*, and translated the passages]. An earthly man namely a temporal man, may not be head of the Church. Notwithstanding, seeing that spiritual men have bodies that must be clothed and have bodily sustenance, the King is their head in temporalities and protector and defender of the same. But that the King should be head in ministering of sacraments, or in incensing, or such other, I deny, and will in any place of the world.

Although he had spoken with some care, a charge of treason could easily have been constructed out of all this. He then tried to move to less dangerous ground: touching the pope, he agreed that his alleged power was 'by man's ordinance' and not by Scripture, and whether or not other countries accepted it, 'this I know well that the whole Council of this realm hath taken this authority from him'.

Here some will say: sir, ye seem to speak against yourself, seeing that your order was confirmed by the bishop of Rome. To this I say that so long as the bishop of Rome was in authority, the fathers Benet, Dominic and Francis did well in going to him to have their rules approved.

Still wobbling very dangerously on thin ice: this sort of thing was not what the government intended when they demanded that preachers support the royal supremacy and denounce the pope's.

The sermon caused some consternation in the large congregation: 'much of the audience was offended and not edified'. The mayor told the prior of King's Langley, who was visiting the city that he and some of the aldermen 'were weary of hearing' Harcocke: why did he meddle in such matters?[1] Cromwell ordered Sir Roger Townsend to arrest the preacher, but Townsend contented himself with getting the mayor to make sure that Harcocke could be produced whenever wanted.[2] This curious evasion of duty, which suggests an explanation of the prior's immunity, was allowed to work, for Harcocke was still in office in 1536.[3] And there he stayed, for in January 1537, John Hilsey, bishop of

[1] SP 1/83, fo. 205 (*LP* vii. 595). This and the next letter are misdated in *LP*.
[2] SP 1/84, fo. 70 (*LP* vii. 694).
[3] F. Blomefield, *Essay towards a Topographical History of the City of Norwich* (1806), iv. 339-40.

Rochester and lately provincial of the black friars, complained about Harcocke in terms which indicate that he was unaware of Cromwell's earlier brush with the man. He had been trying to correct Harcocke's behaviour (seditious preaching, and keeping a nun in his friary) but without success, and even process out of the viceregent's court had availed nothing. Would Cromwell please examine the delinquent himself? He would find him one who 'hath used himself craftily in his preaching against the King's highness and your lordship'.[1] We do not know what happened next, but Harcocke may at last have lost the immunity which attended him in 1535; by 1538, another man was prior of the house.[2] Perhaps he was deposed, perhaps he died; people did, after all, even without assistance from the government. What stands out is the fact that in total safety he could preach a sermon which proved most disquieting and unsettling to the city fathers of Norwich and which hinted at opinions of the sort for which soon after Fisher and More were to die.

And so the tale of disturbing voices mounts up. In September 1535, another friar was despatched by the convent at Kingswood to answer to Cromwell for preaching solidly in favour of the Petrine doctine.[3] In October, the subprior of Lewes admitted a treasonable sermon and involved his prior who had known of it and 'counselled' it. Both underwent examination but nothing worse.[4] In November 1535, a country priest was alleged to have exhorted his parish not to 'follow the saying of evil princes nor evil rulers, but rather put on your harness and fight against them'.[5] In early 1536, Prior Richard Marshall wrote to the black friars of Newcastle to explain why he had fled.[6] Though a loyal subject of the King, he could not declare the royal supremacy or denounce the pope's. He offered seven reasons for his stand: Scripture, the teaching of the Catholic Church, the decisions of General Councils, the interpretation of the Fathers, the opinion of all the Universities except a few 'lately corrupt and poisoned with Luther's heresies', the consent of Christendom in acknowledging the pope, and his friar's oath of obedience to the supreme pontiff. He had been warned to preach according to the King's command, but could not; the result was that in Advent

[1] SP 1/115, fo. 140 (*LP* xii. I. 297).   [2] Blomefield, *loc. cit.*
[3] SP 1/96, fo. 122 (*LP* ix. 315). Nothing further is known.
[4] See below, p. 85.   [5] SP 1/99, fo. 9 (*LP* ix. 786).
[6] BM, Cleo. E. iv, fo. 157 (*LP* x. 594).

and Lent he preached comprehensive treason and decided to flee abroad. Though ready in his heart to die for his opinions, 'I feel my flesh grudge with death'. A solid man, but his witness at Newcastle, however principled and worthy, did not exactly help those trying to keep obedient order in that distant and difficult region.

Even disaffected preachers who stayed in the country made no secret of their views. The story of another sermon takes us back to Herne where William Cobbe, a visiting preacher from St Peter's in Thanet, told the congregation: 'Many men, because the name pope is taken away, have therefore a scrupulous conscience. But as for taking away of his name, it is no matter, for he never wrote himself *papa* but *summus pontifex*. And as for his authority, he hath not lost an inch thereof, I warrant you.' His exercise in linguistic subtlety got him gaoled at Canterbury, there to await the pleasure of King and Council; no more can be discovered.[1] Richard Jackson, a Suffolk parson, also took his general opposition into the pulpit; not only did he refuse to obey the order to preach against the pope but positively denounced the King's supremacy, used the bidding prayer to speak for the pope, and waved the Ten Articles at his congregation, saying, 'Beware, my friends, of these English books'.[2] Past experience did not cure Hugh Payne, once an observant friar and then parish priest successively in two Suffolk livings. Imprisoned and thoroughly investigated in 1533–1534, he submitted and got off; but early in 1537 we find Cranmer still trying to discipline him and to stop his subversive preaching, manifestly with little hope of success.[3]

The patience practised with difficult preachers emerges very clearly from the story of Robert Augustyn, a white friar who in June 1535 preached a sermon at St Bride's, Fleet Street, which so exasperated one of his hearers that he challenged his authority to preach there and then. But Augustyn held the bishop of London's licence and preached there

[1] E 36/120, fo. 49 (*LP* xi. 464).
[2] SP 1/113, fo. 51 (*LP* xi. 1393).
[3] In 1533, Payne, an observant friar, was suspected of a connection with the Aragon interest (Merriman, i. 361); he was then under arrest. In June 1534, he was trying to leave the country from Cardiff where he was caught wearing lay clothing; he had been causing trouble at Bristol and was anxious to get away (SP 1/85, fos. 26, 93 [*LP* vii. 734, 1020]). It seems that his unconvincing denial and submission, addressed to the King himself (*LP* vii. 1652) were accepted, for the Hugh Payne who troubled Cranmer in 1536–7 (SP 1/115, fo. 89 [*LP* xii. I. 256, 1]) was described by him as a friar observant and must have been the same man.

'with the good will of the curate, then being present'.[1] What had especially annoyed the informer was Augustyn's attack on a previous preacher of the opposite persuasion: 'Lately ye had one that preached the gospel in this place which was pseuda [sic] propheta – that is to say, a false prophet and a new prophet – which applied this gospel [the parable of Dives and Lazarus] to women, when not one word of that gospel and place speaketh of women'. This contemptuous dismissal clearly grieved the pseudo-prophet's follower, but more serious was tbe charge that Augustyn had neither attacked the usurped power of Rome nor prayed for the King as supreme head. What was more, Cromwell supposedly possessed information accusing him of extremely dangerous sayings, as for instance that he would regard the author of any uncharitable writings against the pope as 'no other wise than he would a schismatic, paynim or Jew', that 'we should see a new turn of the bishop of Rome, if we did live', and that the present pope was 'a good man' though 'some of his predecessors were evil'. His slanders even embraced the tribe of historians – those persons upon whose testimony Cromwell had, after all, rested his Act of Appeals: when challenged to justify the pope's deplorable behaviour towards King John, 'he said the chronicles of this realm was false and how he was accused maliciously, of malice and of false heretics'.[2] Yet with all this against him, and clearly guilty of upsetting people, he turned up in October 1538 to obtain his dispensation to hold a benefice.[3]

Another who bore a charmed life and refused to learn discretion was William Inold, at one time priest of Rye. Off and on, he had been causing trouble, getting denounced and experiencing interrogation and prison, since 1533. By 1536 he had split Rye into two parties: there was talk of 'insurrection' and that things would 'never be well' until one side or the other had won. Inold had apparently done all this on grounds of religion, calling honest men (honest according to themselves) 'heretics and other opprobrious names' and instigating 'other of his accomplices – drunkards and papists – to fight with them'. He provoked his enemies by keeping the old ceremonies and the abolished holy days. Since in Rye he could no longer get a clear hearing, he rode in August

---

[1] SP 1/121, fo. 84 (*LP* xii. II. 65). Internal evidence suggests the date 1535; *LP*'s 1537 depends on the assumption that he must have preached on a Sunday.
[2] SP 1/92, fo. 127 (*LP* viii. 624), placed also by *LP* in 1535.
[3] *Fac. Off. Reg.* 152.

1537 thirteen miles to Burwash where he preached sedition, telling the people 'to remain and do as of old time they had done'. This, and a bill of charges from the parishioners of Rye accusing him of neglecting his cure as well as disobeying the King's instructions, put him back in gaol. It is clear from these accusations that there were some of the usual troubles at Rye, especially over tithe, but abuse of the pulpit clearly also took place.[1] Inold really displayed unconquerable rashness. In 1535, between leaving Rye temporarily and returning there, he once engaged a stranger, who had just arrived in England, in conversation, 'thinking me to be of his opinion', and complained that the realm was full of heretics. 'And then he took a little book out of his purse, Eckyns Enchiridion,[2] wherein be many false sayings impugning the supreme dignity of the King's grace.'[3] Inold went on for years, denounced again and again, preaching publicly against the new order, provoking disturbances in the town; and in the end he survived to move to the diocese of Canterbury and there, in December 1539, get licence to hold a second living in plurality.[4] Who protected him? Perhaps the fact that at one time at least, though under pressure from Cromwell they withdrew their assistance at any rate temporarily, he had the support of the mayor and jurats of Rye accounts for his immunity.

Less fortunate was John Ainsworth, a bachelor of arts of St John's College, Cambridge, born in Lancashire and round about 1518 rescued from menial employment in London by means of an exhibition from Catherine of Aragon. This exhibition gained him seven years at Cambridge and his degree; and his gratitude to his benefactress thereafter dominated his life. Until 1538 he was variously employed in curacies around Cambridge, but then he went north to York. By this time, it seems that he was no longer quite sane. On the second Sunday in Lent 1538, he approached the incumbent of St John the Evangelist near the Ouse bridge in York for permission to preach in his church. Since he could show no licence, the priest refused, to which Ainsworth rejoined that he must needs show his matter somewhere; if the curate would not let him preach, he would nail his sermon to the church door. This he did, but the sermon was seditious and treasonable, calling Rome 'our

[1] Troubles of 1533–4: SP 1/79, fos. 23–4; 80, fo. 11; 238, fos. 153, 177 (*LP* vi. 1077, 1329; *Add.* 871, 879). Troubles of 1536–8: SP 1/102, fo. 115; 124, fos. 21, 24; 133, fo. 7 (*LP* x. 365; xii. II. 505; xiii. I. 1150). And see below, pp. 85–90.
[2] The notoriously papalist *Enchiridion* of Johann Eck.
[3] SP 1/99, fo. 97 (*LP* ix. 846).   [4] *Fac. Off. Reg.* 202.

mother, Holy Church' and attacking the Acts of Supremacy and Succession; according to the report it ended in 'manifest and frantic ribaldry'. Ainsworth claimed to have preached the same sermon in the summer of 1533 at Teversham near Cambridge. Interrogated by the Council of the North, he made it plain that he was still fighting the battles of Henry VIII's first wife, but also showed signs of a familiar type of religious mania. He said that Holy Church was now blind, 'and therefore God hath altered his Church again in one other woman, which he said was the forenamed Lady Dowager, and by himself whom in the foresaid book he calleth the Spirit, and by his brother' – Oliver Ainsworth, of Jesus College, Cambridge. But frantic or not, he was too much for the Council of the North who had him tried and executed for treason. Their report to the King shows plainly that the whole affair was settled without reference to the government in London: Ainsworth may well have been unfortunate in spreading his preaching within the jurisdiction of a body rendered apprehensive and savage by the recent experience of rebellion.[1]

By 1538, failure to obey the vicegerent's Injunctions was becoming an obvious offence to allege against preachers. Thomas Cowley, vicar of Ticehurst in Sussex, was an oldfashioned man who continued to preach the value of images and miracles. He held up a 'King Harry groat', pointed to the King's image on it, and said:

How darest thou spit upon this face? Thou darest not do it. But thou wilt spit upon the image...Then thou spittest upon God...Hold you there, hold for a while; for once within four years we shall have it as it was again. Therefore do as ye have done: offer up a candle to St Loys for thy horse and to St Anthony for thy cattle.

In a Lent sermon he accused his audience of eating meat in fasting time – 'white meat, and yea, and it were not for shame ye would eat a piece of bacon in the stead of a red herring...I daresay there be a hundred thousand worse people now than there was this time twelve months in England'. These and similar sayings, praising the old ways and foretelling their early return, got him into trouble with his bishop, but he got off with a penance.[2] Cromwell heard of a preacher, claiming to be chaplain to the archbishop of York, who was preaching against the

---

[1] SP 1/130, fos. 28–9; 131, fo. 56 (*LP* xiii. I. 533, 705).
[2] SP 1/133, fos. 51–3 (*LP* xiii. I. 1199).

Injunctions at Beverley. Archbishop Lee at first denied that the man could be his chaplain, but on investigation found him to be an old man, lately his suffragan there, too feeble to travel and so crippled with arthritis that he had great difficulty in writing out the offending sermon on Lee's orders (after the event). The paper was sent to Cromwell, but there the matter ended.[1] Dr John Lusshe, vicar of Aylesbury (Bucks.), got into hot water early in 1539; among his papers were found sermons in praise of Becket and in favour of the pope which had been supplied by another man, as well as several in his own hand so badly written as to be partly illegible. But the investigators could make out a prayer for the pope, an attack on the English Bible, and contempt for serving men and craftsmen who read the Scriptures in English. Nevertheless, Lusshe was not troubled and died two years later, still in possession of the vicarage.[2]

There are other less substantial indications scattered through the record to show that government control of the pulpit was far from complete. It should not be doubted that from the point of view of maintaining peace, obedience and the new order this could be, and usually was, a serious matter. Moreover, the fact that in so many cases in which the allegations were manifestly true the offenders escaped all serious consequences may at once cast doubt upon the traditional story of savage repression. However, in all this preaching against the supremacy and the Injunctions, priests and friars offended against known laws and caused much displeasure among the more conformist of their flocks: these matters could be tackled. Much more difficult, as well as much more frequent, were attacks on innovators in religion, on preachers of reform and Reformation; and yet these attacks always harboured within them the likelihood of trouble and unrest. It is very patent that throughout the 1530's the battles between advanced and conservative clergy were setting people all over England by the ears, gravely affecting the maintenance of good order and the enforcement of the new dispensation.

A good many oldfashioned priests made no secret of their feelings and went about to stir all who would listen against heretics and favourers of the new learning. This sort of thing started as soon as the

[1] SP 1/133, fo. 189; 134, fo. 93 (*LP* xiii. I. 1247, 1317).
[2] SP 1/144, fo. 112 (*LP* xiv. I. 525); R. E. G. Cole, ed., *Chapter Acts of Lincoln Cathedral*, Lincoln Record Soc. vol. 13 (1917), 77.

policy of reform came manifestly to be added to that of supremacy. The liberty of St Albans was alleged to contain but three priests given to 'the truth'; the rest 'smells of their old mumpsimus', especially one Thomas Kyng, stipendiary curate of St Andrew's chapel, who went out of his way to warn his audience against the new books, singling out Luther, Melanchthon, Tracy, Tyndale and Frith, a catalogue in which the third name stands oddly. All these, he said, had been condemned for heresy. Kyng used words which exemplify the dilemma of men who had been trained up one way and were now ordered to adopt another: 'he was brought up so and muzzled so in the old ceremonies that he cannot forsake them'.[1] The ex-curate of St Mary Woolchurch in London inveighed against Robert Barnes, England's best known Lutheran; thinking no doubt of Fisher and More (for he spoke on 1 July 1535), he declared his defiance, no matter what the consequences might be, for 'there were better men that lost their heads now in these days than he was'. Five days later he went so far as to call heretics all those who nowadays preached at the King's commandment, defied informers, and added that 'he cared not a fart' for the Tower; we do not know whether anyone took him up on this challenge.[2] Dr Maydland, a grey friar of London, 'trusted to see every man's head off that is of the new learning and the maintainers thereof to stand upon a stake'; more dangerously, he hoped 'to see the King suffer a violent and shameful death and...the mischievous whore, the Queen, burned'.[3] Since he is not in the list of those in the friary when it was surrendered in November 1538, he may have suffered.[4] The vicar of Eastbourne, whom we have already encountered preaching against the new order, said in private conversation that those who preached 'after the new sect and called themselves children of Christ...were the children of the Devil'.[5] At Sturminster Newton in Dorset, the incumbent, one Mr Lovell, in June 1536 preached for the old ceremonies and warned his hearers against 'these abominable heretics that readeth the New Testament in English...As a scabbed sheep infesteth the whole flock, so these abominable heretics infect the whole company with their new learning'.[6]

[1] SP 1/91, fos. 105, 107 (LP viii. 406–7). For good measure, Kyng was also charged with having 'deflowered a certain maid called Crane's daughter' and of having got his parish clerk 'to convey her away'.
[2] SP 1/94, fos. 1–2 (LP viii. 1000).   [3] SP 1/99, fo. 67 (LP ix. 846).
[4] Reports of the Deputy Keeper of the Public Records, viii (1847) App. ii, p. 28.
[5] SP 1/105, fo. 296 (LP xi. 300 [ii]).   [6] E 36/120, fo. 15 (LP x. 1140).

The Bible in English provided one of the conservatives' main targets, especially but not only after its reading had been ordered by the Injunctions of 1538. As early as April 1537, a Kentish priest, James Fredewell, teased about his book-buying, burst out that 'he had liefer that all the New Testaments in English were burned than he would buy any or look upon any'.[1] That good conservative, Thomas Colley, described any persons that possessed the English New Testament as 'of the new trick – it is but a trick, and lightly it came and lightly it will be gone again'.[2] John Fuller, again in Kent, just after the Injunctions had been received, warned men that they should not look at the Bible before doomsday,[3] while Richard Bush, the parish clerk of Hastings, hoped to see the official translation burned 'because it is set forth with annotations in the margin and also it hath a prologue contrary to the King's proclamation'. Protesting a complete and servile loyalty, he claimed that he had objected to the translation of one passage which might persuade people, falsely, that priests might marry.[4] And when the villagers of Wincanton in Somerset showed an inclination (probably in early 1539) to study the Bible, John Divale, their priest, denounced 'these new-fangled fellows which read the new books, for they be heretics and knaves and pharisees'. He likened them 'to a dog that gnaweth a marrow bone and never cometh to the pith'.[5]

Hostility to the reformers seems to have been strong at Oxford where one Mr Smith, of Merton, in 1536 preached a sermon attacking them which attracted attention.[6] He offended against the Injunctions by praying for souls in purgatory, violently attacked justification by faith alone, defended traditional ceremonies, and made 'many exclamations against the new sect and new masters, as he called them, that would enterprise to dispute of the constitutions of the Church and go about to have any constitutions of the Fathers altered'. Corpus Christi College would appear to have been a stronghold of conservatism where some fellows resisted the order to erase the pope's name from the service books; one of the dons asserted that if he found a scholar with a New Testament he would burn it, and fellows given to the new learning ('as they call it') were allegedly kept from office and from taking part

[1] SP 1/118, fo. 231 (*LP* xii. I. 990).   [2] SP 1/133, fo. 53 (*LP* xiii. I. 1199 [2]).
[3] SP 1/242, fo. 78 (*LP Add.* 1253).
[4] E 36/120, fo. 7 (*LP* xiv. II. 301). For the proclamation, see *TRP*, no. 191.
[5] SP 1/151, fos. 155–6 (*LP* xiv. I. 897).   [6] SP 6/2, fo. 2 (*LP* x. 950).

in College business.[1] As predictable was the conservatism of a monk of Christ Church, Canterbury (John Stone), who in January 1537 sighed over 'these new books' which would be the destruction of King Henry and Prince Edward. Upon investigation he admitted this and other dangerous matters, but he was left in peace in the priory till its dissolution in April 1540.[2] No doubt many who so lamented would have had to confess, as that stormy petrel, Rowland Phillips, did in July 1537, that they could not back their hysterical attacks on the reformers with any specific examples.[3] Such possible scruples did not exist for John Kene who disturbed Bristol in 1536 by publicly despising 'the new preachers, saying they preached new learning with their new books'. He compared the distance between them and real learning to that between 'Jerusalem and Jericho, which is threescore miles and over', and called 'their new learning...old heresy new risen'. 'They say they have brought in the light into the world; no, no, they have brought in damnable darkness and endless damnation. Choose you, go to hell an ye will, for I will not be your lodesman.' Strong stuff to throw into the cauldron that was Bristol at the time.[4]

At Stanmore, in Middlesex, the curate (once a monk of the Charterhouse and of Mount Grace), who claimed to have been in trouble before for such opinions, greatly angered some people by declaring that 'he would not hold with this new doctrine, nor that it would never sink into his heart'. Especially he would not agree to the campaign against images, 'for that was greatly against his profit and ours'. How, with such 'ignorant curates' about (asked the parish), were they to fulfil the requirements of God, King and Council?[5] It was a more serious matter still when Dr Arthur Draycott, mistakenly described as chancellor of Lincoln, continued to adhere to popery and refused to attend to the supply of Bibles in parish churches.[6] He was in fact a newly installed prebendary, who may have been deputising for the chancellor, and he was not deprived, despite the charges against him, until the world had turned several times and Elizabeth sat on the throne.[7] Equal immunity attended Dr Thomas Thomson, vicar of Enfield, a persecutor

---

[1] See below, p. 97.
[2] SP 1/115, fo. 89 (LP xii. I. 251 [1]); LP xv. 452.
[3] T. Cranmer, Works, ed. J. E. Cox (1844–6), ii. 338–40.
[4] SP 1/119, fos. 190–4 (LP xii. I. 1147). For Bristol, see below, pp. 112–20.
[5] SP 1/136, fo. 170 (LP xiii. II. 361).   [6] SP 1/153, fo. 159 (LP xiv. II. 214).
[7] Le Neve, i. 34.

of those of his parishioners who wished to read the Bible in English – a book he called 'the book of Arthur Cobbler'. To him the new learning was 'a green learning that will fade away'.[1] Yet all these examples of resistance come from parts of the country well controlled by the government, not perhaps from the notorious 'backward north' – many indeed from the capital and its immediate environs.

Preaching and public talk could cause trouble enough; perhaps even more serious, because much harder to discover, were signs that conservative priests used the confessional to attack the innovations and innovators. At St Albans, Thomas Kyng was not the only disaffected priest; John Matthew did as well who told a young man come to be shriven that 'when the King...is dead, all these fashions shall be laid down'. But when he discovered his charge to be favourably inclined to reform he first railed at him and then took fright: 'whatever I have said unto thee, repeat it not, but speak like a ghostly child by me and I shall report likewise by thee'. The matter came to light only because the priest was the first to break the confessional seal, spreading it about that the young man 'smelled of heresy'. On another occasion, Matthew inquired whether the man he was confessing believed 'as his fathers did before him, or whether he believed in the new learning'. He believed in Christ, answered Robert Hyx, as he ought to do. This reassured Matthew who again used his common consolation: 'if it fortune the King to die, you shall see this world turned up so down or clear changed'. On a third occasion, he risked real trouble, exclaiming that the sinner 'was the [most] ungracious boy that ever came under his hand and smelled of heresy, and said also our sovereign lord the King took naughty opinions'. The last six words in this letter to Cromwell are underlined, as though marked for investigation, but nothing further is known of the case.[2] The parson of Honey Lane parish in London was comprehensively accused of corrupting his parishioners when confessing them by calling 'these new preachings and new learnings... contrary to God's laws' and telling people 'to stand strongly in their old faith'.[3]

A remarkable conversation was reported by John Stanton who on

[1] SP 1/156, fos. 72–3 (*LP* xiv. I. 796).   [2] SP 1/91, fo. 105 (*LP* viii. 407).
[3] SP 1/99, fo. 97v (*LP* ix. 846: this passage omitted). This parson may have got into trouble, for five years later his living was in the hands of Thomas Garrett (Wriothesley, i. 114).

23 February 1536 went to be shriven by George Rowlands at the Crutched Friars in London.[1] Rowlands appears as an outspoken adherent of the old ways, but Stanton, clearly acting on his own account, seems to have behaved rather like an *agent provocateur*.

First the said John Stanton said Benedicite, and the priest said Dominus. And then the said John said Confiteor, and afterward rehearsed the seven deadly sins particularly, and then the misspending of his five wits. And then the priest said, Have you not sinned in not doing the five works of mercy? The said John said, Yea, forsooth, for the which and all other I cry God mercy and beseech you, my ghostly father, of forgiveness, and give me penance of my sins.

This Rowlands did,[2] but as he was about to pronounce absolution Stanton raised a scruple. He had heard Latimer preach to the effect that no man of himself had power to forgive sins and that the pope had no more authority than any other bishop, and he therefore doubted Rowlands' capacity to absolve him. Rowlands exploded: Latimer was 'a false knave' (repeated three or four times), and his – Rowlands' – pardon was effective. He went on to inveigh against Latimer and to assert that tbe pope's power was as great as ever.

And so I will take him, forasmuch as all other realms be of the same opinion. But here in England, the King with his Parliament hath put him out because of the great sums that was wont to be paid to him; but the King and his Parliament could not deny all such pardons as was granted before the Parliament. . .and therefore Latimer is a false knave.

He urged Stanton to avoid Latimer's sermons, 'for so shall all my ghostly children do' (a useful reminder of a confessor's potential influence), and to reassure him told how he had recently gone to confess five of the fathers of Syon of whom but one was 'of the new learning'. Stanton was not to waver in his faith. 'for these things will not last long, I warrant you; you shall see the world change shortly.'

Stanton refused to be comforted. 'You know,' he said, 'that we be sworn unto the King's grace and hath already abjured the pope.' 'As for that, said the priest, an oath loosely made may be loosely broken,'

---

[1] SP 1/102, fos. 73–4 (*LP* x. 346).

[2] To eat no meat or fish on two Wednesdays between Easter and Whitsun; twice to say the seven spalines with the litany; and before leaving the church to say five paternosters and five aves with a credo.

and illustrated the point with a curious story. Supposing he had an enemy, and a man friendly to them both were to ask him to drink with that enemy, and under pressure he were to promise on his faith to do so and indeed went and had that drink with his enemy, 'trow you that I will forgive him with my heart?' Neither would he abjure the pope in his heart, no matter what oath he had publicly sworn; and he claimed that he had once told Cranmer precisely as much and was answered that he might pray privately for the pope, though not in public.[1] 'We may say nothing openly, for the knaves hath our heads under their girdle'. But the world will change, and the faithful shall have their reward. No doubt remembering the sort of thing that Latimer was liable to say, Rowlands reverted to his duty and enjoined Stanton to stand fast by purgatory and offering to saints: 'offer a candle, a man of wax, or a bowed penny, for God hath given you your health of body for such causes.' Ah yes, said honest John, but he had heard preachers say that these images were 'but stocks and stones and cannot do us no good'. They represent the saints, replied Rowlands, and remind us of them; and good deeds done in such remembrance have their reward. Stanton started to express doubts, but Rowlands interrupted with yet another of his dubious parables:

I put the case that I know that a thief came to me and asked his alms for God's sake, then would I give him alms not because he is a thief but because he asked it of me for God's sake; and so in like manner, whatsoever you give in the honour of God or for any good saint, God shall reward you for it, though it be given to an image of stock or stone. Somebody hath profit thereby, either the parson, parish priest,[2] or somebody.

But Stanton remained obdurate. He did not question that charitable alms even to a thief were a good deed, 'but we may go in the church for long enough or any image of stock or stone will ask his alms'. This did for Rowlands, who said: 'I pray you, make an end, for I must go to

[1] Rowlands spoke of 'the bishop of Canterbury', but since that interview took place at a time when prayers for the pope were already forbidden the archbishop meant must have been Cranmer. The story cannot, of course, be verified; one wonders whether Cranmer's well known double-dealing over his own oath to the pope was sufficiently notorious for tales like these to be attached to his name, or whether he really was so full of untimely liberalism.

[2] In the sixteenth century, 'parish priest' usually meant assistant curate, while the term curate was used to denote the beneficed incumbent.

mass.' So Stanton took his absolution, without it seems believing in it, and went off to write all this down and report it. If there was any truth in his report at all, Rowlands should have been in dire trouble, but there is no sign that the matter was ever followed up. Yet this does not convict Stanton of writing fiction. As he tells it, the story is circumstantial, elaborate and careful, and hangs together; it really does not read like invention. It is more likely that whatever steps were taken have left no evidence behind or that Rowlands was lucky, or well friended, and left alone.

Since we may thus accept it, the story not only graphically exemplifies how dangerous to the success of the government's policy conservative priests, in control of the confessional, could be; it also reminds us that of all the reformers Latimer caused the most trouble. He proved particularly explosive at Bristol where the authorities found it necessary as early as April 1533 to inhibit him from preaching because his sermons were threatening to provoke riots, but that story shall be pursued at greater length below.[1] A little later, another reforming preacher, John Erley, got into trouble at Marshfield in Wiltshire where the local priest, a Mr Key, was of a different persuasion. Erley was called a disciple of Latimer 'which, said he, hath done more hurt in this country than Luther and all his disciples hath done beyond sea'. When Erley replied to this curious exaggeration that Latimer had the King's licence to preach, Key retorted that Latimer 'was admitted by them that were of his own sect' and that he, Key, would not respect the King's letter in such a matter.[2] Latimer's reputation endured, especially as he did enough to keep tempers hot. Thomas Bell, sheriff of Gloucestershire, tried in 1537 to get this 'whoreson heretic' and his chaplains stopped from preaching by petitioning the duke of Norfolk, notoriously no friend to innovation, and the Parliament, not then in session. Other people in those parts felt as strongly.[3] A year later, Richard Cornewell, a priest who had fallen foul of Latimer in his episcopal capacity, was saying loudly that the bishop had no authority to curse him because the rightful bishop was in Rome.[4] Cornewell was a foulmouthed priest who threatened his bishop with the fate of a relapsed heretic and added that

[1] SP 1/75, fo. 228 (LP vi. 411), and below, pp. 112–20.
[2] SP 1/79, fo. 124 (LP vii. 1192).
[3] SP 1/115, fos. 166–7 (LP xii. I. 308); and see below, pp. 35–6.
[4] I.e. Bishop Ghinucci, one of Wolsey's absentee appointments, deprived in March 1535.

'he had set his wench by the bishop's nose...Let me see who dare meddle with her...If he [Cornewell] would marry her, the bishop would be contented that he tilted up her tail in every bush'.[1] No doubt, Latimer had tried to make a wenching priest behave himself, but through the objections to him there always run these charges of heresy and reformed preaching. More than any other man, he represented all they hated to the traditionalists.

As the mention of Thomas Bell shows, hostility to the despised 'new learning' was not confined to the clergy, though most of our evidence involves them. No doubt they were more readily in the way of expressing opinions on the subject, and no doubt also they attracted more informers. There are, however, enough cases extant of laymen talking to much the same effect to demonstrate that not all those exhortations to stand by the old ways and wait for the early arrival of another world (in this life) fell on stony ground. Miles Denyson, a tailor of Kidderminster, whom the examining commissioners described as 'a very seditious person and a very drunkard...and also a disturber of the officers of the town...and also a despiser of the preachers and doctrine of Christ', lived up to all the items of this catalogue when two of Latimer's trained revivalists visited the town on 27 and 28 July 1538. On the latter day, Denyson, meeting a group of his acquaintances, asked them blandly for a pot of ale, there being no sign that he meant to contribute to the cost. One of the men replied that he never drank before mass, while the others, less scrupulous, debated where to go. Lache's place was out since he had got married, but there were Delff's and John Aware's. The conversation turned to the sermon preached on the 27th – preached at the execution of eight men and two women – which had allegedly edified both the criminals and the bystanders.[2] Denyson called the preacher 'a foolish puppy and a boy' who had delivered his new learning standing on the vicar's colt: 'I would that the colt had winced and cast him down.' He added that now there was a 'foolish knave priest come to preach of this new learning, which I set not by'. He was warned to mind his tongue, at which he jeered at the speaker: 'Now thy master and thou be the bishop's servants, we must beware now what we say before you.' However, he came along to church with the rest of them to hear this despised representative of the

[1] SP 1/130, fo. 84 (*LP* xiii. I. 545).
[2] There is no reason to think that the cause of these executions was political.

new learning hold forth; but when asked during the sermon what he thought of it, he would only say, 'I would he were gone that I were at my dinner'. One's heart warms to this reprobate, but he upset people at the time; that he spoke the words alleged is certain enough, for the one witness he brought to support his denial admitted that he had been suborned. Denyson's loose tongue got him a month in prison, awaiting Cromwell's pleasure, but no worse.[1]

An argument at Shelford in Essex, in February 1538, made trouble for William Smyth, one of Sir Roger Wentworth's servants. It took place, as these things so often did, in a 'victualling house' and started when William Hunte, a professional minstrel, advised John Tomkyns, saddler, to 'read and learn' the New Testament. Tomkyns declared himself unlearned; he would not meddle with it. Smyth took Hunte to task: 'though thou be naught thyself, entice none other men to be as bad as thou art.' Askéd what he meant, he challenged Hunte to deny that at a recent wedding he had sung a song railing against saints. Hunte not only admitted it but claimed that, now the King had driven out the pope, saints (who were popish creations) were done with. Smyth had often, he reminded him, heard this 'declared unto thee and other at thy parish church'. 'I pray thee,' said Smyth, 'were there not in times past as wise kings reigning over us as this King is now, and yet they all obeyed the pope's power. And I pray thee, who gave the King leave to put him down?' This very pointed question – the great question of the hour to which to this day no really successful answer has been offered by historians – got Smyth sent up to Cromwell, but again it seems that nothing further happened to him.[2] The same fate befell a Devon man, William Cater, who was denounced for calling a parson 'an heretic, and let him take good heed of his preaching, for the world will not prove as he thinketh it will, and that he will be punished for his preaching'.[3] Perhaps the most striking testimony to an entrenched conservatism in a person of mark comes from the words of a judge, Sir William Shelley, spoken in the Common Pleas to a fellow-judge and fellow-conservative, Sir Anthony Fitzherbert, in November 1534: 'I can tell you news. These new books of heresy shall be called in, and who as doth after keep tbem shall be taken for an heretic.' He mused about some dubiously orthodox people in his own county 'whom he

[1] SP 1/134, fos. 298–300; 135, fo. 237 (LP xiii. I. 1509; II. 194).
[2] SP 1/130, fo. 151–2 (LP xiii. I. 615).   [3] SP 1/154, fo. 181 (LP xiv. II. 540).

would common withal at his coming home', and expressed glee at the manner in which one 'Dr Nicholas the Italian' (Nicholas del Burgo) had routed some Lutherans in a disputation. Though he was at once informed that that disputation had never taken place, he paid no attention but repeated his satisfaction at the heretics' discomfiture and went on to attack Robert Barnes.[1] Nothing, of course, was done about Shelley at this time or any other;[2] of all the Tudors, only Mary ever dismissed a judge for the sake of his private views. But when judges of the Common Pleas were so manifestly unsympathetic to the reform, tradition had plenty of teeth left and could bite.[3]

For, of course, the trouble with all this talk and temper was that it could so easily get beyond words and produce real disorder. Old Dr Benger was a man of testy habit whom the sight of a good fire reminded only of the use to which it might be put against the visiting preacher and other 'new-learned men'; when he got into an argument, he soon promised that this new learning, which had already led to some strife, would 'in time to come...set men by the ears and cause broken heads'.[4] Very similar were the words spoken by Dan William Wynchelsea, a monk of St Augustine's, Canterbury: the gloomy and ominous forecast came readily to mind.[5] Henry Letherand, a vicar of Newark who ultimately, in the long aftermath of the Pilgrimage of Grace, succeeded in getting himself executed, spent four years in bitter battle against innovations, calling in even Scottish friars to denounce all books published *cum privilegio regis*, advising the use of daggers against their promoters, and exciting people to resistance by declaring that whatever King and Parliament and archbishop of Canterbury might do to the contrary of 'the holy pope of Rome' would be heresy.[6] The only wonder must be that he was suffered so long. Thomas Corthop at Harwich similarly declaimed against 'these new learned fellows', 'these new preachers nowadays that doth preach their three sermons in a day', lamenting 'such

---

[1] SP 1/239, fo. 83 (*LP Add.* 953).
[2] He remained on the bench till he died in 1548/9 (E. Foss, *The Judges of England 1066–1870*, 611). Foss records that Shelley was a humourist on the bench; the example he gives shows that this description has the usual ghastly implications.
[3] Cf. the part played by Fitzherbert in the campaign against another advanced preacher, Edward Large (below, pp. 378–9).
[4] See below, pp. 317–18.
[5] SP 1/88, fo. 19 (*LP* vii. 1608); the *LP* dating to 1534 is purely conjectural and probably too early.
[6] SP 1/82, fos. 235–6; 116, fo. 171; 135, fo. 141 (*LP* vii. 261; xii. I. 537; xiii. II. 156).

divisions and seditions among us as never were seen in this realm', while doing his best to keep these divisions in being.[1] One understands his chagrin at having to deal with people who 'would not regard nor believe the sayings of the captains of the Church, but when a newfangled fellow doth come and show a new story, they do believe'. This sounds familiar enough in the twentieth century, but a vicar who was recorded as hammering away at this theme for at least six months, over and over again, contributed little towards keeping the peace. And John Divale, whose conservative passions have already been mentioned, went the whole hog of consistency: applying 'his school of fence', he declared he would fight anyone who proposed to preach the New Testament after the new fashion.[2] Shocked to the core, and deeply frightened by the innovators, the conservative ranks rallied in violent language and every possibility of violent action.

Certainly the promoters of the often despised new learning were a disturbing influence, and it is clear enough that these changes of faith and observance caused even more unrest than the great political readjustment in England's relations with Rome. The many denunciations of bigoted traditionalists testify to their existence, but also to the existence of passionate innovators who did the denouncing and in turn maintained the disturbed state of mind so prevalent in the parishes. The very fact that the changes burst upon the country without much preparation and in the wake of recently revived attacks upon the remnants of Lollardy, to which the new programme bore at least a superficial resemblance, must have helped to create especial consternation. The government's policy, which involved at least a measure of religious reform, utterly confused those who until very recently had been repeatedly taught that any doubting of what were now dubbed superstitious practices amounted to the vilest kind of heresy; at the same time, it helped to advance men whose fervour made them particularly likely to upset more conventional minds. We have come to recognise again that the Reformation of the 1530's was by no means only a political event, an act of state: genuine convictions and real religious feelings manifested themselves from the start.[3] The men promoting an evangelical revival (whether Erasmians or not, and by no means all can be

[1] SP 1/99, fos. 200–4 (*LP* ix. 1059).
[2] SP 1/151, fo. 156 (*LP* xiii. I. 897).
[3] A. G. Dickens, *The English Reformation* (1964).

allocated to that essentially reasonable and moderate group) formed a sizable body influential well beyond their size because they had the effective support of Cromwell and Cranmer. What has not, perhaps been of late stressed sufficiently is the fact that, partly because of Cromwell's difficult position and interrupted career, they achieved less in the way of positive renewal than they accomplished in disturbing the indifference of a people by and large content to live and die in the comforts of an unthinking formalism. Despite the support – itself intermittent and affected by the exigencies of politics – which they received from above, the early reformers had a sufficiently hard time of it (even if one omits the few extremists commemorated by John Foxe who fell foul of everybody and actually died for their religion) to underline the threat to order, peace and obedience which their activities represented. From Cromwell's point of view, the disturbances provoked by these sincere and heedless men must have been particularly exasperating because he shared their faith in the ends in view. Too much of his time was spent in saving his troublesome allies from themselves.

Not unexpectedly, Latimer's little group of zealots proved particularly good at running into difficulties. Their activities, as we have seen, often provoked conservative reactions, and since these could command the support of some of the local gentry the consequences could be serious. In the eyes of respectable men, Latimer's preachers were guilty of 'misorder, crafty and colourable preaching', and the bishop had been indiscreet in his choice of men. Thus he had, allegedly, admitted among the preachers a friar banished before this for 'his abominable living and daily usage of drunkenness', while excluding learned doctors of divinity much respected in the diocese.[1] Three men in particular caused real disturbances. James Asche, parson of Stanton, gave his many enemies a welcome handle when he said in a sermon 'that if the King our sovereign lord did not go forth with his laws as he began, he would call the King Antichrist', and another time that 'the King our sovereign lord was naught, the bishops and abbots naught, and himself naught too', a statement of universal Christian humility which could be made to sound like treason. At least he was presented at Great Malvern Quarter Sessions on 1 June 1536 for such sayings and there bound, in one hundred marks, to appear before the King's Council;[2] at the same time, Sheriff

[1] Thomas Bell to Bishop Stokesley, 9 June 1536: SP 1/104, fo. 157 (*LP* x. 1099).
[2] SP 1/104, fo. 93 (*LP* x. 1027).

Bell urged the bishop of London, a safe conservative, to make sure that the duke of Norfolk would hear of it.[1] The trials of Edward Large show that such charges need not always be believed;[2] at any rate, Asche seems to have been troubled no further.

John Erley, whom we have already met, was another ex-friar promoted by Latimer. He got into worse trouble as early as the summer of 1533 when, at the instigation of Mr Mullins, parson of Trowbridge (Wilts.), he was presented for preaching heretically all round the west country, was handed over to the bishop of Bath and Wells, and underwent the humiliations of public penance.[3] But such things did not put these evangelicals off, and Erley was still active at Salisbury in 1541 when he was one of a group examined for suspected rebellion in religion. The investigators discovered a letter of his to one Mr Mathew, an upholsterer in Cornhill (London), which really removes Erley from the class of suspects into that of unquestionable sectaries. Mathew (Erley wrote) was 'not only associate and in company daily with such manner of men as be favourable to the word of God but also with such as can partly delate whether that it be of any likelihood that God's word shall have free passage or no', and he was to give the bearer any news to 'the comfort and consolation of good willers' so that 'we shall not be without it'. To anyone at all familiar with the atmosphere of sixteenth-century sects, the symptoms of an underground movement are clear enough.[4] Since John Foxe missed Erley, we know no more about him, but by the same token we may presume that he escaped any form of martyrdom. Clearly, however, he had – if anything – grown more radical over the years; the punishment of 1533 had achieved nothing. The best known of Latimer's preachers was Thomas Garrett whom (since he was burned in July 1540) Foxe did include in his book.[5]

[1] See above, p. 35, n. 1.   [2] Below, pp. 375–80.

[3] SP 1/79, fos. 124–5 (LP vi. 1192). Nevertheless, after he had done his penance he dined every day at the bishop's palace and kept his ears open, in order to report all sorts of dubious talk to Cromwell (unsolicited). The bishop's secretary in particular was a ribald: when he told of the Princess Elizabeth's birth he said that 'if he had lain with her [Anne Boleyn] he would have gotten a boy, or else he would have meddled with her till his eyes did start out of his head'. Though this remark distressed Erley and earned its perpetrator a rebuke from the bishop's steward, it went round the household as a great joke.

[4] Erley's activities of 1541 emerge from a report of commissioners and attached papers among the Council archives (St Ch 2/34/28).

[5] Foxe, v. 421 ff.

Throughout the 1530's he followed a much troubled career as an advanced preacher, annoying Bishop Longland by intruding into the diocese of Lincoln in early 1536,[1] upsetting Sheriff Bell in Gloucestershire a few months later,[2] and becoming parson of Honey Lane parish in London, before the whirlpools of Cromwell's fall carried him to the stake, in the company of Barnes and Jerome.[3]

The vigour and recklessness of the advanced preachers, usually described as being light and indiscreet, often enough brought them to the notice of the authorities, and not surprisingly that violent man, John Bale, was amongst them. In November 1536, Bale was compelled to offer a very long excuse and explanation for what he had said from various pulpits.[4] He had upset people by his exposition of the creed and by some less than respectful remarks about St Thomas Aquinas. He explained that his failure to give Aquinas his full title was 'only the overslipping of my tongue', but he admitted going out of his way to attack Thomas's canonisation, for money only, by a pope about whose claimed primacy Aquinas had disseminated so much error. In fact, Bale had said that all who died 'in faith and testimony of the word of God were saints most lawfully canonised or authorised in the blood of Christ' and had clearly preached a lot of inflammatory stuff about ceremonies, prayers and observances which went well beyond the tenor of the 1536 Injunctions; but he denied that his words could be called contemptuous. Nor would he have been John Bale if he had not counterattacked vigorously, accusing his accusers, in much detail, of sympathising with the northern rebels. But in the event it was he who had to answer charges, not they. Of course, the experience did not stop him, and only a few months later more articles were gathered against him when Sir Humphrey Wingfield informed the duke of Suffolk that Bale's preaching was attracting the more volatile spirits on the duke's manor of Thornedon and causing those 'of good opinion' to fear upsets.[5]

There is no doubt that when in trouble such men regarded Cromwell as their best hope. Thomas Netter asked his protection against Ralph

[1] SP 1/103, fo. 304 (*LP* x. 891 [1]).

[2] He was one of those denounced as a 'light person' in Bell's letter to Stokesley (above, p. 35, n. 1), though in fact he was a doctor of divinity, a distinction which in a conservative Bell regarded as proof of excellence.

[3] *Grey Friars Chronicle*, ed J. G. Nichols (1852), 43, and above, p. 27, n. 3.

[4] SP 1/111, fos. 182–7 (*LP* xi. 1111).

[5] SP 1/114, fo. 54 (*LP* xii. I. 40).

Robinson, a Sussex parson. Netter had gone to the alehouse carrying an English psalter published *cum privilegio regali*. Taking exception to this, Robinson had charged him with heresy and had got the constable to put him in the stocks for two days, no light punishment. Robinson had spoken contemptuously of the King's privilege, but Netter, claiming to be too poor to sue his adversary at law, wished Cromwell to call both before him and see justice done.[1] Robert Wisdom, parson of All Saints, Oxford, protested in 1536 that he was being stopped from preaching truly by 'some malicious persons which are aggrieved to lose their glory and to give it to Christ'. He had not the means to seek the help of his distant ordinary (the bishop of Lincoln) and therefore asked Cromwell's; in view of Longland's well known conservatism, distance is not likely to have been the only reason for his choice of protector.[2] Cromwell saved him sufficiently, so that in 1543 Wisdom (who had moved to London) could once more get into trouble through his preaching. This time there was no Cromwell, and Wisdom found himself in the Lollards' Tower where he used his leisure to compose a long defence of his opinions.[3] In fact, he saved himself by recanting and lived to become archdeacon of Ely, dying in 1568.[4]

Cromwell may also have helped Sir Henry Parker's chaplain, persecuted by one of Bishop Stokesley's men and, in his employer's opinion, the only satisfactory promoter of the gospel in his part of Essex.[5] He certainly assisted William Hewytt, vicar of All Hallows, Cambridge. Hewytt had caused an uproar by suddenly offering communion in both kinds to all his congregation, using 'his mother's tongue' to consecrate the elements instead of observing the established custom ('which also, I suppose,' added the informant, 'is consonant with Scripture, or else it would not have been suffered so long time'). Some of Hewytt's people would not bear this and went to other churches, a practice always frowned upon as being disordered in itself and removing individuals from supervision. He explained himself on the following Sunday, saying that despite his natural timorousness and fear of 'worldly punishment' he was 'strengthened by the Holy Ghost so to set forth and bring to light the verity of the gospel'. Communion in both kinds

[1] SP 1/100, fos. 87–8 (*LP* ix. 1130) – probably some date in 1535.
[2] SP 1/105, fo. 104 (*LP* xi. 138).
[3] J. Strype, *Ecclesiastical Memorials*, i, Doc. 115. The document was among Foxe's unused papers.
[4] Foxe, v. 831.   [5] SP 1/106, fo. 226 (*LP* xi. 515).

was, he had become convinced by direct divine intervention, obliga-
tory on Christians, notwithstanding what General Councils (which he
termed devilish councils) might have said. 'He would be judged by no
man's laws.' Cromwell was asked to spare time among his 'busy pains'
to cleanse the Church of such seditious persons, the complainants
adding a straight reminder that people like Hewytt promoted dangers
to the realm by preventing people from being 'all of one mind and all
of one opinion'.[1]

However, Cromwell heard not only from Hewytt's accusers but also
from the man himself who had been treated very roughly indeed.[2] If he
is to be believed, he was writing from 'a deep dungell where all venom
beasts creep about his legs', fettered by the legs and neck, unable to see
the light of day or even move, 'having not so much as a poor stool or
bed to rest upon', starved ('unto this hour no bread hath done me either
good or hurt since my ingression'), always 'alone without company'.
He denied that his actions had caused the sedition alleged and charged
his accusers and the vicechancellor of the University with hostile bias.
Only the compassion of the gaoler, touched by the sight of so maltreated a prisoner tied to a post 'both day and night', had given him
this chance to write. Perhaps so: but the handwriting of this letter is
exceptionally firm and clear. Hewytt claimed to have been Cromwell's
devoted adherent for sixteen years (since 1521?) and prayed his aid. He
submitted himself to the lord privy seal but could not forbear to conclude by demanding, in the effronterous manner common among these
converts to revivalism, that his bishop (Goodrich, a favourer of reform,
but, needless to say, no friend to self-appointed innovators) should
show 'how the horrible sin of sacrilege can be avoided in ministering of
one kind only against both the practice and authority of the primitive
Church'. We need have no doubt that Hewytt was an enthusiast and at
least a potential troublemaker, the sort of assistant whom a reforming
government, trying to shift great masses of conservative opinion, can
afford to do without. However, Cromwell heard him, and Hewytt
returned from his dungeon to his living which he held long enough to
resign only in the reign of Mary.[3]

[1] SP 1/118, fo. 90 (LP xii. I. 876). The informant, a marshal of King's Hall, added that
the vicar of Caxton had last Easter Day ministered the sacrament to the laity by using
ale in place of wine.
[2] SP 1/118, fo. 91 (LP xii. I. 877).
[3] I owe this information to Mrs Felicity Heal.

Another whom Cromwell's favour preserved for even better things was Matthew Parker, troubled in 1538 for his preaching in his pulpit at Stoke by Clare (Suffolk). His enemy was one Dr Stokes, himself recently imprisoned because he was suspected of insufficient ardour for the new order and freed on Cromwell's orders; now Cromwell was called in to stop him hunting down Parker. The case usefully demonstrates that Cromwell was at heart less concerned with advancing this party or that than with preserving the peace and doing reasonable justice to all. Stoke by Clare, a village variously declared to be solidly behind Stokes and solidly behind Parker, seems to have ceased troubling his attention.[1]

That those who disliked the changes could fall foul of the King's law is well enough known; but criminal process could also be used against the innovators. Thus Robert Ward, another of the many friars who followed Luther's example, was indicted of heresy at Chelmsford Sessions in the spring of (probably) 1536, at the instigation of the parson within whose parish he had preached the offending sermon.[2] According to himself, he had only promoted the gospel and attacked idle ceremonies, though he had certainly done so before these practices came under the official disapproval of the 1536 Injunctions; especially he had spoken against holy water because another friar had earlier told people that it 'washed away venial sin'. Altogether, he had really only inveighed against popery and should never have been indicted. But even from what he admitted it is clear that he proclaimed Lutheran ideas.

I say to you: to trust to have forgiveness of your sins for the doing of this penance thus enjoined by man, forgetting the promise of the favour that we have obtained by Christ, it is superstitious robbery of the honour of Christ's blood...[Works are required] not by the way of satisfaction but to the laud and praise of God...Only Christ is our saviour and whole satisfaction and the price that hath bought us from sin and pain.

The words alleged in the indictment were these: that it was wrong to believe 'that satisfaction is necessary and profitable for the wealth of Christian souls; for the truth is contrary, for satisfaction is but a superstition, and that only to believe in Christ is sufficient for our salvation'.

[1] Parker was commended by the bishop of Dover (SP 1/139, fo. 212: [LP xiii. II. 935]). For Stokes's case see below, pp. 140–1.
[2] SP 2/R, fo. 21 (LP viii. 625).

These do sound like a deliberate and well-designed perversion or mis-hearing, charging him with a Lutheranism vulnerable under the heresy laws, but even what he admitted was, by the standards of March 1536, incendiary enough. We do not know whether he was convicted on the indictment or even tried; he certainly survived, presumably rescued by Cromwell, to be a stumbling block to the commissioners who in 1540–1541 were enforcing the Act of Six Articles in London.[1]

In April 1538, Cranmer wrote to Cromwell that six laymen, from two villages in Kent, had been indicted at Canterbury Sessions, for what offence he fails to say; but that the real reason lay in their being 'fautors of the new doctrine (as they call it)'.[2] The archbishop hoped that if the pretended offences could not 'be duly proved' Cromwell would help free the men from this indictment. 'For if the King's subjects within this realm which favour God's word shall be unjustly vexed at Sessions, it will be no marvel though much sedition be daily engendered within this realm.' The point could be taken either way: the favourers of the new doctrine were themselves inevitably liable to become disturbers of the peace and were only indicted because they upset their neighbours. But the approach was surely the right one to take with Cromwell whose chief concern was with sedition, not doctrine, and it looks as though he saved both these six and Robert Ward from the hostility of justices and juries.

As one would expect, the friends of the new order included the characteristic representatives of passion, selfrighteousness and oddity, the sort of men who embraced innovation for reasons more plainly connected with their own state of mind than with any rational attach-ment to Scripture properly understood or to the new learning. Men of this sort always ride on the backs of radical movements and prove an embarrassment to the more balanced and sensible leaders of reform. One such, for instance, was Gervase Tyndale, schoolmaster of Grantham, no relation (so far as I know) to the famous William. In November 1535, Tyndale wrote to Cromwell a pompous and rather nasty letter in Latin, complaining of a local priest, Dr Stanley, who had displeased him.[3] This *doctorculus* had preached in the parish church of Grantham ('in quo oppido humaniores istas artes professus sum') in favour of

---

[1] Foxe, v. 443–4, 447–8. The Robert Ward whose recantation is printed ibid. App. XI, was clearly no friar and not the same person, despite the note, ibid. 831.
[2] SP 1/131, fos. 239, 241 (*LP* xiii. I. 865).   [3] SP 1/98, fos. 190–1 (*LP* ix. 740).

purgatory and masses for the dead, impressing the horrors of purgatory on his appreciative audience by calling in Etna and Vesuvius for purposes of comparison. These classical allusions pleased the schoolmaster less than one might have supposed. He described the sermon at length in very superior fashion, 'et quod maiorem mihi risum movit, suae stultitiae assertorem citavit Augustinum'. Tyndale at the time remonstrated with Stanley, without any trouble arising, but heard later that behind his back the priest was cursing him for being touched by the Saxon contagion ('ut illi vocant') – as indeed he seems to have been. His real grievance was that his schoolboys had gone elsewhere and he had lost his livelihood. He claimed to have done some work for Cromwell and the earl of Rutland in investigating some friars suspected of necromancy, but it is not apparent that either his service or the page of fulsome praise bestowed on the minister for his expected favour to the pure religion got Tyndale anything of substance.

Or there was John Palmes, owner of the parsonage of Bentworth in Hampshire, whose invariable signature, 'your blind man', may as probably have been intended to refer to his spiritual as to his physical state.[1] His trouble was that he had married, yet wished to occupy the benefice and preach, even though by his own admission he had never taken holy orders. He claimed (in January 1539) that by royal letters patent he had been 'clearly acquitted, discharged and delivered from all bondage and encumbrances brought into Christ's Church by the usurped power of the bishop of Rome';[2] yet Bishop Gardiner of Winchester had now cited him for his marriage. Since he was not a clerk it seems more likely that he was cited for improperly exercising clerical functions in the living, of which presumably he only owned the impropriation. He told Cromwell he would resign it if in the lord privy seal's opinion 'a wife and a benefice may not stand together'. By all accounts – and allowing for the fact that the information does not enable one to discover his exact standing and position – he was in the wrong, and his real grievance came out at the end: 'They have both temporal lands and tithes spiritual, yet may no wedded man take one crumb that falleth from their board.' He followed up his first approach with regular monthly letters: he was the only man in Hampshire to

[1] SP 1/142, fo. 135 (*LP* xiv. I. 120).
[2] What this alleged licence might be is entirely obscure. Palmes does not appear in the Faculty Office Register.

preach against the pope; a local priest had lived for twenty years with his concubine and had had children by her, without anyone saying 'black is his eye'; for a year he had bombarded the vicegerent, yet Cromwell's letters had had no more effect on Gardiner than direct appeals. Out of the blue Palmes introduced a quarrel with his cousin John Coke, registrar of Winchester and a follower of Sir John Wallop (an influential conservative courtier). Cromwell again wrote on his petitioner's behalf, but Coke continued the persecution, saying Palmes was no parson and should occupy no benefice. Why should the bishops object to a 'woolman' preaching, seeing that this had been the practice of the primitive Church? But he had now surrendered his earlier ambition actually to preach and only asked to be allowed 'a lecture of Scripture' in Bentworth church or elsewhere, so that he would not have to bury the Lord's talent 'which no man can wrap in his handkerchief without danger of damnation'.[1] The mixture of religious obsession, ingrained private grievance, and the matter of property is characteristic enough; the fact that Cromwell gave him some assistance possibly reflects upon his readiness to promote the new doctrine, but in this case more probably may be suspected to result from his willingness to embarrass his enemy Gardiner. Gardiner won: by late February 1540, Palmes was out of the living and by £14 10s 4d a year poorer.[2]

Hampshire seemed to breed these semi-priests: Robert Vaws, parson of Over Wallop, in 1538 defended himself against the charge that he was 'non sacerdos'.[3] 'If I might see a clear description,' he declared in a formal answer, 'and a perfect definition of where a very priest is in Christ Jesus,' he would admit to falling short. However, the archbishop of Canterbury had instituted him in the living and admitted him to the cure of souls there, and he lacked nothing of the form 'of the making or ordaining of a priest or overseer in Christ's Church which was used in the antique and apostolic Church, not yet fallen to Antichrist, being pure and uncorrupt of all popish ceremonies'. All this has a pretty suspicious air, as does his willingness to have it proved by the word of God

---

[1] SP 1/142, fo. 223; 144, fos. 2–3; BM, Tit. B. i, fo. 80 (*LP* xiv. I. 206, 412, 890).
[2] *Registrum Stephani Gardiner et Johannis Poynet, Episcoporum Wintoniensium*, ed. H. Chitty (Canterbury and York Society, vol. 37, 1930), 70–1, 114, 166. His successor, the ex-abbot of Beaulieu, was presented by the King, the advowson being in his hands during the minority of the owner James Palmes. An odd omplication.
[3] BM, Cleo. E. iv, fo. 153 (*LP* viii. 20). Although he was charged with words spoken in January 1535, the proceedings took place two years later (see next note).

whether he lacked any proper attributes of priesthood. One must conclude that he could not, more conventionally, prove the fact of ordination. As he said, when he was asked for the dispensation which would entitle him to hold the benefice, he exhibited to Gardiner 'the Testament of our Lord Jesus Christ...as a sufficient dispensation for the holding of my spiritual office and the charge and cure of the church of Over Wallop'. Also, he was married. In short, by all the law of the Church, still solely valid, he had no right to benefice or pulpit. His activities and pretensions, and his shrill protests, underline the confusion into which ecclesiastical affairs could get in the situation produced by the upheavals of the 1530's. Vaws' preaching, apart from being unauthorised, was clearly highly radical, against candles and saints and in favour of what he called 'the new law'. It is no wonder that Gardiner was after him, and in this case Cromwell does not appear to have intervened. Vaws, who had occupied the living since October 1531, was deprived of it before October 1538.[1]

In conclusion we may briefly look at the state of mind that could be produced in the laity by all this preaching of new doctrines. In May 1538, information was laid before the mayor and aldermen of Cambridge against one Robert Towson for that he had attacked candles and images. Allegedly he had said: 'The devil blind that rood that cannot see at noonday except he have candles set before him' and that till these last six years 'there was never a good man within the realm of England, and if any were they were burned'. Asked if the King was not a good man, he replied, 'no, all was naught till within this six years'. He also attacked monasteries and hoped to see them all down. There were several witnesses, and upon examination Towson 'obstinately defended' all these sayings.[2] There may be echoes of Lollardy here, or touches of nascent Protestantism, but in reality what he had been guilty of was a muddled outburst stemming from the sort of sermon he was likely enough to hear in Cambridge.

In sum, it is plain that the first decade of the English Reformation produced enough matter 'to set men by the ears' – enough arguments, accusations, scurrility, conviction, abuse and unsettlement to guarantee every possibility of unrest and disturbance in a country always hard to control and impossible to police efficiently. Any thought that the political and doctrinal changes were simply and silently absorbed by

---

[1] *Registrum Gardiner et Poynet*, 71, 113.   [2] SP 1/132, fo. 89 (*LP* xiii. I. 975).

the people must be forgotten. Many resented and, to the best of their ability, resisted the innovations; others who welcomed them were fewer but noisier and by their frequent excess of zeal provoked reactions in village and town which, taken together, could amount to the sort of violence that might endanger the security of the King's government. There was a real problem facing the King and his advisers, a real problem of disaffection, disobedience and disturbance. No doubt the problem can now in retrospect be seen to have been far from enormous, but at the time only its reality could be taken for granted, not its size. What made the situation even more delicate was the presence, behind the effects of real events, of fanciful suspicion and irrational fear.

2

RUMOUR, MAGIC AND
PROPHECY

WITH A NATION so volatile, at a time when even the truth of events
was demolishing concord and threatening all good order, no government could afford to ignore the less rational attacks on the general state
of mind. It was necessary not only to put down disaffection, but also to
prevent the dissemination of false hopes and fears. The revised 'charge'
to inferior courts displayed an urgent, almost an hysterical, concern:[1]

Ye shall also enquire of tale-tellers and counterfeiters of news that import any
hurt or damage to the King's person, or to any of his nobles and councillors,
or to move disorder between his grace and his nobles or nobility, or whereby
any nobleman or any his grace's councillors may incur the infamy and
slander of the common people. These kind of people be to be abhorred
and hated of any honest man. They go about utterly to extirp love, concord
and quiet whereby any commonwealth flourishes, and to sow in their place
sedition, disorder, variance and trouble – as the prophet witnesseth, fearing
whose tongues be full of lying and slandering; their feet be swift to do mischief, kill and slay. It is no way to reform evil if any were meant, but rather
to kindle and increase it, and many times it procureth him that is gentle,
loving and kind to be ungentle and cruel, and to do that that was never intended or thought. Yet it is no means to tame a lion with beating or pricking.
In any wise note ye well such devilish persons and suffer them not to live
among you. Such people God hateth and hath banished them his most
glorious sight for ever and will reward them at length with eternal damnation, as the apostle testifieth. Be not ye, for the love of God, light of credence
of such things. News, if they be naught, such as import hurt to any man,
come they never so late come too soon. If there be or hath been any among
you that hath reported or told any such news, by the oath that ye have made
ye shall present his name, to whom, when and where he spake it.

Such candidates for eternal damnation did indeed abound. The tales,
readily invented and readily believed, did not always have an obvious

---

[1] BM, Add. MS 48047, fos. 63v–64. The 'charge' is discussed below, pp. 337–8.

political purpose, but their effect was rarely free from political implications. Sometimes they could be stopped. In February 1537, the town of Buckingham was visited by a rumour to the effect that Aylesbury church should be pulled down and its jewels confiscated. Since it was market day, many people had heard it; it was 'hotly talked of' and caused much unease. Sir John Baldwin, investigating, traced the rumour through a barber's boy to his mother and thence to the 'common bakehouse'. However, the wife of the parish clerk brought peace by explaining that her husband had 'kept the church all that week and had no such knowledge'.[1] Rumours of an intended reorganisation of parishes with consequent destruction of churches reached also a village in Northamptonshire where the parson wished to evade his duty to maintain a priest in an outlying chapel on the grounds that the King and Council were 'about to convert three parishes into one'; they had made a start, he said (untruthfully) by pulling down a church near Cripplegate in London.[2] He had meant no harm – all he hoped for was to prevent the parish from forcing him to do his duty – but he had upset the locality. Even less political was the story spread by Robert ap Howell at Oxford in March 1537, to the effect that at Abingdon some men had been killed and others badly wounded by the fall of a wall in the church. This brought a procession of wives from Oxford 'with noise enough, to bury their dead husbands and...help them that was hurt', all the makings of a riot; yet nobody was injured and no wall had collapsed. 'So the wives of Oxford were much gladder to see their whole husbands than they were sorry to hear the rumour.' The story ended happily for everyone except ap Howell, in Oxford Castle awaiting Cromwell's decision.[3]

Even more upsetting than simple rumour was any tale of magic or necromancy – and those tales were many, quite independent of any political implications. Sorcery and 'juggling' were widely believed in and too widely practised;[4] and it is surprising how many country priests dabbled in such games. Richard Holland, parson of Yatson (Somerset), was reliably reported to have done so.[5] The friars of Grantham, who had conspired against their warden, were thought to be

[1] SP 1/116, fo. 75 (LP xii. I. 456).   [2] SP 1/134, fo. 29v (LP xiii. I. 1508).
[3] SP 1/130, fo. 95 (LP xiii. I. 555), misdated by LP to 1538.
[4] For a discussion of sorcery in its context cf. K. V. Thomas, Religion and the Decline of Magic (1971), ch. 8.
[5] LP. xiii. II. 815.

47

similarly engaged.[1] A monk named Sheldon involved a whole gang in Huntingdonshire in conjuring; one of them was an old man of Hatfield, outside the informing justice's jurisdiction, which made full detection difficult, but it looks as though Cromwell rightly ignored a fussy and pompous letter.[2] One Threder, a black friar of Oxford, claimed to be able to find lost or stolen goods by divination, with the result that crosses were falling down all over the place as men dug underneath them on Threder's instructions. He was arrested and 'his evil books suddenly...taken from him', to teach him a lesson.[3] Tales of buried treasure found their usual tally of credulous believers. At Ockley (Northants.) Sir William Parr learned of some secret meetings organised by the parson, Henry Cowpar, and investigated, but there was no sedition or plotting, only necromancy and digging for money in places indicated by Cowpar's wizardry. Once he started looking, Parr found another priest in the neighbourhood quite unconnected with Cowpar, who had books of magic but had not so far practised; he meant to do so as soon as he found 'a trusty fellow to accompany him'.[4] I know of no such books surviving now (though the attraction of this sort of thing remains almost as strong), but from another information we learn that they told of such things as 'finding out of treasure hid, consecrating of rings with stones in them, and consecrating of a crystal stone wherein a child shall look and see many things.'[5] Practices of this sort got two men indicted in the King's Bench for cheating three fools at Islington. As usual, they claimed to know of hidden treasure worth £200 to each of their victims, but it needed careful handling. It had been buried by a man whose soul was now in purgatory, for which reason it was being guarded by 'a devil of hell'. Thus there was need of much fasting and praying and offering to saints to release the late owner's soul, after which 'the fiend of hell shall have no power to keep the said treasure'. For this, of course, the necromancers needed money, and they collected 40s. This was their mistake, for mere cozening without money taken was not indictable. There turned out to be no treasure, 'et sic predictos 40

[1] Merriman, i. 415.
[2] SP 1/78, fo. 177 (*LP* vi. 1023).
[3] SP 1/103, fos. 234v, 274, 304 (*LP* x. 804, 850, 891). Cromwell heard of him through Bishop Longland of Lincoln. Threder would appear to have been connected with the University, for Longland asked that he should be dealt with by the commissary of Oxford, 'a scholar'.
[4] SP 1/126, fo. 177 (*LP* xii. II. 1102).   [5] SP 1/97, fo. 128 (*LP* ix. 551).

solidos amiserunt, contra pacem regis etc.'. The jury found a true bill, but there is no record of a trial.[1]

In January 1538, a sinister discovery in a London churchyard resulted in an investigation by a formidable trio – Cromwell's secretary Thomas Wriothesley, an alderman of London (Paul Withipoll), and the learned Dr Thomas Starkey.[2] On Thursday the 3rd, a crowd of people gathered around what seemed to be a half-buried child. Greatly daring, the parish clerk dug it up and found 'a piece of cloth knit like a winding-sheet' and in it the wax image of a child with two pins stuck into it. The witness, Fulk Vaughan, took it to one Pole, a scrivener in Crooked Lane, known to be versed in such matters. Pole not only displayed the required knowledge but also a professional contempt for an amateur bungler: it was, he said, 'made to waste one, but (quoth he) he that made it was not his craft's master, for he should have put it either in horse dung or in a dunghill'. Vaughan expressed surprise, but Pole assured him that the magic would work, though the arrival of his wife prevented further revelations. Pressed by his examiners, Vaughan explained that Pole had long set up as a magician, claiming to be able to do many things and especially to find hidden money. But it seems that an eye was being kept on him: Cromwell had before this interfered with his trade by taking away his books, though this left him able to conjure in various ways. Pole had several times tried to persuade Vaughan to come with him for buried treasure (it seems that two men at least were always required for this magic) and had proffered mysterious talk of having got 'the King's highness' mother's money' as well as assurances 'that he had friends and acquaintance enough for all their purposes'. The wax image seems to have intervened just in time to prevent Vaughan getting in too deep with one whom the lord privy seal was watching – though whether Cromwell's interest had to do with the scrivener's name (there is no evidence that he was connected with the Pole family) or stemmed only from his determination to stamp out these trades in superstition cannot be known.

All this may seem small beer and of little interest either to the reader or to a government engaged in a political and religious revolution. But whatever may be true of the reader, it was matter which Cromwell could not ignore. The line between wild rumour and foolish necromancy on the one hand, and public trouble with treason in the offing on

---

[1] KB 9/539/13.　　　　[2] E 36/120, fo. 71 (*LP* xiii. I. 41).

the other, was tenuous, as the complicated story of William Neville will illustrate. It happened in 1532, just as Cromwell was gathering the reins of government into his hands, and it may well have warned him at an early date that practices of magic and involvements with wizards whom a rational person could only despise might too readily hide possibilities involving murder, ambition and disaffection.

The story is confused and, as the way tends to be in such things, partially obscure; the conflicting and insufficient evidence makes it hard to know the truth.[1] There is quite a list of *dramatis personae*, beginning with three of the third Lord Latimer's fifteen younger brothers – William, George and Christopher Neville. The last hardly appears, and George got only mildly involved, but William was the centre of the storm. On the strength of his *Castle of Pleasure* (published in 1518), the *Dictionary of National Biography* calls him a poet, but his real preoccupations seem to have been an exceptional ambition for a title and an unhealthy interest in magic. The news of a 'bruiter' of Welsh pedigrees and prophecies was just the right sort of bait for him, and at one time he tried to make himself a cloak of invisibility of two layers of linen with one between of buckskin, the whole to be treated with a mixture in which horse bones, skin, chalk, rosin and powdered glass were the chief ingredients. The search for these materials fell to his chaplain Edward Legh who in the denunciation which first revealed the conspiracy feelingly remembered looking for days for dead horses. The wizards with whom Neville got involved included William Wade whom he employed to 'labour in astronomy for him', a certain Nashe of Cirencester (by trade a caulker), and especially Richard Jones, an Oxford scholar deeply immersed in alchemy and sorcery. His chamber

---

[1] The evidence consists of the following documents: Edward Legh's denunciation of William Neville (E 163/10/20: 3 Dec. 1532); depositions upon interrogatories taken on Dec. 30th from William Neville (SP 1/72, fos. 200–3: the marginal notes are not, as *LP* maintain, in the King's hand), George Neville (ibid. fo. 204), Richard Jones (ibid. fos. 206–7: *not* Thomas Wood, as stated in *LP*), and Thomas Wood (ibid. 196–9); a letter from Jones to Cromwell, of early to mid 1533 (SP 1/73, fos. 1–2); the report of Roger Tyler's arrest on 12 Jan. 1533 (SP 1/69, fo. 13, misdated 1532 in *LP*); a letter probably from Tyler to Jones, of about the same date (SP 1/73, fos. 3–4); a report of further discoveries, dated 21 March 1533 (SP 1/75, fo. 38); an appeal from Legh to the King's Council, Feb. 1533 or later (ibid. fo. 39); and a petition from Jones's brother Roger to Cromwell of about mid-1533 (SP 1/238, fo. 119). The denunciation and depositions are listed in the office catalogue of Cromwell's papers (E 36/139, fo. 48v). *LP* references to these documents, in the sequence as listed, are: v. 1679, 1680, 712, 1681; vi. 257–8; *Add.* 863; vii. 923 (xxi).

contained all the usual props – stills, alembics and other glassware, a sceptre needed for the calling up of 'the four kings', a white metal 'image', and a box with a snake-skin inside. Also, of course, books of magic. When he got into trouble, Jones claimed never to have meddled with anything 'save to make the philosopher's stone' and offered within a year and a bit to make the King all the silver and gold he could want. Jones had an accomplice, one Roger Tyler, whom the commissary of Oxford described as a 'simple person and a poor body'. Also involved was Thomas Wood, a close acquaintance of Neville's, and various walking-on parts were played by an aged man of Warwick, by the keeper of the castle there, and by assorted servants. In the wings stood the eldest brother, John Lord Latimer who had succeeded his father in 1530; he never came on stage but in effect dominated the whole play. In assessing the government's concern it is worth remembering that he was a man of influence in the north where he was to play a highly ambiguous part in the Pilgrimage of Grace.

William Neville maintained that he got into the toils of these people in December 1531 when some spoons were found missing in his London lodgings and he consulted Nashe about their whereabouts. This tale, if true, sufficiently reveals his inclinations. Nashe seems to have known his man and took occasion at once to play on his private ambitions. He warned Neville that his present wife would not live long, told him that he would next marry a wealthy heiress of the Graystock family, and prophesied that within five years he would succeed his brother as Lord Latimer. Neville told his two brothers of these prophecies, at which they showed a lively interest which throws some light on relations between the numerous offspring of the second baron. They decided to meet Nashe together and for that purpose rode to Oxford, where Nashe, in conversation, dropped Jones's name, describing him as a good physician. Thus when Neville's wife duly fell ill (a contingency that could be allowed for in the sixteenth century), he called in Jones and predictably took the opportunity to consult him about the future, no doubt hoping to have Nashe's prophecies confirmed. Jones indeed obliged and was careful to make these promises more precise. The first Mrs Neville might be 'patched forth' for ten years, but no more (again quite a safe bet); the second would be under fifteen years of age when he married her and bring him 500 marks in land; he was to be Lord Latimer and indeed one greater than a baron. Such, at least, was Neville's version of his first encounter with Jones; later he claimed that he had found these prophets often quite wrong about his personal affairs. Jones, on the other hand, maintained that at their first meeting his client showed a chief interest in the possibility of having a ring made 'that should bring a man in favour with his prince'. He said that Wolsey had owed his position to such a ring and remembered that 'Master Cromwell, when he and I were servants in my lord cardinal's house, did haunt to the company of one that was seen in your faculty: and shortly after no man so great with my lord cardinal as Master Cromwell was'. Jones possibly made this up in order to turn Cromwell's anger against Neville, but the tale has the sound of truth; Neville was just the sort of man to believe that careers were made by magic. Jones said further that he played up to Neville with talk of the books he had, especially the works of Solomon which gave guidance on the making of such rings. However, no rings were made.

Meanwhile Neville did not feel inclined to put all his eggs into Jones's basket but consulted William Wade, another 'kalcar or a wise man among common people', who also foretold various things about Neville's good fortune. The earldom of Warwick was now mentioned for the first time. Back went Neville to Jones and by speaking well of Wade and disclosing his prophecies stirred the Oxford wizard to better efforts. Pretending ignorance, he asked Neville if he knew how a certain device had got into the Latimer coat of arms, and when told that it derived from the Beauchamp earls of Warwick excitedly gabbled of a dream he had had in which a spirit had taken the two of them to the highest chamber in Warwick Castle and there had delivered to Neville those very arms. He insisted that they should at once go to Warwick to confirm this vision. There things appear to have been well arranged in advance. In the streets of the town, Neville was promptly accosted by an aged stranger who 'bade me welcome to mine own' but would not stop to explain himself. The incident deeply impressed Neville who would not listen later to Wood's sneer that the man had probably just been a beggar looking for alms. As they entered the castle, the keeper – as was his habit with tourists, 'in hope of reward' – showed Neville the sword of the legendary Guy of Warwick and invited him to feel its weight; Jones at once exclaimed at the token. Having thus softened up his man, he exploited the situation on the ride home. He explained that long before he had been assured by a worthy prophet overseas that he would one day be 'chief of counsel with one that should be a great man of the realm' – and now this would come true because he would be chief counsellor to an earl of Warwick. He talked of a battle that was to be in the north in which Lord Latimer would be killed and (since the sister-in-law was not well disposed towards the rest of the Neville brood) advised William to be on the spot when it came to the sorting out of the inheritance. All three Nevilles thought this sound advice.

For the rest of the summer of 1532 Jones and Nashe continued to work upon their victim. They kept him supplied with bits of prophecy, pandered to his interest in serious magic with conversations upon Agrippa's *De occulta philosophia*, and especially kept up the talk of war in the north, the expected battles ultimately rising to three. William Neville later claimed to have realised that Jones wanted to arrange for a cheap trip north because he hoped to get hold of a book of Friar Bacon's now in the church loft at Durham priory, but at the time he clearly lapped it all up. Increasingly his ambitions took hold of him, and he began to talk freely to Wood and Legh who grew very worried at all this confident chatter about what should be arranged once Neville had succeeded to the earldom. It was especially worrying that Neville kept insisting that he would gain the earldom by personal right of inheritance and not by royal grant: indeed, the King was at best left right out of the reckoning. Some of the talk got really dangerous, as when Wood was advised to keep his money in cash that year and not sow any corn, 'for they that sow corn shall not reap in this year, and money should be ready treasure in this season', or when Neville spoke of 'a bear which had been long tied to a stake [which] should arise and make peace and unity' – a reference to the bear and ragged staff, the Warwick device. Neville was talking like a man planning to overthrow the state in his search for what he had come to regard as his proper rights. His delusions were encouraged further by Jones who addressed his patron as earl of Warwick and in terms of high-flown humility; later Jones claimed that these letters had been written to make sport of Neville who was a laughing stock around the neighbourhood. On this point Jones's evidence carries hardly any conviction.

For Neville was now certainly going beyond mere folly. Prophecies and the assertion of claims based on heraldic devices had played their part in the downfall of the duke of Buckingham and Sir Rice ap Griffiths, two recent instances of disastrous treason well remembered by

those who conversed with Neville. The sorcerers had from the first
mixed political elements into their tales, and some of them were very
dangerous. When Henry VIII's intention to cross over to Boulogne
became known in the summer of 1532, Nashe had said that the marriage
to Anne Boleyn would take place before their return, that this would
prove dangerous to the noblemen there, and that Lord Latimer might
die that way instead of waiting for a battle in the north. Jones once
explained that none of Cadwallader's blood (which included the
Tudors) should reign for more than twenty-four years, which would
terminate King Henry's reign by 1533. There was talk of issue from
Prince Edward – presumably Edward V – and of a Yorkist descendant
alive in Saxony; either this person or the king of Scots would succeed
'after the king that now is'. The frequent talk of battles on English soil
was by itself bad enough. George Neville was told that if the King returned from France he would be driven out again by the commons of
England. Wade also talked politics, but in his bitter competition with
Jones he confined himself to pooh-poohing all the wilder prophecies.

William Neville was in due course to make out that he had always
contradicted all dangerous statements and expressed total disbelief. But
Wood and Legh saw him at the time, and they were badly rattled. To
Wood he spoke of inheriting his earldom without having to get it from
the King, 'who shall not reign'; he was very disappointed when Henry
after all got back from France, saying 'he would have laid wagers that
his grace...should not return into this realm'; and, building a new
gallery where at need he could assemble a hundred or two hundred men,
with 'draw-doors and privy doors' to get them in and out, he made
preparations to claim his rights by force. Legh was shocked to hear that
the King should not even last his twenty-four years and that 'he that
was of great blood should have all the rule of the realm and subdue
those that the King had made of low blood', the former evidently to
be led by the future earl of Warwick. Both Legh and Wood later
deposed to these and similar sayings in such detail and at such length as
to make it highly improbable that there was nothing but invention in
it; and indeed, in all William and George Neville's testimony there are
no denials, merely differently shaped statements of much the same sort
of thing. As the year wore on, Legh became ever more apprehensive
and (he said) ever more aware of his loyal duty to his King. When he
found that Wood, too, felt the same and had broken with Neville, he

concerted things with him; and so, on 24 December 1532, Legh wrote on both their behalves to the King's Council.

The matter at once came into Cromwell's hands; he was already the man responsible for security. And he acted fast. Within a week he had detailed statements from Legh, Wood and the two Nevilles; Jones was soon in the Tower writing his account; and Tyler was arrested at Oxford. There survives a letter almost certainly from Tyler to Jones which was torn into small pieces but found and pasted together again at the time. In it Jones was urged to depose in terms identical with those used by the writer who meant to make out that the practice of necromancy had had nothing political about it but was intended to get Jones a bishopric. This letter survives among Cromwell's papers. On the evidence we possess the case looked black all round, but the evidence is not enough to tell us exactly what the Council thought of it all. Thanks to Cromwell's efficiency they had the whole story within two or three weeks of the first information being received, but they clearly did not have all the relevant bodies. There is no evidence that Nashe or Wade were ever arrested, and they may well have melted away; Christopher Neville, too, apparently remained untroubled. Still, the principals were in the Tower, under lock and key. And even if William and George Neville were to be believed implicitly, it was manifest from their own statements that they had dabbled in very perilous matters. They had vaguely plotted – or at least sincerely hoped for – the death of a peer of the realm; they had listened to treasonable talk of the King's early demise; they had planned to revive the earldom of Warwick, last held by a Yorkist claimant, by sorcery or possibly by force.

In the end they proved more fortunate than their idiocy deserved. Nothing was done to the Nevilles: William, who some eighteen months later had the nerve to appeal to Cromwell for the relief of the poverty into which these upsets had thrust him, was back on the commission of the peace for Worcestershire by July 1534 and acted as the King's trusted servant in the aftermath of Bigod's rebellion in 1537.[1] Tyler, Wood, Nashe and Wade vanish from the record. Legh had occasion, probably about February 1533, to remind Cromwell of his loyal services and to ask for his discharge from the burdensome attendance on the Council required of accusers, but thereafter nothing more is heard of him. Jones alone lingers a little longer in our knowledge. Some time in

[1] *LP* vii. 1026 (4), 1649; xii. I. 234.

1533, still in the Tower after the investigation, he wrote to Cromwell in terms which suggest that things were running reasonably well for him – reasonably well for one who had every reason to think that if his employers escaped he would have to be made the scapegoat. Cromwell had shown him great mercy and pity: this was kindness which Jones could never hope to repay. It was now also that he offered to make the royal fortunes by means of the philosopher's stone, but he pointed out that in order to pursue his researches he needed to be at liberty. He offered references – the earl of Worcester and Sir William Morgan. For good measure he threw in a promise to reveal things about Dr London, warden of New College, Oxford, 'that would make him smoke, and others too of his affinity'. (London was one of the customary targets for informers in the 1530's). There are hints that Jones had been busy throwing denunciations about to save himself, but he was careful to exonerate William Neville of all treason, for otherwise he would himself have been guilty of concealing treason. Cromwell does seem to have decided to use Jones, though whether as an informer or an alchemist must remain uncertain. He told him to arrange sureties with the lieutenant of the Tower, and the agreed bonds were duly put up, mainly thanks to Sir William Morgan's services back home in Wales. Despite this, Jones was still in the Tower in July 1533,[1] and it needed a reminder from his brother Roger to secure his release: at least, this is the likeliest explanation of Roger's appeal and Jones's disappearance from the record.[2] In the end, no one seems to have suffered more than temporary discomfort, a bad scare, and no doubt some serious financial losses when this foolish and dangerous conspiracy was exposed. Lord Latimer survived to die in 1543 and be succeeded by his son.[3] The King's finances were repaired from the wealth of the Church rather than the retorts of the alchemist. This branch of the Nevilles gave no further trouble.[4]

[1] LP iv. 873, a curious letter to the mayor of Bristol which with its boisterous air of mingled sense and nonsense suggests that Jones, imprisoned anything but rigorously, was either far from well-balanced or expecting happier days. Perhaps both.

[2] One 'Master Jones' was involved in a big robbery at Oxford in 1535; it could have been the same man (LP viii. 789). At any rate, no Jones was in the Tower later that year when the other suspected robbers, including the abbot of Valle Crucis, had found accommodation there (ibid. 1001 [3]).

[3] LP xviii. I. 802 (28).

[4] Another of Lord Latimer's brothers, Thomas, did get reported for possibly treasonable talk in September 1537. On that occasion it came out that when William had been sent to the Tower Thomas had been recklessly furious, allegedly exclaiming, 'By God's

But the menace that could lie behind such silly-seeming dabblings in magic and sorcery, the perils of superstition close to the centre of affairs, were thoroughly revealed when the Council received Edward Legh's fearful denunciation and asked Cromwell to extract the truth from this bunch of fools and rogues.

Of course, political issues were always more likely to call forth magical practices and ominous prophesying. It was one of the charges against Dr Maydland of London, an inveterate opponent of the new order, that he claimed to know 'by his science, which is necromancy' that the men of the new learning should be put down and the old order fully restored 'by power of the King's enemies from the parts beyond the sea'.[1] Fulk Vaughan's image with pins in it may have had no serious implications, but in 1538 a kitchen porter at Corpus Christi College, Oxford, was retailing at third hand the story of another such wax figure found in London with a knife in it – and this was reckoned to represent Prince Edward.[2] More to the point, practical magic was tried by a group of dissatisfied people in the north late in 1537.[3] The main culprit was a widow of thirty-two, called Mabel Brigge, who suddenly started a three-day fast called 'St Trinian's Fast' which she said would cause the death of the King and 'the false duke' (Norfolk); she had tried it only once before, on which occasion the victim had broken his neck before the fast was done. She claimed to have been put up to it by Isobel Buck who had given her some wheat and linen for it. Mrs Buck maintained that she had asked Mabel's help in finding some money she had lost, and there was also some confusion whether the order had been put in recently or seven years before. Other people in Holderness got pulled in by the enquiry which revealed that Mrs Buck's husband and father-in-law had tried to buy off the chief informant. The charges flew around fast and wild, but the Council in the North, especially sensitive to such treasons at this time, swiftly cut through the tangle. Mrs Brigge was executed at the York oyer and terminer of April 1538; Mrs Buck convicted with her, was reprieved (and probably pardoned); her

blood, if I had the King here I would make him that he should never take man into the Tower, for by the Mass, I know he will not leave a man alive'. The charges were not proceeded with because Lord Chancellor Audley thought the evidence insufficient (SP 1/124, fos. 193–5, 199 [*LP* xii. II. 665, 667]).

[1] SP 1/99, fo. 67 (*LP* ix. 846).   [2] SP 1/141, fo. 67 (*LP* xiii. II. 1200).

[3] SP 1/130, fos. 24–31 (*LP* xiii. I. 487). As usual, the mutual accusations leave some questions of guilt unsettled, but the main outline of the story is clear.

husband and her confessor were convicted of misprision.[1] Mabel Brigge had certainly been guilty of compassing the King's death, though the act of 1352, which applied to her case, had not contemplated the use of magic for this nefarious purpose.

Reports of dangerous prophecies were frequent enough to form a genuine problem to the government, and the more comprehensible cases may be listed here. In 1533, a Warwickshire priest, Ralph Wendon, allegedly spoke of a prophecy 'that a queen should be burned at Smithfield' and trusted it might be that whore and harlot Queen Anne; the investigation suggested malice in the accuser, and the matter dropped.[2] Next year, the parson of Chesterton (Hunts.) was accused by his curate of keeping 'a false and abominable' prophecy in his parlour; the parson was worth £100, and the curate wanted an interview with Cromwell.[3] This case, too, went no further. In 1535, Alexander Clavell, a servant of Lord Dawbeny's, conversed with a servant of Sir Thomas Arundel's. First he lamented 'the stormy weather, and then the world' which 'was like to be worse shortly', telling of a prophecy that the priests should rise up against the King. He thought the time was surely come for this to happen. The prophecy was traced to an old man who neatly blocked further enquiry by admitting having it from his old master, now fifty years dead. The prophecy went on: 'that the priests shall rule the realm three days and three nights, and then the white falcon should come out of the northwest and kill almost all the priests, and they that should escape should be fain to hide their crowns with filth of beasts because they would not be taken for priests'.[4] Fairly characteristic stuff, and no doubt less offensive than usual to Cromwell, though spreading this sort of thing around amounted to a serious attempt at breaking the peace.

In March 1536, William Thwaytes, parson of Londesborough (Yorks.), was acquitted at York Assizes of various sayings including a prophecy that the King would be forced to flee the realm. The jury thought the charges malicious, but the depositions suggest rather that Thwaytes, guilty in fact, had the right sort of friends.[5] In 1537, Robert Dalyvell of Royston (Herts.), who had recently been to Scotland, told

---

[1] SP 1/131, fo. 56 (*LP* xiii. I. 705).   [2] Cf. below, p. 347.
[3] SP 1/88, fo. 56 (*LP* vii. 1624).   [4] SP 1/99, fo. 194 (*LP* viii. 736).
[5] SP 1/99, fo. 20 (*LP* ix. 791) and SP 1/91, fo. 161v (*LP* viii. 457); the second document is placed a year too early in *LP*. Cf. below, p. 358.

of prophecies he had heard there that the king of Scots should rule England before three years were out; those 'railing Scots' had shown him a book of Merlin's sayings, and he had been incautious enough to tell what he had heard. He lost his ears over the business, but a year later was still unrepentantly repeating the same sort of talk.[1] In November 1538, Richard Swann, a young servingman of Hounslow, risked his life by telling of a prophecy touching the birth of Prince Edward, to the effect 'that he should be killed that never was born'; he knew it meant the Prince because a lady had told the King at the time of Edward's birth 'that one of the two must die', whereupon Henry had ordered the child to be saved by being 'cut out of his mother's womb'. Swann admitted hearing this tale from the usual convenient stranger and added two other prophecies he had heard: 'the boar and the bear should play at the base and set all England in a chase,' and 'a stout knight in a stour his bugle did blow, his raches to roche, to slay him that never was born.' This did not apply to the Prince; what it meant he no doubt could no more tell than we can.[2] Outlying parts provided their quota. A grey friar from Plymouth, Robert Elys, told in Cornwall of 'a prognostication that there should be a king of England that should do great wrong to his commonalty', but within two years would repent and do penance; he thought the time of the prophecy had arrived.[3] And a 'lewd' prophecy against the King and Cromwell was reported to be circulating in Ireland in 1539.[4]

The full flavour of these sort of sayings – a mixture of mad obscurity, resentment, and dangerous incitement – may be illustrated more fully from three typical cases. A Mrs Amadas, clearly both something of a wise woman and a virago,[5] was as early as 1533 reported to have issued quite a string of pronouncements.[6] She claimed to have been in the prophesying business for twenty years, 'and this is the year that her matter shall come to pass'. The King, she said, was 'in her book of

[1] BM, Cleo. E. iv, fo. 128*; Calig. B. i, fos. 130–1; SP 1/140, fo. 125 (LP xii. II. 74 [2], 80; xiii. II. 1090).   [2] E 36/120, fo. 58 (not in LP).
[3] SP 1/242, fo. 103 (LP Add. 1370). This matter also petered out: Elys soon after got a dispensation from his vows (Fac. Off. Reg. 167).   [4] StP iii. 131–2.
[5] Probably the widow of Robert Amadas, keeper of the King's jewels, who died in early 1532. Some of the evidence collected precedes his death.
[6] BM, Cleo. E. iv, fos. 99–100 (LP vi. 932). The prophecies collected by Mrs Amadas included several from the old Book of Merlin, ascribed to Geoffrey of Monmouth; some of the vatic extravagances of this compilation recurred as an element in English political history down to the seventeenth century. The moldwarp (mole), originally

prophecies' called the moldwarp and 'is cursed with God's own mouth'. Like Cadwallader he would be banished the realm which before midsummer would be conquered by the Scots; but 'the clobbes of Essex shall drive them forth again, and a bush in Essex shall be worth a castle in Kent'. A monk living on an island, 'who is called the dead man', would come 'and keep a Parliament in the Tower, and it shall be called the Parliament of peace'. 'The blazing star was toward' the dead man's island;[1] 'now this gear begins to work'. There was to be 'a battle of priests' in which the King would die; there would be no more king of England, and the realm was to be divided into four and called the land of conquest. These and other prophecies she had got in an illus-trated roll; and with these ominous sayings she mixed more straight-forward abuse of Queen Anne and other dignitaries.

Poor Mrs Amadas was not entirely sane, as old Master Whitnall concluded who visited her with his son George to ask her and her husband to come to London because the King was there. 'Tush,' she replied, 'the devil's straw; I care not for the King a rush under my foot; it is the king of heaven who ruleth all.' Some of her outbursts suggest a fairly obvious diagnosis. Thus she claimed that the King had often tried her with gifts 'to make her a whore', alleged that Sir John Daunce had attempted to lure her to Sir William Compton's house for the King's evil purposes, and swore by Christ's passion that 'there was never a good-wedded woman in England, but Prince Arthur's dowager, the duchess of Norfolk,[2] and herself'. The common link would seem to have been that all three had bad husbands, for she added that since the King had left his wife 'she suffered her husband to do the same: but the good emperor shall deliver all good wives when he cometh'. Among her *bêtes noires* whom she trusted to see beheaded were Lord Chancellor Audley, Chief Justice Norwich, and Sir John Baker, which rather suggests that she had been also unbalanced by lack of success at law. No doubt her troubles were sufficiently well known to help her escape the consequences of her ravings; but the Nun of Kent had died for less, and Mrs Amadas was lucky. She could certainly have become more

attached to Henry IV, was at this time thought to represent Henry VIII. Cf. for all this Rupert Taylor, *The Political Prophecy in England* (1911), esp. 48 ff., and Thomas, *Religion and the Decline of Magic*, ch. 13. I think that some of Mr Thomas's identifica-tions are a little rash.   [1] The comet of 1534, which dates this paper.

[2] The third duke's lawful wife whom he treated very badly and finally put away to live with his mistress.

than a nuisance with her prophecies, and (as we shall see) there are signs that she was listened to.

Markedly less fortunate was John Dobson, vicar of Muston in Yorkshire, but then he committed the usually fatal indiscretion of saying what he did within the jurisdiction of the Council of the North after the Pilgrimage of Grace. He had frequently prophesied that the King would be driven from the realm and 'flee unto the sea'; he had seen the eagle (the emperor) come to take over the realm; he exulted over 'the cow which is the bishop of Rome' that was to come to England 'jingling with her keys' to restore the true faith. Not obscurely he had recited a verse to the effect that 'when Crumme is brought low, then we shall begin Christ's Cross row'. The moon, he said, shall 'shine kindly again and take the light of the sun', and by the moon he meant the Percies. Next came Lord Lumley's turn: 'the cock of the north shall be billed in the neck and head; and after that he shall busk him and bunch his feathers and call his chickens together, and after that he shall do great adventures.' And 'the scallop shells' (the device of Dacre of Gilsland) 'shall be broken and go to wreck': Lord Dacre had failed the commons in the rebellion. Arrested by the Council, Dobson tried desperately to cast the blame elsewhere, but even in defending himself he had to admit his avid interest in prophecies and the possession of an incriminating roll of them. He added a lot more obscurely worded dooms, supposedly derived from Merlin and Thomas the Rhymer of Erceldoun, all of which had allegedly pointed to 1537 as the year of fulfilment.[1] It is no wonder that a fanatic like Sir Francis Bigod should have decided to exploit the constellations. As for Dobson, the evidence against him was overwhelming, and Tunstall could report to Cromwell that he had a judges' opinion on the case which encouraged him to send the vicar for trial. He was duly tried, convicted and executed at the Lent Assizes at York in 1538.[2]

Dobson's prophesyings had been a very real danger to a peace barely

[1] 'A long man in red shall rise and go over at Darwin Staithes; the rays of the "ceall" shall shine full bright off Berwick walls; the king of England shall have all the keys of Christendom to govern so long as God wills; the eagle shall spread his wings and do much things.' Etc. Dobson's collection of prophecies clearly included bits of Merlin, Thomas of Erceldoun, parts of *The Cock of the North*, and perhaps John of Bridlington (Taylor, *Prophecy*, 48–58, 62–71), but also, it seems to me, some original lines which he may have made up himself.

[2] SP 1/127, fos. 63–7; 128, fo. 124v; 131, fo. 56 (*LP* xii. II. 1212; xiii. I. 107, 705).

restored; the loose talk of John Ryan, a fruiterer and lodging-house keeper of Tower Hill, was a deal more harmless and probably had a happier outcome. In June 1539 he was heard talking of prophecies at supper-time to one Roger Dicons, a seaman staying at the house, by another lodger, John Wessell, a tinker. Dicons drank a loyal toast to King Harry and Prince Edward, trusting to see them both reign to a ripe old age. Ryan agreed that the Prince would succeed his father – the prophecy said so. But it also said that he would be 'as great a murderer as the King his father is, and that he must be a murderer by kind, for he murdered his mother in his birth'. Dicons, interrogated, revealed that the occasion of the talk had been the prospect of war in Ireland. Ryan, a loudmouth, said that the King would never get anywhere with that country unless he followed his (Ryan's) expert advice – which was, to put two armies of 10,000 men each in O'Brien and O'Donnell country, have them burn and kill to their heart's content, and so to move across the island till they met. Dicons hoped that this would not be necessary, after which followed the talk reported by Wessell. In his own testimony, Ryan turned things round: he had gathered that there was a chance of Prince Edward being sent to Ireland, which plan, in view of the Prince's tender age, he had deplored, and there had then been mention of a prophecy that King Henry should be the last crowned king of England. To this he replied that he knew of a prophecy of Merlin's according to which Edward would indeed succeed, but it would be a time of more murders and treasons than the present reign was. This and other prophecies he had got off a man in the King's service who was 'the best chronicler of England'. It then appeared that this chronicler, who mixed historical studies with trust in prophecies, was a pursuivant called Robert.[1] Ryan, under arrest in the Compter in Bread Street, made every effort to get this Robert to come to see him. Told that the man would not come 'for fear of suspecting', Ryan ominously retorted that he had better do so since all he had said and stood accused of came from this man's prophesying. The fact that a real chronicler, the well known Charles Wriothesley, who faithfully recorded all executions in London, makes no mention of this case strongly suggests that Ryan escaped the consequences of his loose tongue, being let go after a spell in prison.[2]

---

[1] Identified by *LP* as Fayery, portcullis pursuivant, but not known to history as a chronicler.   [2] SP 1/153, fos. 5–6, 50, 74 (*LP* xiv. II. 11, 73, 102).

Prophecies could upset the peace; false stories of what was alleged to have happened or be happening were almost sure to do so. It was, of course, too much to expect that a decade so full of strange events should not produce its crop of relevant rumours. Once the lesser monasteries had been dissolved, it was soon being said that other houses would come down; Hugh Latham said so, at large, early in 1536 and got himself gaoled for it,[1] and William Barnard was reported for similar talk in October 1537, though in his case it looks as though the letter to Cromwell ended the matter.[2] The rumour played its part in provoking the northern risings and was the more uncomfortable because it was essentially true. Some time, probably in 1538, Cromwell thought it necessary to send a circular letter to the heads of still remaining monastic houses, assuring them that there was no plan to suppress them and that only voluntary surrender or political crime would end the life of any house; he asked the persons addressed to arrest anyone who reported otherwise.[3]

The risings themselves naturally provided wild stories of all kinds, all of them likely to disturb hearers and infringe security. In January 1537, Richard Stanold spread a rumour at Rochester that the earl of Cumberland was defying the King, keeping his castle from the royal forces, refusing a summons to come to London, and not letting his son come either. The King was preparing to besiege him. Stanold claimed to have had all this from a man of Kendal who in turn denied saying any such things, but it must be remembered that according to the evidence 'of truth the Kendal man was very drunk' when he talked to Stanold.[4] Well over a year later this sort of news was still live, as Richard Oversole, a young man of seventeen, found when he came south to Kent from Northallerton, to live with his aunt Isobel Forest, single-woman, his mother Joan's sister, in service at Dover. Lodging on his way in a house at Sittingbourne, he was overcome by self-importance and told all who would listen that if the rebels had won 'Lord Cromwell would have fled this land'; also that all the Percies were dead

---

[1] SP 1/101, fos. 5–6 (*LP* x. 5–6). He knew Richard Cromwell and other men of influence, and may thus safely be assumed to have been set free.

[2] SP 1/125, fos. 90–1 (*LP* xii. II. 800). He spread a rumour that all houses of religion beyond Trent 'except one' would be suppressed.

[3] J. Strype, *Ecclesiastical Memorials*, i, Doc. 56. Though not included by Merriman, this is manifestly a draft circular emanating from Cromwell and written in his name.

[4] SP 1/114, fo. 74 (*LP* xii. I. 63).

except one that had fled to Scotland, but he would 'cause England to shine as bright as St George' when he came with Scottish assistance to take over the kingdom.[1] In 1539, stories of forthcoming musters and of the earl of Shrewsbury having been captured by rebels (rather belatedly) were causing unrest at Tiverton in Devon.[2] The south was clearly always on edge where reports from the north were concerned, but so far as we know none of these people suffered any ill consequences for their tale-telling. As usual, things worked out differently for two men (Richard Howthwaite, subprior of Carlisle, and John Humphrey of Scaleby in Cumberland) who plied the rumour-monger's trade in the north. Both were tried and executed at Carlisle on 1 December 1538 for putting it about that the commons had risen in the south – an original variation on the more usual tale.[3]

The northern risings in fact provided a fine example of rumour-mongering and its dangers. Apart from the few who prophesied the trouble and the many who later said how right the northerners had been, there were some who used the occasion to spread alarm. A Kentish weaver, Christopher Norman, 'cast from him his shuttle' when he first heard of the rising and went for more news to the vicarage. There he found Ralph Elderton, himself from the north, buckling on his armour. Asked if he proposed to fight against his countrymen, Ralph replied: 'Ho, I am here, and leapt, and then leapt again and said, Ho, I am here now.' The vicar intervened with a warning: if the southern levies did not go over to the rebels once they went up against them, 'all we be cast away'. This roused Norman to defiance; he expressed the desire to 'tussle with some of the northern knaves'. 'There be ten men against one,' replied the vicar, 'and when ye have a rap upon the pate and shake your legs, how tussle you then? For there be great men and mighty men of war which be but children here to them.'[4] The same note was struck in Sussex by a visitor from Lincolnshire, George Brantwheat, who tried to dampen a local man's loyal ardour by warning him to stay at home: 'if ye come there ye shall find them there one man good enough for two of the best should come out of this country.'[5] The con-

---

[1] SP 1/140, fo. 33 (*LP* xiii. II. 996).

[2] SP 1/118, fo. 245 (*LP* xii. I. 1000). For the possibility that the *LP* dating is wrong, cf. below, p. 80.

[3] SP 1/138, fo. 89 (*LP* xiii. II. 739); BM, Calig. B. iii, fo. 157 (*LP* xiii. II. 1101); *LP* xiii. II. 1129.

[4] SP 1/120, fos. 250–1 (*LP* xii. I. 1318).   [5] SP 1/110, fos. 24–5 (*LP* xi. 920 [1]).

viction that the mysterious north breeds special men goes a long way back. As Marmaduke Neville, another of Lord Latimer's dubious brothers, put it after he had got involved with the rebellion: 'We are plain fellows and have shown our minds. Ye southern men thought as much as we, though you durst not utter your minds, but if it come to battle you would have fought faintly.'[1] Two months later he was singing a different tune from the Tower,[2] but he had contributed his bit towards the general apprehension that the northern men were giants as well as barbarians who, if ever they crossed the Trent, would carry war and destruction through the realm.

Less obviously designed reports also got their tellers into a little trouble. Thus John Rede of Ewelm (Surrey) was called 'a seditious tale-teller, a spreader abroad of tidings, news and rumour' because in March 1539 he reported that the workmen at Hampton Court park had been discharged, that a new building was being started at Nonsuch, and that the navy was being got ready for war: 'there came one cart laden with harness through the town of Ewelm to London ward this last week.'[3] He was in fact at worst embroidering slightly upon the truth, but all hints of war had a way of creating disquiet and were therefore likely to bring out the authorities' displeasure. More drastic was the curious behaviour, in May 1534, of Richard Stopes, clearly a man deranged, at Hereford. He had announced that 'he himself was king, and he was of the name of Henry the Heddeysson of Henry late earl of Wiltshire, and that he was proclaimed king of England on low Easter eve last past at Charing Cross in the suburbs of London by the name of Henry king of England'; and he went on, somewhat illogically, to hope aloud that Queen Catherine would be again 'queen of England in his old place'. This mad talk, too reminiscent of quite recent false claimants to the crown, was reported to Cromwell, and it is difficult to believe that nothing more was done about it; but there is no evidence of proceedings, and it may be that obvious insanity saved Stopes from further action. Yet his outburst could have been the cause of real disturbances.[4]

In those years, when men looked with either hope or fear across the Channel for some reaction to the fierce doings of the English govern-

[1] SP 1/112, fo. 245 (*LP* xi. 1319).
[2] His appeal to Cromwell for the King's mercy (*LP* xii. I. 28) proved successful.
[3] SP 1/144, fo. 89 (*LP* xiv. I. 499).
[4] SP 1/84, fo. 172; BM, Tit. B. i, fo. 171 (*LP* vii. 802). Henry, earl of Wiltshire, brother to the traitor Buckingham, had died in 1523.

ment, rumours of international affairs and possible war were particularly serious. They began to flow from 1537 onwards, as imperial and papal action became more likely. A curious conversation took place in April 1537 at West Malling in Kent, between a priest, James Fredewell, and the local schoolmaster, Adam Lewes.[1] After some drinking and card-playing, the talk turned to the New Testament (Fredewell, as we have already seen, being against the English version).[2] They then adjourned to John Domeright's shop to look at the copies of the acts for apparel and unlawful games, put up for sale there. Lewes, fresh from the cardtable, hoped to see them better enforced, but Fredewell remarked, mysteriously, that the King was likely to be otherwise employed. 'Why so,' asked Domeright, 'his grace hath overrun his enemies of the north, for they hang at their own doors.' Ah, retorted Fredewell, there was 'another bird a-breeding' which would appear before midsummer and give the King such a time as he had never yet had. When he would not explain himself, Lewes piously hoped for no such thing. Thereupon Fredewell appeared to change the subject: 'The emperor hath given the king of England Flanders.' His companions stared at him and clearly did not take his point, so that he enlarged it: 'If the king of England take part with the emperor, then shall he have the French king and the king of Scots in his neck, for the French king hath made the king of Scots admiral of the sea.' Nobody questioned his bogus news, but Lewes laughed at the threat and, anticipating Shakespeare, boasted that 'if we be true within ourselves they can both do us little hurt'. Warming to it, he proceeded to bait Fredewell: 'And moreover, I said, if we go beyond the sea, it is best that we cut off a great many priests' heads before we go, for they will betray the King while he is absent, I fear.' Fredewell answered, 'it is soon said, cut off their heads, but it will not be so soon done'. To which Lewes replied, 'ye say truth, for by St Anne there is a shrewd sort of you if you be together'. Domeright confirmed the story in every detail, but again we know no more.

These dark hints of war and invasion were a good deal less innocent than they seemed. By 1539, there was a genuine invasion scare along the south coast, as Cardinal Pole travelled about France on his mission against England, while the English government fed the rumours by its necessary measures of defence. Thus it was most unwise of Christopher Batermay, a Frenchman resident in Sussex, to spread the tale that

[1] SP 1/118, fo. 231 (LP xii. I. 990).   [2] Above, p. 25.

Cromwell and his son were in the Tower just as the neighbourhood buzzed with rumours of a French landing in Hampshire.[1] In Hampshire itself a little earlier, a rumour spread very fast that Sir Geoffrey Pole had only by his sudden arrest been prevented from sending a force to assist his brother Reginald, the cardinal. The earl of Southampton had the greatest difficulty in tracing the rumour. He got Lawrence Taylor, who had been the first man denounced for spreading it, and he understood that Richard Eyre, a surgeon, whom Taylor finally accused, was in custody; along the road he found two women, a mother and a daughter, whom in the end, since the originator was known, he hoped he might let go – one of them an old woman and a midwife, and the other a young woman 'having a child sucking on her breasts'.[2] The business was part of the general investigation connected with the Pole and Exeter conspiracies and had wider implications;[3] what we must note is the manner in which circumstantial stories about likely rebellion and contacts with the King's enemies were adding to the ferment in the countryside. A little later these rumours travelled further along the coast: in March 1539, Edward Loxton, drinking a pot of ale in an inn at Otley (Somerset), said when asked for news: 'we shall have war...and that the Lord Cromwell was gone away'.[4] The rather obscure tale running round Salisbury in April 1538 that the King, having been ordered to do so by an angel and by the ghost of Queen Jane, was about to go on pilgrimage to St Michael's Mount must be read in this context, too:[5] St Michael's Mount played its part in the endemic prophecies, pilgrimages denoted repentance, and the King's movements were linked to war. Just then the whole south was alert for signs of trouble with foreign enemies, and given any sign, however dim, made the most of it, to add to the general sense of unease.

Much the most common, and the most troublesome, rumours touched fears of financial exactions and reports of the King's death. Either could lead to immediate disturbance by creating excitement, disaffection and fear which, once unleashed, would be hard to restrain, and it is a tribute to the authorities' vigilance that (Lincolnshire apart) so little serious trouble occurred. Henry had put so many new charges

[1] SP 1/150, fo. 174 (*LP* xiv. I. 823) – April 1539.
[2] SP 1/136, fos. 200–5 (*LP* xiii. II. 392–3).
[3] Cf. Dodds, ii. 304 ff.   [4] E 36/120, fo. 55 (*LP* xiv. I. 557).
[5] SP 1/135, fos. 53–6 (*LP* xiii. II. 62).

on the clergy that stories of imaginary taxes for everybody are not, perhaps, surprising; people may also have recalled Wolsey's levies in the years 1523–1525 which had resulted in a widespread taxpayers' strike. Early in 1538, Brian Woodcock, a Yorkshire husbandman, made the point very forcibly when, coming from Malton market, he told two friends that the earl of Westmorland had promised to collect 'plough nobles and poll groats' for the King from all his tenantry; he was sure this would lead to 'more business and rising than ever there was'. Challenged as to the source of his information, he spoke like a true Yorkshireman: 'If I could not tell where I heard them I were a fool to speak them.' And warned to say no more, he muttered, 'why then, let it rest where it is'.[1] He was arrested: perhaps things went as ill for him as for Richard Fish who in December that year was condemned at York for saying that commissioners had arrived at Lincoln to levy 6s 8d for every plough and the same sum for every christening.[2] This was barely two years after rumours and facts of taxgathering had started the rebellion at Louth in Lincolnshire; Fish was asking for trouble.

Many rumours clustered around the Injunctions of 1538 for the keeping of parish registers which were widely interpreted as a tax-gathering device.[3] This was said in Gloucestershire by Lewis Herbert, returned from London, in September 1538, just after the Injunctions had been published: all burials, baptisms, weddings and ordinations, he said, were to be registered, and people thought it would mean pay-ments. At least that was the talk at Abingdon in the inn there, where he had also heard that angels (10s) were to be devalued to 8s and cross groats (8d) to 5d. He vehemently denied being responsible for the further embroidery that no pig, capon or goose was to be eaten 'but they should pay tribute to the King', but what he had to admit was admirably calculated to produce a violent reaction.[4] In March 1539, William Hole, the smith of Horsham in Sussex, spread it about that 15d was to be levied for the King for every wedding, christening and burial, and the same sum for the lord of the franchise. This time the rumour was traced back, by stages, to Margaret Ede of Horsham who admitted having started the tale: on Sunday she had heard the priest say various things from the pulpit, but being sixty years of age and 'lacking

---

[1] SP 1/128, fos. 124, 126 (*LP* xiii. I. 107). [2] *StP* v. 143–4.
[3] See below, pp. 80, 259–60, 330. [4] SP 1/136, fos. 226–8 (*LP* xiii. II. 413).

a great part of her hearing' she had it all wrong, as she had later discovered.[1] The silliest tale of this sort was spread earlier, in January 1537, and at London – in fact, in a boat from London to Greenwich – by Richard Birch, glover of Southwark, who claimed to know that no christening was to be performed hereafter in the north without payment to the King. Evidently, no injunction about registers was needed to start this line of thought. Everybody, Birch asserted, was telling this: he could bring a hundred men to prove it true (though none was found afterwards). Indeed, many children up there had remained unbaptised for two or three weeks because their parents could not raise the money. He thought this a bad thing, but what was really bad was his inventing it for his four fellow-travellers who promptly reported him.[2]

The idea, too, that ploughs or cattle might offer a handy object for taxation sprang up in various places. In the summer of 1538 the whole of Norfolk and Suffolk was loud with the story that the King would take all cattle left unmarked after midsummer. Cromwell drew the duke of Norfolk's attention to the matter in a letter which hinted that 'the spreading of such a bruit in your own country and in your absence from hence' might be misinterpreted, and the duke, duly scared, went into action, only to discover that the local gentry had found the rumour so widely spread that in despair they had done nothing.[3] About the same time, similar talk was heard in Sussex whence a conversation was reported between Ralph Adyshede and Edward Atote, collectors of the fifteenth granted in Parliament, and Nicholas Apsley, gentleman and taxpayer. The collectors had tracked Apsley to a coney-burrow where he was ferreting, and when they explained their errand Apsley said, 'I trust to be in rest for a while and pay no more'. Adyshede agreed that there would be no more fifteenths for the present, but he had heard it said in Kent that a poll tax was planned 'as hath been paid in times past'. According to Apsley, there was also talk of horn money, or a cattle tax. Various other people were involved, but the remarks did not amount to much. The earl of Southampton, who investigated, in fact told Cromwell that all the men were very sorry for what they had said and that only Adyshede could be to blame, if anyone was; it looks as though Cromwell took the hint and did nothing.[4] The story had been

[1] SP 1/144, fos. 93, 135 (*LP* xiv. I. 507, 553).   [2] SP 1/114, fo. 73 (*LP* xii. I. 62).
[3] SP 1/135, fos. 47, 49 (*LP* xiii. II. 52, 57).
[4] SP 1/129, fos. 216–18; 130, fos. 4–8 (*LP* xiii. I. 440, 475). The story throws light on the

stopped in good time. The rumour of another even more devastating tax – a 10% property tax on every man's goods – reached Boston in Lincolnshire in April 1540.[1] Of course, one often does not know whether these stories travelled about or were invented where they were first detected.

More particularly, the financial attack on the clergy and clerical property called forth a crop of rumours. A Cornish priest was presented at Bodmin in January 1539 for loose talk which included an allegation that by royal decree all holders of benefices were from henceforth to receive no more than an annual stipend of £6 13s 4d, that tithe should cease to be paid, and that instead men were to sell their corn and pay the King a tenth part of the money received. This invention, which reflects some rather advanced thinking on a stipendiary clergy and the standing grievance of tithe, got him into Launceston gaol, where he disappears.[2] The dissolution of the monasteries led many to think that parish churches were at risk, too. In 1537, 'common false tales and sayings' were current in Norfolk to the effect that the King would have all church and gild lands not 'put away' before May Day.[3] Some of the parish of Aylesham, hearing these stories, promptly sold the lands of their parish church to their own benefit and tried also to sell the cross and jewels (improbably valued in the information at £500); if this is true, as apparently it was, we have here not the spreading but the exploitation of a rumour and an example of the sort of irresponsible action which this tale-bearing could produce.[4] Much the same trick was tried by Robert Johns at Thame (Oxon.) who gave people to understand that the King would have the crosses and jewels of their church and proposed that 'four or five of the best of the town' should organise a quiet sale, 'and thus the King shall not have all his mind'.[5] The same rumour also reached Wigmore (Salop.) in 1537 where three townsmen got very worried to think that the number of parish churches was to be halved

status of people appointed collectors of parliamentary taxes. According to Southampton, Adyshede was a Lancashire man and a smith by trade, but his brother, the parson of Pulborough, had leased the parsonage to him where he lived 'like a gentleman, not occupying his craft or science'. He was reputed to be an honest man and a good neighbour.

[1] SP 1/159, fo. 169 (*LP* xv. 592).
[2] SP 1/142, fo. 92 (*LP* xiv. I. 87).
[3] SP 1/91, fo. 216 (*LP* viii. 518). The *LP* date of 1535 is out by two years.
[4] SP 1/120, fo. 247 (*LP* xii. I. 1316).
[5] SP 1/123, fos. 120–2 (*LP* xii. II. 357).

with but one chalice in each. They came to Nicholas Holte, an outsider now resident there and seemingly of higher status, and said:

The honesty of the parish do will you to speak with them at our church. Forasmuch as you have taken a house in our parish, they would have your advice touching the treasure of our church.

He refused to meddle and warned them against believing such stories, but they said the news had come all the way from London. In the end he could only warn them once more and inform the authorities.[1] In June 1539, the mayor and jurats of Dover were troubled about a Frenchman who was telling his countrymen how the king of England had pulled down all abbeys, would destroy all parish churches, and had had twenty cart-loads of gold and silver carried from Canterbury to London. They thought he might be a spy busy spreading disaffection.[2] The wildest stories met credence, as when one William Wodlow spread it about Gloucestershire in 1540 that the King had had two horseloads of plate from Winchcombe abbey and a portion of every rich man's goods of that town, and that two malt-sieves full of private persons' plate were brought to the toll-booth at Tewkesbury. Since he added, 'Sirs, now beware and take heed, for all will be away', he was clearly guilty of incitement.[3] No government, and especially none which remembered the part played by rumour in stirring up the northern risings, could afford to let such tales go unchecked.

Beyond all other rumours, reports of the King's death could undermine public order and cause the kind of frightened bewilderment which would leave government helpless. At the same time, it was an obvious brand of story to peddle. Occasionally, men even dared prophesy the King's death, though in law this was manifest treason. Thus Thomas Syson, or Sheston, abbot of the Leicestershire house of Garendon, was reported to Cromwell in 1536 for a comprehensive set of prophetic utterances.[4] The Church would have a great fall in 1535 but rise again in 1539 to be as high as ever it had been. He asked his companion

---

[1] E 36/120, fo. 105 (LP xii. I. 808). The information reached Cromwell directly, whereupon he rebuked Bishop Lee, president of the Council in the Marches, for not discovering the offence (SP 1/158, fo. 170 [LP xv. 447, there misplaced into 1540]).

[2] SP 1/152, fo. 31 (LP xiv. I. 1073).   [3] SP 1/157, fo. 155 (LP xv. 183).

[4] SP 1/81, fo. 175 (LP vi, App. 10: misplaced into 1533). The correct year appears from the letter cited below, p. 72, n. 5; the information came belatedly, some two years after the words were spoken.

whether he knew who was meant by the eagle,[1] but himself would only say, without explanation, that 'the eagle shall rise with such a number that the King shall go forth of the realm, and the King shall come in again when he is at most highest and be slain at a ford'. And who was the mole? Again, the other man had no idea. So far as he knew, said the abbot, it was the King,[2] and he was 'cursed of God's mouth, for he roots up the churches as the mole roots up the molehills'. Also, 'when the Tower is white and another place green, then shall be burned two or three bishops and a queen': which sounds as though the prophet could not quite remember his book, evidently another copy of Merlin's sayings.[3] 'And after all this is past we shall have a merry world.' Nothing happened to the abbot who was to see his house dissolved in 1536 and in September that year got a dispensation from his habit,[4] but the ominous sayings set on foot by him were still circulating in Leicestershire in 1537 and undermining people's loyalties.[5] Round about the same time, the prior of Launceston (Cornwall) claimed, on the authority of an unnamed Oxford scholar, that the rebellion in the north would lead to the King's death unless he fled the realm before the end of March.[6] A good many people knew of these prophecies and thought they had ideas on how to apply them; the Pilgrimage of Grace especially was readily supposed to be the occasion foretold.

Some prophesied the King's death, some (as we shall see) reported it, one man only wished for it. Adam Fermour, an Essex man, hearing early in 1536 the true story of Henry's fall from his horse in a tourney, enlarged the King's actual bruises into some broken ribs and expressed the view that 'it should have been less loss that he had broken his neck'; at least this would have stopped all those laws being made which disinherited a man at his death (a tendentious rumour about the forthcoming Statute of Uses) and made sure that 'his wife and children shall go abegging'. He offered to 'shoot forth' the two sheaves of arrows he had to prevent any more such laws, a clear case of treason. But we know no more of the case; just possibly the accusation may have been invented, though the depositions sound convincing.[7]

---

[1] Usually the emperor.   [2] Cf. Mrs Amadas' concurrent opinion, above, pp. 59–60.
[3] This bit about the Tower (a tower?) was known also to Mrs Amadas who, like the abbot, relied on Merlin.   [4] *Fac. Off. Reg.* 74.
[5] SP 1/125, fos. 90–1 (*LP* xii. II. 800).   [6] SP 1/115, fo. 141A (*LP* xii. I. 298).
[7] SP 1/136, fo. 109 (*LP* xiii. II. 307). There were three witnesses to his words, but the report was some two years late.

Prophecy apart, that the King was actually dead was several times bruited about during those years. Simon Wylkynson spread the tale at Donnington (Lincs.) in September 1536; he alleged that the news was being kept dark until 'my lord privy seal has levied the tax' (the subsidy granted in 1534). The story originated with one Maud Kebery who denied it until her own mother 'before her face' convicted her of lying.[1] Again, in November that year, a prisoner in Exeter gaol was told by a fellow-sufferer the happy news that they would soon be out. How so, asked the first. The bearer of the good tidings replied: 'Is there not a general pardon given at the change of a head?...Thou shalt hear this man gone within a short space.' What man, asked number one. The King, replied the other, who would shortly leave the realm, come back and be killed. The report is suspect, being rendered several months after the event and forwarded by a mad goldsmith who rambled on about treasons he knew without telling any, but it may well be that the Exeter prisoners had taken too seriously rumours of the prophecy already mentioned.[2]

However, it was in late 1537 and early 1538 that the country was suddenly buzzing with the news of the King's death. The first report came from Nottinghamshire in October, apparently then occasioned by 'the hasty riding of the duke of Norfolk through Newark'.[3] This shows the state of mind along the route to the lately subdued north: of all the things that might cause the duke to hurry away from both London and his county, the King's death would normally come pretty low in likelihood. After a short lull, the rumour revived without any such inducement as a galloping duke. In December it was round Sussex,[4] Northamptonshire and Leicestershire,[5] and also all over Berkshire and Oxfordshire.[6] In the following month it had reached Kent[7] and Gloucestershire,[8] as far east and west as it might go. In March a man was put in the stocks for repeating it in Warwickshire; by this time it was

---

[1] SP 1/106, fo. 109 (LP xi. 417). The year must be conjectural because the collection of the 1534 grant was spread over the years 1535–7, but the tone of the denunciation suggests that it should be placed before the Lincolnshire rising in October 1536.

[2] E 36/122, fo. 34 (LP xii. I. 685).   [3] SP 1/125, fo. 337 (LP xii. II. 935).

[4] SP 1/127, fos. 38, 161; 128, fo. 20 (LP xii. II. 1185, 1282; xiii. I. 16).

[5] SP 1/127, fo. 59; E 36/120, fo. 57 (LP xii. II. 1208).

[6] SP 1/127, fos. 57, 81, 120, 123, 126–35 (LP xii. II. 1205, 1220, 1252, 1256).

[7] E 36/120, fo. 176; SP 1/128, fos. 61, 86; BM, Cotton App. L, fos. 73–4 (LP xiii. I. 6, 57, 76).

[8] SP 1/128, fos. 62–3 (LP xiii. I. 58).

getting stale.[1] In the last week of March, Agnes Davy was indicted at Ipswich for telling it on February 12th last at Carleforth in Suffolk. She had claimed that the King was dead and the Prince as good as dead, and that 'the king of Scots would enter the north parts of the realm and the French king the south parts', thus comprehensively using the false news to create a panic. However, no action seems to have been taken on the indictment which was belatedly, in October 1539, called by *mandamus* into King's Bench, usually a proceeding intended to end in a quashing.[2]

This wildfire spread of a rumour, based (it seems) on nothing at all, naturally had the authorities badly worried, but their investigations rarely got very far. Nor is this surprising; what does surprise is that the government really thought itself able to track down an originator at all when the story was reverberating through whole counties and people honestly could not remember from whom they had first heard it. But action was ordered and taken. In Northamptonshire, two magistrates, Edward Montague and Robert ap Rice, traced the story to one John Petyfer, a husbandman who had gone to Leicester to consult 'a wise man' about some stolen property. On the way back, he baited his horse at Lutterworth where one Harrison, a harper, told of the King's and Prince's death. He stilled doubts by saying, in his best harper's manner, that 'a great deal of wheat will not stop the mouths that say it here'. Petyfer (who asserted that he had not at first believed the tale) heard it again at Theddingworth; this time it was said that an informant thrice removed had seen the sad news in a letter from London. So now Petyfer believed it, and on his return home he told his wife and another man who spread it further. Since so many of the rumour-mongers lived outside his jurisdiction, Montague had merely taken a bond from Petyfer and awaited the issue of a commission to investigate further. What he had been able to report already showed the manner in which such a report could scurry through two shires.

In Sussex, they discovered two quite separate sources: three friars at Lewes who were punished by being forced to confess their lying inventions publicly, and some very little people at Horsham who spoke vaguely of information received from London and do not seem to have been punished at all. In Gloucestershire, the investigating justices found that the rumour had come out of Dorset; here, as in Lincolnshire the

[1] SP 1/130, fos. 81–2 (*LP* xiii. I. 543).
[2] KB 9/545/85–6.

year before, it was said that the authorities were keeping things dark till they had collected more tax money. Rather more energy went into the search in Kent. The rumour had got there about New Year's Eve and was soon all over the county, being variously reported from Aylesford in the west, Wingham in the east, Cobham in the north, and Dover in the south. Here, too, some people concentrated on the effect the news might have on outstanding tax-payments, so much so that one might suspect that hopes of avoidance or (in one report) even repayment lay behind the invention. There were some handsome embroideries, the best being the tale that 'as the King sat upon his horse, he saw God's marks upon his hand and kissed them and said *laudes Deo*, and after he lay twenty-four hours in a trance and departed'. An old labourer at Higham had aggravated things by having to have the tale yelled a second time into his deaf ear. Lord Cobham, ever alert for trouble, quickly collected depositions without being able to make much headway, while in the east Cranmer managed to track the tale to a wandering fisherman and some of his acquaintance. Selling his fish around back-doors, the man had thrown in the rumour for free. There is no sign that either Cobham or Cranmer went beyond investigating and reporting.

The most vigorous pursuit took place in the central region affected by the rumour – Berkshire and Oxfordshire – where, to judge by the dates, it quite possibly originated. It would appear that there it got such rapid credence because the abbot of Reading was involved, the only man of quality who ever seems to have believed it. Indeed, the abbot at once displayed a revealing measure of nervous apprehension, writing to Cromwell on December 12th – the minute he heard the tale – to report that the death of both the King and the marquess of Exeter was being confidently announced. He indicated his belief by calling it 'the most lamentablest and heaviest tidings that ever was heard to any man now living', but at this point he also stated his ignorance of its origin. As the investigation was to show, this was not quite true, though Dr Tregonwell, writing from Oxford on the 23rd, telescoped things confusingly when he thought that the whole business started with a letter to the abbot from some member of the King's Court. Cromwell at once ordered an enquiry, and on the 18th Sir Walter Stonor, Sir William Essex and Thomas Vachell started a perambulation of Berkshire, the results of which they communicated at length on the 24th. The chains of passage were traced. Thus Stonor opened the proceedings by writing his own experience into the record: he had heard the tale from his servant Nicholas Thorne, who had had it from George Barton, parson of Broadfield, who had it of William Turner, husbandman of Broadfield, who had passed it also to John Cordrey, ditto of ditto, from whom it travelled through John Lawrence, tiller of Yattendon, to William Cryppes, weaver also of Yattendon. In Cryppes several streams met. He had also heard the rumour on the 8th from Edward Lyttleworke, a fuller of Newbury, who had allegedly got it from two innkeepers there. Furthermore, Cryppes's son-in-law Nicholas Wilkinson had brought independent confirmation from Sir John Norris's butler, John Sowthen, who had asked him to inform the abbot of Reading. This the abbot confirmed, adding that (as he understood) the news reached the Norris household in a letter from John Norris, gentleman usher of the King's Privy Chamber. Now the search was getting somewhere, though somewhere pretty dangerous; the Norris family, whose leading member, Sir Henry, had suffered execution in the fall of Anne Boleyn, could not afford such suspicions. In fact, the commissioners realised that in Wilkinson they had reached the crux of their matter; they called him back and worked on him some more, till he admitted having invented John Norris's letter. He also now added more to the story. The talk had been that the King had been poisoned. Later it came out that some rather ghoulish speculation as to the manner of it had taken place, the favourite theory apparently being that a priest saying grace could most easily drop the poison from his fingers where it would do most good.

In fact, Wilkinson had clearly been over-enthusiastic. When he talked with Sowthen a second time – on which occasion the latter was alleged to have suggested that the King was killed because he was in love with the late Sir Henry Norris's daughter and meant to marry her – the butler took real fright and denied that he had ever heard the tale from his master (as Wilkinson had believed and said); he now blamed two people called Thomas Hynde and John Mylch. Mylch, interrogated, said that he had first heard the rumour from 'a foolish beggar' but that, having recently seen the King alive and kicking, he had given no credit to it. However, he then got a sort of confirmation from Hynde who silenced scepticism by claiming to have it direct from Sir John Norris, his master. This was firmly denied by Sir John himself; he had in fact warned Hynde to cease telling lies. Norris discovered Wilkinson's lively embroideries when the abbot of Reading, warned by Wilkinson, got in touch with the knight. Things were narrowing down towards Hynde who, after some wriggling, admitted everything, including the talk of poison. But it soon appeared that Hynde was not the sole source, and therefore not the end of the search. In addition, the investigation uncovered at least two quite independent lines of transmission. One ran back through four people completely separate from the Norris household: the last man in that chain had started it all by saying that 'we should have a cradle king'. A second terminated in John Boxworth, an almsman, whose son's daughter was told by two strangers that the great wind of November 30th had brought down the greatest oak in England – a remark which Boxworth promptly interpreted to mean that the King was dead.

Perhaps for some people the rumour really originated in some such innocent misunderstanding, but the more sinister possibilities suggested by the Norris household clearly existed separately and additionally, and this was the line which the investigation explored most thoroughly. Mylch, questioned once more, further implicated Sowthen who, allegedly, was the first to mention poison and also said that if the story was true 'my lord privy seal would have all'. A number of other people were interrogated whose stories tied in with this particular tangle. The only man who refused absolutely to say where he got the rumour from was Edward Lyttleworke. The commissioners clearly did not believe the stuff about two anonymous innkeepers, and since they could not budge Lyttleworke they made him pay heavily for his obduracy. He was ordered to be pilloried at Wallingford, have his ears 'cut off by the hard head', to be tied to 'a cart's arse' naked to the waist and to be whipped about the town, and then to have the punishment repeated at Reading. Evidently the investigators thought him to be the origin of the whole outburst of rumouring, and the mayor of Wallingford agreed; but after all was done they found that there might be deeper roots still because Thomas Hynde, having thought some more, suddenly remembered another teller of the tale. Though they promised Cromwell to pursue this new line further, it does not look as though they did; and indeed the chances are that Hynde was trying to wriggle out of his very awkward situation by inventing further links in the chain behind himself.

However, enough had been uncovered to show what had happened. Loose and idle talk had gained quick credence because the name of a local worthy with Court connections had been falsely invoked. It had also been clearly established (which is of concern to us) how the story had spread rapidly from mouth to mouth, and even into neighbouring shires, all within a few days. The commissioners had orders to punish the guilty parties and took it out on Lyttleworke; in addition they warded three other people (unnamed) to await Cromwell's pleasure. Only Boxworth's granddaughter Joan, being 'great with child and looking every day her time', was expressly let go without punishment, but it does not look as though all the various bearers of the tale had occasion to rue the day. Most probably the three persons imprisoned were the three most dubiously involved – Sowthen, Wilkinson and Hynde, all closely connected with the eminent people touched by the investigation. The commissioners had really behaved very well by Tudor standards: while careful to free Sir John Norris and the abbot of Reading from serious implication, they had not shirked the duty of interrogating them thoroughly and did not protect their dependants. By all accounts, there were no further consequences to this odd outburst, except that – as the reports coming in from other shires proved soon enough – it had been too late to arrest the further spread of the story. Tregonwell suggested to Cromwell that a public statement about the King's good health might be advisable, but the lord privy seal wisely refrained from providing the further fuel for hostile rumour which any such disclaimer would assuredly have been.

The government did not, however, have to be reminded of the menace represented by this kind of rumour; on the contrary, it went out of its way several times to express its appreciation of the point. The first positive step taken was a proclamation of late October 1536, at least in part provoked by the Lincolnshire rebellion, which inveighed against 'divers devilish and slanderous persons' who had spread the tales about the King's intention to collect all the gold in the realm, to tax christenings and so forth, and to levy money for the eating of pigs, geese and capons: we have encountered the rumours which set off this blast. The people were adjured to pay no heed to 'any false forged tales' and to do all they could to capture the tellers of them.[1] Another

---

[1] *TRP* i. 244–5. There are difficulties about dates here. The rumours specified are exactly those spread about Glos. in 1538 (above, pp. 74–5), that date being confirmed by

proclamation, of which no copy survives, seems to have been issued in early 1538 when it reached John Wellesbourne at Abingdon (Berks.); that this was a different one is borne out by his reference to its attacks on people who 'brought up new rumours'.[1] Cranmer may have been acting in response to it when in late January that year he punished two rumour-mongers at Canterbury and Sandwich.[2]

Cromwell soon took personal steps to reinforce the campaign. Late in 1536 he drew up, with his own hand, sets of interrogatories to be administered to Richard Fletcher of Norwich who had acquired and broadcast a newsletter full of false reports,[3] and for the examination in the Tower of Robert Dalyvell;[4] and at the end of the Hilary term 1538 he took care to have the lord chancellor assemble the justices of the peace in the Star Chamber 'specially giving them charge for bruiting of news, vagabonds and unlawful games' – a revealing combination which shows that what was at stake for him was a whole social policy.[5] It was also about this time that he drafted the circular to heads of religious houses urging them to prevent talk of more suppressions.[6] This more energetic drive from 1536 onwards no doubt accounts for the fact that nearly all the reported cases belong to the second half of the decade. In the end Cromwell resorted to a favourite device of his to suppress rumour, namely solemn circulars ostensibly coming from the King. One such, now lost, went out in early 1538 and was probably linked with Cromwell's personal letter because it, too, dealt specifically with the spreading of stories that the King intended 'to put down more religious houses'. We know of it because in May it elicited from Thomas Pope, abbot of Hartland in Devon, the reply that such talk 'hath been so common among great estates and low that it is impossible for me to call to remembrance the principal author'. Though he promised to

the mention of the 1538 Injunctions. Yet the date of the proclamation seems certain from both internal and external evidence. It is surprising that rumours about the consequences of parish registration should circulate two years before the registers were ordered, but one can only conclude that stories of exactions were readily invented and, once invented, had a long life despite being nailed in a public proclamation.

[1] SP 1/130, fo. 95 (LP xiii. I. 555).
[2] LP xiii. I. 141, 171.
[3] SP 1/240, fo. 197 (LP Add. 1146); the examination at the Tower by Thomas Bedyll and Richard Layton is noted in SP 1/112, fos. 169–74 (LP xi. 1260).
[4] See below, p. 384, n. 4.
[5] SP 1/141, fo. 210 (LP xiii. II, App. 5).
[6] Above, p. 63.

write again if he learned anything fresh, one cannot help but regard the early dissolution of his abbey (with a large pension for the abbot) as a suitable retribution for this piece of deliberate insolence.[1] In January 1539, another circular order in the King's name was sent to a wide range of local administrators which once more rehearsed the particular troubles and policies it was their duty to prevent and enforce. Prominent among them was the injunction to apprehend 'tale-tellers...and speakers of rumours, and false inventors of news'; it was alleged that this evil had recently revived after a period during which official vigilance had kept people quiet and prevented them from being misled by 'false lies and most untrue rumour'.[2] Oddly enough, the only responses we have to this circular also came from Devon. In April Sir Thomas Denys reported receipt of the letter and the arrest of rumour-mongers at Tiverton;[3] and in August Sir Piers Edgecombe replied by informing Cromwell that men in Devon dreaded the financial exactions which they felt would result from the keeping of parish registers.[4] This can by then hardly have been news to the lord privy seal.

A very particular difficulty attended upon the suppression of incon-venient rumour and disturbing false tales. Talk of this sort, seditious or not, carried no known penalty. If the tale told could be construed as treason under the statute the teller might suffer as a traitor, but this (as we have seen) happened in these years only in the north where after the Pilgrimage of Grace any story of this sort could have had incal-culable consequences, and where the Council of the North, anxious to repair an earlier remissness, specifically got a judicial decision that such rumours could be treasonable words under the act of 1534.[5] Even northern offenders did not suffer death automatically. In February 1537, Norfolk expressed regret that he could not hang a sheriff's officer who had been disseminating an invented prophecy extremely slan-derous of Cromwell; the duke had been able only to put him in the

---

[1] SP 1/132, fos. 2–3 (LP xiii. I. 893). The LP date (1538) must be right because the abbey was dissolved on 22 Feb. 1539 (LP xiv. I. 341), so that Pope's letter cannot have been in response to the later and extant circular.

[2] Below, p. 259.

[3] SP 1/118, fo. 245 (LP xii. I. 1000). LP put this into 1537, but Denys's reference to the King's letter makes 1539 a likelier date. Talk about fighting in the north, also men-tioned in the letter, would have been out of date in late April 1537, too.

[4] StP i. 612–13.

[5] See the cases of Brigge, Dobson, Houthwaite and Humphrey, above, pp. 57, 61, 64.

pillory and deprive him of office for life.[1] We have seen that the commissioners investigating rumours of the King's death could inflict savage penalties on a man whom they concluded to have been the cause of it all,[2] but even they felt obliged to keep other people they wanted punished until they had further instructions and to let the bulk of the offenders go. One of their number, Sir William Essex, had the year before spent a spell in the Tower 'for writing and publishing of news';[3] he knew what could happen, and also how hard it was to discover anything triable at law in rumour-mongering. The offence was much too vague – though by no means new – for precise definition; and Tunstall, president of the northern Council, may well have been disappointed in his desire to know 'the full minds of the judges what such false seditious rumours do weigh unto and what punishment shall be used therefor'.[4] Unless it was possible to construe treason – and mostly it was not – the law knew of neither offence nor punishment.

In this situation, driven on by their own resentment at these needless disturbers of the public mind and by Cromwell's pressure, magistrates and investigators generally either referred themselves to Cromwell for instructions (which they seem rarely to have received) or acted summarily, using public disclaimer, the pillory and the whip as fancy took them or the seriousness of the offence seemed to warrant. Probably the satisfactory experience with the three friars of Lewes, much chastened after being made to confess their inventions in public, was characteristic enough. Cromwell never attempted to provide a more precise or savage end to these proven charges of loose or seditious talk. Not for nothing did he handle the business in a proclamation, which could add no fresh penalties in law, rather than a statute: and from so determined a maker of statutes that omission may be regarded as significant. Even the proclamation specified only that offenders should be detected and held in prison until the King's further pleasure was known.[5] These rumours and tales varied so much in their import and effect that the flexibility of 'the King's pleasure' rather than the rigour of the law seemed the best way to deal with them. Right towards the end of Cromwell's career

---

[1] SP 1/115, fo. 175 (*LP* xii. I. 318). No doubt Norfolk enjoyed telling Cromwell what nasty things were being said about him, but there is no need to question his anxiety to prove himself energetic in the pursuit of such evildoers: he could not afford reports that he was a 'papist or favourer of traitors nor rebels'.

[2] Above, p. 77. [3] SP 1/240, fo. 203 (*LP Add.* 1151).

[4] SP 1/128, fo. 124 (*LP* xiii. I. 107). [5] *TRP* i. 245.

Roger Townsend, reporting that he had used the stocks and a paper (declaring the offence) to punish a woman who had spread a rumour about a miracle of our lady of Walsingham, added: 'I know no law otherwise to punish her but by discretion, trusting it shall be a warning to other light persons in such wise to order themself.'[1]

He was quite right: there was no law, and Cromwell wanted magistrates to use their discretion. Only after he had left the scene did his successors, allegedly so much more mild, bring rumour-mongering within the compass of the death penalty, by the act of 1542 which made it felony without benefit of clergy or sanctuary to erect tales and prophecies of a political nature upon talk of heraldic devices and similar things.[2] In Cromwell's day, rumours were sought out more energetically, but discretion was allowed to apply. And while very occasionally magistrates were very severe in its employment, they seem generally to have been content to put the fear of retribution and a recognition of the consequences into idle talkers and let them go. Cromwell's purpose was to have rumours stopped and to have tale-bearers exposed locally where their tales had been told; beyond that he was not concerned to pursue the matter unless real treason might lurk behind it. But there need be no doubt at all that rumours and prophecies posed a special problem to the enforcement of policy, and that people's credulity was a burden to King and government. Cromwell said so often enough, and the rulers of the countryside agreed with him.

[1] Ellis, iii. III. 162–3.   [2] 33 Henry VIII, c. 14.

3

IN EVERY PART OF THE REALM

THE TRUTH OF THE SITUATION can become clear only from a detailed survey of the sort of events which could take place among a people always ready to look for trouble, at a time when this readiness was fed by new causes of disunion superadded to existing ones. Private feuds, disputes among gentle families striving for local ascendancy, the latent dislike of parishioners for their priests – and of priests for their parishioners – all gathered fresh strength from the impact of the government's revolutionary policy. Soon the reports started coming in of denunciations and counter-denunciations, quarrels and disturbances, and plots were hatched and discovered. The events to be described varied from the ridiculous to the ominous, but all had to be given attention, and all got it. We shall here be concerned only with England south of the Trent. I am well aware that the supposedly profound difference made by that line is now recognised to be something of a myth, but in the north endemic troubles were to burst into open rebellion, involving in turn all the counties to the far side of that river, which posed quite different problems to the Crown. The truth about the situation there is well known and has been often discussed,[1] whereas there exists a general notion that the main and 'settled' part of the kingdom gave hardly any cause for anxiety. How insufficient that superficial opinion is I propose to show by taking a clock-wise tour through the country, starting in the south-east. The events to be described are only the more notable or better documented cases of dispute and disaffection. Nor, by omitting several counties do I mean to suggest that all was restful peace there. The tally of tales could easily be enlarged, though respect for human patience advises otherwise. A good many further examples have also been noticed already, and more still will appear in the remainder of this book.

[1] Cf. especially Dodds, and A. G. Dickens, *Lollards and Protestants in the Diocese of York* (1959); also C. S. L. Davies, 'The Pilgrimage of Grace Reconsidered,' *Past and Present* 41 (1968), 54–76, and M. E. James, 'Obedience and Dissent in Henrician England: the Lincolnshire Rebellion 1536,' ibid. 48 (1970), 3–78.

I

We start with Sussex, always a shire given to its own secret ways and troublesome to its bishop who, moreover, throughout the 1530's was himself but doubtfully attached to the new order. At first the see of Chichester was occupied by Robert Sherburne, in his eighties when he resigned, early in 1536, to be succeeded, at Cromwell's promotion, by Richard Sampson, dean of the Chapel Royal and an important King's councillor. But Cromwell solicited Sampson's appointment because they were both members of the government, not because the new bishop shared his own way of thinking; Sampson, a lawyer, was known to be a conservative and to need an eye keeping on him. Both bishops nevertheless tried to do their duty,[1] but the county, so dangerously exposed to the threat of invasion and a major area of concern in time of war or the likelihood of war, was never particularly quiet. There was nothing that could be done about a mad-sounding denunciation from a disgruntled student whose exhibition had been cut off by his benefactors, the priory of Christchurch, Canterbury, and who sought to curry favour by attacking an eminent divine, Dr Richard Boorde, lately living in Sussex but 'now [ca. 1535], fearing of likelihood attachment, . . . departed his country'.[2] Boorde was alleged to have declared that he 'would rather be torn with wild horses than assent or consent to the diminishing of one iota of the bishop of Rome his authority'. He would flee the realm 'if any jurament and oath were required of him' against the pope. This threat he carried out, but from whatever place he had got to he (it was claimed) tried to stir trouble at Lewes by writing to one of the monks there, Dr John Senocke, urging him to join in flight, for 'no Christian might abide the company of so arch-heretics as were under our most noble sovereign his governance'.

The story was probably roughly true, for the informant vouched two other monks of Lewes to warranty to whom Senocke had shown the letter. And while an absent doctor of divinity could only be ignored, stirs at Lewes – where, as we have seen,[3] some friars were later respon-

[1] Cf. below, pp. 89, 232.

[2] SP 1/99, fo. 229 (*LP* ix. 1066). The date is conjectural but must be before Cromwell's elevation to the peerage and after the oath of supremacy. Unfortunately almost nothing seems to be known about Boorde who makes this single appearance in *LP*. That he was an M.A. of Oxford and D.D. of Paris is the extent of the information supplied by Foster's *Alumni Oxonienses*.

[3] Above, p. 74.

sible for starting the rumour of the King's death – required more careful consideration. For at about the same time that this denunciation was received, Richard Layton, visiting the priory, had uncovered serious disaffection there.[1] 'At Lewes,' wrote the notorious visitor, 'I found corruption of both kinds – avowterers [fornicators] and sodomites – *et quod peius est*, traitors.' The subprior, Anthony Bolney, had preached a treasonable sermon, as he himself confessed in a statement which Layton made him sign. He involved the prior, Robert Croham, who had known of his intention and had encouraged it. The prior's denial only got him harsh words from Layton who called him a perjurer and a 'heinous traitor, with the worst words I could devise'. Croham begged on his knees that the matter be not reported to Cromwell but was ordered to appear before the secretary on November 1st. We do not know what had been said, for Layton promised to tell Cromwell in person all the details 'and the tragedy thereof', so that the minister might do with the prior 'what ye list'. But in likelihood Layton's rage had been excessive, at least for Cromwell, for Prior Robert and Subprior Anthony were still in office when their house was dissolved in November 1537, and both got decent pensions. In December 1538 they also, with the rest of the house including John Senocke, obtained the usual dispensations to hold livings.[2] However, though Cromwell was somehow appeased, that influential monastery clearly stood far from well affected and needed watching. And even as he let the offending monks go, Cromwell watched to such good purpose that he acquired the priory at the Dissolution, the biggest thing he made out of that upheaval.[3] The new lord of those manors might keep Sussex in better obedience than the old.

Happenings at Rye and Winchelsea were more disturbing still because those towns formed part of the realm's defences in the south. The troubles were connected with William Inold, vicar of Rye, whom

---

[1] SP 1/98, fos. 26–7 (*LP* ix. 632).

[2] *LP* xii. II. 1101; *Fac. Off. Reg.* 119–20. Prior Robert had been in office for some time – certainly since 1531 (*Sussex Star Chamber Proceedings*, Sussex Record Society, vol. 16 [1913], 56). The story is needlessly complicated by T. W. Horsfield in his *History and Antiquities of Lewes* (1824), 182, who dates the surrender to 1538 and calls the prior Thomas. Croham died peacefully in 1555 (L. Salzman, 'The Last Prior of Lewes,' *Sussex Archaeological Collections*, lxxvi [1935], 178–82).

[3] *LP* xiii. I. 384 (74). There is absolutely no reason to link the monks' escape with Cromwell's acquisition of the property. Apart from the time lag, Cromwell got a grant of the lands out of the King's hands after the Dissolution; he needed no favour from the late owners.

we have already encountered.[1] Inold first caused a disturbance in (probably) 1533,[2] and for the rest of the decade news of him kept coming to the minister's ears. In September 1533, he was denounced for disturbing the parish by talking of the consequences of papal displeasure. If 'our holy father the pope' were to excommunicate the realm, England would be in the same sort of trouble as had been brought upon her by the interdict in King John's time when 'there was neither corn, grass nor fruit growing'. His hearers called the pope's curse 'but words' and opined 'that no like effect will follow in our days'. However, if the pope made war upon the King – 'were we not bound to resist in defence of our prince and realm?' 'No, marry,' replied Inold, 'for the pope is above all kings and princes of the world.' Talk of this kind was also being spread by local friars who threatened the people with destruction, oddly enough by 'the emperor and the Danes'. After his second marriage, they said, King Henry would find no helpers except heretics. People, Cromwell was told, were getting upset and beginning to murmur.[3]

This, of course, was the point that mattered, and so action resulted, but confused action. The mayor and jurats of Rye examined Inold and sent the result to Sir Edward Guildford, warden of the Cinque Ports; Sir Edward re-examined the witnesses, sent the priest to ward in Rye, and reported to Cromwell on October 6th.[4] Meanwhile Cromwell had apparently been informed of the denunciation in some other way; as he heard it, two men were involved – Inold and one Sir James, an Austin friar. On the 7th he therefore ordered the mayor of Rye to have both arrested. The letter did not get to Rye till the 17th – a most unusual delay, if true – and provoked two answers. The mayor and jurats replied on the 23rd that the warden was taking care of the matter.[5] Guildford wrote on the 25th to explain that Inold had been in gaol for three weeks now 'by my commandment and at my cost and charge'. He had not before said anything of the friar because he had not been aware of his existence, but now the friar had joined the priest in ward, though since the main witnesses were at sea, returning from Yarmouth, further action would have to wait.[6] In fact, no more action of conse-

---

[1] Above, pp. 20–1.
[2] The dating by *LP* vi. 1077, 1329 was confirmed by the discovery that Sir Edward Guildford was involved: he died in late 1533 or early 1534 (*LP Add.* 871).
[3] SP 1/79, fos. 23–4 (*LP* vi. 1077).   [4] SP 1/238, fo. 153 (*LP Add.* 871).
[5] SP 1/80, fo. 11 (*LP* vi. 1329).   [6] SP 1/238, fo. 177 (*LP Add.* 879).

quence was taken at this time. If other cases may be used as guides, the difficulty was that such utterances as Inold had allegedly been guilty of were not yet treason by statute.

Possibly Inold received a warning; at any rate, he went free – free enough to talk rashly to John Maydwell in 1535.[1] At that time he also crossed John Yonge who said 'that as good men, as true men and better than the said Inold had been hanged within this month' because they would not take the oath of supremacy, while Inold had taken it but always acted in breach of it. Inold complained to the mayor who thought it his duty to go into the matter but could not discover any grounds for this implicit charge of treason.[2] Anyway, again nothing happened, but in 1537 the rumbling dispute got out of hand and needed serious attention. In the summer of that year, Inold's enemies gathered themselves together and prepared an accusation against him.[3] It appears that Inold had been away from the town for some time, but on July 14th he returned to occupy the cure of souls till August 8th. In those few short weeks he succeeded in stirring up plenty of strife by his attacks on some of the parish, calling them 'heretics and other opprobrious names' and inciting his papistical and drunken followers to start fights. It was claimed that there had been six or seven affrays since his coming back. He talked freely about the return of the old order and kept several of the holy days lately abolished, 'with solemn ringing, singing, procession and decking of the church', contrary to the Injunctions. Also he had taken his seditious preaching to Burwash where he had attacked those who favoured the new learning. Apparently his enemies succeeded in getting a summons against him from the King's Council which they served on him on August 7th; this, no doubt, was the reason that he once again deserted his cure on the following day, though no other consequence seems to have resulted for the moment.

Inold, indeed, fought back, and he had the local authorities on his side. On August 12th, the mayor and jurats wrote in his support to Cromwell.[4] The lord privy seal had no doubt heard from Inold's accusers, not a new tale, of course, for these rumblings against the priest had been going on for a long time. However, in truth most of those men 'be very simple and of small substance, rude both in their communication and behaviour not only against him but also against the

---

[1] Above, p. 21. [2] SP 1/92, fo. 224 (*LP* viii. 776).
[3] SP 1/124, fo. 23 (*LP* xiii. II. 505 [2]). [4] SP 1/124, fo. 21 (*LP* xii. II. 505 [1]).

estate of our town'. Cromwell's favour was sought for Inold and the worthy men of Rye, seventy-five of whom joined their signatures to this petition. Probably by way of underlining the character of his enemies, Inold started to throw charges of heresy around which were brought to Cromwell's notice by the people accused. The paper in which they are collected is headed, 'articles untruly surmised against the persons hereafter named, which they and any of them deny'.[1] Among the persons named appear Inold's leading enemies from Rye and Winchelsea: Thomas Bispin who had denounced him in 1533, John Yonge who had slandered him in 1535, Robert Coke who had delivered the Council summons on August 7th, Thomas Fongler and others who were present on that occasion. For good measure, four priests were subjoined who preached the new learning and new doctrine, including Thomas Garrett, the well known chaplain and follower of Latimer, and Thomas Lawney, a chaplain of Cranmer's whom we shall meet again in the story of Dr Benger.[2] It looks as though Inold, perhaps in association with others, was trying for a clean sweep.

The charges against the villagers did indeed make them look like men 'rude in their communication'; they reeked of Lollardy and ribaldry. Men may swear by the mass because 'it is not of God's making'. Images were 'idols and mammets' to which no one should offer candles. The mass was 'of a juggler's making, and a juggling cast it was'. 'The divine service sung in the church of God is of no more effect than the bleating of a cow to her calf.' 'If our lady were here in earth, I would no more fear to meddle with her than with a common whore.'[3] One man would rather 'have a dog to sing for him than a priest'. Also included were some very Lutheran remarks about every man being a priest and that there were but three sacraments; that of penance in particular was allegedly denied by several people (a hallmark of heresy in the 1530's). The four priests were charged with denying penance, purgatory, the worship of the Virgin Mary and the saints, all very probable things for these particular men to have attacked. But whether the men of Rye and Winchelsea were guilty of utterances they vigorously denied cannot be determined: instead of going after these

[1] SP 1/113, fos. 106–9 (LP xi. 1424). The names identify the purpose and date of this otherwise unassignable document.
[2] Below, pp. 317–18.
[3] A much later hand, possibly of the early eighteenth century, wrote against this in naive indignation: 'No man would say so, and therefore a forgery to make them odious.'

heretics, Cromwell now stepped in to end the immunity which Inold had enjoyed thanks to his friendship with the upper classes of the town. It is clear enough that the divisions here ran not only between adherents of the old and the new way in religion, but more especially also between the rulers of Rye and the poorer sort, entrenched old conflicts being given a religious and political dressing for the purpose of the moment.

What persuaded Cromwell as to the truth of the situation is not known, but it seems that he also had information about the parson of Winchelsea which clinched matters. Two disaffected priests in those two towns was too much, and although he was usually careful not to encourage the lower orders against their betters he now sent unequivocal instructions to Sussex. In February 1538, a servant of his, John Prouse, was at Rye and able to report to Miles Coverdale that Cromwell's letter had taken effect.[1] Both priests were in prison; at Rye, the arrest of Inold had put an end to a situation which was very close to 'insurrection', with two parties sure that things would 'never be well' until either one or the other was put down. Admittedly, there was little haste in the matter, but that was because Cromwell decided to deal with Inold through his bishop, and Sampson's chancellor did not arrive at Rye until June 1538. On the 8th of that month, the mayor and jurats were finally persuaded to send up to the lord privy seal all the books and papers found in Inold's house, while the positive steps against the priest himself were embodied in a bill of charges presented by some of the parish to the visitor.[2] The accusations really concerned themselves with his behaviour in his cure of souls, not in matters political: for five years he had neither resided nor provided a substitute, he had failed to carry out earlier visitatorial injunctions, he frequently offended against the royal orders touching ceremonies and the keeping of feasts, he failed to preach or read the gospel in English, he kept bad company and behaved irreverently.[3] Although the opportunity was taken to include charges against two other clerics in the parish and to accuse Inold also of disrespect for the *Bishops' Book* and of failure to preach against the pope, nearly all the bill dealt with matters cognizable in a Church court and not remotely touching treason. Presumably, despite the loose talk

[1] SP 1/102, fo. 115 (*LP* x. 365). The date in *LP* (1536) makes no sense.
[2] SP 1/133, fo. 7 (*LP* xiii. I. 1150).
[3] A charge of sorcery: he had, 'as a witch', given a child three drinks from the chalice 'for the chyne cough'.

earlier on, treason could not be proved against Inold, only dislike of innovation, and it was no doubt for this reason that Cromwell did not personally engage himself further in the affair. As we have already seen, Inold came to no harm, though he was finally removed from Rye. From Cromwell's point of view – since there were no politics in it – what mattered was the restoration of peace and good order at Rye and Winchelsea, and this was achieved, without shedding of blood, after years of tiresome quarrelling.

2

We move north-west, into the southern Midlands. Berkshire and Oxfordshire, as we have seen, formed the centre of the great rumour of 1537 that the King was dead. Other things also occurred in those counties to attract the government's attention.

In April 1538, information was received which charged treason against Richard Lawson, parish priest of Windsor, and his assistant, known to us only as Sir Peter.[1] The possibility of treason on the very doorstep of the King's castles seems to have stirred the authorities deeply; action resulted with quite unaccustomed speed. The events which brought the local trouble into the open occurred in the evening of April 3rd; by the 5th, commissioners were taking evidence from all involved. Not so long before, in October 1536, there had been a notorious case at Windsor when a priest, egged on by a butcher, preached support for the northern rebels, in the presence of the King's army, with banners displayed. In those circumstances, treason was properly triable by the law martial, and both men were hanged on the spot.[2] It is quite likely that even eighteen months later the town was still a bit on edge. Lawson's accuser was Robert Guy, a singing-man of the College and evidently a supporter of the reform; the two priests, beyond question, viewed the innovations with alarm; behind these respectable disagreements lay the usual petty personal dislikes and small-town squabbles. Statements were taken from accuser and accused, as well as from various other people at Windsor, on the basis of which I shall attempt a coherent reconstruction of what took place. One peculiar aspect of this story are the ages of the men concerned: Guy, at thirty-six, was the youngest of them. This is not a tale of irresponsible youth.

[1] All we know of the story comes from depositions collected by commissioners appointed to investigate: SP 1/131, fos. 23–31 (*LP* xiii. I. 686).
[2] Hall, 823.

About five o'clock in the afternoon of April 3rd, Guy was leaning against the doorpost of the fuller's shop kept by Robert Leche, whittling 'a piece of box' with his knife. Two bakers, Robert Orchard and John Tyle, coming into town, stopped to watch him. Guy must have known them and their views and, remembering the recent proclamation permitting the eating of white meat and eggs in Lent that year,[1] decided to annoy them. 'How say ye now, my two masters,' he said, àpropos of nothing, 'to a good salt eel? I could gladly feed thereof and not charge my conscience. Yea, masters, how say ye to a dish of buttered eggs?' Tyle took the bait, swearing that 'by the grace of God, no eggs shall come into my belly before Easter'. Anyway, eggs were now so dear that a penny would buy but eight instead of the usual dozen. Ah, replied Guy, in effect quoting the proclamation, the law against eating white meat in Lent was but a popish tradition which the bishop of Rome had regularly allowed men to buy exemptions from; now 'the King – God preserve his grace – hath freely given licence to all his subjects, and without money'. Here Leche's servant, Edmund Knight, interposed that he had heard the proclamation read at Uxbridge, together with a warning to people not to 'murmur ne grudge' at any who took advantage of it. Tyle, alarmed, said, 'I would thou knowest, knave, I do neither murmur ne grudge at it'. Knight protested that he was accusing no one, but his master intervened, 'peace, apply thy work'.

Having got a nasty situation under way, Guy switched to his pet hate, Richard Lawson. 'We have,' he said, 'a curate here: a certain woman, married, being with him in confession, he demanded of her whether she had accompanied carnally with any other beside her husband.' When she said no, Lawson remarked that 'many women in this town have done'. Also the parson's assistant – 'the morrow mass priest' – had told another woman not to be ruled by her husband, 'for he is naught and if ye be he will make thee naught also'. There was something in these tales, but Guy had rather distorted them in order to slander the priests and make them appear active in slandering the parish. Lawson admitted telling Alice Merbeke: 'If ye have not offended beside your husband, ye have cause to thank God; many other have

---

[1] *TRP* i. 260–1, proclamation of 11 March 1538. The dispensation was justified on the grounds that fish was scarce and dear that year, and also that the Lenten rules were but 'positive law' which kings could vary if they 'shall perceive the same to stand to the hurt and danger of their people'.

done – the more pity!' And Sir Peter, who resented Guy's making him out an 'undiscreet ghostly father', had warned Agnes Wilson against eating meat in Lent merely because her husband did so. There was also talk of his having solicited offerings contrary to the royal Injunctions. To Guy all this was proof that the priests would not obey the King's orders and were 'privy traitors'. All, he said to Tyle, would come out one day. Tyle angrily expressed confidence in Lawson and went off.

By this time, however, the day was only forty-eight hours off, for on the 5th Guy stood before investigators to tell all he knew of Lawson. His accusations fall into two parts. In the first place, Lawson was guilty of superstitious practices condemned in the *Bishops' Book*. He had used a piece of wick to measure the church and churchyard, and had then had it made into a wax-candle called 'a tryndell' the light of which, he told the people, would 'mitigate and assuage the plague, the high indignation and displeasure of God'. Leche confirmed that Lawson had done this, but Lawson maintained that, the old trindle being spent, he had merely asked the churchwardens to provide a new one; of any measuring done he knew nothing, and he claimed to be supported by many honest men of the parish who had already deposed before the commissioners. There are no such depositions in the bundle collected and certified by the commissioners, which must reflect upon Lawson: Guy's accusation would seem to have been essentially true.

Similarly, there was sufficient truth in his much more serious charge that Lawson had not been warm enough in support of the royal supremacy. About January 10th he (Guy) had privately warned Lawson to be more careful in praying for the King and the Prince, and more convincing in declaring the King's title to the people, as his duty was. Lawson retorted, 'meddle ye with that ye have to do'. So, on February 3rd, in the presence of the mayor and one of the worthies of the town (who confirmed this), Guy repeated his warning. He also pointed out how often he had tried to get Lawson to preach the Ten Commandments and to teach the Paternoster, Ave and Creed in English (as required by the Injunctions), only to be told that 'I have no such commandment from mine ordinary'. The mayor added his urgings to Guy's, but Lawson, by his own account, turned surly: 'Mine ordinary can teach me mine office – meddle ye with that ye have to do.' He had been priest at Hatfield before, and both there and at Windsor he claimed to have discharged his duties properly, even before, very lately, he had at last received instructions from his bishop about denouncing the bishop of Rome – a really incredible statement by this date.[1]

We do not know what happened further – almost certainly nothing. Guy was evidently pursuing a private vendetta, but Lawson manifestly – to put it no stronger – had been less zealous than he should have been in his advocacy of the new order. Guy's talk of treason was absurdly extravagant, and there is no sign that anyone took it seriously. It may be conjectured that the experience of being denounced sufficed to mend Lawson's ways. But it also appears that in a place so close to the centre of government passive resistance to the most important royal decrees could persist as late as 1538.

At Oxford, as one might expect, arguments reached a higher level of intellect and also, predictably, of academic passion. Oxford, in fact, was something of a problem to Cromwell; as John Parkins discovered in 1537 when he accused two abbots of treason and was instead treated as the party accused, the authorities there leant towards the old ways and proved far from active in assisting the promoters of the new.[2] One of the men who had come out quite strongly against Parkins was William Bannister who as mayor of Oxford in the following year found himself involved in more of these quarrels and again gave some indication of his opinion. On three occasions in 1538, the lord privy seal was troubled with information about characteristic exchanges of academic courtesies, and on a fourth he had to look into a matter of ecclesiastical discipline reported by the bishop of Lincoln. Yet at no time could he feel sure that the policy of the government commanded the ungrudging support of the people on the spot on whose exercise of authority he had necessarily to rely.

The first trouble arose out of the break-up of the friendship between two of the chaplains of 'the King's College' (Christ Church to be), Henry Spicer and John Hatley.[3] Hatley inclined to the new, Spicer to

---

[1] Windsor was in Salisbury diocese in which admittedly until early 1535 the bishop, Cardinal Campeggio, had been a permanent absentee. But his successor was Nicholas Shaxton, a reformer, who cannot be supposed to have been negligent in so elementary a duty. If he had indeed been, he was in trouble, for just before these events he had got on Cromwell's wrong side by protesting against some vicegerential interference in his diocese, only to be firmly rebuked (Merriman, ii. 128–31).

[2] Elton, 'The Fool of Oxford,' *Star Chamber Stories*, 19 ff.

[3] SP 1/130, fo. 74; 132, fos. 13, 15; E 36/120, fos. 142–6 (*LP* xiii. I. 529, 904, 905, 845).

the old, and Spicer was not a man to watch his words: 'a perilous fellow of his tongue,' Hatley once told someone, 'and one day will babble so far that he cannot pull in his tongue again.' 'Ye be my friend,' said Hatley to Spicer when the dangerous talk first began, 'and hath been, but if ye speak such words as these be I cannot abide you.' The final break between them came on 16 March 1538 at dinner at the house of David Pratt, apothecary,[1] when Hatley completely lost his temper and called Spicer a traitor whose treason he would prove on him. He assured Pratt that he had witnesses to substantiate the charge, and the apothecary thereafter felt obliged to press harder even than Hatley who once admitted that but for Pratt's urging he would never have taken matters to extremes. He would certainly have been wiser to let his temper cool. As it was, two Oxford aldermen reported to Cromwell on the 17th that they had arrested both men and proposed to send them up. Cromwell hurriedly, on the 20th, instructed the mayor to deal with the business at Oxford instead, and Bannister, assisted by other men, proceeded to take evidence. Hatley did not make much of a case. At first he could do no better than accuse Spicer of having 'a traitor's heart', but, given time to collect evidence and witnesses, he prepared himself a little better. He now produced twelve articles against Spicer as well as fourteen witnesses, but the latter all denied any knowledge of the first eleven articles which included charges of speaking well of More and Fisher, attacking the preaching against images, and such-like suspicious stuff. The only thing that could be proved against Spicer on this occasion was some rather loose talk about abbeys: he had certainly regretted their coming down and expressed the view that they would all fall and even so their wealth would not satisfy the King.

Seeing the way things were going, Hatley intervened to say that there were three other witnesses to support him who could not, however, be present before the Friday in Easter week (April 26th, a fairly long adjournment). The commissioners agreed to put things off till then, but Hatley's real purpose in asking for time was different. He evidently recognised that Spicer would escape him; he may well have remembered Parkins's fate the year before; and he was sure that one of the commissioners, Robert Carter, a canon of his own College,[2] was

---

[1] Pratt played a part in Parkins's story where he is called stationer to the University and a bailiff of the town (Elton, *Star Chamber Stories*, 26, 40: miscalled Daniel there). He favoured the innovators.　　　　　[2] *LP* v. 1207 (38).

violently prejudiced against him. So he wrote to Cromwell instead, complaining of this partiality and asking for aid. Cromwell responded with a letter ordering Bannister to abandon the examination of the case, a somewhat strange proceeding which suggests that he now saw the inanity of Hatley's accusations but wished to save him from the consequences of false delation. He, too, was likely to remember Parkins. When the commissioners reassembled on April 26th, Hatley greatly astonished everyone by delivering to them Cromwell's letter 'of discharge of further examination' and, while they were still trying to make it out, reading a copy of it aloud to the company, 'which like thing we had not seen before'. He improved the occasion with some slanderous remarks about the commissioners and complaints about the way his witnesses had been treated. All this Bannister reported to Cromwell on May 5th, asking huffily in the end that the matter might be committed to some other gentlemen. Not that Cromwell had any intention of allowing further proceedings, but he was mistaken if he thought he had heard the last of Hatley. A little later he received a new complaint. The end of the commission had only unleashed Carter's full rage upon the chaplain: Carter was warning off Hatley's friends, withholding his wages, and in general making life miserable for him. So Hatley begged Cromwell to get him his pay and also to continue to investigate Spicer, suggesting that Dr Cave, a canon of King's College and chaplain to the lord privy seal, would make a suitable examiner. So far as we know, Cromwell ignored this appeal; he may well have felt that he had done quite enough for Hatley. This is not to doubt, however, that Spicer had talked actively against the innovations and caused at least some foaming at the mouth in others.

Oxford soon enough re-appeared on Cromwell's plate. On 25 June 1538, Bannister wrote that the warden of New College (Dr John London) had brought in two men – John Emerson, a young fellow of the College, and Robert Croft, one of the chapel priests – because there had been an argument between them touching the supremacy. The mayor forwarded the statements taken from them and from a witness, Matthew Goodryke; meanwhile, the warden was keeping the parties safe.[1] In fact, Emerson had charged Croft with speaking treasonable

---

[1] SP 1/133, fo. 203 (*LP* xiii. I. 1257). The depositions are SP 1/92, fos. 267–8 (*LP* viii. 799), misplaced by *LP* into 1535. None of these members of the University appears in the known lists.

words. The story rambles rather, and some complications – especially the intrusion of an auger and some nails which Emerson wished to borrow from Croft to mend his garden gate with – are best ignored. According to Emerson, Croft had in the evening of May 19th forced his company upon him as he was walking in the garden and had then talked in favour of the pope. There was a long argument, in the course of which Croft offered a non-accademic reason as well for abandoning newfangled ideas:

There shall be £40 given to the College, and I assure you, none that be of these new opinions shall get a farthing, and I know that ye be a poor man having need of exhibition. Wherefore it shall be most expedient for you to leave this new trade.

He also offered to show Emerson a book which conclusively proved the papal supremacy to be true. This once again turned out to be Eck's *Enchiridion versus Lutheranos*, still the standard refutation of Reformed doctrine. There was some argument about the familiar passage touching Christ's giving the keys of the kingdom – 'to the whole congregation of Christian people,' said Emerson; 'nay, nay,' said Croft, 'but to some spiritual men'. Emerson loyally affirmed that 'the King's grace was the head of our congregation and under him the bishop of Canterbury'. To this, 'he, making a mad gesture, said no more'. Croft, of course, denied it all. They had talked of Scripture and the Church's authority in deciding which gospels were canonical, but there had been not a word spoken of the pope's primacy. Emerson was simply moved by malice: malice occasioned by Croft's action in reporting him to the warden some time before for denying transubstantiation and saying that Frith had been wrongfully put to death. In his 'simple judgment', added Croft virtuously, this last remark was seditious, inasmuch as it tended 'against the King's majesty and his laws'.

Unfortunately, it was just one man's word against another's, for the alleged witness, Goodryke, while admitting that he had been there at the start of the two conversations in question, said that he had left on both occasions before the argument got to the crucial points. Even if Cromwell had wanted to investigate Croft further, this was a dead end. But at least he had proof that yet another College harboured men of violently opposed views and some who, from the Crown's point of view, could not be trusted. The most weighty demonstration of this dispiriting fact reached him a little later, in October, when Cranmer forwarded statements he had received against certain members of Corpus Christi College who were accused by some of their fellows of a dangerous unwillingness to cooperate with the new order.[1]

On the one side – the old side – stood two masters of arts and one bachelor, John Donne, Thomas Slater and Hugh Turnbull. On the other were men of the same age or a little younger: Richard Marshall, Gregory Stremer, Edmund Mervyn, Hugh Goode and others.[2] They produced a short compendium on their three enemies to which Marshall added a separate list of articles. Some of the stuff reported is typical of the pettiness of academic communities, as when Marshall took offence at the insufficient punishment of one man who had tried to prevent the erasing of the pope's name from certain books: he was deprived of his commons for a fortnight but in fact 'had his meat and drink given to him'. But much of it was serious. Donne, it was alleged, had violently objected to erasing the pope's name from what he called 'profane books' (that is, anything but service books: in this case the works of St Gregory); in preaching he had defended the bishop of Rome's right to be called *papa* on the grounds 'that it was but a foolish fantasy of men to make so much about the name *papa*, because divers bishops beside the bishop of Rome were so called'; in particular, he had refused to give instruction in the way now approved. Stremer had urged Donne 'to teach the youth why the bishop of Rome was expulsed' since 'none of them can tell why it is done'. 'No more can I,' said Donne. 'No?,' said Stremer, 'what mean you, Master Donne? Bear record, masters.' But Donne was not a don for nothing; he thought a moment and then said that he could not understand the need for any expulsion because 'he never knew of any authority he had here'. This explanation had satisfied the bishop's commissary – and it may be added that, with less justification, it has satisfied certain historians since.

The trouble really was the usual one: Stremer and Marshall, zealous reformers, had got very unpopular in the College by calling loudly for obedience to the order to remove the pope's title wherever found, while Donne loved the old time when 'good men were wont to build and

---

[1] SP 1/137, fos. 141–3 (*LP* xiii. II. 561).

[2] Mervyn and Marshall had graduated B.A. in 1537, but Goode (1524) was the oldest of the people involved. The dates of rest were: Donne 1526, Slater 1528, Turnbull 1536, and Stremer 1529. For these and the details mentioned in the next note see Foster, *Alumni Oxonienses*.

maintain churches, and now they be more ready to pluck them down'. Turnbull, a reader in logic, had offended the younger men by forcing the 'good questions' propounded by the undergraduates into the strait-jacket of 'Duns' quiddities'. It exasperated Marshall to find that books supporting the pope, including the treatise of Alexander of Hales, had not been removed from the library. The older men objected to students studying Scripture – 'a subversion of good order' – and equated the new learning with adultery and knavery. The young men preached rather too excitingly. The College was deeply divided, and in that close community tempers flared and words flew. But there was no matter of treason or triable sedition, nothing to get hold of for action, only a good deal of disquieting indication that the undergraduates of Corpus Christi might very well not be brought up in the right way. Cromwell was always exercised over the state of both Universities; he needed sound seminaries to supply the clergy for his reformed Church and the intellectuals whom he meant to employ in the state. He needed to know about such ominous internal disputes as those reported from New College, Corpus Christi and the future Christ Church; but beyond filing the information there was nothing that he could or would do.[1]

So far Oxford had provided news of troublesome men of the old faction. In the spring of 1539, as Cromwell got ready for the battle to maintain the Reformation, he heard, inconveniently, of men there whose excessive zeal on the other side had enabled the conservatives to strike back. On 5 April 1539, Bishop Longland reported, not (one may suppose) without glee, that a gang of people had been caught at Oxford who had eaten meat in Lent.[2] They had in fact been interrogated by the mayor and others on the previous 3rd.[3] The discovery centred upon the house of Horman Men (presumably a German or Dutchman), a book-seller, where unlawful Lenten feasts seem regularly to have taken place. He, his wife, family and visitors had since the beginning of Lent (Ash Wednesday falling on February 19th that year) got through a sub-

[1] All these fellows of Corpus continued their careers. Donne transferred himself to New College in July 1539, but such moves were far too common for anything to be read into this. It would seem that the youthful ardour of the reforming party did not endure: both Marshall and Mervyn, who made their peace with the changing order under Mary, were deprived under Elizabeth – Marshall of the deanship of Christ Church, a College he had joined on its foundation in 1544.
[2] *LP* xiii. I. 811 (misdated there).
[3] SP 1/146, fo. 252 (*LP* xiv. I. 684).

stantial stock of meat: about twenty legs of mutton, five rounds of beef, and six capons. Their visitors included fellows of New College, All Souls, Corpus Christi (Stremer and Marshall inevitably among them), Oriel, Canterbury College and Alban Hall, several black monks, and at least three bookbinders with their families. Men admitted knowing that all this fast-breaking – he had heard of it going on elsewhere as well – was contrary to the King's injunctions.

So it was, but the detected persons rallied and appealed to Cromwell.[1] They called themselves 'the whole number of your scholars in Oxford, those only which are the favourers of God's word', confessed that they had secretly eaten meat in Lent, but claimed that they had intended to cause no offence and had acted thus only because they feared 'the evident infirmity of their bodies'. Hardly the stuff of which revolutionaries are made, though anyone recalling that the Reformation in Zürich had announced itself with an allegedly secret breaking of the Lenten fast was no doubt likely to watch such goings-on with apprehension. Certainly the conservative bishop of Lincoln did so watch: there had been a traitor among the meat-eaters, bought with Longland's money, who had revealed the affair. The petitioners said that they were compelled to flee from Oxford and begged Cromwell to give them the consolation of a decision, or at least to commit the matter to upright men and not to such 'as will strain a gnat and devour a camel'. All these papers reached Cromwell at the start of the parliamentary session which witnessed the passing of the hard-fought Proclamations Act as well as the Act of Six Articles; small wonder that he did nothing about Oxford's legs of mutton and rounds of beef. But he was not allowed to forget them. After the conservative triumph of that session, Longland was not likely to let slip a chance of stamping on the Oxford radicals, and in August, when the court was at Oatlands in Surrey, the bishop urged that the minister's proximity to Oxford (it *was* nearer than London) should enable him to do something about those breakers of Lent.[2] He had his own spiritual instruments, of course, but he wished to push the lord privy seal into action against his own supporters; at Cambridge, he said, similar offences had led to indictments for Lollardy and public penances. Cromwell still did nothing, and Longland stopped pestering him.

[1] SP 1/141, fo. 232 (*LP* xiii. II, App. 19), also misplaced by a year.
[2] SP 1/153, fo. 46 (*LP* xiv. II. 71).

4-2

The southern Midlands were not in uproar, but neither were they at rest. Few real traitors were reported. The neighbouring county of Buckinghamshire yielded one, an unfortunate tailor of Newport Pagnell, George Baburney, who stood trial and presumably suffered execution for as comprehensive a treason by words as it is possible to imagine. In February 1535, in front of witnesses, he was carried away by some fury to the extent of saying: 'King Henry VIII was a heretic, a thief and harlot, and a traitor to God and his laws; and before mid-summer day next coming he trusted and would play football with his head, and that our sovereign lord King Henry VIII was not of right king of England and had no title to the crown of England.' The true king was the king of Scots who would wear the crown of England before midsummer. And he wished 'that the sword of vengeance might light upon' the King and all his Council.[1] However, such rash men were on the whole more easily dealt with than sullen opponents who stopped short of treason and yet spread disaffection – and did so in spots as sensitive as the royal borough of Windsor and the University of Oxford.

3

The city of Salisbury provides a splendid example of a very typical situation in the England of the early Reformation.[2] Here, the municipal officers had for long been at daggers drawn with the bishop and his officers over rights of jurisdiction and the bishop's claim to be ruler of the city. Under letters patent granted by Edward IV, the bishop enjoyed the right to appoint commissioners of the peace and gaol delivery in Salisbury, an unusual delegation of royal powers which Campeggio had exercised.[3] Nicholas Shaxton in April 1535 at once revived the quarrel, especially as Shaxton's under-bailiff (his chief agent

---

[1] KB 9/531/11. He was tried by a special commission of oyer and terminer. One cannot be sure that the sentence passed on him was carried out since the return of the record of a trial into King's Bench at this time usually implied an attempt to get the case quashed; but since nothing appears on the plea roll, the chances are that the attempt failed.

[2] The story is briefly and not quite accurately told in Fanny Street, 'The Relations of the Bishops and Citizens of Salisbury between 1225 and 1612,' *Wilts. Archaeological and Natural History Magazine*, 39 (1915–17), 185–257, 319–67. The article adds a little information from the city records. The evidence involves some serious dating problems, and I here relate events in the best order that I can devise.

[3] E 135/8/38, 25/25, commissions of the peace and of gaol delivery dated respectively 23 December and 20 March 1532.

in the city) was soon to be another tactlessly eager reformer, John Goodall, who stepped up the policy of asserting the bishop's rights of franchise in order to employ them to overcome conservative resistance in matters of religion.[1] Goodall later claimed to have greatly laboured 'in the last two Parliaments by writing, speaking and spending his goods for the extirping of the fucated and usurped authority of the bishop of Rome', and to have had nothing but malice in return.[2] By late 1538, and probably much earlier, he had formerly entered Cromwell's service,[3] and he owed his appointment at Salisbury to the minister. This fact gives a certain problematic quality to a draft bill of Parliament intended to limit the jurisdictional powers of the under-bailiff and to make sure that he was always a man sufficiently learned in the law.[4] The draft is heavily corrected by Cromwell, and it was he who replaced a generalised complaint about bailiffs' courts with a reference to the present holder of the office as one 'who can neither write, read ne hath any manner knowledge in the laws of the land', a remark which he knew could not apply to Goodall who wrote him only too many letters. Though possibly the description may have fitted Thomas Chambers, in office until the autumn of 1537, it is much more likely that this bill belongs to the days of Cromwell's private practice; in which case the city started attacking the bishop's officer in Campeggio's tenure, round about 1529–1531. However, Shaxton and his men certainly called forth a more determined activity.

All the old causes of friction notwithstanding, it was the Reformation which provoked the first serious clash. In February 1537, the bishop's Scottish chaplain John Madowell (McDougal?) preached a sermon so hostile to the old ways that the city was up in arms. In late March,

[1] One John Goodall, servant to a London printer, was involved in the clandestine distribution of Lutheran books in 1528 (*LP* iv. 4004, 4017, 4073). Although the Salisbury Goodall also favoured the reform, it is far from certain that the two men are one; the chances are against it. The record yields one other person of the same name who is assuredly not connected with either of these two (*LP* xiii. I. 306).

[2] SP 1/140, fo. 224 (*LP* xiii. II. 1178). He does not appear in the members' list for 1529 (*Official Return*, i. 368 ff.), and there is no list for 1536. I conclude that either he entered the Reformation Parliament at a by-election and was re-elected in 1536, or he merely wished to point to his active promotion of the new order during the time the two Parliaments sat.

[3] He is called Cromwell's 'vigilant servant' (SP 1/137, fo. 196 [*LP* xiii. II. 606]).

[4] SP 1/238, fos. 46–7 (*LP Add.* 824). Cromwell advised his clients to proceed by private rather than public bill: he altered the opening phrase from 'Prayen the Commons' to 'Prayen the mayor, aldermen and the poor commons of the city of New Sarum'.

Madowell thought it wise to appeal to Cromwell and Shaxton in self-defence.[1] He produced a long list of charges against the people of Salisbury who had torn down the King's proclamations relaxing Lent that year, had imprisoned a man who had protested against the unsound preaching of an old-fashioned friar, had tried at the last Sessions to promote indictments for heresy against the bishop (a manoeuvre which Shaxton's counsel got quashed in King's Bench), had failed to remove the pope's name from books as ordered, and had done all this and more with the connivance of the city fathers. At the same time the mayor informed against Madowell. Cromwell reacted in his customary manner, by ordering that the complaints be investigated. He told the mayor to bind Madowell in sureties and to release on bail the man who had been imprisoned for attacking the friar;[2] and he ordered Thomas Benet, a prebendary of Salisbury Cathedral, to examine Madowell. This Benet did on April 4th, forwarding the result on the 8th.[3] The questions asked were so framed as to treat Madowell as a disturber of the peace. He admitted his incendiary sermon and his accusations touching the pulling down of the royal proclamations, but did not know who was responsible; he denied ever saying that the mayor 'would be the King's officer and not the bishop's', though he felt inclined to think that the mayor behaved like neither's; and he asserted that he only regretted the disputes between mayor and under-bailiff which had had the consequence that no one had tried to find out who had illtreated the Lenten proclamation. The tone of the interrogation is hostile, as is Benet's covering letter. Though at this point Madowell disappears from the story, he had served to consolidate opinion at Salisbury behind the municipal officers and against the bishop. One of the things that had displeased the mayor about him was, needless to say, his Scottish birth.

[1] SP 1/117, fos. 153, 158–9 (LP xii. I. 746, 755–6). Madowell referred to the King's proclamations permitting meat in Lent, and the only one known to us is that of March 1538. But Madowell's later examination is dated to the year 1537. Either this date is wrong, which is possible, or Lent was also relaxed in 1537, though we are otherwise ignorant of this. I have adhered to the 1537 dating, but with some misgivings.

[2] SP 1/117, fo. 272 (LP xii. I. 838), the mayor to Cromwell on April 6th. The mayor refers to Cromwell's complaint that with respect to one William Ferreys things had not been done as they should have been and reports that Ferreys was now bound to appear before Cromwell. The suggestion in the text makes the most likely sense of this obscurity.

[3] SP 1/117, fos. 257–9; 118, fo. 82 (LP xii. I. 824, 868).

The city, learning that Shaxton was seeking renewal of his charter, now went over to the attack. On June 7th, they dispatched a petition to Cromwell in which they attacked Chambers and asked that if the charter were renewed it should be in less generous terms than hitherto.[1] At the same time they raised two special complaints with Lord Chancellor Audley: the commission of the peace and the mayor's oath.[2] They claimed that the Act in Limitation of Franchises[3] had cancelled all such grants as that by which the bishop appointed justices of the peace in his liberty, and they pretended to believe that the ancient oath (which bound the mayor to the bishop as well as the King) was an innovation introduced by Chambers the previous November. This line of attack was well chosen, for on both counts Cromwell's policy of strengthening the Crown's exclusive authority in government seemed involved. However much the minister might suspect that a specious case was being made out against those who supported his religious policy, he could not readily overrule these politically acceptable pleas. Thus he compromised by ordering the justices of assize to investigate, and on August 8th the city appointed a committee to watch its interests at the enquiry.

This attempt at settlement failed completely. The judges – Sir John Fitzjames, L.C.J., and Sir Thomas Willoughby – heard the arguments on the 10th, but were unable to do more than order both parties to put their case in writing to be delivered to Cromwell. According to Shaxton this was because, when things looked like going right for the bishop, one Thomas Caffyn, 'having the personage of a sober man and nevertheless the most importune and seditious person of them all', interrupted by affirming that the city would have its will one way or another, and if they failed on this occasion they would look to the lord chancellor instead.[4] As it happened, Fitzjames did not go up to Westminster to attend the Michaelmas term which he thought would have to be put off because of the plague, so that Cromwell received no report and the enquiry did no good at all. Nor did the one step possibly taken in response to the mayor's complaints, the replacement of Chambers by Goodall. For Goodall proved a good deal more active still, and

[1] R. Benson and H. Hatcher, *Old and New Sarum* (1843), 237–8.
[2] Street, 'Bishops and Citizens of Salisbury', 324–6.
[3] 27 Henry VIII c. 24; Street gives the wrong regnal year.
[4] SP 1/126, fos. 186–7 (*LP* xii. II. 1114).

in November two citizens denounced him for attacking the authority of the mayor. Goodall was claiming all rights of government for the bishop, and for himself as the bishop's agent; he had contemptuously said that the mayor was just another officer like the catchpole or the bellman, and was 'but as a May king'. Told that the mayor could arrest him for misbehaviour, he had wished 'a turd in thy teeth, and in the mayor's teeth also'. And he had promised that the quarrel would soon be settled in the bishop's favour. This was a reference to the forth-coming swearing-in of a new mayor at which the disputed oath would come up again, as the mayor explained in forwarding the denunciation to Cromwell.[1] Aware that the paper delivered to Fitzjames had never reached the minister, the mayor enclosed another set of articles stating the city's case.

At this point, Shaxton at last intervened to defend his officer.[2] He praised Goodall, an exception in a world 'wherein well nigh every man goeth about to oppress us poor men of the King's clergy *indignissimis modis, per phas et nephas*', not the most tactful line to take with Crom-well. He went on, quite correctly, to explain that the city was simply trying to destroy the bishop's lawful franchise; Chaffyn in particular had done so frequently, for instance by setting free people attached by the bishop's officers for trespass or debt. They claimed that 'the city is the King's city, the mayor the King's mayor and the King's lieutenant'; but, as Edward IV's charter proved, 'the city is the bishop's city, and the mayor is the bishop's mayor and hath none authority within the city but the clerkship of the market', though Shaxton admitted that 'now' the commission of the peace must run in the King's name. Evidently, the act of 1535 had done its work there. The real authority, the bishop went on, was the bailiff's and in his absence the under-bailiff's, 'your servant Goddall'. But Goodall's efforts to defend the bishop's rights produced only cries of 'the bishop is a heretic' and 'we trust to see him hanged'. This pointed the problem: the ancient quarrel over jurisdiction, which had nothing to do with the new order at all, exploited the religious divisions. Shaxton assured Cromwell that he was being patient beyond belief, but he could hardly be asked simply to give in on everything. He had heard it reported that Cromwell had accused him of having 'a stomach more meet for an emperor than for a bishop', but this was really not so. His patience was marvellous.

[1] SP 1/126, fo. 84 (*LP* xii. II. 1026).   [2] SP 1/126, fos. 186–7 (*LP* xii. II. 1114).

Put in the position of having either to reassert clerical claims or weaken the progress of the Reformation, Cromwell hesitated. In October 1538, he heard from Lord Fitzwarren that the subdean of Salisbury, Giles Hakluyt, was working for the old order and had the favour of various people, including the mayor's. An attack on him had been suppressed by the mayor, and Fitzwarren, suspecting 'bearing' ('as there is in every other matter saving only in the cause of a poor wretch that hath no man to speak for him') promised the radical party to let Cromwell know.[1] The report underlined the need to back up the reforming clergy at Salisbury. Soon there was evidence that the minister's failure to act had greatly encouraged the city: late in 1538, Goodall, Cromwell's servant or not, found himself in prison. He claimed to have been put there by the 'unjust and malicious complaints of his papistical and seditious adversaries' who resented his doing his duty in his offices of undersheriff, stewart of the court leet, and bailiff of the liberty, in all which capacities he had endeavoured to enforce the law against the pope and against idolatry. Rather rashly he promised that, if delivered, he would never again meddle in such matters; at least he asked to be set free on bail.[2]

To this extent Cromwell did assist him; on 11 January 1539 the mayor reported that Goodall had been bound to appear at the Sessions to be held on the 22nd and asked what was to be done about the choice of a jury. The panel was Goodall's responsibility: would Cromwell please instruct the justices to see fair play? The mayor used the opportunity to press the city's case once more: Goodall had been guilty of 'extortion and bribery' and would ruin the city unless soon deprived of office. He asked that he might wait upon Cromwell to present grievances.[3] We do not know what happened at the Sessions, but we do know that Goodall remained unabashed and soon meddled again. Another of his characteristic exploits, on Easter Day (April 6th) 1539, provoked a protest to the Council and a hasty letter from Shaxton.[4] Seeing people kissing the image of Christ on an altar, and unaware that the eucharist had been put in that altar, he ordered the priest to remove the image because such kissing was contrary to the Injunctions. His

[1] SP 1/137, fo. 196 (*LP* xiii. II. 606).
[2] SP 1/140, fo. 224 (*LP* xiii. II. 1178). The date of this undated document is fixed by a reference to the proclamation of 16 November 1538 (*TRP* i. 270).
[3] SP 1/128, fo. 72 (*LP* xiii. I. 64); misplaced by a year in *LP*.
[4] Only the second survives: SP 1/150, fo. 140 (*LP* xiv. I. 777).

point was that kissing was permitted only on Good Friday and the morning of Easter Day, whereas by that time it was three of the afternoon! This story tells a good deal about the reasons for people's dislike of Goodall. When the priest hesitated, Goodall had his servant take the image down and put it behind the altar. But his loyal action was now being described as contempt of the sacrament; Goodall was called a sacramentary (a Zwinglian or Anabaptist), which most certainly he was not.

Goodall also wrote himself, explaining that he had done his duty by the proclamations and saying that one of the people doing the kissing deserved special punishment, 'he being a graduate of the University'. His appeal was to Cromwell as the single-handed destroyer of bad religion: 'your calling of God,' he wrote, is to be 'the only suppressor within this realm...of all idolatry and popishness'.[1] What is more, this line of argument seems to have worked. When some men of Salisbury brought an action against Goodall in Star Chamber, charging him with sacrilege, the move apparently collapsed at once.[2] The last document surviving from these troubles is another letter from Goodall to Cromwell to the effect that while the under-bailiff might have got much personal disfavour out of his zeal, his reports to Cromwell had done some good. At least the Cathedral clergy were now doing their jobs properly. But the Injunctions were not being obeyed further west, nor would they be till Cromwell instituted proper enquiries, 'the King to bear the charge'.[3] Goodall really was indefatigable, but, of course, times were turning against him. In July Shaxton resigned his see on account of the Act of Six Articles; he was succeeded by John Capon, an ex-abbot and a rather disagreeable conservative. Significantly enough, the city – for the moment – ceased to quarrel with its bishop. The next trouble to blow up at Salisbury was, so to speak, the other way on: in July 1541, Capon certified the Council of the discovery of what looks very much like a group of real sacramentaries or belated Lollards.[4]

On the face of it, the problem of Salisbury remained unsettled in Cromwell's day; certainly, nothing was done to resolve the issue over the bishop's charter and the city's claims. In practice, as subsequent

---

[1] SP 1/150, fo. 142 (*LP* xiv. I. 778).
[2] Only Goodall's answer now survives: St Ch 2/24/408.
[3] SP 1/151, fo. 152 (*LP* xiv. I. 894).   [4] St Ch 2/34/28.

events were to show, the bishop was in full retreat.[1] Shaxton had, indeed, been ill-advised to attempt a revival of his most pompous claims at a time when priests were so much under attack and the Crown was so active in reducing franchisal pretensions. It is probable enough that Cromwell really, in exasperation, suspected him of having an imperial 'stomach' – a taste for high rule – and Cromwell seems to have been right. But the manner in which both sides exploited their strong points – the city its anticlericalism and the bishop his reformer's zeal – made a definite resolution impossible: it looks, interestingly enough, as though Cromwell's own passion for the reform alone prevented him from putting Shaxton down. At any rate, he saw to the appointment of Goodall, his servant; Goodall from first to last made no bones about his zest in promoting the new order and thereby caused very special annoyance; and Goodall in the end enjoyed Cromwell's protection.

4

Somerset, too, provided the usual crop of dubious denunciations and dangerous speeches. There was the prior of the Charterhouse at Henton, Dr Horde, reported in May 1533 by a discontented inmate of the neighbouring Charterhouse at Witham (*quia nunquam deformata?*) for attacking Anne Boleyn and swearing that he would never consent 'to so unjust and unlawful a deed' as the King's second marriage.[2] The same informer a year later was telling Cromwell that all the Somerset Carthusians were disaffected and would prefer martyrdom to obedience to the King.[3] Cromwell, for once, did not oblige; and in 1535 Dr Horde could thank him for his 'old benignity'. They had been friendly at Sir Walter Hungerford's house in the quiet times, and that good will, the prior noted with pleasure, was 'not utterly extinct'.[4] Yet it was alleged against him that he had seen seditious visions – and he the head of a house from which prophecies had emanated that had played their part in the fatal charges raised against the duke of Buckingham.[5] The prior continued in office till March 1539 when memories of the fact that the lord privy seal had ever been his 'especial good lord' persuaded him to

[1] Street, 'Bishops and Citizens of Salisbury,' 328 ff.
[2] The monk informed Lord Stourton who passed the matter to Cromwell: SP 1/76, fo. 84 (*LP* vi. 510).
[3] SP 1/83, fo. 192 (*LP* vii. 577). [4] SP 1/91, fo. 103 (*LP* viii. 402).
[5] Cf. J. Bowle, *Henry VIII* (1964), 103.

accept the necessity of surrendering his house, reluctantly but peace-fully.[1] Less amenable was Thomas Sprent, vicar of Paulet, who in May 1539 allegedly said 'that if the King do set forth any new laws contrary to God's law we ought not to follow them'. He was also charged with praying for the pope as late as this. He cleared himself before the bishop of Bath and Wells, but his enemies revived the accusation as late as April 1542 when the Council once more investigated: they discovered the usual internecine enmities of the village and let the matter drop.[2] William Cruche, a layman and possibly a gentleman of Laventon, had a harder time of it. Cromwell ordered him to be examined, and he spent a spell in the Fleet. Yet what he was accused of was not so heinous: if he had money enough, 'he could buy and sell the crown of England'. He had forcibly abducted and ill-treated his chief accuser, which no doubt weighed against him.[3] However, he got off: the man who had dreamed of wealth enough to buy all the lands he wished and even the King's crown did purchase a messuage from the earl of Hertford in June 1541.[4]

These are the common coin of the police reports of the 1530's; more could be cited for Somerset as for any other county. But Somerset also offers one of the most serious and just about the most absurd cases of trouble requiring investigation: a major riot at Taunton, and a report of treason emanating from Ilchester gaol.

The Taunton riot of early April 1536 was a nasty business – nasty because it could have become really dangerous, nastier because of its consequences, nastiest because it sprang up without any substantial cause. It certainly had nothing to do with either the political or the religious changes of the time, but it demonstrated the ease with which an unsettled situation could get explosive.[5] So far as we can tell, the affair was sparked off by the activities of a commission 'to take up corn', at a time when 'the poor people doth much complain them of the scarceness and dearth of grain'. Resistance was offered by a group of

[1] Ellis, ii. II. 130, a letter from his brother Alan.
[2] St Ch 2/31/120.
[3] The offence predated Michaelmas 1539; the investigations took place in February and May 1540: SP 1/157, fo. 146; 160, fo. 51 (*LP* xv. 167, 689 [1]).
[4] *LP* xvi. 947 (45).
[5] The evidence consists of four letters sent to Cromwell from Somerset: SP 1/239, fos. 287–8, 292; 240, fo. 5 (*LP Add.* 1056–7, 1063, 1075); an entry on the King's Bench plea roll (KB 27/1102, Rex, rot. 9); and a mention in Wriothesley, i. 61. It is, as usual, confusing; I have tried to amalgamate what can be discovered into a coherent story.

people led by one Thomas Powell, who were put in ward. Thereupon an armed mob of about sixty, including men and women, sallied forth, yelling imprecations against various magistrates and shouting to have the prisoners released 'or else we will die for it', or again 'it shall cost a thousand lives'. In itself this was hardly serious, but there are signs that the authorities nearly panicked in the face of the rebellious lower orders. Henry Long, alerted at Frome, in the direction of which the mob was moving, dashed twenty-six miles to meet them, but all was over before he got there, his son-in-law Robert Liversiche having dealt authoritatively with those poor people. Clearly their courage evaporated fast: 'they delivered their weapons to him and was contented to obey at the first word'. Long knew of only twenty-eight rioters, but that does seem to have been an underestimate. On April 7th, Cromwell wrote sharply to have the rioters dealt with. He wished them to be warded, for trial, in Nunney Castle, but was told that the place was 'much used and employed with the business of husbandry, and no perfect divisions of strong rooms there for the safekeeping of them without watch night and day'. His information on Somerset castles was clearly out of date. He also asked how things were in general, and to this he received a reassuring reply.

However, riots of this sort needed quick repression, however futile they had actually been; before the end of the month, a commission of oyer and terminer, presided over by the lord chief justice, sat in judgment. They showed little mercy: the law was clear about people caught in the act of a seditious uprising of this kind. Twelve were sentenced to death and executed in three different places, *in terrorem*;[1] the remaining approximately fifty were also condemned, but, being very penitent and not ringleaders, were reprieved to await the King's pleasure. In the end they were pardoned: or rather, had to buy their pardons. Each of them was bound for his fine in a personal recognisance of £20 and sureties of £10 each, a fact of which we know because John Wiles of Wilton failed to make his appearance, so that the King's Bench had to initiate the laborious process of extracting this debt from him. The court seems to have failed.

The ease and rapidity with which the riot was suppressed left various effects behind. Old Sir Nicholas Wadham, one of the commissioners for corn whose activities had provoked the outburst, thanked Cromwell

[1] Twelve was Fitzjames's figure; Wriothesley's information inflated this to fourteen.

in early June for the delightful news that the King strongly approved their doings; he had had, he said, more praise than he deserved, but tried to capitalise on it by asking for some substantial token of the King's good will, 'to help me withal now in my later days'. The local people, on the other hand, deeply resented the severe repression and especially blamed a servant of Sir John St Loe's for it: typically, and sadly, they persuaded themselves that this man had acted contrary to the King's desires and spread a rumour that the King's fury had nearly cost him his life.[1] Wadham's information was the more accurate: Henry VIII was only too pleased to have a dozen rioters hanged and the rest fined for their transgressions. And in essence he had a point. The Taunton riot turned out to be a flop, but six months later very similar causes led to the vast uprising in the north. Armed assemblies were no joke in the England of the 1530's.

The antics of the prisoners in Ilchester gaol, early in 1532, on the other hand, were a joke and little else. There was talk of treason involved, but behind it there lay nothing but a set of dubious plots among certain professional criminals tired of this particular gaol and anxious to get out.[2] As the authorities first heard it, one of the prisoners, John Ashwood, had asked for a justice of the peace to whom he would reveal knowledge of treason. But this was a misunderstanding, and Ashwood was a man somewhat wronged. Four prisoners (Thomas Cheeselade, Peter Aleyn, Michael Bury, and William, a Devon man) had earlier plotted a prison break which Ashwood had betrayed. Cheeselade, the ringleader, in consequence threatened his life, but for the moment Ashwood talked himself out of this tough spot. Thinking to be safer still and not confident of the keeper's promise to protect him, Ashwood asked for a justice, a request which Cheeselade, who overheard it, at once interpreted to mean talk of treason: 'if it were not for treason, he should have no justice of the peace there'. There is evidence elsewhere that Cheeselade was something of a barrack-room lawyer who with good reason prided himself on his knowledge of the law's technicalities. Ashwood, overawed by this display of learning, mumbled, 'perchance I do'.

This gave Cheeselade and Aleyn an idea. If they could not break

[1] SP 1/120, fos. 73, 77 (*LP* xii. I. 1194–5).
[2] The main information comes from depositions taken by Fitzjames on 5–8 February 1532: SP 1/237, fos. 121–7 (*LP Add.* 768).

prison, perhaps they could get out of Ilchester another way. So Aleyn asked to be taken to see a justice of the peace, but the keeper, fearing another attempt at escape, instead brought a clerk to the gaol to write two letters on Aleyn's behalf in which he told the King's Council and Lord Dawbeny that he wished to inform on a traitor. While this went on, the other prisoners were removed to an upper chamber. Aleyn had chosen his victim, a fisherman named Robert Wescote against whom he bore a grudge. It appears that at his trial at Bridgewater Sessions Aleyn was convicted but was lucky enough to be reprieved into custody, not so uncommon an experience for sixteenth-century felons as the legend supposes, but his hopes to get bail were dashed by Wescote's refusal to stand surety for him. This was the reason for Aleyn's continued imprisonment, though on the evidence it looks as though Wescote was wise to have nothing to do with him. Hearing the plot, Ashwood naively asked how Wescote could possibly have committed treason, to which question Cheeselade replied: 'Thou art but a baby; may not he poison the King's fish?'

At any rate, the plot worked well at first. Aleyn was taken to London where on 28 January 1532 four highpowered commissioners – the earl of Oxford, Sir William Fitzwilliam, Sir Henry Guildford and Thomas Cromwell – interrogated him in the Tower; the record is in Cromwell's hand.[1] If Cheeselade could have been present he would have been disgusted at the performance put up by his pupil. All that Aleyn could say was that Ashwood had several times asked for a justice of the peace to report treason and that there had been a break-out at Ilchester: not a word of Wescote or any of the matters he had told the Council he meant to reveal. Meanwhile, from February 5th to 8th, Sir John Fitzjames, on orders from the Council, investigated at the gaol itself and uncovered the conspiracy. He also got news of yet another kind of treason, alleged now by Cheeselade who reported another prisoner, John Richards, for retailing a number of politically charged prophecies among his fellows. Since these included forecasts of the King being driven from the realm 'and killed at Paris gates', the offence was manifest. Other inmates confirmed this part, and all agreed that Richards claimed to have had the sayings from one Horlock some six years earlier. Cheeselade naturally got in some more digs at Ashwood. It appeared that the talk of treason had started among the prisoners

[1] E 36/120, fo. 76 (LP v. 759).

when news of Rice ap Griffiths' fate filtered through to them. Fitzjames dutifully collected all this stuff, though oddly enough he did not interrogate Richards himself. In any case, he expressed his opinion forcibly in a report to the King which, though addressed to Henry, came first to Cromwell's hands. In the judge's view, there was nothing in it at all – just Aleyn's invention. Cromwell, of course, showed the letter to Henry who, as usual, hesitated to believe that any reports of treason could possibly be untrue; he demanded more work, and Fitzjames was forced a second time to assure Cromwell that the investigation had drawn a blank. Aleyn was a villain and a rogue, but the treason he talked of did not exist.[1]

This, of course, was perfectly correct, though the plot demonstrates how readily men's minds ran on talk of treason even at this early date. It also shows with what absurdities the King's busy councillors had to waste their time, especially when the King got to hear of the details. The fertile mind had evidently been Cheeselade's, as Aleyn's poor performance in the Tower indicates. There is no further news of either man, though Aleyn certainly did not stay in the Tower; he never appears in later lists of inmates there. Perhaps he succeeded in the ambition he had shared with Cheeselade to 'bring themselves more at liberty'; he may have vanished into the London underworld. The real irony of the story became apparent in July 1533 when a big prison break did occur at Ilchester, with prolonged repercussions very awkward for the sheriff.[2] Not one of the people involved in the Ashwood–Aleyn story was among those who broke out on that later occasion.

5

At Salisbury, religion served to complicate old problems of the relations between clergy and laity. At Bristol, religion turned out to be the sole cause of lengthy upheavals.[3] For some reason, this town was the only one in England to provide the setting for an event familiar in the European cities of the Reformation: violent exchanges from the pulpit between old and new. The most probable reason, in fact, was the presence of Hugh Latimer, well known as a preacher by the early thirties. His sermons had upset the hierarchy before he moved to the

[1] SP 1/69, fos. 115, 136 (*LP* v. 793, 830).
[2] *LP* vi. 914. [3] For Bristol, cf. also above, p. 30.

west country to become rector of West Kington in January 1531.[1] His fame soon spread, and in early 1533 the mayor of Bristol appointed him preacher for Lent and Easter.[2] He started off with three sermons in two days, on March 16th and 17th,[3] and at once the town was humming. According to Latimer, the local priests, perceiving how well his preaching was liked, at first pretended to agree with him, but on the 18th one Richard Browne wrote to Dr Thomas Bagarde, chancellor of the diocese and then attending Convocation in London, to protest at sermons which had attacked the Virgin Mary, pilgrimages and other traditions; 'the good catholic people of the town do abhor all such his preaching'.[4] Bagarde reported this to Convocation because it appeared that Latimer had broken a promise made at his submission the previous year to keep off such contentious matters, and Convocation, censuring him again, resolved to send a copy of his submission to Bristol so that the local people might know where they stood.[5]

This, of course, had no effect, and the Bristol conservatives decided on positive counter-measures. They may well have been moved by the fact that at Bristol the town authorities favoured the radical preacher, an unusual thing in the England of the early Reformation. Latimer was to be preached out of existence, and for this purpose three high-powered traditionalists were imported for Easter. Dr Edward Powell and Dr Nicholas Wilson, two notorious adherents of the old order who from this day onward were to be mostly in trouble until Wilson submitted and Powell died a traitor's death soon after Cromwell's fall, attacked what Latimer was alleged to have said; they had some of the local clergy to help them, including John Hilsey, prior of the Bristol Dominicans.[6] What really got things moving, however, was the

---

[1] The story of Latimer's troubles at Bristol has been told several times, especially by H. S. Darby, *Hugh Latimer* (1953), ch. 5. While that account makes it unnecessary for me to go at length into the doctrinal disputes, it sees everything too much through Latimer's eyes. Much of the evidence for this affair is in print, some of it in the appendix of documents in Cattley's edition of Foxe which is not paginated. The material is in vol. vii, App. of Docs., No. IX; it will here be cited as Foxe, vii, App.

[2] As Latimer reported to Ralph Maurice (*Remains*, 358). This letter is clearly of later date than March where it is placed in *LP* v. 247; it covers so much of the story that it cannot have been written before May/June.

[3] Wright, 8–9.   [4] Foxe, vii, App. (*LP* v. 246).

[5] *LP* v. 276; Foxe, vii, App.

[6] SP 6/1, no. 19, item iii (*LP* vi. 433). Printed in Wright, 11 ff., where the addressee is given in error as Cromwell; it was Bagarde. Also *LP* vi. 433 (vi).

arrival of William Hubberdyne, a preacher almost as popular as Latimer who got his effects by eccentricity and drama in the pulpit.[1] Hubberdyne preached two sermons on Easter Eve and Day (April 12th–13th), and from this moment the town was noisily divided into two factions. The details of the heresies alleged and Latimer's quite convincing explanations of what he had really said need not trouble us;[2] what matters is that peace had ceased to be possible. As Hilsey soon after wrote to Bagarde, 'our crying one against another is not fruitful'.

Bagarde, in fact, took the obvious steps by inhibiting both Latimer and Hubberdyne from further preaching. This earned him an enquiry from Cromwell to which he replied with apologies.[3] His purpose had been to avoid 'rumour and sedition', and he had been under the impression that he had had Cromwell's counsel 'and consent' to the inhibition. Probably Cromwell had indeed agreed before fully realising who was involved, for he would have wanted in the first place to put an end to the stirring up of conflict; but the conservative preachers were notorious partisans of Queen Catherine, and it was undesirable that they should be put on a footing with Latimer. Bagarde at once withdrew his ban from the latter and could report, with what frankness we cannot know, that his preaching in Rogation week had been satisfactory. The conservatives, in fact, were in retreat, and the radicals decided to mount a full-scale attack on Hubberdyne. They scored a notable success when Hilsey changed sides: he had talked to Latimer and found him hostile only to the abuses of the truth and not to the truth itself. Evidence was collected – articles extracted out of Hubberdyne's preaching in Easter week and a summary of Powell's sermons on April 25th and 26th.[4] The initiative in this was taken by townspeople who reminded the authorities that Hubberdyne's sermons had offended 'the commons'; they displayed a quite professional appreciation of the finer points of theology which argues some spiritual counsel in the background. Hubberdyne's opinion of the new learning is manifest from a letter which Latimer

---

[1] Foxe (vii. 478) tells a splendid story of Hubberdyne's end. To illustrate a point he jumped about so much in the pulpit that the structure collapsed and he broke a leg, from which injury he died a few days after. The churchwardens, accused of negligence, replied 'that they had made their pulpit for preaching, not for dancing'.

[2] Cf. Darby, *op. cit.* 86 ff., based on Latimer's analysis in *Remains*, 225 ff.

[3] SP 1/75, fo. 228 (*LP* vii. 411).

[4] Foxe, vii, App. This contains two papers against Hubberdyne; I here mean the second one, presented to mayor and town council.

wrote to him on May 25th in defence of Scripture which, said Latimer, could hardly be called 'new' since it was surely older than all the popish authorities (Duns, Aquinas, etc.) alleged by Hubberdyne.[1] Someone remembered hearing at several removes that a little earlier John Floke, the dean of Bristol, had secretly advised a parish priest not to offer prayers for King and Queen from the pulpit, a charge touching nigh to treason.[2] The ground for battle was being prepared.

On June 5th, the offensive started in earnest when thirteen men of Bristol, including four priests (Hilsey among them) forwarded to the King's Council a set of articles against 'the behaviour of the sinistral preaching' of both Powell and Hubberdyne.[3] Only those against the latter survive, no doubt because they finished up in Cromwell's papers.[4] According to them, Hubberdyne had placed the pope above all kings and asserted that he could not err; he had also made some extremely conservative statements on the authority of the Church and declared that 'the gospel in English bringeth men to heresy'. Although Hubberdyne at once put his side of the case to Cromwell, claiming that he had been the victim of malice and would be able to disprove the charges if once he were given details,[5] things quickly went against him. By July 4th he was in the Tower.[6] This did not silence him: on the 19th, Richard Jones, the Oxford wizard, wrote from the Tower to the mayor of Bristol, warning him that Hubberdyne ('no friend of yours') was continuing his popish talk.[7] On the 10th, the mayor had in fact written to thank Cromwell for acting upon the townspeople's petition.[8]

In this letter there is also a reference to the positive step taken by Cromwell, the appointment of a commission to investigate and report.

[1] Ibid. The letter was provoked by a new sermon of Hubberdyne's, still preaching even though Cromwell had been told that the inhibition against him stood.

[2] Ibid. It is not known that anything was done about Floke, but by June 1539 the deanship was in the hands of one John Kerell (LP xiv. I. 1095). Of course, anything could have happened in six years.

[3] SP 1/76, fo. 183 (LP vi. 596).

[4] E 36/139, fo. 48. The articles are, I think, the first of the two sets printed in Foxe, vii, App., a series of heads extracted from the sermons.

[5] SP 1/75, fo. 229 (LP vi. 412).

[6] SP 1/94, fo. 3 (LP viii. 1001), a list of prisoners of mid-1535 which gives dates of admission.

[7] SP 1/78, fo. 21 (LP vi. 873). For Jones see above, pp. 50–6. Hubberdyne was still asserting that the pope and the Church could not err, so that the Bristol bill of articles is likely to have been true.

[8] SP 1/77, fo. 208 (LP vi. 796).

The violent disputes at Bristol clearly demanded this, though by his removal of Hubberdyne Cromwell had already given a broad indication of where he stood in the matter. The instructions reached John Bartholomew, customer of Bristol, at 6 p.m. on July 5th.[1] They were rather odd. Bartholomew was to choose five or six 'honest men' to help him sort out the accusations against both Latimer and Hubberdyne. At any later date, Cromwell would himself have named the commissioners, and he would ordinarily have sent his instructions to a chief magistrate, probably the mayor. The arrangements he made for Bristol suggest on the one hand that he was not yet well acquainted with the people there, so that he (chancellor of the Exchequer since 12 April 1533) found himself resorting to an Exchequer official as his only local contact, and on the other that the known partisanship of the mayor and town council made it inadvisable to have them sit in judgment. Bartholomew acted in good faith and avoided using any of the men known to be involved. He chose the abbot of St Augustine's, three ex-mayors, and one gentleman of the town; and on the 6th, he and his fellows sat in public to receive information against both the embattled preachers. Plenty of people came forward to testify at several sittings from July 9th to 11th, but, despite the heading which mentions also Latimer, they all deposed only against Hubberdyne.[2] Their main complaint was that the preacher had spoken of the presence of twenty or thirty heretics in the town; and it seems that apart from commonplace revilings of the men of the new learning and new order he had also made a dangerous statement that denial of the pope's authority was heresy.

In forwarding these depositions, the commissioners were less one-sided than their witnesses; they described the uproar that had been current throughout Bristol since Latimer first preached there. Though bad enough before Easter, it had been much worse since: 'for many that favoured Latimer and his new manner of preaching, and other many that favoured Hubberdyne in his old manner of preaching, both the said parties hath been more ardent now since Easter than they were before'. Unless the King provided a remedy, 'much more incon-

---

[1] What we know of the investigation comes from the report written by Bartholomew in the first person but signed also by the other commissioners (Wright, 7–9; LP vi. 799).

[2] LP vi. 799 (2), printed in Foxe, vii, App. (the penultimate document in the volume).

venience is like to ensue'. They hinted that some pressure had been exercised to bias the evidence against Hubberdyne. Immediately, as so often, nothing happened. Presumably the removal of the offending conservative – Hubberdyne remained in the Tower for at least two years – quietened Bristol; if the two parties were really as well matched in numbers as the commissioners suggested, the fact that the mayor and council favoured Latimer may well have subdued the conservatives. Bristol was certainly exceptional in this respect: as John Erley discovered, preaching about Wiltshire, being linked with Latimer would get a man nothing but ill words around the countryside.[1] Latimer for the moment ceased to preach at Bristol and by the latter part of 1533 had effectively abandoned his cure to work for the Reformation in London, under Cranmer's direction. Cromwell, whose purposes he had served so well, did not forget him. In August 1535, the friends of reform at Bristol learned with delight that their Lenten preacher of 1533 was to succeed the absent Ghinucci as bishop of Worcester. This elevation was to have further repercussions, for Latimer was never a man around whom peace settled easily.[2] As for Hubberdyne, he also in his way had served Cromwell's purpose. In March 1538 he was probably still in the Tower,[3] but about a month later his name appears in Cromwell's memoranda in such a way as to suggest that his fate was under consideration.[4] In the event he was released, for by 1541 he once again caused an uproar with his preaching, this time by attacking the heresy called psychopannichia (the soul's sleep after death till the last judgment).[5] Thereafter, except for the odd manner of his death recorded by Foxe, he disappears from sight.

At Bristol, however, trouble was to recur, and Lent 1537 had some of the makings of another 1533.[6] Things started with a sermon preached on February 18th by Robert Sanderson, the warden of the Franciscan friars there, which smacked somewhat of the old learning, with a heavy stress on the special respect due to his order: friars were among the kind of Christians most like Christ and John the Baptist, and men of religion deserved 'a greater penny than laymen for because they kept both precepts and counsels'. This provoked the warden's opposite number,

---

[1] SP 1/79, fos. 124–5 (*LP* vi. 1192); cf. above, p. 36.
[2] Cf. the remarks of George Rowlands or Miles Denyson, above, pp. 28, 31.
[3] *LP* xiii. I. 627; the Christian name given there (John) is likely to be just a mistake.
[4] Ibid. 877.   [5] St Ch 2/34/28.
[6] SP 1/116, fos. 119–20; 119, fos. 184–90 (*LP* xii. I. 508, 1147).

Hilsey's successor as prior of the Dominican house, Friar William Oliver (of whose conversion to modernity we have already had occasion to speak),[1] to devote his sermon the following Sunday to an exposition of rather advanced thinking. He defended justification by faith alone (citing all the standard texts used by the Lutherans, from *Romans*, *Galatians* and *Hebrews*) and denounced any attempt to set friars apart from the body of Christians: 'a whole shipload laden with friars' girdles and a dung-cart full of monks' cowls' would avail nothing without faith. He then turned to more temporal matters, deploring seditious bills that had suddenly appeared and trusting that the magistrates would not 'wink at it'; he prayed God 'there were no privy northern hearts nor close festered stomachs' among them. Finally, perhaps not very sincerely, he professed apprehension at being called to account for his words but took comfort from the fact that the scribes and pharisees would not have sought Christ's death so eagerly if he had not 'so sharply rebuked their abominable living'.

Apart, perhaps, from the charge that he had renewed contentious preaching, Oliver had nothing to fear, but the matters to which he had alluded were serious. The bills of which he spoke seem to have been seditious and slanderous parodies of the Paternoster, the Ave and the Creed. There was talk of seditious preaching this last half year. In particular people had been loosing off at Latimer again. Once more, turmoil seemed likely, and Cromwell acted as soon as he received information. On May 7th, a commission headed, this time, by the mayor sat to investigate and report. They had also been instructed to punish if necessary. The two sermons were proved by witnesses, but no steps were taken against the two friars.[2] Others fared less well. John Kene, parson of Christ Church, Bristol, was proved to have frequently attacked the new learning and to have abused his hearers as 'heretics, heretics and newfangled fellows'. One of his choicer sayings was this: 'There be some women do say, they be as good as Our Lady: for we have born four or five children and know the fathers of them, and she bare but once and knew not the father.' The old allegation that Latimer

---

[1] Above, p. 14.

[2] Sanderson was apparently a pluralist, being also warden of the Grey Friars of Richmond (Yorks.), a fact which provides his name (*LP* xiv. I. 96). He continued at least moderately stubborn and resisted pressure to surrender his house; he was hard to move because he was reported to be in favour – with whom? However, he gave in in September 1538 (*LP* xiii. II. 200, 321).

had despised the Virgin Mary and induced others to deny her died hard. Kene had expressed a wish to speak with the King 'mouth to mouth', and though he knew he had but seven men 'of the old fashion' with him and 'twenty-seven with a captain' on the other side, he trusted to be heard and reckoned he had done some good in the parish. However, in actual fact he had offended the parish by not praying for the King when the northern rebellion was on and by railing at them. For these offences – ominously distant in time – the commissioners sent him to prison for twenty days.

Kene had also attacked Latimer in private conversation, calling him a false harlot and a heretic who should have been burned, but this the commissioners ignored. Yet they gave three days in gaol to the parson of St Lawrence, John Rawlyngs, for saying precisely the same thing, and four to William Glaskeryon for wishing 'a vengeance upon the bishop of Worcester: I wish he had never been born: I trust or I die to see him brent'. Glaskeryon had supposedly welcomed the Pilgrimage of Grace, and Piers Baks had replied to one who rejoiced at the end of the rebellion that 'it was a shrewd downing, for I hope they will rise again and that a little stronger than they did before, and I will be one of them myself'. All these and others who had spread abuse of Latimer had before this been in prison for their misbehaviour.

The commissioners had certainly been far from savage, and the story contains hints that Latimer, and the Reformation, were less popular at Bristol than they had been. The long delay after Kene's offences no doubt played its part in provoking Oliver into hoping that the magistrates would not ignore disaffection, but it took those remarks and a royal commission to produce action. If the charges against Kene, Rawlyngs and the rest were true, a few days in prison constituted a very light punishment for seditious slander and plain treason. Yet Cromwell and the Council seem to have been content. At least order was being maintained at Bristol, and if the spreading of the Word, in Latimer's fashion, was costing the bishop more trouble than had seemed likely during his triumph of 1533, that was no doubt his business. The town was not 'reformed' in the continental sense. In 1539, the authorities made no effort to protect the Scottish reformer George Wishart whose preaching at Bristol offended the clergy and led to a denunciation. He had allegedly declared that Christ 'neither hath nor would merit for him no yet for us', which was even for Wishart improbably way-out stuff: he was sent to be examined by Cranmer and returned to carry a faggot in two Bristol churches.[1] The crude and violent abuse showered upon the authorities by Wishart's supporters explains something about the attitude of the worshipful men of Bristol on this occasion, nor did all the praise poured by these vilifiers on 'my good lord privy seal' make any difference.[2]

6

As we move north from Bristol, we enter the general domain of the Council in the Marches of Wales, a body which should have been able to bring hom the power of the state to that locality, despite its distance from the centre.[3] But perhaps because, after the appointment of Bishop Rowland Lee to the presidency, that Council concentrated most of its efforts on the pacifying and subduing of Wales, the border counties do not appear to have been much troubled by the commissioners at Ludlow and yield sufficient instances of dubious or dangerous behaviour. A rather striking example of obstinacy occurred at Ashlower in Gloucestershire in the autumn of 1534 as royal commissioners went the rounds to swear the realm to the oath of succession decreed by statute. Before coming to Ashlower they sent an order to the constable of the parish to assemble the whole village at a stated time and place to take the oath. Since the constable 'was and is a man not learned', he took the precept to the local vicar, John Knolles, and asked 'in the King's name' to have it read out in church. However, despite repeated urgings Knolles 'utterly refused' to do any such thing, and when pressed to read it in the King's name and also the Queen's replied crudely 'that he would not publish it either for King nor Queen, but said he would it had been brent or ever it came there, with many other rebukeful words'. In the end he added further insult to his resistance by agreeing to publish the order solely for the sake of one of the people urging him to do so, a remark which so annoyed the constable that he forbade him to read on such terms since he would not do his duty for their majesties' sake. The

---

[1] SP 1/152, fo. 61 (*LP* xiv. I. 1095); *The Maire of Bristowe his Kallender*, ed. L. Toulmin Smith (Camden, New Series, vol. v, 1872), 55.

[2] *LP* xiv. I. 184, three anonymous bills which, among other things, called the vicar of St Leonards a 'shiting and stinking knave' and the town clerk a 'grinning knave'.

[3] Strictly speaking, the Council's authority extended over only Shropshire and Herefordshire, but Cromwell expected it also to keep a distant eye on Gloucestershire and Worcestershire.

constable reported the matter to the commissioners who, taking it to be treason, put the vicar in ward. Local favour intervened, and a justice of the peace was soon found who bailed Knolles. This upset certain men of the parish who – not certain whether the vicar's behaviour was treason and afraid 'that they in not uttering of it should not do their duties according as your true subjects ought' – complained to Lord Chancellor Audley and asked his advice.[1] It does not look as though further steps were taken; the rather sanctimonious tone and the details of the complaint suggest that some local backbiting was probably involved, but the complainants cannot have invented the detail about the commissioners' suspicion of treason. Knolles had evidently behaved contumaciously in one of the touchiest matters of all, and he looks to have got away with it.

The city of Gloucester itself had its local trouble-maker in Hugh Rawlyngs, alias Williams, parson of Trinity church there, a supporter of the new order who upset people by his brash advocacy of reform. In March 1537 he was banished from the diocese by the bishop's (Latimer's) visitor, and two of his friends wrote in protest to Latimer.[2] As they had heard, Cromwell had been informed that the punishment had been imposed for four offences: censing at the high altar in his close cap (when he was 'diseased in the head', that is had a cold), refusing a penny from a woman, sleeping out of the college, and being a seditious person and sower of strife. Only the first two charges were before the visitor; so far from being seditious, Rawlyngs was a witness against Robert Pole, himself very rightly (they said) accused of seditious words. Also Rawlyngs had been 'showing God's word'. When Latimer's chaplain Thomas Garrett wrote for information against ex-sheriff Bell, also suspected of sedition,[3] Rawlyngs's adherents painted a picture of deep rifts and disturbances at Gloucester. They could not understand why after three bills on the subject and other information Garrett should need to know more about Bell, but they would oblige: and they did, at length, involving half a dozen men or more in their denunciations.[4] Manifestly, the quarrels at Gloucester stemmed from the looming presence of the bishop of Worcester. Bell had repeatedly called Latimer

---

[1] St Ch 2/21/120. This is all we know of the business.
[2] SP 1/117, fo. 91 (*LP* xii. I. 701).   [3] For Bell see above, p. 30.
[4] SP 1/115, fos. 66–7 (*LP* xii. I. 308). This letter should be placed after the last one, not before.

a heretic; there were many witnesses to prove this, including a group of Germans from the Steelyard who had visited the town a little while before. He had boasted of trimming the bishop by means of bills preferred to the duke of Norfolk and the Parliament (presumably that of 1536) till 'none of his chaplains durst in manner come to Gloucester'. Bell was so loud because he had solid support, including his brother, the recorder of Gloucester, and the bishop of London (Stokesley). But he was not the only one. There was a gentleman described as 'old brawling Barker' or 'babbling Barker' who, together with one Jurden, 'strieth and marreth all the parish'; there was Mr Mayor who said of Latimer, 'well, my lord might be an honest man, but it was much unlike, for he kept none but heretic knaves about him;' there was John Dull, a butcher, who spoke 'foolish proud words'. If 'they had not been altogether brutish mad, Pole's trouble had been sufficient warning for them'. Instead they had attacked Rawlyngs, a good and loyal man. Above all, they had expressed themselves very improperly about Cromwell's 'most honourable and gentle letters' intended to make peace.

For Cromwell had intervened by restoring Rawlyngs to his cure at Gloucester, no doubt at Latimer's request; wherever Latimer went in those years, the reforming party exploited their ascendancy without scruple. There was soon trouble again at Gloucester, and this time Cromwell sought information from Thomas Evans, a Worcester gentleman whom he trusted.[1] Evans told a very different story. In March 1538 he forwarded a bill of complaints from Rawlyngs's parishioners against their priest, as well as the priest's answers in which he 'could void never a one [complaint] but qualified some'. Evans assured Cromwell that he was not trying 'to renew any matter against the priest' whom he had tried to help (earning a rebuff) after Cromwell had restored him, but he wanted the lord privy seal to know that more and worse was charged against Rawlyngs than Rawlyngs's party had let on. Nearly all the respectable people of the parish were against him, and the whole place was 'far out of frame'. But the accusations were not pursued, nor did Latimer's resignation in July 1539 silence Rawlyngs. In February next year he overreached himself, preaching sedition by attacking 'the King his book of articles' – that is, the Act of Six Articles. He was joined in this deed by John Erley, once a friar and later

---

[1] SP 1/127, fo. 223 (*LP* xii. II, App. 13); this letter is misdated in *LP*.

a hermit, whose activities in Latimer country on behalf of the Reformation we have already encountered several times.[1] Once again, Gloucester was in uproar with 'the best of the town...one in another his top'. Evans had examined the matter and resolved to make peace. By Cromwell's authority he discharged Rawlyngs and Erley from what should have been a very serious accusation; if this is true as told, one can begin to see why Cromwell five months later could be credibly accused of having protected heretics and traitors. But Evans had also banned both men from the diocese, unless Cromwell would let them back in again.

Were there two priests called Hugh Rawlyngs? A man of that name sat in Convocation in 1540 and put his signature to the dutiful resolution against the Cleves marriage.[2] Perhaps the parish priest of Trinity church in Gloucester could hardly have sat there; but somebody had to represent the diocese, and why not he? The point matters because one Hugh Rawlyngs, by that time vicar of Tenby (a perfectly possible move and promotion), is found pursuing the bishop of St David's, Robert Ferrar, in both the reigns of Edward VI and Mary, a quite remarkable achievement probably possible only in Wales.[3] Ferrar then described him, admittedly in self-defence, as a multiple pluralist and total non-resident who, ever eager 'to work mischief', wandered to and fro, spending his life 'to the hindrance of other men'. He was chosen as an instrument by the bishop's enemies just because he was a known rogue.[4] There are here echoes of the Gloucester Rawlyngs's behaviour; if the two were identical, Cromwell was much deceived in him by his friends. At any rate, the Gloucester Rawlyngs had caused much trouble, though his second removal had done the trick; Evans finished his report with the cheerful boast that afterwards he got 'divers of the worship of this town to drink together that did not drink together this three quarters of a year'.

The authorities in Worcestershire had no occasion to worry much when Edmund Brocke, an 'aged wretched person' from Cowle (he was eighty), was reported to have blamed the shocking summer weather of 1535 on the King: while Henry reigned, Brocke continued, there would never be an end to such bad weather, 'and therefore it makes

---

[1] Evans to Cromwell, 18 Feb. 1540: SP 1/157, fo. 155 (*LP* xv. 183).
[2] *StP* i. 634. The next man to sign was Richard Cox.
[3] Foxe, vii. 3 ff.; *APC* iii. 313.   [4] Foxe, vii. 17.

no matter if he were knocked or patted on the head'. Confronted with this accusation, Brocke could not believe that he had spoken the dangerous last words; if he had, 'he was mad or drunk and wist not what he said'.[1] But the news of treasonable talk at Worcester priory, in the same year, was quite another matter, and here for once the government tried very hard to get a conviction. The story has been told before but very much from the point of view of one side; for the light it throws on the problem of enforcement, it will bear re-examination.[2]

Worcester priory had not been a haven of peace for some time. Prior William More owes his fame to the survival of his journal (account book) which displays him as a comfortable country gentleman, undistinguished but harmless, void of spirituality or vigour but well acquainted in the neighbourhood. The qualities which secured him the friendship of the local gentry still, somewhat surprisingly, earn him the indulgence of the modern historian.[3] As a head of his house he was handicapped by frequent absences. In about 1528 he added to the divisions among his monks by transferring the office of cellarer, which included the management of the priory's estates, from William Fordham to Thomas Sudbury. In consequence there were two parties, a larger one supporting the prior and the new cellarer,[4] and a smaller one behind Fordham which included John Musard, long at odds with the prior, and Roger Neckham, himself some time before replaced as subprior by John Lawarne. Fordham claimed that the 'saddest' (most considerable) men of the house were on his side,[5] and since both he and Neckham held doctorates he may well have been right. The simmering troubles burst forth after Cromwell's visitors had attended to Worcester in July 1535, but they had started before. On March 2nd, Musard denounced a fellow monk, Richard Clive, for treasonable words. He made the accusation before the subprior and other senior monks, but (as so often) the accuser was the man to suffer, and Musard found himself imprisoned. Cromwell's visitors were not impressed by him, and he was still not at liberty on August 8th when he succeeded in getting off a letter of appeal to the secretary. About the same time he also dispatched an appeal to Henry VIII, recalling his own and his ancestors'

[1] SP 1/95, fo. 76 (*LP* ix. 74). The covering letter is misplaced by *LP* into 1534: SP 1/85, fo. 125 (*LP* vii. 1062).
[2] Cf. Knowles, iii. 342–5.   [3] Ibid. 108 ff.
[4] A letter from this party attracted twenty-nine signatures: SP 1/98, fos. 50–1 (*LP* ix. 653).   [5] *LP* ix. 6.

services to the house of Tudor;[1] when later examined, he composed memorials outlining the alleged treason to Cromwell, the King and the Council in the Marches.[2] From these papers the charge appears, as does Musard's prolonged attempt to explode a mine under Prior More's feet.

The special words alleged against Clive ran: 'that it was as lawful to appeal to the weathercock as to the Chancery'. This referred to the clause in the Act of Dispensations (1534) which had directed appeals from archiepiscopal courts to go to special commissions out of Chancery, later known as the High Court of Delegates, so that the remark amounted to a denunciation of one aspect of the royal supremacy. The particular occasion for Clive to speak thus had been Musard's attempt (which in fact would seem to have been out of order) to escape his imprisonment by appealing over the heads of the ecclesiastical hierarchy. But Clive had allegedly also railed for a long time against the Boleyn marriage and spoken in support of the pope. In the course of his examination, Musard dredged up grievances extending over sixteen years, accusing the prior of bribing himself out of difficulties with Wolsey, of abusing his office as a justice of the peace, and of generally oppressing the monks of his house.

Since Cromwell's visitors, and Cromwell with them, had originally ignored Musard's denunciations and petitions for release, it may be conjectured that what produced action was his appeal to Henry. Pushed on by the King, Cromwell now took steps. He at once wrote to one of his Worcestershire contacts, Sir John Russell, to know what was going on. Russell replied that last March the subprior had been to see him and seek his advice about a quarrel between two monks – he could not remember their names, though we know them.[3] Clive had accused Musard of sodomy, and Musard had retaliated with an accusation of treason. At the time Russell advised keeping both men in ward and informing the Council in the Marches. Nobody ever told him what the words amounted to. Cromwell next questioned Fordham who expressed great delight at the turn of events but could not really discover what Clive's treason might have been.[4] One difficulty seems to have

[1] Musard to Cromwell, SP 1/95, fo. 54 (*LP* ix. 51); to the King, SP 1/95, fo. 55 (*LP* ix. 52 [1]).

[2] SP 1/95, fos. 154–8 (*LP* ix. 52 [2]).

[3] SP 1/95, fo. 106 (*LP* ix. 108).   [4] SP 1/96, fo. 8 (*LP* ix. 204).

arisen because depositions drafted by Musard were stolen from his cell.[1] It all sounds pretty thin, though certainly, if the charges against Clive were true he had spoken treason under the statute, while More and possibly Lawarne were guilty of misprision for concealing the offence. At any rate, Cromwell went ahead and instructed the Council in the Marches to have the monks indicted. Here he hit a snag: Rowland Lee had to admit that the business was unfamiliar to him and that he hardly knew what to do. He wanted the King's learned counsel to draw up the indictments and dreaded the partiality of juries in those parts; also he wished to know whether he was to proceed at once to trial and, in case of convictions, whether any persons were to be reprieved.[2] At the same time Cromwell moved in on the priory. Neckham was instructed to collect the prior's plate and other property and deliver them to Russell. Sudbury received a letter charging him with selling reversionary leases of the priory's estates, a letter which caused much uproar among the monks who blamed Neckham for telling tales.[3] Both Sudbury himself, and the main part of the house on his behalf, wrote hurriedly to deny that the cellarer had done anything improper since Prior More's troubles began and Fordham had been put in charge by Cromwell.[4]

More, in fact, was by this time sequestered at Gloucester, while the government went about the task of dealing with him. This was more easily spoken of than done. Audley, asked his opinion, doubted if the words about appeals to Chancery were really treason, while the un-doubtedly treasonable words about the King's marriage had been spoken before the act of 1534 came into effect.[5] And the locality began to rally round. Only one letter survives to exemplify the pressure put on Cromwell, from Lady Margery Sandes, an old friend of More's, but it shows the kind of thing that was thought to be effective.[6] More, she reckoned, was 'a true man to God and the King', and he should be allowed to enjoy his place to which he was properly elected by the

[1] SP 1/97, fo. 91 (LP ix. 497).

[2] SP 1/97, fo. 94 (LP ix. 510): 1 Oct. 1535.

[3] As Neckham reported on Oct. 14th, in reply to Cromwell's letter of the 3rd: SP 1/98, fo. 8 (LP ix. 609). His charge against Sudbury, admittedly a little obscure, was mis-represented by LP. He did not say that he (Neckham) had many fair children, but that Sudbury had granted reversions 'for affection on their heads that have many fair children'. On the same day, he also wrote in very similar terms to Sir Francis Bryan (SP 1/98, fo. 9 [LP ix. 610]).

[4] SP 1/98, fos. 50–1, 53 (LP ix. 653–4).   [5] StP i. 442.

[6] SP 1/98, fo. 54 (LP ix. 656).

whole convent 'and the gift of the bishop of Winchester, Dr Fox'. Lady Margery thought to persuade Cromwell best by very offhandedly promising that More would 'give you as much in ready money as any other man will', and historians have since, of course, supposed her attitude to be justified. In fact, there is no sign at all that Cromwell got a penny from these proceedings. He initiated them, against the better judgment of his visitors, probably because Henry had decided that there was treason there. He abandoned them, as now he did, not because he was bribed but because the case would not stand up in court, especially after local influence had manifested itself to remind him of Bishop Lee's warning about the difficulty to get a jury that would convict the prior. So far from being anxious to exploit divisions in the monastery for his own ends, he was driven to take seriously some very doubtful accusations of the kind he often ignored, until he got himself, his agents and his supporters in the priory into a markedly false position.

This false position probably lies behind the stance he now took up. On 8 January 1536, Latimer replied to a letter from the secretary about More.[1] It appears that Cromwell had informed the bishop of the King's desire to be merciful and to restore More to his office, while expressing a conviction that 'great crime was not alonely detected but also proved against him', information which led Latimer to think that a pardon would be a mistake. But that point apart, Latimer thought ill of the plan to return More to the priory: his age and character were not, the bishop reckoned, up to the task. Thus it seems that, forced to abandon a case which he had first been forced unwillingly to start, Cromwell took the odium, pretended real discoveries, and resolved all by referring all to the King's special mercy. It might be thought that this was actually the real picture if Latimer had not destroyed it by his concluding words. Earlier on, he said, he had once tried to intercede for More with the King, but, finding that 'there was no hope to speak for this man', had suggested alternative priors. Before the investigation had run its course, and while even Latimer, now so hostile, had tried to help More, Henry had thus already decided against the prior's restoration. This exposes as pretence the notion that Henry was now, against everybody else's better judgment, about to forget all that had been charged and discovered and shows that instead he had been persuaded to accept the facts but meant to gain some unmerited credit.

[1] *Latimer's Remains*, 371–2.

Early in 1536 Cromwell thus let More and Clive go; on February 11th they were back at Worcester, and they lost no time before rubbing in their victory. The immediate victim was Neckham, once again deprived of control and publicly 'baited 'by the prior and his servant. Neckham refused to believe that Cromwell would not reward his loyal service and at once trotted out some fresh charges about More's behaviour in the house,[1] but Cromwell had had enough. All he could now hope to do was to restore some semblance of order until the house was dissolved, and to rescue his partisans. He would not permit More to enjoy his triumph over his enemies for long; before February was out, the prior had resigned, possibly under pressure.[2] But he extracted quite exceptionally generous terms, including a goodly country estate, a solid pension, a discharge of all his debts, and the right to carry quantities of personal belongings away with him.[3] Vows of poverty had never bothered More and did not trouble him in his retirement. He was close on sixty-five years old by this time, and his resignation, which ended the vexatious interference of his office with his pleasures, can have been nothing but a relief. His chief accuser was also removed before very long: on 20 May 1538, John Musard obtained a dispensation to change his habit, 'gratis quia pauper', probably a small and final token of favour.[4] He had had enough of the life religious. The troubles of 1535 did have some slight long-term effects. In January 1540, when the priory was suspended, the commissioners pensioned off 'divers superfluous persons late religious' whom it was not intended to retain as prebendaries when the priory was converted into a cathedral chapter;[5] the eleven persons ejected on these humane terms can be identified as being of the old prior's party and included Sudbury and Clive. But there was no clean sweep; Lawarne and other friends of Sudbury's were there to receive prebendaries' stalls in January 1542, still in uncomfortable harness with Roger Neckham.[6]

---

[1] SP 1/102, fos. 43–4 (*LP* x. 311). Neckham replied that he would forsake Martha's part and follow Mary's. He also expressed confidence because Cromwell had signed his letters as his friend; but 'your assured friend' was Cromwell's standard formula.

[2] The licence to elect his successor was dated 7 March 1536 (*LP* x. 597 [8]).

[3] Ibid. 1272.   [4] *Fac. Off. Reg.* 133.

[5] *LP* xv. 81. I cannot find that Worcester priory was ever fully or formally dissolved before being refounded as a cathedral chapter in 1542, but this action proves that the intention to convert existed long before the deed.

[6] *LP* xvii. 71 (29).

St Mary's, Worcester, was not the only monastic establishment in the county to attract attention from those charged with vigilance over the King's affairs. The abbot of Pershore, John Stonywell, a bishop *in partibus* since 1512, was several times informed against in the 1530's, without any consequences.[1] He had, of course, behaved with due conformity, but on one occasion at least the reports against him sounded very serious. In April 1538, William Harrison, groom of the King's Chamber and therefore a member, though a minor member, of the inner royal administration, laid information before Cromwell concerning a conversation he had overheard during a visit to Pershore.[2] There had been talk of dissolutions which Harrison, talking to someone else, had little heeded till he heard Stonywell say, 'the King will have all'. This alerted the groom who thought 'that surely the abbot would dote, as he was wont to do'. Ralph Sheldon, to whom the abbot was speaking, provoked him deliberately by praising the King's actions against the monasteries and against Rome. 'Ah,' said Stonywell, 'be ye come thereto? And I have loved you so well and taken you for so true a man and so substantial a man. Well, well, I will love you no more. But whatever you say, I wot what I think.' Sheldon teased him further: 'I trust,' said the abbot, leaning across the table, 'that I may die one of the children of Rome.' He went on, in effect, to assert that the pope still ruled: 'Omnis potestas a deo est quia a deo ordinata sunt [*sic*].' 'Ye wot what I mean,' he added. 'No, my lord,' replied Sheldon, 'I understand no Latin.' At this Harrison intervened: 'My lord, I wot what you mean, and under your lordship's correction I deny your argument.' All power was not given of God, for God would give no false power: 'ergo, the usurped power of Rome was not given by God.' Besides, it could be proved from Scripture that God had given supreme power to princes 'and to no other spiritual person'.

The abbot replied only with a scornful smile and wisely changed the subject, though his new choice was not so wise. He turned to John Marshall to ask if it was true that there was no plague north of Doncaster. Yes, said Marshall, it was, but in the eighty miles from Doncaster to Pershore not a place had escaped. 'Yea,' said Stonywell, 'you died fast enough in the north last year; and as for us in this country, we

---

[1] Stonywell's earlier troubles are well described by Knowles, iii. 340–2. From his see of Pulati he was known as Politensis.
[2] SP 1/131, fos. 181–2 (*LP* xiii. I. 822).

be stricken with the plagues of David for David's offences.' This allusion to the executions in the wake of the Pilgrimage of Grace really annoyed Harrison who hotly maintained that the King had been very merciful to the rebels: 'his grace might justly have put 4000 more to death.' As for David, 'my lord, who is David now?' The abbot had sense enough not to reply, but Sheldon asked Harrison not to be so quick: there was no such meaning. Harrison answered shortly that, meaning or none, this matter 'may be commoned of', and the company again changed the subject, to 'a mine of coals'. Harrison did common of it to Cromwell, and in this case the information could not be written off as the product of the usual petty squabbles inside a monastery. If Stonywell said these things he deserved investigation at least. Yet nothing was done, though Cromwell did try to get the old man to resign, without success; Stonywell came very cheerfully out of the Dissolution and died in very advanced years in 1551.[1] This tale underlines the strangeness of the treatment accorded to Prior More whose supposed misprision was markedly less serious than the other man's possible treason. But in Stonywell's case, of course, no one involved King Henry.

Naturally, the border counties also provided examples of malicious informing, or at least the sort of political reports which really disguised private quarrels. Henry Horton, of Northfield (Worcs.), was in August 1537 denounced to Latimer for calling Cranmer, Latimer and Hilsey knaves, heretics and Lollards whom he would gladly see burned.[2] He was arrested by the sheriff, but the sheriff died and Horton went free, not surprisingly breathing fire against the informers. These, therefore, revived their efforts next April when the Council in the Marches once more interrogated Horton.[3] He denied all charges and asserted that he had gone untroubled the year before because Latimer, on investigation, had found nothing to pursue. He also took serious exception to most of the witnesses against him, conveniently demonstrating the realities behind these disputes: one was the son-in-law of his chief accuser, William Baker, another's daughter had married Baker's son, a third was Baker's nephew, a fourth was William Baker himself, a fifth

---

[1] E. A. B. Barnard, 'John Stonywell,' *Transactions of the Worcestershire Archaeological Society*, 1937, at p. 43. At the Dissolution, Stonywell got the enormous pension of £160 p.a., plus part of the abbey's buildings for his lodgings (*LP* xv. 92).

[2] E 36/120, fos. 69–70 (*LP* xii. II. 530).   [3] SP 1/131, fos. 64–70 (*LP* xiii. I. 715).

owed Horton a grudge because the latter had recovered a debt from him on behalf of a Lincolnshire client, a sixth would swear to anything and was bound to a seventh who had spoken for him in a suit 'in the spiritual court about two women'. In actual fact, he would have been wiser not to cast quite so much doubt because the witnesses did well enough by him; from their testimony it appears that he may well have talked a little loosely but in the main reported things he had heard in London rather than expressed personal views. The Council nevertheless sent the depositions to Cromwell and held Horton in ward, but he came to no harm; in April 1539 we find him in a list for the musters of Worcestershire.[1]

Among the Shropshire denunciations, that of John Brome, vicar of Stanton Lacy, deserves brief mention. In September–October 1535 he was examined by the Council in the Marches on a charge of having failed to erase the pope's name from his service books. In some he had touched nothing; in one he had covered the offending word 'with small pieces of paper set on with barm' which, being removed, displayed the *papa* 'as fair as ever it was and as legible'.[2] His accusers were two priests and a clerk. While on this point and on his excuse – that 'they are but fools that so will destroy their books, for this world will not ever last' – the evidence seems solid, the witnesses disagreed on the more serious question whether he had properly declared the royal supremacy from the pulpit and prayed for King and Queen; some confusion arose from the negligence of the vicar's deputy one day when Brome, after a fall from his horse, had not himself performed. The accused man put everything down to the malice of William Heynes, a big man in the village who had allegedly coerced or suborned the witnesses and even gone so far as to tamper with a witness summons by inserting another name in it. Rowland Lee sent up all the papers,[3] but no more was heard of what on the face of it looks like a typical enough village dispute taking advantage of Brome's incautiously oldfashioned opinions.

Cheshire posed an altogether more serious problem. There the authority of the Council in the Marches did not run, though Lee tried to do something about the frightful murder rate which at one point he claimed was higher in one year than for any two years in Wales, about as severe a standard as could be applied.[4] The shire was distracted by

---

[1] *LP* xiv. I, p. 309. [2] SP 1/96, fos. 210–13 (*LP* xi. 408).
[3] SP 1/97, fo. 99 (*LP* ix. 510). [4] *LP* xiii. I. 1042.

battles for ascendancy between the families of Brereton and Dutton, a situation fully dominant in the events attending upon the dissolution of Norton Abbey, which are related elsewhere.[1] In general, Cheshire behaved more like the northern counties: independent, backward, ill governed, it somewhat resembled Lancashire rather than the border or Midlands regions with which it might seem more obviously linked by geography.[2]

7

The northern Midlands, as it happens, provide little evidence of serious disturbance, but there are two extraordinary cases which throw much light in their different ways. One of these revolves around the persecution of Edward Large, incumbent of Bishop's Hampton (Hampton Lucy, Warw.), which reveals the interaction of village rivalries, quarrels among the gentry, favour at Court, and sincere religious disagreement.[3] The other occurred at Coventry. But before we turn to that, a glance may be spared for William Dragley, an elderly prebendary of Southwell Minster. He misconducted himself in March 1534 by abusing the King to a visitor, Chester herald, who, shocked, reported that he had never heard anything like it in over thirty years of service to the Crown.[4] Dragley had taken hold of the gold scutcheon the herald wore on his breast and asked what it was. The following exchange then took place:

'It is the King's arms.'

'Marry, I love it the worse.'

'Sir, wot ye what ye say?'

'By God's passion, I love him not, for he takes our goods from us and makes us go to the plough; I have been at the plough this day myself.'

'Sir, ye need not for necessity, for ye have enough if ye be content; but I fear ye will rather [im]pair than mend – so much have ye said now. The King's grace covets no man's goods wrongfully.'

[1] Below, pp. 321-5.
[2] For the problems of the north-west see C. Haigh, 'The Reformation in Lancashire to 1558,' unpub. Ph.D. dissertation, Manchester, 1969. Dr Haigh shows conclusively how little control the central government had over any part of Lancashire; even the aftermath of the Pilgrimage, which did on the whole subdue the north-east, left the remote and sparsely populated north-west still very ill managed.
[3] Discussed at length below, pp. 375–80.
[4] SP 1/82, fos. 266–71 (*LP* vii. 298).

'God's passion, I think no harm; God save the King.'

'Marry, amen, but whatsoever you think, your saying is naught.'

'I pray you, Master Chester, be content, for if ye report me I will say that I never said it.'

'Sir, that will not serve you, for I am one of the King's heralds, wherefore I must needs report all such things as is anything prejudicial to my sovereign lord the King, either to his most gracious highness or to his most honourable Council.'

But Chester was mistaken, for Dragley went scot-free, dying in possession of his prebend in October 1538.[1] He may have owed his immunity to his accuser's garrulous reminiscences, for the herald went on to say that the nearest case he remembered occurred in 1499, the day Perkin Warbeck was hanged, when he (Chester) took a railing fellow in Cheapside and put him in the Tower; but within a fortnight the fellow was, for his continued railing and jesting, set free as a fool. Cromwell might have thought this a fair precedent. What is more likely is that Dragley was saved by making his remarks before the Treason Act came into force.

To return to Coventry. This capital of the Midlands might be expected to have been troublesome. The city had declined from its great days; its population was decaying and its manufacture in a bad way, ready enough material for disturbances. Moreover, it had a persistent history of religious radicalism. Lollards here suffered frequent persecution, with many burnings in 1485, 1488, 1511–1512 (a major assault), 1519 and 1521.[2] In 1542, ten men were indicted there for offences against the Act of Six Articles, in a prosecution arising out of a serious rift in the city.[3] The accused secured a *certiorari* for the return of the indictments into King's Bench, on the grounds that some of the jury would testify that the indictments read differently from what the inquest had found, but the mayor (who privately admitted that the charge would never have arisen if the men had not first accused the vicar of something or other, and who induced the city council to finance the prosecution – which was maintenance) disobeyed the writ. The accused petitioned the Star Chamber and, since the indictments are found among the State Papers, presumably won and had the charges quashed.[4]

[1] Le Neve, iii. 448.

[2] Foxe, iv. 133–5, 557–8; J. Fines, 'Heresy Trials in the Diocese of Coventry and Lichfield 1511–12,' *Journal of Ecclesiastical History*, xiv (1963), 160–74.

[3] *LP* xvii. 537.   [4] St Ch 2/3/61.

A decaying town full of radical religion should have proved difficult in the storms of the early Reformation, especially as most of the time the bishop was an absentee: Rowland Lee, busy in the marches of Wales. Yet the only case to be recorded, and very poorly at that, is one which reduces the whole problem of treason, disaffection and security to its final absurdity.[1]

In the morning of 25 November 1535, Coventry was humming with the shocking news that overnight someone had torn down the proclamations and statutes posted up in the market place, a manifest act of sedition at the very least. John Robbins, a tailor of the town, came to his friend George Wakefield and told him in horror that he had been 'in company the last night' with those who had done the deed. What was he to do to clear himself? Wakefield replied that, now he had been told of it, it was his duty to inform the mayor; he would advise his friend thereafter; but the result of the information was that four men – Robbins, William Apreston of Windsor, Henry Heynes of Allesby (Warw.), and Robert Knottesford of Lutterworth (all yeomen) – were called to be examined before the mayor, the recorder and eight aldermen. This solemn assembly heard the following tale. On the night of the 24th, the four of them (presumably stimulated by the rare chance of all meeting together) went out drinking. About ten at night, being by this time 'overseen with drink', they wandered from Rogers's tavern to 'the inn at the sign of the pannier'. After a further spell of drinking, they staggered forth from there to the cross in the market place where fate overtook them: 'they all untrussed them and did their easement at the cross'. One of them – probably Apreston – seeing the proclamations and so forth nailed to 'tables' (notice-boards) in the market place, pulled some off 'and cast the same to the said Heynes and bid him wipe his tail with them'. In their drunken state, 'they tore down part of the tables and tore in effect all the papers, but what further they did with the tables or with the rest of the said proclamations and acts' Robbins, at least, could not tell. The others were even vaguer; quite clearly, memories of the night before were extremely hazy, and while they admitted that the treasonable offence had been committed for the hygienic reason stated they could not exactly recall who had done what.

[1] The only evidence is a set of depositions of 21 November 1535: SP 1/99, fos. 101–2. They are censored in *LP* ix. 883, for reasons which will become apparent, with the result that the calendar makes the affair sound serious.

They only remembered staggering around for a while before returning to the Pannier to sleep it off.

No more is known. It is not likely that these defilers of the King's legislative instruments got off without penalty, but one trusts (with some confidence) that their punishment was light. The authorities will hardly have wished to give wide publicity to this story. It is to be hoped that the ten worshipful men to whom it was revealed by the bedraggled crew before them had a sense of humour. What shines most clearly through the depositions is that fourfold monumental hangover.

8

While things remained pretty peaceful in the Midlands, East Anglia had a very different story to tell. The ascendancy of the Howards, headed by the duke of Norfolk, supposedly controlled this region for the King,[1] though Henry VIII had for some time been pursuing a policy of promoting the counterbalancing interest of his close friend, Charles Brandon, duke of Suffolk. Both dukes tended to pride themselves on their rule of a notoriously volatile area, and the presence of numerous gentle families was supposed to complete the protection of the Crown against disaffection among the lower orders. Certainly Howards and Brandons remained securely loyal at this time, even when radical policies and upstart ministers like Cromwell put ducal noses out of joint, but it is to be remembered that before the 1540's were out Norfolk was convulsed by one of the more dangerous uprisings of the Tudor century – Ket's rebellion of 1549.[2] This took the authorities completely by surprise; yet even in the 1530's the signs of possible unrest were plentiful, though no one could perhaps have predicted so markedly Protestant a rebellion ten years before. The complacency voiced several times by the duke of Norfolk had less to support it than he thought.[3]

[1] For the Howards and Norfolk, cf. Neville J. Williams, *Thomas Howard Fourth Duke of Norfolk* (1964), ch. 5.
[2] It should, however, be noted that Ket's rebellion occurred after Henry VIII had interfered with the balance of forces by temporarily destroying the Howards.
[3] There is a rather elementary review of the troubles in the shire in T. H. Swales, 'Opposition to the Suppression of the Norfolk Monasteries,' *Norfolk Archaeology*, 33 (1962–5), 254–65. The article adds nothing to the *LP* evidence, confines itself to cataloguing, and commits such errors as to suppose that treasons were tried at Quarter Sessions. However, the map on p. 263 usefully indicates how well distributed protests were.

Norfolk provides one of the few cases of a strictly non-political treason in the crime committed by Robert Sharpe, a Franciscan of Norwich. Anxious to escape the life religious, and stupidly unwilling to pay the necessary fees for one of the licences which at the time were granted readily enough, Sharpe had forged an archiepiscopal capacity and the royal confirmation, cutting off the seals from genuine documents and attaching them to his spurious ones.[1] For this he was tried and condemned on 16 July 1538, his crime being treason under the act of 1352 (forging the great seal). However, Cromwell ordered the sheriffs of Norwich to put off Sharpe's execution and hold him in safe custody until further notice, an instruction which scared the sheriffs since, as they pointed out on August 27th, they were liable to a fine of £100 if they failed to dispose of their prisoner before they left office at Michaelmas next. Cromwell ignored the protest – and presumably saw to it that the fine was not exacted; and in January 1542, the case, called into King's Bench nearly two years earlier, was annotated to the effect that Sharpe had produced his pardon, which was in fact dated 4 July 1541. It must be said that there is something suspicious about the reprieve of a prisoner held for so long under a sentence of death which could still have been carried out; and when it is remembered that (as we shall see) the authorities were anxious just before Sharpe's conviction to know what went on in Norwich gaol, it may confidently be conjectured that he bought his life by turning stool-pigeon.

Of course, the more conventional problems also arose in Norfolk. In June 1534, Cromwell's old friend Reginald Lyttylprow informed on William Ysebelles, parson of St Augustine's church in Norwich. Ysebelles had spoken incautiously both in private and in the pulpit and had several times been examined; in the end he was put in the mayor's ward. Lyttylprow sent up the depositions and also asked what he was to do about the priest's movables, worth some £40 and kept in his chamber to which the mayor had the key; did Cromwell want an inventory taken to prevent these goods – which might after all come to the King – from disappearing? Not even the prospect of £40 could, however, overcome Cromwell's adherence to the law which at this time did not yet make words treason, and Ysebelles, having transferred to another parish, died peacefully in 1540 when his will, bequeathing

[1] KB 9/541/107; SP 1/135, fo. 139 (*LP* xiii. II. 154); KB 29/172, rot. 6d; *LP* xvi. 1056 (22).

those movables, was proved.[1] Other persons who spoke what by then was treason were lay people. In 1535, Margaret Chaunseler (of Suffolk) gained enduring fame by calling Queen Anne 'a goggle-eyed whore', a description which has got into a good many textbooks. She also hoped that the Queen would never have a live child and blamed the King for marrying within the realm, but she penitently pleaded drunkenness and 'the evil spirit' which caused her to say such things; she looks to have got off.[2] The case of Nicholas Came, a husbandman of Bockenham Ferry in Norfolk, poses difficult problems of dating. He was indicted for the theft of a man's violet gown worth 40s on 11 January 1536, but when the justices of gaol delivery sat to try him they were told that Came could not appear because he was held in the King's prison, by the sheriffs of Norwich, 'forte et dure'.[3] One would suppose that he was held for treason so that he could not be produced for the felony, but the only treason reported of him was allegedly committed on 7 October 1537: there is no doubt about the year.[4] Although his accuser then was the gaoler of Norwich Castle, this must be a coincidence, for the offence took place at St Faith's fair: clearly, Came had got out of prison since the day that the gaol delivery had failed to try him. Asked if he knew when the lead of the abbey roof was to be melted down, he replied: 'No, the church shall stand, Rome shall be up again, and purgatory is found.' When examined, he admitted the words but ascribed them to the parish clerk of Lavenham (Suffolk) who had allegedly spoken them to his priest, a grey friar 'who wagged his head saying he would meddle in no such matters'. Both priest and clerk denied it all. We do not know what became of Came, but a man so frequently in touch with the law is unlikely to have escaped permanently.

A good deal more dangerous was a vagrant singer, John Hogon, who in early 1537 went about the county 'with a crowd and a fiddle'. At Diss, in the butcher's house, he obliged with a song that bothered the men that heard it:

> The hunt is up, the hunt is up.
> The masters of art and doctors of divinity
> Have brought this realm out of a good unity.

[1] SP 1/84, fos. 130, 165 (*LP* vii. 779, 796); *Norfolk Record Society*, vol. 16, part 2, p. 215.
[2] SP 1/89, fo. 158 (*LP* viii. 196). [3] KB 9/535/47–9.
[4] SP 1/125, fo. 163 (*LP* xii. II. 864).

Three noblemen have take[n] this to stay:
My lord of Norfolk, Lord Surrey, and my lord of Shrewsbury.
The duke of Suffolk might a made England merry.

He was warned not to sing this song in Suffolk, but asked why not:
'I have sung this song twice afore my lord of Surrey,[1] at Cambridge and
Thetford Abbey.' Another man refused to believe this; Surrey would
have set Hogon 'fast by the feet, for thou slanderest that nobleman'.
Anyway, what did the line about the duke of Suffolk mean? Hogon
replied he meant that if Suffolk had allowed the men of Lincolnshire to
join with the men of the north, 'they together should or this time a
brought England into a better stay than it is now'. Besides, Suffolk had
broken his promises of pardon to the rebels. After this, he went from
house to house, singing the same song.[2]

The usual disputes arising from differences in religion are also found
in Norfolk, though in the absence of a Latimer or Shaxton, and despite
the relative proximity of Cambridge, the diocese ruled in succession by
two determined conservatives, Richard Nix and William Rugge (or
Reppe), produced no serious clashes. Actually, the most serious nearly
backfired on Bishop Rugge. On 23 February 1539, he preached a sermon
at Norwich in which among other things he accepted a measure of free
will in man which 'holpen by the grace of God' may assist the workings
of grace 'which else should be received in vain'. This had struck one of
the audience, Robert Watson, as dangerously Pelagian. He called on the
bishop next day and 'very arrogantly and in a great fume' altogether
denied the existence of free will in man. Rugge was afraid of the state of
opinion in Norwich and tried to put the discussion off to a later date
and different place, but this produced rumours that he dared not face
Watson in the city. So he decided to return there and settle the dispute.
He was warned that Watson's followers would assemble in strength
and therefore asked a body of gentlemen, including the mayor and
headed by Lord Fitzwater, to attend him so that their presence should
prevent 'ill fashions'. He had hoped to find just a small discussion group
when he got to Norwich; instead there was a crowd who sympathised
with Watson; and as Cromwell heard it, Watson could have been
plotting a seditious assembly. Hence this letter of 15 March 1539.[3]

[1] Norfolk's son, the poet, executed for a very different treason in 1547.
[2] SP 1/116, fo. 30 (*LP* xii. I. 424).
[3] SP 1/144, fo. 114 (*LP* xiv. I. 526).

But Rugge was to find that, even in this year which was to see the so-called conservative reaction, Norwich and Cromwell remained on the other side. Even before the bishop wrote, Fitzwater examined Watson, and though he bound him in a recognisance to appear at Thetford Assizes to explain himself, he hinted that he thought the man innocent of sedition. He also reported Watson's opinion, which was that 'a natural man destitute of the spirit of God cannot receive the grace of God when it is offered by the gospel'.[1] Apparently this soundly Protestant view intrigued Cromwell who decided to see Watson himself. So Watson went up to Court, with a letter from Fitzwater who by now (March 16th) had no doubt that no sedition had been intended and asked the lord privy seal to be a good lord to this worthy man.[2] Cromwell complied with an expedition which was even for him remarkable: early in April he wrote to the mayor of Norwich to recommend an earlier suitor for the next vacancy of the town clerkship (the present holder being aged) and Watson for anything else going. The mayor and corporation did even better; acknowledging the letter, they explained that Cromwell's nominee for the clerkship was a stranger, and that therefore they proposed to appoint Watson, one of themselves, as soon as the office fell vacant.[3] They described him as well learned in Scripture and in the laws of the realm, qualities which he had indeed displayed in his quarrel with the bishop. Manifestly, Watson's religious inclinations were shared by the city authorities of Norwich; any inference from Rugge's reliance on the gentry to support him in his dispute with this radical to the effect that religious and social divisions coincided would be quite false.

Rather similar consequences had attended an earlier effort of Rugge's to arrest the Reformation. This was provoked in 1538 by the preaching of Matthew Parker, the future archbishop, then dean of the College of Stoke-by-Clare in Suffolk.[4] Parker delivered a radical sermon at Clare

[1] BM, Vesp. F. xiii, fo. 201; Cleo. E.v., fo. 409 (*LP* xii. I. 588). These notes are misdated in *LP*; they belong to the same business which is fixed for 1539 by the name of the mayor.

[2] SP 1/144, fo. 119 (*LP* xiv. I. 531).   [3] SP 1/150, fo. 101 (*LP* xiv. I. 721).

[4] The story was first told by John Strype, *The Life and Acts of Matthew Parker* (1711), 11–12. He dated the start into 1537. The editor of Parker's *Correspondence* (Parker Society, 1853), 5, opted for 1539, on the ground that Audley was elevated to the peerage in that year and that Parker's memorial addressed him as Lord Audley. In the case of a lord chancellor, the point is not conclusive, but in any case Audley was ennobled on 29 November 1538. The most recent moderately serious life of Parker

on November 17th which upset some people. To counterbalance this, the bishop despatched one Dr John Stokes, prior of the Austin Friars of Norwich. This was an unfortunate choice because Stokes had been in trouble before. In the summer of 1535 (or 1536), Cromwell had summoned him to explain a report that he had failed to preach the royal supremacy. On that occasion Stokes had cleared himself by producing a Latin sermon addressed to a gathering of the Norfolk and Suffolk clergy in which he claimed to have proclaimed the King's title even before the duty was imposed by the act of Parliament.[1] Cromwell commanded him from henceforth to preach the matter every Sunday and holy day in English, and he received similar instructions also from his diocesan. Then, in the spring of 1538, Stokes again misbehaved himself, though in what fashion is not known.[2] He later reminded Cromwell that a sermon of his had been complained of, presumably at Norwich, for which reason he was imprisoned from 28 June 1538 till brought before Cromwell on November 3rd.[3] Once again Cromwell was kind to him and let him go.

However, this was a mistake. Four months in prison had not cooled

(V. J. K. Brook, *A Life of Archbishop Parker*, 1962) accepts the date of 1539/40 and speculates about the part played in the story by the reaction exemplified by the Act of Six Articles (pp. 18 f.). Mr Brook appears never to have heard of *LP*. Actually, the calendar assigns one relevant document to 1536 and the other to 1538. That 1538 is the correct date is proved by the part played in the story by the bishop of Dover who visited East Anglia in that year, but some difficulties remain.

[1] These details emerge from Stokes's letter to Cromwell of Nov.–Dec. 1538 (SP 1/112, fos. 64–5), misplaced by *LP* xi. 1216 into 1536. He there refers to this previous encounter, but the date is not certain. Stokes says he preached as stated 'fifteen days before the abrogation of the usurped power of the bishop of Rome', which could refer to the Act of Supremacy (1534) or the Act Abolishing the Pope's Power of July 1536. He also states that on that occasion he was summoned by the 'bishop of Dublin'. In late 1534, there was no such person, John Alen having been murdered in March 1534 and his successor George Brown not being appointed until January 1536. But it does not look as though Brown was ever in England in mid-1536, and it is more probable that the whole business really belongs to 1535, the summons being delivered in his then capacity as provincial of the Austin Friars; by 1538 Stokes could well have used Brown's later title even when referring to a time before his elevation.

[2] Strype's story, with the whole affair in the spring of 1537, is wrong. As Parker's letter to Stokes of 23 Nov. [1538] shows, which Strype himself prints (*Parker*, App., Doc. III), it was only on that date that Stokes came from Norwich to reside at Clare and engage the dean of Stoke in battle.

[3] E 135/8/39; SP 1/112, fo. 65. *LP* ix. 1216, summarising the second document, refers in error to the interview with Cromwell as taking place on the Sunday before All Saints; it should read 'after'.

Stokes's ardour, and he at once and willingly undertook the mission against Parker which Rugge (very probably) suggested to him. On November 17th, Parker, as has been said, caused some murmuring at Clare where he visited from his deanery to deliver a reformist sermon. Stokes arrived post haste, and although at once inhibited from preaching by the bishop of Dover, Cromwell's special visitor to all the friaries of England, who had just reached East Anglia on his travels through the realm, nevertheless decided to attack on the 24th. The day before Parker wrote him a long letter warning him not to provoke strife and explaining that he himself had not preached the doctrine alleged,[1] but Stokes went ahead. He later affirmed that he had done nothing but proclaim all the proper things about King and pope, and even that he had specially praised Parker's previous sermon, but this was not the general impression at Clare, even though Stokes got twenty-two men to append their seals to his defence.[2] He was at once reported to Cromwell, but at the same time his supporters – described by the bishop of Dover as men of 'no good judgment' – prepared an accusation against Parker on the basis of his sermon on the 17th.[3] To this paper Parker replied in December with a long justification addressed to the lord chancellor.[4] Despite Stokes's anxious letters, and despite the twenty-two seals, Cromwell, in this familiar situation, believed his visitor and accepted Parker's explanations. Stokes found himself again in prison from where he wrote once more to say that he had done nothing wrong.[5] But he had had enough: at the same time he begged the lord privy seal to allow him to cast off his habit. Cromwell approved of friars who felt like that, and although the incomplete registers list no dispensation for Stokes he may well have had his wish. His friary at Norwich had been dissolved in August, during his first imprisonment.[6]

In these kinds of dispute, East Anglia essentially followed the pattern discernable elsewhere, except perhaps for the hint that the reform found more general support here, despite a conservative bishop, than it

---

[1] Strype, *Parker*, App., Doc. III.

[2] This is E 135/8/39, not calendared in *LP*. Further details emerge from his other defence (SP 1/112, fos. 64–5 [*LP* xi. 1216]) which is annotated by the bishop of Dover to the effect that Stokes had broken the inhibition, had angered even the priests there by his sermon, had attacked Parker, and had preached sedition.

[3] SP 1/139, fo. 212 (*LP* xiii. II. 935): the bishop of Dover to Cromwell.

[4] *Parker's Correspondence*, 7 ff.   [5] Strype, *Parker*, App., Doc. IV.

[6] *LP* xiii. II. 282. Not all dispensations were registered.

commanded in the west even under Latimer's rule. These hints are in accord with what is usually held about those eastern parts, with their ready access to continental influence. However, what really distinguishes East Anglia are the signs of social dissatisfaction, an undercurrent of trouble in which neither religion nor politics played any significant part. In September 1536, the duke of Norfolk, alerted by Cromwell, with the aid of five powerful members of the local gentry investigated two 'lewd fellows', one an organ-maker of Norwich who, it seems, intended 'to have made an insurrection', while the other was just a common criminal. The lawyers had their doubts about the case, but the duke, 'speaking as a man unlearned in the laws', thought the organ-maker should be hanged. At the same time he smugly noted that Norfolk was the last shire in which a rising would succeed: 'we be too many gentlemen here to suffer any such business'.[1] Less than a year later, a major conspiracy was uncovered at Walsingham (which I shall discuss in a moment), an event which can be read as either proving or disproving the duke's confidence. It helped to inspire Richard Bishop of Bungay in Suffolk who, in conversation with a man he had never met before, committed himself to some very dangerous remarks.[2]

After a word about the weather (very hot), they fell to talking of the present time. Bishop complained that in his village things had reached such a point that if two or three people were walking together 'the constable come to them and will know what communication they have, or else they shall be stocked'. He alluded to the affair at Walsingham and spoke of a prophecy (the prophecy of the mole) according to which the people should rise 'this year or never'. It was said that the earl of Derby had turned traitor and that the duke of Norfolk was so tied up in the north 'that he might not come away when he would'. This was the day of opportunity. People would not long bear all this living under suspicion and control. All this he later admitted: the only words he denied (and could not 'by fair means nor by foul' be induced to confess) ran, 'if three hundred good fellows were together that they should have company enough to subdue the gentlemen'. The informant swore they were spoken, and Bishop's parting words, on which the depositions agreed, make plain that more was intended than idle talk on a hot afternoon: 'Farewell, my friend, and know me another time if you can, and God send us a quiet world.'

[1] SP 1/106, fo. 183 (*LP* xi. 470).   [2] SP 1/120, fos. 100–4 (*LP* xii. I. 1212).

Bishop's amalgam of prophecies, rumour, sedition and hostility to the ruling classes had in it all the makings of a plot for the commons to rise, and the duke of Suffolk, who investigated, took the matter seriously. He had also been told of a May Day play with suspicious overtones, a play 'of a king how he should rule his realm'. The actor playing the part of Husbandry 'said many things against gentlemen, much more than was in the book of the play' – and the man had vanished. Suffolk warned all justices to watch out, especially 'at games or plays where any number of idle persons shall meet', and suggested that during that sultry summer the King might prohibit all such events.[1] This talk against gentlemen certainly needed watching, and this was the year after the Pilgrimage of Grace when people might well feel inclined to copy the northern men. A slump in the textile industry added to the difficulties: in March 1537, John Cokke, a worsted weaver of Norwich, complained that he could not pay the tax assessed on him 'for I can sell no worsted nor receive no part of my debts'; the only remedy that he could see was that 'poor men do rise'.[2] Together with his journeyman Richard Toll he was put in gaol by the mayor until the matter should be fully discovered; Toll, whose loose tongue had first revealed it, denied retelling Cokke's words but 'if he did that, he knoweth he was drunk at the time'. Their excuses were soon accepted: when the Walsingham conspirators came to be tried, the names of Cokke and Toll were added to the original list of jurors.[3] Bishop's fate is unknown.

However, this sort of undercurrent continued. In June 1540, John Walter of Griston in Norfolk was denounced for planning a full-scale insurrection, though the plan was pitiful.[4]

If two or three good fellows would ride into the night, with every man a bell, and cry in every town that they pass through, 'to Swaffham, to Swaffham': by the morning there would be 18,000 assembled at the least. And then one bold fellow to stand forth and say: sirs, now we be here assembled; you know how all the gentlemen in manner be gone forth, and you know how little favour they bear to us poor men. Let us therefore now go home to their houses, and there we shall have harness, substance and victual, and so many as will not turn to us, let us kill them, yea even the children in the cradles. For it were a good turn if there were as many gentlemen in Norfolk as there be white bulls.

[1] SP 1/120, fo. 100 v. (*LP* xii. I. 1212).   [2] SP 1/121, fo. 23 (*LP* xii. II. 13 [3]).
[3] KB 9/538/7.   [4] SP 1/160, fo. 157 (*LP* xv. 748).

He named the first to be dealt with. 'And, sirs, if you will take upon you to play this act with the bells, you shall have horse of me and no man shall know you.' He had been trying this revolutionary talk on his neighbours 'at dinner, supper and other times' unceasingly through the month of October (the informers were pretty late).[1] Sir Roger Townsend, one of the victims named, ordered Walter's arrest and sent the denunciations to Cromwell,[2] but when the papers reached London the lord privy seal was on the eve of his fall, so that his correspondence tells us nothing further.

All these strains and stresses – religious, political, social – came together in the most serious plot hatched anywhere south of the Trent in those years, the Walsingham conspiracy of 1537.[3] The first the authorities heard of it was on April 26th when John Galant laid information before Sir John Heydon against certain men of Walsingham and thereabouts who had been trying to get him to join a scheme to 'raise the country', to capture and behead any gentleman who would resist, and to redistribute their property 'to maintain their people of their parts'.[4] Heydon got in touch with Sir Roger Townsend, and they acted fast. On the same day they secured five of the accused (George Gisborough, his son William, Thomas Howse, Robert Hawker, and John Semble), took depositions from them,[5] and sent the papers together with the two Gisboroughs to Cromwell.[6] They reported that Ralph Rogerson, thought to be the man who first involved George Gisborough, had so far escaped capture. On the 29th, the two Gisboroughs were examined in Cromwell's house at Stepney,[7] and on the 30th, Richard Southwell (whom Cromwell had despatched to Norfolk the moment he had

[1] Walter's remark about the gentlemen absent from the shire might place the event into 1537 or even 1536, but the depositions are precisely dated. It is of course possible that the revelations were extremely stale when made.

[2] SP 1/160, fo. 172 (LP xv. 755).

[3] The affair has been noticed before, but insufficiently (e.g. VCH Norfolk, ii. 256-8, a miserable account, or J. C. Dickinson, The Shrine of Our Lady of Walsingham [1956], 63-4, necessarily brief). Only Gasquet saw the court records (Henry VIII and the English Monasteries [ed. 1910], 315); characteristically he marred his short account by inventing an additional canon of Walsingham, Roland Vowell, among the victims. Vowell, prior there throughout this period and to the Dissolution (Fac. Off. Reg. 153) was not involved. Gasquet also conflated two different trials and gave a wrong date to the product.

[4] SP 1/119, fo. 30 (LP xii. I. 1045 [2]).

[5] SP 119, fo. 33 (LP xii. I. 1056), erroneously dated April 28th.

[6] SP 1/119, fo. 29 (LP xii. I. 1045 [1]).   [7] SP 1/119, fos. 37-8 (LP xii. I. 1056 [2]).

heard of the plot) wrote back to the lord privy seal to report his arrival and his intention to seek out the remaining culprits.[1] He told Cromwell that Heydon thought the whole affair very minor, the work of a dozen people at the most ('all very beggars and men neither of honesty, wit or conduct'): there was no danger of any 'commotion'. Walsingham was not the start of another rebellion on the Lincolnshire or Yorkshire model, a possibility which had obviously been in Cromwell's mind. The county was in 'as good and due obedience as ever it was', so that Southwell proposed to return to London when he had caught the missing conspirators and lodged the lot in Norwich Castle.

Three days later he could report full success. To those previously suspected and caught he had added Nigel Mileham, the subprior of Walsingham Priory, of whose complicity he had received only very belated information. He thought that more might be squeezed out of the prisoners.[2] But on May 10th, replying to Cromwell's instructions received two days earlier to 'execute upon all such persons without sparing anyone as hath offended in this conspiracy', he and Townsend explained that in their opinion there was nothing further to 'bolt out of any more of that confederacy'; they thought 'the deepness thereof fully ensearched'. In consequence they were forwarding all the depositions, keeping only copies, and would act as soon as Cromwell had worked through them and sent precise instructions about all the people involved.[3]

What, in fact, had happened? The depositions agree reasonably well, especially if it is remembered that the Gisboroughs made it plain from the first that they 'would not accuse or confess till they needs must'.[4] In consequence, they did not involve Rogerson before Townsend and Heydon, but explained his part to Cromwell, for when they were examined at Stepney Rogerson had been taken. And they never mentioned Mileham, who was subsequently denounced, a fact which raised Southwell's suspicion that more was yet to be discovered, though in the end he decided – prematurely, as we shall see – that this was not so.[5]

[1] SP 1/119, fo. 51 (LP xii. I. 1063).
[2] SP 1/119, fos. 141–2 (LP xii. I. 1125).
[3] SP 1/120, fo. 24 (LP xii. I. 1171).
[4] SP 1/119, fo. 141 (LP xii. I. 1125). George Gisborough was twice interrogated at Stepney; his second signature is much more shaky than the first, which suggests that torture was used on him.
[5] The story is here pieced together from the letters and depositions already mentioned.

The whole conspiracy had blown up very fast. About the middle of April, Rogerson, a singing-man at the priory, approached the elder Gisborough, also a singing-man there but mainly a yeoman peasant in the parish. Thanks to its attraction to pilgrims, Walsingham Priory had been one of the most lucrative establishments in the kingdom, and Rogerson complained about the putting down of abbeys and the consequent decay of 'our living'. Walsingham would soon suffer the fate of other houses, he thought. He also spoke of the misdeeds of gentlemen who 'had all the farms and all the cattle in the country in their hands, so that poor men could have no living by them'. He called for resistance and proposed to raise a company for the purpose. Gisborough agreed to help, his real grievance evidently being against the gentlemen – against enclosers of commons and engrossers of farms – rather than against the disappearance of monasteries. They decided to prepare themselves for a major rising in north Norfolk on St Eligius' Eve (June 24th). They would fire the beacons to gather their company and at once march across the county into Suffolk, attacking the gentlemen as they went. At this time, 'they were not at a full point but a communication'; the next step was to recruit followers. This proved less easy than they had hoped. Even William Gisborough (who lived in Wells and is described as a yeoman and merchant) hesitated but in the end agreed to come in. Thomas Howse, who claimed throughout to have done nothing but warn of the dangers, was coerced into compliance by threats to his life. The conspirators certainly took a good many risks in beating up support, and, as we have seen, when they tried to bring in John Galant they lost the game altogether. They used a shooting-match at Binham to co-ordinate their efforts, a discovery which moved Southwell to suggest that another such occasion on the Suffolk border ('for which the prizes were proclaimed last May Day at Wymondham' and elsewhere) had better be watched because a great crowd from both shires was sure to assemble there.[1] At this point, of course, the whole plot blew up. In the outcome, the total number of arrests ran to twenty-seven, sufficient to show that a very serious danger had been averted only by early discovery. The motives were mixed, but hatred of the exploiting landlords

---

[1] Townsend and Southwell had taken it upon themselves to warn the duke of Suffolk. They were worried about being charged with excessive zeal but pleaded that they would rather 'suspect too much upon light likelihood than to have our suspicion undisclosed' and cause 'inconvenience' by their 'oversight'. Heydon's confidence in the pettiness of the business does not seem to have influenced his colleagues.

of the shire stood paramount, whereas defence of abbeys and fears of the King's doings weighed much less in the scale.

By May 10th, all the people involved were in Norwich Castle. While Cromwell and the local authorities reviewed the facts and decided what to do, further material accumulated in the gaol, though this did not become known until early June, after the Walsingham conspirators had been dealt with.[1] Rogerson in particular tried to involve more people in his own fate, accusing one John Smith and Mr Robert Griggs alias Dobedo of inciting him to rebellion, in support of the northerners. He and Mileham, the subprior, also tried to stir the felons and suspects amongst whom they found themselves into a proper appreciation of their rights, talking somewhat mysteriously of distributing sheep to all and sundry, and drawing up bills which they then tore into tiny pieces. Old Gisborough seemed inclined to follow Rogerson's lead again, but his son said, 'Father, there is no remedy but death with us, and for us to put any more in danger it were pity'. These activities got mixed up with various attempts by the ordinary criminals to get back at their own accusers. Once the authorities heard of this mingle-mangle (perhaps from Sharpe?) they investigated; but since clearly there was nothing there but malice and invention, especially on Rogerson's part, the matter went no further.

On May 25th, the conspirators were indicted at Norwich Assizes.[2] The grand jury threw out the charges against eight men who were therefore 'delivered by proclamation' and (as was customary) merely bound to good behaviour. Fourteen men were indicted of treason: Mileham, Rogerson, the two Gisboroughs, Howse (husbandman), Semble (mason), John Pecock (Carmelite friar), Richard Henley (plumber), Andrew Pax (parish clerk of Wells), John Grigby (rector of Langham), Thomas Manne (carpenter of Langham), John Sellers (tailor of Langham), Thomas Penne (husbandman of Houghton), and John Punt (rector of Waterdon). William Gibson (another Carmelite), Richard Maryot (mariner of Wells), and Robert Hawker (butcher of Walsingham) were charged with misprision for concealment. The wives of Pax and Malyot, both called Agnes, are mentioned as sharing

---

[1] Depositions taken from prisoners in the Castle on 8 and 9 June 1537: SP 1/121, fos. 70–2, 86–9 (LP xii. II. 56, 68).

[2] There is an annotated list of all the persons involved in SP 1/120, fo. 226 (LP xii. I. 1300 [2]); the indictments are in KB 9/538/4–8.

Hawker's misprisionary knowledge but do not seem to have been indicted on this occasion. The charges against all the alleged traitors except Punt were that they had conspired to make an insurrection 'as well for staying of abbeys' putting down as for reformation of gentlemen for taking of farms' and had plotted to hold the bridges at Thetford and Brandon against the King. Punt's offence was that on May 18th he had supported the rebels in words, saying that 'what they did was for a commonwealth'. The jury was chosen with care: it consisted of five knights and seven esquires. These gentlemen could be trusted to protect their kind, and all the accused were found guilty as charged. The three misprisioners were sentenced to life imprisonment; of the convicted traitors, Grigby and Punt (for reasons unknown to us) were remanded in gaol without sentence;[1] the rest were to suffer a traitor's death. The sentences were carried out the following day on all except Penne who, again for reasons unknown, was left in gaol. As was usual, the executions were distributed around the shire the better to impress the people: five men died at Norwich, two at Yarmouth, two at Walsingham, and two at Lynn. All except Rogerson made the good end expected of sixteenth-century criminals, expressing their remorse and exhorting the bystanders to obey the King in all things; only the originator of the whole affair remained true to the temper he had shown throughout by starting to express 'his cankered stomach' on the scaffold, but he was stopped.[2]

However, these deaths did not end the matter. First of all, Elizabeth, wife of Robert Wood of Aylesham, spoke much too freely of her fury at what had happened. On May 12th,[3] in conversation with two men at a tailor's shop, she said: 'It was a pity that the Walsingham men were discovered, for we shall never have good world till we fall together by the ears; and with clubs and clouted shoon shall the deed be done; for we had never good world since this King reigned'. On the 28th she stood before Heydon to answer this charge of wanting to make a peasants' war. There were two witnesses against her, and so she went to Norwich gaol.[4] Thomas Wryght, a carpenter of Houghton, was also

---

[1] This sort of thing was as a rule decided by the King's Council or Cromwell, on the basis of the evidence and before the trial, the judges having their instructions in case the jury convicted.

[2] SP 1/120, fos. 224, 227 (*LP* xii. I. 1300 [1, 3]).

[3] The indictment (KB 9/538/13) says July 12th, but this must be a mistake since she was delated before that date.   [4] SP 1/120, fos. 228, 230 (*LP* xii. I. 1301).

reported for incautious words in conversation about the trials at Norwich. A friend told him that when the sentence was pronounced the wife of one of the accused had fainted and remained in a swoon for a whole hour; Wryght remarked that 'the judges had never the more pity upon her for all that'. 'Her husband,' said the other man, 'had as he deserved.' On the contrary, asserted Wryght, 'they that died for the commonwealth were hanged up'. The last thing the government would want to see was a crown of peasant martyrdom bestowed on the Walsingham rebels, and though Cromwell was informed he did not pursue an accusation which Wryght firmly denied.[1]

A good deal more serious was a report, received very belatedly on June 27th, of a further intended insurrection, not this time at Walsingham but in the village of Fincham, twenty-five miles away to the south-west. The man accused, a husbandman called Harry Jervis, had clearly thought along much the same lines as Rogerson, though there was no apparent link between them and the conspiratorial talk in which he had indulged occurred in April, before the Walsingham conspiracy had been betrayed. He told his fellows of his plan.[2] At mass time in the church, he would raise the cry that Fincham Hall was on fire. This would bring out the squire, John Fincham, and in the confusion they would capture him and force him to do as they bid; if not, 'they would make a cartway betwixt his head and his shoulders'. Then he proposed to ring the bells in every town 'to raise the commons'. The informant failed to tell Fincham because he feared for his life, especially as others were involved such as Thomas Stilton who agreed that the commons of Norfolk should follow the example of their friends in Yorkshire. He had been there during the Pilgrimage and had seen 'that they rose for the wealth of the commonalty'. Jervis in effect admitted everything, but Stilton vainly tried to make out that the words about seeing things in Yorkshire were also Jervis's who had served there during the suppression of the rising. These two also made the journey to Norwich Castle, where they were joined by John Hubbard who on July 10th[3] had said that 'the Walsingham men have risen, and it is a pity that they went not forward and set the beacons on fire'. All four persons – Harry Jervis, Thomas Stilton, Elizabeth Wood and John Hubbard – were tried

---

[1] SP 1/121, fos. 19–22 (*LP* xii. II. 13).
[2] SP 1/121, fos. 173–6 (*LP* xii. II. 150), and the record of the indictment (KB 9/538/13).
[3] Probably the date of the denunciation: as in the case of Elizabeth Wood, the indictment surprisingly gives a very improbable date.

and condemned for treason on July 26th.[1] At the same time, three people faced indictments for misprision: William Gibson, Richard Maryot and William Younger, all sentenced to life imprisonment.[2] Gibson and Maryot, of course, already stood in like case for the Walsingham conspiracy; if they concealed anything further, we do not know what it was. They may have known about Wood or Hubbard; but if the offence touched Fincham, this would be the only positive hint at a connection between the two plots.

The four people condemned for treason no doubt died, though there is no positive evidence; and unless we hear of it, it is never absolutely certain that such sentences were carried out. This left seven men in prison: four misprisioners with life sentences (Gibson, Maryot, Hawker and Younger), two men convicted of treason but not sentenced (Grigby and Punt), and one man sentenced for treason but spared (Penne). None of these men suffered long. Poor William Younger, described as a chaplain, unfortunately died a prisoner in Norwich Castle, aged only thirty, of the French pox, as the coroner's inquest testified on 21 January 1538.[3] The other six, however, obtained their pardons on 27 November 1537 and pleaded them in the King's Bench in the Hilary term of 1538. At the same time they produced an order to the Bench to bind them in sureties for good behaviour, and this being done they all went free.[4] They can hardly be said to have been treated badly for their share in a potentially most serious treason. Agrarian grievances, exacerbated by fears about the fate of abbeys, had been behind it all: just the ingredients that had made their appeal in Yorkshire the previour year. The rebels had clearly remembered the Yorkshire example. The discovery revealed much bitter resentment against the ruling classes, and the success of Ket's programme twelve years later now need not surprise. By then the religious inspiration was of the other kind, but on both occasions the real troubles had little enough to do with religion. Fifteen people died for these intended disturbances, easily the biggest tally anywhere in the

[1] KB 9/538/13; 29/170, rot. 33.
[2] KB 9/538/11; 29/170, rot. 33d.
[3] KB 9/539/134.
[4] LP xii. II. 1150 (38); KB 27/1105, Rex, rot. 2. There remains the problem of Agnes Pax and Agnes Maryot, recorded on the controlment roll as being charged with treason and misprision, but never, it seems, tried (KB 29/170, rot. 33). Their troubles ended with the cessation of the court's interest in April 1539, but what happened to them in the interval remains unknown.

realm during the 1530's, open rebellion and dynastic strife excepted. The fact that it was discovered in time saved the government from having to suppress yet another rising, but does not prove that no rising could have come out of these plots.

9

As we return to the home counties, we leave such excitements behind. This is an area which might be supposed to rest more peacefully under the eyes of the government, and on the whole this is what happened. It was also an area – Essex perhaps in particular – in which resistance to the new order was less likely to occur, for here there was sufficient both of old Lollardy and of new Protestantism.[1] Compared with the very conservative west country and the largely unmoved Midlands, one might expect that 'progressive' county to provide hardly any striking cases of disaffection or opposition. Yet even here trouble was encountered. In 1534, Henry Fasted of Colchester reported to Cromwell the presence in that dubiously orthodox town of at least two clerical resisters.[2] John Wayne, the incumbent of St James's church and an official of the bishop of London, had refused to have anything to do with the propaganda issued by the King's Council: he would neither read out the materials provided nor let anyone else see them. Dr Thysell, another cleric, had in a sermon likened these writings to the fig tree cursed by Christ which would bear no fruit. Over a year later, the parishioners of Harwich produced a long set of articles against their parson, Thomas Corthop, who had disobeyed royal instructions, tried to bind the parish clerk with an oath to himself personally, abused individuals as knaves and churls, repeatedly failed to erase the pope's name as ordered, refused to allow a preacher licensed by Cranmer to use his pulpit, attacked the new learning and cast doubt on the King's claim to supremacy, and generally fallen foul of opinion at Harwich by his rough words and surly behaviour.[3] His misbehaviour extended over some six months, and the witnesses against him, though clearly forming a coherent clique, were numerous. In none of these cases is there any

[1] A good summary of the prevalence of heresy in Essex (in 1527) is given in Strype, *Ecclesiastical Memorials*, i, ch. 7.
[2] SP 1/83, fo. 38 (*LP* vii. 406). For Wayne see also below, p. 209.
[3] SP 1/99, fos. 200–4 (*LP* ix. 1059); though placed by *LP* into Dec. 1535, this document cannot be earlier than the latest occasion recited in it, which was 2 January 1536.

indication that Cromwell took action, but it is clear that not everybody, even in Essex, could be trusted to support his policy; the public attack on official government propaganda was really, from his point of view, intolerable.

On the other side, there were always suspicions of sacramentarianism in Essex, and Bishop Stokesley of London, himself a rigid conservative, worked at suppressing these new heresies. It was complained of him that even after being ordered by the King to set some suspects free he only removed them from gaol in London to gaol in Colchester.[1] All his vigilance did not suffice, and even towards the end of his life he was still receiving news of people charged with heretical behaviour, like John Varley, the parish clerk of Colchester, who had offended by refusing to confess and compounded the offence by refusing the bishop's jurisdiction: he would explain himself to Lord Chancellor Audley, the county's foremost reforming magnate.[2] At Langham, the disadvantages of a Bible-reading laity came home to the priest there when on 24 October 1534 he mentioned in his sermon a 'little or small king' who would not believe when Christ told him his son was safe, until he had confirmed the news by means of his servants. The priest went on to say that a poor man in need could lawfully break into a rich man's house if he was refused help. It was probably this last, rather extraordinarily radical notion – quite out of step with the priest's other opinions – that provoked John Collins to challenge him afterwards. 'You spake not this day,' he said, 'sincerely after the gospel,' for in truth Scripture stated expressly that the king believed without hesitation. As for his advice to the poor, it was 'contrary to all good laws of God and man'. The priest flew into a passion and called upon the churchwardens to bring Collins before the ordinary, though it is by no means clear what he might have been accused of.[3]

The two outstanding cases in Essex in these years both concern monasteries and in consequence have been discussed before. Nevertheless they deserve re-telling here from the point of view of the government's involvement. In the first place, there are the events at Coggeshall

[1] LP ix. 1115.
[2] BM, Cleo. E. v., fos. 410–11 (LP xiv. I. 1001). There is a mystery about this letter from Stokesley. LP date it 1539 and suppose that it was addressed to Cromwell. But since it mentions 'your mastership', it either belongs to before July 1536 or was sent to someone else.
[3] E 36/120, fo. 59 (LP vii. 145).

Abbey in 1536.[1] In early January that year, some of the monks produced accusations against the abbot, William Love, which were repeated to the earl of Essex. Calling to him the earl of Oxford, Essex examined the matter but concluded that there was nothing in it: the accuser was a simple person and had the support of Love's predecessor, resentful at having been deprived (round about 1530 or earlier),[2] while Love was 'a true subject'.[3] But the earl's attempts to protect his friend failed, for the discontented monks had taken the precaution of addressing a further protest to Thomas Legh, Cromwell's visitor, who went through Essex in November 1535.[4] This raised seven charges. The abbot had continued to support the power of the bishop of Rome. When the visitation was approaching, 'the fame went' that he hid some of the house's jewels. He had used divination to discover matters concealed: he takes 'a key and a book and the man's name that he has suspicion unto, and puts the key and the name in the book, and says certain verses with a psalm of the psalter with other superstitious ceremonies, and this done, if the book fall, then believes he the matter to be of truth'. He got his office by simony, boasting that it cost him 300 marks. He claimed that the house owed him a further 300 marks that he had spent on it, though none of his accusers 'did ever see the house so evil maintained nor smaller hospitality kept'. He always avoided seeing any of the King's servants visiting Coggeshall, which showed his mind, for if he favoured the King he would favour his servants, 'according to the common proverb, he that loveth me loveth my hound'. Lastly, he was ruining the monastery to his own profit, selling farm produce, cheating sick monks out of their proper sustenance, oppressing poor men, and grabbing what he could. He had betrayed many confessions and (discussing Lutheranism) had said 'that the maintainers of all heretics and heresy were Mr Cromwell and Friar George Brown'. They asked that he be replaced by someone else – anyone Legh thought right, 'so it be one of our house', and prayed for the King, Queen Anne, the Lady Elizabeth and Mr Cromwell, the

---

[1] For a brief account cf. J. E. Oxley, *The Reformation in Essex to the Death of Mary* (1965), 102–4. The abbey is ignored by Knowles.

[2] Oxley, *op. cit.* 102, is in error in identifying the *quondam* mentioned as an ex-abbot of Beeleigh; he has misread the document.

[3] *LP* x. 94.

[4] SP 1/103, fo. 215 (*LP* x. 774), placed much too late in the year by *LP*. For Legh's movements, see Knowles, iii. 280.

visitor-general of all the religious in the realm, 'most worthy', as well as for Legh.

This altered matters, especially since a charge of treason, however ill supported, had been made, and Legh (or Cromwell) investigated. Articles were drawn up only partially based on these general charges, and answers secured on 23 January 1536 from two of the younger monks.[1] If their evidence is to be believed, Love had behaved very badly but dangerously as well. On the eve of the visitation (that which collected the evidence for the *Valor Ecclesiasticus*) he had advised hiding some of the plate 'because the King's grace should not have it to do him pleasure with'. He had made some very suspicious leases and payments which concealed personal profit. He never prayed for King or Queen. He had cited from a book he possessed which 'told him...of all the trouble that the clergy had and should sustain, and what punishments should follow, and how in the end there should be a new pope chosen by God'. He was allegedly 'in familiar company with a mystery woman which he gave drinks unto to destroy generation'; on one occasion he procured an abortion on a woman who nearly died, and if she had he and his cronies would have buried her in the woodyard. About ten years before he had 'unlawfully used' Robert Goswell, now a monk of the house, who had told of this more than once in the abbot's presence. And he used magic to discover hidden things, in the manner already described.

It was a comprehensive indictment of Love's conduct, as abbot, monk, man and subject. How true it was is hard to say. Goswell was indeed a monk of Coggeshall and stayed there till the suppression of the house;[2] it is hard to believe that the charge involving him could have been made unless there was more than a little in it. From what followed it is clear that Cromwell reconised the weight of the evidence and over-came the protection which Love enjoyed, but, on the other hand, he behaved with extraordinary restraint if indeed he thought that here was a disaffected man who had called him a friend to heresy. It looks as though he decided that Love had committed no political crime but that his record rendered him unsuitable to continue in his position. In August, Cromwell received a suggestion from Anthony Knyvett, to

[1] SP 1/101, fos. 153–61 (*LP* x. 164 [i–iii]). The relationship of the two documents has to be conjectured, but this seems the most likely sequence of events.
[2] *Fac. Off. Reg.* 124.

whom the abbey owed money, that Love should resign and Henry More, abbot of St Mary Graces by the Tower, should be appointed his successor; More was so likely to die soon that the King would before long have the abbey in his hands again, to bestow elsewhere.[1] This was the solution adopted. On August 31st, Love obtained a dispensation to hold any benefice (for which he had to pay £4 10s 0d) and More was granted the office to hold *in commendam* with his own abbacy.[2] The dispensation for this grant cost More a thumping £125 11s 0d.[3] But Love, surprisingly, did not use his licence; instead he stayed on at Coggeshall. Both he and his accusers continued in the monastery, to see it suppressed and to obtain the usual licences for secular employment in February 1538.[4] Contrary to what one might expect, the new arrangement seems to have worked peacefully; thus Love joined his successor in investigating dangerous words spoken by the abbey's porter,[5] and in due course he became one of the three living ex-abbots of Coggeshall to receive a pension.[6]

The Coggeshall affair had little political significance, though some of the more precise things alleged touched the safety of the realm quite closely. The fact that a man like Love could have the favour of two earls must have caused some misgivings. Essentially, however, it was a case of a common kind: a state of enmity within the monastery. Cromwell's solution deserves to be called generous, and if he had hopes of Henry More's early demise he was to be disappointed. So far as we can tell, his concern was to establish peace rather than destroy a possible enemy of the new order. His behaviour in the matter of Thomas Beche, alias Marshall, abbot of Colchester, was very different – but so were the circumstances.

Marshall, as is well known, was one of the three Benedictine abbots executed in late 1539, a sudden outburst of violence so much at variance with the government's previous behaviour that it requires explanation and has received a variety, including, wrongly, that these tragedies were

---

[1] *LP* xi. 392.
[2] *Fac. Off. Reg.* 90; *LP* xi. 385 (37).
[3] *Fac. Off. Reg.* 75 (4 Sept. 1536).
[4] Ibid. 124.
[5] SP 1/106, fo. 77 (*LP* xi. 393). *LP* identify the Dr Heryng mentioned as 'my late predecessor' listed next, but this is not correct; no abbot of that name ever ruled at Coggeshall.
[6] *VCH Essex*, ii. 128.

quite in step with the normal policy of Henry and Cromwell.[1] This familiar story is worth reviewing once more, partly because it throws light on the state of opinion with which the government was faced, but partly also because the versions so far available are not entirely satisfactory. As Professor Knowles has recognised, there is no link except that of accident between the events at Colchester, Reading and Glastonbury; what distinguishes Colchester is simply abundance of information. We know far less about the background to Hugh Cooke's and Richard Whiting's fates. I do not propose to tell it all once again, but certain salient points need bringing out.[2]

The abbot had never really reconciled himself to the new order, though like nearly all his brethren he had taken the oath of supremacy and forsworn the pope. What ended his outward obedience, however reluctant, was the threat of the Dissolution. A year before his trouble started he had told Sir John St Clere:

I will not say that the King shall never have my house, but against my will and against my heart. For I know by my learning that he cannot take it by right and law, wherefore in my conscience I cannot be content, nor he shall never have it with my heart and will.

St Clere warned him against relying on the learning he had acquired 'in Oxford when ye were young' – it could get him hanged. Marshall, however, continued to put no restraint on his tongue, and at last, in November 1539, his rather surprising immunity came to an end. Earlier reports of treasonable words had been ignored; now, a whole series of accusations were quickly dug up. There is no doubt that Marshall talked altogether too much: one of his oft-repeated sayings was, 'well, well, this world will boil no water'. Once when warned about his loose tongue he replied, 'hold thy peace, fool, for my nay-say shall be as good as thy yea-say'; on another occasion he boasted of having 1200

---

[1] Cf. Knowles, iii. 376–82, 483–91; Oxley, *op. cit.* 125–30; J. E. Paul, 'The last abbots of Reading and Colchester,' *Bulletin of the Institute of Hist. Research*, xxxiii (1960), 115–21. Knowles prints some of the documents in Marshall's case, and Paul his indictment.

[2] The documents in the case are these: Sir John St Clere to Cromwell, 22 Nov. 1538 (SP 1/139, fo. 178 [*LP* xiii. II. 887]); the examinations of Edmund Troman, 1 Nov. 1539 (SP 1/154, fos. 101–6 [*LP* xiv. II. 438 (2), 439]); the depositions of Thomas Nuthake, 9 Nov. 1539 [*LP* (SP 1/154, fos. 115–18 [*LP* xiv. II. 454]); the deposition of Robert Rowse, 4 Nov. 1539 (SP 1/154, fos. 124–5 [*LP* xiv. II. 458]); Marshall's answers to an interrogatory (SP 1/154, fo. 128 [*LP* xiv. II. 459]: cf. Knowles, iii. 486); the record of the trial, 1 Dec. 1539 (KB 9/545/34–41); a report on the execution from Christopher Jenney (SP 1/156, fo. 183 [*LP* xiv. II, App. 45]).

marks to buy himself out of anything, 'and therefore my friend hangeth always at my girdle'. But he was not prosecuted for being a bore and a braggart. Nor did it signify too much that he had apparently often spoken of the Divorce as the sole reason for Henry's rejection of the pope; this was at worst corroboratory detail. The crucial charges were more specific. In bulk, the evidence builds up a striking picture of a man who, whatever his outward conformity might signify, had for six years consistently and in other people's hearing talked and railed against every aspect of government policy.

Yet what finally brought him down was, in fact, the intended suppression of his house. Cromwell's agents suspected the abbot of improperly disposing of assets for whose preservation he had become responsible after the visitation of 1535, and when looking into this possibility they soon heard of other charges, raised one way and another, which ran as follows. Marshall had refused to contemplate surrendering the abbey and wished others would follow his example; this was deposed by his servant Edmund Troman. He had denied the supremacy, both during the passing of the relevant statutes and since then; this was affirmed by Thomas Nuthake, physician and mercer, and by Robert Rowse, mercer, while Troman had never heard any such sayings. He had asserted the truth of the papal primacy 'next immediate under Christ' by the law of God; this rested on Nuthake's testimony, but Troman had again heard no such words. He had called Cranmer, Audley and other councillors 'archheretics' who went 'about to destroy the Church and the law of God' (Nuthake). He had lamented the deaths of Fisher, More and the Carthusians, speaking of 'tyrants and bloodsuckers' who had 'put to death and martyred[1] those blessed clerks and best learned men...They died martyrs and saints, in my conscience, for holding with our holy father the pope, for the right of all Holy Church' (Nuthake and Rowse; Troman heard him only regretting the pity of their deaths, no more). He had praised the northern rebels who would prevent the putting down of abbeys, according to Nuthake and Rowse; Troman reported words so obscure that they seem to hide the opposite meaning.[2] He had expressed a wish that Cranmer, Audley and Cromwell were taken by the rebels: this would put an end to all these

---

[1] Not 'murdered', as *LP* has it.
[2] 'The same northern men were "goad" men, mokyll in the mothe [large in the mouth?], great crackers [boasters] and nothing worth in their deeds.'

proceedings (all three witnesses). There were other dubious sayings: certain councillors had made the King so greedy that 'if all the water in Thames did flow gold and silver it were not able to quench his grace's thirst' (Troman); 'ye may see to what end the King's fervent love of Queen Anne is come to: he began with a hot love, and now it is soon quenched: God give grace that the other come not to the same pass' (Nuthake); Audley, Cromwell and two or three bishops were making laws 'to make all England heretics' (Nuthake).

Thus, embroideries apart, Marshall stood accused of treason in that he had spoken explicit words against the royal supremacy, for the papal power, and in support of the Pilgrimage of Grace. If the charges were true, the law left little doubt about his fate. But all three rested on the testimony of the two outsiders; Troman, who had denied nothing concerning the disposal of property or Marshall's general dislike of the new order, would not testify to the more precisely treasonable items. And Nuthake and Rowse had to admit that they had always been alone with the abbot when he made these indictable statements. Nevertheless, the government decided to go all out against him. Someone set to on Nuthake's deposition to extract the formal charges from it, marking off the various points and drawing a line (with *finis* against it) after a pro-papal statement, so as to exclude some slightly embarrassing further words about the Divorce being the cause of it all. By November 20th, Marshall was in the Tower[1] where he was examined on a set of articles charging him with six specific treasons: speaking against the King's supremacy, supporting the bishop of Rome's usurped authority, the bit about the waters of the Thames and the King's covetousness,[2] saying that God would take vengeance for the suppression of abbeys, speaking as he did about the victims of 1535, and speaking as he did about the pilgrims of grace. In his answer, Marshall tried to wriggle out of the conclusive charges, the first two: he now gave it as his opinion that the papal power was not *iure divino*, had arrogated too much to itself, and the King had 'good authority' to be supreme head. All the rest he simply reversed, alleging that in each case his remarks had been the opposite and so entirely proper. On abbeys he really humbled himself:

[1] *LP* xiv. II. 554.
[2] The only article based on Troman's deposition: was that why it was included? It amounted to slander of the King but could hardly have been brought within the compass of the 1534 Treason Law.

he would certainly, though regretfully, have given up his house if it had been demanded, but he thought by a little resistance to increase the size of his pension. This is a sad document, but normal by the practices of the time. The prisoner did what he could to save himself and finished with the usual appeal for the King's mercy.

He was not believed; and indeed it is difficult to see why Nuthake and Rowse, whose relations with Marshall had, by their own account, been perfectly friendly (witness his free speech in their presence and their constant anxious warnings), should have invented this record of some six years of treasonable sayings. There is no sign that they got any benefit whatsoever out of their action.[1] They had not denounced him before when he had said those things, in itself a dangerous omission to confess which makes their depositions the more credible; once the investigation began they had to do their duty by telling the truth. It is not really possible to doubt that Marshall was guilty of those treasons, and it was for them that on December 1st he was indicted at Colchester under the Treason Act of 1534.[2] He pleaded not guilty, but was convicted by the jury and sentenced to a traitor's death, the sentence being carried out the same day.

Two questions remain: what did Abbot Thomas die for, and why was he treated with such severity when other men denounced (including abbots) so often escaped? The first point arises because Professor Knowles denies him the right to be thought a full-scale martyr for the papacy. He had, we are told, weakened: he retracted his denial of the supremacy, and on the scaffold, according to the report received, had begged the King's forgiveness and effectively acknowledged the truth of the indictment. The abbot of Glastonbury, similarly judged to be inferior to such as More and Fisher in steadfastness, is in a different case because he was tried for felony, not for treasonable denial of the supremacy. But the abbot of Reading is to be reckoned superior to his brother of Colchester because he died for asserting the papal primacy and did not weaken.[3] The debate is of no interest to the historian, but

---

[1] Troman, with other servants of the abbey, obtained on Oct. 30th a very small 'reward' from the King, together with outstanding wages and expenses for the journey to London in the course of the investigation (LP xiv. II. 416). There is no indication that the other witnesses were ever paid anything, even expenses.

[2] For the details see Paul, 'The last abbots of Reading and Colchester', 121. The articles of the indictment repeat the main treasons as put to Marshall at his examination.

[3] Knowles, iii. 378, 491.

this analysis of the case will hardly do. We happen to have evidence of Marshall's behaviour; for Cooke we have neither a record of his examination nor a report of his scaffold speech. Marshall may have wavered in the Tower, but he acknowledged at the end that he had adhered to the authority of Rome. Indeed, he broke with convention by refusing to retreat, even at this last, from 'his own conceit that the suppression of abbeys should not stand with the law of God'. Marshall was a tough old man. Formally he died for treason committed in denying the royal supremacy, and he had committed that treason. In inner reality he died for his absolute conviction that the King had no right to take his abbey from him. In a sense, he was the only martyr (so far as we know) for the monastic institution as such that the Dissolution threw up. And almost certainly this was also the reason for the vigour with which he was persecuted. His stubbornness on the point finally brought him into trouble and then drove the government to take matters to extremes. Marshall had been no threat to peace or order. He had uttered his convictions only in private. Colchester was not in turmoil because of him. But he had made it very plain that he would not surrender his abbey, and when means were sought to put pressure on him the search turned up such plain and rank treasons that there could be only one end to the story.

10

Of all the places in the kingdom, London seemed almost the least distracted, but this was because it harboured the King's Court and administration and could not escape constant vigilance. Of course, there were the usual reports of radical opinion or dubiously loyal preaching, as well as the minor irritations and quarrels resulting in denunciations which everywhere absorbed time and energy. George Rowlands's unsatisfactory behaviour in the confessional, for instance, occurred in the capital.[1] It will here suffice to display two problems of very different kinds encountered at both ends of the religious spectrum.

The bishop of London, John Stokesley, was the only southern bishop to be given a bad time during those years. After Stephen Gardiner's temporary disgrace in 1532, Stokesley was in a manner the leader of the conservative hierarchy and therefore always rather exposed. He made

[1] Above, pp. 27–30.

no secret of his dislike of the Reformation, but he usually behaved with sufficient circumspection to avoid the worst: no one preached the royal supremacy more zealously, deceiving the many who thought 'that sugar would scarcely have melted in his mouth'.[1] However, in 1538 the government encountered resistance at Syon monastery and found occasion to blame Stokesley for it; it was decided to teach him a lesson. On May 29, the attorney-general laid an information against him in the King's Bench for *praemunire* (under the acts of 1393 and 1536), a challenge which, if successful, would have destroyed him as it destroyed Wolsey.[2] Joined with him were several inmates of Syon and a number of his secular clergy. The intention clearly was to break a knot of resistance, but it is not so clear who may have initiated the move. Stokesley does not seem to have thought Cromwell responsible, though he may have been pretending. As soon as the information was entered, he did the only possible thing by appearing to confess his guilt, making a total surrender of everything, and throwing himself on the King's mercy.[3] On the very day that his trouble started he wrote to Cromwell to inform him of his decision, to recall his faithful service to the King, and to beg his aid in terms which indicate that he regarded the lord privy seal as neutral in the issue.[4] He also saved what he could of his pride by explaining that he had yielded when he knew himself to be innocent because 'I would not be seen to contend with my sovereign lord'.

His surrender worked as it was meant to: the court bailed him in swingeing sureties (10,000 marks of his own and six others of 500 marks each) and postponed judgment, knowing, of course, that the King would decide what to do. On July 3rd Stokesley received a comprehensive pardon which ended his persecution.[5] There need be no doubt that the attack on him originated in difficulties encountered in the imposing of the new order on a diocese whose bishop, an expert canon lawyer, was adept at putting up passive resistance, and it seems improbable that Cromwell was not behind it; at any rate, the trick worked. Stokesley had only just over a year to live, but during that year he ceased to champion the cause nearest to his heart. His apparent conversion did not

[1] So said a pamphleteer of 1539: cf. below, p. 162, n. 1.
[2] KB 9/539/7.
[3] KB 27/1105, Rex, rot. 20.
[4] SP 1/132, fo. 204 (*LP* xiii. I. 1096).
[5] *LP* xiii. I. 1519 (3).

convince one of Cromwell's pamphleteers who after his death accused him of having been instrumental in seducing the abbot of Reading from his allegiance: had he lived, 'I fear he should have stretched a rope'.[1] There is no evidence to support this allegation.

An obedient bishop of London was the more desirable because the capital contained too many religious radicals whose existence gave the conservatives a chance of disguising opposition to the official policy as protection of the truth against officially unacceptable extremism. The point may be illustrated from a peculiar story which matters here because it produced unrest, even though the occasion was absurd rather than important. The culprit was John Harrydaunce, a bricklayer of Whitechapel, who could not be got to stop preaching in and out of season. The city authorities first interested themselves in him in 1537.[2] On August 26th, he delivered himself of a sermon 'out of the window of his mansion house', causing thereby 'a great conventicle and unlawful assembly'. The lord mayor, himself a friend to moderate reform, committed him to prison and a few days later, at Cromwell's request, sent him along to the lord privy seal. They had gaoled Harrydaunce because he admitted his unlicensed preaching, a confession which left them no alternative, and because there was bad blood between the bricklayer and his parish priest. The priest denied the charge that he had caused annoyance by denouncing Harrydaunce from the pulpit as a heretic and offered to prove this by the voice of the parish, for which reason the lord mayor had let him go. There need be no doubt that Harrydaunce in fact was something of a heretic, probably of Lollard inclinations. He told his interrogators that though he could not read or write he had for thirty years endeavoured 'to learn the Scripture', claimed to have no followers or associates, and there and then began to preach his sermon again. Beginning 'In nomine patris et filius and spiritus sanctus [sic]', he gave the city fathers a summary which he offered to expand for anyone who wished to hear it; and he had 'the New Testament ever about him'.

Perhaps Cromwell heard all the sermon; at any rate, he did nothing about the man. At some date in these years, an angry conservative threw Harrydaunce into a list of people allegedly teaching heretical doctrine, thus showing how useful an eccentric extremist could be when sensible

[1] SP 1/155, fos. 65r–v (LP xiv. II. 613).
[2] SP 1/124, fos. 118, 155 (LP xii. II. 594, 624).

reformers were to be attacked.[1] Being included along with Latimer and Bale did Harrydaunce too much honour, but the name with which he was more specifically linked was that of Lawrence Maxwell, another bricklayer who had certainly got into trouble for dissent.[2] Perhaps Cromwell had persuaded the preacher to hold his peace for a while, but in August 1539 Harrydaunce was once more before the city authorities, denounced this time by his parish priest William Longford, a new man since 1537 but no more happy with this particular soul in his cure. Longford had been asked to report any man in his parish who was causing disorder and had been able to think only of Harrydaunce with his preaching from his window.[3] He himself had never heard the sermons because they always took place at inconvenient hours, very early or very late. Thus on the night of Sunday, July 20th, Harrydaunce had held forth from ten at night till midnight. Two days later two people complained of being kept awake by the noise. Longford had meant to seek his bishop's advice, but Bishop Stokesley had been too ill to see him. He seemed rather at his wits' end to know how to stop the performance, especially since Harrydaunce had simply ignored a Council order to cease his preaching. When challenged by a local baker why he would not stop, the bricklayer replied, 'it is as fit for me to be burned as for thee to bake a loaf', and another passage was remembered in which he seemed to glory in persecution.

The investigators found one man who had heard the preaching, Lawrence Clark, a barber-surgeon. He remembered two occasions, the one already mentioned when about six or eight people were present, and another time when he was playing bowls with Robert Silvester in the garden next to Harrydaunce's. The bricklayer, raising himself above the fence, proceeded to exhort the players, but he had small success with Silvester who told him to stop his preaching or 'he would cast his bowl at his head'. Harrydaunce himself admitted that he had 'declared in his garden the Word of God' on some twenty occasions since midsummer (about six weeks), there being some half dozen of his neighbours present to hear him. On July 20th, he felt moved to do better and opened the casement of his window overlooking the king's highway to address an

---

[1] BM, Cleo. E.v, fo. 398 (*LP* ix. 230). There is no sign of the right date, but the fact that Bale is mentioned as preaching against convention about four years earlier makes the *LP* dating of 1536 improbable. Since Barnes is included, the date cannot be later than early 1540. My guess is 1538 or 1539.

[2] Foxe, iv. 585.   [3] E 36/120, fos. 133–5 (*LP* xiv. II. 42).

unknown number of passers-by. He claimed to have spent no more than half an hour in this way, but somehow Longford's two hours sound more convincing. The bricklayer also agreed that he had put on similar performances 'upon the backside of his garden'. He was clearly a worthy, exalted nuisance, annoying people by his braying but also (it seems) attracting some who thought he had something to say. Perhaps he was one of the sights of Whitechapel. So far as the evidence goes, his preaching ceased after this; since we know that at some unknown date he abjured his opinions, he may at this time have made his peace with authority.[1]

II

This circuit through the realm has picked up examples of resistance, attack, disturbance and disquiet both serious and unimportant; it has shown that there was no region and no year in which the government could take obedience or even reluctant conformity for granted; it has shown something of the vigilance required by, and the labour involved in, a phrase like 'the enforcement of the Reformation'. I must stress again that I have presented a very far from exhaustive tally, and especially that the shires unmentioned (not to speak of outliers like Calais) also provided their quota of denunciations and investigations. If, however, the character of the Crown's problem is to become graphically patent, it will be useful to show how the stream of reports and requests looked from the receiving end – how it affected the person most concerned. I propose to look at three separate months in the life of Thomas Cromwell and string together day by day the information of trouble as it passed across his desk, remembering that by no means everything has left evidence behind. It needs to be stressed that the matters that here interest us were in life mingled with a great many other necessary occupations: foreign policy, defence of the realm, finance, administration, managing the King, private affairs, and especially the laborious details of patronage on the effective use of which Cromwell in great part depended for his power and survival. I shall assume that letters reached him between two and three days after they were written, except that reports from the far north took longer and those from overseas (Ireland and Calais) longer still.

In March 1535, the first consequences of the revolution were begin-

---

[1] Foxe, iv. 586.

ning to make themselves felt. The King's new title had been proclaimed in the new year, the Treason Act had come into force on February 1st, and Cromwell was preparing for the investigation of the Church's property which occupied so much of his time that year. On March 1st, he received information of political trouble in Essex, a guarded promise of loyalty from the archbishop of York, and news of treasonable talk in Buckinghamshire which, Sir Francis Bryan advised, called for a commission of oyer and terminer to try and despatch the traitor. About the 2nd, the recorder of London showed him a letter in which the inmates of a Cistercian house in Essex doubted their abbot's loyalty. Next day he was studying a long and highly confidential document reviewing the march treasons and other offences committed by Lord Dacre's retainers in the west march over against Scotland. On the 6th or 7th, he considered the plea of a suspect felon imprisoned at York who claimed to be only the victim of his own devotion to justice. On the 8th, he learned that his order to put some fear of his displeasure into the abbess of Malling (Kent) had been carried out, and that the interest there of his friend Sir Thomas Wyatt was being pressed home; also he had to consider what to do about the abbot of Merevale (Warw.) who was refusing to pay any attention to his letters. On the 16th he had before him Cranmer's denunciation, with supporting papers, of Dr Benger, and decided to send for the man and interrogate him himself. That day also he wrote into Huntingdonshire to order the investigation of suspect traitors. On the 19th, the prior of Henton Charterhouse acknowledged receipt of a letter which concluded Cromwell's serious attention to that house, a business which a little earlier had involved a personal interview with plain speaking all the way in Somerset. On the 23rd, Cromwell learned of a tiresome delay in the work of the commissioners for the *Valor* in Norfolk. On the 23rd, a really delicate matter arose: Catherine of Aragon decided to keep Maundy Thursday in the old way, despite the King's orders to the contrary the year before, and Cromwell had rapidly to inform Henry who, after consultations, agreed that she could do so provided she kept the observance totally private. On the 18th, Cromwell knew that his order to the Huntingdonshire magistrates had been carried out, but it only meant that he now had information to study in order to decide upon further action in the case. On the 30th he probably received an important letter from Ireland where the usual intermittent warfare and the usual hunting of a Fitzgerald traitor were going on, as well as a four-page account of what had been achieved there in the last six months. On the same day, he had to give attention to a long report on the felonies dealt with at York Assizes and on matters there outstanding – an escaped murderer, a suspected pro-phesier, and treasonable talk among the clergy. And when at the end of the month he collected together the business that he had to discuss with the King, he noted among other things the problem of Anabaptists infiltrating into the country, suspicions entertained of the vicar of Halifax's loyalty, the need to dispose of persons needlessly imprisoned on the word of a known traitor, letters to conservative bishops from whom more fervent abjurations of the pope were required, the King's plans for the Charterhouses of London and Richmond, and the inten-tion to set up a commission to revise the canon law.[1]

September 1536 was a month of spurious peace after the fall of Anne Boleyn and the death of Catherine of Aragon; as it ended, the rising in Lincolnshire broke out. On the 1st, Cromwell faced the unwelcome task of deciding whether the bishop of Lincoln should be allowed to burn a heretic. On the 3rd, the newly appointed abbot of Coggeshall proved his zeal by informing against the abbey's porter for suspicious words. The following day, the abbot of Abingdon (Berks.), who had coerced his tenants to cease troubling one of Cromwell's clients, demonstrated his good will in another way. About this time, Cromwell also confronted the consequences of everybody's failure to judge Regi-nald Pole aright and supervised the drafting of the letter in which Pole's ex-friend Starkey broke off relations with one who was now to be treated as a traitor; this was a very worrying matter because Cromwell had shown favour to Pole's associates and could easily have stumbled into trouble with the King. On the 7th, he learned that the commis-sioners for the lay subsidy had run into tiresome difficulties in Norfolk, information to which he replied on the 9th with unfeeling exhortations to do better; but on the 8th, there was more cheerful news from Corn-wall where seditious suspicions of Cromwell's visitors had vanished and people were glad to know that they owed the relaxation of the new rules against their favourite holy days to Cromwell's intercession with the King. One matter recurred through the rest of the month. On the 7th, he received information, with a deposition, against a Worcester-

[1] *LP* viii. 268, 277–8; 297; 310; 320; 349, 351; 386–7 (cf. below, p. 318); 450; 402; 420; 427, 435; 450; 397, 449; 457; 475.

shire priest who had talked treason; having consulted the King, he replied by return, ordering a more stringent investigation especially of the effect which the priest's talk might have had on others and authorising the use of torture, if necessary. On the 28th, a statement arrived from the accused on whom the torture authorised by the King had indeed been used, but Cromwell was so busy with 'affairs of greater importance' that he could only write on October 8th to ask that the matter be kept on ice till he could attend to it. He never could.[1]

On the 9th, he heard that the King's death was being rumoured in Lincolnshire and read the examinations certified from there. Next on that day he had to deal with Sir Thomas Cheyney's tedious unwillingness to execute his office as warden of the Cinque Ports against certain known pirates without special instructions. On the 11th, the backwash of a dispute between two curates at Warwick, complicated by disputes among the local gentry, landed on his desk: would he authorise bail for the imprisoned party? He also had the abbot of Vale Royal's firm refusal to surrender his house, at least until pressed harder. On the 12th, he once again had to listen to the duke of Norfolk's ruffled feelings, a common experience throughout his years of power, and to extract from the letter the one piece of information that it contained, concerning two seditious persons and their intended punishment. On the same day, he wrote into Oxfordshire, ordering three justices to investigate complaints about a mill which at intervals caused flooding. Next day he learned that there was a parson in Romney Marsh who would not delete the pope's name from his mass books. Kent appeared on his plate again on the 20th, with depositions about treason talked by the vicar of Herne. On the 21st, Norfolk wrote again to explain that the troubles about the subsidy assessment were far from over and to sweeten the pill by producing evidence of his zeal in pursuing disaffected persons (the tale of the organ-maker). On the 23rd, Cromwell's mind switched back to Kent as he read William Petre's report of investigations at Canterbury into matters obscure to us.[2]

On the 24th, there was news that the brethren of Walsingham did not get on together; the prior needed Cromwell's support in exercising the authority of his office. Next day, the lord privy seal was asked to do

[1] *LP* xi. 369; 393; 397; 402; 404, 434; 405; 407, 495; Merriman, ii. 30, 32 f.
[2] *LP* xi. 417; 418; 431; 433; 434; 446; 447; 464; 470 (cf. above, p. 142); 476.

something for an honest tallow-chandler of Southwark, in trouble because he had stood surety for a debtor who had run away to Spain. On the 28th he had an urgent report from Ralph Sadler at Court: the King was angry because his order to remove the London Carthusians from their house had still not been carried out, he was talking of putting off Jane Seymour's coronation on account of the plague, he expected his councillors to come to Court on Michaelmas day, despite the holiday. Right at the end of the month, several troublesome matters came in: the lieutenant of Guernsey reported difficulties in the disposal of foreign friars whom he had been told to remove (though he had succeeded), Lord Dacre wrote to say that the earl of Cumberland would not abide by the award that Cromwell had made between them, Sir Francis Bigod intervened on behalf of some of his servants removed by force from sanctuary at York, and the commissioners for the Dissolution reported on the armed resistance they had encountered at Hexham. A suitable end to the month and a suitable overture to the events of October and November 1536.[1]

In November 1539, a good many troubles (especially the attempt to unseat Cromwell by attacks on his religious policy)[2] lay in the recent past, but the lord privy seal, up to his neck in the arrangements for the Cleves marriage, was still struggling to keep his feet on the slippery rocks of Court politics. On the 1st, he was asked to make sure that two murderers should be punished: it looked as though one of them might escape by using the tricks of the law. On the 3rd, the earl of Derby reported that he had carried out Cromwell's instructions touching two suspects in Lancashire and sent up the men themselves to be examined by the lord privy seal. On the same day, Lord Russell asked for a letter to speed a marriage. About this time, Cromwell's notes of things to be done were full of the plans for new bishoprics and the dying affairs of many monasteries, but there was also the problem of the gypsies, which touched security. It was disquieting to hear that the men of Tynedale were once again showing signs of their ancient disloyalties and trouble-making. Right through the month, at intervals, Cromwell was busy with the attack on the abbot of Colchester. On the 4th, he had a letter from Cranmer, forwarding information on the highly complex troubles at Calais – treason, sacramentarianism and popery – which

[1] *LP* xi. 480; 490; 501; 473, 477, 503, 504.
[2] Cf. my reconstruction in *Cambridge Hist. Journal*, x (1951), 164–9.

recurred steadily down to Cromwell's fall. On the 9th, there was the always disturbing news of an officer who had left Ireland without licence and was now in ward at Chester. Less urgent but rather nagging was the problem of finding a master for Balliol College, Oxford, which bothered Cromwell several times between the 9th and the 18th. Around the 10th, he set out long lists of things to be done in which the welcoming of the Lady Anne jostled with the usual items of patronage business, with the gypsies (still unsettled), the catching of some robbers in London, the treason of Giles Heron (difficult to deal with because there was but one witness) a present of canary birds for the King (would he accept?), various decisions required by foreign policy and the defence of the realm.[1]

On the 12th, Cromwell studied the inconclusive reports of the two bishops and four doctors of law who were investigating serious charges of heresy and treason, centring on Calais but with ramifications even at Court. Next day, he was confronted with evidence that one of his own servants had committed the major crime of unlawful hunting in Essex. On the 15th, there was the happy relief of being able to turn briefly to the more constructive and satisfactory work of providing a good English Bible. But on the 18th it was back to the usual grind, to read Lord Russell's report of all the men executed in Somerset, including the abbot of Glastonbury. On the 19th, a reply arrived to his order to investigate an accusation of heresy made in Devon against a man of the new learning; the man who had uttered the words was on his way to be examined by Cromwell. On the 20th, he received from one of his own servants an appeal on behalf of the mayor of Rye, allegedly a sound man whom the warden of the Cinque Ports and other officers of the King's Household had imprisoned at Dover. Behind the obscurity of this report there may lurk some very serious power struggles at Court. About this time, Cromwell found it again necessary to draw up lengthy memoranda of business, as mixed as before and containing some of the same detail not yet dealt with. On the 20th he wrote to Bishop Longland to take the case of a woman accused before the bishop out of his hands; Longland replied huffily that he saw no reason why he should be made to appear before the whole county as one who would not do justice. And towards the end of the month, Cromwell ordered two persons familiar with Ireland to set down their views of the dangerous

[1] *LP* xiv. II. 407; 417; 319; 427; 431; 446; 471; 477, 498, 543 (ii); 495–6.

split in the Irish Council between the deputy, a Cromwell nominee, and other officers who relied on Cromwell's enemies.[1]

Such was the situation in the realm in the years during which the revolution of the 1530's was to be enforced upon it, and such the position of the man chiefly charged with carrying that policy into effect. Unquestionably, there was a problem, one requiring constant and unending attention and deliberate methods of action. The passing of statutes, the proclaiming of titles, the decision to suppress the monasteries: these striking deeds meant nothing unless they were for ever followed up, in petty matters as well as large, in the repulsive disputes of men who used the great events to discharge their private spleen, in the conflicts of conscience and passion as well as the meannesses of greed and revenge. It all had to be heard, sifted, decided upon. Above all, resistance and disaffection had to be discovered and exterminated. The tasks of enforcement, from clarifying the new truths to dealing with the irreconcilables, not only existed; they were pressing, constant and pervasive.

[1] *LP* xiv. II. 496; 503; 516–17; 530; 540; 546; 548–9; 563; 617–18.

4

PROPAGANDA

IF THE PUZZLED NATION of England was to accept Henry VIII's new order, it would have to be told what truth was now proclaimed and why. That the government, in fact, undertook a full-scale propaganda campaign, using both the printing press and the pulpit in most intensive fashion, has long been recognised, and several historians have given their attention to some of the pamphlets produced. Thus Pierre Janelle, Philip Hughes and J. J. Scarisbrick used the official writings of the day to elucidate the King's purposes;[1] Gordon Zeeveld has much to say on the relevant labours of his Padua–London coterie;[2] and Franklin Baumer has written a whole long essay on the campaign itself which might be supposed to make further discussion superfluous.[3] However – quite apart from the remarkable tendentiousness which especially Janelle imparted to his influential pages – the first four writers were really interested only in the arguments put forward, not in the part played by the propaganda campaign in the government's policy of enforcement, while Baumer has been insufficiently precise: his list shows him unconcerned whether a piece of writing can really be assigned to government initiative at all. For in this last point there lies a necessary distinction. Granted that Henry VIII and Cromwell discovered the use of printing as an instrument for convincing the people of their claims, they neither invented printing nor controlled everything that came to the printer. They soon managed to prevent the publication of positively hostile writings,[4] but that is not the same thing as being responsible for everything written in their favour. In the first instance it is necessary to establish the canon of relevant works.

For this present purpose, Baumer's list is inflated in three different

---

[1] P. Janelle, *L'Angleterre Catholique à la veille du schisme* (1935), chs. 6 and 7; P. Hughes, *The Reformation in England*, vol. 1 (1950), esp. 249–69, 330–41; J. J. Scarisbrick, *Henry VIII* (1968), esp. chs. 8 and 9.
[2] W. G. Zeeveld, *Foundations of Tudor Policy* (1948), esp. chs. 6 and 7. His demonstration that Cromwell guided the campaign is conclusive.
[3] F. Le Van Baumer, *The Early Tudor Theory of Kingship* (1940), 211–24.
[4] Below, p. 256.

ways. He includes writings sponsored by the Crown which concerned the prospective General Council of the Church. This was indeed propaganda material (and deliberately devised), but it does not belong to a study of the domestic enforcement of the revolution.[1] Secondly, Baumer notes the survival of a good many tracts and treatises which were never printed. It is, indeed, true that any student of opinion or doctrine, or even of the government's religious policy, would be well advised to read these manuscripts, but to say that 'without a glance at these, the extent and nature of the king's propagandist campaign cannot be fully understood' is misleading.[2] The campaign consisted of *publishing* books and pamphlets, not just of writing them; unless a manuscript bears directly on published work or clearly formed an early stage of intended publication, it cannot be used to describe the government's organisation of their appeal to the world to believe in the justice of their proceedings. And lastly, Baumer introduced a serious confusion when he claimed that 'a propagandist campaign...means a literary offensive sponsored by the government *in alliance with all the sympathetic people of the nation*'.[3] Yet surely people must be allowed to have even strong views on the great issues of the day without running the danger of being called propagandists. If one is concerned to understand the government's campaign – the degree to which they planned and managed persuasion from above – one cannot include in the material considered these happy windfalls which resulted from the eager support for the new order available in some quarters. Cromwell and his men were not the only people anxious to put their thoughts on paper. Cromwell's zest in this matter was sufficiently known for people who wished to curry favour to offer up exercises of their own, as the prior of Kingswood did who had written a little book on the supremacy (dedicated to the minister), or John Plackett, a monk of Winchcombe, who announced that he would shortly forward an attack on the pope's claims.[4] Cromwell's papers contain a good many pieces so received,

---

[1] For Henry VIII and the General Council cf. the valuable papers by P. A. Sawada who employs these propagandist publications: 'The abortive Council of Mantua and Henry VIII's *Sententia de Concilio* 1537,' *Academia* (Nanzen University, Japan), vol. 27 (1960); 'Two anonymous Tudor treatises on the General Council,' *J. of Eccl. History*, xii (1961), 197–214; 'Heinrich VIII. und die erste Phase seiner Konzilspolitik,' *Reformata Reformanda: Festgabe für Hubert Jedin* (1965), 476–507.

[2] Baumer, *Kingship*, 218. [3] Ibid. 215 (Baumer's italics).

[4] *LP* viii. 79, 321.

and further independent initiatives made their appearance between boards. The government's campaign cannot be argued from such things: what matters is the material put out on its initiative, however it was produced in the first instance.

In fact, I think it wise to include only two kinds of printed works: those specifically known to come from government-employed pens, and those published by the King's printer, Thomas Berthelet.[1] Most relevant productions qualify under both tests. But both tests exclude Baumer's favourite author, Christopher St German. St German, who had turned seventy before the clergy recognised King Henry as their supreme head, had long cherished and expressed doubts about the claims of the spirituality; he had tangled with Sir Thomas More; and, as the revolution progressed, this vigorous, septuagenarian lawyer, coming more and more into the open in defence of the royal supremacy, was certainly to be a most useful ally for the King's propagandists. But there is no sign at all that he and his writings were sponsored by Henry or Cromwell, or that he was in any way connected with the government.[2] On one occasion, in fact, Cromwell's men tried to get his help in the settlement of certain legal questions which Cromwell had asked them to debate, but St German excused himself several times and never appeared.[3] Nor does his being listed by the northern rebels among the heretics they hated make him a government man (as has sometimes been supposed), unless Luther and Hus and Melanchthon deserve the same classification.[4] The fact that he offered an opinion on the Bishops' Book only over two months after it was published positively discourages any supposition that he was closely connected with the makers of policy.[5]

[1] Berthelet formally succeeded to Richard Pynson's patent on 15 February 1530, and the bulk of his work thereafter was 'official', i.e. supplied by the government (E. Duff, A Century of the English Book Trade, 1948, 11).

[2] Baumer (Kingship, 215, n. 8) relies on Janelle's statement to the contrary. Janelle (L'Angleterre, 150) admits that he could find no proof of St German being retained in service, but argues that the coincidence between his treatise on the Spiritualty and Temporalty and the Commons' Supplication of 1532 proves him to have been in paid employment. This rash assertion, which relies on similarities liable to occur in any two sets of complaints against the clergy, is further undermined by the fact that the Supplication was being drafted two years before St German's book appeared and was not official in origin (G. R. Elton, 'The Commons' Supplication of 1532,' Eng. Hist. Rev. lxvi [1951], 507–34). It is thus not impossible that St German picked up the lines of his argument from the Supplication, but Janelle's point falls down in any case.

[3] LP vii. 1008.   [4] LP xi. 1246.

[5] LP xii. II. 1151; for the date of publication see ibid. 703, 818.

Unlike Cromwell's known writers, St German virtually never appears in his correspondence.[1] His books were published not by Berthelet but by Thomas Godfray, a somewhat mysterious figure who has mistakenly been identified with Berthelet's office; there is no justification for this confusion, and Godfray was not used by Cromwell and the government.[2] It must be concluded that St German worked independently. No doubt, King and minister were pleased to have this prolific author defend the King's new title and the subjection of the Church, especially as he produced arguments clothing the innovations with the antiquity and authority of the common law, but his books do not belong in a discussion of official propaganda.

The reduced list is still sizable, but not now so large that the supposition of planning and control becomes hard to credit. By the nature of the propaganda problem to which they address themselves, the writings fall into three categories. First of all, there are the pieces which defend the revolution currently and proleptically, step by step as it went forward. Secondly, a group of works concentrates on defending the completed achievement; this group includes also the production of men who hoped by defence of the new order to avoid becoming its victims. The third body of pamphlets was called forth by resistance: these are concerned to preach obedience and to denounce rebellion.

The whole campaign started very quietly, but more especially it started rather late. The first issue arising on which the world needed to have its views formed was, of course, the King's Great Matter, his divorce from Queen Catherine. Since for some five years, however, this business was supposed to be secret, there could be no question of writing pamphlets about it, at least not until January 1531 when the prevalence of largely accurate rumours persuaded Henry to publicise the situation in both Houses of Parliament, by means of his reluctant lord chancellor, Sir Thomas More.[3] Once the nation was officially seised of the issue, it had quickly to be persuaded to see it in the right light, but the government's first effort shows little skill and less success. Some time in the summer of 1531 it was decided to explain the royal

---

[1] If the Christopher St German who in 1539 briefly corresponded with Cromwell on a private lawsuit (*LP* xiv. I. 1349) is the same man, the lawyer and the minister were at least distantly acquainted; but the identity is not certain (*the* St German, close to death, was a bit old for private practice), and the tone and substance of the letter tell against rather than for a closer connection between the two men.

[2] Duff, *Century of Book Trade*, 56.   [3] Hall, 775 ff.

point of view on the two crucial and technical questions – the validity of a marriage to a brother's widow, and the pope's power to dispense from the law of Scripture – in a laborious pamphlet of 154 folios which at length rehearsed the scriptural, patristic, early conciliar and medieval authorities on the King's side. Prefaced to the book were the favourable opinions of eight foreign Universities, collected in the course of 1530; these, rather misleadingly, provided the book's title.[1] Even attempts to brighten the discourse by dwelling at length on the filthiness of carnal copulation condemned by the Mosaic law cannot disguise the tedium of this production which is likely to have been the work of theologians and canon lawyers on the King's Council. It was first put out in Latin but quickly translated into English. The most remarkable thing about it is the fact that it never once mentions King or Queen or the particular marriage in dispute. A stranger coming upon it would have to regard it as a peculiar academic exercise. However, no one was by this time likely to be deceived by such reticent delicacy which reflects rather an enduring unwillingness to have the Great Matter bandied about in alehouses, a reluctance which in turn reflects on the sense of realism prevalent at this point in Henry's circle. Least deceived were his opponents: the *Determination* has the distinction of being the only one of Henry's propaganda tracts to elicit an answer of which a complete copy still survives. Catherine's chaplain, Thomas Abell, succeeded in getting his reply, to which he gave the resounding title *Invicta Veritas*, published abroad;[2] in it he removed the decent obscurity preferred by Henry's writers and used an equal array of very fusty learning to support the Queen's case rather than argue a nameless issue.

Before the debate could be smothered under the weight of such dead learning, something happened in government circles – perhaps the arrival of Thomas Cromwell, perhaps a more general recognition of what needed doing. At any rate, the next publication to appear was a

[1] *The Determination of the most famous and excellent Universities of Italy and France, that it is unlawful for a man to marry his brother's wife and that the pope hath no power to dispense therewith*. Printed Berthelet, 7 Nov. [1531]. *STC* 14286–7; BM, 228. c. 38 (1).
[2] Printed Lüneburg, May 1532. *STC* 61; BM, G. 12. 36. Abell was soon imprisoned, though he survived in the Tower till after Cromwell's fall. His book was certainly not the only one to appear in support of Catherine of Aragon, but it seems to be the only to have escaped the government's destructive vigilance. Even so, the BM copy is unique, unless more is to be found in continental libraries. The *Determination* survives in some ten or so copies, an unusually large number for this type of thing.

very different thing and a vastly more effective instrument of propaganda. This was *The Glass of Truth*, justly famous in its own day and rendered more enduringly famous nowadays by being reprinted in the last century.[1] Despite some debate, there is no doubt about its date: it was written in 1532, as the mention of the 23rd year of King Henry shows,[2] probably before Archbishop Warham died in August that year because in one place there is a reference to both metropolitans which would read oddly if written while Canterbury was vacant.[3] Besides, by early September Berthelet had it in hand, at a stage when improvements in proof were still thought possible, but by the 23rd of that month copies were being given out at Oxford.[4] Another of Catherine's chaplains, William Peto, tried his hand at a reply of which part was also printed at Lüneburg,[5] but no one seems to have managed to refute it comprehensively.

The Glass of Truth acknowledged no author, but there are some firm hints that the King had a personal hand in it. Richard Croke, distributing it around Oxford, could not persuade people that his majesty, though no doubt skilful and learned enough, could possibly have had the time for such a task, but he himself in correspondence with Cromwell (who must have known) clearly thought so.[6] Nicholas Hawkins at Mantua, engaged upon possible translations, called the book 'your highness' Dialogue'.[7] The inclusion of intimate family details about Catherine's first marriage has sometimes been supposed to suggest the likely author; it is, at least, manifest that they could not have been put in without Henry's knowledge and approval. Yet it is also pretty clear that Henry was not the only author of the book, or at least had a good deal of expert advice. He was apparently a difficult co-author, for when Thomas Goodrich, a learned divine soon to gain the see of Ely, drew the printer's attention to some matter that needed amendment and asked him to tell the King, Berthelet demurred: 'he had moved the

[1] Printed Berthelet, [1532]. *STC* 11918–19; BM 228. c. 38 (2). The *STC* dating is wrong, being taken from the correct date written on the last page of the book now bound ahead of the *Glass*. Also, in spite of *STC*, there was only one printing of which four copies survive. The *Glass of Truth* is reprinted in Pocock, ii. 385–421, and that version is cited here.

[2] Pocock, ii. 401. *LP* v. 547 (1531) is in error; so is Janelle (*L'Angleterre*, 238) who for no stated reason opts for early 1533; all his comment on this book is sadly out of true.

[3] Pocock, ii. 418.   [4] Ellis, iii. II. 196, 198.

[5] *LP* vi. 901.   [6] Ellis, iii. II. 198.

[7] *StP* vii. 389, 404.

King in such matters aforetime and perceived that his grace was not content therewith.' Cromwell was therefore advised 'to get out by policy the things that Mr Goodrich noteth', an appeal which shows who supervised the production.[1] Clearly there was some team-work involved, but the King – an established author, after all – would seem to have been willing in private to claim the book for himself.[2]

The *Glass of Truth* is a successful piece of propaganda – readable, clear, lively, short enough but seemingly full of meat. Its whole argument is directed very much by the theological and canonistic exposition one finds in the *Determination*, but where that was heavy and dull, though learned, the *Glass* provides a surface-skimming and popularised version of the official views on the Levitical law and the limitations of the pope's dispensing power. Newly added is the lengthy story of Prince Arthur's boasts about his wedding night which, intended to prove that the first marriage had been consummated, was originally obtained from witnesses for the legatine trial in 1529, and which now proved useful in cheering up a dry discourse. The dialogue form – between a theologian and a canon lawyer – makes possible both the

---

[1] Ellis, iii. II. 196–7. We cannot tell whether Cromwell succeeded in putting the text straight without offending the King.

[2] A claim tacitly rejected by his latest biographer, J. J. Scarisbrick, who has nothing on the point. Some fascinating problems are posed by the BM copy of the *Glass of Truth*, bound up with the *Determination*. The present binding is of the period 1840–60, but there are signs that the two books may have been so joined in the seventeenth century (I owe this information to Mr Howard Nixon, of the Department of Printed Books). The double volume is part of the royal library, presented by George III. The copy of the *Determination* bears marginal notes in a Henrician hand – notes of the kind a man might make who was collecting material for another production. They were certainly made in about 1531–2, as the one personal remark among them shows. On fos. 32v–33, across the foot of the open pages, the annotator, commenting on Gregory I, has scribbled: 'That good pope disdained not to answer St Augustine to all his questions, but the pope now will rather keep in his courts seven years matters asked of him than do as holy Gregory did without such foolish lawing.' His hand bears a strong resemblance to Henry VIII's, but some letters are formed so differently that I cannot propose the identification, though the King may have had a 'scribbling hand' for such purposes, his normal writing being manifestly slow. I have not been able to find this hand elsewhere. If the notes were the King's they would support the notion that he collaborated in the *Glass*; the fact that they cease on fo. 37 (out of 154) answers to Henry's habits – curiosity rather than stamina ever marked his intellectual exercises. The remnant of Henry VIII's library came to the BM as part of the old royal library, the gift of George II; George III's donation is not supposed to contain any volumes that had belonged to Henry VIII's collection. However, the 1542 catalogue of the King's library lists the *Determination* (E 315/160, fo. 109v.).

breaking up of the argument into manageable chunks and a very useful pretence at debate, as though all opinions were given their chance before the conversation ends with a solemn approval of the King's case. The book is further made more attractive reading for its intended audience by having the theological and canonist arguments placed against a background of patriotic fervour and king-worshipping loyalty. The stress on the need for a male heir to save the realm from disaster, on the duty of obeying the King and of refusing to listen to the lying rumours which evil-wishers spread about him, especially the clangingly chauvinistic conclusion – all these show to whom the work is addressed. It was written to be read in England and to defend to Englishmen both the King's desire for a divorce and his refusal to submit to papal jurisdiction, and it does this work extremely well.

The book is as notable for what it does not say. There is not one word against the pope's headship of the Church, nor a single word of rudeness against one who is invariably referred to by his traditional title. All that is stated, again and again, is that the pope has no power to dispense from the law of Scripture and moreover no right to insist on provoking a case to Rome when, by the law of the Church, it should be heard in England. This was the line taken ever since Wolsey's failure in 1529 to hold his fellow-cardinal to a settlement in England. The tone of the book has nothing drastic or ominous in it, and to all outward appearance the *Glass* marks no change in English policy.[1] However, there is one important qualification to this. The treatise does not confine itself to re-asserting the justice of the King's position; it also, very briefly, offers a solution for resolving the deadlock. Parliament, we are told, if it would exert its 'wits and good will', would soon find a way, and that way in effect should be an instruction to the 'metropolitans of this realm (their unjust oath made to the pope notwithstanding)' to bring the affair to a satisfactory conclusion.[2] Not that this sort of talk was new, but it must be remembered that on previous occasions talk of Parliament had always ended in inaction as it was decided that there

[1] Janelle (*L'Angleterre*, 238–9) makes the *Glass* mark a transition to a purely anti-papal position by seeing too many things in the book which only later events enable one to cast backward into it. Thus even the argument against divines who hold other views (Pocock, ii. 397–8), which to Janelle is simply against the pope and heretical, in fact carefully avoids attacking the pope's authority and speaks out only against the perverse obstinacy of some clergy.

[2] Pocock, ii. 418–19.

was nothing that Parliament could do to help. By contrast, some three months at the latest after the *Glass* was published, Cromwell was at work on the Act of Appeals by means of which Cranmer in May 1533 could issue a final sentence ending the marriage. A draft bill specifically empowering the archbishops to proceed fits the words of the *Glass* better than the Act of Appeals which in the winter of 1532 took its place (because it was decided to turn the settlement of the specific issue into the opening shot of the new revolutionary course of action), but either way Parliament would at last have shown itself able to intervene.

It is surely not extravagant, therefore, to see these future events forecast in the one positive proposal for action contained in the *Glass*. And from this it follows that the book was in measure intended to serve two purposes: to defend the justice of the King's demands, and to prepare the ground for the new and stronger line already decided upon. The passage in the *Glass* makes real sense only in the light of what immediately followed and on the supposition that its authors knew what was coming forward next. Ever since Thomas More had resigned the great seal in May 1532, the radical policy espoused by Thomas Cromwell had dominated the Council; evidently, by the time that the *Glass* was being written, the decision to ignore Rome had already been taken, though possibly the decision that the moment for the declaration of a major break had come was still to be hammered out. But that the pope would not be allowed to stand any longer in the way of the Divorce is what those few words in the *Glass* discreetly indicate – as indeed does the very fact of the book's publication. Thus the events of early 1533 were preparing by the third quarter of 1532, and the view frequently expressed that things either happened much more unexpectedly and without long preparation, or had long since been intended by the King, seems inadequate. There was a new policy, and it triumphed in May–July 1532.[1]

---

[1] For these events, and the argument about them, cf. G. R. Elton, 'The Evolution of a Reformation Statute,' *Eng. Hist. Rev.* lxiv (1949), 174–97, and 'King or Minister? The Man behind the Henrician Reformation,' *History* xxix (1954), 216–32; Scarisbrick, *Henry VIII*, chs. 9 and 10 (and my review in *Hist. Journal*, xii [1969], 158–63). The hints in the *Glass* seem strongly to favour the view that the Act of Appeals was not suddenly produced because of Anne Boleyn's pregnancy (which could not have been known before early January 1533), but that on the contrary the second marriage, with all its consequences of Anne, was in effect made possible by policy decisions taken not later than the late summer of 1532. Scarisbrick, 309–13, makes all the events of 1533 flow from that pregnancy; it looks as though they were more planned than that.

One effect, however, of the speed of events in 1533 was to render the *Glass of Truth* rapidly out of date; a new official statement of justification and purpose was required within the year. When it came, it proved to be a very different piece of writing. Late in 1533,[1] Berthelet printed a short pamphlet of nine *Articles devised by the whole consent of the King's most honourable Council*, intended – as the title-page obligingly states – 'not only to exhort but also to inform his loving subjects of the truth'.[2] The pamphlet may well have been linked with the important Council meeting of 2 December 1533 at which the government agreed on a variety of devices for spreading the new truths,[3] and it was the only piece of propaganda in the whole decade that firmly proclaimed its official origin. The origin determined its tone. In the preface, the Council somewhat condescendingly explained 'to the residue of his loving subjects' their duty to preach the virtues of true obedience; the people are taught to resent all injuries, including verbal ones, to the King, and to earn God's favour by their loyalty. The articles themselves are quite brief assertions of fact, with very little attempt to expound or persuade. No man can dispense from the law of God, and the Divorce is therefore lawful and necessary; General Councils have laid it down that problems of the law should be settled in the locality in which they arise; the pope has contravened the law by refusing to admit the King's *excusator*; General Councils are superior to all bishops; by the law of nature, an appeal would lie from Rome to a General Council, but the pope has refused this; such an appeal having been made by the King, the pope was not entitled to proceed further, and his excommunication of Henry is therefore not lawful; popes have in any case abused the sentence of excommunication; Cranmer's action was not only correct but, as the state of the realm proves, pleasing to God; the present pope deserves no respect. All this is stated rather than argued.

The *Articles* are marked by a special regard for Parliament whose consent is used to give weight and authority to the government's actions, and by a notable disregard for the pope, very different from the attitude expressed in the *Glass of Truth*. Not only do they violently attack Clement VII in particular – 'a man neither in life nor learning

---

[1] The pamphlet is dated to the year, and the mention of the Princess Elizabeth places it after mid-September at the earliest.

[2] *STC* 9177; reprinted Pocock, ii. 523–31.

[3] *LP* vi. 1486–7.

Christ's disciple, a man also, though the see apostolic were of never so high authority, contrarious, unlawful also by their own decree to occupy and enjoy his usurped place';[1] for the first time also the title of pope is rejected and replaced by that of bishop of Rome. The few citations are all from the Bible, but there is really no attempt at all to base assertion upon learned authority. The sole approach to anything resembling an argument occurs in Article 8 which adduces God's approval as shown in the early issue of the second marriage, the fine weather 'with great plenty of corn and cattle', the peace moves on the European scene, and the absence of epidemic disease. Fears of divine retribution expressed in failed harvests and bubonic plague were prominent among the arguments put forward by the other side, especially after Clement VII's excommunication of the King had revived tales of King John and the disastrous effects of that interdict; and the framers of the *Articles* thus show themselves well aware of what people were hearing. In general, however, the Council preferred a highly didactic, even authoritarian, note. The *Articles* were intended to lay down what people should believe and to do so in straightforward terms; the absence of argument, of learned authorities, of theological debate produces a pervasive air of absolute conviction and calm assurance, a firm basis from which to attack the problem of dissent.

The basis naturally reflects the state of affairs in late 1533, with the Divorce and re-marriage achieved and papal censure by-passed by means of an appeal to a General Council. The *Articles* were in the main designed to counteract general doubts about those proceedings and the fears current in the wake of the papal excommunication. But, like the *Glass*, this pamphlet, too, hints at further matters. The mention of Parliament and the obedience obviously due to its statutes becomes even more significant when it is remembered that though the Acts of Appeals had passed (and authorised the settling of the Great Matter) no other statute of significance had yet attacked the foundations of the old order. That was to be the work of the following year. In the *Articles* there remains no trace of any willingness to seek accommodation with Rome, and anyone willing to read – not even really between the lines – could see that the attack on the pope would go further. Though there is no word of the royal supremacy and no explicit dismissal of papal authority (subject only to the authority of a General Council), the tone and tenor

[1] Clement VII's birth was illegitimate.

of the *Articles* make sense only on the assumption that the moves of
1534 – the First Succession Act, the Act of Supremacy and all the rest –
were already firmly on the government's programme. Again we see a
piece of defence and justification used to prepare the ground for the
next step.

The next step was the royal supremacy in the Church, and that
certainly needed defending. So far as published propaganda went, the
work was done by two eminent men among the King's clergy: his
almoner, Edward Foxe, and the dean of his Chapel, Richard Sampson.
Both men got bishoprics for their services, Foxe succeeding to Hereford
in 1535 and Sampson to Chichester the year after. Interestingly enough,
they represented rather different persuasions. Foxe was a reformer and
Cromwellian much used in the negotiations with the German Lutherans,
Sampson a conservative Henrician whose arrest by Cromwell in April
1540 precipitated the final crisis in the minister's life. But in 1534 they
were at least able to agree on Henry's claim to supremacy, and before
the year was out Berthelet had printed pamphlets from both their pens.
Foxe's *De Vera Differentia regiae potestatis et ecclesiasticae...opus eximium*
offered little more than a sizable collection of passages from the usual
sources – Scripture, the Fathers, and the writings of suitable medieval
controversialists – intended to demonstrate that the rule of the Church
belongs to kings; it was so useful as an armoury of arguments that it was
reprinted in 1538, the only one of all these pamphlets to enjoy that
fortune.[1] Sampson called his little piece an oration or sermon, and it
may indeed originally have been delivered from the pulpit; it is certain
shorter than some of the sermons that were later printed and reads
rather homiletic.[2] Taking as his text *John* xiii. 34 ('A new commandment I give unto you: that ye love one another; as I have loved you,
that ye also love one another'), Sampson went on to found the love of
God upon obedience to princes. The people must reject the pope's
usurped authority because the King has so ordered; in this instance the
King was (of course) right, but he would in any case be entitled to
exact obedience. Both Foxe and Sampson wrote in Latin, addressing
especially the clergy in the realm. Their pamphlets evince none of that
sense of popular involvement which distinguishes the English tracts;

[1] *STC* 11218–19; CUL, C*. 5. 41 (D) and Syn. 8. 53. 30.
[2] Sampson's *Oratio* (*STC* 21681) is reprinted in Strype, *Eccl. Memorials*, vol. 1, Doc. 42;
it is discussed sufficiently in Hughes, *Reformation*, i. 336–7.

characteristically the work of scholars, they are but moderately competent as works of propaganda and not surprisingly were replaced as the learned defence of the supremacy by Gardiner's *De Vera Obedientia*, to be considered in a moment. Nevertheless, here were useful arguments for the learned to persuade themselves into the new ways, and useful points for preachers to memorise.

At much the same time, the unlearned were also once again taken in hand. Some time in the course of the year, Cromwell produced a memorandum drawing attention to the need to combat opposition to the second marriage: 'though they forbear to speak at large, for fear of punishment, yet they mutter together secretly.'[1] He especially had disaffected priests in mind, regretted the special obloquy which had fallen on Cranmer – since everybody, of course, thought Henry 'the gentlest prince and of the most gentlest nature and the most upright that ever reigned among men' – and offered explicit advice on how the clergy ('most dear brethren in Christ') were to be addressed for their own good, but the little book that resulted from the memorandum, though directed specifically against popish priests, spoke to a wider audience. This was *A Little Treatise against the muttering of some papists in corners*, another lively English pamphlet designed to gain recruits for the revolution.[2] The booklet has not much new to say – thus it repeats the usual arguments against the Petrine claim and the point from the *Articles* concerning appeals to General Councils – but it notably reflects the government's awareness of what was being said around the country. The muttering it sets itself to discredit consisted particularly of the doubts raised by innovation after so many centuries of unquestioning obedience to Rome, the alleged slander that the King had turned against the pope only because he could not otherwise rid himself of wife no. 1, hankerings after the good old days, and apprehensions of God's displeasure expressed in rainy seasons and rotting crops. All these things, as depositions testify, were indeed being muttered among the people. The *Little Treatise* copes very well with its task. It uses

---

[1] Printed in Pocock, ii. 487–9, and there dated 1533. I regard mid-1534 as a more likely date because (*a*) speaking against the Boleyn marriage carried no specific punishment until after the First Act of Succession, and (*b*) tbe paper is endorsed as 'reasons to clear the clergy for condescending to the King's second marriage and for abolishing the pope's supremacy', a phrasing also more probable after that act. The paper is in the hand of one of Cromwell's clerks (*LP* vii. 738).

[2] Printed Berthelet, 1534. *STC* 19177; BM, C. 95. a. 18. Reprinted in Pocock, ii. 539–52.

reason where reason will do, as when it maintains that custom, however ancient, must give way to the truth (that is, the truth about the usurpations of Rome, though it is alleged that in any case Rome had never had more authority than kings were willing to admit into their realms). It employs flattery of its readers and abuse of the opponent without overdoing the abuse. Thus the pope gets his ancient title, rather belatedly for English conditions, as well as many hard words. It employs the usual authorities including the by now rather shop-worn opinions of the Universities, without boring the reader with tedious learning. Those who blame worldly troubles on the attack on Rome are told that their argument is as sensible as that which says 'since Tenterden steeple was builded, Sandwich haven hath ever more decayed'.

They say it was merry before such matters were moved, but they tell not what time it was, with whom, nor wherein it was merry. And if they mean that the nobility and the commons of England had more riches and greater plenty of food and victual, and lived in much more wealth and more at their heart's ease in lawful liberty; then let them consider that this was before the pope and his clergy were grown so great, so strong and mighty, and to so huge possessions and riches as they wield at this day. For before that time they preached the gospel truly; they were meek and lowly spirited, and sufficiency was to them abundance: they were charitable, they were mild and merciful and gave good example, and men gladly followed them; then reigned love and liberality, then there was peace and unity that caused great plenty in every place. But after they were once endowed with possessions and their minds inordinately drowned in them, and that covetousness began to creep in among them, after that (I say) followed all mischief and misery, all wretchedness and penury.[1]

A very neat turning round of those sighs for the old days which are for ever loud in times of change. The *Little Treatise* introduces a new note into these somewhat solemn labours, a note of light scurrility, rapid ease and stylistic elegance. In these respects it improves distinctly on the *Glass of Truth* which in substance certainly carried the heavier metal. No author offers his name, but whoever he was he knew how to write so as to be read. And that, after all, is the first condition of successful propaganda.

The machine churning out defence and persuasion was by this time

[1] Pocock, ii. 549.

running quite smoothly. Not everything got as far as print, but some of the things suggested show how the printed works were prepared. We have seen that the *Little Treatise* was inspired by a Cromwellian memorandum. Another, more detailed, proposal outlined fourteen points to be covered in a treatise which would comprehensively attack the papal claim to supremacy; it goes over some old ground such as the early Councils and the powers of General Councils nowadays, but also wants to remind the Church that the pope augmented his power at the expense of other bishops and to argue that in view of the Annates Act (early 1534), which had affirmed the realm's continued orthodoxy, the later Act of Supremacy could not be regarded as a declaration of schism, a tortured and not very convincing argument.[1] The more interesting ideas come at the end. One forecasts a future policy when it deplores the special obedience to Rome sworn by monks taking their vows; the other insists that Englishmen 'are bounden in conscience to obey the Parliament' since its acts do not contravene the law of God, the issue over which More was to die. The problem of the supremacy exercised another writer who feared that two scriptural texts (*John* xx. 21 and *Acts* xx. 28) could be used to prove the superiority of bishops over princes and wanted an authoritative pamphlet from some leading clergy to expound the texts in a more convenient manner. This he hoped to see done 'before the breaking up of the Parliament' – possibly the last session of the Reformation Parliament in February–April 1536.[2] These ideas came to nothing, as did also Richard Morison's proposals for more intensive anti-papal propaganda techniques which he inserted into his treatise on the law, written in about 1535/1536.[3] Morison regretted the popularity of plays of Robin Hood which not only led to 'lewdness and ribaldry' but taught people disobedience: 'these good bloods go about for to take from the sheriff of Nottingham one that for offending the laws should have suffered execution'. He wanted to see them replaced by plays demonstrating the pope's wickedness with his 'monks, friars, nuns and such like' and teaching obedience to the King. 'Into the common people things sooner enter by the eyes than by the ears.'[4] No doubt he was right, but one may feel some relief at the

[1] SP 6/6, fos. 87–90 (*LP* viii. 295); evidently produced soon after the session which ended on 18 December 1534.

[2] SP 1/105, fo. 56 (*LP* xi. 83).

[3] For the date cf. my remarks in *Proceedings of the British Academy*, liv (1968), 178.

[4] BM, Royal MS 18. A. 1.

thought that the prehistory of the Elizabethan stage was not littered with pope-hunting plays commissioned by Thomas Cromwell.[1]

In fact, Cromwell continued to put his faith – and his money – in printing and in some writings hardly suitable for the common people. William Marshall, one of his circle, advocated the publication of translations useful to the new order and himself produced the only two undertaken – an edition of Valla's *Donation of Constantine* in 1534 and what was actually the first printed edition of Marsiglio of Padua's *Defensor Pacis* in 1535.[2] These were, indeed, the outstanding anti-papal tracts of relatively recent times; to have them in English print gave the campaign a solid, respectable, scholarly, European backing. Nevertheless, in the main the government continued to look to contemporaries for support, and especially to men whose known standpoint made them far from obvious propagandists in the King's behalf. It looks rather as though special steps were taken to involve such people in public statements of adherence which could then be effectively used to demonstrate the unity of the realm and to silence the voices claiming that only heretics and schismatics would agree with what had been done. The group of writings produced to consolidate the revolution came mainly from that source, though both of Cromwell's leading pamphleteers, Thomas Starkey and Richard Morison, also brought out comprehensive treatises upon which the regime could take its stand.

The best known of the conservative pamphlets – thanks to its modern edition the best known of all Henrician writings – is Stephen Gardiner's

[1] Jesse W. Harris, *John Bale* (1940), 103, bases the view that Bale was 'the official playwright of the Cromwellian period of the English Reformation' and that his plays formed part of Cromwell's propaganda campaign on somewhat slender grounds. Still, Bale, who certainly had Cromwell's favour, came nearest to fulfilling this demand of Morison's.

[2] Marshall undertook Valla entirely on his own; it was printed by Godfray. Marsiglio was approved by Cromwell before publication (Cromwell advanced the money needed to produce it) and printed by Richard Wyer. In all this, however, Marshall took the initiative: he was not officially employed as a translator, a fact which underlines the value of Berthelet's imprint to prove official action (and payment). For Cromwell's involvement see Marshall's letters, SP 1/83, fos. 57, 58 (*LP* vii. 422–3: arranged in the wrong order). They were written at perhaps a few weeks' interval before 1 April 1534 (*tenebrae* Wednesday – the day by which Marshall wanted his money). From them it emerges that the translation of Marsiglio had been ready for a year but kept from the press by lack of money, and that Cromwell's hitherto neglected promise to lend £20 towards the costs also lay some time in the past. He had clearly been long aware of the plan to publish Marsiglio.

De Vera Obedientia.[1] It was not the only piece of propaganda he wrote at this time, but his tract attacking Fisher was never put in print, though manuscript copies were allegedly shown round the French Court.[2] The *Oration of True Obedience*, on the other hand, was reprinted several times, but not by the government. Berthelet was responsible for the first printing in 1535;[3] early in the following year, the pastors of Strassburg were so delighted with the book's anti-papal arguments that they arranged for another printing locally, with a new preface (probably by Bucer) praising England's bishops and saying nasty things about their own pseudo-bishops;[4] and also in January 1536 the book seems to have been sent for reprinting by the Council of the Schmalkaldic League in Hamburg, though of that edition no copy survives.[5] Gardiner, on embassy in France, received twelve copies for distribution there as early as November 1535, though Cromwell rather tactlessly also included a dozen of Sampson's *Oratio* in the package.[6] The bishop of Winchester had laboured quite long over the work and could be pleased with the reception, which up to a point was deserved. Not that there is anything very original in it, but it remains the most careful and most powerful exposition of the 'high' view of the King's supremacy. The argument – for obedience to divinely appointed princes – has been so often analysed that it would be absurd to go over it once more.[7] The tone is learned, severe, occasionally savage, and unambiguously anti-papal. As propaganda it scores by its weight of argument and the high seriousness of its thought, but also perhaps by the piece of autobiography with which it starts: Gardiner renders what follows a good deal more persuasive by his frank admission that he, who had not always known this truth, had now seen the light. Never translated until Gardiner's enemies dug it out against him in 1553, it was addressed, once again, to the learned, but more than any other work of the period it was designed to persuade readers outside England. Henry hoped to convert the king

---

[1] The only edition now to be used is P. Janelle, *Obedience in Church and State* (1930), 67–171. My remarks here are much indebted to Janelle's introduction.

[2] 'Si sedes illa': ibid. 21–65.

[3] STC 11584; BM, T. 811 (2).

[4] CUL, I*. 6. 47 (F). The flyleaf of this copy bears the signature 'Thomas Cantuarensis' in a contemporary hand, but it is not Cranmer's usual signature.

[5] *LP* x. 303.   [6] Merriman, i. 434.

[7] Hughes, *Reformation*, i. 337–41; J. A. Muller, *Stephen Gardiner and the Tudor Reaction* (1926), 61–5.

of France with its aid. Its chief success, however, did not lie there but in the restoration to favour which it brought to its author.

Other conservatives were given the chance of putting the words of convenient sermons in print, probably at Crown expense. The series started off with the sermon which Simon Matthew preached at St Paul's on 27 June 1535 and Berthelet published on July 30th following.[1] Although this undistinguished piece of writing contains some acceptable stuff about the irrelevance of popes and the obedience due to kings, what secured its publication was no doubt the following passage:

Of late ye have had experience of some whom neither friends nor kinsfolk, neither the judgment of both Universities...nor the universal consent of all the clergy of this realm, nor the laws of Parliament, nor their most natural and loving prince, could by any gentle ways revoke from their disobedience, but would needs persist, giving pernicious occasion to the multitude to murmur and grudge at the King's laws: seeing that they were men of estimation and would be seen wiser than all the realm and of better conscience than other.

He went on to mention Fisher and More by name, to share the widely felt regret at their fate, but to affirm that they were traitors and that their treasons had cancelled all their excellent qualities.

Such a public statement was assuredly welcome, for the execution of More and Fisher had really shocked opinion not only abroad but also at home. Cromwell had at once seen the need to dress the story suitably. He had instructed Sir John Wallop, in France, to expound the treasons committed and to express the King's displeasure at the readiness with which the French Court had believed lying tales about the event; to Sir Gregory Casalis at Rome he wrote a long Latin letter for public consumption which rehearsed the allegedly treasonable opposition offered by Fisher and More through five long years.[2] But propaganda against their memory had to continue, nor was it to be very effective even in the short run, as several reports from the later 1530's testify. In the long run, of course, it did not work at all.

[1] STC 17656; BM, 114. a. 31. The date of publication may account for the fact that the sermon treats as accomplished events which when it was preached still lay in the future. Matthew was a prebendary of St Paul's from 1533 till his death in 1541 (Le Neve, v. 62). His conservatism is proved by his preaching for souls departed, unlike (he says) his predecessor the previous Sunday.
[2] Merriman, i. 417–18, 427–31.

Matthew owed the services of the King's printer to saying the right thing at the right moment; others – bishops all – owed them to their personal eminence. Bishop Stokesley of London rather unexpectedly preached so acceptable a sermon on 11 July 1535 (at that late date still on the invalidity of the first marriage) that Cromwell drew Henry's attention to it; and it was agreed to print. Unfortunately, Stokesley was forced to explain that he never wrote his sermons but preached free: he disliked using a script because he habitually departed from it, nor could he afterwards remember exactly what he had been saying. In any case, he wrote, the gist of his argument was in the book which he and Edward Foxe and Nicholas del Burgo had put together, and which Cranmer had translated into English – a book, possibly unpublished, of which we know nothing.[1] The bishop's excellent lecturing habits lost him a title in his bibliography and Cromwell a useful pamphlet; all the minister could make of the occasion was a word to the imperial ambassador, wishing that Charles V could have heard that splendid sermon. One suspects irony.[2]

Other men of the old opinion did better. Two of the sermons preached before the King by Bishop Longland of Lincoln on Good Friday were printed, but not for the same reason. That delivered in 1536 had no politics in it, and the general get-up (there is neither title-page nor colophon) suggests that Berthelet was not involved. Very likely, Longland himself was responsible for seeking a wider audience for his edifying discourse on Christ's passion.[3] But two years later he knew his duty better, and Thomas Petyt printed a sermon on the bishop's office which turned into a stern denunciation of the pope's arrogant and money-grubbing ways.[4] More weighty still, and also even more useful because of the author's reputation and his well known opposition to the Reformation, was Cuthbert Tunstall's sermon preached before the King on Palm Sunday 1539, which at once appeared from Berthelet's press.[5] This was a long discourse which possibly tried the endurance of the congregation, but in what Tunstall said there was nothing but convenient doctrine. He chose to speak on

---

[1] SP 1/94, fos. 50, 110 (*LP* viii. 1043, 1054). Cromwell noted that he would order Stokesley to write the sermon out nevertheless (*LP* viii. 527: placed there too early in the year) but he seems to have been unsuccessful. Was the book the *Determination*?

[2] *LP* viii. 1105.

[3] *STC* 16795; BM, C. 53. bb. 7.   [4] *STC* 16796; BM, C. 53. k. 14.

[5] *STC* 24322; BM, 1026. a. 7.

Phil. ii. 5 and therefore on humility – Christ's humility, the disobedience of men 'by pride done to man against God's law', and the further disobedience done to God. It was the second part of the sermon that justified the printing of it, for this included a long passage exhorting all to obey 'princes and governors'. More particularly Tunstall attacked the mission against England which Cardinal Pole was just then conducting across the Channel and which was causing much disturbance in the country. He admitted the danger:

> But for all this, thou Englishman, take courage unto thee and be nothing afraid. Thou hast God on thy side who hath given this realm to the generation of Englishmen, to every man his degree, after the laws of the same; thou hast a noble, victorious and virtuous King, hardy as a lion, who will not suffer thee to be so devoured by such wild beasts. Only take an English heart unto thee and mistrust not God.

The hardy lion, sitting under the preacher, promptly called for his printer.[1]

Such testimonials from political opponents were useful, but Cromwell did not rely only on windfalls when he wished to put out a reasoned defence of the new order. There are three very different pieces to be noted coming from his stable, as well as two projected works which would have provided comprehensive statements of his position if they had ever been completed. The diversity is interesting: it reflects the good propagandist's recognition that different targets need different arrows, though also, of course, the diverse talents of those writers. Richard Morison displayed his controversial skill in his *Apomaxis Calumniarum Convitiorumque*, an answer to John Cochlaeus' attack on Henry's Divorce in February 1535; Thomas Starkey in his *Exhortation* addressed himself more constructively to the consequences of the revolution; and an anonymous lawyer produced a dull *Treatise proving by the King's Laws that the Bishop of Rome had never right to any supremacy within this realm.*[2] This last, which needs no extended notice, assembles the medieval case and statute law touching control of the clergy by the king's courts and thus represents a common-law counterpart to Foxe's

---

[1] Tunstall was by way of being an expert at combating Reginald Pole. In 1536, he and Stokesley had jointly written a severe letter to the cardinal, upbraiding him for deserting King and country (*STC* 24321; CUL, Syn. 8. 56. 13: not printed until 1560 and therefore no part of the propaganda campaign of the 1530's).

[2] Printed Berthelet, 1538. *STC* 24248; there is a seventeenth-century manuscript copy of this very rare book in CUL, Dd. 14. 27 (2).

De Vera Differentia, supplying ammunition to others. The first two books, on the other hand, are major works of propaganda.

Morison's *Apomaxis* did not appear in print until 1537 or 1538, though it had been writing since the middle of 1536; the chief cause of the delay was probably the northern rebellion which, as we shall see, took both author and printer off to other things.[1] In any case, it came rather too late to be no more than an exchange with Henry's German adversary; instead, Morison produced – in Latin and for the European market – a

---

[1] The genesis of *Apomaxis* (*STC* 18109; CUL, Syn. 7. 53. 30) presents difficult problems which have not all been solved by Zeeveld, *Foundations*, 158–60, 165–6. Morison was in Cromwell's service by Oct. 1535 (*LP* ix. 687), though it was not until the middle of 1536 that he finally came home from Padua to join the minister's household (*LP* x. 660 of 12 April 1536, when the question was still not finally settled, despite Morison's statement on March 4th [ibid. 418] that Cromwell wanted him back in England). Since he evidently did not know Pole's mind concerning the King's doings until he saw a manuscript of Pole's *De Unitate* in England, he presumably left Pole's household before May 1536 when that work was sent to Henry VIII. Thus he was very close to Cromwell, as his letters show, for some nine months while still at Padua, and his pleas for money and favour are those of a retainer feeling neglected by distance rather than those of an applicant seeking service. I do not believe that Morison visited England in Sept. 1535 or that he was the 'M. . .' of Bedyll's letter of July that year. Zeeveld, who so supposes (p. 158), has his man hopping about quite impossibly: in England in late July and early September, but in Padua on Aug. 27th and Oct. 26th. The only sensible explanation of the evidence is that Morison remained in Padua till he finally came home ca. May 1536, and that Cromwell in effect scooped him up abroad, having (probably) heard of his quality from Starkey. Where did Morison start *Apomaxis*? On 22 July 1536 he announced to Harvel in Venice that he had been set the task (*LP* xi. 328). By then or soon after the book was with the printer, so that the actual beginning was earlier; but in view of the terms employed by Harvel, who knew Morison well in Italy, Morison cannot have had his instructions before he arrived in England. On the other hand, in order to be able to discharge Cromwell's commission he must have read Cochlaeus earlier: i.e. he had been preparing himself. Harvel's words show clearly that the actual idea for the book was given to Morison, not invented by him. Then, at a point when *De Unitate* was known in England in manuscript and the question of whether it would ever be printed remained open, but before the northern risings (Aug.–Sept. 1536), Berthelet on Cromwell's instructions stopped printing *Apomaxis*, and Morison offered to switch his attack from Cochlaeus to Pole, if the minister wished (*LP* xi. 1481). In the end the book did appear, but when? Berthelet's colophon has the date 1537; Morison's dedicatory letter is dated 20 June 1538 (not July 12th, as per Zeeveld, p. 159 n. 7: Morison used the classical form '12 Cal. Julij'!). *LP* xi, p. 584 n., concludes from the form of address that the letter was written before Cromwell became lord privy seal in July 1536. Two explanations are possible: either Morison, writing in Latin, cannot be pinned down to a precise description of Cromwell's office, so that the letter was written in 1538 and added belatedly to a text already printed, or 1538 is a misprint for 1536. The latter seems to me much the more probable, and it therefore looks as though Morison wrote this substantial Latin treatise in May–June 1536.

major review and defence of all that had happened in England since Henry first discovered doubts about his marriage. The book is pure propaganda, not only for what had been done but also, exceptionally, for Thomas Cromwell. One might expect a dedicatory letter to be fulsome; what is interesting are the specific terms in which Cromwell is praised, namely for his sheer business capacity. 'Res est plane incredibilis, unius hominis ingenium, memoriam, uim, tot, tantia, tamque inter se dissidentibus rebus sufficere posse.' Anyone who has ever read Cromwell's correspondence must agree with that astonishment. Everybody's begging letters, every man's complaints, says Morison, come to you and are answered: 'qui tibi notus, non aliquot tua beneficia senserit?' Even in the body of the work he goes out of his way to offer praise (fo. 71): there was no affair of any kind that Cromwell could not manage by his skill, protect by his integrity, or bring to conclusion by his ingenuity. Moreover he was the most loyal of men, a quality he proved he possessed during Wolsey's last year of adversity. There is no doubt who Morison thought was in charge of the government, and it is of interest to find that Cromwell's faithful service to the fallen cardinal, a matter in which he behaved so differently from the rest of Wolsey's clients, was noted at the time.

In the main, however, the *Apomaxis* is a full-scale review of the past seven or eight years in the course of which all the crucial charges are refuted by means of the propaganda devices built up from the *Determination* onwards. Morison sets out the official versions of all the *causes célèbres* – the Divorce, the Nun of Kent, Fisher and More. He contributes details of his own, as for instance a characteristically lively, even frivolous, description of the Nun's trances, or a neat argument to show that real scholars are on the King's side. You people opposite, he notes, draw attention to the stand made by More: but who is More, compared with Gardiner, Foxe and Tunstall (three of the King's propagandists, as it happens)? Look at the difference in scholarship! Not that it was More's fault: always busy with the law (*forensibus negotiis*) he had no chance to equal such as Tunstall in learning; and his writing under a pseudonym – the reference is to More's defence of Henry against Luther – shows that he did not expect to find favour with real scholars. The last point comes oddly from one who did not put his name to his book at all, but that need not disguise the fact that Morison had hit upon a truth about More which later generations have too readily forgotten.

Morison was writing unashamed propaganada and proving that even the use of Latin could not suppress his natural combative ebullience. Starkey, a much more serious, even a solemn, man, proved rather more difficult to fit into the government's scheme of things, but in the end he was persuaded to write a book which repaid the expense of printing. He had originally written, in effect, his political testament, centring his argument on the notion of the middle way in religion and politics, a tenet which owed something to Bucer but much to Starkey him-self, so that with justice he has been seen as the first specific advocate of the Anglican *via media*.[1] With justice, that is, if one goes by what was written down. After criticism by Henry (who found the argument too little scriptural), some divines (who missed in the treatise their own commitment to one side or the other), and Cromwell (who, seeing the point, wanted even more stress laid on the middle position which he himself had first pressed on Starkey), he re-wrote the book so that it might have some propaganda value, by stringing his argument upon the main chord of the duty of obedience. In this form it was pre-sented to the King in September 1535, at which time Starkey had no thought of putting it into print. The government decided other-wise, and by April 1536 the book was out.[2]

Despite these revisions, the title misrepresents the book. Its real purpose remained unaltered from the first: the exposition of a middle way in policy, justified by a theological system of things indifferent – *adiaphora* – which sensible men can agree are not doctrinally necessary and may therefore be varied from place to place and time to time with-out endangering the unity of Christendom. Some matters are in them-selves good or evil, right or wrong, but

things indifferent I call all such things which by God's word are neither prohibited nor commanded...but left to worldly policy whereof they take their full authority; by the which as time and place requireth they are some-times good and sometimes ill.[3]

Philosophy supports propaganda when Starkey goes on to state that the doctrine of papal supremacy belongs among these indifferent things,

[1] Zeeveld, *Foundations*, 152 and n. 69.

[2] Thomas Starkey, *An Exhortation to the people instructing them to Unity and Obedience.* Printed Berthelet; only one extant copy; title-page missing, colophon undated. STC 23236; BM, 4103. aaa. 28. The prehistory of the book is worked out by Zeeveld, *Foundations*, 147–9; for an analysis of Starkey's thought cf. ibid. 149–56.

[3] *Exhortation*, fo. 6 v.

and this slightly uneasy admixture of the government's purposes to Starkey's continues throughout the book. Starkey lists two kinds of spiritual blindness which prevent the middle way from being adopted, superstition and arrogance. He takes time off to point to More and Fisher as being afflicted with the first which made them stand so stiffly on the pope's authority and therefore suffer their sad fate.[1] Arrogance turns out to be radical extremism, but Starkey does not bother with examples, though his description shows him to have had the godly kingdom of Münster in mind. He demonstrates that life is different from Scripture, but is careful to blame the very fact of the papal supremacy for this rather than any form of mere abuse. We then get a long excursus, sitting uneasily in the argument, which presses the Bible and history into service to disprove the Petrine claims. The real Starkey in his sensible moderation comes out in a final remark: Indians, Armenians and Greeks do not recognise the primacy of Rome and yet are Christians – are they thus damned or do they not prove the papacy to be a matter indifferent in God's eyes?[2] Starkey's discussion of particular *adiaphora* is also geared to the needs of the moment: he deals with those ceremonies and practices – such as pilgrimages or praying to saints and for the dead – which the government was trying to modify or suppress, but his concern throughout is with moderation, not with taking stands: thus prayers for the departed are declared to be useless to the dead whose state, damned or saved (there being no purgatory), they cannot alter, but they please God by proving the presence of charity and kindness. There is remarkably little in the book about the obedience dutifully mentioned in the title; what concerns Starkey is unity, and though he laments the dissidence and disobedience he sees all around him, he is more insistent upon the duty of princes to maintain 'the order and redress of their commonalties, by the providence of God to their governance committed',[3] than upon the subject's duty to obey. Starkey's thought is impressive – as is that of the minister who first urged him to advocate the middle way – but as a propagandist he did less well. The task came hardly naturally to one who wanted to think clearly and charitably, and who at his best commanded an unexciting style.

Nevertheless, he had provided a philosophic and highly constructive

[1] Ibid. fo. 18.
[2] Ibid. fo. 44v.   [3] Ibid., Preface to the King.

defence of the new order, as Morison had provided a defence of the actions which had produced it. Cromwell evidently thought money well spent that went to the publishing of such books, and on at least two later occasions plans existed to compose further comprehensive works of propaganda. The execution, in 1539, of the three abbots manifestly seemed to call for some downright statement; memories of the effect that More's and Fisher's deaths had had four years before should by themselves have been sufficient to suggest as much, though that occasion had also demonstrated the limits of successful propaganda. Thus a pamphlet was drafted in thirty-three pages but never published.[1] It consists simply of a violent attack on treason in general and the traitors in the case in particular, and the style suggests that Morison may have had a hand in it. There are some characteristically artificial constructions – 'merciless monks, false friars and uncharitable canons, and other fools of feigned religion' – as well as some furious phrases about Reginald Pole, all of which calls Morison to mind. But the pamphlet also presents several rather strange features which may account for the fact that it was put aside. Perhaps at that date at the end of 1539 Cromwell would not have minded an attack on four conservative leaders of the clergy now dead – Bishop Stokesley, Bishop Standish of St Asaph, Archbishop Warham, and Rowland Phillips, vicar of Croydon – though he had himself been responsible for treating three of them gently when they had got into trouble. But the pamphlet also committed the solecism of hitting hard at two of the traitors' associates whom the government had decided to reprieve.[2] Clearly it was not well worked out so far, and clearly it was much too reformist in sympathy to suit the moment.

More interesting is a long paper which at first sight seems to be a detailed exposition and official account of the work achieved since 1529; internal evidence dates it to the early part of 1539, before the parliamentary session of that year which enacted the Act of Six Articles.[3]

[1] SP 1/155, fos. 55–72 (*LP* xiv. II. 613). The earliest date of composition would be Dec. 1539, and the paper does seem to have been written about the time of the executions – perhaps even a little earlier in the expectation of the outcome, since it denounces as traitors persons later reprieved.

[2] William Moore, 'the blind harper', was still receiving his wages in January 1541 (*LP* xvi. 1489, fo. 164b); Richard Manchester, who died peacefully before Nov. 1540, still received an Augmentations pension at Michaelmas that year (ibid. 92, 1391 [17]).

[3] *LP* xiv. I. 402, printed in Jeremy Collier, *An Ecclesiastical History of Great Britain* (2 vols., 1708–14), Doc. 47.

It is in the hand of Thomas Derby, clerk of the Privy Council and a member of Cromwell's staff, a fact which together with its contents can leave no doubt of its official origin. But there is no need to think Derby the author, nor to think this is any way a finished product. On the contrary, it is manifestly at quite an early stage of composition, consisting as it does of four separate parts some of which are insufficiently worked out. It rather looks as though we get here a glimpse of how Cromwell's team worked in producing what were in effect official handouts. Derby presumably copied a collection of notes into a form which would make a proper literary working up possible. At any rate, the four sections differ so much in content and elaboration that several authors (different specialists) are much more likely than one hand.

The first two sections – which deal respectively with 'a summary declaration of the faith, uses and observations in England' and with abuses there reformed – are no more than a succession of lapidary assertions of fact, intended to prove that the country, so far from being heresy-ridden, has seen the light of true religion. There is a thumping start: 'Englishmen have forsaken Satan, his satellites, and all works of darkness, and utterly dedicate themselves to Christ, his words, faith and the works of light;' and the next five paragraphs similarly start with the word 'Englishmen', explaining what other spiritual benefits these now own. Englishmen believe in the Trinity, the Apostolic and Nicene Creeds, both the Old and the New Testament ('fons aquae salientis in vitam aeternam'), the Councils and the Fathers; they abhor Anabaptist and similar heresies; they worship in their churches and 'pay their tithes and offerings truly as ever they did'; preaching of the gospel is better than ever; Englishmen have the Bible in hand in place of 'the old fabulous and fantastical books of the Table Round, Lancelot du Lac, Huon de Bordeaux, Bevy of Hampton, Guy of Warwick'. They continue to observe the ten commandments, Sundays and holy days, 'confession and communion at Easter at least', ember days, Lenten fasts, weekly fast days; and Parliament has provided a law to put down vagabonds and take care of the impotent poor. This last point, oddly inserted in an illogical place, again demonstrates that this is a draft, not a finished product. The point of this first section, and in a way the main point of the exercise, is stated in a rhetorical question: how in view of all this can anybody think the English heretics or schismatics or 'slander them as infidels'?

The second section recites the evils in the Church which the Reformation in England had removed. These include the abuses dealt with in 1529 (probate and mortuary fees, pluralism, non-residence, clerical engagement in secular employment), in 1533 (appeals) and 1534 (appointments of bishops, peter's pence, dispensations, the commission for the reform of the canon law). In this recital of statutory reform, hardly any of the bare statements receive any elaboration, with the result that there is rather less abuse of Rome than one might have expected and than, no doubt, the finished product would have provided. Section three turns to the fact that the clergy of England have 'of their own free will and common assent' accepted the King as supreme head. This is a good deal more worked out; after all, the team were on familiar ground here. The draft refers to Foxe's book for a full exposition of monarchic rights, but spells out at length the tried and trusty arguments against the Scripture-based primatial claims of the pope. Parts of this section, too, would have needed elaborating and tidying, but with its recital of texts and more rounded sentences it shows how the whole thing might have looked in the end. This is also true of the last section which attempts the portmanteau task of controverting accusations based on 'other proceedings'. It gives the official version of the Dissolution, stresses the reform of various 'superstitious practices' (excessive holy days, indulgences, images and shrines), and especially tells the revised version of Thomas Becket's fate according to which he died in a private quarrel with the see of York and in a scuffle in which he had struck the first blow. Becket, as we have seen, needed to be exorcised;[1] to represent him as a violent, selfish man, really killed by his own fault, a man whose real record shows him to have been 'a great warrior, a burner of towns, an encroacher of benefices, a hunter and hawker, proud and seditious', and one who by his own confession obtained the archbishopric corruptly, was to do a thorough job of blackwashing on England's holy blissful martyr. Modern research inclines to endorse some of this propaganda judgment.

Lastly, in this section, the writer turns to our special concern, executions for treason. He can see no reason why a bishop or abbot should not die for treason, despite his anointing, when thiefs and lay traitors, though Christians baptised, are hanged every day.

[1] Above, pp. 16, 23, and for the official re-writing of the Becket story, cf. below, p. 257, n. 1.

Should the King's highness have suffered those traitors to live – Thomas More, the jester, Fisher of Rochester, the [vain]glorious hypocrite, both the champions of superstition and abuse; the Carthusians and friars obstinate,[1] and other wool-clothed wolves who attribute more to their cowl and habit than to the precious blood of Christ?

Was it wrong to deal with the Nun of Kent, intent on using her false prophecies for the King's destruction; with the northern rebels, rebellious a second time after their pardons; the traitors in the Exeter conspiracy? But – and this point is heavily stressed – the real proof of propriety in all this is legality: the King 'never put to death any man *authoritate absoluta*, but by ordinary process'. Open trials, by all the rules of law, have found these people to be traitors. The point, unlike some of the rest, happens to be objectively true and needs to be remembered. The document ends abruptly with a paragraph on General Councils which is still in somewhat ungrammatical form and unfinished.

This embryo pamphlet could have become very interesting: a firm, assertive, detailed statement of the government's view of the revolution and its position on all the controversial deeds of the decade. Essentially it must have been intended for use abroad, as especially the first section shows; it was abroad that the sort of accusations against 'Englishmen' were likely to be made. Presumably, therefore, it needed not only a good deal of development and polishing, but also translating. As things turned out, no time was found to complete the job. One may hazard the guess that the so-called Catholic reaction, by taking a good deal of steam out of the Cromwellian machine, played its part in relegating the whole idea to the filing-drawer. After May 1539, it would at the very least have been necessary to change crucial passages in the text so as to play down the changes and play up the traditionalism of the English Church, not the most agreeable of tasks for the people likely to have been involved in drafting the pamphlet. In the upshot no such comprehensive defence was offered until William Thomas, reformer and clerk of the Privy Council and at last an executed traitor himself, did the job, by private enterprise, in his *Pilgrim*.[2]

[1] A pun on 'observant'.

[2] William Thomas, *The Pilgrim*, ed. J. A. Froude (1861); first published in Italian in 1552. The tract is a defence of Henry VIII's reign against Italian calumniators. For Thomas, cf. E. R. Adair in *Tudor Studies...presented to A. F. Pollard* (1924), 133–60.

All the propaganda so far considered was, so to speak, active: in it government writers asserted the truth of the government's aggressive actions and defended them against hostile opinion. Once, however, the revolution had been accomplished, the chances were that the propagandists would find themselves writing what may be called passive pieces – pamphlets against the positive action of others. The change of line came in October 1536, with the outbreak of rebellion in Lincolnshire, and for the rest of the decade the main propaganda effort was governed by the need to resist very positive attempts to destroy the new order. There were two phases – rebellion in the realm (1536–1537) and a threat of foreign invasion linked with domestic treason (1538–1539) – both of which are reflected in the output of the press. In actual fact more was written than reached print, but while the contents of unpublished manuscripts are interesting for the study of the government's ideas and plans they remain irrelevant to a discussion of the propaganda effort in this phase, too. There is no sign at all that those manuscript tracts circulated outside the innermost ring of government, that anyone else read them, or that they were ever employed to influence opinion. On the contrary, it looks very much as though several members of Cromwell's propaganda staff received orders to deal with rebels and traitors, so that the minister had a choice of pamphlets for publication. Thus the difference between print and manuscript is in this case likely to reflect a deliberate decision to use some pieces but not others. In the choice he made, Cromwell demonstrated his competence: the events of 1536 brought to the fore the man who wielded far and away the best propagandist pen in Henrician England. Richard Morison's contribution stands out for sheer skill in writing and vigour in controversy, and significantly it was his work that Berthelet received for publication.[1]

However, the first propagandist to turn his attention to the rebels was the King himself, or those who drafted for him his *Answer to the Petitions of the Traitors and Rebels in Lincolnshire*. A little later he issued a similar *Answer made by the King's Highness to the Petition of the Rebels in Yorkshire*, and since they came hard upon one another (and are bound up together in the only extant copy) they may be considered together.[2]

[1] Zeeveld, *Foundations*, 176–8, considers the rejected manuscripts and gives some idea of their relative feebleness.

[2] *STC* 13077; CUL, SSS. 17. 29. *STC* fails to note that this volume contains also the reply to Lincs. Both printed by Berthelet in 1536, in identical style. In fact, Berthelet used the same border for the title pages of all the material put out in the autumn of

Their contents have often been described: a vigorous denunciation of the impudence of the commons in rising up against their anointed head and a total refusal to listen to any of their complaints. That the King was not solely responsible for these 'letters' is suggested by the long passage in the second which carefully explains that the Privy Council is now fuller of nobles than it was at Henry's accession when 'the most were lawyers and priests'. This looks like a personal defence produced by the councillors attacked in the rebels' demands, indeed like the personal defence of two particular men:

And for because it is more than necessary to have some of our Privy Council learned in our laws and acquainted with the policies and practices of the world, we, by the advice of our whole Council before named,[1] did elect and choose into our Privy Council, and also into their rooms, Sir Thomas Audley, knight, our chancellor, and the Lord Cromwell, keeper of our privy seal.

So much for the worldly wisdom and practical knowledge of dukes and bishops.

The *Answers* were in effect policy statements and widely distributed.[2] But they were not designed to create a proper climate of opinion. For this purpose Cromwell turned to Morison who proved his competence but even more his speed. According to himself he wrote his first piece, *A Lamentation in which is showed what ruin and destruction cometh of seditious rebellion*,[3] 'in my boots', in one afternoon and night,[4] and it has to be confessed that the pamphlet reads like that. *A Lamentation* was written when only Lincolnshire was up, and it suffered the fate of much propaganda in disturbed times of being overtaken by events before it was even published.[5] It is a rather wordy piece, by Morison's standards, with too few points to make and those repeated several times. The

1536, but this does not prove him to have been working under extreme pressure (Zeeveld, *Foundations*, 180). In the 1530's Berthelet used three types of title-page, showing himself economical rather than pressurised in this work for the government: one round about 1531–5 (*Determination, Glass, Little Treatise*, Matthew's *Sermon*); one in 1536; and a third round about 1539 (Tunstall's *Sermon*, Morison's *Invective* and *Exhortation*). Wear and tear presumably account for these changes.

[1] I.e. the ten noblemen and knights and four bishops just listed.
[2] Cf. *LP* xi. 1406, where it also appears that the rebels' demands, though not printed, became available in London in manuscript.
[3] Printed Berthelet, 1536. *STC* 15185; BM, C. 38. d. 7. For the attribution to Morison rather than Sir John Cheke cf. Zeeveld, *Foundations*, 174. There is certainly no doubt about it.
[4] *LP* xi. 1482.   [5] Cf. Zeeveld, *Foundations*, 175 and n. 49.

general tenor is given by some of Morison's characteristic epigrams: 'Obedience is the badge of a true Christian man;' 'dissension, dissension, hath been the ruin, the venom, the poison of all great estates.' The style is exclamatory and full of rhetorical questions; the reader is left in no doubt that the author disapproves of rebellion, but he gathers no sense of any recognition that rebellion has its causes or its remedies. There is a typical Morison touch in the praise bestowed on the King for dissolving the monasteries rather than executing the inmates for the sodomy proved against them, as the law demanded, and another in the exculpation of Cromwell:

What cruel and blind malice is this, to lay in one or two men's necks as evil done that which was thought by the whole counsel and consent of the three estates of England to be most to the honour of God, discharge of the King, and weal of his realm and subjects of the same!

A Lamentation is not an attractive pamphlet, and Morison had reason to be ashamed of it, as he said he was,[1] but as an immediate and passionate denunciation of miserable rebels it served a purpose.

The spread of the rising to Yorkshire intensified the government effort and the pressure on Morison, but he had a little more time to write *A Remedy for Sedition* (published soon after October 26th) and did a good deal better.[2] The argument was reviewed at some length by Zeeveld who rightly draws attention to the learning displayed – and carried lightly – and especially to Morison's acquaintance with Machiavelli.[3] The *Remedy* avoids the hysteria and emptiness of the *Lamentation*. It has a theme: the benefits of order and hierarchy. There is no other way, claims Morison, in which a commonwealth can be successfully run. The theme is developed with logic and conviction and plenty of historical examples (here the influence of Machiavelli is patent); the style has the usual easy speed and attractive touches without the descent

[1] *LP* xi. 1482.
[2] Printed Berthelet, 1536. *STC* 20877; CUL, Syn. 7. 53. 57.
[3] Zeeveld, *Foundations*, 180–9. He also discusses the evidence of Morison's drafts, relevant here only in showing the speed with which Morison could produce and revise several stages of a substantial pamphlet. But Zeeveld's argument regarding Cromwell's 'machiavellianism' will not stand up. His own evidence indicates that it was Morison who introduced Machiavelli to both England and Cromwell, and here the fact that Morison stayed later in Italy than anyone else involved becomes important. He had the chance of reading Machiavelli in print after the book had become famous in Italy.

into Billingsgate which was always close to Morison's heart. His main proposition, and also conclusion, is stated soberly:

A commonwealth, as I think, is nothing else but a certain number of cities, towns, shires, that all agree upon one law and one head, united and knit together by the observation of the laws. These kept, they must necessarily flourish; these broken, they must needs perish.

This mixture of legalism, authority and consent really did form the basis of the Tudor state especially in the political philosophy of which Cromwell was the most active exponent, and Morison's *Remedy* succeeds in turning a successful piece of *ad hoc* propaganda into a convincing statement on political order. Where before he had only lamented, he now knew how to remedy.

The collapse of the northern rebels made it unnecessary to continue the work of propaganda, but the war-scare of 1538–1539, and especially the threatening mission of Cardinal Pole, summoned the writers once more to the barricades. We have already seen that Tunstall's sermon reached print in part at least because he went out of its way to attack Pole and reassure his readers about the realm's chances of survival. These were also the main themes of Morison's two most substantial pamphlets. *An Invective against the great and detestable vice of treason* was regarded as so important, or was selling so well, that two editions appeared in one year.[1] The work found favour with Henry who recommended it as a 'pretty book' to Sir Thomas Wyatt, ambassador with the emperor; there may have been some intention to bring out a translation for use abroad which was never accomplished.[2] Morison followed it up with a second barrel, *An Exhortation to stir all Englishmen to the defence of their country*, written probably in March 1539, a month or so after the *Invective*.[3] The two books go together: between them, they constitute Morison's (and the government's) message to the people at a time when deep-seated disaffection had been discovered in high places and domestic

---

[1] Printed Berthelet, 1539. *STC* 18111–2; BM, 521. b. 7 and 292. a. 33 (1). It does not look as though the second printing was freshly set up: the deterioration in the title border and the type in general suggests otherwise. The only evidence of separate printing appears in the fact that the space between the last line and the colophon is larger in one copy than in the other.

[2] Zeeveld, *Foundations*, 229 and nn. 15–16. *LP* xiv. I. 233 shows that Wriothesley, not Cromwell, supposed that a translation might be in hand.

[3] Printed Berthelet, 1539. *STC* 18110; BM, C. 54. aa. 8. For the date, cf. Zeeveld, *Foundations*, 231, n. 10.

traitors were alleged to be plotting with foreign enemies. England was beleaguered: but England, Morison explained, had nothing to fear and much over which to rejoice.

In *An Invective* Morison employed the technique he had learned in *A Remedy*. The chief purpose of the pamphlet was served in a violent attack on the lately discovered traitors, the Poles and Courtenays, but this was set in the framework of a general treatise on treason. This general discussion, intended to prove that treason never prospers, persuades the reader with a quite impressive array of learning: examples are piled up from the Bible, the civil law, the laws of Macedonia and Athens, and Cicero's correspondence. Even if Morison got this at second hand, his mind was well stocked. Henry VIII's escape, we are told, was more remarkable than David's who at least knew that Saul was out for his blood. This sets the tone of both pamphlets with their strident proclamation of England's special favour at the hands of God. But the bulk of *An Invective* is just that, a furious assault on individuals. Morison is particularly savage about Pole, lately his friend and patron – 'archtraitor...whom God hateth, nature refuseth, all men detest, yea, and beasts too would abhor if they could perceive'. He uses his long personal acquaintance with the cardinal to make points about the man's honesty: did he not falsely call himself the King of England's nephew when first he got to Italy, in order to cut a better figure? 'Thou art now a Pole of little water and that at a wonderful low ebb.' Playing on the name Reynold, he calls him Reynard (the fox) and constructs laborious conceits around the pope's 'godly sowers of treason'. From Pole he switches to Lords Exeter and Montague whose treason, like Pole's, is made worse by their notorious indebtedness to the King's kindness. The marquess was for ever threatening the King's loyal servants, promising 'one day to give them a buffet', and his real beliefs are shown by the fact that he dismissed from his service any man found with the New Testament in his hand. As happens to Morison at intervals, imagination carries him into absurdities, as when he draws an incomprehensible comparison between the death of Exeter and Adam's expulsion from paradise. But he cannot for long forget his deep resentment of his erstwhile patron, and we are soon back at abuse of Pole.

At this point Morison shows his skill and rescues his pamphlet from defeat by switching to a more positive line. These traitors plotted in vain: England is stronger than that. He pictures the pope and Pole 'that day that the news was brought of the end of our hurly-burly in the north'. And why is England strong? Because the King has seen the light.

Of all the miracles and wonders of our time, I take the change of our sovereign lord's opinion in matters concerning religion to be even the greatest. There was no prince in Christendom but he was far liker to have changed than our sovereign lord; he was their pillar and bore them up a great while; they gave him fair titles for his so doing and honoured his name in all their writings; was it not a wonderful work of God to get his grace from them to Him?

There is rather more frankness than tact in this manifestation of Morison's very genuine Protestantism, which is further underlined by much praise for good preaching and new doctrine. How can treason hope to succeed against one whom God had taken so much trouble to convert to the truth? The pamphlet ends with a few more examples of the protection enjoyed by King and realm, as shown by the fact that those treasons lurking unsuspected for years among men for ever close to the King yet failed of their purpose. The passage on Sir Geoffrey Pole, the cardinal's feeble brother, with its tale of nervous breakdowns and attempted suicide, is very nasty but highly effective.

The theme of England's strength and good fortune is taken much further in the *Exhortation*. The specific purpose of this tract was to make the warlike preparations of 1538–1539, which were causing much apprehension, acceptable to the nation, and Morison used three chief arguments: the duty of subjects to assist a prince who prepares the defence of his people, the wickedness of the pope and his minions, and the martial valour of England as proved by her history. Perhaps the pope believes that Englishmen are so divided that 'his true friends' will prevent the realm from supporting the King. On the contrary, the wicked, money-grubbing bishop of Rome needs to fear his own destruction: 'he writeth, he sendeth, he calleth, he crieth for help unto all princes.' The only thing that can possibly harm England is her own pusillanimity. Morison cites from a report allegedly made of late by an ambassador returned home from England (he probably had Chapuys in mind who was recalled in February 1539):

The activity of Englishmen hath been great, if historians be true, but if I may judge by my conjectures it is nothing so now. I see neither harness ne weapons of manhood amongst them. They have been of good hearts, courageous, bold, valiant in martial feats; but those Englishmen are dead.

Morison grows indignant and trusts that his readers will share his feelings. If 'we be not blinder than beetles' we can now see the point of the commotion in the north: it made England arm herself with weapons which shall now be used against external foes. A note of quite un-Henrician exultation intrudes: 'some trust in chariots, some in horses, but we in calling upon the Lord.' There follows a powerful evocation of England's heroic past, of Crecy and Poitiers and the rest. 'We may forget the battle of Agincourt, but they will remember and are like never to forget with how small an army...King Henry V vanquished that huge host of Frenchmen.' Numbers need not trouble the English who have always won against the odds. The King is nobly spending his substance on building splendid defences from Berwick to Cornwall. The King is the lion of prophecy who will destroy the popish eagle. 'Let us fight this one field with English hands and English hearts: perpetual quietness, rest, peace, victory, honour, wealth, all is ours.'

The *Exhortation* thus adopts a distinctly exalted tone, and we should be sure that Richard Morison really felt something of this mixture of Protestant religion and patriotic fervour: he was an early example of a type familiar later. But he was also too good a propagandist not to know the advantages of varying his pace. Thus in the midst of a serious assessment of England's chances in war he deviates (ostensibly in order to prove the vileness of Rome) into a long irrelevant story about a homosexual rape committed by his guest upon a young Roman bishop: but then that guest, a captain of soldiers, came of a bad stock, for his mother gave birth before marriage and (punchline) his father is now the bishop of Rome. Nor can Morison forget his obsession with Reginald Pole, though he manages the introduction smoothly. When Pole first came to Italy, he meant to spend six months at Rome, but his first impressions (as I, says Morison, have often heard him say) drove him out of the city after a few days. Yet what do we hear now? Nothing but 'Roma mihi patria est'. These were the last pamphlets of the 1530's, and also the last political tracts that Morison was to write. With Cromwell's fall, an age of both dynamic reform and active propaganda came to an end. In this work, the pamphleteer displayed superb skill, mingling abuse and exhortation, low comedy and high seriousness, passion and cynicism in a well written and most effective appeal to reason and the emotions.

Several things thus emerge about the propaganda campaign conducted by Henry and Cromwell. In the early stages in particular, while policy was rapidly developing, the writings were clearly 'official' – produced by the government and intended to declare what was being done, to explain the reasons why, and to prepare the ground for the next step. The *Glass of Truth* implicitly announced the forthcoming legislation on appeals, the *Articles of the Council* foreshadowed the statutory transfer of the supremacy to the Crown, the *Little Treatise* announced the policy of extirpating the pope in England. The propaganda tracts thus serve to underline the systematic and planned purpose which lay behind government action at this point. Once the real revolution had been achieved, its defence against external and internal enemies, and the desire to justify things done, called for a less planned sequence of writings, both from men specifically employed for the purpose and from possible waverers whom it was thought advisable to tie in print to conformist statements and who could be the more persuasive abroad on account of their known hesitations. Then, when the new order came under attack, Cromwell employed his special staff to blast the opposition (on paper) off the face of the earth. Throughout the press was used, intensively, carefully and purposefully, to back up political action.

On the whole, the work was done with considerable and augmenting skill. The principles of sound propaganda are well observed, in various ways, in the smooth persuasiveness of the *Glass* or the stern, confident edicts of the *Articles*, in the solidly tendentious scholarship of Gardiner and the mixture of mace and stiletto employed by Morison. All the English treatises are eminently readable, and the Latin ones reached that high level of humanist competence which prevented them from being ridiculed. Erasmus had not in vain set the pace here. Care was taken to leave out no possible audience. English writings for home use and the guidance of the generality appeared side by side with Latin writings (over names respected for their eminence in theological and legal learning) directed at scholars, clergy and foreigners. The tone varied as much as the language, as a comparison of the *Glass* with its source-collection in the *Determination* shows as clearly as anything. How astonishing this high degree of competence was can be properly appreciated only if it is remembered that this was the first such campaign ever mounted by any government in any state of Europe. Not that propagandist writing was new, but an intensive and government-organised campaign of printed propaganda was. The activity threw up only one propagandist of genius, a point quite apparent to Cromwell who in 1539 secured Morison's election to Parliament, so that he might there be 'ready to answer and take up such as would crake or face with literature of learning or by indirect ways, if any such shall be'.[1] The record of that Parliament, which passed the Act of Six Articles and amended the Act of Proclamations, may suggest that Cromwell made the common mistake of thinking that an effective pamphleteer would necessarily also be an effective speaker in the House of Commons. The activity also produced two enduring writings in Gardiner's *De Vera Obedientia*, still a classic statement of Christian divine-right kingship, and Starkey's *Exhortation*, a much more original though less well finished piece of political theory.

How successful was all this propaganda? That, unfortunately, is a question to which no very precise answer can be given. We have no idea at all how widely the writings were distributed and no idea even of the number of copies printed. Like all propaganda, this was very perishable material.[2] The *Articles* must have been produced in hundreds, yet only two copies have survived. Gardiner handed around twelve copies of his book in Paris alone: of that printing, only three now exist altogether. Of Sampson's *Oratio*, of which a like number went to France at the same time, two are the sole survivors. The story is the same throughout, and rarity of present survival therefore proves nothing. Perhaps because it was partly the King's work, the *Glass of Truth* seems to have got the most concentrated promotion. We have noted Richard Croke's efforts to spread it at Oxford. As soon as it reached him in Italy, Nicholas Hawkins set to work to carry out instructions for the production of a Latin translation, to make the book usable in continental countries. He worked fast but offered one criticism: would it not be wiser, in a version intended for foreigners, to omit various scathing references to the 'unkindness and unnaturalness' of the English?[3] These passages, which lamented the nation's failure to take everything humbly at their King's hands, are as likely as any part of the book to have been Henry's handiwork, and if Goodrich's experience was typical Hawkins's humble suggestion will not have pleased. When

[1] Merriman, ii. 199.
[2] The following statements are based on the first edition of *STC*, but even if since that date a few more copies have turned up they do not affect the argument.
[3] *StP* vii. 389.

he had finished he was only partially satisfied.[1] He could have made a version in 'English or French Latin', but he thought the English version enough for the home market and understood there was to be a French vernacular translation. The Germans were already half persuaded of the truth. He had therefore addressed himself to the Italian taste in Latin which was particularly fastidious, so much so that they had difficulty in swallowing the Vulgate; he hoped this was all right.[2] This informed view on the different national uses of Latin in the sixteenth century is interesting, but what matters is that of all these intended translations no single copy is known to exist in print.

If we try to look for people's reactions, we find almost nothing said about any tract except the *Articles*. According to Croke, the *Glass* had by general consent 'done more to the preferment of the King's cause' than any books so far published or sermons preached; at Oxford it had, he swore, converted many of the most stubborn opponents.[3] But Croke, writing to Cromwell at Court, thought he knew who the author was. Oxford does, however, seem to have been unexpectedly convertible: at least Dr John London's young nephew Edward, a student there, claimed that his eyes were opened to the truth by the *Articles of the Council*.[4] Other reported reactions turned out to be more resistant to persuasion. Dan John Frances, a monk of Colchester, on 22 January 1534 reckoned that the *Articles* proved the King and his Council 'to be all heretics, whereas before, he said, they were but schismatics'. He admitted saying this, though he professed to have spoken generally, not against King and Council.[5] Friar Thomas Charnock was more judicious but no more impressed. He could not really believe that the King's Council was responsible for the *Articles*, 'because of the slenderness of the matter'. Interestingly enough, he supposed that if the government really wanted to put these ideas across and get them accepted, the document 'should be ratified by the next Parliament'; and he reckoned

[1] Ibid. 404.
[2] Hawkins had made some minor changes without authority, but he had marked them for the King's attention. He asked that Cranmer and Goodrich should insert quotations from the resolutions of General Councils since he lacked the books to verify the phrasing.
[3] Ellis, iii. II. 198.
[4] SP 6/6, fo. 6 (*LP* vii. 146), printed Janelle, *L'Angleterre*, 339–40.
[5] SP 1/82, fo. 151; SP 2/P, fos. 160–1 (*LP* vii. 140, 454). Frances had a rough tongue; he also said that when Henry went to Boulogne in 1532 'the Queen's grace followed his arse as the dog followeth his master's arse'. This is bowdlerised in *LP*.

that then 'the heads and doctors of all religious houses, and especially those that were nighest London, should be called to the Parliament House' to be instructed in the truths they were to preach. Since he expected to be one of the scholars so summoned, he had prepared a discourse proving that there could be 'but one principal head of the Church of God under whose obedience every Christian man ought to live', which discourse he intended to rehearse before King, Council, bishops and Commons 'and to all Christian people good and bad'. He was in trouble because this memorial had been found, so that he was suspected of preparing anti-government propaganda for printing abroad.[1] John Wayne, parson of Colchester, was accused of refusing in March 1534 to accept 'certain books of the King's print' (probably the Glass and the Articles) in which action he allegedly emulated a good many 'holy fathers of the spiritualty, as they call themselves'. When the informant brought him the books and asked him at least to read them before he condemned them, Wayne shouted, 'Hence, hence, away with them, they be naught, I say.'[2] About the same time the parishioners of Langham (Essex) complained of their questman, John Vigorouse, because he had tried to prevent them from reading certain books 'printed and openly sold' with the King's privilege.[3]

More exalted persons also do not seem to have been clear about their duty in this kind of business, as Lord Lisle's agent, John Hussey, discovered in an embarrassing scene with Cromwell. They were talking of Lisle's affairs when Cromwell suddenly whispered in Hussey's ear, 'yonder cometh a man whom my lord hath put out of wages, wherein he hath not done well'. Apparently Lisle had dismissed a member of the garrison at Calais for reading government publications. Hussey stammered some excuse, but Cromwell waved this aside and warned him:

Well, I would you advised my lord to meddle in no such light matters; for what is passed by books or otherwise by the King's privilege must be common, and it is lawful for every man to occupy them, and that all such books are set out in furtherance of the King's matters, in derogation of the pope and his laws.[4]

When even the deputy at Calais needed such instruction, the propaganda campaign clearly was both necessary and meeting much difficulty.

[1] SP 1/82, fo. 234 (LP vii. 259).   [2] SP 1/83, fo. 38 (LP vii. 406).
[3] E 36/120, fo. 59 (LP vii. 145).   [4] SP 3/5, fo. 93 (LP vii. 182).

It is likely that things improved as people got more used to these handouts and sponsored explanations. But there is certainly not much explicit evidence of success, though such pointers as Edward Hall's reaction to More's execution or John Foxe's dubious opinion of Becket indicate that among the well disposed the official versions took hold.[1] They certainly did so in the long run, for much of what was put about by Henry's pamphleteers became accepted opinion till the rise of revisionary historical studies in the nineteenth century, but it is probable that this sort of diffused success owed far more to the Marian reaction and Foxe's *Book of Martyrs* than to the *Glass of Truth* or *A Remedy for Sedition*. If one may offer a mere general impression, it would be that the campaign did reconcile most people to the justification of the Divorce without ever destroying Catherine's popularity or Anne's unpopularity; that it supplied much material to those who did the direct persuading on the issue of the supremacy and was successful there; that it made no impression abroad; and that it played its part, a part of modest significance, in creating that feeling of loyal obedience which so clearly marks the last years of Henry VIII. Gardiner's book greatly excited Protestants at Strassburg and in the Council of the Schmalkaldic League, but it is less certain that it pleased the French who had no reason to welcome its doctrine. Marshall vainly tried to convert some London Carthusians by presenting them with the formidable arguments of Marsiglio.[2] Such men, of course, were proof against persuasion. It may in general be supposed that so much effort, and especially so much money, would not have been spent without some evidence of profitable returns.

Perhaps the most effective form of printed propaganda is found not in the tracts but in the printed statutes which, embodying highly propagandist preambles, were on occasion distributed throughout the realm for public display.[3] However, like all propaganda campaigns by

[1] Hall regarded More very much as 'the jester', as the 1539 draft pamphlet did, and disliked him for it (Hall, 817); for Foxe and Becket, see *Acts and Monuments*, ii. 246–9.

[2] *LP* ix. 523. Mr Zeeveld has doubted the truth of the story (*Foundations*, 133, n. 14). He was mistaken, but not for the reason which I, equally mistaken, gave years ago (cf. *Econ. Hist. Rev.* 2nd Series, vi [1953], 65, n. 7). Not all the London Carthusians were executed in 1535, and Marshall was, of course, working on the survivors (twelve monks and six lay brothers); while the John Rochester mentioned was an inmate of that name, not John Fisher, bishop of Rochester.

[3] The Act of Appeals was ordered to be so published (*LP* vi. 1487) and others probably were, too, like the posters damaged at Coventry (above, p. 134). The propaganda

the printed word, this pioneer effort of Cromwell's is also less likely to have been immediately effective than direct addresses could be. The government knew this well enough: to them the pulpit mattered even more than the printing press, which latter may indeed in part be seen as playing the role of supplying the right kind of arguments to the preachers. It does not matter so much that we cannot tell how many men may have read the pamphlets when we find preachers proving by the contents of their sermons that they had done so. Although the actual organisation of the preaching campaign needs to be seen in connection with the general policy of sending instructions to the clergy which is discussed in the next chapter, it will be advisable to glance briefly here at the place which the pulpit occupied in the government's propaganda plans.

We have already seen how important sermons were both in conveying new notions to the people and in stirring up discontent, and it is therefore no wonder that the government made efforts to control the licensing of preachers. This duty lay really with the bishops who could license a man within their particular diocese, though in the past one bishop's licence had usually been accepted elsewhere. The Council meeting of 2 December 1533, which debated various means of propaganda, especially concerned itself with ways of securing the right kind of preaching, but on the assumption that the task would lie in the bishops' hands; four months later, Cranmer revoked all existing licenses and ordered new ones to be issued with instructions embodying the Council's resolutions.[1] There are signs that Cromwell tried to go further and to operate through royal licences with nation-wide effect, a device not always received with acclaim. Even in London, an obstreperous parson could refuse to lend his pulpit to a man carrying the King's licence, though he would have accepted the bishop's authority,[2] and we have seen how hard Latimer's band of preachers, all licensed by Cromwell, found it to get a hearing.[3] George Lazenby, a monk of Jervaulx, who was to die for a treasonable vision, in July 1535 caused a rumpus by interrupting a preacher 'having there the King's licence to preach'.[4] Richard Croke obtained a licence from Cromwell and

sermon preached at the Nun of Kent's recantation formed the basis of the preamble in the Act of Attainder and this must have been intended for wide consumption.
[1] *LP* vi. 1487; vii. 463.   [2] E 36/120, fo. 178 (*LP* xiii. I. 1492).
[3] Above, pp. 35–7.   [4] SP 1/94, fo. 25 (*LP* viii. 1025).

used it to preach in thirty-seven separate churches around Northamptonshire, Oxfordshire, Hertfordshire and Buckinghamshire, more than once at several of them. He proudly informed the lord privy seal of the highly loyal and satisfactory content of his sermons which incidentally illustrates the manner in which the arguments of the propagandist pamphlets could be disseminated further. Thus Croke emphasised the familiar points against the Petrine primacy and the edicts of the Council of Nicea which recur in several of the writings but would in this way become familiar to many who never read the *Glass of Truth* or *De Vera Obedientia.*[1]

Of course, episcopal licensing had not ceased. In July 1536 Bishop Longland had occasion to reprove the curate of All Hallows, Oxford, for preaching without his licence, and the rector of Lincoln College (owners of the appropriation) for permitting him to do so. This curate was 'neither graduate nor learned, neither yet student of divinity, but a man that hath forsaken his religion', that is, an escaped monk. He was told to do some serious work on theology before 'that ye take upon you to preach the Word of God', while the rector was told to see to it that he himself or some learned fellow of the College carried out the duty.[2] Longland was a conservative in religion, which explains his worry. Altogether, while there were bishops of his views Cromwell's administration could not leave the licensing of preachers entirely in their hands. Longland underlined this point in 1536 when he complained about one John Swynnerton, 'the preacher', whose frequent sermons were 'not fruitful but rather seditious'. Swynnerton was a radical who was upsetting the simple people – who 'leave their worldly labour and fall all day to reading of English books' – but Longland's real complaint was not this social disturbance (nor perhaps the robberies allegedly committed by Swynnerton's adherents) but the fact that he was preaching about doctrines which had not yet been officially decided one way or another, and discourse upon which had therefore for the present been inhibited. Yet Swynnerton held a King's licence, and the only way the bishop managed to prevent him from preaching at Woburn on Holy Rood day was by occupying the pulpit himself. On this occasion Cromwell seems to have thought that one of his men had

---

[1] SP 1/117, fo. 160 (*LP* xii. I. 757). A vicegerent's licence to preach was held by one Cardmaker from January 1536 (BM, Add. MS 48022, fos. 88r–v).

[2] SP 1/105, fos. 102–3 (*LP* xi. 136–7).

indeed overstepped the mark and authorised the bishop to apprehend him, but Swynnerton had vanished to London or Essex.[1] Another whose authority to control preachers could be awkward was Gardiner who in 1539 was complained of for protecting one Wigg whom Wriothesley suspected of disloyal preaching.[2]

Thus Cromwell did what he could by way of personal action to fill the pulpits with right voices. He by-passed Longland in January 1535 when he got Goodrich, bishop of Ely, to instruct a competent preacher at his manor of Somersham (Herts.), which happened to lie in the neighbouring diocese. Goodrich thought this very necessary in those parts, and the priest was ready to do whatever Cromwell commanded, 'so it be not contrary to Christ'.[3] Cromwell was anxious to know what was being said at the main centres, and Edward Leighton, who in 1534 preached in St Paul's Cathedral, was horrified to learn that the minister had received a very adverse report. He was sure he could clear himself.[4] From the point of view of propaganda, however, the only pulpit that really mattered was that at the Cross outside St Paul's, a location used regularly and for a long time before to deliver major statements of views, usually official.[5] Until the onset of the Reformation, Paul's Cross sermons were as a rule intended to declare some policy and were in measure supervised, but there was nothing like the control which Cromwell introduced. If he needed any inducement he received it in mid-1532 when one Father Robinson, of the Greenwich Observants, publicly declared his intention to preach there in refutation of an earlier sermon which had supported the Divorce.[6] It looks as though Cromwell acted upon the information and prevented the friar from using Paul's Cross to attack official policy, but evidently the filling of that pulpit was still far from well ordered.

Though in December 1533 the Council instructed the bishop of London to be careful about the preachers appointed,[7] the situation at the Cross remained confused throughout much of 1534. It was awkward when John Rudd, in March, mingled a dutiful condemnation of the

---

[1] SP 1/103, fos. 234v–5, 274 (LP x. 804, 850).
[2] SP 1/150, fo. 138 (LP xiv. I. 775).   [3] SP 1/89, fo. 71 (LP viii. 105).
[4] SP 1/85, fo. 61 (LP vii. 981).
[5] There is a useful list of sermons preached there in Millar Maclure, *The Paul Cross Sermons 1534–1642* (1958), 184–9. Despite some errors and misunderstandings, it forms the basis of what is said here. The explanations are my own.
[6] *LP* v. 1142.   [7] *LP* vi. 1487.

Nun of Kent with some uncalled-for comments on the false and slanderous stories spread about her, and Cromwell sent him to learn discretion with a spell in the Compter.[1] By May, Cranmer was trying his hand at the task of appointing preachers, but his nominee proved difficult to bring to the point.[2] However, throughout the important parliamentary session of November–December 1534 the government took over the pulpit; it seems that they put up a bishop every Sunday for six weeks to preach the royal supremacy, finally settled in that session.[3] But there were still difficulties, mainly caused by the jealousy of Bishop Stokesley who by rights should have been responsible for this most famous pulpit in his diocese and greatly resented interference from his metropolitan. Not that Stokesley wanted to use the Cross for anti-government propaganda: it was here that in July 1535 he preached the sermon which Cromwell wished to print but of which no written text existed.[4] All he asked was that he should not be shamed to his face by having to attend a sermon hostile to his theology. Thus he substituted Simon Matthew, whose recent sermon in the Cathedral had after all been printed by the government, to preach on 18 July 1535, in place of Friar John Hilsey, provincial of the Dominican Order, the government nominee, who he was sure meant to attack both bishops and purgatory. Let Hilsey preach the Sunday after when Stokesley would have left London.[5]

Cromwell took a rather characteristic revenge: on 20 October 1535, he granted a commission to Hilsey to license and silence preachers, and this included appointments to preach at Paul's Cross.[6] Hilsey was instrumental in arranging for the recalcitrant Carthusians to attend there every week from December 1535 onwards, in the hope that

[1] *LP* vii. 303. [2] Ibid. 616.
[3] Foxe, v. 68. [4] Above, p. 189.
[5] *LP* and Maclure between them have created some confusion here. Stokesley explained his position on 17 July 1535 (*LP* viii. 1054); he refused the pulpit to a provincial of friars whom *LP* needlessly identify as George Brown, the Austin friar. It is clear from *LP* vii. 1643 (undated, and for no reason placed in 1534) that the man in question was Hilsey. That the 'Mr Symons' of Stokesley's letter was Simon Matthew emerges from *LP* viii. 1043: on July 15th Bedyll explained to Cromwell that Mr Symon was prevented from forwarding the sermon he had preached earlier (i.e. the sermon in the Cathedral, preached on 27 June 1535 and later printed) because he now had to prepare a sermon to be preached at the Cross 'tomorrow' (really on the 18th).
[6] BM, Add. MS 48022, fos. 87–8. However, he continued to consult Stokesley, too: in July 1536 he asked the bishop for a list of suitable preachers for himself to choose 'a convenient mixture' from (*LP* xi. 186).

homiletic propaganda would achieve what Marshall's translation of Marsiglio had failed to do; and Hilsey, now bishop of Rochester, himself appeared as a preacher twice in early 1536.[1] We know the preachers for ten of the eleven Sundays between 23 January and 2 April 1536, and everyone of them was either a firm supporter of the government or, if more backward in his views, took care to preach conformably.[2] Among those honoured with an invitation were Cranmer, Longland, Tunstall, Shaxton, Latimer and Capon – bishops all. Clearly Hilsey proved a very successful programme secretary. Though thereafter the evidence gets more patchy, the policy evidently continued, even though zealous Protestants sometimes found the official preacher distinctly too conservative for their taste.[3] Perhaps this was the reason that in the autumn of 1537 Cromwell for a time decided to attend personally to the selection. There survive two form-letters of his, sent to Dr William Sandwich, dean of Canterbury College, Oxford, and Dr Matthew Parker, dean of Stoke-by-Clare, in which both were told that 'for the honest report of your learning in holy letters and incorrupt judgment in the same' the lord privy seal had appointed them to preach on August 19th and September 23rd respectively.[4] It would seem that, characteristically, Cromwell organised the business thoroughly: he first told a number of people that they were on a roster of preachers, so that they could prepare themselves, and in due course gave them the particular day on which they were to perform. Also characteristically, his form-letter included words of exhortation to do well with promises of favour which did not conceal the likely consequences if the preacher misbehaved.

Nevertheless, Hilsey remained his agent in this aspect of propaganda and himself occupied the pulpit at intervals. Things went well for a time, and Hilsey scored his last success when he chose Tunstall to preach the sermon of 30 March 1539 which was printed. The crisis of 1539 and the revival of the conservatives effectively destroyed Cromwell's control of Paul's Cross, though not, of course, the control of the government as

[1] *LP* ix. 989; Maclure, 185. [2] Ibid. 185–6.

[3] The sermon on 6 August 1536 displeased the censorious Marshall who, mistakenly, blamed Stokesley; that on 25 February 1537 struck an anonymous reporter as much too backward and legalistic (*LP* xi. 325; xii. I. 530). On the other hand Hilsey could cause annoyance to conservative hearers who on occasion railed against him at the Cross as a 'knave bishop and heretic' (SP 1/131, fo. 65 [*LP* xiii. I. 715]).

[4] Merriman, ii. 67–8; *Parker's Correspondence*, 5–6.

such. After the parliamentary session which enacted the Six Articles, Hilsey found that he could not get anyone to accept invitations to preach there except himself and his chaplains, and the man who preached on July 20th was promptly cited before Stokesley to answer for his sermon.[1] The bishop of London had clearly decided that his chance had come to revenge himself on his interloping brother of Rochester. Nor was Cromwell ever able to regain control of the pulpit which was to play an ironic part in his fall. For it was here that, in February–March 1540, Stephen Gardiner and the group of Protestants who were to be burned in July to satisfy the bishop of Winchester's ruffled feelings conducted those violent exchanges which undermined Henry's trust in his vicegerent's orthodoxy.[2] The break-up of the Cromwell administration, like so much else of the decade's doings, was publicised at Paul's Cross.

It might be a moot point whether Cromwell's interest in preaching, including his unmistakable favour to such as Latimer, reflects only a concern with the political function of the pulpit or also the characteristic attitude of the religious reformers with their passion for bringing the Word to the people. A possible answer may suggest itself when we have looked at the intensive campaign to get the right things said in the right place. Preaching was a form of propaganda: so much was recognised. At Paul's Cross one could attain direct control, but nothing like the same degree of supervision was possible in the rest of the realm, licences or no licences. Indeed, it was not certain whether the bishops could be trusted. Because of this dilemma, Cromwell had to incorporate the management of the pulpit in the general system for supervising the work of the clergy, and in the outcome the propagandist activities of the preachers became an aspect of the actual enforcement of the new order.

[1] *LP* xiv. I. 1297.
[2] Maclure, op. cit., 188–9; cf. Scarisbrick, *Henry VIII*, 381.

5

MEASURES AND PRESSURES

EARLY-TUDOR GOVERNMENT had several instruments at its disposal for bringing information and instruction to the nation at large. Among them, proclamations were the commonest, as they are the most familiar to historians; they could both announce some new situation and initiate some forms of administrative action. Proclamations, of course, were public, which could have its disadvantages; if one wanted to reach a large but selected number of people one used royal circular letters, by this time always letters sealed with the signet and signed with a stamp of the King's name. As Cromwell discovered, similar letters could be sent out by a minister of sufficient official standing; later these were replaced by Privy Council circulars, never used in the 1530's. A well tried method employed the King's judges on their circuits to make announcements at the Assizes where a fair part of the county's leaders could be expected to attend, but such exhortation would be useful only after the necessary details had become reasonably familiar. Lastly, the transfer of ecclesiastical authority to the Crown gave the government the opportunity of using the Church's established procedure of visitations, that is journeys of enquiry and investigation followed by corrective orders called injunctions. In the 1530's, Cromwell's administration used all these, but it did so in a fashion so much more systematic and intensive than had ever been used before that it transformed the traditional methods of a loosely hierarchic state into innovations suitable to a consolidated and dynamic state. In particular, it gave a great deal more weight to the most direct and most authoritative method, the circular letter, and rather less to proclamations. This government legislated by statute, and its proclamations were far more subordinated to parliamentary supremacy than had been the case before.[1] In addition to issuing some relevant proclamations properly so called, it also arranged for the proclaiming of the most important acts of

[1] See the table in *Hist. Journal*, viii (1965), 269. In the Cromwell era, some 40% of proclamations were statute-based, as against 9% of Henry VII's and about 19% in Wolsey's years.

Parliament themselves, but that is an aspect of its propaganda effort which had already been mentioned.[1]

I

Considering the extent of the changes promoted, the government was surprisingly sparing in its use of proclamations. Throughout the decade only nine were issued which in any way touched the great affairs of the day, and of that total four appeared before July 1533, before Cromwell's administration really got going.[2] The proclamation of that month, in fact, was the first to result from the revolution: following up Cranmer's sentence of divorce, it announced Catherine's new title of Princess Dowager (as widow to Prince Arthur) and reminded the nation of the penalties attached to the Act of Appeals.[3] Before that there had been three proclamations that need looking at here; their contents underline the changes that came over policy in 1532. In September 1530 the King prohibited the purchasing of papal bulls 'containing matter prejudicial to the high authority, jurisdiction and prerogative royal of this his said realm, or the let hindrance or impeachment of his grace's noble and virtuous intended purposes'.[4] The prohibition was expressly intended only for the protection of the recent reform legislation against papal interference, but since it tilted at a shadow there is little significance in the action.

More interest attaches to two proclamations against heretical books, issued early in 1530 and on June 22nd that year, which represent Lord Chancellor More's attempt to save the realm from heresy, the sum total of his contribution to government policy during his tenure of office.[5] In his opening speech to the Parliament of 1529, More had made

[1] Above, p. 210.
[2] *TRP* i, nos. 122 (misdated), 129, 130, 140, 155, 161, 168, 186, 188. No. 158 (discussed below, p. 238, n. 5) is a circular letter; nos. 145 and 192 are letters patent. Nos. 153 and 177, though relevant to the management of religious and ecclesiastical problems, seem to me of no concern to the problem of enforcement. No. 191 never got beyond the draft stage.
[3] *TRP* i. 209–11. [4] Ibid. 197–8.
[5] Ibid. 181–6, 193–7. The first of these is misdated 'before 6 March 1529' in *TRP*. As the headnote says, Foxe dated this proclamation into 1530, and (as the headnote does not say) William Rastell knew that More was responsible for it (Harpsfield, 223). The list of books includes several that either were in manuscript at the time or printed in now lost editions; but one of them, Tyndale's *Practice of Prelates*, was certainly not written

his intentions plain: he had announced his conviction that Wolsey's laxness had allowed dangerous new notions to spread in England and hinted at changes to come.[1] He meant to step up the campaign against heresy, but, Parliament and especially the Commons being unsympathetic, he resorted to prerogative action to construct a system for bringing offenders into the hands of the Church's machinery. The first proclamation denounced the spread of Lutheran heresy and commanded all men bearing authority right down to village constables to help prevent deviationist preaching and teaching. It imposed imprisonment for suspected heretics and ordered the sheriffs to assist the bishops in carrying out sentences against any found guilty. A general inquisitorial campaign, seeking out Lutherans and Lollards, was to be undertaken by the Council, the judges and the justices of the peace, but More demonstrated his tenderness for the liberties of the Church by subordinating all these activities to the penal power of the bishops. In fact, this proclamation created the nearest thing, the Elizabethan and early-Stuart High Commission possibly apart, to an Inquisition that England was ever to know. Lastly there was a list of books declared unlawful, which added an embryonic *Index Librorum Prohibitorum* to the embryo Inquisition. A few months later, a second proclamation filled in some gaps by adding more works to the proscribed list, urging further vigilance upon the authorities, and especially fulminating against English translations of the Bible which, 'having respect to the malignity of this present time, with the inclination of people to erroneous opinion', could lead only to a further disastrous increase in heresy. There was a promise added that an officially approved translation would appear as soon as the nation had eradicated all traces of heresy from within itself, but this small seed of future things (representing the King's partial disquiet with the repressors)[2] cannot, in the midst of so firm a restoration of the past, disguise or alter the proclamation's real purpose.

This policy of repression stood in line with that which some governments elsewhere found themselves adopting wherever the Reformation spread in despite of the temporal power. Charles V in the Netherlands

before late 1529, soon after Wolsey's fall (J. F. Mozley, *Tyndale* [1937], 167). The confusion has arisen from an elementary mistake: Pynson's warrant of payment for printing the proclamation was dated 5 March, 21 Henry VIII, which is 1530, not 1529 (*LP* v, p. 311).   [1] Hall, 764.

[2] Scarisbrick, *Henry VIII*, 253, who pays attention to only one sentence in this long proclamation and entirely omits the drastic earlier one.

and Francis I in France acted very similarly, in method and purpose. The policy has had little attention, partly because it was so soon to give way to a different one, but partly because it reflects upon Sir Thomas More's standing as a liberal intellectual. In fact, More meant what he said, and for some two years episcopal attacks on heresy, encouraged by the chancellor who alone of the officers named took the active part called for in the proclamation, certainly increased somewhat. It would be an error to suppose that these proclamations were simply connected with the King's campaign at Rome, perhaps as a proof of orthodoxy needed to make the conflict with the papacy seem respectable, though that is not to say that the King disapproved of them. In practice, the effect of these proclamations vanished with the policy that had inspired them; though never withdrawn, they also ceased to be regarded.

The one aspect which the contrary policy might have borrowed from these moves was also not regarded with much attention. The regime which presideed over the revolution from January 1533 onwards also faced the existence of books it disapproved of and indeed did its successful best to suppress opposition writings. But it avoided the construction of an *Index*, perhaps in the knowledge that this would only help to advertise the enemy. A proclamation of January 1536 ordered the surrender to Audley or Cromwell of any publication spread abroad 'in derogation and diminution of the dignity and authority royal of the King's majesty and his imperial crown'.[1] As the terms of the proclamation went, it gave the government all necessary powers over hostile products of the press, but the terms seem to have proved confusing. At least, Bishop Stokesley found them so, but then he had heard them only at second hand. On January 16th he told Cromwell that he would have sent 'my books of the canon law and schoolmen which favour much the bishop of Rome', but he had been credibly informed that Cromwell was interested only in Bishop Fisher's sermon against the Divorce (the only book mentioned by name in the proclamation) and recent writings supporting the pope 'against the opinions of the Germans and other'. 'I do not send them,' he wrote, 'until I know your further pleasure; which known otherwise, I shall forthwith send them and all other books that I have rather than keep one that peradventure (me unawares) does defend or maintain that intolerable and exorbitant

[1] *TRP* i, 235-7. Rather incongruously, papal indulgences and the activities of pardoners were attacked in an afterthought.

primacy.'[1] There is an air of subtly insolent virtue about this letter: no one at this point intended the confiscation of all pre-Reformation writings in support of the papacy. In November 1538, a major proclamation, marking a retreat from a reformed position and imposed on Cromwell rather than devised by him, again inveighed against dangerous books, but it too included no *Index*; instead it attempted to control the printing and sale of books.[2] Though at the time the endeavour proved overambitious, this was the beginning of an effective censorship, a policy continuously maintained, with varying success, till after the revolution of 1688. In fact, 'heretical' books, some of them promoted by Cromwell, were spreading fast in the 1530's,[3] and the censorship planned (by the King himself) in 1538 could not stop them because the machinery did not yet exist for enforcing it. More's system, had it endured, could easily have been more formidable.

For the rest, the Cromwell era used proclamations almost exclusively (so far as politics were concerned) to combat the extremer kinds of radical reform. Their presence always threatened the progress of the moderate reform which Cromwell favoured because it enabled conservatives to raise emotional resistance and especially because it was the one thing that Henry himself hated beyond measure. Thus, on 25 March 1535, foreign Anabaptists were expelled on pain of death if found in the realm twelve days after.[4] The same point was made more fiercely in the proclamation of 16 November 1538 just mentioned when the King promised death to those already arrested and told the remainder to get out fast.[5] There were, in fact, some burnings for heresy in consequence of this proclamation,[6] but the government soon showed that they were not of one mind on the issue. On 23 February 1539 another proclamation announced a general pardon for all such heretical offences before that date.[7] We shall see in due course what these contradictory actions meant.

[1] SP 1/89, fo. 32 (*LP* viii. 55; misplaced into 1535). Thomas Bedyll suggested a different purpose for this hunt after Fisher's writings: he delivered what he could find to Cranmer so that it might be used in answering Cochlaeus (*LP* viii. 1125).

[2] Below, p. 256.

[3] Cf. J. K. McConica, *English Humanists and Reformation Politics* (1965), ch. 6.

[4] *TRP* i. 227–8.   [5] Ibid. 272–3.

[6] Wriothesley, i. 90, mentions three, two in London and one in Colchester, all 'Dutch persons'.

[7] *TRP* i. 280. Thomas Broke, the Protestant burgess for Calais, who was in a good deal of trouble in 1539–40, at least managed to fight off some of his enemies by suing a pardon under this proclamation (SP 1/153, fo. 11 [*LP* xiv. II. 14]).

In any case, proclamations could serve only a very limited purpose for a government intent on enforcing a new policy in the realm; they could announce, order and threaten, but they could not secure coherent obedience, the more so because the question of their effectiveness remained wide open.[1] What was needed were measures to bring home to everybody where their duty – and convictions – now lay and then to follow up by pressures upon the instruments of authority to hold the nation to its new path. Immediately after the first steps had been taken which created the real schism, the government initiated the necessary moves. As usual, they employed methods which can be called traditional, but in so strikingly novel a fashion that the traditional veneer looks very thin. In the first place, it was decided to bind people with general oaths. Oaths of fealty and oaths of allegiance had long existed, of course, and formed useful precedents for this swearing-in of the realm, but the oath-taking of 1534 was really something new – the first employment, though certainly not the last, of a spiritual instrument of commitment as a political test. When Thomas More refused the oath of succession in April 1534 he opened a chapter in history which did not close until the abolition of the Test Act in 1828.

The first, and the most comprehensive oath emerged from the First Act of Succession, passed in the spring session of 1534 to secure the Boleyn marriage.[2] The act provided that all subjects of the Crown were to take an oath 'that they shall truly firmly and constantly, without fraud or guile, observe fulfil maintain defend and keep to their cunning wit and uttermost of their powers, the whole effect and contents of this present act'. There has been some confusion over the terms of the oath actually offered.[3] The failure to include it in the act itself was a piece of inefficiency, perhaps produced by inexperience, perhaps by pressure of time, or else a piece of sharp practice designed to smuggle through a more ominous oath than might have found favour in Parliament. But this second explanation is the one less probable, for by 30 March 1534,

---

[1] Cf. G. R. Elton, 'Henry VIII's Act of Proclamations,' *Eng. Hist. Rev.* lxxv (1960), 208–22.

[2] 25 Henry VIII, c. 22 (cf. Gee and Hardy, 232–43; for the oath see ibid. 242). This act was also proclaimed in order 'that the people may not make themselves ignorant thereof' (*LP* vii. 420), but the general exaction of an oath served that purpose more effectively.

[3] Cf. Hughes, *Reformation*, i. 270, n. 1: he alleges that 'what the oath declared exactly we do not know' and then goes on to show that we do.

when the Parliament was prorogued, the Crown presented the fully worked out form of the oath to members of both Houses who took it without question.[1] Then, however, the government ran into the legal ingenuity of Sir Thomas More who on April 13th, before commissioners at Lambeth, refused to swear.[2] Though he declared himself willing to swear to the succession, More maintained that he could not accept the oath as tendered 'without the jeoparding of my soul to perpetual damnation'.

What precisely did More object to? It is commonly said that he could not stomach the preamble to the act because it would have committed him to an anti-papal point of view. However, this notion came originally from Cranmer who thought that it might be possible to obtain obedience from More by allowing him to swear to the enactment only – a simple acceptance of the succession. The idea was turned down by the King.[3] It seems probable that Cranmer did not quite grasp More's objections, for More, who had been permitted some prolonged private study of the form of the oath and a copy of the act, apparently argued that the oath went beyond the demands of the act.[4] Yet since the act plainly states that an oath to 'its whole effects and contents' (which includes the preamble) was required, the point raised by Cranmer would not have satisfied More any more than Henry. In any case, the preamble has nothing very anti-papal to say: it merely charges the bishop of Rome with interfering in the jurisdiction 'given by God immediately to emperors, kings and princes',[5] and while this phrase might imply a wider denial of the papal supremacy it strictly leaves the foundations unattacked. Thus, if More had really objected only to the preamble he would have been neither correct in his legal objection to an oath which exceeded the provisions of the act, nor right in spirit about the jeopardy of his soul. But if the oath as offered to him included the clause

[1] *Lords' Journals*, i. 82.
[2] This famous scene was described by More himself in a letter to Margaret Roper (Rogers, 501–7).
[3] Merriman, i. 381. Cromwell reported that Henry explicitly insisted on the preamble.
[4] According to Roper, More told Margaret that the cause of his imprisonment was 'his refusing this oath not agreeable with the statute' (Roper, 240). More's letters did not make this plain; all the argument there turns on whether he could swear an oath of his own devising by which he would simply accept the succession as a fact. The notion that it was the preamble which stuck in his throat is Cranmer's alone; no word of More's supports it.
[5] Gee and Hardy, 233.

touching 'all other acts and statutes made in the present Parliament' which is in the form sworn by both Houses, More had a solid case. The present Parliament meant all sessions since November 1529, and such an oath would not only have demanded more than the statute authorised but also committed More to such statements of the royal supremacy as are enunciated in the Acts of Appeals and Dispensations.[1]

The point was taken. In the next session, the government remedied the defect of the First Act of Succession by an amending statute which recited the oath particularly and repeated the duty of all subjects to swear it, with further details about enforcement. But though it says that the tenor of the oath is the same as that taken by the Parliament, the dubious clause about the other acts is missing: takers of the oath are to swear only to the Act of Succession and other acts 'made in confirmation or for the execution of the same'.[2] We do not know when the offending words were removed from the oath, whether at once in April or only in November when Parliament reassembled. Something depends on this because without the words the oath in no way constituted a recognition of the royal supremacy; it really confined itself to an admission that statute can settle the Crown and that such matters must be determined in the realm. Since other oaths were applied throughout 1534 in which the supremacy was explicit, it may be conjectured as more probable that the succession oath did not include the offensive phrase about other legislation, once More had drawn attention to the implications. Very likely the government were content at this stage to bind the realm to the security of the succession only, confining the interest in the more formidable assertion to a selected number of people.[3]

At any rate, the oath was immediately and widely administered, and there are virtually no signs of opposition. The sort of sullen refusal displayed by the vicar of Ashlower[4] may have been met with more

---

[1] I here agree with Hughes, *Reformation*, i. 270, n. 1. There is no reason at all to think that the form of the oath offered to More differed from that registered in the *Lord's Journals* only a fortnight earlier.

[2] 26 Henry VIII, c. 2 (Gee and Hardy, 244–7). Possibly More might still have objected to the passage which bound the swearer to refuse 'faith truth and obedience...to any other within this realm, nor foreign authority and potentate', but since there is no word of pope or supremacy he would have had trouble raising a legal or conscientious objection.

[3] Hughes, *Reformation*, i. 271, confuses two different oaths when he includes the clergy's renunciation of the pope in the administration of the oath of succession.

[4] Above, p. 120.

frequently, but no evidence exists to say so. The commissioners at Lambeth, who failed with More, Fisher and also with Nicholas Wilson, got compliance from everybody else, including all the clergy of London.[1] Precisely a week later, on April 20th, the city followed suit,[2] after which commissions issued into the country. On May 5th, Gardiner reported the first stage of successful accomplishment in Hampshire where a large and mixed assembly of lay and clerical persons had 'very obediently' sworn as required.[3] By June 10th, the business was likewise discharged at Norwich where priests and monks had been dealt with earlier.[4] There was no trouble in Yorkshire, either.[5] How thoroughly the orders were carried out is shown by the exceptional survival of a commissioners' certificate for the village of Waldringfield in Suffolk where on May 18th three gentlemen presided over the administration of the oath to ninety-two people, though it is not absolutely certain that all the ninety-two were there to take it.[6] Bureaucratic inefficiency produced the occasional small difficulty. The Chancery seemed unaware that the cities of York and Hull and the wapentake of Ainstey were 'shires' of their own, apart from the Ridings and therefore requiring separate commissions;[7] while in Northamptonshire, Sir William Parr failed to receive some important government papers. The messenger who arrived there about May 1st had brought copies of proclamations and similar things for all Parr's neighbours but could find none directed to himself despite searching his satchel.[8] Parr had a copy of the Act of Succession and a 'copy of a commission under the King's broad seal' with the oath attached, but he lacked the order to proclaim the act, a matter of importance in the circumstances. Even so, he was making an unnecessary amount of fuss.

The government clearly made an all-out effort to swear all males

---

[1] Rogers, 503–4.   [2] SP 3/5, fo. 95 (*LP* vii. 522).

[3] *The Letters of Stephen Gardiner*, ed. J. A. Muller (1933), 56–7. Gardiner organised the business by getting a complete census of males over fourteen years of age; he wondered whether the King wished women to be sworn, too. It looks as though in the end the operation was confined to men.

[4] SP 1/88, fo. 170 (*LP* vii, App. 29).   [5] SP 1/88, fo. 166 (*LP* vii, App. 26).

[6] E 163/10, fo. 23. The names were written out beforehand; one gentleman, two clerks and nine others signed their names, thirty-four men made their mark, against one the word 'impotens' (sick) is written. My count differs from that of *LP*. Does this mean that the remaining forty-eight refused or were absent, or not even capable of making their mark? The last is the most probable, since the certificate claims to be a list of people sworn.   [7] *LP* vii, App. 23–5. Apparently this mistake had been made before.

[8] SP 1/83, fo. 21 (*LP* vii. 656).

in the realm to the oath of succession, as the act demanded. All that writing and sealing of commissions was a big enough task – at a time when a good many other things had to be done in the secretariats – but it was done. One hardly knows whether to be surprised or not to find that it was never repeated. The act of November 1534 which exemplified the oath clearly supposed that much oath-taking would still continue to occur in the future: after all, passing time would qualify more people for inclusion. It is hot about the intention that 'every subject should be bounden to take the same oath'. It speaks of further commissions and provides that certificates testifying to refusal shall have the force of indictments at law.[1] But so far as we know, no commissions ever again issued for this purpose, and after the summer of 1534 the oath of succession effectively departs from the story of events. The Second Act of Succession, necessitated by the fall of Anne Boleyn and the King's third marriage, also – naturally – provided for an oath (identical with that of 1534, except that for Anne we now read Jane) to be taken generally by all the King's subjects.[2] Yet the signs that anyone took notice or action are extraordinarily slight and dubious – nonexistent by comparison with the evidence for 1534.[3] The more selective oath of supremacy, ordained by another act of the same Parliament, very probably superseded the succession oath.[4] It would, of course, be rash to argue too categorically from the absence of evidence, but there can be no doubt that nothing like the formidable efforts of the first occasion was ever attempted again. And yet, in the theory of the oaths such events as the replacement of Anne and her issue by Jane and hers raised very large problems.

The facts indicate what the real purpose of the 1534 succession oath is likely to likely to have been. What Henry, and Cromwell, wanted was the country's sworn acceptance, not so much of the legitimacy of the issue to be expected from the Boleyn marriage, but rather of the major policy which that marriage symbolized – the political revolution and the religious schism. Unlike other oaths used, that to the succession applied to everyone and in effect worked to commit everyone to the

---

[1] Gee and Hardy, 246–7. [2] 28 Henry VIII, c. 7 (SR iii. 661–2).

[3] There survive copies of lists of people sworn to the 1536 act at two manors, taken apparently from the fly-leaf of an MS gospel (LP xi. 105), and the draft of the oath to be taken by future wardens and scholars of All Souls College, Oxford, which mentions allegiance to the heirs of the third marriage (ibid. 291). This latter, however, is not really an application of the 1536 statute. [4] Below, p. 229.

new order. More was quite right in practice: whatever the legal meaning of the oath, those who took it implicitly renounced the papal jurisdiction and supremacy, and they may well have done so the more readily because on the face of it no such drastic statement was required of them. That is to say, the government used the oath of succession in lieu of a universal oath of supremacy on the one dramatic occasion – at the start of the new order – when the nation's submission needed to be spectacularly registered. Those who saw clearly, with More, must have known what they were doing or refusing to do, but those who saw less clearly could readily agree to the parliamentary declaration concerning the inheritance of the crown without having to feel the full sense of the revolution that lay behind the statute. However, there were sectors of the nation in whose case such implications were not enough, men of whom because of their special place in society and between the contending parties a special and explicit recognition of the revolution was required. Thus even while people in general swore the oath of succession the government began to apply more drastic oaths to those whose adherence to a royal supreme head was necessarily most doubtful, the clergy and especially the regular clergy who when taking the vows had sworn particular allegiance to the pope. And of all the clergy, the bishops came first, since on their dutiful obedience depended the government's control over the clergy at large.

Thus, as soon as the spring session of 1534 had at long last clarified the situation, immediate steps were taken to make sure that the bishops would plainly abandon the pope and as plainly accept the King. Two men who achieved promotion in March–April 1534 Rowland Lee of Coventry and Lichfield, and Thomas Goodrich of Ely – both swore not only to be faithful and true to King Henry VIII and to maintain his imperial crown, but also to recognise him 'under Almighty God to be the chief and supreme head of the Church of England'. They acknowledged that they had received their bishoprics 'wholly and only of your gift' and promised to enforce the laws against 'the reservations and provisions of the bishop of Rome, called the pope'. Finally they swore to the Act of Succession.[1] This oath, which thereafter came to be

---

[1] Lee (Burnet, vi. 290–1) and Goodrich (SP 1/83, fos. 59–60 [*LP* vii. 427]) swore in identical terms; both documents are headed, 'this is the oath which every person elected or presented to any archbishopric or bishopric within this realm or in any other the King's dominions shall swear to the King's majesty'.

generally demanded of new bishops, left no loophole, even though it was not until the first half of 1535 that formal renunciations of the papal authority were obtained from all existing occupants of sees (including, incidentally, those already sworn in on the new terms).[1] Meanwhile the government turned its attention to the whole order of the clergy. It was clearly intended to secure from them some binding oath breaches of which could be made the basis for penal action, and though in the end the Treason Act of November 1534 superseded all other methods for maintaining the new order the oaths sworn now did occasionally play their part in the charges that began to fly about as opposition began to manifest itself.[2] But in tackling the clergy, the government made a distinction which, though probably in the main the result of administrative convenience, had certain deeper implications. They distinguished between the corporate clergy and the rest.

Between the middle of 1534 and early 1535, 168 separate institutions – abbeys, priories, hospitals, cathedral chapters and colleges (including those of the Universities) – set their seals and the signatures of their members to a long Latin declaration which marked their full, unreserved and individual acceptance of the royal supremacy in its complete form. The number does not exhaust that of all such bodies in the realm, but it is much more likely that some documents are lost than that anyone was left out.[3] The terms put before the signatories turned their assent into a corporal oath by which they swore obedience to King Henry second only to Christ. The oath of succession was included, but beyond that the document denounced the bishop of Rome who had usurped by his bulls the name of pope and arrogated supremacy to himself; he had no more power in England than any other foreign bishop. The signatories swore never to call the bishop of Rome pope or to pray for him by either name; to renounce obedience to the canon law in so far as it contravened the laws of God or Scripture, or the law of the realm; to preach the Word truly – 'catholice et orthodoxe'; and to

---

[1] Seventeen survive (*LP* viii. 190, 311, 494, 803). Cf. Foxe, v. 71.

[2] E.g. in the case of Dr Benger, below, p. 318.

[3] These declarations are printed by Rymer and calendared in *LP* vii. 665, 921, 1024, 1121, 1216, 1347, 1594; viii. 31. The text of the formula may be read in Rymer, *Foedera*, xiv. 495. Perhaps it was originally planned to involve only the friars (*LP* vii. 590), though that document could also be read as showing an intention to add the friars to the rest.

pray for the King as supreme head, for Queen Anne and for their issue. A comprehensive acceptance indeed, with nothing left out at all.

Much less, in form at least, was expected of the secular and parish clergy who, mostly deanery by deanery, signed only the plain declaration (no word of an oath) that 'the bishop of Rome has no greater power conferred on him by God in this realm than any other foreign bishop'. Again, we possess no complete lists of names, but again it is clear – so much does survive – that the signatures were collected generally.[1] The secular clergy were really asked to do no more than individually to agree with what the Convocations had already formally resolved on behalf of all the clergy of England, in March and May respectively,[2] but, of course, the government's action turned a mere resolution into a universal understanding. Yet it remains true that at this time no one exacted a sacramental adherence to the royal supremacy from the bulk of the clergy, but only from the regulars and similar bodies. After 31 July 1536, a formal oath of supremacy was demanded of all newly appointed office-holders, both spiritual and lay, as well as of all men who sued livery of their lands or accepted a Crown fee.[3] Presumably this selective oath was thereafter applied, but the only occasion on which it seems to have been used as a test seems to have been in 1537 when the King's venom against the London Carthusians achieved its final victory.[4] The realm as a whole was never sworn to the supremacy. In Henry's reign the concept of an oath as a political test was still both new and undeveloped. To the succession, everybody swore – but only on one of the several occasions when, thanks to the King's matrimonial history, it should have been required. To the supremacy no one swore explicitly before 1536 except the bishops and the corporate clergy, those that is whose influence in the Church and among the people was exceptionally important. The clergy in general were allowed to do no more than declare that the bishop of Rome had

---

[1] *LP* vii. 1025. The original declaration was, of course, in Latin. The only names to occur in both lists (full oath and brief renunciation) are those of the cathedral clergy of St David's and St Asaph. Anything could happen in Wales, and what seems to have happened here is that the Welsh commissioners preferred to make doubly sure.

[2] Gee and Hardy, 251–2. In the south four brave men voted against the motion, a fifth (still brave enough) expressed doubts. York was unanimous.

[3] 28 Henry VIII, c. 10, sects. 6–8. Some blank forms of this oath survive (*LP Add.* 914, placed too early).

[4] *LP* xii. I. 1233; BM, Add. MS 48022, fo. 95 v. That Henry and not Cromwell wished to continue the persecution of the Carthusians is shown in *StP* i. 459.

no authority over them, and to do so without the swearing of formal oaths. From 1536, office-holders and tenants in knight's service committed themselves by oath to the supremacy, but no one else. Oaths, then, were at this time used selectively and almost tentatively, partly no doubt because in the circumstances of the revolution universal applications caused endless labour and overwhelming practical problems, but also perhaps because by themselves oaths could not achieve very much. These dramatic weapons had their uses, of course; but it was the less dramatic instruments that got lasting results. While it was useful to have people solemnly aware of their new duty, it was more important to organise the pressures which would ensure that they did it.

2

By this time, few men with any sort of authority in the realm were not aware that the actions of the Crown called for further action from them. They knew that Henry VIII had broken with the pope and that support for the pope could no longer be permitted. However, what they actually could or should do to signify their loyalty was much less clear. As Sir Piers Edgecombe so rightly complained as early as May 1533, when one John Mayow was reported to him for seditious speech: 'My duty bends me to disclose it,' but he had 'no further authority in that behalf to take direction'.[1] It was not until after the parliamentary labours of 1534 had created the law of the new order – succession, supremacy, treason and all the rest – that Cromwell found the time, and had the foundations, for actual enforcement. He could well have supposed that before that time nothing existed sufficiently worked out to be enforced. In the summer of 1534 Cranmer instructed all bishops to preach about the justice of the Divorce and the pope's usurpation of power, but at that time, before the Act of Supremacy and the proclamation of the King's new title, nothing was said about instructing the people in the truths of the supremacy.[2] However, after the turn of 1535

[1] SP 1/76, fo. 74 (*LP* vi. 503). The date depends on the assumption that a letter addressed to Cromwell as merely 'of the Council' must predate his appointment to the secretary-ship. However, the appointment might well have been still unknown in Cornwall only a month or so after it had been made, and on the face of it the tone of the charge against Mayow makes 1533 a less likely date than 1534. Mayow was a trouble-maker: in November 1530 the attorney-general had sued him in the King's Bench for interrupting a right of way (KB 27/1080, Rex, rot. 9).

[2] Ellis, iii. II. 326.

things had changed, and from April Cromwell went into action. His preferred instrument now was the circular letter, a laborious and expensive device which, used as he used it, must have put a severe strain on the secretarial organisation, but which also better than any other method could mobilise the whole force of the state in support of the King's policy.

The series started with a signet letter under the King's stamp sent on 16 April 1535 to both lay and ecclesiastical authorities, a letter which effectively resolved the sort of doubts that Edgecombe had earlier expressed.[1] It conveyed the plainest of instructions. Various persons spiritual, both regular and secular, had continued to 'set forth and extol the jurisdiction and authority of the bishop of Rome...praying for him in the pulpit and making him a god'. The recipient was therefore ordered immediately to arrest any such seditious persons that he heard of and to keep them in ward without bail 'until upon your advertisement thereof unto us or our Council ye shall know our further pleasure in that behalf'. This order thus initiated such organised police system as Cromwell felt able to operate, and in essence it was effectively used through the rest of his administration, as his correspondence shows.[2] The people charged with the peace of the countryside and the enforcement of the law could confidently proceed to the catching of the disaffected and the imposing of conformity, and letter after letter, reporting the arrest of suspects and asking for Cromwell's 'further pleasure' testifies to the fact that the instructions were followed precisely. The essential purpose of the circular was not to punish but only to make potential offenders available, so that it would become possible to investigate each case and to deal with it on its merits.

In April 1535 Cromwell thus took care of the immediate problems posed by opposition; in June, in the most intensive period during his career that he devoted to the fastening of the new order on the realm, he turned to the more positive task of ensuring that the necessary propaganda and persuasion would be widely and regularly disseminated. He

---

[1] Two copies survive – those sent to the earl of Sussex (BM, Cleo. E. vi, fo. 217 [*LP* vii. 494: printed Burnet, vi. 110]) and Cranmer (BM, Harl. 6148, fo. 81 [*LP* viii. 623: copy in Cranmer's letter book]). They are identical in every way except for the form of address. The earl is properly called 'right trusty and well beloved cousin', but Cranmer apparently received one starting 'trusty and well beloved', quite improper for an archbishop. However, this form confirms that the letter went to J.P.s in general. While *LP* place one copy in 1534 and the other in 1535, the contents make plain that the second date is right.   [2] See below, ch. 8.

began with a letter to the bishops, sent out on the 3rd.[1] This ordered each diocesan to preach, every Sunday, not only the Word of God but also the King's new title of supreme head, and further to give instructions to do likewise to 'all manner abbots, priors, deans, archdeacons, priests, parsons, vicars, curates, and all other ecclesiastical persons' in his diocese. He was also to make sure that schoolmasters took care to teach the same doctrine. Lastly he was to ensure the removal of the pope from all religious services, by having the name (*papa*) erased whever it occurred in any 'mass books and other books used in the churches', so that it 'be nevermore (except to his contumely and reproach) remembered but perpetually suppressed and obscured', a consummation to be further achieved by leaving out in the general sentence read in church all articles which might tend to glorify the pope. These instructions were justified by reference to the formal recognition, by Parliament and both Convocations, of the King's new title, and the letter expressed regret that the bishop addressed had not, despite his earlier consent and subscription to the supremacy, done enough to get 'the foresaid truths ...imprinted and rooted in the hearts of the ignorant people'.

This circular represents the foundation of the whole positive policy of persuasion and coercion, and it was clearly received in that sense by the bishops who hurriedly wrote in to acknowledge receipt and promise action. Cranmer had it on the 4th, but rather surprisingly felt some unspecified doubts which unfortunately he sent by the mouth of the messenger.[2] On the same day, Shaxton, characteristically more definite, congratulated Cromwell on the tenor of the letter.[3] Old Robert Sherburne of Chichester replied, carefully, to both Henry and Cromwell on the 6th; his letters suggest strongly that Cromwell may have sent a covering letter of his own along with the official circular.[4] Patrolling the Welsh border at Gloucester, Rowland Lee acknowledged the instructions on the 7th; he promised at once to return to his diocese and to do what he had never done before – actually preach in person.[5] Tunstall in the far north received his copy at the hands of Sir Francis Bigod on the 9th but confined himself to the merest acknowledgment;

---

[1] This circular has not survived, but its date and purport are known from the replies of recipients and from a later circular to lay authorities (Ellis, iii. II. 324–6; *TRP* i. 230–1).

[2] *LP* viii. 820. This proves, usefully, that the archbishop had no hand in the letter. Cranmer's part in all the administrative activities of the decade is usually obscure and debatable.

[3] Ibid. 821.   [4] Ibid. 835–6.   [5] Ibid. 839.

Bigod also promised to keep an eye on Edward Lee of York who was always regarded as not totally reliable.[1] Lee himself wrote on the 14th directly to the King, his letter expressing in its length and tone the anxiety he felt at the opinion entertained of him.[2] He took the criticism of episcopal inactivity to be meant for himself personally and penitently recalled Cranmer's earlier orders. But he exculpated himself: he had followed the instructions to preach the fact of the pope's usurped power and the justice of the Divorce, and if he had not before this proclaimed the King's supremacy that was because at that time nothing had been said of it. He had always preached straightforwardly, sticking to the plain expounding of the gospel as had been demanded in the formula presented to the leading clergy in 1534.[3] He offered evidence that at least some of the things now enjoined had been done by stages, and he described the zeal with which he had at once carried the latest instructions into effect. Not until the 25th did Longland of Lincoln write to say that he had further received from Cromwell a form of declaration to be made from pulpits of which – since in his vast diocese he needed so many copies – he had had 2000 printed; he hoped it would be all right to use those.[4] Goodrich of Ely did not need to assure the minister of his loyalty, but he, too, acted. On June 27th, he communicated the gist of the King's orders to all his clergy and commanded them to inform their flocks: they were to say that the royal supremacy was true not only by their own knowledge but also because it was 'certified... from the mouth of mine ordinary, the bishop of Ely, under his seal'. Also, they were to expunge the pope's name from their books.[5]

It is only from Longland's letter that we learn an important fact: Cromwell went beyond sending mere instructions, however pressing, and took care to provide the right sort of material to be declaimed from the pulpit. Some evidence of the labours that went towards that

---

[1] Ibid. 849, 854.

[2] Ellis, iii. II. 324–32 (*LP* viii. 869).

[3] The insistence that all preaching should be a simple, truthful and orthodox exposition of the Scripture recurs time and again in these years. This strand in Cromwell's reform programme represents the humanist reaction against the allegorical and analogical artificialities of late-medieval preaching. Cf. J. W. Blench, *Preaching in England in the late Fifteenth and Sixteenth Centuries* (1964), ch. 1; Blench has missed the government's campaign in support of the radicals' preferred style.

[4] Ellis, iii. II. 335–6 (*LP* viii. 922).

[5] Ely Diocesan Records, G/1/7, fos. 125r–v. None of the few printed bishops' registers preserve such evidence, but more may exist in manuscript.

specimen sermon has survived. In fact, the paper that Longland sent to the printer may be the 'articles for priests unlearned' of which we possess a draft.[1] This political sermon, starting 'Ye shall understand that I am commanded by mine ordinary to declare unto you...specially two things', embodies all the instructions given to the bishops. The preacher would proclaim the King's supremacy in the Church, rest it upon the authority of 'the King's high court of Parliament' as well as 'of all the clergy of this his realm assembled in both the Convocations of the province of Canterbury and York', and support the case by citations both from the New Testament (*Rom.* xiii and I *Peter* ii) and the Old (a recital of the sovereign things that the kings of Judah and Israel had at various times done to their priests). But if this was the discourse which Longland received in mid-June, Cromwell was not satisfied that he had yet got the best possible version. He had help from some of the bishops who were eager to inform him of the thorough manner in which they were carrying out the instructions of the 3rd. Clerk of Bath and Wells sent a copy of the orders he had circulated to all the clergy of his diocese; but these were not very useful because they did no more than simply repeat precisely the details of the King's circular.[2] Edward Lee, on the other hand, composed a long set of articles which were to be declared from every pulpit, such as were able to do so being required to expound them further in their preaching, and he sent a copy to Cromwell.[3] His articles were much fuller than Clerk's and added matter to the contents of the King's letter, but the substance was the same. Lee took care to include scriptural passages in support of the authority of princes (much the same ones as in the draft sermon already noticed), to deny at large that papal authority rested on Scripture, and to incorporate the point from the *Little Treatise*, that only royal sufferance had in the past permitted the exercise of the pope's jurisdiction in England. Cromwell, it seems, was impressed. He had the articles copied out in a form capable of being revised and himself went over them, inserting the necessary phrases which turned Lee's third-

[1] SP 6/5, fos. 165–72 (*LP* viii. 294); printed with some slightly misleading comments in *Complaint and Reform in England 1436–1714*, ed. W. H. Dunham Jr. and S. Pargellis (1938), 130–4.

[2] SP 6/3, fos. 85–8 (*LP* viii. 293 [i]).

[3] SP 6/3, fos. 149–54; Ellis, iii. II. 337–42 (*LP* viii. 292 [i], 963). Lee made the point that he was trying to combine the recent instructions from the King and the previous instructions from Cranmer.

person structure into the address form required in a discourse from the pulpit. The hand that had drafted the articles for unlearned priests also made some alterations and added a long paragraph extolling Henry VIII and exhorting to obedience. The most significant new sentence stated 'that it is no less offence to deny the said title [of supreme head] to the King than to deny him to be King of England, which is high treason'. At the end Cromwell scrawled 'for priests unlearned', but we do not know whether this longish disquisition was ever distributed for that purpose.[1]

That such labours were necessary need not be doubted. It was one thing to issue an order, another to see it carried out. And with the best will in the world the bishops would have difficulties in getting the right things preached simply because they lacked the right men to do the preaching. As Lee explained when he forwarded his articles: he had to rest content with parish priests who were of sufficient moral standard, could read, and knew how to 'minister sacraments and sacramentals, observing the due form and rite', without asking for more. He knew of barely a dozen secular priests in his large diocese who could preach at all, plus a few friars and hardly a monk. So many of the benefices carried a starvation income that he had no hope of attracting more learned men. He did his best by instructions to those under his authority and by personal supervision, 'but you know I cannot be in all places'.[2] Nor could he always be sure of ready conformity among his clergy. Thus four parsons from the archdeaconry of Cleveland had reported themselves unable to make any such declaration as had been ordered, for fear of what their congregations would do to them.[3]

Though no doubt York and the north were both worse off for learned priests and more likely to produce recalcitrant clergy and troublemaking parishioners than the south, a similar picture existed elsewhere. The clergy of the early Reformation may not have been so deficient in general education or so insufficient for their charge as tradition supposed; but neither were the incumbents of most benefices

---

[1] SP 6/8, fos. 221–42 (*LP* viii. 292 [2]). The corrections made in this document do not appear in the last one cited, which gives us their proper order; a correction by the copying clerk on fo. 235 proves he had the other one before him. It is quite possible that the sermon, discussed above, which starts 'Ye shall understand', was composed after the work done on Lee's paper and represents a replacement of it. In that case we do not know what it was that Longland had printed.

[2] Ellis, iii. II. 338–40.   [3] Ibid. 342.

brought up to think of themselves as preachers.[1] That task had hitherto been left to specialists; parish clergy were supposed to conduct services and administer the sacraments of the Church. In addition, of course, there was resistance. One man's conscience drove him to confess his error spontaneously and to promise a better behaviour in the future.[2] Those less sensitive and those driven by their conscience in the opposite direction had to be sought out, corrected and punished. Robert Augustyn's offensive failure to preach as required has already been noted.[3] A monk of the Charterhouse at Sheen accused the vicar and prior (Henry Ball and Henry Man) of failure to read the renunciation of the papal supremacy and the confirmation of the King's every Sunday, as instructed – Ball telling the brethren in the chapter house, and Man attending to conversi and servants in the church; but since neither alleged delinquent suffered, the charge was very possibly malicious.[4] The villagers of Oxhill in Warwickshire took a while to wake up to their curate Thomas Burley's deficiencies; only when talking to people in other places did they discover that the new order was to have been proclaimed regularly from the pulpit. At Oxhill this had been done only once, when the bishop's instructions had first arrived. Nor had Burley erased the pope's name in the books, even though the rural dean had shown him how to do it at the beginning of the missal and ordered him to complete the job. Burley's excuse was that his master, the parson, after making the initial announcement, had taken the document away and would not suffer him to do his duty. When the investigating justices asked for the parson, he had made himself scarce.[5] In general, inadequate preaching by the standards of the new rules –

---

[1] For the revisionary discussion cf. P. Heath, *The English Parish Clergy on the Eve of the Reformation* (1969); Margaret Bowker, *The Secular Clergy in the Diocese of Lincoln 1495–1520* (1968).

[2] Oliver Bromley, curate of Exton (Som.) who in August 1535 admitted of his own volition to the vicar-general of Wells 'that he had not fulfilled my lord of Bath's commandment...in declaring of the usurped power of the bishop of Rome, ne had put out the name of the pope in the mass books'. So far he had believed that the deaths of Fisher and Reynolds for the papal supremacy must dictate his own behaviour, but now (under some pressure) he hoped to amend. His bishop thought him 'very lewd, fond and foolish' (SP 1/95, fos. 97. 107 [*LP* ix. 100, 109]).

[3] Above, p. 20.

[4] SP 1/93, fos. 209–10 (*LP* viii. 959). Ball, who had been involved with the Nun of Kent and had got a pardon, was on Cromwell's good side in 1535; Man was to become the second dean of the new see of Chester (Knowles, iii. 237, 392).

[5] SP 1/101, fo. 9 (*LP* x. 14).

both political bias, oldfashioned artificiality, and too frequent omission – occurs often in the charges against conservative priests.

As Burley's case shows, another offence was failure to erase the pope's name from the service books. Especially since adherents to the pope were more likely to retain a quasi-superstitious reverence they often felt extremely uneasy about the physical act of scratching out the word. The order to do so was one of the few which could be precisely applied, but for that very reason it remained a headache. Cromwell took it seriously: when the bishop of St Asaph on one occasion told him of a priest expelled from the diocese for disobedience in this respect, he insisted on knowing the name which was sent to him later.[1] The offence rarely occurred in isolation and was more commonly used to clinch a charge of disaffection than as the regular basis of any prosecution. Thus Christopher Michell, a Yorkshire parson, had attracted enquiry by incautious talk in consequence of which it was discovered that he had tried to evade the test by using wax to stick bits of paper over the offending word. In his subsequent indictment, nothing was said of this.[2] Thomas Corthop, of Harwich, had in fact attended a conference at Manningtree at which the assembled clergy were given their instructions, and in July 1535 had been warned by the bishop's inspectors; yet in the following January the pope still stood clear in his mass books.[3] One in Wales thought he had done well enough by putting a single stroke of the pen through *papa*, only to find his dean disagreeing with him.[4] The same dean, John Barlow, reported that William Norton, who offended in the same way and on top of that had a copy of Fisher's forbidden book, escaped indictment despite Cromwell's knowledge of the matter because he enjoyed the local protection of Lady Anne Berkeley.[5]

The reports continued over the years, but for a time nothing much was done to offenders.[6] Hilsey of Rochester found the books untouched

---

[1] SP 1/113, fo. 157 (*LP* xi. 1446).

[2] SP 1/94, fo. 18 (*LP* viii. 1020); KB 9/233/45. All this happened in early June 1535, almost immediately after Michell could have known of the order.

[3] SP 1/99, fos. 200–4 (*LP* ix. 1059).   [4] SP 1/104, fos. 207–8 (*LP* x. 1182).

[5] SP 1/111, fo. 62 (*LP* xi. 1041).

[6] Among those accused were Robert Brachie of Dymchurch, Kent (SP 1/106, fo. 161 [*LP* xi. 447]); Richard Jackson of Witnesham, Suffolk (SP 1/113, fo. 51 [*LP* xi. 1393]); a monk of Abingdon who called his brethren accursed when they started erasing (SP 1/129, fo. 50 [*LP* xiii. I. 275]); William Dyvers of Stoke Dry, Rutland (SP 1/132, fo. 45 [*LP* xiii. I. 938]); and a French priest in Essex (SP 1/152, fo. 79 [*LP* xiv. I. 1126]).

when he preached at Paul's Cray in Kent in May 1538; his investigation discovered a murky mess of accusations of treason flying about between the parson and the curate, but nothing happened.[1] At Croydon, un-corrected books were found in June 1538, a whole year after Cranmer had warned the incumbent to do his duty.[2] In the end it was decided to proceed more drastically against those who for years had refused to obey. James Thayne, a Northamptonshire chaplain, was indicted in the autumn of 1539 for merely covering the name with wax; he pleaded guilty and was sentenced to the penalties of *praemunire*, so that he must have been tried under the 1536 Act for Extinguishing the Bishop of Rome's Authority.[3] William Trevelyan, vicar of Kingsbury (Som.) was also indicted, in April 1540, for this offence, but in his case it looks as though the indictment was not pursued.[4] Evidently, isolated cases of this readily ascertained form of disobedience continued to occur all round the country.

Cromwell was well aware that issuing orders to the bishops, even if they hastened to demonstrate their own obedience, was not enough because the effort to enforce the Reformation was bound to take time and therefore needed continuous supervision. Six days after the letter to the bishops, on June 9th, another circular went out, this time to the lay officers, the sheriffs and justices of the peace. It was certainly a circular meant for the recipient's eyes only, though in London at least they seem to have posted it up publicly, an action which has caused considerable confusion.[5] Part of its purpose was to convey to the secular

[1] BM, Cleo. E. vi, fos. 265–6 (*LP* xiii. I. 987).

[2] *Cranmer's Letters*, 369–71 (*LP* xiii. I. 1171).

[3] KB 9/544/191; 27/1113, Rex, rot. 12.   [4] KB 9/544/43.

[5] One sample of this letter survives, addressed to the justices of Salisbury, dated, sealed with the signet, and signed with a stamp: SP 1/239, fos. 168–9 (*LP Add.* 990). A contemporary copy, probably from a letter-book, with one page missing, is in BM, Add. MS 32091, fos. 119–20. The document is printed in Foxe, v. 69–71, and *TRP* i. 229–32, both of whom call it a proclamation. This it was not: it was addressed 'trusty and well beloved' and had none of the marks of a proclamation, a fact disguised by *TRP*'s habit of leaving out the common-form parts of documents. The matter is put out of all doubt by a later document which describes this circular as being addressed to J.P.s (below, p. 241). The cause of the trouble would appear to be the printed copy in the possession of the Society of Antiquaries (accessible as no. 13 of their *Facsimiles of Tudor Proclamations*, 1897). But contrary to what is said in *TRP* i. 229, this was not printed by Berthelet (no printer's name appears at all), nor has it a year date, nor can I find the precept to sheriffs there mentioned. This printed copy recites the letter but adds, proclamation-fashion, 'God save the King'. It is headed 'Yet again by the King to the

authorities the information which had already gone out to the Church, namely that the pope's power had been extinguished in England and the King was now recognised as supreme head, but it is interesting to note that the laity were referred only to what had been done in Parliament: there is no mention of the Convocations. It then goes on to recite the gist of the letter to bishops, again for information. The real point of the circular comes in the next paragraph: recipients are charged 'upon pain of your allegiance' to make 'diligent search, wait and espial in any place in your sheriffwick whether the said bishop do truly, sincerely, and without all manner cloak, colour or dissimulation, execute and accomplish our will and commandment'. If they discover the bishop to be acting 'coldly' or using 'any manner sinister addition, wrong interpretation or painted colours', they are at once to inform the King and Council.

Thus Cromwell decided to set the sheriffs and justices as watchdogs over the bishops, and the important reversal of roles – the laicisation of the realm – could not have been more plainly demonstrated. The letter achieves solemnity by the sort of verbosity one expects in official communications; everything seems to be said three times. Yet two things are left starkly unambiguous: the new duty to watch over the bishops and to see that the ecclesiastical order does as it is told, and the mixture of flattery and ominous majesty applied to the officials themselves. The letter ends by assuring the addressee – each addressee – that

we, upon singular trust and assured confidence which we have in you, and for the special love and zeal which we suppose and think you bear toward us and the public and common weal, unity and tranquillity of this our realm, have especially elected and chosen you among so many for this purpose, and

Sheriffs'; a much later hand has written above this 'a proclamation for the abolishing of the usurped power of the pope' and added the year (27 H. 8) at the bottom. The printing is peculiar – very much worse in style and competence than Berthelet's standard way of setting up proclamations. But it is in effect identical with that of facsimile 11, the Oct. 1534 proclamation concerning butchers (*TRP* i. 218–19). Both have the same decoration, too: a crude woodcut of the royal coat of arms, which recurs nowhere else. No. 11 is stated to have been sent to the sheriffs of London. It therefore seems most likely that no. 13 (our circular) was put into print by these same officers (which explains the exasperated sound of the heading supplied) and proclaimed by them on their initiative, or by a misunderstanding, an explanation which also accounts for Foxe's conviction that the document was a royal proclamation. Although, in view of its contents, publicity must have seemed unfortunate, there is no sign that anything was done to the sheriffs for their misplaced zeal. The text in *TRP*, unlike the headnote, is satisfactory.

239

have reputed you such men as unto whose wisdom, discretion, truth and fidelity we might commit a matter of such great weight, moment and importance as whereupon the unity, rest and tranquillity of our realm doth consist and is established.[1]

But if these expectations were to be disappointed – if these wise and worthy men should turn out to be negligent and 'slack', 'or halt, stumble or wink' at any deficiency in the bishops' behaviour,

be ye assured that we like a prince of justice will so extremely correct and punish you for the same that all the world besides shall take by you example.

A proper discharge of the duty laid upon them would not only advance the honour and glory of God and 'set forth the majesty and imperial dignity of your sovereign lord' but also bring the greatest good to the commonwealth 'whereunto both by the laws of God, nature and man you be utterly obliged and bound'. There is no hypocrisy in these last words: Cromwell's whole policy looked towards that improvement of the commonwealth within the operation of the laws divine, natural and of England. At the same time, the reminder could no doubt serve to make a duty palatable which to some willing to brave the vague threats of the letter might seem distasteful.

The labours of Cromwell's writing clerks were, however, to be called for again before the month was out. No possible device was neglected for getting the new order advertised as quickly and as widely as possible, and round about June 20th Cromwell resolved to write 'special letters...to justices of assize throughout the realm, touching the unity of the people'.[2] Of these, sent on the 25th, there survive two copies.[3] The first part of the letter goes over the ground already covered: it recites once more the facts of the revolution, the consent of Parliament, the assent of the bishops both in their Convocations and by

[1] It is this passage in particular which makes the proclamation of the letter in London so extraordinary. *TRP* i. 232 renders 'stablished' as 'stabilized'.

[2] BM, Tit. B. i, fo. 475 (*LP* viii. 892). The date of this collection of 'remembrances' poses difficulties. The paper seems to have been drawn up before Fisher's execution on June 22nd and after Matthew's sermon on June 27th, which cannot be. Part of it are additions in Cromwell's hand. Most probably it was put together over a period of days.

[3] The copy in SP 1/93, fos. 168–71 (*LP* viii. 921 [1]) is addressed 'to our trusty and well beloved councillor', correctly for a judge. The other extant copy (BM, Cleo. E. vi, fos. 218–19), printed several times, is most conveniently found in Burnet, vi. 106–9. Both are signed with a stamp and have the dating clause added later, just before despatch, as was normal practice.

dint of their personal subscriptions, the orders issued to them, and the further orders (expressly stated to be to justices of the peace) by which the bishops had been put under surveillance. The justices of assize were being brought up to date in every detail. Therefore, 'considering the great good and furtherance that ye may do in these matters in the parts about you, and specially at your being at Assizes and Sessions', the addressees are instructed 'within the precinct of your commission and authority' to find out whether the bishops are doing their duty and to report any negligence discovered. All this is dressed up with a good deal of earnest urgency about the faithful service to be expected and the splendour of the cause to be served – 'setting before your eyes the mirror of truth, the glory of God, the right and dignity of your sovereign lord' (climactic or anti-climactic?), but in substance it simply adds the assize judges' labours to those of J.P.s. One new thing, however, they are to do: to declare to those assembled at the Sessions

the treasons traitorously committed against us and our laws by the late bishop of Rochester and Sir Thomas More...but also of divers others who lately have condignly suffered execution according to their demerits.

The interaction of propaganda and enforcement emerges very power-fully from these instructions, and it was a good move to have the King's judges, the guardians of the law, explain that the executions punished proven breaches of the law. There is subtle attention to fact in the dis-tinction between the late bishop (executed on the 22nd) and the yet living More, but since More was not even tried until July 1st, we have here another reminder that the age saw nothing improper in pre-judging a case – or, if one feels inclined to put it that way, that More's case was so well arranged that the conclusion could be called foregone.

This letter, too, ends with a mixture of commendation and threats, taken in abbreviated form from that sent on the 9th. Altogether, the King is made to address his judges in much less lush fashion than the generality of local officers, a sensible awareness of differences in the target. At any rate, the first task was now completed and the net strung over the realm: bishops active in proving themselves and moving their clergy, justices of the peace everywhere keeping an eye on the bishops, judges of assize adding their authority to that labour and also using their place on the bench to disseminate propaganda. Cromwell could justly suppose that in one short month he had, without the need for any new machinery and merely at the cost of the mass of paperwork involved, created a system which could render the revolutionary purposes of the King's government at the centre effective in every part of the realm. We need not doubt that the assize judges did as instructed, while some of the justices have left evidence to prove that the King's letters remained effective for quite a while. From Yorkshire, Sir Marmaduke Constable hastened virtually by return to report what the archbishop had done on receipt of the royal letters.[1] He confirmed Lee's own account in many particulars and should thus have reassured the government, though they were always likely to listen to Bigod who distrusted Lee. Actually, in Lee's case Cromwell applied the principle of the June 9th letter individually, asking Bigod to report at intervals what was going on – instructions received by Bigod together with the letter of June 3rd which he himself delivered to the archbishop.[2] It is ironic that in the end Bigod and not Lee turned out to be a traitor.[3] Most justices, of course, reported suspicions and allegations from their locality actively enough without specially referring to the letters received, but the two magistrates in Warwickshire who investigated Burley made the careful point that they were acting 'according to our duties and allegiance, and according to our sovereign lord the King's most dread letters to us and all other justices of the peace in that behalf directed'.[4] One cannot expect to find reports on the bishops' negligence since none of them was being particularly negligent. The fact that not all their clergy proved equally zealous was another matter, but it did not arise under those special instructions. It may be conjectured that some of the bishops at least behaved more diligently than they liked because they knew themselves observed.

Once Cromwell had discovered the great virtues of circular letters and the manner in which this occasional device of tradition could assist in the task of enforcement, he was not likely, being the man he was, to prove sparing in its use. Throughout the 1530's official circulars of varied purpose and importance continued to go out to remind people that they remained under authority, and a very active authority at that. Very occasionally the stream was broken by the boulder of a proclama-

[1] SP 1/93, fo. 245 (LP viii. 994).
[2] SP 1/94, fo. 42 (LP viii. 1033).
[3] For Bigod and his extraordinary career, cf. A. G. Dickens, *Lollards and Protestants in the Diocese of York* (1959), 53 ff.
[4] SP 1/101, fo. 9v. (LP x. 14). For Burley see above, p. 236.

tion, and on two occasions Cromwell varied the procedure by exploiting his ecclesiastical office of vicar-general and vicegerent. Nearly always he professed to be acting in the King's name, though twice at least he wrote in his own, but that the drive for this extremely vigorous activity (unknown before and much reduced thereafter) came from the minister both the documents and the probabilities make plain. One can speak with less assurance of the mind behind the developing policies. However, there are general signs that in the four years or so from mid-1535 Cromwell applied himself to the building of a new commonwealth on the basis of the consolidated polity which had been created in the revolution of 1533–1535. This is no place to discuss that general policy, though I hope one day to do so elsewhere. In many ways, the task of enforcement became much more difficult. The Divorce had called forth contempt and ribaldry, but no one really wished to die in order to save Queen Catherine from the title of Princess Dowager. The break with Rome had found a good deal of willing acceptance; unrelenting supporters of the pope were few, and the many who continued to adhere to him in relative silence or occasional furious outbursts were material for the treason law and the malice of their neighbours. But by 1535 policy began seriously to intrude upon large numbers who would readily keep out of politics. Changes in doctrine, changes in ceremonies, attacks on monasteries and purgatory and superstitions, the promotion of the English Bible, positive moves towards a better education for laity and clergy alike, the institution of parish registers – these and other manifestations of Cromwell's relentless reforming zeal brought real disturbance to the people at large. Never content merely to decree, always conscious of the need to apply and make real, Cromwell continued to bombard the country with exhortations to act.

3

The first thing that appeared to need attention was preaching. We have already seen that Cromwell involved himself in the licensing of preachers whose activities could make so much difference to the acceptance of the new order as well as to the general peace of the country. We have also seen how real the problem was becoming, as, in the wake of the revolution, representatives of both extremes in religion battled things out in the pulpit and caused uproar among the faithful.[1] Thus, in January 1536, the government undertook to deal with this confusion. On the 7th of the month, a royal letter went to all the bishops.[2] It complained that despite all attempts to provide better instruction and stop 'the temerity' of those who continued to defend the jurisdiction of Rome and those, on the other hand, who 'treat and dispute such matters as do rather engender a contrariety than either touch things necessary or apt to be spoken and declared to their audience', precisely these evils were continuing. 'There swarmeth abroad a number of indiscreet persons which, although they be furnished neither with wisdom, learning ne yet good judgment, are nevertheless authorised to preach and permitted to blow abroad their folly.' The King is made to express his ominous regret at the bishops' failure to 'stop the mouths of such as rather sow sedition than with wisdom travail to remove out of men's hearts such abuses as by false doctrine... have crept into the breasts of the same'. Considering

that it appertains especially to our office and vocation, unto whose order, cure and government it hath pleased Almighty God to commit this part of his flock to be ruled and conducted, to foresee and provide with all policy, counsel, wisdom and authority that the same, being educated, fed and nourished with wholesome and godly doctrine, and not seduced with filthy and corrupt abominations of the bishop of Rome or his disciples and adherents, ne yet by the setting forth of novelties and the continual inculcation of things not necessary brought and led to inquietness of mind and doubt of conscience, might have their instruction tempered with such mean and be taught with such discretion and judgment as little by little they might perceive the truth,

the King orders the bishops to call in and examine all licences, with an eye to removing unfit persons. The letter ends with the usual threats – dire consequences for those who fail to act.

There is a strong reformist air about the tone of this circular; especially, heavy stress is laid on the middle way, the 'mean' that was to charac-

[1] Above, pp. 13ff.
[2] SP 1/101, fos. 33–4 (*LP* x. 45). A draft (SP 6/2, art. 18) was misplaced into 1534 by *LP* vii. 750. The extant copy is addressed to the bishop of Llandaff and probably survives because it was never sent. The bishop, George de Athequa, was Catherine of Aragon's confessor and in personal attendance upon her in early 1536 (*LP* x, p. 51); besides, he had been effectively suspended by Cromwell's visitors in the previous November (*LP* ix. 806).

terise instruction. As if to remove any doubt who was really behind this move, Cromwell sent the circular enclosed in a covering letter of his own.[1] 'Ye shall herewith receive,' says the minister, 'the King's highness' letters...to put you in remembrance of his highness' travails and your duty.' He again urges the need for the middle way and expresses his confidence that the bishop will be eager to carry out the effect of the King's orders. However, 'forasmuch as it hath pleased his majesty to appoint and constitute me in the room and place of his supreme and principal minister in all matters that may touch anything his clergy and their doings', the vicegerent thinks it his duty to add his own exhortations to repress both 'novelties without wise and discreet qualification' and 'the temerity of those that...would advance the pretended authority of the bishop of Rome'. All this is mere repetition; the point of the letter comes at the end:

As I be not for my discharge both enforced to complain further and to declare [i.e. to the King] what I have now written unto you for that purpose,[2] and so to charge your own fault and to devise such remedy for the same as shall appertain – desiring your lordship to accept my meaning herein tending only an honest, friendly and Christian reformation for avoiding of further inconveniences – I write frankly, compelled and enforced thereunto both in respect of my private duty and otherwise for my discharge, forasmuch as it pleaseth his majesty to use me in the lieu of a councillor whose office is as an eye to the prince, to foresee and in time provide remedy for such abuses, enormities and inconveniences as might else, with a little sufferance, engender more evil in his public weal than could be after redubbed with much labour, study, diligence and travail.

The last phrase, one of the few occasions on which Cromwell recorded a view of the theory of government, has its wider importance for an understanding of the man, but 'I write frankly' is not a phrase that a

[1] Merriman, ii. 111–13; also Burnet, iv. 394–5. The fact that this letter, dated January 7th, was sent with the King's circular which is dated to the year, resolves Merriman's hesitation between 1536 and 1538, but in the direction opposite to his own choice. Of the two surviving copies (LP x. 46 and xiii. I. 40) one is an unused blank, the other meant for the bishop of Llandaff, presumably not sent for the reason stated in the previous note.

[2] Note the device, characteristic of Cromwell's circulars, by which the recipient is made to feel that he is being personally, perhaps solely, addressed. Whether one should take seriously the suggestion that the King knew nothing of this covering letter is more than I can tell.

reading of this letter brings to mind. However, whether the recipient bothered to unravel its complex sentences or not, he could not mistake the vicegerent's earnestness or the certainty that disobedience would bring retribution. The measured weight of the message stamped with the King's signature combines with the urgent and personal note of his minister's covering letter into a powerful instrument of persuasion and pressure; and the second manifestly saves the first from being treated as just another of those by now familiar general addresses.

No doubt all this took some effect, though the problem of diverse preaching continued. Cromwell fully realised that little of the desired restoration of conformable peace could be hoped for until more positive decisions on disputed points could be promulgated. Favourers of the pope could be dealt with by the law, but preachers of 'inconvenient' innovation needed to have the proper lines drawn for them. The task was put off for a few months while Parliament met, in February 1536, to pass (among other things) the Act for the Dissolution of the Lesser Monasteries. The summer of that year was therefore occupied with the organising of that dissolution, an activity which also, by the way, called forth a short circular letter. This, addressed to the heads of the houses affected, has unaccountably escaped the attention of all the historians of the Dissolution, though it well fits their feelings about Cromwell and his methods.[1] As the commissioners went into the country they carried with them individual signet letters, dated May 10th, which urged their intended victims to cooperate in every way in the accomplishing of the work decreed 'in this session of our High Court of Parliament'. The letter mentions the usual stick – obey 'as ye will answer to the contrary at your extreme peril' – but also an unusual carrot: obedience will enable us 'to judge you worthy to be otherwise advanced and in the mean season to deal the more liberally with you in the assignment of a convenient stipend for your honest sustentation'.

This, however, was the last circular for the moment. The definition of a suitable and agreed theological position required other methods which were promptly adopted. On 11 July 1536, the Convocations, with the King's active assistance,[2] agreed on a formulary of the faith known as the Ten Articles, 'devised by the King's highness' majesty to establish Christian quietness and unity among us and to avoid conten-

[1] SP 1/239, fo. 298 (LP Add. 1068).
[2] Scarisbrick, Henry VIII, 409–10.

tious opinion'.[1] They were intended to be the answer to the problem of the innovations so much deplored in January. As is well enough known, these Articles marked a clear advance towards a reformed position, especially in that they confined the sacraments to the three accepted by the Lutherans – baptism, penance and the eucharist – though they effectively endorsed the doctrine of transubstantiation without saying so explicitly.[2] They also initiated the campaign against superstitious attitudes to images, saints and various ceremonies. In all this, and also touching purgatory, they followed the adiaphoristic teaching of Starkey's *Exhortation* by retaining 'laudable' uses but removing magical elements and devotional abuses. They were printed and distributed, but they also needed enforcing, and this was done by the First Royal Injunctions for the Clergy, issued by Cromwell by virtue of his vicegerential office in August 1536.[3]

The Injunctions have always been treated simply as the general set of orders that they are, but if Cromwell's methods are to be fully understood it will be briefly necessary to consider their technical character. Injunctions are orders issued by bishops or other visitors at the conclusion of a visitation, to remedy defects discovered and promote reform. The Injunctions of August 1536, a product of Cromwell's formal office as the King's deputy in matters spiritual, were indeed technically justified – even made possible – by the fact that from September 1535 onwards Cromwell had been carrying out a general visitation of the Church of England. For lack of record, Cromwell's vicegerency has remained something of a mystery, but the discovery of the copy of a register kept by William Saye, principal registrar for ecclesiastical causes, now makes it possible to assert that the formal organisation of

---

[1] Printed Burnet, iv. 272–90. Discuss Hughes, *Reformation*, i. 349–52; Smith, *Henry VIII and the Reformation*, 365–7. For the date cf. Wriothesley, i. 55.

[2] I am aware that the *Bishops' Book* of 1537 (*The Godly and Pious Institution of a Christian Man*) marks a very modest drawing back from the advanced position of the Ten Articles. But, though temporarily licensed for study in 1538, the *Bishops' Book* never received authority from either King or Parliament or Convocation; it thus plays no part in the enforcement problem of a policy which it may have done something to confuse (cf. Smith, op. cit. 158–64, 386–90).

[3] Gee and Hardy, 269–74. The version printed by Burnet, iv. 308–13, mistakenly (allegedly in reliance on Bonner's register, but this sounds improbable) adds the paragraph concerning a Bible in English which belongs to the Second Injunctions of 1538. The headnote in Gee and Hardy ascribes a remark about 'the first act of pure supremacy' to the chronicler Wriothesley; it was in fact a footnote addition by the Victorian editor of the chronicle and is footling.

the vicegerential court, employing a special seal for causes ecclesiastical and probably presided over by Dr William Petre, lasted at least from 14 October 1535 to 2 February 1540. The office issued licences to restore some parts of their spiritual jurisdiction to the bishops, deans and others superseded in September 1535 by the general inhibition (a normal measure) when Cromwell first embarked on his visitation. It also produced licences to preach, to deprive a prior and instal a bishop, to celebrate a marriage although the banns had been called only once, to try a petition for divorce, and to take the oath of succession and obedience from the London Carthusians in May 1537.[1] Cromwell thus treated the vicegerency as he treated all his offices – actively and with the hand of a bureaucratic reformer. He used its powers, large and small,[2] and having held his visitation he very properly issued the necessary and customary Injunctions.[3]

[1] The vicegerency is discussed by S. E. Lehmberg, 'Supremacy and Vicegerency: a re-examination,' *Eng. Hist. Rev.* lxxxi (1966), 225–35; for Petre cf. F. E. Emmison, *Tudor Secretary* (1961), 324 n. 2. Some of Lehmberg's questions are answered by the new evidence which comes from BM, Add. MS 48022, fos. 83–96, a volume from the collection of Robert Beale, Elizabethan clerk of the Privy Council. It is not clear whether Beale copied all he found or only extracts from a register kept by William Saye (for whom cf. also *LP* xii. I. 1232–3). There is a draft citation before the vice-gerent's court (for probate) in Cromwell's papers (SP 1/162, fo. 96 [*LP* xv. 1029, 5]). Quite evidently the vicegerency was more formal, enduring and active than Lehmberg, or anyone else, had supposed.

[2] Lehmberg (op. cit. 233) supposed that Cromwell's purpose in inhibiting episcopal authority but quickly restoring most of it was to demonstrate the King's autocratic control of the Church which would always be waiting in case of need, and this is supported by the advice that Cromwell received from his canon-law experts (*LP* ix. 424). However, it now looks as though Cromwell meant the vicegerency to be both permanent and real, not only a threatening potential; in effect it was to replace the papal court in its relation to the two provinces of England. The powers restored by stages from about a month after the inhibition onwards (Lehmberg, 231–2) did not include powers of visitation which seem to have remained suspended while the vicegerency lasted; the purpose of a universal inhibition varied by partial concessions seems to have been both administrative (the best way to carve out the reserved powers of the vice-gerency) and financial (to extract compensation from the bishops, as Lehmberg shows). One other interesting point emerges from the new evidence: the office copied Chancery style in its documents, not the notarial practices of ecclesiastical secretariats and especially of Rome. It would be good to know whether this was also true of Wolsey legacy – possibly a pattern for Cromwell's vicegerency – but the evidence for that is even thinner.

[3] Though in general historians have treated the visitation as though it concerned only the regular clergy, it covered in fact the whole Church. Evidence that seculars were also visited survives at least from Wales (*LP* ix. 806; x. 215).

In this light, the Injunctions do not appear as 'a fundamentally secular document',[1] but rather as a deliberately ecclesiastical document embodying a programme of spiritual reform. That is to say, however unspiritual or sober their general tone may seem to us – and in this they do not differ from the usual episcopal injunctions – they intended to deliver a set of orders relevant to the spiritual improvement of the Church of England, the nation in its spiritual aspect. Their technical roots and form are assurance of this. They have been so often described and analysed that a lengthy discussion would be out of place here, though it should be noted that they did exactly what visitation injunctions usually did, only on a special scale. Thus the clergy's misbehaviour is corrected by orders to attend better to their duty to instruct the people in the Christian faith, to see to the education of the young, to make proper provision for the administration of the sacraments, to provide sufficient substitutes when licensed for non-residence, to avoid scandalous behaviour like tavern-haunting and the playing of dice or cards, to study Scripture, to distribute alms, and to maintain exhibitioners at the Universities according to their incomes, on a scale specified. In all this, there is not much originality, except that no one had so far found the opportunity to make an official programme of these familiarly 'Erasmian' reforms. Even more traditional is the injunction to repair the fabric of the buildings in their care. Naturally, in Cromwellian Injunctions issued in the year 1536, heavy stress was laid on maintaining the anti-papal legislation and the regular preaching of the royal supremacy – every Sunday for three weeks, and thereafter at least twice a quarter. And naturally also, the Injunctions enforce the doctrinal position recently defined. The clergy are to preach and expound the Ten Articles, to announce and observe the reduction in the number of holy days, and to conform to the new rules about prayers to saints and the use of ceremonies.

A solid, moderate and rather necessary reform programme, for the first time giving effect to the often expressed desire for an improvement in the moral and spiritual state of the people. Not everybody, therefore, received the Injunctions with joy.[2] One Thomas Jennings, a London

---

[1] A. G. Dickens, *Thomas Cromwell and the Reformation* (1959), 145. He also calls them 'a characteristic and mundane programme of decent practical reform'. That is true, but not quite enough.

[2] For other examples of resistance to both sets of Injunctions cf. pp. 250–1, 258–9.

rector, was unwise enough to speak 'contemptuous and abuse words against the Injunctions' in the hearing of twenty-two people.[1] In some places purgatory continued to be preached, contrary to the Injunctions. At Wimborne in Dorset, Edward Thorpe asserted 'non semel sed bis, ter, quarter' that the souls of men departed could be rescued from it by means of money, thus reaching back across the years to the first beginnings of the Reformation.[2] In Worcestershire, one Dr Smyth seems to have run amok in his prayers in the pulpit:

We shall pray for our sovereign lord the King, supreme head of the realm, and Lady Jane, late Queen, and for the archbishop of York, and for the bishop of Lincoln, and for our most holy father bishop of London, a founder of the faith of Christ, and for my lord of Evesham, and for my lord of Hailes, and for my lord of Winchcombe, and for my lord of Abingdon, and of the fourth part for all the souls that are departed out of this world abiding the mercy of God that lie in the pain of purgatory.

His inconvenient choice of notoriously conservative bishops and abbots to pray for will have compounded his offence in maintaining the existence of purgatory, but he got away to Oxford, out of the informant's jurisdiction, and vanishes.[3] Holy days caused confusion. In Bishop's Stortford (Herts.) the clergy kept Holy Rood day, contrary to the Injunctions, 'high and solemn, with ringing and singing', which provoked some anger among those who obeyed the order to work that day.[4] John Barrett, the parson of Monkston (Hants.), thought he could explain his error in celebrating St Mark's day (April 25th) which had been demoted because of its proximity to St George's day on the 23rd. After the celebration of this last he was going to do nothing about St Mark when one John Egge, 'a poor and simple person', told him that at Winchester the day had been ordered to be kept as a holy day and day of fast. 'Astonished and much more light of credence,' Barrett instructed his curate and chapel priests to follow suit, but it was a genuine error, not an arrogant flouting of the Injunctions.[5] One party in a Star Chamber action thought to help itself by accusing the defendants' village (Holfleet in Lincs.) of generally using 'papistical ceremonies and the usurped power of the bishop of Rome', not an impossible story from that part of the country, though such super-

[1] SP 1/113, fo. 110 (*LP* xi. 1425).   [2] SP 1/109, fo. 196 (*LP* xi. 876).
[3] SP 1/124, fo. 56 (*LP* xii. II. 534 [2]).   [4] SP 1/106, fo. 228 (*LP* xi. 514).
[5] SP 1/119, fos. 115–18 (*LP* xii. I. 1097).

imposed charges must always be treated with caution.[1] Nor need it be supposed that the Injunctions at one blow repaired the clergy's moral standards: John Divale will not have been the only one who continued to devote himself 'to dicing, carding, bowling and playing at the cross wafter'.[2] Since he called Scripture-reading heresy, his surname may have been highly suitable. Lancelot Pocock, a curate in Kent, used ale-houses and in fact slept there though he was welcome at the parsonage, but his really serious offence consisted in refusing to read out the Injunctions in church, a year and a half after he himself knew that they had been published.[3] Naturally, the Injunctions were no more than a start on the long road of reform and its enforcement, but they were a well considered start firmly based on a proper constitutional practice in a revolutionary situation. In this they fitted into the general methods of Cromwell's government; and they offered him yet another means for getting a message across.

Cromwell used his favourite device to follow them up. Late in 1536, the bishops received one further circular letter from the King, dated November 16th.[4] This started characteristically with a comprehensive reminder of all that had already been urged on them (they who had been made bishops for their good qualities and thus endowed 'with great revenues and possessions'!): the orders about moderate preaching and avoidance of contention, and the Ten Articles. The King had supposed – or so he was made to say – that after all that care taken no one would presume to disobey or be remiss, but from what he heard his 'labours, travail and desire therein is nevertheless defeated'. There is a lot of talk against the Articles and worse, and witness the recent insurrection. And so the bishops are given several specific orders. They are themselves to declare the Articles every holy day that they spend in their diocese. They shall personally travel the length and breadth of their diocese and every holy day preach plainly from a proper scriptural text as well as proclaim the supremacy. They are warned against privately uttering words of dissent and must send up for punishment anyone around them 'that will not better temper his tongue'. They shall once more instruct all their clergy in the proper reading of the Articles and the full exposition of the new teaching regarding super-

[1] St Ch 2/2, fos. 152–3. [2] For Divale see above, p. 25.
[3] *LP* xiii. I. 921.
[4] Burnet, iv. 396–9.

stition, and shall also once more review all licences to preach, including those issued by the Crown. Lastly – quite a new point which indicates that the government were beginning to be worried by the speed with which some people were adopting reformed ways – the bishops were secretly to search out any priests that had had the effrontery to marry, for the rumour went about that some had done so 'contrary to the custom of our Church of England',[1] and send offenders to be dealt with by the Council. There is a mild note of desperation about this letter, understandable enough in the situation created by the northern risings; what effect it had we do not know.

In any case, the cause of ordered reform, so well launched in 1536, now had to wait until internal peace was restored. Besides, the rebellion unquestionably caused some apprehension in high quarters that perhaps things had gone too fast and too far. For the rest of Cromwell's time, a closer control over public order became a major preoccupation. At the outbreak of the trouble, the government used a proclamation to impress on the realm the need to behave itself. The Lincolnshire rising had shown what could happen, and 'considering that there is nothing more odious to God nor more pernicious and hurtful to the commonwealth than the contempt and inobedience of people against their sovereign lord', the King adjures his loyal subjects to avoid rebellion, to stop spreading rumours, and not to assemble in any unlicensed gathering. He will punish disobedience by withdrawing his 'eye of mercy' and proceed against rebels with full force of war, destroying 'them, their wives and children, with fire and sword, to the most terrible example'. This excited document, which sounds like Henry's own composition, went out together with the King's *Answers to the Rebels* to restore the desired atmosphere of obedience.[2] A follow-up circular to justices, of October 20th, emphasised the urgency of the campaign against rumour-mongers.[3] In the south, at least, the policy worked. The rebellion did not spread, and by the spring of 1537 it was all over in the north, too.

[1] I.e. clerical marriage is here treated as forbidden not by the law of Scripture but only by the sort of local custom which adiaphoristic teaching regarded as alterable.

[2] *TRP* i. 244–5. Though in the form of a royal letter, this was proclaimed and intended to be. That it was sent out with the *Answers* emerges from Cromwell's letter to Audley of Nov. 11th (Merriman, i. 390: following *LP* vii. 1415, Merriman misdated this letter – endorsed as sent by Lord Cromwell! – into 1534).

[3] SP 1/240, fo. 146 (*LP Add.* 1117).

Yet evidently greater vigilance than ever seemed called for, a point only confirmed by such discoveries as the intended rising at Walsingham. Thus, on 3 April 1537, the Council agreed to send letters to all justices of the peace, 'to have vigilant regard to all the parts about them, specially for the apprehension of seditious persons',[1] and the resolution was carried out by means of a royal circular. In May, two justices in Cornwall and the mayor and corporation of Cambridge, reporting some actions, expressly referred to the recent letters received.[2] Since both these replies mention that the letter commanded the enforcement of acts of Parliament, it is very probable that the document in question survives now in an otherwise unidentified draft circular.[3] This urges the destruction of 'the privy maintainers of that papistical faction' and complains that too many people 'retain their old fond fantasies and superstitions, muttering in corners as they dare'. These are 'the most cankered and venomous worms...in our commonwealth, both for that they be apparent enemies to God and manifest traitors to us and our realm'. This language sounds more like Cromwell's than Henry's. Secondly, the justices are to be on the lookout for those who raise and spread rumours touching the King's honour and the interests and laws of the realm. The laws against vagabonds – especially the penal act of 1531, too often neglected – are to be strictly enforced in the interests of better security, and lastly, justices are to employ themselves more actively in the hearing and settling of private suits.

In fact, Cromwell seems now to have resolved to make such letters to justices an annual event. None survive, but that they went out is certain. In July 1538, Lord Sandys acknowledged receipt of an order touching the right execution of justice, the observation of the laws, and the performing of previously and repeatedly urged duties.[4] Twelve months later, in July 1539, yet another circular letter carrying similar exhortations went the rounds, seemingly in still stronger terms since two magistrates, who must have been getting used to these missives,

---

[1] *StP* i. 547.

[2] BM, Cotton App. L, fo. 75 (*LP* xii. I. 1127); C. H. Cooper, *Annals of Cambridge* (1842–52), i. 387 (*LP* xii. I. 1182).

[3] SP 1/166, fos. 81–6, placed for no reason at all into 1541 by *LP* xvi. 945.

[4] *LP* xiii. I. 1459. The year is confirmed by the place of despatch, Sandys's house of The Vine, Hants. In 1537 and 1539 he was at Guisnes. The same circular letter is alluded to in the further circular printed in Burnet, vi. 223.

thought the last one 'so fearful'.[1] The policy of regular reminders does, therefore, seem to have had some effect, to repay all the effort involved.

It was not until the autumn of 1538 that Cromwell felt free and secure enough to resume the work of pushing on with the reform. When, however, he once more turned to it he displayed more even than his accustomed energy. On September 5th he published a second set of Injunctions,[2] and a few weeks later, after they had been printed in sufficient quantity, he sent them to the bishops. The covering letter – that to Cranmer, dated September 30th, survives – explained that the Second Injunctions were made for the enforcement of the First and commanded their distribution to every beneficed priest.[3] The bishop could 'send, whereas they be printed, for as many more as will serve to give to every curate within that diocese'. The Second Injunctions, in fact, differ technically from the First in that they were not the product of a new visitation; they were meant to be the second half of the reform orders consequent upon the original visitation. Their contents, too, are well known enough. In every way they continued the policy of the First Injunctions; there is no sign at all that doubts about the progress of the Reformation had touched Cromwell, whatever may have been true of Henry VIII. Apart from again enjoining obedience to the orders of 1536 and adding specific detail to the earlier commands to teach the people the rudiments of the faith, to preach Scripture, and to war against superstitious ceremonies, they introduced two new points which became famous: the placing of an English Bible in every church, and the keeping of parish registers of baptisms, marriages and burials. The services of the Church were to be increasingly purged of the excesses of the past, and the Injunctions further promoted distinctly Protestant teaching on such topics as images and prayers to saints. Under the two sets of Injunctions, which parsons were ordered to read from the pulpit once every quarter, the Church had gone a long way to satisfy the demand for moderate reform and to achieve the shape which Cromwell evidently desired.

[1] SP 1/159, fo. 258 (*LP* xv. 633). The writers comment on trouble caused by the chief chanter of the late monastery church of Carlisle. Carlisle was dissolved in Jan. 1540 (*LP* xv. 44) which dates the letter to that year (May); it mentions the King's circular sent from Cobham the previous July, which therefore cannot be the one received by Sandys in July 1538.

[2] Best read in Gee and Hardy, 275–81 (taken from Cranmer's register). Merriman, ii. 151–5, prints the PRO copy which gives the date of promulgation. Discussed in Hughes, *Reformation*, i. 360–1.   [3] Merriman, ii. 156–7.

The main difference, however, between 1536 and 1538 concerns enforcement. Clearly, Cromwell had learned lessons; he now employed a much more intensive follow-up procedure. The bishops were encouraged to produce diocesan injunctions of their own, grounded upon the vicegerent's, to press the instructions as vigorously as possible upon their clergy. Cranmer issued a general mandate to the archdeacons of his province on October 11th;[1] he was also responsible for supplementary injunctions in the diocese of Hereford which, *sede vacante*, rested in his charge.[2] Archbishop Lee similarly produced a set of orders for his diocese which, true to his habit, was long and detailed.[3] Rowland Lee and Nicholas Shaxton did likewise for Lichfield and Salisbury; they used print, to simplify the task of distribution.[4] Very likely other bishops acted in the same fashion, and more such subsidiary injunctions may still be discovered in unprinted registers. Very much later, on 21 October 1541, Goodrich of Ely still thought it necessary to institute orders against the worship of relics and the offering of candles, described as being 'against the King's Injunctions'; he also wished to discover 'all those that doth not observe and keep the said Injunctions according to the meaning of the same'.[5] At long last, the bishops had been fully mobilised.

However, these Injunctions, with their Protestant hue, had barely been published when the King issued a major proclamation which quite clearly announced the existence of divided counsels or else a certain hedging of bets.[6] For the only time in this story of circulars and other instruments, the King's personal intervention appears in the record: the draft of part of the proclamation was substantially corrected by him.[7] On this occasion, therefore, Cromwell's influence was not even paramount, let alone unrivalled. That part of the proclamation which the King corrected was published in the form in which he left it, and his corrections are significant: they display his reluctance to go further in the direction of reform and also his characteristic leaning to

---

[1] D. Wilkins, *Concilia Magnae Britanniae* (1737), iii. 837.
[2] Burnet, iv. 392–3. Hereford was vacant from 8 May 1538, when Edward Foxe died, to Oct. 26th or rather Dec. 12th, the dates of Bonner's election and confirmation respectively.
[3] Ibid. vi. 199–205.   [4] Ibid. 206–15.
[5] Ely Diocesan Records, G/1/7, fos. 141r–v.
[6] *TRP* i. 270–6, 16 Nov. 1538.
[7] Printed from BM, Cleo. E. vi in Stype, *Memorials of Cranmer*, App., Doc. VIII (where the King's corrections are shown).

savagery.[1] The proclamation was manifestly designed to deal with a number of security problems conceived of as arising out of the relatively rapid advance of the Reformation. These were: 1. The import of English books from abroad, now forbidden except under royal licence. 2. Printing in England, from now on to be licensed by the Privy Council; and printers were ordered to add *ad imprimendum solum* if they claimed to be printing *cum privilegio regali*, the omission having been a device for suggesting that the contents carried the King's approval. 3. Bibles printed or imported, whose preface and notes must be approved by King or Council. 4. The sale of Bibles which was restricted to versions so approved.[2] 5. Anabaptists and sacramentaries, who with their helpers were to be executed or expelled (as already noted).[3] 6. The eucharist, discussion of which was forbidden. 7. Rites and ceremonies not abolished but now neglected because of the general attack on 'superstition'; these were to be strictly observed. 8. Clerical marriage, which is declared contrary to Scripture and the Fathers (no longer merely against the custom of the Church of England); married clergy are to be deprived and declared laymen. 9. False superstitions, the product of inadequate instruction, which the clergy are once more urged to do something about. 10. The erroneous regard for Thomas Becket as a martyr, denounced by means of a rewriting of history. The King's draft ends with number 8, which even in the finished proclamation begins with the word 'finally'; the last two items are introduced with a second and internal preamble.

Thus this proclamation falls into two parts. The original eight points amount to a repression of the reform: they institute a stricter censorship, hedge the English Bible about with severe reservations, insist on an unquestioning traditionalism on the central point of doctrinal dispute (the sacrament of the altar), retain a good many 'popish' practices and beliefs, and by disallowing the marriage of priests attack another hall-

---

[1] It was Henry who added 'wrong teaching and naughty printed books' to the 'sundry contentions and sinister opinions' of the preamble; who remembered that Anabaptists disputed not only about the eucharist but especially about baptism; who recognised the ambiguity of licensing books *cum privilegio* without explaining in full; who not only wished to stop Englishmen from adopting Anabaptist views but insisted on having converts to heresy sought out and reported; and who added the pedantic scriptural and patristic authorities to the passage touching clerical marriage.

[2] The possible effect of this paragraph was reversed, nearly a year later, by the issue of an order to printers which put the control of Bible production and sale solely in Cromwell's hands.

[3] Above, p. 221.

mark of reform. But the last two points, evidently added, work the other way: no. 9, though it adds nothing to what had several times been enjoined, somewhat neutralises point 7's respectful attitude towards the remaining ceremonies and breathes the spirit of Cromwell's Injunctions, while the last point fills a gap in the propagandist structure.[1] The restrictive main part bears the King's physical imprint; the part appended seems as clearly to come from Cromwell whose convictions and preoccupations it reflects. How those disparate pieces ever came to be joined together is a mystery, though one may conjecture disputes in the Council ending in a compromise: the main part of the proclamation represents a victory for the conservative faction, but the reformers managed to add a second part which, though harmless on the surface, would remind people that things had not changed right round again. But there is no doubt that the proclamation marks a retreat from the Second Injunctions and demonstrates the existence of a stream of opinion hostile to Cromwell. However, the reformers were not beaten

---

[1] Cromwell's revision of the Becket story makes an interesting example of his use and abuse of history. There are three relevant bits of evidence, in the main identical but with some small variations: the proclamation of Nov. 1538 (*TRP* i. 275–6), the circular of Dec. that year (Burnet, vi. 224–5), and the draft treatise of early 1539 (Collier, *Eccl. Hist.* 171–2). Becket, it seems, did not die in a quarrel with Henry II at all. He had indeed caused the King a lot of trouble by resisting 'wholesome laws established against the enormities of the clergy', but all that was in the past when Becket brought upon himself a death 'which they untruly call martyrdom'. The occasion of it was a quarrel over jurisdiction with his brother of York. In the course of it a servant of Becket's was quite properly arrested, but the archbishop attempted a rescue, an unlawful liberation of a person attached at the King's suit. This led to a riot in the course of which he gave 'opprobrious words' to a group of his opponents. One of them he called a bawd, another (Tracy) he took 'by the bosom and violently shook and plucked him in such manner that he had almost overthrown him to the pavement of the church'. Anxious to save Tracy, one of his companions struck at the archbishop, 'and so in the throng Becket was slain'. The story had in it just enough psychological truth about Becket and enough evasion as to inconvenient detail to make it perfectly credible; moreover, it would appear to derive from tales put out over the past century by Lollard heretics (J. F. Davis, 'Lollards, Reformers, and St Thomas of Canterbury,' *Univ. of Birmingham Hist. Journal*, ix [1963], 1–15). Mr Davis also accepts the tale that Henry and Cromwell organised a formal 'trial' of Becket, and he has persuaded others to believe it, too (e.g. F. Levy, *Tudor Historical Thought* [1967], 86). He spurns J. H. Pollen's argument that the alleged documents, first printed in Chrysostom Henriquez' *Phoenix Redivivus* (1626), 199–212, are spurious (*Month*, cxxxvii. 330–2). Pollen is assuredly right here: the summons and judgment are manifest forgeries and full of howlers. Since the proclamation of Nov. 1538 makes no reference to a judicial decision against Becket, I see no reason to think that any such trial ever took place.

yet. A mere three months later, on 26 February 1539, yet another proclamation appeared which not only pardoned the Anabaptists, as already mentioned, but also modified the worst anti-Reformation effects of its predecessor by explaining the proper practice with regard to the ceremonies retained.[1] All the explanations were designed to emphasise that ceremonies served only as aids to remembrance and edification, not as necessary means of salvation or aspects of sacerdotal magic: here surely the revising hand of Cranmer – and Cromwell – had been at work, and some recovery could be noted from the conservative victory of the previous November. Of course, the situation was to be once more reversed by the forthcoming session of Parliament and the Act of Six Articles.

These toings and froings did not assist a coherent policy of either reform or stand-still, nor did they help at all in the task of enforcement. Until November 1538, the government had always spoken with that one voice which at least left the local authorities, lay or spiritual, in no doubt what was expected of them. Now there could be confusion, a confusion accurately reflecting the divisions in the Council itself. And some there certainly was. Thomas Tyrrell, parson of Girlingham in Suffolk, refused to stop saying the service of Thomas Becket until he had specific instructions from his bishop, even though one of his parishioners, who before Christmas had heard the proclamation read at Bury, had told him all about it.[2] Since he still stood by his opinion in mid-January, he clearly had heard nothing from Bishop Rugge, but it was not, in fact, the bishop's job to confirm or enforce a proclamation which the parson should have obeyed without further orders. About the same time, Sir William Walgrave, also writing from darkest Suffolk, complained of the 'great heartburning' he had in promoting the Injunctions.[3] He was almost isolated and treated with suspicion by many who had inkling of the fact that 'all things shall be as it hath been'; unless Cromwell sent him particular orders he dared not meddle further. He especially resented old Lady Walgrave, 'my grandam', under whose protection a papistical chaplain preserved the Becket story unchanged, 'for all proclamations and injunctions'. Not that objections to the Injunctions were always of a high doctrinal kind. One feels some sympathy with a Warwickshire curate, Robert Mawde, who found the

[1] *TRP* i. 278–80.   [2] SP 1/142, fo. 62 (*LP* xiv. I. 76).
[3] SP 1/140, fo. 225 (*LP* xiii. II. 1179).

frequent reading aloud of them too tedious to bear. On 2 March 1539, he told his congregation that

this must needs be conned, for by God's bones I have read this out to you a hundred thousand times, and yet ye be never the better. And it is a matter that is as light to learn as a boy or a wench should learn a ballad or a song. And by God's flesh (he swore), here is a hundred words in these Injunctions where two would serve, for I know what it meaneth as well as they that made it. For lo, it cometh in like a rhyme, a jest, or a ballad.

He had a point, but he enjoyed his mockery altogether too well; and since his way of dealing with vagabonds included having them stay in his house two days long playing cards, he was not perhaps the most worthy of parsons, just an exceptionally unstuffy one. If he really added, 'A vengeance upon him that printed these Injunctions, for by God's bones there is never one in Westminster Hall that would read thus much for twenty nobles', he spoke truth but truth dangerous to his neck or at least his well-being.[1]

Evidently, then, the disputes were becoming public property and giving fresh heart to the enemies of reform: no wonder, since they so manifestly appeared in the government's own edicts. However, Cromwell was still in charge and took the steps that Walgrave desired. In the first place, in December 1538, he secured one more extraordinary (non-routine) circular to justices and other officers which went a long way to dispel the confusion.[2] In exceptionally strong terms, this recalled the orders issued on earlier occasions: to defend the supremacy, attack followers of the pope, seek out and punish rumour-mongers, and enforce the laws against vagabonds. Some, the letter says, have done their duty so well 'that our loving subjects have not been disquieted for a long season', but of late 'some ungracious, cankered and malicious persons' have stirred up trouble again. Especially some parsons have done their best to sabotage the Injunctions by 'hemming and hacking' the Word of God as well as the royal orders they read from the pulpit. Very likely many conservatives, forced to proclaim highly distasteful doctrine, had used such tactics of passive disobedience. These men, the letter goes on, have also suborned rumours concerning parish registers, putting it about that new exactions were intended. This is quite untrue: the real reason for the introduction of registers is 'for the avoiding of sundry

---

[1] SP 1/144, fo. 128 (*LP* xiv. I. 542).   [2] Burnet, vi. 223–7.

strifes, processes and contentions rising upon age, lineal descents, title of inheritance, legitimation of bastardy, and for knowledge whether any person is our subject or no'. An interesting explanation – even though. less candidly, 'also for sundry other causes' is added – which throws much light on aspects of Cromwell's social policy. But those priests had allegedly pretended that the newly intended payments were just what 'Becket of Canterbury, which they have tofore called St Thomas', died for. The letter therefore once more repeated the new version of the Becket story, correctly pointing out that Becket's quarrel with Henry II was never over taxes on the people but only to prevent the clergy from being tried in the courts of the realm. He was a traitor to his king and so to be proclaimed. The justices are therefore once again and without any ambiguity ordered to suppress all such sedition and to see all In-junctions, laws and proclamations ('as well touching the sacramentaries and Anabaptists as others') enforced to the full. The letter contains a last sentence not found in any other circular: recipients are to inform other justices in the shire and give them two copies of the letter. It there-fore appears that only one person in each shire received a copy from the government, a sign of the haste with which this circular was drawn up and despatched. Unable to make sure that everybody, as usual, got his orders, Cromwell was clearly acting at speed and for once in an unplanned situation. He was hurrying to save both the reform and himself.

Apart from getting the November proclamation modified in February, Cromwell took one more step to secure a proper cooperation with his policy, before the situation finally began to escape from his control. Some time in 1539 and probably quite late that year, he again circularised the bishops to remind them of the general reform that had been going on ever since 1535.[1] He recalled his visitation, his Injunc-tions, the various orders issued and letters sent, and complained that in spite of everything too many people continued 'in their old ignorance and blindness'. Speaking in the King's name but playing his own tune, he reiterated his demands for more diligent and urgent enforcement and

---

[1] Merriman, ii. 144–7. There dated June 1538 because *LP* xiii. I. 1304 placed this undated document in a collection of similarly deficient pieces after that month in the calendar. The conjecture is thoroughly improbable: the letter makes a special point of the English Bible and its availability in all churches and must, therefore, be later than the Second Injunctions. Most probably it was written as copies of the approved Bible became available, in Nov. 1539 (*StP* i. 589–90).

called for punishment for all clergy 'found negligent, remiss or stubborn'. Especially he stressed the King's interest in the English Bible, an interest which the previous November's proclamation had clearly shown to be Cromwell's rather than Henry's. The bishops were to make sure that it always lay open in their houses, and in their churches all incumbents were to make like provision, at their own costs.[1] And, recognising that mere injunctions to expound Scripture would serve little purpose in the light of so many priests' disabilities, Cromwell enclosed a form of address to be delivered in church. This stressed the King's goodness in giving people the very Word of God and his desire that they should read and receive it properly. They were to remember 'that all things contained in this book is the undoubted will, law and commandment of Almighty God, the only straight way to know the goodness and benefits of God towards us, and the true duty of every Christian man to serve him accordingly'. Men were to learn virtuous and pious behaviour from their reading and thus by their example to encourage their wives, children and servants 'to live well and Christianly according to the rule thereof'. If doubts or difficulties arose, they were not to give 'too much to your own minds, fantasies and opinion' nor argue about it 'in your open taverns and alehouses', but rather resort to 'such learned men as be or shall be authorized to preach and declare the same'. Thus they would prove to the King that they could use 'his most high benefit' in the right way – 'and God save the King'.

This exposition of Cromwell's belief in the Bible as an instrument of social peace and moral improvement constituted his last word to the nation he was trying, under King Henry, to lead into new ways. There were, it seems, to be no more circulars; at least none survives, not even in allusions. From April 1539 onwards, Cromwell's control of affairs became intermittently precarious, and from the end of the year he had his hands full with attempts to avoid the disaster that in the end overtook him. But he had in any case done enough in six years to bring home the facts of the new order to a country that was often reluctant and mostly slow to accept them; certainly, by late 1539 the arrival of yet another circular or commission or proclamation or public injunc-

---

[1] The Injunctions divided the expense of acquiring a copy equally between the parson and the parish, and this demand of Cromwell's may represent a recognition that the laity would never make the necessary contribution. On the other hand, it may be no more than an inaccuracy produced by compression.

tion had become one of the more familiar experiences of magistrates the nation over. It was by these means that Cromwell laboured to overcome the most serious difficulty facing Tudor governments, the difficulty of transforming central resolve into local action. His constant shoulder-charges, followed up by pressure on individuals found wanting, achieved more success than has often been supposed. As the two decades after his death were to show, the beginnings of the Reformation, religious as well as political, had taken partial but firm hold in England during his administration.[1] In this achievement, his policy of circulars, time and paper consuming though it was, played a very considerable, indeed an indispensable, part.

Circulars could urge action and conformity; they could and did stir the indifferent and the moderately backward. The problem of positive opposition and disaffection they could hardly touch. For that there existed the law – the law of treason – and its machinery; for that there was need of continuous police activity.

[1] Cf. A. G. Dickens, *The English Reformation* (1964), esp. 135 ff., 179 ff.

6

THE LAW OF TREASON

ON THE EVE of the Henrician Reformation, the law of treason was markedly less well developed than one might suppose.[1] Over a century of dynastic war, party violence, and the vigorous extermination of opponents had left strikingly little deposit in the law which was still essentially defined by the famous act of 1352, the first, and to this day the basic, treason statute.[2] Minor attempts to vary the law may here be ignored, and the only serious statutory alteration – the act of 1397 which omitted the demand for an 'overt deed' – was repealed in 1399. The reasons for what might at first sight seem a surprising reluctance to extend the grasp of the treason law are not obscure. For one thing, most of the so-called traitors of the later fifteenth century were men who had had the misfortune to fight on the losing side in a civil war. Their treason grew out of the see-saw of politics and was committed in open war. They were therefore commonly amenable (if not already killed in battle) to the summary procedure of treason trials under the law of arms and did not come within the purview of the law of England at all.[3] This method of dealing with the vanquished had one disadvantage: conviction by a constable's or marshal's court did not involve the forfeiture of lands.[4] The Crown therefore had recourse to the authority of the High Court of Parliament, and Acts of Attainder followed each turn of the wheel in the civil wars. Between them, the laws of chivalry and Acts of Attainder coped adequately with most of those whom law or policy wished to designate traitors. As for the few others who for one reason or another could not be dealt with under the law of arms – because they were not knights, or because their treasons had not been committed in open warfare – and who yet did not simply fall under the terms of the 1352 statute, they could be caught by judicial interpretation of the old act. Thus fifteenth-century judges could construe a good many things,

[1] J. G. Bellamy, *The Law of Treason in the Later Middle Ages* (1970).
[2] 25 Edward III, st. 5, c. 2, printed in *Select Documents of English Constitutional History 1307–1485*, ed. S. B. Chrimes and A. L. Brown (1961), 76–7.
[3] M. H. Keen, 'Treason Trials under the Law of Arms,' *TRHS* (1961), 85 ff.
[4] G. D. Squibb, *The High Court of Chivalry* (1959), 25.

including mere treasonable utterances, as constituting an overt deed within the meaning of the statute.[1]

The last man in England to be tried for treason under the law of arms was, apparently, John Tuchet Lord Audeley, the leader of the Cornish rising of 1497.[2] The earl of Warwick in 1499 and the duke of Buckingham in 1521 faced a bastard institution, a sort of invention, in the Court of the Lord Steward and were seemingly tried under a mixture of chivalric and common law.[3] This might do for great men, but even for them it was a method not well established in the law, doubtful during times of political upheaval when a nobleman's peers might not necessarily be reliable from the Crown's point of view, and of course useless against lesser men. Moreover, it added only a procedural variety: the law itself – the offence called treason – was not thereby enlarged. For all charged with treason not committed in open war, that remained as defined in 1352.

Edward's statute had laid down five specific treasons: to compass or imagine the death of the king, his consort, or his eldest son and heir; to violate the king's consort or his eldest daughter, being unmarried, or the consort of the king's heir; to levy war against the king in his realm or adhere to the king's enemies within the realm; to forge the king's great or privy seal, or counterfeit his coin; and to kill the chancellor, treasurer, or a justice of either Bench, of Eyre, of Assize, or of Oyer and Terminer, in the execution of their duties. Of these, the last two need not concern us here; the fourth was elaborated in 1536 to include forgery of the king's signet or sign manual,[4] an extension obviously demanded by administrative methods new since 1352, while the last did not occur or cause comment. But the first and third grounds might well be thought insufficient to deal with opposition arising out of Henry VIII's anti-papal policy. To object to the King's attacks on the liberties of the Church, or to quarrel with his matrimonial policy, could certainly amount to serious resistance and could cause great difficulties to the government; but it could not be brought under any definition of compassing the King's death or levying war upon him, unless opposition

---

[1] Bellamy, *Law of Treason*, 116 ff. It has been denied (e.g. W. S. Holdsworth, *History of English Law*, iii. 292–3) that the medieval law knew a doctrine of constructive treasons, but Bellamy has settled this question.

[2] L. W. Vernon Harcourt, *His Grace the Steward and Trial by Peers* (1907), 414 f.: the commission appointing a constable and marshal for the trial of Lord Audeley.

[3] Ibid. 429 ff.   [4] 27 Henry VIII, c. 2.

turned to violence and conspiracy – by which time it might be too late to act. True, the act of 1352 was expressly passed to define treason within the larger area of conflicting opinion as to what constituted the offence; by implication, it left the door wide open for other treasons at common law, and it is now widely held that in the fifteenth century it was not regarded as exhaustive.[1] But the sort of opposition or difficulty produced by the early stages of the Reformation was naturally neither in the minds of the makers of the statute, nor could it conceivably be interpreted into some residue of undefined treasons still left in existence by it. Even those most hostile to the activities of Henry's government will probably agree that the most deplorable thing of all would have been to encourage the judges to treat all attacks on the King as treason, irrespective of the law; and even they might agree that Henry VIII had reason to provide himself with protection against attack. In sum, no conscientious minister could hold that the law of treason, as it stood in 1530, would serve; and it is not at all surprising that from the first that law should have been drawn under review. For some three years the makers of government policy concerned themselves with the problem, until a new treason statute emerged in 1534, the first comprehensive statement since 1352.[2]

The first attempt to draft a new law was made towards the end of 1530, in preparation for the parliamentary session of January–March 1531: the draft mentions 6 March 1531 as the date on which certain treasons should become operative.[3] A pretty rough effort, it was put together by two scribes and left incomplete. It has no preamble or enacting clause; in fact, it is simply a list of new treasons. These are defined to include: (1) contemptuous withdrawal, after lawful summons

---

[1] This is denied by Bellamy, *Law of Treason*, 101. However, some of the judicial construction which he himself shows was applied to the act suggests strongly that a view of further treasons not in the statute continued to exist.

[2] The history of the 1534 statute was analysed by Isobel D. Thornley, 'The Treason Legislation of Henry VIII,' *TRHS* (1917), 87 ff. However, that article is mistaken in quite a few particulars, a fact which makes another detailed examination necessary here. Above all, Thornley was quite wrong in supposing that all the corrections on the various drafts were in the hand of Thomas Cromwell. The larger part is in that of Thomas Audley. While the two hands have certain similarities, the differences are clear enough; doubts may be set at rest by comparing Audley's draft of an additional clause (SP 1/65, fo. 95) with Cromwell's transcript of it (ibid. fo. 94).

[3] SP 1/65 fos. 87v–89 (A₁ in Thornley's numbering, minus the last folios which belong to her A₂).

to appear before the king, to any of the king's castles in England, Wales, Ireland or the town and marches of Berwick (Calais and its environs being added at a later stage), and forcible maintenance of resistance there; (2) contemptuous departure from the realm by any natural subject of the Crown ('of his own malice engendered in his heart against the king's highness'), and the taking of an oath to any foreign prince involving renunciation of native allegiance; (3) malicious activities on the part of any of the king's subjects living in another realm, designed to hinder or annoy the king, his ambassadors, messengers or servants in the execution of the king's business; (4) bringing into the realm 'any manner of writing or commandment brought from any outward parts which shall extend or be in dishonour or slander of the king's most royal person, or be to the damage or diminishing of his crown or majesty or jurisdiction royal'.

These four points are revealing: they are manifestly intended to prevent interference in one specific form of policy, namely the government's campaign to put pressure on the pope; they in no way extend treason to those great innovations – the King's new powers which, it is often asserted, were already part of the government programme at this time. At the very moment when this draft was being prepared, the Church was being got ready for the acceptance of that supposedly revolutionary description of the King as supreme head; and yet the planned additions to the treason law included nothing that would in any way assist in the revolution or protect anything resembling the royal supremacy as finally established. The contrast with the law actually passed in 1534 surely supports the view that the ultimate constitutional revolution was not at this time government policy.[1] In 1531, there was no thought to protect the King against attacks on any new titles or claims; the draft simply wishes to equip him with power against any who actively hamper the diplomacy and negotiations that filled the years down to 1532, and it further assisted by a last clause which provided that offences committed outside the realm 'where the king's writ runneth not' shall be tried by jury in any shire of the realm and according to the common law.

[1] Cf. my remarks on these stages in the political Reformation in *History* (1954), 221 ff. My views on this have been attacked by G. L. Harriss and P. H. Williams, 'A Revolution in Tudor History?,' *Past and Present*, 25 (1963), esp. 18 ff.; and cf. my reply, ibid. 29 (1964), 26 ff.

The draft bears a few corrections, all in the hand of Thomas Audley, speaker of the Parliament but also King's serjeant-at-law from 14 November 1531. It is perfectly obvious that this patchy and incomplete draft was never before the Parliament, a fact which together with Audley's appointment to the King's legal council, the professional drafters of government legislation, confirms what is in any case probable: the corrections were made not at this stage but a few months later when the attempt to draft a treason law was resumed. Audley crossed out the first clause, perhaps because (as Miss Thornley conjectured)[1] it really added nothing to the law: holding the King's castles against him would amount to levying war on him in the realm. However, refusal to obey a summons was not treason in the act of 1352, and it therefore causes no surprise to find the clause restored at the next stage. No journals of either House are extant for the session of 1531, and we cannot tell whether a treason bill was introduced at this time; the very primitive state of this surviving draft makes it very improbable. No one was yet ready to legislate on treason.

But the matter was not put by for long; Henry VIII himself soon signified his interest. At the beginning of the Michaelmas term 1531, Cromwell received instructions from the King 'to be declared...to his learned counsel and indelayedly to be put in execution', which included an order that the bill 'for augmentations of treasons' be got ready 'and engrossed' for the next session.[2] It was to include a new clause 'that the first accuser of any manner treason shall have his pardon and a certain sum for his labour, for the detection of any such treason'.[3] The drafting of the act now took on an air of energy and purpose. After Audley had briefly looked at the earlier effort and found it unsatisfactory, two different drafts were apparently made whose relationship to each other is not entirely clear since one of them contains corrections put into the other but also in some respects seems to come first. It is most probable that two people re-drew the bill on slightly different lines, and that Cromwell decided to use one of these versions but inserted into it certain verbal improvements taken from the other.[4] Each of these drafts

---

[1] *TRHS* (1917), 92.   [2] *StP* i. 381.

[3] This order proves that SP 1/65, fo. 89v, attached to the first draft in *LP* v. 52 (1) and so accepted by Thornley, really belongs to the second stage of drafting.

[4] These drafts are SP 1/243, fos. 149–50 (*LP Add.* 1480), which was unknown to Thornley; and SP 1/65, fos. 92–5 (Thornley's A₂). The difficulty of putting them in order arises from such facts as that the former looks to be earlier, e.g. because in the clause

started from the abortive version of 1530–1531 but added to it in different ways. In the one discarded by Cromwell, a new and rather odd offence was inserted after the reference to people who renounced their allegiance: it was also to be high treason if any natural-born subject of the Crown not only swore an oath to a foreign power but also were to 'consent or agree, privily or openly, to contribute or pay any sums of money to any foreign prince or other estate, contrary to the prerogative royal or in prejudice of the king's highness and this his realm'. Just what specific fear may have provoked this clause can only be guessed: perhaps it was thought that English merchants in the Netherlands might continue to pay dues to the emperor, even if Charles V took practical steps to assist his aunt. In this draft, the last clause, permitting trial in England of treasons committed abroad, was struck through, but this meant no more than the cancellation of the first clause in the very first draft of all. Both reappear in the version which Cromwell took over and corrected.

This version was clearly that used in the further preparation of the bill. It also contained a new idea: it was to be treason to flee the realm after proclamation had been made in a man's neighbourhood ordering him to appear before the king. This tightened up the attempt which runs right through this phase of policy towards treason, to make sure of disaffected men's persons. There is also the new clause, required by the King's orders, which offered a pardon and reward to any who would betray a treason; this shall be considered by itself in a moment. Cromwell's corrections in this draft, in so far as they do not amount simply to a borrowing of improved phrasing from the discarded parallel draft and to minor verbal amendments, are of some interest. The draftsman had spoken of proclamations 'under the king's great seal or under the king's privy seal': Cromwell, seemingly better aware of what would legalise a proclamation, crossed out the second alternative. In the clause dealing with unlicensed departure from the realm, Cromwell demonstrated his conviction that treason was an offence against the king only – that is, the state – by removing words which extended the malice implied to 'any nobleman of his realm'. On the other hand, he added 'or noble person' to the foreign princes to whom a traitor might transfer his

which contained a specific date (at this stage, 6 Feb. 1532) it has only 'from henceforth', as though at the time of writing the session in which it was to be introduced remained uncertain; on the other hand, some corrections made in the latter appear in the text of the former.

allegiance, an addition which shows a good understanding of the political map of Europe.

But the main drafting problem concerned the new clause, soliciting information from people themselves implicated in treason. As originally drawn, this offered total exoneration and a reward of £20 to anyone who, knowing that an offence had been committed which this act or the act of Edward III (the first reference to the 1352 statute) declared treason, should disclose it to the king, his chancellor, treasurer, keeper of the privy seal, steward or treasurer or controller of the Household, or to the chief justice of either Bench. This formula, clumsy in itself and not really useful because it would not help a man who had got involved in treason but later developed cold feet, clearly did not please, and Audley set about improving it. His draft, with many crossings out and interlineations, displays the difficulties he found in the task;[1] it got so messy that it was given to a clerk to copy fair before incorporation into the working draft.[2] As recast, the clause offered a full pardon and a quarter of all lands and goods forfeited by a traitor to any man who, being involved in treasons plotted or committed by more than one person, was the first to give information to the King or to any of his Council upon which convictions against the rest could be secured. This version Cromwell transcribed on to the working draft, with two significant alterations. He would not go so far as to deprive the King of a whole quarter of the profits from forfeiture, but since clearly the committee could not agree on what would constitute a sufficient inducement to an informer he crossed out 'twenty' and left for the moment undecided what actual sum should be offered. And where Audley had concluded his addition with a surprising phrase limiting the proposed act's duration to the time till the next Parliament, Cromwell, omitting this, signified his view that a new Treason Act should be a permanent addition to the law.

The committee had not yet finished with this draft, for Audley wrote in one more clause which would resolve one of the main uncertainties of the law. It provided that any convicted traitor should forfeit all property held to his use as well as what he had in possession. At common law, and under the act of 1352, a traitor forfeited only what he held or possessed in his own name, and this limitation was unquestionably one chief reason why the landed classes of the fifteenth century had so

[1] SP 1/65, fo. 89v.   [2] Ibid. fos. 90v–91.

enthusiastically practised enfeoffment to uses, the device by which the legal estate in land and other property was vested in a person different from him who enjoyed the benefits. On conviction at law such property remained untouched since, so far as the law was concerned, it did not belong to the traitor himself. These lands could be kept in the family, even if its head misjudged the course of politics. Hitherto the only way of getting round this trick had been by Act of Attainder, a parliamentary statute which, declaring a traitor's whole blood (family) 'corrupt' and incapable of holding land, confiscated also estates held to his use. Audley's clause abrogated the necessity for these clumsy and savage instruments; it would also in the future have made it easier to reverse such forfeitures because the King could then have restored the property to the heirs by letters patent without calling upon Parliament to repeal the attainder.[1]

The substance of the act seemed now ready, and the time had come to make another copy for further consideration.[2] In particular, the act required a preamble. That none had been in hand so far is proved by the interesting point that the preamble now devised did not lead straight into the first clause, as was customary in acts of Parliament, but ended by declaring that to offend 'in any of the articles underwritten' was to be treason; there then followed the heads as previously worked out. The drafters took the existing list of points and stuck a preamble in front of it.[3] This preamble, which Cromwell further revised extensively without, however, adding or deleting anything of substance, displays a conviction that points of propaganda cannot be too fully, clearly and firmly stated. It takes its start from the 1352 statute and demonstrates the government's awareness that what was proposed was part of the historical development of the law. Cromwell referred to the clause in the old act which, admitting that new treasons not yet thought of by man might later occur, provided that in such cases the judges should refer the case for decision to the king in his Parliament; he went on to

---

[1] The enabling act of 1523 (14 & 15 Henry VIII, c. 21: *SR* iii. 259), which authorised the King to repeal attainders by letters patent, extended only to attainders passed between 1484 and the end of the current Parliament.

[2] SP 2/Q, fos. 103–9 (Thornley's A₃).

[3] That this was at the time a not uncommon method of preparing statutes is shown by the survival of the form in some enacted legislation, e.g. the Act for the Court of Augmentations (27 Henry VIII, c. 27) and the 1543 Statute of Wales (34 & 35 Henry VIII, c. 26).

claim that 'the noblemen of this realm and the Commons in this present Parliament assembled' had come to the conclusion that the time was ripe to put this purpose into effect. There is some vigorous denunciation of the abominable consequences of treason, its danger to the King and to the peace of the realm; but this one would expect. More surprising, and somewhat revealing of Cromwell's principles in parliamentary management, is the pretence, in a statute which beyond all others concerned the Crown and represented an act of state, that the whole business sprang from the two Houses' recognition of a need and their determination to prove themselves 'as fervently disposed and as greatly affectionate' as their predecessors had been in 1352. Needless to say, there is no word of fervour or patriotic concern in Edward III's act which justified itself on the sober grounds that the confused law of treason needed clarifying. Henry VIII's Parliament was to be made to display its love and care even to the point where a Treason Act, of all things, was to appear as arising out of the unsolicited initiative of Lords and Commons.

The substance of the bill was also further corrected. Audley left his mark in only one place: he inserted the clause, new in the discarded draft at the second stage, which punished allegiance and financial support given to foreign powers. The fact that this clause had not been incorporated in Cromwell's working draft and was now resuscitated by Audley suggests that the discarded draft had been his; presumably he and Cromwell had begun work separately, for convenience' sake, but the minister had then taken charge of the joint labours. Cromwell himself made only minor verbal corrections at this stage, with one exception: he deleted the clause offering a reward to informers. The evidence is strong that the idea for this had come from Henry himself; at any rate, it was first mooted in the instructions which are expressly stated to have been given by him to Cromwell. We have seen that it proved far from easy to shape the idea into a practicable clause; Cromwell was clearly unhappy about the potential loss of profit – at this time he was busy trying to undo the effects of Wolsey's financial extravagance – while his colleagues, and especially Audley, seem to have held that only a truly substantial reward would work. It may also have seemed doubtful whether it would in practice be possible to distinguish between first and later betrayers of a plot, or even whether the safety of the informer in the courts could really be guaranteed. One may further conjecture some doubt in Cromwell's mind concerning the reactions of Parliament to a rather lavish Treason Act which, to top it all, virtually invited false accusations. The clause went out.

The act was now ready 'against the Parliament', as Henry had ordered; according to his request, it should also now have been engrossed, which (if the technical sense was implied) meant written out fair on parchment. The request surprises. For obvious reasons of economy and convenience, parliamentary bills were normally introduced on paper and not engrossed until they had been considered in the House which saw them first; yet the King's order plainly envisages engrossing before the Parliament assembled. There is at least a possibility that it was done, for round about 1533 Cromwell's archives contained two paper copies and one on parchment of a bill of treasons.[1] These could have been the two drafts for the 1532 session which have just been discussed, and the engrossed form demanded by the King. If so, the date of the archive entry supports the view that the bill was never in fact introduced; Miss Thornley's opinion that Parliament saw the bill and 'refused Henry the vote of confidence he demanded' rests on no evidence.[2] Of the surviving drafts only the last, which had a preamble and enacting clause, was remotely ready for Parliament, and even this shows in its largely verbal – and extensive – corrections that it was still in an unfinished stage of drafting. In the absence of a trace of evidence that the 1532 session of the Reformation Parliament considered a treason bill, we are not entitled to assume, with Miss Thornley, that the

[1] E 36/143, fos. 21, 21v (LP vi. 299).
[2] TRHS (1917), 100. Thornley treated all the surviving drafts as though they had been discussed and amended in Parliament. Quite apart from the internal evidence provided by the kind of corrections made, this is in itself highly improbable. The drafts have very large spaces between lines (i.e. are evidently prepared for major revision), whereas there is some evidence that when ready for Parliament bills were copied out fair without such spacing, as indeed one would expect (G. R. Elton, 'Parliamentary Drafts, 1529–40,' Bulletin Inst. Hist. Research, xxv [1952], 117 ff.: esp. 120 f.). Moreover, there is good reason to think that at any rate by the later sixteenth century, and by the laws of probability even before then, paper bills in Parliament were kept in the clerks' offices, so that the presence of these drafts in the State Papers supports the view that they were never before Parliament. Giving evidence before Select Committees in the early nineteenth century, certain officers of the House showed that they possessed papers, including early stages of bills, 'from the earliest times', though this may in practice have meant not earlier than the reign of Elizabeth; petitions were preserved from 1607. They suggested that those masses of paper might be otherwise disposed of, and their wish was granted in the fire which destroyed the old Houses of Parliament (H.C. Accounts and Papers, 1823, iv. 97–8; 1828, iv. 495–6; 1831–2, v. 266–7).

extant drafts, which on the face of them are very plainly pre-parliamentary, were seen and revised in either House. The probabilities are, overwhelmingly, that the government abandoned its intention to legislate for treason in this session.

Why? No doubt, the honest answer would be that we do not know. However, legitimate speculation yields some interesting results. In the first place, this was an extremely busy and rather difficult session when there was quite enough to do without adding a possibly controversial treason law to the boiling pot. The government had difficulty in getting the first Act of Annates through the Commons and entirely failed in its endeavour to legislate for uses and the King's feudal rights. At least the second half of the more than fourteen weeks of this session – there was a recess of about a fortnight over Easter – was preoccupied with the discussions and negotiations arising out of the Supplication against the Ordinaries.[1] And if time had been found for the treason bill, one may fairly enquire whether it would have been worth it. On closer inspection, this first attempt to bring the treason law up to date looks pretty pointless and inadequate. Some of its contents added only flourishes to the existing law; thus, holding the king's castles against him certainly amounted to levying war within the realm under the 1352 act, and transferring one's sworn allegiance to a foreign potentate could matter only if it was equal to adhering to the king's enemies. The proposals did a little to augment treason, but that to little purpose, when they included unlicensed departure from the realm: that was already an offence, probably felonious, at common law. Disobedience to proclamations which summoned a man to the king's presence was an existing crime for which this bill sharpened the penalties; and introducing foreign (papal) documents to the prejudice of the king's prerogative, already punishable with perpetual imprisonment and loss of movables under the law of *praemunire*,[2] could usefully be made worse by being called treason. The strange clause attacking those who hindered the king's ambassadors abroad, which no doubt seemed purposeful in the atmosphere of those years with their feverish negotiations and intrigues,

---

[1] Hall, 784 ff.; G. R. Elton, 'The Commons' Supplication against the Ordinaries,' *Eng. Hist. Rev.* lxvi (1951), 507 ff.; J. P. Cooper, 'The Supplication against the Ordinaries Reconsidered,' ibid. lxxii (1957), 616 ff.; M. J. Kelly, 'The Submission of the Clergy,' *TRHS* (1965), 97 ff., who argues that the history of the Supplication reveals less planning and more confusion, and consequently even more demands on ministers' time, than I have supposed.   [2] Thornley, *TRHS* (1917), 93 f.

never even after all improvements looked particularly sensible or clear; it would have been a crime singularly hard to prove and a law singularly difficult to enforce. The bulk of this bill therefore either tinkered with detail or made rather impracticable new provisions. In fact, the first treasons bill of Henry VIII's reign was not a very good one, and this was so because it had got off to a poor start. It rested on no coherent principle but from first to last presented something of a collection of ideas, almost as they might have come into someone's head casually and in the passage of time. It may not be without meaning that this form was determined for it before Cromwell arrived in full power, that the King himself seems to have been a main mover behind it, and that in the end it was abandoned despite the firm intention, a few months earlier, to put it before the Parliament.

If anything had been required to demonstrate the bill's insufficiency, the events of 1533 would have done so. In January, the Act against Appeals to Rome radically altered both the constitutional doctrine on which policy proceeded and the terms of the conflict with the papacy; in April, the matrimonial issue, from which so much had sprung, was settled, as far as the law was concerned, by Cranmer's judgment at Dunstable. A war had now been declared in which the existing weapons of the law were at best doubtfully adequate. Proof of this was not long in coming. By the summer of 1533, the government had cause to worry about the activities and influence of that deluded prophetess, Elizabeth Barton, the Nun of Kent,[1] and by September she had been arrested. From Henry's and Cromwell's point of view, the offences of the Nun and her supporters were manifest: she had declaimed against the second marriage, incited people to opposition, and threatened the King with imminent death at God's hands if he did not desist. But none of this was treason in the law; though the Nun might be prosecuted as a seditious person and punished, perhaps, by public exposure and recantation, she could not be successfully tried for treason. Though Henry pressed for a treason trial and Cromwell, under his instruction, made a note that he was to draw indictments 'for the offenders in treason and misprision concerning the Nun of Canterbury', the judges took the line that no such offences had been committed.[2] Since, apparently, they

[1] Cf., e.g., Knowles, iii. 182 ff.
[2] *LP* vi. 1445; vii. 48. These memoranda should be dated a little earlier than the date of January 1534 assigned by *LP*.

refused to follow the precedents for a generous interpretation of the 1352 statute, no more was heard of any process at common law.

One need not be an unthinking admirer of Henry VIII to agree that the lesser penalties would hardly have sufficed to remove the threat to obedience, harmony and public order which the Nun's activities had constituted. In any case, the King and his minister were not men of gentle kindness. They were riding a revolution and they needed drastic instruments of repression. The case of Elizabeth Barton proved that the only such instrument which they possessed lay in the very dubious expedient of an Act of Attainder in lieu of trial. This was duly employed against the Nun and five of her followers,[1] and the act provided an opportunity, taken with both hands, to publicise her offences and sterilise them by every device of denigration and propaganda.[2] But the method had grave drawbacks. It was certainly cumbersome and wasteful of time. It also lacked that air of legality which was so important to sixteenth-century opinion and usually so marked in the activities of Cromwell's administration. Assuredly, the Parliament could, as it did, recite the Nun's doings and enact that she and others 'for their several offences above rehearsed...shall be convict and attainted of high treason, and shall suffer such execution and pains of death as in cases of high treason hath been accustomed'. Given the power of statute, this was legally valid, nor (despite contemporary and later statements) was an attainder without previous trial something new in 1534.[3] But it was not good propaganda and an uneasy method at best. It amounted to the retrospective condemnation of offences hardly established at the time of their commission, and it embodied the highly unsatisfactory principle of sentence without trial or 'due process of law'. As a method it was not only unhappy but also unwise, and (it seems to me) instinctively repugnant to the whole cast of mind brought to the business of government by all the main actors involved, with the possible exception of the King.

At any rate, that Cromwell, now in charge of affairs, felt the need for proper legal provisions, the events of 1534 demonstrated to the full. By late 1533 he had again begun to reconsider the treason law and contem-

---

[1] 25 Henry VIII, c. 12 (*SR* iii. 446–51).

[2] Sect. 2 of the act provided that it should be proclaimed in full in every part of the realm.

[3] For attainder cf. Bellamy, *Law of Treason*, ch. 7. From 1459, at any rate, conviction at law no longer formed a necessary preliminary.

plated an act under which it would be treason to support the pope's attempts to contest the second marriage.[1] The thought took full shape in the First Succession Act (25 Henry VIII, c. 22) which, passed in the spring session of 1534, regularised and secured the situation produced by Henry VIII's marriage to Anne Boleyn. Its main sanction consisted in an expansion of the treason law. The drafting of this very long and complex act caused some difficulty of which a small indication survives. This (which has always been misinterpreted) is a note in Cromwell's hand of objections raised by the drafting committee considering the bill, objections which he had to report to the King.[2] The Council Learned suggested that 'the opinion of the levitical law[3] ... were better out' because it was sufficiently explained in other acts already passed or prepared for the forthcoming session;[4] they considered a proposed clause 'for his heir to be rebellious or disobedient' unsuitable because 'a rebellion is already treason and disobedience is no cause of forfeiture of inheritance'; and they held that 'the king of Scots should in no wise be named, for that it might give him either a courage or else cause him to take unkindness'. That these are manifestly suggestions and revisions proposed at the preparatory stage, and not in Parliament, emerges especially from the first two points; it is once again worth notice how careful of the law the government's advisers showed themselves to be. A fourth demand of theirs has attracted historians' attention to the exclusion of the rest. 'To touch the "word, writing or deed": they be content that deed[5] and writing shall be treason and word to be misprision.' That is to say, Cromwell had proposed to make it treason to attack the marriage and succession not only by some overt act, of which 'writing' would be one form, but also in words only, and the advisers shied away from this drastic step.

[1] BM, Tit. B. i, fo. 161 (*LP* vi. 1381).

[2] BM, Tit. B. i, fo. 425 (*LP* vii. 51). Taking one of the points out of context, Pollard (*Henry VIII*, 263, n. 1) supposed that the report referred to parliamentary discussions of the 1534 Treason Act; and though Thornley (*TRHS* [1917], 103, n. 1) and K. W. M. Pickthorn (*Early Tudor Government* [1934], ii. 236, n. 3) correctly ascribed the event to the Succession Act, they too thought that the argument occurred in the Commons. The full note can leave no doubt that Cromwell was reporting a discussion that took place while the bill was being prepared.

[3] I.e. the scriptural justification of the King's divorce.

[4] The Act of Appeals (24 Henry VIII, c. 12); the acts for Queen Anne's jointure and declaring Catherine to be but Princess Dowager (25 Henry VIII, cc. 25, 28).

[5] Here Cromwell was guilty of a significant slip. He first wrote 'word' and had to substitute 'deed'.

All these emendations were accepted, as the enacted statute shows.[1] This created several new treasons. In the first place, it expanded the old treason of compassing the king's death by adding to it attempts to imperil the king's person, attacks on the security of his crown, activities 'to the prejudice, slander, disturbance and derogation' of the marriage with Anne Boleyn, and interference with the order of the succession as defined in the act. All these treasons could be committed 'by writing or imprinting, or by any exterior act or deed'; that is to say, the 'overt deed' of 1352 was now defined to include incitement to opposition by the written word. The statute brought hostile propaganda within the compass of the treason law and thus assisted the government's determination to maintain its monopolistic hold on opinion. On the other hand, as the drafting committee had advised, purely verbal attacks on the King's second marriage, 'without writing or any exterior deed or act', were to be misprision of treason only, punishable by imprisonment at pleasure and loss of all possessions. The same penalties were appointed for failure to take the oath of succession.[2] However, the provisions made for the government of the realm in the event of a minority were protected by the penalties of treason. The King's subsequent matrimonial adventures necessitated a reconsideration of this act in 1536, and the Second Act of Succession had the awkward task of adjusting treason to new circumstances.[3] It did this with a characteristic blandness. The repeal of the First Succession Act was stated to make no difference to treasons committed under it before the beginning of the 1536 Parliament; on the other hand, the act offered the King's free pardon to any who had, by remarks about Anne Boleyn and her 'daughter illegitimate', incurred the dangers of the law but were now shown to have had only the truth and the King's best interests at heart. Thus the act of 1536 preserved the treasons defined in that of 1534 which did not touch directly upon the cause of it all, but showed proper thought, if little gentlemanly feeling, by retrospectively endorsing the common description of Queen Anne as a whore.

The positive treasons of this Second Act of Succession protected the new marriage and its heirs, but there was now no longer any sort of milder attitude to certain offences. Misprision had disappeared, and

[1] SR iii. 471 ff.; Gee and Hardy, 232 ff.
[2] For the oath cf. above, pp. 222–6.
[3] 28 Henry VIII, c. 7 (SR iii. 655 ff.).

both words only and refusal to take the oath were full treason. In this the statute only accepted the victory of the drastic party which, over-ruled by legal scruples in early 1534, had won through in the autumn session of that year. There is no reason to think but that both Cromwell and Henry wanted the most potent weapons available. As a matter of fact, the treasons of the First Succession Act might not have sufficed to catch the Nun of Kent whose own offences were all in words only. Moreover, by the middle of 1534 it had become clear to Cromwell that the King's doings were causing enough loose and hostile talk in the country to trouble the man charged with preserving public order, protecting the security of the crown, and holding the nation together through a revolution. This was the revolution's crucial year when it had not yet become clear that the main part of the people might accept the new order with sufficient zeal or apathy to make disaffected talk rela-tively unimportant. In July 1533, William Ap Lli, a priest in Wales, picturesquely but dangerously 'wished to have the King upon a mountain in North Wales called the Withvay, otherwise called Snow-don Hill...He would souse the King about the ears till he had his head soft enough.'[1] In the same month, James Harrison, parson of Leigh in Lancashire, reacted violently to the proclamation of Queen Anne: 'I will none for queen but Queen Catherine; who the devil made Nan Bullen, that whore, queen?'[2] Across the country, in Essex, John Ward (another priest) said bluntly in November 1533 that 'King Henry VIII is no king of right'.[3] At Cambridge, in May 1534, Henry Kilby, engaged in looking after his master's horse during a journey home to Leicester, got involved in an argument with the ostler of the White Horse Inn, that hotbed of Lutheranism. The ostler, who had kept his ears open, remarked that 'there is no pope but a bishop of Rome'. Kilby retorted that those who said so were 'strong heretics'. The ostler triumphantly reminded him that 'the King's grace held of his part', and Kilby (presumably still rubbing down that horse) threw back that in that case 'was both he an heretic and the King another and...that this business had never been if the King had not married Anne Bullen'. 'And therewithal they multiplied words and waxed so hot...that the one called the other knave, and so fell together by the ears, so that this examined broke the ostler's head with a faggot stick; and so he was

[1] SP 1/77, fo. 203 (LP vi. 790, i).   [2] Ellis, i. II. 42–4.
[3] SP 2/O, fo. 321 (LP vi. 1492).

deprehended and led to prison; and more words that were spoken there he remembers not.'[1]

He had remembered enough and incidentally had shown how easily these political arguments could lead to a disturbance; but no matter, though he had said all this and more, he had, as the law stood, spoken no treason. Neither had Dan John Frances who early in 1534 declared that their latest doings had turned King and Council from mere schismatics into heretics;[2] there is no sign that either of them came to grief. Dan John was still free in July when he signed the acknowledgment of the royal supremacy.[3] The terms used by these rash speakers may be remembered. Others delated at this time also got off, so far as we know. In the case of Mrs Burgyn of Watlington in Oxfordshire, it may be that the sheer absurdity of the story carried its own corrective.[4] When in labour, she called in the midwife, one Joan Hammulden, and was so pleased with her attentions that allegedly (as Joan later told her cronies) she remarked that 'for her honesty and cunning...she might be midwife to the Queen of England, if it were Queen Catherine, and if it were Queen Anne she was too good to be her midwife, for she was a whore and a harlot for her living'. Mrs Burgyn, solemnly interrogated before three justices, denied it all and counter-accused Joan for saying a few months earlier that there would soon be fewer than the three queens whose presence in England a Mrs Dolphin had regretted.[5] These words Joan in her turn denied, but she admitted that she would never have reported Mrs Burgyn if the latter had not on an earlier occasion threatened 'that she would burn the said Joan Hammulden's tail and do her other displeasure'. It is possible that the story ends there; certainly the record does. Other instances of similar disaffected talk have already been noted.

None of these people could be proceeded against under the Succession Act, but even in cases to which the act applied the government might find its hands tied. Some clearly enough offended under it. Thus Gervase Shelby, in Kent, refused in June 1534 to take the oath of succession because 'his grace has broken the sacrament of matrimony';[6] he was thus liable to the penalties of misprision on two counts. We do not

---

[1] SP 1/84, fos. 111–12 (LP vii. 754).   [2] Above, p. 208.
[3] Deputy Keeper's Reports, vii, App. ii. 284.   [4] SP 1/84, fo. 213 (LP vii. 840 [2]).
[5] Catherine, Anne, and the 'French Queen' (Henry's sister Mary, widow of Louis XII of France).
[6] SP 1/76, fo. 230 (LP vi. 634: the date in LP – 1533 – is wrong).

know what happened to him.[1] Dr Gwynbourne, a grey friar of Beverley, had really put his foot in it by composing writings against the King's second marriage; he even sent one to Henry himself. This, of course, was treason by the act. Nevertheless, when Brother George Brown, engaged upon administering the oath in the northern friaries, came to Beverley in July 1534, Gwynbourne was there and ready to swear. Brown, who knew about his earlier attitude, refused to accept the oath from him. Gwynbourne then pleaded ignorance, but Brown easily extracted from him at least the knowledge that Queen Anne was crowned and the Lady Elizabeth born. Why then had he written so shamefully against the marriage? 'I wrote, said he, as my conscience served me.' 'And does your conscience serve you now to forswear all this writing?' 'Yea, truly.'[2] Despite the friar's confessed offences, there is no sign of further action. The hesitancy of the statute would have involved John Snappe, of Buckinghamshire, in misprision only for saying that he would spend £2000, if he had it, on defending the Lady Mary's title to the succession.[3]

We do not know if he got into trouble, but William Copley, a lay brother of Roche Abbey, provides evidence that the statute did not remain a dead letter. On 16 September 1534, he was indicted, under the act, at Spalding in Lincolnshire, for saying: 'If there be no pope there can be no bishop, and if there be no bishop there can be no priest, and if there be no priest there can be no saved souls...The archbishop of Canterbury is an heretic, for he came not in by the pope...The said archbishop did unlawfully marry the King and Queen together, and that they live in adultery because it was not done by the pope's consent ...The Queen's grace should not be called Queen Anne but Anne the bawd, and that they were married underneath a "guysshyn" [cushion?] and that he would justify, to die for it.' It seems that he was convicted of misprision and sentenced to imprisonment, for in May next year he is found in the King's Bench prison, still unrepentant; a fellow-prisoner there denounced him for saying 'it was pity the King's grace's head were not from his body'. But perhaps he never said this, for the

---

[1] In 1549 there died one Alice Shelby, widow, of the same parish (*Index to Wills preserved in the Probate Registry at Canterbury*, ed. H. R. Plomer, Kent Records [1920], 430). If, as is quite possible, she was Gervase's widow this still does not tell us how or when he died, but the fact that she had something to leave suggests that her husband had not forfeited all his possessions.

[2] SP 1/85, fo. 46 (*LP* vii. 953). [3] SP 1/83, fo. 96 (*LP* vii. 497).

marshal, to the informer's disgust, made light of it, and no more is heard of the matter. It is to be supposed that if a prisoner in the King's Bench had been convicted of treason (as by then this utterance would have been) the evidence would be available.[1] Another who showed the Succession Act in operation was Christopher Plummer, canon of Windsor. Charged with the wrong sort of words in May 1534, he was at once committed to the Tower where he still lay a year later; but in March 1536 he was pardoned, a few months before he would have been in any case released under the Second Act of Succession.[2]

The difficulties caused by the distinctions made in the First Succession Act are illustrated by one Simon Morton, though his offence, for once, had nothing to do with the changes in religion. He was arrested at Leicester in June 1534 and examined on four articles of which he admitted the first and third, while witnesses would swear to the last. He admitted that he had served with a company of Scots for nine months and drawn twenty nobles in wages; against this there is a marginal note, 'If this were in time of war, as me seemeth it is treason'. He also admitted saying that if the king of Scots came to England he 'would bring a knot of good fellows and some of them should be found shrews or they go'. Witnesses had heard him say that the king of Scots would come with 40,000 men and by the time he reached Leicester 'the king of England should have little power'. But these two bits of posturing were not treason. Neither was the charge that he had said that anyone willing to serve in the Scots army should have twelvepence a day and meat and drink in peace time, 'and if there were war, to have twenty pence by the day and to find himself'; the examiner noted that 'the speaking of these words only is misprision'.[3] Thus, if he was to be got on a treason charge it would have to be proved that, an Englishman born, he had served the king of Scots in war, an offence under the act of 1352; and yet his mixture of threats and recruiting propaganda for a foreign power had been truly dangerous in a country always readily disturbed by rumours of foreign invasion and threats to the King's policy from abroad.

No doubt, all this loose talk looks far from devastating, and it may well be thought that the penalties of misprision would serve to keep it

---

[1] KB 9/529/39; SP 1/83, fo. 59 (misdated by *LP* vii. 678 into 1534).

[2] SP 1/84, fo. 97; 94, fo. 3 (*LP* vii. 828; viii. 1001); *LP* x. 597 (36).

[3] SP 49/4, fos. 48–50 (*LP* vii. 847).

in check. But, for one thing, some of it could not be brought under the law as it stood in mid-1534 because attacking the King's policy was punishable only if the accused specifically spoke against the marriage, and by this time the consequences of the break with Rome had extended well beyond the reputation or fate of Anne Boleyn. And for another, it is always worth remembering that the task of governing England through a revolution was not an easy one; we have seen how problematic order and obedience could become in so ill-policed a country. At any rate, that the government were not content with the weapons at their disposal became apparent in the autumn session of 1534, the session which, among other things, passed the Act of Supremacy and effectively completed the work of transferring the papal supremacy in the Church to the King. And before we assume too readily that only the government felt this way – that a severe treason law was something imposed on the country by the King and Cromwell – we might take note of the sort of opinion expressed by the earl of Essex, not one of the King's councillors, who in reporting John Ward's statement that the King was not king of right had added that these were 'as heinous words as ever I heard... There were no death that could be imagined sufficient for his offence, as I think'.[1] But in November 1533 it was far from clear whether the law agreed with the earl. The Treason Act of November 1534 settled this and many other questions.[2]

Two drafts survive of this act,[3] and it is of some importance to decide whether they reflect debate in Parliament or belong to the preparatory stage of drafting, especially since the last draft with its corrections is identical with the act as passed. Miss Thornley apparently took it for granted that these paper drafts were before the Parliament (indeed, she meant the Commons in particular), and she thought so the more readily because there is evidence that the bill caused trouble there. It is admittedly rather poor evidence for the sort of assertions that have been built on it.[4] In 1535, Bishop Fisher deposed during interrogation that his brother Robert had visited him in the Tower and told him of the act then 'in hand in the Common House' which would make words treason. 'And because it was thought by divers of the said House that

[1] SP 2/O, fo. 321 (*LP* vi. 1492).
[2] 26 Henry VIII, c. 13 (*SR* iii. 508 ff.); printed also in Gee and Hardy, 247 ff.
[3] SP 1/65, fos. 97–103; SP 2/Q, fos. 90–6 (Thornley's B₁ and B₂).
[4] H. A. L. Fisher, *Political History*, v. 346; Pickthorn, *Early Tudor Government*, ii. 249 f.

no man lightly could beware of the penalty of the said statute, therefore there was much sticking at the same in the Common House, and unless there were added in the same that the said words should be spoken maliciously, he thought the same should not pass.'[1] Robert Fisher sat for Rochester in the Reformation Parliament,[2] and this report must therefore carry quite a lot of weight. Nevertheless, it is doubtful. The bishop's servant, Richard Wilson, interrogated on the same point, stated that the vital visit took place in February 1535, not during the session at all; his version is otherwise similar enough, though more racy.[3] The real problem touches the fate of 'maliciously' in the statute. It is in both the surviving drafts and looks to have been there from the beginning; unless these much corrected drafts were preceded by at least one other in the House, it was not the Commons who insisted on the inclusion of the word. Here it may be noted that if Wilson's memory was better than that of his old and very sick master, the Commons possibly insisted on keeping the word in, not on putting it in: 'they stuck at the last to have one word in the same, and that word maliciously'. This could also be the way the story came to Fisher's early biographer who said that the Commons were loath to pass the act 'except due proof would be made that the words were spoken maliciously'.[4] It is therefore quite as possible that the Commons' debates turned upon the safeguard provided by the requirement of malice to make words treason, as it is that the word was added by way of amendment; and this fits the evidence of the drafts much better. In any case, 'maliciously' had been used to qualify words made misprision of treason in the Succession Act: the government did not need the Commons to suggest this adverb to them.

This is not to say that there was not much doubt and some consternation when the bill was introduced, only that it could well have been introduced in the form in which it finally passed. And that is certainly what the two extant drafts suggest. The corrections on them are nearly all in Audley's hand; one or two small ones suggest that Cromwell looked it over after his colleague had done the main work. This was an act which needed the full application of legal expertise, and of the two

[1] BM, Cleo. E. vi, fo. 165 (*LP* viii. 858).
[2] *Official Return of Members of Parliament*, i. 369.
[3] SP 1/93, fo. 52 (*LP* viii. 856): men should come to the Tower 'thick and thriff'; it had never been 'heard of before that words should be high treason'.
[4] *The Life of Fisher*, transcribed by R. Bayne, E.E.T.S., extra series, cxvii (1921), 102.

Audley, lord chancellor since January 1533, was certainly the more eminent lawyer. And since it is so largely his hand, and not only Cromwell's (as Miss Thornley supposed), which appears on the drafts, the point is quite clear. By this time Audley sat in the Lords, and the corrections cannot therefore have been made in the Commons. Nor can they have been made in the Lords, or there would have been no chance of Cromwell's hand appearing at all. That the Commons did not touch it is quite clear. The bill was introduced first in the Lords.[1] The Upper House either despatched, or much more probably received and despatched, the final version; the Lower, however much they were disturbed by it, passed it as they received it. The drafts belong to the preparatory stage, and the Parliament did not alter the act in any way.

This is also the impression that emanates from the sort of corrections that appear on the drafts and the lines of thought they suggest. The 1534 Treason Act did not simply pick up from the abortive attempts of 1532; essentially it marked a fresh start, though the earlier efforts were looked at again and used. The preamble is quite new: markedly shorter, lacking all those justificatory references to the statute of Edward III and the nation's demand for a law, and firmly assertive of a single principle. The act is made because 'it is most necessary both for common policy and duty of subjects...to prohibit...all manner of shameful slanders, perils or imminent danger' to the King, the Queen and their heirs. All good subjects will agree on this, since on the monarchy 'dependeth the whole unity and universal weal of this realm'; they will also accept that 'cankered and traitorous hearts' must not have 'too great a scope of unreasonable liberty'. Hence this act. A comparison with the earlier preamble brings out clearly the new spirit of single-minded determination and clear purpose which had come to the government. Audley's corrections in the preamble are only stylistic, but he made a more necessary change when he altered the clumsy and unusual enacting clause first drafted (which spoke of the consent of the King and of 'the Upper and Nether House of this his present Court of Parliament') to the by now pretty well standard formula of King, Lords and Commons 'in this present Parliament assembled, and by authority of the same'.

The date by which the act was to come into force gave difficulty. It was first put down as 'the first day of the beginning of this present

[1] The Original Act (Record Office, House of Lords) bears the correct formulae: 'Soit baille aux Communes. A cest bille les Communes sont assentz.'

Parliament', but that would have made it retrospective to November 1529. The trouble was that statutes were normally effective from the start of the Parliament which passed them, but a Parliament with so many sessions made the usual formula useless. The drafting clerk's attempt to clarify things by inserting 'the last session of' before 'this present' did not improve matters, and one of the very few corrections made by Cromwell changed it to January 1st next (1535). At the next stage, Audley put the date back one month, which suggests that either the introduction of the act was delayed beyond the government's expectations or it was decided to give sufficient time for it to become known. 1 February 1535 did, however, become the date fixed by the statute; words treason thereafter were not statutory treason before, a fact which explains something about the incidence of prosecutions. In the body of the draft, most of the corrections did little more than clean up the phrasing and make clauses more precise. Audley deleted a section which made it treason to attack the succession; this had, after all, been dealt with in the earlier act. He also removed a very comprehensive phrase which would have made it treason to speak words which might have caused 'derogation of the King's honour, the Queen's or their heirs', unsurety of their person, division in the realm, infamy to their names', or which might have brought the royal personages 'in hatred or evil opinion as well of outward princes as of his own people'. It is true that some such treason (that of bringing the king into hatred with his people and thereby stirring up division and strife) seems to have existed at common law and was to be employed against the earl of Strafford in 1641;[1] nevertheless, embodied in statute this would have made all talk of politics not plainly adulatory of the King a possible treason. As we shall see, some men were to have cause to bless the excision of this sentence when they were charged with words which by it would have been treason, without it were not.

The act includes the old treason concerning the King's castles and munitions, only better worked out; this, originally a separate section, was revised and then transferred to its present place as the second half of the first section. The last phrase of section 2, giving the reason why

---

[1] C. Russell, 'The Theory of Treason in the Trial of Strafford,' *Eng. Hist. Rev.* lxxx (1965), 30 ff. As Bellamy points out (*Law of Treason*, 210), the notion of such an offence underlay the charges of treason brought against Empson, Dudley, and Elizabeth Barton.

sanctuary was abolished for traitors, originally included a curiously embarrassed reference to the fact 'that (though not in such specialty) it is already by the whole Parliament condescended that they that offend against the Act of Succession shall be esteemed as traitors in some part and that no sanctuary shall serve them'; all this was ringed by Audley and it then appears in the next draft in its final brief form. At the end, Audley drafted an additional clause to replace that comprehensive one struck out by him: words 'other...than such which by this act are limited to be treason' but which are dangerous to royalty or the unity of the realm were to be misprision, carrying the penalties declared in the Act of Succession. At the next stage, this addition, still savage enough, was again removed, a fact which suggests that Audley's was not the directing, only the drafting, hand; instead, the chancellor wrote in the clause saving certain rights with which the act was in the event to conclude. His other corrections in the second draft are again simply of the improving kind and reflect no policy changes. Altogether, the prehistory of the statute demonstrates that its purposes were nearly all clear from the first; the only substantial alteration removed one really pernicious clause by first reducing the penalty for generally obnoxious talk from treason to misprision and finally by cancelling the whole idea; for the rest, Audley was in the main engaged in tightening and cleaning up. The act was not his specifically; he worked on a draft which he altered hardly at all in substance. It may well have been Cromwell's, as people in general seem to have thought; at any rate, it represented the considered policy of the government and, despite much doubt and some 'sticking' in the Commons, went through unaltered.

The Treason Act of 1534 contained the first major redefinition of treason since 1352, and its import was wide; on the other hand, it was really quite a short act – a good deal shorter than the proposed statute of 1532. What it lost in length it gained in precision and directness. How this worked out for the preamble has already been shown. Some of the quainter notions of the earlier drafts disappeared, especially the clause protecting royal ambassadors and messengers from being interfered with. The new treasons were essentially three. Where in 1352 it had been declared treason to attempt the death of the king, queen or heir by some overt act, this was now enlarged to include any desire or attempt even if expressed (maliciously) in words or writing to cause bodily harm to those persons or attempt to deprive them of their dignities and titles. Secondly – a new principle altogether – it was to be treason to call the King, in express writing or words, slanderously and maliciously, a heretic, schismatic, tyrant, infidel, or a usurper of the crown. As we have seen, words of this order were being applied to Henry by those who objected to his policy. This short clause was the real core of the act; it embodied the full purpose for which it was designed and served to catch most of those who suffered under it. Thirdly, the earlier extension of levying war to include detention of royal castles, ships, ordnance and munitions, within six days of proclamation made, was preserved in the act; it is not quite clear what this was intended to do or whether any particular occurrence provoked the clause, nor do we know of anyone against whom it was applied. It has a somewhat oldfashioned air about it, a reminder that civil war and noble rebellion were by no means yet out of the question; no doubt the lawyers felt that they had stopped a gap. The really interesting thing about the clause is that the gap was one which the laws of war had hitherto filled well enough: this is one of the many signs about this legislation that this government preferred to rely exclusively on the ordinary law of the realm, the common law codified, expanded and amended in statute.

These new treasons have traditionally had a bad name, and the Protector Somerset partially swept them away in the search for popularity with which he initiated his regime in 1547. Nor have historians' attempts to drain passion from comment been altogether successful. Miss Thornley, while admitting that the changes made were considerable, called them 'neither unreasonable nor unprecedented',[1] but this has not prevented a fairly general feeling that the act contained at least the potential of tyranny. That it was fierce, and intended to be fierce, should not be questioned. It stood manifestly as the legal protection of a revolution whose acceptance was so far distinctly in the balance. Yet at the same time, it will not do to let indignation have too free a rein or to overlook the situation, and the century, in which it was made. When Cromwell fell, the Treason Act was remembered against him by his enemies; but its repeal in 1547 was regretted by some men charged with the task of governing mid-Tudor England, nor did even Somerset entirely abandon the principle that words alone might constitute treason.[2] Robert Fisher may well have been right and the

[1] *TRHS* (1917), 105.   [2] Ibid. III, n. I.

Commons may have worried about the implications; but they passed it unaltered, and Henry VIII's Commons were not unable to alter acts they did not like.[1] In any case, Miss Thornley's adjectives are in the main valid. The first and third of the new treasons simply elaborated the existing details of the law; like so much else in the legislation of the 1530's, they advanced the cause of certainty in the law at the expense of judicial manipulation and interpretation of statute,[2] and this is a form of legal progress rather than an abuse of power.

The crux of the matter lies in the introduction of treason by words only. Now it is certainly true that cases have been found from Henry IV's reign onwards in which the courts interpreted mere words as proof of treason; to Miss Thornley's and Mr Bellamy's examples,[3] we can add the unhappy fate of the men condemned in 1451, at Quarter Sessions held at Canterbury in saintly King Henry VI's presence, 'for hyr talkyng a gayne the Kyng' in favour of the duke of York.[4] On at least one occasion, Henry VII's councillors interrogated men suspected of treasonable utterances.[5] It has been argued that these are not good precedents because in these cases words were interpreted to constitute the overt act proving the existence of treason which the 1352 statute demanded; 'conspiring was the treason; words were the overt act'; there was no 'construction' of treason by words, merely an expansion of 'the more fundamental idea that as regards the king the mere compassing of his death amounted to treason'.[6] But this is at best a quibble. The point is that the judges could declare that a man might commit treason by speaking it, even if they preferred to support the charge with

---

[1] Cf. my discussion of 'Henry VIII's Act of Proclamations,' *Eng. Hist. Rev.* lxxv (1960), 208 ff.

[2] See my remarks in *Tudor Constitution* (1960), 233 f.

[3] *TRHS* (1917), 107 ff.; Thornley, 'Treason by Words in the 15th Century,' *Eng. Hist. Rev.* xxxii (1917), 556 ff.; Bellamy, *Law of Treason*, 116 ff.

[4] *Historical Collections of a London Citizen*, ed. J. Gairdner (Camden New Ser. xvii, 1876), 196. I owe this reference to Dr J. W. McKenna.

[5] Elton, *Tudor Constitution*, 61.

[6] S. Rezneck, 'Constructive Treason by Words in the 15th Century,' *Amer. Hist. Rev.* xxxiii (1928), 544 ff. Rezneck wished to deny the existence of 'constructive treasons' left over by the side of the 1352 statute and argued that what appears to be judicial discretion in accepting proofs of treason not mentioned in the act amounted to no more than a characteristic use of the power of interpretation applied to the act. Even if this somewhat metaphysical point is true, it does not affect the fact that on occasions before 1534, and without explicit statutory sanction, words were quite often treated as equivalent to overt deeds in trials of treason.

some other overt act if they could find one. Whether they held that words, in the abstract, might be treason, or that words proved the existence of a physical danger, cannot have been material to the accused and is of remarkably little significance to the law. This is not to deny that in spite of all the precedents the definition of such a treason in the act of 1534 gave a powerful and mainly new weapon to the Crown, or that some men were to die for speaking rash words without plotting anything. But it is to assert that treason by words was not so unprecedented or outrageous as indignant opinion, then and since, has liked to maintain. Moreover, many of the cases of treason by words did in the circumstances amount to an excitement to violence and resistance and even rebellion. There was cause for Henry VIII and Cromwell to take up and develop the well attested notion that men who confined their rebellious activities to talking at large were far from harmless to the state or to public order.

The act thus enabled the govenment to attack actual or suspected opponents with the most devastating of all legal weapons, and it underlined this purpose in the three proccdural details which followed upon the additions to the substantive law. In the first place, traitors were deprived of the privilege of sanctuary. This was clearly part of a general policy which sought to remove this particular obstacle to law-enforcement, a policy which went back at least to the early days of Henry VII and was pursued in several acts of Henry VIII.[1] Especially the existence of the abbot of Westminster's liberty, where a criminal could live undisturbed to his death, was a major problem to the King's ministers, and Cromwell several times demonstrated his opinion of it. In 1533, one John Wolf and his wife, who had brutally murdered two foreigners while ferrying them across the Thames, had apparently taken refuge there; it took an act of Parliament to dispose of them,[2] and Cromwell's notes show how determined he was to get them.[3] Again, in January 1539, a Cheshire feud exploded in St Paul's Churchyard when one John Mainwaring, assisted by four Welsh thugs, beat up and killed one Roger Cholmley.[4] The murderers promptly took refuge in the Westminster sanctuary where they registered with the keeper,

---

[1] I. D. Thornley, 'The Destruction of Sanctuary,' *Tudor Studies...presented to A. F. Pollard*, 182 ff.   [2] 25 Henry VIII, c. 11.   [3] *LP* vi. 742; vii. 48.
[4] KB 9/541/85–6; KB 27/1112, Rex, rot. 9. Both Mainwaring and Cholmley are described as Londoners, but the quarrel originated in Cheshire. Ralph Mainwaring of Cheshire was indicted there but ultimately acquitted at his trial.

William Webbe. However, a coroner's jury indicted them on February 10th, and on the 15th they were tried at Newgate gaol delivery, before a commission which among others included the lord mayor, Thomas Cromwell (lord privy seal), Sir Richard Riche (chancellor of the Augmentations) and Baron Hales of the Exchequer. All the accused pleaded the privilege of the sanctuary. Mainwaring claimed that he had been 'fetched out' by Cromwell's order, but three of the others admitted that they thought themselves immune: they were not taken out of sanctuary against their wills 'but came...at my lord privy seal's commandment, according to my oath that I made in the sanctuary'. All pleaded not guilty and asked 'to be tried thereof by the King's grace's privilege of Westminster'. The attorney-general, prosecuting, argued that the plea was insufficient in law, and the court, agreeing with him, sentenced all five to be hanged. Clearly opinion had set firmly against the whole principle of the thing, but in strict law the felons should almost certainly have been protected; it was not until the next session that an act abolished sanctuary for serious felonies.[1] Mainwaring's case may have been the cause of the act; at any rate, in March 1540 Cromwell recorded his intention to secure the termination of sanctuary.[2] The case demonstrates very plainly how the whole out-dated principle could be used to hinder the most obviously necessary enforcement of the law, though it also illustrates the determination of Thomas Cromwell to suppress crime at all costs. The abrogation of sanctuary in the Treason Act was of a piece with past development and present purpose, and part of the policy to destroy sectional privilege.

The 1534 act further included clauses which made treason committed out of the realm triable within the country, and which ordered the forfeiture of all the estate of a traitor, including that held to his use. These points, as we have seen, had been part of the earlier proposals. Audley's saving clause at the end had the curious but possibly intended effect of depriving rather than safeguarding a particular class of owners. It protected the rights of all persons, their heirs and successors, except actual traitors, their heirs and successors. By including this last word, 'successors', it made possible the confiscation of the property of a monastery whose head had been executed for treason.[3] Before the act, only heirs lost their rights; and bishops and abbots had no heirs. The

[1] 32 Henry VIII, c. 12. [2] *LP* xv. 438.
[3] Cf. Thornley, *TRHS* (1917), 118 f.

suspicion that the effect was intended is supported not only by the superfluity of the clause, but also by the existence of an earlier plan for an act expressly designed to achieve the same end.[1] The provision for the trial of treasons committed abroad seems never to have been brought into use while the act lasted.

This act, short, sharp but comprehensive, bears the characteristic marks of Thomas Cromwell's legislation; though Audley was charged with the final drafting, though the King no doubt wanted it, and though the whole government was in a way responsible for it, there is no need to doubt the conviction of contemporaries that he stood behind it. We have seen that a few months earlier a slip of his pen had betrayed some disappointment at his failure to get words made treason in the Succession Act. The contrast, specifically, with the draft of 1532 is revealing enough: the earlier proposals were diffuse, piecemeal, ill directed, not based on a recognisable policy, where the act itself breathed purpose, force and coherent thought. From 1 February 1535, the Crown certainly had a totally sufficient weapon against any who spoke, wrote or acted against the King's new titles and powers: that is to say, against any who opposed the revolution.

However, there was still a gap in the law: what about people who, without attacking the King, defended the pope? This could be done quite easily, for instance by failing to follow the order to remove the pope's title from all mass books and the like. Interestingly enough there appears to have been no thought that this might be comprehended within the Treason Act by some species of judicial interpretation; instead, in 1536, the Act Extinguishing the Authority of the Bishop of Rome legislated against any who 'by writing, ciphering, printing, preaching or teaching, deed or act' in any way maintained the jurisdiction and authority of Rome.[2] But the punishment appointed for this was to be that of *praemunire* only – imprisonment at pleasure and loss of all property. This may be thought severe enough, and the act seems to have been used quite frequently against disaffected persons; nevertheless, it represents some relaxation in attitude compared with the Treason Act of 1534. However, the 1536 statute did not forget about treason: it also ordained the oath of supremacy already mentioned and made refusal to comply treason, in accordance with the principle that all denial of the royal supremacy amounted to just that.

[1] *LP* vi. 1381 (3). [2] 28 Henry VIII, c. 10 (*SR* iii. 663 ff.).

This completed the legal armoury of repression, and there is no doubt that it now covered all eventualities.[1] Even supposing that the law was to be interpreted strictly – and as a rule it was – no one against whom hostile acts or sayings, however casual, could be proved now stood a chance of escaping. But they had to be proved. One further point about this treason legislation is never mentioned, but it deserves careful attention. The preamble to the last draft of the first, and abortive, stage of planning includes a statement of real significance: people offending in the details enacted were to be treated as traitors, provided they 'thereof be lawfully convict according to the common laws of this realm'.[2] This was the draft which bears most corrections by Cromwell, but he did not touch this point. The 1534 act repeats this as 'being thereof lawfully convicted according to the laws and customs of this realm', and virtually the same phrase occurs in the 1536 Act against Rome. Here was an end to all trials of treasons in such courts as that of the constable, by any law of arms, upon notoriety or the king's information, expedients which all had been freely used in previous centuries. The common law had triumphed: treason was to be tried solely by the rules which governed it. The most heinous offence of all, so often political in its implications, had been firmly reduced under the supremacy of 'due process', with all its technicalities, with its use of indictment and jury. This was not the work of the fourteenth century when yet it had been common in other acts to insist on the laws and customs of the realm:[3] the act of 1352 had simply spoken of an offender being 'convicted by proof'.[4] It was the work of the sixteenth century, the supposed century of *raison d'état* – the work of Henry VIII's councillors, labouring to bring all England and all matters under the rule of law, and that law the common law of the realm. The full meaning of those few words cannot appear until 'due process' as applicable in treason trials is understood and until the problems it could pose to the enforcement of policy have become clear.

[1] The only other treason created in this period concerned those who by fleeing the country hoped to escape punishment for breaches of proclamations (31 Henry VIII, c. 8, sect. 7: printed *TRP*, i. 545 ff.). No cases are known.

[2] SP 2/Q, fo. 105. In the very first draft, Audley had inserted the words 'thereof lawfully convict' only to strike them out again.

[3] Cf., e.g., F. M. Powicke, in *Magna Carta Commemoration Essays*, ed. H. E. Malden (1917), esp. 119 f.

[4] Chrimes and Brown, *Select Documents*, 77: 'et de ceo provablement soit atteint'.

TREASON TRIALS

ALTHOUGH THE CRIMINAL LAW of the early sixteenth century was
in many ways primitive and undeveloped, it followed a known and
quite rigorous procedure – those laws and customs of the realm under
which, as the act of 1534 demanded, a lawful conviction must be
obtained. This required a competent and properly constituted court
before which offenders were presented or indicted by the presenting
(grand) jury of the shire. A presentment is an accusation made by the
jury from their own knowledge, in response to the 'charge' given to
them by the court after they have been impanelled. The charge requires
them to name any persons suspected of certain listed crimes; depending
on the competence and purpose of the court, these may range from
treason, heresy, murder and felony at one end to trespasses and failure
to remove a nuisance at the other.[1] Indictment requires a bill of accusation put before the jury on behalf of the Crown and either approved by
them (when it is annotated 'vera billa') or rejected. If the jury reject the
bill, the person accused is set free: he is 'reprieved by proclamation'.
Thus in 1530, Thomas Pytwey, concerning whose standing and fame
enquiry was made of a Hereford jury 'pro suspicione prodicionis'
allegedly committed at Westminster, for which suspicion he was imprisoned in the Marshalsea for three years before the inquiry, was freed
when the jury returned that he was 'bonorum nominis, fame et gestus'.[2]
Several of the Walsingham conspirators owed their liberation by
proclamation to the jury's refusal to find a true bill against them.[3]

[1] Cf., e.g., the form of a charge to be given to the jury in a court leet (SP 1/156, fo. 186
[LP xiv. II, App. 47]). This included inter alia various forms of high and petty treason;
offences under the Act of Six Articles (false opinions of the eucharist, married priests,
etc.); murder, rape, robbery (with a note that these felonies are not clergiable – 'the
book shall not save'); burglary; allowing a suspected felon to escape; fishing in a
man's ponds or fish-stews (a felony); routs, riots and unlawful assemblies; outcries
against the king's peace; assaults and affrays; victualling offences; withdrawal of rents
and services from the lord. The Ancient Indictments (KB 9) are full of London presentments for keeping offensive matter in the streets, failure to maintain the highway,
breaches of sales regulations, and similar things.

[2] KB 9/514/84.　　　　　　　　　[3] Above, p. 147.

A man indicted of a crime was either already in custody (especially if the court was one of gaol delivery), or after indictment was sought for and arrested by the sheriff. He then had to be arraigned for trial by jury, usually in the same court before which the presentment or indictment had been taken. Arraignment was not automatic but at the discretion of court and prosecution; sometimes it might prove useful to keep a man in custody while inquiries went on or the implications were sorted out.[1] At the trial the Crown's case had to be proved. Although rules of evidence differed greatly from those in use today, and although the accused could neither command the services of counsel nor have his witnesses sworn to their testimony, it would be wrong to suppose that this stage was a mere formality; the trial jury played a genuine and vital part in the business. If they found a verdict of guilty, the convicted person was given a chance to speak; and it was apparently either at this point or before arraignment that he might succeed in postponing his fate by securing a review of his trial in King's Bench (appeal in the proper sense there was none). This is a very obscure point: cases were constantly called up by writs of *mandamus* or *certiorari*, so that technical deficiencies might be exploited or pardons produced, but how defendants managed to do this remains uncertain. Occasionally the court intervened at this stage. Roger Waters of Newmarket was in 1536 indicted for heresy at Ipswich Assizes and convicted by the jury. However, 'quia judiciarii hic se avisare volunt de et supra premissis priusquam judicium inde reddunt', they bound Waters to appear before King and Council to receive judgment. The result was a *mandamus* out of the King's Bench, and after the indictment had been certified into the court the record, and the case, terminated. The judges' action, which arose from doubt whether the offence as charged was heresy, saved the accused.[2] The Crown side of the King's Bench plea rolls records at this time little except cases called up and quashed. In any case, sentence would not be pronounced by the trial judge until the prosecution had asked for it; and sentence was followed by execution, which in treason cases meant the ghastly business of drawing on a hurdle, hanging, cutting down alive, disembowelling and castration, decapitation and quartering. All these stages of a trial were governed by technicalities

---

[1] In 1535, Bishop Lee asked if Cromwell wanted some suspects arraigned at once if indicted, and if any 'shall be reprieved' if convicted (SP 1/97, fo. 94 [*LP* ix. 510]).

[2] KB 9/545/86; 29/170, rot. 31.

which set limits to the power of the Crown and caused occasional difficulties. It is no wonder that a really speedy trial caused surprise: in 1538, Christopher Hales, master of the rolls, congratulated himself and others on the condemnation of William Knell, 'attainted this day of high treason with such acceleration as I have seldom seen'. He was indicted and arraigned before noon and tried by four o'clock; even so it was several weeks before he was executed.[1]

By no means all the King's courts could try treason, and in particular none but common-law courts could; their ability was governed by their specific competence and by the rule in law that crimes must be tried in the shire in which they were committed. The King's Bench was the central court for criminal offences, but it acted as a court of first instance only for those committed in the shire in which it sat, that is Middlesex. Elsewhere, courts had to be specially constructed by commission. Though commissions of the peace included all major crimes except treason, and though many misdemeanours as well as some felonies were tried at Quarter Sessions, most criminal trials in the shires were held before commissioners of oyer and terminer or of gaol delivery. Regularly issued to justices of assize when they went on circuit, these two commissions empowered the judge, usually associated with two or three local magistrates, to try respectively indictments taken before them and persons already indicted and held in gaol awaiting trial. In ordinary times, this local jurisdiction in criminal matters sufficed – it is still the basis of criminal trials today – but difficulties could arise, as in the case of Carpissacke, indicted of treason in Cornwall. The gaol delivery declared itself incompetent to hear a case of high treason, and an Assize session (equipped with oyer and terminer) was put off at Launceston because of plague. This annoyed the King, but the defaulting judge, Sir John Fitzjames, explained matters to Cromwell. Himself troubled by his 'old disease', he had asked his fellow judge to take the Assize at Launceston; on his way there this man ran into plague and turned back. Nor could the Assize be held elsewhere because the civil pleas sent down from Westminster on *nisi prius*[2] 'have

---

[1] SP 1/131, fo. 142; C 82/744 (*LP* xiii. I, 783; II. 491 [18]). Sixteenth-century usage still sometimes employed 'attaint' to mean 'convict'.

[2] The main purpose of county Assizes was to try civil pleas remitted from the Westminster courts by process of *nisi prius*: the local commissioners were instructed to send a jury to Westminster to try the dispute unless the matter had been settled elsewhere before. Clumsy as the phrasing was, it amounted to a perfectly effective way of securing

their day and place given them at Westminster, and in like wise have the commissioners of gaol deliveries their place limited in the commission'. Carpissacke had apparently tried to revive the Pilgrimage of Grace in the south-west: he had, early in 1537, commissioned a painter friend to make a banner with the five wounds of Christ, and he had done so at St Kevern where the 1497 rising had taken its origin. There was already some unrest in the shire about the abolition of cherished holy days, so that it is no wonder to find Sir William Godolphin, Cromwell's informant, seriously perturbed and demanding that Carpissacke be hanged in chains, for a warning. After the failure to hold the Assize he noted that the matter would have to stand over till the next one, unless a special commission of gaol delivery were obtained. Godolphin had Cromwell's instructions to see the traitor tried and executed: how was he to do it? In fact, there is no evidence that Carpissacke was ever tried; possibly he was, but at any rate the technicalities of the law made it impossible to use his death for overawing the local unrest.[1]

In the 1530's, the use of Assize sessions for treason trials, though common, was on the whole rarer than the issue of special commissions of oyer and terminer to selected individuals, or groups of judges and justices of the peace. The commission might be particular, like the 'oyer and terminer for the priest in Wales' which Cromwell reminded himself of in 1538.[2] Alternatively it could be general, like that issued on 4 July 1538 to twenty-eight commissioners (with a quorum of three of which the two Westminster judges included had always to be present), to perambulate the Midland shires and towns to try treasons, rebellions, felonies and other matters. In the five sittings of which record survives, they secured the conviction of four traitors and the acquittal of two more as well as of three misprisioners.[3] A man likely to encounter

trial in the locality where the jury could be got together, rather than at the centre where the courts often patiently sent out repeated writs for years for the elusive panel. These stages and their adjournments had become formalities in civil cases at Westminster, and most suits in Exchequer and Common Pleas were likely to end at *nisi prius*.

[1] *LP* xii. I. 1001; SP 1/119, fo. 143, and 124, fos. 119, 224 (*LP* xii. I. 1126; II. 525, 690); BM, Cotton App. L, fo. 75 (*LP* xii. I. 1127).

[2] BM, Tit. B. i, fo. 462 (*LP* xiii. I. 877).

[3] KB 9/542/2-3. Their commission covered Northants., Warw., Rutland, Leics., Notts., Derbs. and Lincs., the cities of Lincoln and Coventry, and the towns of Leicester and Nottingham; they sat at Northampton Castle, Derby, Nottingham, Lincoln Castle and Leicester.

treason in his work on behalf of the Crown could be given a general commission in readiness: thus Lord Chancellor Audley thought the duke of Suffolk should carry one as he prepared to move north against the Lincolnshire rebels, 'to the intent that forthwith upon the apprehension of the traitors the chief ringleaders may be put to execution according to their merits, for the terrible example of all others'.[1] It is interesting that Audley should have automatically assumed the necessity for a trial at common law even when men had been caught in an active state of rebellion. This lawyer's opinion was not shared by the duke of Norfolk during his clearing up after Pilgrimage of Grace. Writing from Carlisle in February 1537, he expressed his conviction that 'in these parts of force I must proceed by the law martial; for if I should proceed by indictments, many a great offender might fortune [to] be found not guilty, saying he was brought forth against his will'.[2] The duke had a point there; it says a good deal about the principles and powers of Tudor governments that they should even have contemplated trying rebels before a jury of the rebellious shire, and – as we shall see – this did not always work out. The law of arms was available when rebels had been caught in the act; here the issue was not complicated by the King's earlier pardon because these northern offenders were to be punished for rebellion renewed after the pardon; martial law could be and was used. But even in the suppression of the risings only Norfolk employed it, and he by no means always; the government preferred commissions of oyer and terminer with indictment and trial by jury. And indeed, unless (as in one case at Windsor) treason was committed in the presence of the King's army with banners displayed,[3] these processes of the common law were the only ones available; those charged with treason under the statute were invariably handled by these methods.

The commissions themselves posed problems and could be inadequately drawn. Norfolk, again, was in trouble in March 1537 when he presided over the Council of the North sitting as a commission at Durham. After the jury had been summoned it was discovered to everybody's embarrassment that the county palatine had been left out of the instrument. The duke and his fellows were 'driven to the extremity of our simple wits, what we should do'. Since everybody was

[1] SP 1/106, fo. 280 (*LP* xi. 559).   [2] SP 1/116, fo. 83 (*LP* xii. I. 468).
[3] Above, p. 90.

297

got together to take the indictments and proceed to arraignment the following day, the duke decided to charge the jury, 'keeping secret from them our lack of authority, and I...thought tomorrow to have proceeded by the law martial and to have taken the indictments but as evidence'. But then he found that since the offences had been committed before the date of his warrant as King's lieutenant he could not use martial law against them, either. Nothing was left except to explain the embarrassment to the King and Cromwell and to complain of the Chancery officials whose negligence had caused the trouble and who should for their fault have had 'as ill journeys as I have had this month'. They 'shall cause me hereafter to call counsel unto me to peruse my commission'.[1] In March 1540, the president of the Council of the North did read his authority in time to discover that he lacked power to enforce the Act of Six Articles properly within his area because the commission spoke only of the three ridings of Yorkshire, which did not include the city and shire of York and that part of the archdeaconry of Richmond which lay in Lancashire.[2] These local Councils had no power to try treasons and heresies unless specially commissioned; that this was a matter of policy and not accident is demonstrated by the instructions of 1539 for the newly erected Council of the West which ordered action against such 'as shall speak any seditious words, invent rumours or commit any such offences, not being treason, whereof inconvenience may grow'.[3] Only courts and commissions under common law could try treason.

The commission of the peace by itself conferred no authority to take indictments for treason or try such cases. Sir Simon Harcourt, the Oxfordshire magistrate, knew this when informed by the bailiff of Bampton that the local shoemaker had talked treason: he committed the accused to ward but sent the informer to Cromwell.[4] The justices could formally receive information: in June 1536, Worcestershire Quarter Sessions recorded that James Asche, parson of Stanton, had been accused of treasonable words spoken in the pulpit, but the only action they could take was to bind Asche and his sureties in a hundred and forty marks respectively to appear before the King's Council to

---

[1] SP 1/116, fos. 236, 238 (*LP* xii. I. 615–16).
[2] SP 1/158, fo. 22 (*LP* xv. 362).   [3] BM, Tit. B. i, fo. 174 v (*LP* xiv. I. 743).
[4] SP 1/85, fo. 2 (*LP* vii. 902); misplaced into 1534 by *LP*, for the depositions show that the alleged offence was committed in June 1536 (SP 1/104, fo. 225 [*LP* x. 1205]).

answer if summoned.[1] If they had gone further and received an indictment they would have exceeded their powers and caused trouble, as the earl of Northumberland did in December 1535 when he convened a session of the peace to indict Anthony Heron of treason, only to find that 'the learned men's opinion is that my lord of Northumberland had no authority to sit upon him, wherefore their opinion is that the indictment is void'. Heron had been improperly indicted for saying 'that the King's highness is not supreme head of the Church of this his realm of England, and sayeth that his conscience will not so take his grace, but expressly sayeth that the bishop of Rome by the name of pope is the very head of the Church'. He admitted these manifestly treasonable words, and though he was apparently 'a simple personage' for whom both Northumberland and Bigod interceded with the King and Cromwell, it may be doubted whether he would have escaped but for this error in procedure. As it was, he was released after a spell in York Castle.[2]

Others were as fortunate. Henry Marpurley, a gentleman of London, was indicted at Nottingham Sessions in October 1537, under the act of 1534, for saying: 'I set not a pudding by the King's broad seal, and all his charters be not worth a rush.'[3] Harry Weston of Hanham (Glos.) was indicted in May 1538 for instigating a priest to tell the people to disregard all preaching of new fashions, 'for the old fashion will come again'.[4] George Robinson, a London mercer who tried to become a country gentleman in Staffordshire, got into trouble in February 1536 by throwing his weight about. Apart from letting a horse thief escape

---

[1] SP 1/104, fo. 93 (*LP* x. 1027). Asche was charged with saying 'that if the King our sovereign lord did not go forth with his laws as he began, he would call the King antichrist', and also 'that the King our sovereign lord was naught, the bishops and abbots naught, and himself naught too'. The accusation was part of the campaign against Latimer's innovating preachers (SP 1/104, fo. 157 [*LP* x. 1099]).

[2] Cf. Dickens, *Lollards and Protestants*, 83. The description of Heron was Northumberland's: SP 1/101, fo. 59 (*LP* x. 77). The details concerning the indictment come from the letter of Heron's enemy, Anthony Brackenbury, to Cromwell (SP 1/102, fo. 5v [*LP* xi. 878]). Brackenbury had confidently anticipated the outcome of the indictment by entering upon Heron's lands in the King's behalf; now 'they have put me clear from it'. His appeal to Cromwell to get Heron in some other way met with no response. Heron's indictment (SP 1/97, fos. 72–4 [*LP* ix. 491]) is a good example of an indictment under the Supremacy and Treason Acts.

[3] KB 9/540/25–6; 27/1109, Rex, rot. 2.

[4] KB 9/539/152–6; 27/1109, Rex, rot. 2d, 13. The priest, Robert Danyell, escaped through the general pardon of 1540 (ibid. 1117, Rex, rot. 12).

(which annoyed his neighbours and was also felony) he spoke treason ('modo proditorio') when he told them:

Sirs, all ye here of Drayton lordship, now that I have it in farm may be glad that ye have me among you. For if the King should fortune to have any business or wars, as to go over the sea himself about any such his affairs, then ye know that as long as I am farmer here I am your head and a Londoner and will at all such times go to London, and you shall tarry here at home and not one of you stir forth with him one foot, howsoever the world go.[1]

Marpurley, Weston and Robinson all succeeded in getting their indictments called into King's Bench where they pleaded that these were void because they were taken before justices of the peace who had no authority to act; in all three cases the court agreed and quashed the indictment. Very probably the same technicality saved Thomas Jackson, a Yorkshire chantry priest, who in June 1535 was indicted for saying that before his second marriage the King had lived in adultery with Queen Anne 'and so doth now still continue, putting away from him his lawful wife'; the King had kept first the mother and after the daughter, 'and now he hath married her whom he kept afore and her mother also'. Sufficient grounds, indeed, but the sheriff had reason to enquire anxiously of Cromwell whether justices of the peace in fact had authority, without special commissions, to take presentments for treason.[2] As we know, they did not, and there is certainly no evidence that Jackson suffered for his words.

Difficulties might also be caused by the rule that trial must take place in the shire in which the offence charged was committed, though this does not seem to have interfered much with the holding of trials. Normally the government, if it had investigated a case and found grounds for conviction, did not forget to remit the man to the locality, as Cromwell did with a hermit of Chesterfield whom he sent to the earl of Shrewsbury for trial at the next Assizes, 'to be punished according to right and the King's laws'. On that occasion he himself had the indictment drawn up on the basis of his examination of the prisoner and forwarded it at the same time.[3] But Thomas Tye, a priest of Haver-

---

[1] SP 1/102, fos. 20–1 (LP x. 272); KB 27/1100, Rex, rot. 6.
[2] Pocock, ii. 468; the correct date is given in LP viii. 862.
[3] Merriman, i. 384–5. The hermit 'could not tell whether he ever spoke the same traitorous words or no'. Even if convicted he would – since the letter belongs to July 1534 – have been guilty of misprision only, under the Act of Succession.

fordwest, could exploit this aspect of the law when in 1540 he was charged with seditious and slanderous preaching. The justices of assize for Herefordshire decided that they could not try him because the words were spoken in Wales, but they put him into Hereford gaol till the matter could be sorted out. He seems to have been on good terms with the sheriff's deputies who first permitted him to go home, forty miles and more out of their sheriffwick, to collect money to help his case; later they took him with them to London and elsewhere, without the knowledge of the Council in the Marches who were responsible for the prisoner. He turned up next year at Calais where he was once more suspected of treason, but in July 1541 he got a pardon for all offences committed before May 1540.[1] In his case, the rule seems to have saved him for long enough to mobilise help. If so, he was luckier than William Barret, a Yorkshire tanner, who in February 1537 spread seditious rumours at Manchester. Sir Anthony Fitzherbert, the judge, not only declared that 'the said words spoken be no words whereupon the law can put him to death' but also that he could not be indicted 'in one shire for an offence committed in another'. The earls of Derby and Sussex wanted him hanged since he was disturbing the precarious peace barely restored in the region, and their representations to the King seem somehow to have got round the law, for a few days later they could tell Norfolk that Barret would be hanged in chains at Manchester. No doubt he was.[2]

Fitzherbert's opinion introduces a serious problem in the pursuit of treason. Even if the court was properly constituted and empowered, it had always to be established whether the offence alleged was really treasonable. The statute had attempted to define what words and deeds might amount to treason, but in practice this was often less straightforward. It would be quite wrong to suppose that anything would do, or that the decision to proceed depended on the mere whim of the men in power. On the contrary, if there was any doubt at all whether a supposed offence amounted to treason there was only one authority which could decide – that of the lawyers and especially the judges. The official attitude – a mixture of strict legalism and such politic reserve as the law permitted – is well brought out in an opinion given by Lord Chancellor Audley in 1535:

[1] SP 1/159, fo. 145 (*LP* xv. 562 [2]); *LP* xvi. 518, 531–2, 1056 (81).
[2] SP 1/116, fos. 113, 253 (*LP* xii. I. 520, 632).

The words spoken in March last...touching appeals will hardly bear treason, but misprision; for there is no express mention made of the King or the Queen. And the words spoken of the King and the Queen...at Christmas last or afore February 6th last had been treason without doubt if they had been spoken since the first day of February [when the act took effect]; but afore that day they be no treason by the act, they be misprision by the Act of Succession. But it were best to have them indicted truly upon the fact [that is, of misprision]...and then let them remain in ward till further opinion be known.[1]

Expert opinion of this kind was no mere formality, and the duke of Norfolk, in his favourite pose as the plain man trying to enforce a complex law, provides good instances of this reliance on the lawyers. In September 1536 he heard of two men of Norwich accused of treasonable conspiracy and went at Cromwell's request to investigate. He had the assistance of five friends, including two judges and one serjeant-at-law whom he subsequently asked 'to look on their books and to advertise me how their offences would weigh in the law'. He forwarded their opinion but went on with a hint that he did not like it: he himself, 'speaking as a man unlearned in the laws', felt that one deserved death because he had planned an insurrection; the other, 'a right ill person', had no such plans. His lay opinion does not seem to have prevailed, and neither accused seems to have suffered.[2] Just about a year later he was at Newcastle, cleaning up after the rebellion, and troubled to know how to deal with a priest awaiting him in prison who had retorted upon his accuser the charge he stood accused of. The duke leant against the priest but sent the evidence to Cromwell, to hear 'how learned men do think the same will weigh against the said priest'.[3] Rowland Lee, trying in 1535 to manage a complex treason trial involving several persons, complained that such cases 'be in these parts rare and no form of indictment known' (nearly a year after the Treason Act had passed!); he asked that the King's learned counsel might draw him some indictments and that then 'the opinion of all the judges to be known against whom the matter shall weigh to be treason and against whom the matter will bear to be misprision'.[4] Some judges seem to have been willing to use a high hand. Fitzherbert, as we have seen, opposed legal scruples to the trial of a dangerous spreader of sedition,

---

[1] *StP* i. 442.
[2] SP 1/106, fo. 183 (*LP* xi. 470).
[3] SP 1/125, fo. 21 (*LP* xii. II. 741).
[4] SP 1/97, fo. 94 (*LP* ix. 510).

though probably without avail; and Sir John Porte, trying treasons at Worcester in August 1537, reprieved two men convicted by the jury 'because it was doubtful to me whether the words were treason'.[1] Since these two 'light persons' were accused only of seditious and slanderous speech against the earls of Shrewsbury and Derby, his doubts would appear to have been justified.

Of course, the matter was not always handled with such firm attention to the sovereignty of law. The lawyers themselves might feel uncertain, as did Christopher Jenney, serjeant-at-law, when he reported in 1535 that at York Assizes some men had been indicted of treason, 'but for that the words were to us doubtful whether they were high treason or not, we would not therefore proceed to the arraignment of them' until Cromwell and the King's Council had sent advice.[2] If practice was followed, as no doubt it was, the Council will have referred the matter to the judges. A man could solve the government's dilemma by committing a second and indubitable treason while the question whether an earlier offence would suffice was being pondered. Thus one Hutton had called a meeting in a barely pacified Yorkshire in early 1537, 'to make a supplication'; and although the King and Council reckoned that this probably 'weighed no less than high treason' and would have been willing to proceed against Hutton for it, Henry was glad to be able to tell Norfolk that fortunately 'this new matter' had occurred 'whereby he may without doubt or ambiguity receive his demerits'.[3] On another occasion, however, it looks as though the men on the spot had acted too hastily and may have been in the wrong. On 11 March 1537, Richard Estgate, a monk of Sawley involved in a rising after the pardon issued to the pilgrims of grace, was reported executed at Lancaster. Yet on the 21st, the earl of Sussex, who had presided over the commission, acknowledged Cromwell's request for the words with which Estgate was charged and had to admit that 'we could never, either afore nor after their condemnation, get anything of him'. And on the 24th, the King himself ordered Estgate – presumably by this time dead – to be sent up in safe custody. Whether Cromwell doubted the monk's guilt or wished to interrogate him further, Sussex's zeal had been untimely and he seems to have stretched the law to secure

[1] SP 1/124, fo. 34 (*LP* xii. II. 375).
[2] SP 1/95, fo. 38 (*LP* ix. 37 [i]).
[3] SP 1/117, fos. 17–18 (*LP* xii. I. 666). We do not know what the second offence was.

Estgate's condemnation.[1] Altogether, such aberrations seem to have been confined to the north, after the rebellions, when the Council of the North often acted in ruthless panic. In March 1540, for instance, they tried to get round the assize judge's opinion that a man charged with treason was covered by the recent pardon by transferring the trial to the next Assize; we do not know if the trick worked.[2]

In general, however, what matters is the evident fact that charges were weighed and the distinction between words treasonable by the statute and other words at best seditious was observed. Since denunciations could be wild and vague, while the act was comprehensive enough, a good deal of essentially harmless talk could be dangerous, but a good deal reported could also be extremely hard to assess. The charges brought against John Lacy, bailiff of Halifax and son-in-law of Sir Richard Tempest, in July 1537 may serve to show the sort of thing that conscientiousness came up against. His accuser was examined by three men, including Sir Henry Saville, Tempest's bitterest enemy, and Dr Holdsworth, vicar of Halifax, who at the time was pursuing Lacy with subpoenas in an attempt to recover property allegedly taken from him during the rebellion. The informer, one William Middleton, told Holdsworth that Lacy had composed a 'rhyme' against the King the quotable part of which ran, 'That as for the King, an apple and a fair wench to dally withal would please him very well'. But when Holdsworth asked him next day in Saville's presence to repeat his accusation, Middleton said he had got it wrong, 'for I told my wife when I come home how I showed the vicar of the rhyme that was made by Lacy of the King, and she said to me again that I told the vicar a wrong tale, for it was by [against] the bishop of Canterbury'. Holdsworth, suspicious of this alteration which left no charge of treason against his adversary, later sent a servant 'to drink and make good cheer' with the Middletons 'and bade him spy a time' to ask the wife at whom the verse had been directed. 'Nay marry, said she, it was made against the King and my lord privy seal.' Her husband interposed, 'Dame, it is not so'. But she insisted 'it was so indeed, against the King and my lord privy seal, by God, without fail'. A few days later Saville tried to persuade Cromwell into action against Lacy who was going about saying 'if they will have my head they shall fetch it'. He called two of his servants after two of

[1] SP 1/116, fo. 253; 117, fo. 77 (LP xii. I. 632, 695); StP i. 541.
[2] SP 1/158, fo. 147 (LP xv. 428).

the King's ministers and mocked that he would do well enough, 'for he had with him of counsel both the lord chancellor and Crumwell'. That verse he made did include the King, 'with such words as any honest man would abhor to hear spoken or see written'. There were broad hints that Lacy had favoured the rebels in the late commotion.[1] What was an overworked minister, who yet could not allow true treason or contempt of the King to pass unnoticed, to do with such stuff? How was he to draw an indictment from it? As far as the evidence goes, he did nothing.

Indictments had to be prepared with care; as has been seen, it was a task sometimes left to the King's legal counsel rather than risk error resulting from local ignorance. In the notorious note in which Cromwell reminded himself that the abbots of Reading and Glastonbury had to be sent to their country 'to be tried and executed' – a note which has often been taken to represent a characteristic prejudging of the case – he also wrote: 'To see that the evidence be well sorted and the indictments well drawn against the said abbots and their complices', which suggests that so far from regarding the trials as a formality he was concerned that his own assurance of the accused persons' guilt should be properly transmitted to the jury.[2] The technicalities of an indictment were formidable, and errors or omissions could cast a good case away. Discovering technical mistakes in the indictment was a favourite trick for escaping from the consequences of a crime; the rolls of King's Bench are full of such dubious avoidance of justice on the part of murderers and robbers. But it still comes as something of a surprise to find that the device could work for men caught under the severe legislation of the 1530's. Harry Weston, who successfully claimed that Quarter Sessions could not try him for treason, also secured the King's Bench's assent to his plea that an indictment which did not give the day, year and place on and at which he was alleged to have committed the offence was not good in law.[3] And Robert Lenton, charged under the *Praemunire* Act of 1536 because he possessed pro-papal writings, got off because his indictment did not repeat the place and county of his domicile when reciting the offence, though the information was given earlier in the document.[4]

---

[1] SP 1/117, fos. 192–5; 123, fos. 91–2 (*LP* xii. I. 784; II. 339). The conflict was tied up with the complex story of Dr Holdsworth's alleged attempt to withhold £300 of treasure trove from the Crown, claiming it to be his own savings.

[2] BM, Tit. B. i, fo. 441 (*LP* xiv. II. 399).

[3] KB 27/1109, Rex, rot. 13.   [4] Ibid. 1113, Rex, rot. 14.

On what grounds William Thacker of Norwich escaped is not clear, but some technicality was involved. He was indicted in 1538 for these words: 'The Council which was about the King [were] naughty harlots, and that he that began to set forth first this new law against pilgrimage and such like, he would that his sword were through the heart of him, and that the marriage was the first setter forth of the new learning.' He was arrested by the sheriff on suspicion of high treason upon this indictment, but the case was for some reason certified into King's Bench where in Hillary 1540 Thacker was bailed. That was the end of the case.[1]

Even a good indictment, technically correct, could be thrown out by the presenting jury, and several men thus escaped trial, generally because they were in fact innocent. Of the twenty-five men indicted for the great Walsingham conspiracy, eight were so set at liberty: in their case, the Crown failed to make the indictment stick. Not that such delivery fully ended the matter: it seems to have been customary to keep an eye on persons once accused if the jury would not indict them. In view of the evidence that cases were not usually brought without preliminary investigation, and of the further fact (discussed below) that juries could behave very oddly, this does not strike one as unreasonable, especially as no case is known where a man so freed but kept under observation was ever again prosecuted. Late in 1537, for instance, Richard Norres, parish priest of Cheadle (Staffs.), was carefully examined on a charge of treasonable words, but when the matter was put to the jury 'they could not find the said surmise to be true'. The commissioners took bonds of both accused and accuser to be ready to appear if further investigation should yield results; no more is heard of the matter.[2] Another priest, John Neale, arrested for suspicion of treason in 1538, was delivered by proclamation and bound to appear before King and Council; he disappears from the record.[3] John Revell, a grocer of Norwich, underwent the same experience; and yet he was a notorious dissident if the John Revell of the Lodge, Shirland (Derb.) is the same man.[4] The date, name and matter fit so well that the difference in

---

[1] KB 9/538/18, 541/110; 27/1114, Rex, rot. 5.
[2] SP 1/127, fo. 172 (*LP* xii. II. 1299).   [3] KB 9/541/110.
[4] Ibid.; St Ch 2/26/194. The accuser brought in the Star Chamber bill on 14 June 1538. The Derbyshire John Revell had two sons, one also called John; perhaps it was the younger man who escaped at Norwich. This John junior (as his father admitted) on one occasion expressed his opinion of the parish priest by bringing a pudding into

domicile may well be accounted for by the supposition that either one of the descriptions is wrong or he was rich enough to have two habitations. This second Revell was accused to Cromwell of being the chief obstacle to the new order in his parish by having bells rung on days forbidden and through his chaplain preventing the parish priest from proclaiming the King's Injunctions. Not everybody whose indictment failed got off scot free. John Welshman, a servant to Lord Hussey, was freed by a Bridgnorth jury early in 1538. However, Sir William Parr, the local authority, kept him in ward to know the King's pleasure and later pilloried him 'for his seditious words'.[1] Still, this was a good deal less than a successful indictment would have done to him.

The fact of the matter is that a trial for treason required quite solid proof; one must forget the very special case of Sir Thomas More, pursued to the death by a vengeful King, and pay some heed to the evidence that the government did not think every charge sure to come to a standard conclusion. Cromwell showed himself aware of this in the very note in which he referred to the forthcoming trial and execution of the abbots of Glastonbury and Reading, when he carefully listed three and two councillors respectively who were to give evidence at those trials.[2] When one Edward Conysby was arraigned in the Guildhall in July 1538, for a treason committed by forging the King's signet and privy seal, the lord mayor, Sir Richard Gresham, who presided over the commission, was very dissatisfied with the evidence supplied and complained to Cromwell. The forgeries to be put to the jury were all dated before 4 February 1536, the date of the statute under which

church and forcing a piece of it down the priest's throat at the communion time, which understandably enough ended mass for the day. John senior claimed that his only interference with the priest consisted of saying, very softly, 'fac finem', when the priest was very long dealing with the gospel and it was already eleven o'clock.

[1] SP 1/120, fo. 106 (*LP* xii. I. 1213); St Ch 2/27/141. This assumes that the two John Welshman are the same, in which case the date in *LP* is wrong: but this is entirely possible. The Star Chamber bill arose out of a slander according to which a servant of the earl of Derby had admitted Welshman to an almshouse, knowing him to be 'apeached of treason'; the person slandered claimed that in fact he had thrown Welshman out of the almshouse when he 'heard tell of his exclamation'. However, Welshman, destitute after his acquittal, had apparently persuaded the bailiff of the village to let him return to that refuge together with his family.

[2] BM, Tit. B. i, fo. 441 (*LP* xiv. II. 399). Strictly, these councillors could testify only to what the abbots had admitted during interrogation; they would doubtless not be admitted in a modern court, but there was nothing unusual about such witnesses in the sixteenth century.

Conysby was to be tried. The indictment spoke of offences committed since the statute, but for these no proof was before the court. Gresham asked for some, as well as for the accused's confession which Cromwell allegedly had; he had adjourned the Sessions for five days to obtain them. On the later occasion, it would seem, the case was better presented, and Conysby was duly convicted and later executed.[1]

Although the law permitted traitors to be convicted on the testimony of a single witness – another fact made notorious by the trial of Sir Thomas More – it would seem that as a rule the government did not like to proceed on so slender a basis. Considering the undoubted traitor Giles Heron in 1539, Cromwell asked himself 'what shall be done with him, forasmuch as there is but one witness'.[2] However, he found the notorious way round this: in a later note, which first read 'the indictment to be drawn against Giles Heron', he changed 'indictment' into 'bill for the Parliament'. Heron was in fact attainted, though like others attainted during Cromwell's ascendancy he was not executed until after Cromwell's own death.[3] At other times, the single-witness problem resolved itself more happily for the accused. A priest, Peter Bentley, was accused by another, John More, of a serious offence (as the time reckoned) against the King's authority. Confronted with a faculty under the royal seal, he had allegedly exclaimed: 'Hold thy peace, man, I set not by this seal nor by him, tush, not this much (making a fillip with his two fingers), for I trust to see the day that all this shall be turned up and done; a man may say what he will in his own house.' The matter came before Lord Sandys who, uncertain what weight to attach to it and feeling that it was but one man's word against another's, asked instructions from Cromwell. He got the answer that 'in respect there is but one witness and that the matter...is not of any great importance' he was to please himself, either discharging Bentley or keeping him a few days in prison. Sandys, now convinced that it was all just malice, let him go.[4] Ordinarily, therefore, Cromwell would appear to have

---

[1] SP 1/134, fo. 247; 135, fos. 7, 57 (*LP* xiii. I. 1462; II. 13, 72). After sentence, Conysby tried to prolong his life by pretending to know something 'for the King's advantage', but Gresham soon got him to admit that he knew nothing. 'So I have put him to execution, and God pardon him.'

[2] E 36/143/28 (*LP* xiv. II. 494). On the problem of witnesses cf. L. M. Hill, 'The Two-Witness Rule in English Treason Trials,' *Amer. Journal of Legal History*, xii (1968), 95 ff.

[3] E 36/143, fo. 33 (*LP* xv. 598 [i]); *LP* xv. 498 (56); Wriothesley, i. 121.

[4] SP 1/133, fos. 1, 160; E 36/120, fo. 98 (*LP* xiii. I. 1141, 1229).

been as careful in such matters as was Audley when confronted, in September 1537, with the long and complicated charges of treasonable words raised against Thomas Neville, brother of Lord Latimer. Looking at the depositions, he reported that the part of the accusations 'whereof there is no witness but one woman' seemed treason to him; the rest, for which there were two witnesses, 'I doubt whether be treason or not'. He would do nothing till he had Cromwell's opinion; Neville was left in peace.[1] The quality of the witnesses had also to be considered, a fact which helped Nicholas Whelocke, vicar of Biddulph (Staffs.) in August 1537. 'The great inquest' indicted him of treasonable words, but the judge wrote that he 'durst not take upon me to proceed in his trial because such as gave evidence said there remain certain writings of his accusement' with Cromwell. This gave Whenlocke a chance of appealing to the lord privy seal; he protested his innocence and called his accusers 'persons of evil name, fame and credit. . . common vexers, perturbers and oppressors of sundry the King's subjects'. He claimed that when the indictment was taken the accusers could not be found, having fled the town; Whelocke, sure that a trial would acquit him, had insisted on the indictment being taken nevertheless so as to end his half year's imprisonment. The judge later talked to Cromwell, and at the next Assizes, on December 30th, before another judge, Whelocke was duly acquitted.[2]

The importance of really preparing a case and of assembling credible witnesses was most clearly stated by Bishop Lee when he contemplated the unwelcome task of bringing Prior More to trial. He thought it very necessary that some who had attended the examination of the accused should be at the indictment and arraignment to testify to the truth of the matter.

For assuredly in these parts juries cannot be found as with you about London. And as ye know, the party is here a great possessioner, and the matter weighty also by reason that the Sessions and Assizes for the shire of Worcester have been always used to be kept at Worcester, by occasion whereof the number of the gentlemen of the shire have been used to be familiarly entertained in the said priory.

Good witnesses were therefore essential, to overcome old memories and long acquaintance.[3] The bishop's doubts may have been too forcefully

---

[1] SP 1/124, fo. 199 (*LP* xii. II. 667).
[2] SP 1/124, fos. 34, 154; 127, fo. 172 (*LP* xii. II. 515, 622, 1299).
[3] SP 1/97, fo. 94 (*LP* ix. 510).

expressed: More was never in fact tried.[1] Lee also erred in supposing
that only Welsh or border juries could not be trusted to behave themselves, though another case within his jurisdiction may be cited to
support his jaundiced scepticism. As we have seen, no jury could be got
to indict William Norton because he was a retainer of Lady Anne
Berkeley.[2] In the last resort, trials for treason, as for all other crimes,
came up against the fact that juries, whether in the interests of justice or
not, could frustrate the plainest purposes of policy and ignore the
clearest evidence.

The problem of the trial jury in Tudor England – the problem of
local influence and prejudice – is a familiar one, but it will bear being
illustrated at some length from unfamiliar material, to underline the
situation confronting a government intent upon enforcing the law.[3]
As Lee suggested, the problem of local corruption and influence was
possibly particularly severe in Wales. In the early 1530's, Sir Roland
Velavyll, constable of Beaumaris Castle, told the King's Council that
information against men who had broken sureties of the peace was
regularly thrown out by juries despite 'pregnant evidences' and that
'very few matters in such case where the King is party' were 'truly
found for his grace'. He also listed a number of oppressors and extor-
tioners among whom Dr William Glyn, vicar-general of Bangor, stood
high.[4] But, despite Lee's confidence in London juries, the capital was no
more free of the evil. A coroner's jury was accused in April 1540 of
failing to indict a known murderer; some of its members were willing
to tell the truth, but others had been 'so specially laboured by the
friends' of the killer that they used every device to delay the verdict,
simply in order to 'fatigue and make weary' the rest.[5] In 1526, a jury
at Newgate, having convicted a burglar who successfully pleaded his
clergy, refused to deal likewise with an alleged accessory; but justice
may here have been done, for the burglar's victim found himself in
King's Bench, accused by the supposed accessory of conspiracy, and the
jury in their answer to his Star Chamber bill pointed to this pending
action as proof that they had acted fairly in the earlier case.[6]

[1] Above, p. 127. [2] Above, p. 237.
[3] Cf. e.g. my *Star Chamber Stories*, 99 ff. The State Papers contain many casual references
to troubles with juries, but the following examples from the Star Chamber proceedings
are both less accessible and rather more detailed.
[4] St Ch 2/17/347. [5] Ibid. 31/159.
[6] Ibid. 24/211.

Juries were certainly open to corruption by interested parties. When one Henley was to be indicted at Guildford Assizes he had the valuable support of a local worthy, Sir Matthew Browne, many times a justice of the peace.[1] Browne asked the sheriff to impanel a favourable jury, offered its members bribes and favours, and appeared at the trial to speak for the accused and impress the jury by his presence. The existence of the interrogatory from which these details are taken shows that he was successful.[2] In the 1530's an informer claimed that his attempt to prosecute the vicar of Andover (Hants.) for breach of the 1529 statute forbidding clergy to hold lands to farm failed because the undersheriff secured a partial jury which he also entertained to dinner between the giving of the allegedly conclusive evidence and the rendering of the verdict.[3] Not that local opinion always favoured the accused: in August 1546, a Lincolnshire jury could not agree in a case of murder because the accused man's fellow-villagers among them were sure he had done it, while the remainder had been got at by his friends and refused to convict.[4] Either way, however, the evidence tended to be ignored. If Lawrence Porter told the truth – and it sounds as though he did – he was maltreated by a jury at Derby who denied him repayment of a bond owed by Henry Bothe, even though Porter produced a letter from four gentlemen testifying to the sealing of the bond as well as a live witness to that fact, and even though he could show that in a bill in Chancery Bothe had admitted giving the bond.[5] Even the attorney-general could come up against juries intent on defending a vested interest against all the law and the facts. In about 1531, Sir Christopher Hales complained to the Council that an inquest at the Guildhall refused to admit that certain lands, granted to the Merchant Tailors by a late member of the company in the form of a use which the Court of Chancery had declared invalid, were not still held in use to the grantor and his heirs, as a result of which perverse verdict the King had lost his rights. They had done so in fear of setting a precedent against the property rights of other London corporations. The jury could only reply that they had several times been troubled for this verdict and asked to be left alone; they did not attempt to controvert the evidence, conclusive in law, recited by the attorney-general.[6]

---

[1] He was so from early in the reign (*LP* i, p. 1545), and the case cannot be dated.
[2] St Ch 2/22/50.   [3] Ibid. 17/95.
[4] Ibid. 5/16.   [5] Ibid. 17/224.
[6] Ibid. 17/349.

On the other hand, it will not do to suppose that juries in such disputed cases always behaved with simple effrontery or under the persuasion of influence, bribery or pressure. The truth is more complex than this and more clearly underlines the special difficulties posed by trial by jury; for juries were thinking men and could take a line of their own. One quest told the Court of Star Chamber firmly that the man who complained of them had ignored an act of Henry IV to the effect that judgments in the King's courts could not be examined 'in the Courts of Chancery or elsewhere' and that 'he hath an ordinary remedy by the common laws of this realm...and ought not to impeach these defendants [the jury] of their said verdict in any extraordinary court'; one wonders how the Council took this.[1] And one may sympathise with a jury trying that notoriously difficult thing, a case involving an alleged rape, or near rape, in the marches of Wales. According to the report of one juror, an issue was tried between Anthony Welsh and Jane Powell. Welsh's witnesses 'did not tell their tale by mouth but it was read unto them and thereupon demanded whether it were true and so affirmed it, and yet but men of small reputation'. Jane, seeing that no evidence was given on her behalf, asked the president of the Council in the Marches, who sat as chief judge, where the bills were that she had given him at Hereford, 'and he, laying his hand upon his breast, said they were gone'. So she asked to be heard and told her tale upon her knees. After her husband's death she had gone to stay with Welsh 'as to her friend', but found that Welsh wished to force her into marriage to one of his servants. She disliked the man and refused him, so Welsh 'spied his time' to lock both of them in a chamber, calling out 'Now play the man – get her if thou can'. Her cries alerted Mrs Welsh who got her husband to unlock the door, no harm having apparently been done. But Jane found a little later that Welsh had 'sold her to a man of the country there' for £5. At this point, Sir John Porte, also on the bench, intervened with a characteristic lawyer's remark to ask if Jane was Welsh's ward (in which case the selling of her marriage would have been lawful), but Welsh had to admit that she was not. In some despair, Jane got an acquaintance to go to Caerleon to Roger Morgan 'and have me commended by this token – and took a ring off her finger – and show him that if he love me, as I do him, let him fetch me away by Friday next, and I will go with him; for I am sold to another

---

[1] Ibid. 24/10.

man'. This was her touching story, but the jury had reason to think that the whole quarrel was less straightforward and involved only the money to be paid for Jane, for Morgan had originally refused to give as much as £5 for her, whereupon Welsh sold her 'to an old man' for £30, but she would not agree. There is not enough here to make the matter clear, but whatever the jury made of it in their verdict produced a protest to Star Chamber; yet it is hard to blame them for not getting things right on this occasion.[1]

That juries could do their own thinking was shown in somewhat surprising fashion when one of them was examined by the Court of Star Chamber for failing to convict a gang of breaking a dovecote in spite of the clear evidence produced against them at the trial.[2] The original case was probably heard at Lewes Assizes during Wolsey's ascendancy,[3] and the plain fact of the matter is that the jury refused to accept accuseds' own confessions put in by the prosecution. One Lowle, they thought, was not present at the crime although he had so 'surmised and confessed', because they preferred the sworn testimony to the contrary given by two priests and a layman before commissioners at Lewes. From this it followed that they could not believe Thomas a Milton when he similarly confessed because he had accused Lowle of being present, which they had already decided was untrue: 'forasmuch he is, as we think, forsworn in this matter, we ought to think of conscience all those that he hath accused are not guilty, for we ought not to give credence to a perjured man'. They thought one Norles was lying in accusing Stephen Rotys since several people had given evidence to acquit him. They could not believe one Sage because 'he hath been racked in the Tower' till he admitted being present, as the jury were told by the lieutenant of the Tower; and Sage had accused one Edmund Bocher who could prove an alibi by witnesses. This muddle of evidence (which in part they had created by the dubious premise of their very first step in the argument) left them, they went on, unable to act. If they convicted those who had confessed, they would have to convict those accused by them despite 'the substantial evidence...the which proveth them not to be there'. If they found them not guilty, 'their confession

---

[1] Ibid. 24/34.
[2] Ibid. 30, fragments.
[3] The document refers to the Star Chamber as 'your grace and this most honourable court'.

is against us and so we should do, we think, contrary to the law'. They therefore remitted the situation to the Star Chamber. It may be that their explanation hides more dubious things, and their asseverations that in conscience they could not do otherwise have an air of protesting too much. Yet there is sound sense in their refusal to accept self-incriminating confessions, one of them at least obtained after torture during the preliminary investigation, against sworn depositions on the other side; though we might doubt the honesty of those witnesses, the jury had seen and heard them. Plainly, a jury trial was at least on occasion a real trial, neither a simple matter of form nor a simple and invariable obstacle to justice.

One might suppose that in trials for treason local prejudice and influence would operate less successfully than in mere felonies, disputes over land, or prosecutions under statutes concerning trade and industry. Yet in the eight years with which we are concerned over thirty men were acquitted by the jury after being arraigned on charges of treason, and it would be as rash to assume that this outcome demonstrates false prosecutions as it would be to take corruption and perversion of justice for granted. Not surprisingly, perhaps, such evidence as survives suggests rather overfriendly juries than unjustified accusations; no doubt, if the acquittal was manifestly correct, there would be little said and no investigation. John Welshman who (as we have seen) was acquitted of treason though later punished for sedition owed his escape to the refusal of two juries to indict him on the rather general grounds that they 'have not known nor heard by him any corrupt heart or deed that he hath borne or done towards the King's majesty'.[1] William Thwaytes was acquitted at York Assizes in March 1536 because the jury preferred to believe the charges malicious.[2] And two cases of which rather more is known deserve to be described at length because they tell a good deal about what went on at trials for treason in the reign of Henry VIII.

The first case is that of William Levenyng who was involved in Bigod's rebellion of February 1537 and therefore forfeited the advantages of the pardon granted to the pilgrims of grace. With others he was

---

[1] SP 1/120, fo. 106 (*LP* xii. I. 1213).

[2] Above, p. 58. At the same Assize the judge bound a jury in £100 each to appear before the Council in Star Chamber because they had acquitted a man accused of an especially nasty murder, clean contrary to the evidence. Yet the sheriff assured the judge that except for one disinterested man the jury were, if anything, of the murdered man's party! (*LP* viii. 457, misdated by a year).

tried at York and acquitted on 24 March 1537.[1] This caused consternation, and the Council ordered an investigation. What happened in the jury room was told by one of their number, Thomas Delaryver, a King's man thought so reliable by Norfolk that the duke had put him on the jury even though he had not been on the sheriff's panel.[2] With four others, Delaryver had been convinced by the evidence that Levenyng 'was worthy to die', but the remaining seven said that Levenyng was their neighbour and they 'knew better his conversation than we did', for which reason they wished to acquit. They stuck, 'beating the matter', from nine in the morning of Friday the 23rd till Saturday night. The leader of the majority, a member of the influential Wentworth family,[3] claimed that Sir Ralph Ellercar's testimony had been given of malice and that Ellercar had secured a grant of part of Levenyng's lands. To this Delaryver replied that the King would not grant lands to anyone till after the owner had been 'attainted by the law'. They ought to find him guilty 'for they knew not what could come upon the matter', and besides, he *was* guilty. The others argued that in that case all those in company with Bigod should be worthy to die. Yes, said Delaryver, if they had been 'inquired upon' (that is, indicted), and so they should have been but that the King was 'so noble a prince and merciful'. Levenyng was guilty, and so they must find him, 'for if they did not it would be a final destruction for us all'. No, said the other side: if Delaryver knew Levenyng as well as they did, 'he would not be so extreme against him'. Levenyng was a sound man: 'at the first insurrection he did nothing against the King's grace nor never taken upon him to be a meddler against the King's grace.' Before Bigod had forced him into complicity, he had never done 'hurt or spoil' to any man. Wentworth argued, very properly, that 'we ought better to favour life than death unless we had evidence given of more persons than one', besides which Ellercar was a personal enemy of the accused.

By about noon on Saturday, the duke of Norfolk got tired of waiting and sent his gentleman usher to ask 'whether they were agreed or no, and to send him word thereof, for if they were agreed he would come and take their verdict'. The majority said they were agreed, at which

---

[1] The date of the trial is given in Norfolk's letter of next day: *LP* xii. I. 730.

[2] So Norfolk (SP 1/118, fo. 184 [*LP* xii. I. 952]); Delaryver's report is in SP 1/117, fos. 133–7 (*LP* xii. I. 731).

[3] Probably Thomas Wentworth of Ganton, gent. (cf. *LP* xiii. I. 970).

point Delaryver gave in: 'if he could see no other remedy he would do as they did'. But he warned them that 'it would be an utter destruction to us all and our blood for ever' and cursed the mischance that had caused him 'to be impanelled with such a rude sort that would in no wise be informed by no manner of means but to go upon their rude wills'. As they were about to come before the duke, Delaryver heard one of the majority say in selfsatisfied tones that Sir Marmaduke Constable the elder, a well established leader of Yorkshire society, 'would not for £100 that the said Levenyng should have been found guilty'. At this evidence of underhand influence, Delaryver, already seriously worried by the King's probable reaction to an acquittal, blew up in a 'fury and fume', swearing that now he would rather die than acquit. They were stuck again, and Norfolk, angry at the palaver, now ordered them to be treated more harshly; all the 'gear' they had for keeping themselves warm was taken away, but they sat on arguing till nightfall. At this point, the duke once more sent to them, advising them to agree. Delaryver tried desperate means: he fell on his knees and prayed, 'beseeching Almighty God to give them grace that they might take that way which might be to His pleasure and the King's, and safeguard of their souls'. But when he got up the majority calmly stuck to acquittal, and the minority gave in.

Yorkshire stubbornness and private favour had won, for Levenyng had been manifestly guilty. The duke thought so and learned a lesson; when he had to hold another trial in May he wrote that he now knew the gentlemen of the shire better and could name a compliant jury, as he wished he had been able to do in Levenyng's case.[1] His words carry the more conviction because he went on to agree that one Lutton, acquitted at the same time, had indeed been innocent. Sir Marmaduke Constable played the innocent, writing to Cromwell for protection against those who slandered him by saying that he had looked after Levenyng.[2] The acquitted man had not apparently thought himself entirely safe even after the jury had done their best for him. A year later, when the recent sheriff of Yorkshire was under investigation for extortion, one John Thorpe told how he had been in the castle yard at York during the 1537 sessions of treason when he was accosted by Thomas Wentworth about Levenyng whom both of them knew. Wentworth said: 'I hear say he is a good gentleman and therefore I would he should do well. He is now

---

[1] SP 1/120, fo. 26 (*LP* xii. I. 1172).   [2] SP 1/120, fo. 163 (*LP* xii. I. 1255).

acquitted, but there will be new matters laid against him at the next Sessions, wherefore I would he should have the sheriff good for him.' The two of them talked to the sheriff, and Levenyng paid over some £20 or twenty marks at the next sheepshearing.[1] In fact, there is nothing to show that Levenyng was ever troubled again. His treason would seem to have been manifest, and Sir Francis Bigod, his principal, died for his, despite all his good service to the King in earlier years. The undercurrents of local opinion and influence had saved Levenyng, though it had been a close-run thing.

In Levenyng's case, the disturbed condition of the north and the aftermath of serious rebellion help to explain the difficulties of getting a conviction, even as they underline the supremacy of the rule of law even in such circumstances. The persistent immunity of Richard Benger, LL.D., is less understandable, and even though his case will take us beyond the ordinary limits of this study into the year 1542, it is worth discussing in full. Benger was a man of substance, learning and standing.[2] Born in Wiltshire about 1484, he was educated at Winchester and New College, Oxford, where he remained as a fellow until 1521. During that time he held College office as bursar and subwarden; furthermore, he proceeded through the degrees of bachelor in both laws to the double doctorate. One would expect a man of his equipment to seek promotion in the service of bishops and King, but instead he followed a career of conventional success in the Church by obtaining a College living in Kent, adding to it as time went on another living, the canonry of Wingham, and the prebend of Womenswold. He achieved all this and preserved it, even though he hated the events of the 1530's, a feeling he did not trouble to hide.

The first time he got into danger was in March 1535 when Cromwell sent for him. What had happened was this.[3] Thomas Lawney, Cranmer's chaplain, preached a sermon at Wingham in the presence of Archdeacon Cranmer, the archbishop's brother, in which he did his duty by attacking the pope. Afterwards he was refreshing himself in the archdeacon's house when Benger, who had attended the sermon, came in. The sight of a pleasant fire put an idea into his head, and he said to the preacher: 'This fire is good to warm on and it is good to seethe

[1] SP 1/132, fo. 88 (*LP* xiii. I. 970).
[2] A. B. Emden, *Biographical Dictionary of the University of Oxford to 1500*, i. 167–8.
[3] This part of the story is derived from SP 1/91, fos. 89–92 (*LP* viii. 386–7).

meat and to roast, but no men, Sir Thomas, I trow; how say you?'
Lawney tried to evade the obvious insinuation by replying: 'Marry,
and if they deserve it, why should they not?' 'Marry,' said Benger,
coming into the open, 'I would all this new learned men were burned
in as good a fire as I could make.' Lawney asked whether by new
learned men he meant those who spoke against the pope. 'There is no
good man', replied the doctor, 'will speak against the pope, for I will
never while I live.' Lawney reminded him of his oath to the King's
supremacy, to which Benger retorted that he knew as well as the
preacher what he was sworn to. 'Yea,' said Lawney, 'ye are sworn to
rhe Church, but it is the Church of England and not of Rome.' So
Benger asserted that no good man would speak against the Church of
Rome and went off 'in a fume'.

When this matter was reported to Cromwell the investigation turned
up another occasion on which the canon of Wingham had let himself
go dangerously. On 20 September 1534, dining at the archdeacon's
house, he had defended the pope's authority to make law. In the course
of a long argument he said 'that by what authority we denied the pope,
by the same authority he would deny the Scripture and say that Christ
is not yet born'. Finally he spoke words of the kind that many men at
the time found led to trouble with the law: 'these new laws may be
suffered for a season, but in time to come it will cost broken heads and
set men together by the ears.' Archdeacon Cranmer warned him:
'Master Doctor, take heed what you say, for I am sworn to the King's
grace and neither may nor will conceal anything contrary to his
majesty.' At this Benger at last took fright and said repeatedly, 'I mean
not here but somewhere else, out of the realm'.

The charges were specific enough and serious, but spoken when the
Treason Act was not yet in force; and so Benger not only survived
them without further trouble or trial but the very next year obtained
his prebend and continued to flourish, known though he was as 'a
marvellous enemy to God and his Word' (as Lawney called him) and an
outspoken opponent of the royal supremacy. It was not until September
1540 that he once again gave his enemies a chance to tackle him. On the
third of that month, in conversation with the archbishop, he criticised
the King's taxing of the clergy, hinted darkly that the profits of the
suppressed abbeys did not all come to the King's hands, denied the
King's authority to tax the clergy at all, and blamed the archbishop for

letting the King go on as he did: for 'the archbishops of Canterbury were wont *opponere se tamquam murum pro domo Israel'*. These words sounded to be an incitement to resistance and rebellion. At least, they and more like them were put to his charge when Cranmer, taking the precaution of associating three other men of substance with himself, formally interrogated him on the 22nd.[1] Benger refused to remember the worst remarks, such as that the King had no authority to tax the clergy and should have been told by Cranmer that 'he should be damned for taking God's part [the money of the Church] and so would he have told the King if he had been archbishop of Canterbury, for it is against God's law'. Cranmer claimed to have told him that 'he was brought in blindness and error by the decrees'. To this justifiable jibe at his legal learning he had allegedly replied 'that he would die in that blindness and no man should make him revoke or recant the same', thereby demonstrating that inveterate stubbornness in crime which the age regarded as justifying the withholding of the royal mercy; but he denied this, too. However, he admitted enough of the conversation to show that he had criticized clerical taxation and expected Cranmer to oppose it with the King, and to suggest that the rest of the charge was true enough; it is much easier to believe, since we know the sort of thing he was capable of saying, that the remainder of his remarks was as Cranmer remembered it, than it is to credit the archbishop with the deliberate invention of long and precise speeches of the kind alleged, against an innocent man.

This was also the Privy Council's view who on November 1st instructed Cranmer to send Benger to the Tower.[2] This time he was not to escape, and in due course he was tried at Kent Assizes before a commission presided over by Sir Thomas Willoughby, judge of the Common Pleas, and Sir Humphrey Browne, justice of assize. He was acquitted, and the Council demanded to know why. In consequence we have an account of the trial rendered by some of the commissioners.[3] The prosecution was in the hands of Sir Thomas Moyle, a noted lawyer and administrator of the day.[4] He explained the indictment to the jury

---

[1] St Ch 2/8/77: Baron John Hales of the Exchequer, his son James (serjeant-at-law), and one John Boys, gent. The *DNB* would seem to be in error in dating Baron Hales's death to 1539; however, as these papers show, he was dead by 1542.

[2] *PPC* vii. 74.   [3] St Ch 2/24/163.

[4] Moyle was a leading official of the Court of Augmentations (cf. index entries in W. C. Richardson, *History of the Court of Augmentations* [1961]).

by citing the relevant statutes and proved it to be true by putting in evidence various letters from Cranmer to the Council, with two examinations of Benger held before the archbishop and others, one of them being the document of 22 September 1540. There was also a record of Benger's treasonable utterances signed by Cranmer and some of his servants. Moyle expounded all this 'fully and clearly' to the jury and reminded them that Cranmer was 'one of the King's most honourable Council and primate of all England, with diverse and much other circumstances for the enforcing of the same, which at the present time is out of our remembrance'. Moyle would be able to tell more.

Next Benger spoke in his own defence, and it is clear that he made a skilful speech. He concentrated on the remark he had admitted making about Cranmer's duty to oppose himself as a wall for the house of Israel and argued from the scriptural context that this did not mean incitement to rebellion but a search for one who would intercede with the King to ask him, of his kindness, to remit the taxes. He accused Cranmer of malice and ill will towards himself: the charges were invented, nor was it the first time that the archbishop had 'wrongfully accused and troubled him', no doubt a reference to the time that Benger had persuaded Cromwell to let him go. He began to quote legal tags at the jury: 'favendum est reo quam accusatori' – the accused rather than the accuser must have the benefit of any doubt – and 'in omnibus gravioribus delictis probationes debent esse luce clariores', in all serious offences proof must be clearer than daylight. It was 'against conscience' that he should be condemned upon Cranmer's unsupported statement, for their conversation had been in private and there were neither substantial witnesses nor proofs. He took exception to the deposition countersigned by Cranmer's servants: these deserved no credit because they 'for fear of losing their service and in trust to obtain higher promotion would say and speak whatsoever it pleased my lord'. He further undermined the evidence by claiming that neither his examiners nor anyone else were sworn to the points that they had put their names to. At this Browne interrupted him, saying that a man of Cranmer's standing should have his word properly respected; he did not know whether Cranmer had been sworn to his testimony but (turning to the jury) 'if you be in doubt, lean rather to life than to death, but herein there is no doubt, and therefore take heed to your evidence and do as God will put in your minds'. These words proved to be a mistake.

That ended the arguments, and Willoughby proceeded to sum up. He told Benger that the King was 'a prince of mercy and justice and would the death of no man wrongfully'. Then he went over the ground covered by Moyle, once more explained the indictment and the law on which it rested, and showed that if the words alleged were proved true 'the said doctor was within the compass of the said statute'. Finally he hammered home the evidence, the care taken by Cranmer to interrogate Benger in detail and get others to sit with him at the examination, as well as the fact that Benger, in a letter of his own, had practically admitted the accusation. 'So these are great evidence to induce your conscience to prove and to find him guilty.' Another hand added a note, probably conveying the opinion of the other commissioners, to the effect that they, too, had thought the evidence 'sufficient matter for the jury to have found the said Dr Benger guilty'. As far as we can tell at this distance of time and with only part of the evidence before us which the jury saw, this seems true enough; whatever exactly Benger may have said or meant, he clearly said enough for the generous Treason Act to catch him. The jury thought otherwise. Whether they were bemused by Benger's legal learning, convinced of Cranmer's malice towards the accused, sidetracked by the judge's incautious suggestion to opt for life rather than death if they had any doubt at all, or simply thought that Benger had the right of it in his attitude to the King's doings, they set him free. He died a few years later, after a decade of successful and far from silent opposition to the might of a state intent upon enforcing a revolutionary situation. And he died peacefully at home, instead of horribly upon the scaffold, because a jury of Kent, despite all that archbishop, Council and judges could do to prepare and prove the case, would have none of it.

One more story will bear telling because it illustrates, in rather garish colours, how a combination of legal technicalities and local influences could frustrate the purposes of government – purposes which, as the law stood, must be called the ends of justice, too. In the late summer of 1536, royal commissioners dissolved the Augustinian abbey of Norton in Cheshire, an action which set in train a somewhat remarkable series of events. The commissioners were about to leave when the dispossessed abbot arrived with some of his canons and a large force of townspeople, compelled the commissioners to take refuge in a tower, encamped his army, and set about a victory celebration adorned with ox-roasting. Before the night was out, however, he himself had been captured with a few others by Sir Piers Dutton, sheriff of Cheshire, who had rapidly gathered a posse; the several hundred other rebels had escaped in the darkness.[1] This was only the beginning of it. On August 3rd, Dutton reported to Cromwell that he had seven men in custody (including Ralph Brereton, an officer of the Exchequer at Chester) and was pursuing his enquiries.[2] Soon after, he would seem to have reported the situation also to Audley who told the King; Dutton received a reply from Henry which Audley had corrected.[3] 'As it appeareth', wrote the incensed monarch, 'that the late abbot and canons have most traitorously used themselves against us and our realm and moved insurrection against the common quiet of the same', they were at once to be executed. The first draft had, very properly, ordered them to be 'indicted and straight thereupon arraigned and so without further tract put all to execution', but Audley, no doubt recalling the permitted treatment of rebels caught in the act, had replaced the whole phrase with the one word 'hanged'.

However, while Dutton had alerted the lord chancellor, his rival for the control of the shire, Sir William Brereton, deputy-chamberlain of Chester, who had a relative at stake in the affair, had written to Cromwell. The King's letter (addressed to both of them jointly) was received in Cheshire towards the end of October, by which time the commons were up in Yorkshire and the whole regime seemed on the edge of collapse. The dangers of the situation were well demonstrated by local reactions to rumours of the King's orders for the abbot. On November 8th, another Cheshire knight, Sir Thomas Boteler (whom Cromwell, aware of the state of the shire, wished to use as an independent source of information) wrote to intercede for the monks of Norton. 'The common fame of the country doth...impute to them no fault at all': since Dutton was proposing to 'put them to execution without any manner examination at all', Cromwell was to intervene quickly to prevent a bad miscarriage of justice.[4]

---

[1] Knowles, iii. 324, and *LP* xi. 681, for a brief summary.
[2] Wright, 52, placed into 1534 by *LP* vii. 1037. The letter is addressed to Mr Cromwell, principal secretary, and by August 1536 Cromwell was lord privy seal and a baron. But Dutton might well have slipped up over a change in his correspondent's status only a few weeks old. In early Sept. 1534, Ralph Brereton was in no sort of trouble (*LP* vii. 1135).
[3] 20 Oct. 1537: SP 1/112, fo. 60 (*LP* xi. 1212 [2]); the draft is SP 1/106, fo. 218 (*LP* xi. 787).   [4] SP 1/111, fo. 28 (*LP* xi. 1019).

In fact, Dutton had already decided to avoid trouble, though this meant ignoring the King's explicit orders. He took advantage of the news, learned in the first days of November, that the Yorkshire rebels had stopped their advance and that the forces of the earl of Derby, on whose support he had meant to rely in his own shire, had dispersed, to put off the execution for which he and Brereton had apparently agreed to fix a date.[1] At this point, particulars of the law and the shire rivalries fused to protect the abbot. The King's order had been addressed to Dutton and Brereton, so that neither could act without the other. Yet Brereton, as Dutton complained, refused to sign a report of their joint action in first preparing and then putting off the execution, while further progress was allegedly blocked by Dutton's refusal to join Brereton in the full investigation which Cromwell now entrusted to both of them together. On January 18th, Brereton once more wrote to the lord privy seal to complain of the sheriff's tactics and for a new commission which would add 'other discreet and worshipful men of the shire' to the two of them and enable a quorum, which need not include Dutton, to proceed.[2] Brereton certainly pretended to be eager in the King's service, but there is reason to think that he was working for the rescue of the accused.

Dutton, on the other hand, had determined to prove his loyalty as well as score off his enemy by achieving the execution; however, it appears that once summary action was out of the question he found difficulty in providing evidence for a formal trial. But as it happened he had a convenient weapon to hand, in one Piers Felday who had been convicted of coining and so forfeited his life. This man Dutton intended to use both in his campaign against Brereton and for the destruction of the monks of Norton. He promised to obtain Felday's pardon if he would accuse eight of Brereton's party of coining and be Crown witness against the abbot and canons.[3] But the plot miscarried when Brereton got the secret into the open. Felday was sent to Newgate for examination and then returned to Cheshire, a step which once again revealed the local feud, for Cromwell authorised his despatch to Brereton, but Audley succeeded in letting Dutton have him first.[4] Dutton needed to

[1] SP 1/112, fo. 29 (*LP* xi. 1212).
[2] SP 1/114, fos. 175–6 (*LP* xii. I. 130).
[3] This appears from Felday's confession: SP 1/121, fos. 75–82 (*LP* xii. II. 58).
[4] SP 1/120, fo. 200 (*LP* xii. I. 1282).

get his hands on Felday and carry out his sentence before too much was revealed, which he did in mid-August 1537, despite another effort of Brereton's, supported by Cromwell, to take Felday out of the sheriff's hands.[1] As it was, the coiner told enough of the truth on the scaffold.[2] He repeated his confession of false witness-giving that he had made in May to Brereton, but did not mention the instigator because he would not 'set debate among the gentlemen of the shire'. His opinion of them was another matter: 'Masters,' he said to the crowd come to watch him die, 'never trust to knight, esquire or gentleman. For I was fair promised; howbeit, it is an old saying, fair words make fools fain.' Since he was going to tell more, Dutton's men quickly pushed him off the ladder. Brereton could do nothing but complain and demand that Cromwell do something about Dutton's dangerous arrogance in the shire.

And what of the abbot of Norton and his canons? Their fate has been regarded as uncertain; Professor Knowles would go no further than this, while the prejudiced historians of the Pilgrimage of Grace felt sure that the monks did not escape execution.[3] Yet on 26 May 1537 Audley wrote to Cromwell that Brereton must not get hold of Felday whom he would otherwise save as he had saved the abbot of Norton, 'being I dare avow a traitor'.[4] There is a hint in this touch of defiance that Cromwell, listening to Brereton, had had his doubts about the treason, while Audley, pushed on by Dutton (and the King), had from the first pressed for drastic action. Because the shire was unsettled, summary execution was put off; then, because the commission of inquiry contained the two shire rivals, nothing was done; in the end Dutton's witness was revealed as suborned and perjured. The abbot got off: in December 1537 he obtained the usual dispensation from the life religious.[5] Since his action during that hectic night in August certainly took place – since he drove Cromwell's commissioners into hiding and raised a large riot – he may be accounted very lucky. No doubt (as Audley believed) he owed his good fortune to Brereton's feud with Dutton. But it may be added that his offence posed problems. Was it treason and could it be proved? All the armed men had melted away

---

[1] SP 1/124, fo. 122 (*LP* xii. II. 597).
[2] Ibid. fo. 124.
[3] Knowles, iii. 324; Dodds, i. 214.
[4] SP 1/120, fo. 200 (*LP* xii. I. 1282).   [5] *Fac. Off. Reg.* 117.

before the sheriff's people could catch them, and in the local state of opinion to which Boteler had testified it would no doubt have been quite impossible to impanel a hanging jury or find evidence to put before it. Hence Dutton's clumsy attempt to rig the evidence. It was one thing to hang the rioters out of hand, quite another to secure an indictment and conviction; and Audley's corrections on the King's letter in October had shown a proper understanding of that fact. Once Dutton had had to give up the first idea of execution without trial at common law – execution as rebels caught in rebellion – the abbot was really safe. Guilty as he was, he stands as a solid example of the advantages to be gained even at the height of the northern troubles from the principle that the law ruled all.

Now no one need suppose that the Crown always, or even usually, failed to secure convictions. Most of the men put on trial for treason suffered the consequences of the law. The point of this discussion is different. It is that the prosecution of dissidents and disaffected men was a matter for the law, a matter of proper trial before duly constituted courts of common law, upon real evidence presented in the technically correct way, and decided by the genuine verdict of juries. Unless men were taken in open rebellion, the government had no means of circumventing these necessary conditions; and even in such cases, as the fate of the Taunton rebels shows, they preferred to use the ordinary machinery. Only one clause in one of the relevant statutes provided for the possibility of trying a man in some way not known to the common law. Section 4 of the 1536 Act Extinguishing the Authority of the Bishop of Rome declared that spiritual persons, found by their ecclesiastical superiors to have offended against the act, should be bound in sureties to appear within fifteen days before the King's Council in the Star Chamber, and that the sentence of *praemunire* might be pronounced against any found guilty 'by confession or witness' either by his bishop or archdeacon, or in the Star Chamber. This method of trial deliberately avoided all the forms of the common law. It is very interesting to note that the procedure is reserved for the clergy only – laymen were to be tried at Assizes or Quarter Sessions in the ordinary way (section 3) – and that it was devised for an offence which did not carry the death penalty. It is even more interesting to find that not a single case is known or even suspected in which the Court of Star Chamber exercised the powers thus conferred, while even a priest like Robert Lenton was properly indicted under the act as though he were a layman.[1] Whether the Church Courts ever acted under this clause must remain an open question until their records have received the study which their condition renders problematic rather than probable.

It has also been shown that care was taken to establish the treasonable content of an allegation. Men were not, it would seem, dealt with upon mere suspicion, charges were properly investigated, and every effort had to be made to ensure that the indictment was sound in law and convincing in detail. All this applied once a man's alleged treason became known. The enforcement of the policy embodied in the statutes of the Reformation depended on the rules of the law: indeed, it submitted to the rule of law. In the discovering of offences, the law put up few obstacles, but that is not to deny that from the government's point of view the problem was, if anything, even greater.

[1] Above, p. 305.

8

POLICE

BEFORE A MAN could be put on trial, his offence had to become known; if order was to be maintained, disaffection and discontent had to be discovered. In the absence of anything like a police force, how was it done? The traditional answer is very simple and bears the authority of Cromwell's biographer: the minister created 'a system of espionage, the most effective that England had ever seen', an 'organized method of reporting treason'.[1] This can only be taken to mean that the flood of reports reaching Cromwell came from people employed by him as spies, and in his index Merriman listed no fewer than forty-four letters of Cromwell's in which he thought the system was illustrated. Unfortunately, his examples evaporate on inspection. Ten of them are unsolicited reports of common crimes, and fifteen touch civil plaints of private people in which Cromwell's help was invoked. Of the remainder, at best eleven concern possibly seditious matter, but they offer no evidence of spies. Three letters refer to international espionage: two report on traitors who had fled abroad and one on suspects who had re-entered England. That Cromwell maintained some foreign intelligence is certainly true – not to do so would have been neglect of duty – but irrelevant here. There is one single instance known in which Cromwell employed paid agents at home, probably servants of his own. In July 1533 he reported to Henry that he had caught two Observant friars who had lately attended Catherine of Aragon. They 'were first espied at Ware by such espials as I laid for such purposes, and having good await laid upon them were from thence dogged to London, and there (notwithstanding many wiles and cautels by them invented to escape) were taken and detained till my coming home'.[2] In all Cromwell's voluminous correspondence this is the only indubitable reference to men explicitly employed as his spies. Another such instance was suggested by the abstract in the Calendar of a letter of 1535 where one Edward Bestney, addressing Cromwell as his master, seems to be saying that the minister had comforted him by 'willing me to spy

[1] Merriman, i. 99.   [2] Ibid. i. 360.

327

out, and ye will help me'. The full text shows that Bestney was being encouraged to look around for a piece of monastic property that he might like to acquire.[1]

There are a few signs that Cromwell may occasionally have placed a man in a strategic position, somewhere where he could suppose that he ought to know what was going on. An unsigned scrap of paper, powerfully redolent of a spy's message, reported on the household of the earl of Derby.[2] The writer had before this written to say that the earl was as true to the King 'as any man in England', and so he was still.

But how he doth take your lordship, in that I am in doubt, for I hear light words among his servants. Or your lordship should be there as they would have you to be, I had liever to be in Jerusalem, to come home on my bare feet.

No doubt Derby's men had consigned Cromwell to hell. 'At my coming to London I shall show your lordship more.' Perhaps this man was planted. More certainly, men were deliberately introduced into suspected monastic houses. Jasper Fyloll, Cromwell's agent at the London Charterhouse, was one such, though there was nothing sufficiently clandestine about the appointment to justify calling it spying. Fyloll was much more of a caretaker.[3] Other eager reporters from religious houses, like the friars John Lawrence and Richard Lyst who kept up a stream of letters denouncing their own Observant community at Greenwich,[4] quite manifestly had taken the initiative in bringing themselves to the minister's notice. Nevertheless, the atmosphere in many monasteries explains, if it does not lend substance to, the jibe with which the abbot of Peterborough greeted the news that one of his servants wished to move into Cromwell's service: 'What will ye do with him? Be one of his spies?'[5] Perhaps some people believed that Cromwell used agents – even had agents everywhere – but there simply is no evidence to support this. When Merriman wrote that 'it was impossible to tell who the government spies were',[6] he spoke much

---

[1] SP 1/98, fo. 222 (*LP* ix. 761).   [2] SP 1/109, fo. 91 (*LP* xi. 859).

[3] Cf. e.g. Wright, 67–9; BM, Cleo. E. iv, fos. 43–4 (*LP* ix. 523).

[4] Knowles, iii. 208–9.

[5] SP 1/242, fo. 94 (*LP Add.* 1363). It must be added that the abbot wrote to protest against untrue reports that he was hostile to Cromwell and soon after could offer thanks for Cromwell's care in evaluating and dismissing the slander (SP 1/241, fos. 289, 294 [*LP Add.* 1299, 1305]: these letters are misdated in *LP*).

[6] Merriman, i. 116.

more truly than he meant to. The general and organised espionage system, improbable enough when one remembers the government's financial resources, is a figment of the hostile historian's imagination.

The point is underlined by the surprising discovery that in the whole mass of papers concerned with reports and instructions there is not one piece of evidence to suggest that any informer was ever paid or rewarded in any way. Even thanks are extremely rare; Cromwell's surviving letters include only one in which he expressed his gratitude – to the earl of Shrewsbury – for his 'good zeal, diligence and dexterity in repressing and apprehending such pernicious and detestable felons'.[1] In all these many delations and informations, whether one looks at Cromwell's own letters or those of others, nothing is more striking than the calm assumption that people will, of course, do their loyal duty in reporting instances of disaffection.

Curiously enough, there is better evidence that Cranmer believed in a systematic practice of surveillance than that Cromwell did. As early as 1534, the archbishop told the secretary that he was about to visit Rochester, 'where if ye have any special matters to be enquired of, I will be glad to do my endeavour in the same', no doubt a delicate allusion to the problem of Bishop Fisher.[2] And it was Cranmer who was responsible for recruiting a regular reporter when in 1539 he told one John Marshall, of Little Carlton (Notts.), to send Cromwell information on the state of people and country in his shire and in Lincolnshire as far as Newark. This produced three long letters from Marshall to Cromwell, written in February, April and June 1539, in which the minister was reassured about the local situation.[3]

In February all was very well and the region in the control of 'the worshipful'. No maintenance, quarrels, vengeance 'for old matters', malice or ruffling disturbed the peace. The common people called it 'a good world, for poor men may now live in peace by the great men'. News of the measures against the pope's enormities caused a little stir: 'then they a little whisper and rown one to another, and bless them thereat, but little they say and soon that is sunken out of their heads and forgotten...The last act of redress is most in memory.' The English

---

[1] Ibid. i. 384. These triple nouns and double adjectives are very characteristic of Cromwell's style.

[2] *Cranmer's Works*, ed. Cox, 294.

[3] SP 1/143, fo. 81; 150, fo. 187; 152, fo. 59 (*LP* xiv. I. 295, 839, 1094).

paternoster is gaining ground 'since the uniform translation came down'. 'Abbeys be nothing esteemed or pitied, for the commons say they now perceive more common wealth to grow to them by their suppressing', as 'many good farms and benefits' reached new users. 'They were but bellymonds and gluttons of the world, and the most vicious persons… saving they think there is much and great losses of their prayers.' People are a little perturbed by the institution of parish registers; they fear that the reform will in the end mean their paying more to the King. There was headshaking over the treason of Lord Montague and fear that his brother, the cardinal (Reginald Pole), would one day 'make business'. While the better sort are keeping the abrogated holy days as work days, 'the poor will not labour of those days as yet'. Valiant beggars are gone and unlawful games with them. The main local complaint touches the ill-maintained highways, impassable after 'every small flood'.

In April, Marshall was a little less complacent. 'Men here say nothing against anything the King doth so long as peace followeth; howbeit, where they hear of war (as was said here at our late musters we should have had) then methought the common people but meanly courageous'. 'How now,' they would say, 'an we have war, then God have mercy upon us all.' But they accept the assurance of their betters that all is well. 'The haveless, poor and needy people' do not care whether it be war or peace, as long as they 'may have the King's wages'. The tale ran much the same two months later. Marshall knew of no rumours or other 'superfluous and lewd fantasies', except that some people, convinced now that there would be no war, were darkly saying that no doubt they would soon be paying 'some money towards the defence and keeping out of our enemies'. Everybody allegedly spoke well of Cromwell who was good to poor men and advised the King to 'take nothing but of them where it may well be spared'. Priests are as ostentatious as ever but behave better; fearing to be caught out by the laity, they 'flee much the occasions of carnal sin, as lewd and suspect places of resort of light women'. The locality's main interest was in a proposal to clean up parish churchyards by act of Parliament, and there was a good deal of hope that the present Parliament would reduce tolls, the chief burden on 'the common and mean sort' with the exception of 'mortuaries in their old fashion taken'. The few remaining abbots were awaiting the visitors coming to dissolve their houses; having sold up everything, they were buying their food in the market and using up their money, for which reason they were now of a sudden anxious to have the visitors come. The picture presented by Marshall is reassuring enough, though not exactly idyllic; it also rings true, with its harping on money worries, though no doubt he could not know everything. There is nothing comparable to his three letters in the Cromwell correspondence, though a good many people wrote occasionally and briefly on some concern or condition of their region. Marshall's energies, too, flagged after six months. Cromwell, who was certainly in reasonable touch with the different parts of the realm, must have regarded himself as exceptionally well informed about the north-east Midlands in the first half of 1539. What Marshall did not provide were informations and delations about suspected people.

There is thus no evidence that the vast majority of the many who brought informations were in any way organised from the centre or agents of the government. This was not the way things worked: information came and did not have to be sought for. Hardly any names recur among informers: just about every man or woman reported for dangerous talk owed the experience to someone who is not known to have inflicted it on anybody else. The informers were not only not government spies, employed and organised in Cromwell's 'system'; they were not even professional enough to make a practice of informing. Certainly, some names do recur in letters to Cromwell on this subject. Some magistrates and local worthies reported quite a few cases to the lord privy seal and sought his instructions. But these were not the informers and did not report first-hand knowledge: they acted as the channel, receiving information from those who had allegedly heard or witnessed the treason and passing the information on for action to the King's minister. Delations almost always followed a common form. Someone – a relative, friend, acquaintance, or almost stranger – heard treason spoken, called upon bystanders to bear witness, took the tale to whoever carried authority in those parts – a man of some substance, a knight, even a peer if one was available – and so discharged his duty. Examples to prove this are plentiful indeed; one or two will suffice. David Leonard, hooper, an Irishman, was in gaol in 1535 awaiting investigation on a charge of having said: 'God save King Harry and Queen Catherine, his wedded wife, and Anne at his pleasure for whom all England shall rue.' He had got there by these stages: John Horsey and Robert Hill, smiths of Bridgewater (Som.), and Robert Alwen of Lyme Pesham, husbandman, who claimed to have heard the words, informed John Gilling, high constable of the hundred of South Brent, and John Burkett, tithingman of East Brent. They in their turn informed two justices of the peace, William Vowell and Thomas Clerk, who ordered Burkett to arrest Leonard, informed Cromwell, and requested instructions.[1] The whole business had taken only a few days. In 1536, Lawrence Holland, gent., and Richard Tumber, fuller, accused of 'heinous words', were reported by one Edward Ryland to two of his betters who in turn went to Sir Thomas Neville, the local magistrate, who took the informer's statement and sent it to Cromwell together with accused and accuser, in the custody of one of his own servants and the constable of the hundred where the accused lived.[2] Even when it looks as though Cromwell's informant was acting on his own, closer inspection of the letter shows this not to be so. William Saunders, of Northamptonshire, denounced John Macok to Cromwell in December 1537. The treasonable words alleged were pretty strong, so strong that Saunders hated to write them, but Cromwell must know what had been reported to him; there were two witnesses.[3] In other words, the information was brought to Saunders by two men who were the real informers.

These cases are the more interesting because they provide evidence of the element of organisation which did exist. The old officers of the countryside – constables and the like – could at times live up to their names, though they are met rarely enough in the story. As for the two Somerset justices, Thomas Clerk was brother to John, bishop of Bath and Wells, who on one occasion described Thomas as Cromwell's servant.[4] And Saunders, at the end of his letter, suggested that Cromwell should send instructions through his servant Edward Saunders, the writer's nephew. How formal these servancy relations were cannot be established, but the normal usage of the time would not have employed the term without some real meaning to it. Thomas Clerk and Edward Saunders stood to Cromwell in a closer relationship than did magistrates and gentlemen not called his servants. The patron–client structure of Tudor society must have proved useful to Cromwell in extending his eyes, ears and hands across the realm, but it would once again be wrong

---

[1] SP 1/95, fo. 137 (*LP* ix. 136). [2] SP 1/105, fo. 109 (*LP* xi. 140).
[3] SP 1/127, fo. 149 (*LP* xii. II. 1269). [4] SP 1/95, fo. 107 (*LP* ix. 109).

to read too much system into this. There is no sign whatsoever that he set about constructing a network of 'servants'; on the contrary, the initiative usually came, in Cromwell's case as in all others, from the man who wished to attach himself to a superior, or from his family. Men who, however loosely and without benefit of retainder, regarded Cromwell as their good lord (for the present) will have been more zealous than others to serve him by passing on information and taking actions against suspects; and the minister thus had a chance beyond the ordinary of hearing about trouble if one of his 'servants' was locally influential. Though it remains an important part of the answer to the question how Cromwell could expect to know what was going on, there is no more to it than that; and moreover, the ranks of his servants did not extend downward to include those who did the actual denouncing.

A few more examples may be given of the varied manner in which men were 'detected'. In December 1537 William Wytham, gent., of Darnton (Co. Durham) informed the Council of the North that he had matter against the prior of Newburgh.[1] On his way to York he had stayed at the priory and after mass had gone to pray in the chapel there, when he was approached by Brian Boye, late keeper of the chapel, with the words, 'If you will not hurt me, I will tell you a thing.' Wytham reassured Brian who then related how he had overheard a conversation between the prior and one of his tenants, a Mrs Margaret Fulthorp, who had come to pay her rent. Somewhat tactlessly, Mrs Fulthorp had started to praise the duke of Norfolk, saying he had done the King good service in the north, to which the prior allegedly retorted that 'it makes no matter if one were hanged against the other'. The prior, accuser and witnesses were at once summoned to York and there interrogated at length on 7 December 1537.[2] Boye repeated his charge but now made it look very odd by two details. In the first place, he claimed to have heard the words charged while standing at the foot of the stairs below the chamber in which the conversation took place; he supposed that they had been spoken too softly and too much out of the side of the prior's mouth for anyone but himself to hear them, though Mrs Fulthorp, one of her sons, one of her servants and two canons of the priory were all in the room. Secondly, he admitted that the prior had dismissed him out of his service last Martinmas. He had before this failed to report the words (allegedly spoken at Lammas, in August)

---

[1] SP 1/127, fo. 22 (*LP* xii. II. 1181).   [2] SP 1/127, fos. 23–30.

because he had feared dismissal; asked if he would ever have disclosed them if he had not been sacked, he replied he 'would have showed it to my lord president if he had come thither or unto some other to whom his fantasy would serve him'.

The suggestion that Boye was lying is confirmed by the other depositions. It seems there had been trouble between the prior and his tenants, the Fulthorps, which Norfolk's coming had resolved in the tenants' favour. When paying her rent, Margaret had thanked God for Norfolk and wished he had come seven years earlier; she and her husband would have saved 200 marks spent on contesting the prior's claims. The prior only said, 'Yea, my lord of Norfolk was good to you'; they had shared a piece of boiled beef and a venison pasty called for by the prior, though the argument had continued. Her son John added that he would certainly not have concealed any treason he had heard the prior speak, 'not only for the truth that he beareth towards the King's majesty, but also for that the prior was so ill towards his said father and mother'. The prior himself defended his innocence with a somewhat improbable totality. He had not only made Mrs Fulthorp welcome but declared himself deeply grateful to Norfolk for settling the dispute against him. Various other witnesses had heard either nothing or only non-seditious matter. Not surprisingly, the lord president, Bishop Tunstall, reported that there was nothing in the charge, but to this Cromwell replied that the King felt sure of a cankered and malicious heart in the prior:

Wheresoever any such cankered malice shall either chance to break out or any to be accused thereof, his highness would have the same tried and thoroughly pursued with as great dexterity and as little favour as their demerits shall require.[1]

Cromwell did not normally hesitate to send his own instructions and opinions in such cases, and it is entirely probable that he here really transmitted an outburst of his master's.

Driven on in this manner, the Council of the North re-examined the charge. They had the prior in again, told him that they regarded the charge as 'fully proved', that his accuser had not the wit to invent such a saying, and that he clearly had so much resented Norfolk's decision in

---

[1] SP 1/128, fo. 123 (*LP* xiii. I. 107), Tunstall to Cromwell, 19 Jan. 1538, reciting the effect of Cromwell's letter.

the Fulthorps' favour 'that his stomach could not but utter what was in it'. They tried every trick, hinting at knowledge of ill behaviour during the late rebellion and suggesting that he could help himself only by a confession. But the prior stuck so nobly to his guns, lamenting himself for a man falsely slandered and explaining how by pretending a leg injury he had managed to keep out of the Pilgrimage of Grace, that his credit clearly rose. Boye simply repeated his earlier statement without varying a word. It is manifest that Tunstall thought Prior Robert innocent but that the King's wrath prevented him from letting the man go. Instead he sent him to Pontefract Castle in case the King wished 'to have him tried by his laws upon these evidence[s]'. It would appear that Henry forgot his first reaction or accepted the truth; Prior Robert went home to die peacefully in his bed three months later.[1]

The denunciation of Robert Oldeham, parish priest of Pluckley in Kent, also helps to bring out some of the stranger realities of this so-called police system. What happened appears from a letter of Sir Edward Guildford's to Cromwell, of May 1534.[2] Guildford defended himself against a charge of negligence brought by John Dranner, Oldeham's first accuser, in that he had allegedly first arrested the priest and then set him free. But this was not true. When Guildford was out hunting, some men brought Oldeham before him 'in the highway', Dranner not being present. As far as Guildford could make out, the only charge was that Oldeham 'had named the pope unadvisedly in his beads', which he promised never to do again; Sir Edward felt it was but a silly oversight. He was in a quandary: the accuser was not there and 'I wist not how to rid the said priest out of my hands, I being in the highway and nigh no house'. So he let him to bail on the spot and ordered some reliable bystanders to act as sureties. This action he defended with some warmth, hinting that Dranner bore the priest malice for another cause and asking that the investigation be committed to himself with two other local justices. He was, he said, sworn of the King's Council and a justice of the peace, and Cromwell had before this asked him to 'take direction and order within mine office and rule'. If he were to have no discretion to let men to bail, 'as other justices do', he might as well be out of the commission 'for any good that I should do'. Guildford was an old man of standing and Cromwell still fairly new to his position; such vigour came to be increasingly rare in letters

[1] *LP* xiii. I. 743.   [2] SP 1/83, fos. 163–4 (*LP* vii. 630).

to the minister. There is no sign that Oldeham, so oddly produced before a hunting squire in the open road, was further troubled, and it is probable that he died peacefully in 1537 when the will was proved of Robert Oldeham, clerk, of Stanford, some ten miles from Pluckley.[1]

Another case shows that at times the so-called authorities of the locality could act upon suspicion, without waiting for a denunciation. William Rede, a baker of Oxford, was travelling home from Lancashire in February 1537. The abbot of Whalley had given him sealed letters for the monastery's scholar at Oxford and for the abbot of Hailes, saying:

Recommend me to the abbot of Hailes and tell him that I am sore stopped and acrased, and pray him to send me word when he purposeth to come over to this country; for I would be glad to see him once ere I depart out of this world, seeing I brought him up here as a child.

On his way Rede stopped at the schoolmaster's house at Knutsford in Cheshire where his host gave him a packet of letters for his son Philip at Oriel, with strict instructions to keep it sealed till delivered. However, Rede next broke his journey 'and warmed himself' at the house of the constable of Wootton, and while he stood by the fire he blabbed what he was carrying. At that time letters from one abbot to another were enough to rouse suspicion; the constable demanded to see them and then took them to Mr Flemock at Kenilworth Castle, reading them on the way, with Rede tagging unhappily along. Flemock took one look at the letters – of whose contents we remain ignorant since the story was told by Rede who never saw them – and put the unfortunate messenger in prison. Rede assured Cromwell of his innocence.[2]

To reinforce these relatively haphazard methods of detection, a scheme was considered for mobilising a traditional instrument, presentment in local courts of criminal jurisdiction. Early in 1538 it was decided to draw up a new standard charge to be delivered at 'inferior courts of inquisition', that is at sheriffs' tourns, leets, law-days, hundred courts and similar institutions. The date is fixed by the mention of 25 March 1538 in the draft and an earlier note of Cromwell's to study

---

[1] *Index of Wills in the Prerogative Court of Canterbury*, Kent Records, 1920, 352.

[2] E 36/119, fo. 67 (*LP* xii. I. 389). The abbot of Whalley, tried for treason in March, was already under suspicion at this time, which accounts for the constable's alertness. For the abbot's fate cf. Knowles, iii. 332, and articles cited there.

this massive document covering forty good-sized pages and every conceivable crime and misdemeanour.[1] Admitting that 'those things only in time past have been used to be given in charge and inquirable' at these courts 'as be punishable by the same', it goes on to explain that the situation has changed: 'the ignorant and unlearned people' need to discover their duty towards God, the King ('God's vicar and minister on earth') and the commonwealth. Ignorance needs dispelling, but it would be unkind to make people travel far from home to learn the truth. Therefore the King, by the advice of his Council, has ordered this new form of charge to be used. The jury is instructed to present the following offences: denial of the basic truths of the Christian faith as well as sectarian heresy; denial of the royal supremacy, and specifically breaches of the 1536 Succession Act and the Treason Acts of 1534, 1352 and 1536 (forging lesser seals); misprision of treason, for once clearly defined as 'where any person knoweth that another intended to offend in any of the cases before rehearsed, the same did keep secret and not disclose or utter before the act done'; blackmail with threat of arson;[2] treason by poisoning (the act of 1531); petty treason; false rumours and counterfeit news to the hurt of the King, nobles and councillors, or 'to move disorder'.[3] There follows a long list of more conventional crimes, from murders and felonies, breaches of the statute of Winchester and extortion, to regrating, waifs and strays,[4] and omission by any person over twelve years old to be sworn to 'the King's assize',[5] but including also rather casually the act of 1536 extinguishing the authority of Rome, with its *praemunire* penalties.

Certainly a great part, and that the most serious, of this list was not triable in the inferior courts, and the most interesting section of the

---

[1] BM, Add. MS 48047, fos. 59–79. This paper belonged to Robert Beale, clerk to Walsingham and the Privy Council. The volume contains several of Sir Thomas Smith's writings, and at least one of its parts had certainly belonged to Walsingham. Though the paper would thus appear to have survived from the office of the principal secretary in the reign of Elizabeth, it is an original document of the reign of Henry VIII. For Cromwell's note cf. *LP* xii. II. 1151.

[2] Made treason by an act of 1429 (Bellamy, *Law of Treason*, 131).

[3] The charge gets very eloquent on this. See above, p. 46.

[4] Waifs are defined as goods dropped by a felon after the commission of the crime; strays as beasts of unknown ownership found in one place for a twelvemonth.

[5] 'To bear true faith and obedience to his majesty, to live and die with his grace only, to behave himself honestly and truly against all people, and to live after the laws of the realm.' Did the whole nation – or anyone – ever take this oath?

charge deals with the action required. When any offences are presented 'whereof the correction and punishment do not by his grace's law appertain to the court where it is found', the quest must certify it by indenture sealed with the seal of the presiding magistrate or steward to the King and Council in the Star Chamber within forty days, or at the next term if the Star Chamber does not sit within forty days. Moreover, the charge was to be used extensively for purposes of propaganda, quite apart from the sittings of the court at which presentments could be made. All incumbents are ordered to acquire a copy by 25 March 1538 and to read it from the pulpit four times a year (Palm Sunday, the Sunday before the Nativity of St John the Baptist, the Sunday before Michaelmas, and the third Sunday in Advent) between evensong and compline. In order to ensure the effectiveness of these public readings, the charge concludes by demanding that any man be presented who, belonging within the court's jurisdiction, has failed to do his duty, 'viz. to serve the King's highness and the commonwealth at this court', or who had not attended church on the four Sundays listed.

This machinery deserves attention. It ought to have covered the realm with a network of investigating bodies very close to the ground and thus secured a steady flow of information to the Star Chamber sitting as a court in term time. It is, however, not at all clear whether the machinery (reminiscent of that created by the Statute of Retainers of 1504) was ever put into operation, or whether we have here a bright idea that came to nothing. Quite possibly Cromwell decided, after looking over it, that so lengthy an introduction to the sessions of petty courts would bewilder rather than instruct. There is no evidence that the procedure was ever used. No trace survives of those regular public readings; there is no single presentment from an inferior court which can be shown to have resulted from it; and the Star Chamber never, to our knowledge, found itself concerned with information so obtained. However, the state of the evidence makes it impossible to speak categorically. Since this document survives among the papers of the Elizabethan secretaries of state it may be that at some time an effort was made to use this charge. However, the fourfold proclamation from the pulpit ought to have left some traces behind. There are none, nor is the requirement referred to in the Injunctions of 1538. This tends to support the conclusion that the whole idea was quickly abandoned. So far as they are known, the facts indicate that this attempt to organise the discovery of offences yielded no profit and was probably never put into effect; it was private delation rather than jury presentment which brought to light actions dangerous to King and commonwealth.

As a rule, therefore, the government heard of cases only if someone close to the accused brought information. All it could do was to co-ordinate the police effort from above by insisting that all suspicious cases should be referred to it, and this was done in the circular of 16 April 1535.[1] In practice, Cromwell's position was manifestly crucial. It is true, of course, that the survival of his correspondence, when that of others has nearly all vanished, may distort the picture, but this is not likely to be a serious complication. Many men from the shires, informing him of a suspect, supposed that the lord privy seal and perhaps others of the Council would look further; that is, they assumed that even though other councillors might take an interest Cromwell was the man to write to. Moreover, such leading councillors as Cranmer, the duke of Norfolk or Sir William Fitzwilliam, earl of Southampton, in such matters constantly referred themselves to him. In July 1534, Fitzwilliam sent him a dubious Scotsman, explicitly by the King's orders, to examine him and do afterwards as he saw fit; Fitzwilliam respectfully offered his own opinion that the man was 'of the same sort and fashion as the Maid of Kent was'.[2] Cromwell's letters to the King are full of reports on political cases and investigations. There is no need to question the traditional belief that he was responsible for internal security in the England of the early Reformation. His attitudes and methods are therefore of some interest.

He was constantly asked for instructions, as when a set of depositions touching John Vigorouse's attempts to arrest the progress of the new learning and new order in Essex was endorsed with a heartfelt 'Sir, I beseech your mastership', seeking to know what do do: 'it is matter touching God and the King my master'.[3] Others wanted to be given general orders. In July 1535, Lord Conyers and Sir John Bulmer (later hanged for his part in the northern rebellion) reported that at Gisburn in Yorkshire a man had taken the King's injunctions (presumably the orders of June 3rd) from the hands of the priest about to read them in church, had torn them in little pieces, and had run away. So far the

[1] Above, p. 000. [2] SP 1/85, fo. 22 (*LP* vii. 930).
[3] E 36/120, fo. 59 (*LP* vii. 145).

search had been fruitless: but what were they to do if they caught him, and with others like him?[1] In 1537, Sir Walter Stonor enquired from Oxfordshire about a case he had in hand. A poor man, one who 'axeth from door to door', was charged with treasonable words by another, both being very simple people and the accuser admitting that the accused was drunk at the time. There was, however, a more ominous possibility behind this: the accused confessed to carrying a letter from Lord Darcy to the marquess of Exeter in his cap, which letter – damaged when the cap was cut open – Stonor was enclosing. Could he have general instructions about such cases – as though the country was crawling with drunken beggars carrying incriminating letters.[2]

To such requests Cromwell never hesitated to respond, and the interesting thing is that his answers are in no way stereotyped: they vary with the case. He might order an arrest, as that of Robert Lawe, vicar of Sproxton (Lincs.), charged with treason by some women, or of Richard Wilcok, curate at Cardiff, who, however, could not be found.[3] Or he might order a man released since he had found sureties to be ready to answer when required.[4] Men's papers were searched on his orders.[5] When William Bird, vicar of Brodford (Wilts.), was charged in June 1538 by the bailiff, William Williams, with abominable treasonous words, Sir Walter Hungerford reported the matter to Cromwell and explained that the bailiff had long delayed before giving the information because the vicar was his uncle;[6] but lately Bird had charged him with stealing a horse and some money, so that he had decided to have his revenge by disclosing this old treason. Hungerford cursed the informer for a wretch, and Cromwell seems to have taken the same line, for he ordered Bird's release on bail; the result was, said Hungerford somewhat inconsistently, that he continued to go about the village denouncing the King 'as unthriftily as ever he did'. Cromwell's scepticism seems to have been misplaced, for in the Parliament of 1540 Bird was attainted of this treason, ironically enough in the act which also condemned Hungerford for protecting him, for conjuring against the

[1] SP 1/94, fos. 22–3 (LP viii. 1024).
[2] SP 1/117, fo. 226 (LP xii. I. 797).
[3] SP 1/128, fo. 141; 241, fo. 229 (LP xiii. I. 125; Add. 1263).
[4] SP 1/100, fo. 93 (LP ix. 1136); Merriman, ii. 62.
[5] E.g. those of Dr John Lusshe, for whom see above, p. 23.
[6] The words alleged were spoken in November 1536.

King's life, and for buggery.[1] Hungerford was also involved when Nicholas Balam, late monk of Henton, declared in June 1539 that he would not take the King to be supreme head of the Church of England 'but only the pope...and so would he die in his opinion'. Though Hungerford reported that Balam had 'been distracted out of his mind and as yet is not much better', Cromwell ordered him held until the Assizes; but he seems to have got off, for in April 1540 he still appeared in the list of pensioned monks.[2] Cromwell could order a man's punishment to be reduced, as in Thomas Croft's case,[3] or after reading a report he could order a man to be indicted and to be made 'a terrible example' of.[4]

Since evidently everything depended on the facts of each case Cromwell was always busy investigating individuals. Nothing could be ignored, not even such absurdities as the case of Baynam, the town drunk of Burford in Oxfordshire, whom Thomas Thomson, one of the bailiffs, charged with treason in April 1538.[5] Thomson had asked his fellow bailiff, John Jones, to arrest Baynam; Jones had allegedly done so, only to let the man go again. The true story was this. Late one evening Baynam had created a disturbance by trying to stop Thomson from shutting the door of the town gaol. Thomson had fetched Jones to help him, and one of their constables threw Baynam out of the gaol. However, he armed himself with a bill and came back to continue the fight, whereupon Jones had him put in the stocks. Thomson, on his high horse, called it treason to resist the King's officers, but Jones said, 'Let him alone in ward till tomorrow.' That was the reason for Baynam's 'imprisonment'. But Thomson continued to say that it was petty treason to treat the watch and bailiffs so, until to appease him the other officers enquired of the nearest justice, whereupon Thomson dropped his talk. But the matter rankled, especially as clearly he and Jones did not get on too well: the whole story had to be investigated and the details sent to Cromwell. In this case the lord privy seal no doubt felt no need to proceed further (all the witnesses supported Jones), but the

---

[1] SP 1/133, fo. 80; 141, fo. 257 (*LP* xiii. I. 1241; II, App. 43); 31 Henry VIII, c. 61. Hungerford, a friend of Cromwell's, was a victim of the minister's fall. The charge against Bird was that he had talked treason in trying to dissuade Williams from joining the King's forces against the northern rebels and had called the King a heretic.

[2] SP 1/152, fo. 100 (*LP* xiv. I. 1154); Merriman, ii. 234; *LP* xv, p. 543.

[3] Below, p. 384.   [4] SP 1/141, fo. 254 (*LP* xiii. II, App. 39); Merriman, ii. 155.

[5] SP 1/131, fos. 84–7 (*LP* xiii. I. 735).

principle that every hint of treason must be looked into was one which he firmly maintained.

He was also always careful to investigate the connections of any traitor and the possible ramifications of treason. In October 1534 he asked the Council to postpone the execution of 'a very evil disposed person' found guilty of treason 'till we may know the whole and profound bottom of his cankered heart'.[1] He will have approved the zeal shown by Norfolk and Sir Roger Townsend who in July 1538 took steps to prevent Anthony Brown, lately an Observant at Greenwich and now a hermit in Norfolk, from being immediately executed after he had been convicted at Norwich Assizes of denying the royal supremacy. They first respited him for ten days, for the characteristic reason that they wanted the bishop of Norwich to preach edifyingly at the execution, but then found that Brown had not been interrogated about his associates and friends. So they had him up, when he agreed to deny the papal supremacy but would not affirm the King's: 'no temporal prince was ever capax of that name and authority.' Further attempts to move him also failed, even though the bishop's words would have persuaded anyone 'not given to wilfulness as this fool is, who in our opinion is smally learned and as little reasonable'. They returned him to the sheriff for disposal, but even so enquired whether the King and Cromwell would wish him to be examined in the Tower under torture.[2]

Cromwell's constant personal activity is impressive. Busy as he was in all sorts of things, he not only demanded to know what was going on but spent much time himself on this sort of police duty. He would write direct to people accused to him, rather than commit the matter locally,[3] and a good many men must have received ominous letters of summons from him of which only two seem to survive, one of them addressed to John Harding, a priest in Leicestershire:[4]

I commend me unto you. Letting you wit the King's pleasure and commandment is that, all excuses and delays set apart, ye shall incontinently upon

---

[1] Merriman, i. 389.   [2] KB 9/541/104; Ellis, i. II. 85-9.

[3] E.g. David Pole and Richard Strete who in September 1534 defended themselves against a report made of them to Cromwell that they favoured 'the bishop of Rome and his wicked laws and practices' (SP 1/85, fo. 211 [*LP* vii. 1188]).

[4] Merriman, ii. 22. The original (SP 1/105, fo. 17) bears a note of Harding's showing that he received it on July 23rd. His trouble need not have been connected with treason, but Dr Robert Dyngley, similarly summoned in Sept. 1537 (Merriman, ii. 78) in a more kindly letter beginning 'In my most hearty manner' and signed 'Your friend' had been unsound on the question of the pope (SP 1/127, fo. 244 [*LP* xii. II, App. 40]).

the sight hereof repair unto me wheresoever I shall chance to be, the specialties whereof ye shall know at your coming. Without failing thus to do, as ye will answer at your peril. From the Rolls, the 8th day of July [1536].

Thomas Crumwell.

This summons is modelled on the standard form of the Council sub-poena. And whether so summoned, or sent up for examination, like the parson of Wednesbury (Staffs.), allegedly a Scot born, who well handled ('either by compulsion or by fair words') would be able to reveal the names of many papists,[1] men then underwent the ordeal of interrogation by Cromwell. There is no need to doubt that it was a tough one. The setting would be adapted to the occasion. When Cromwell was trying to break the resistance of the Carthusians and had before him Robert Lawrence, prior of Beauvale, and Augustine Webster, prior of Axholme, he staged a very formal scene at his house at the Rolls, calling in Edward Foxe, the King's almoner, Doctors John Bell and John Tregonwell, Thomas Bedyll, archdeacon of Cornwall, Richard Riche, solicitor-general, and Ralph Sadler, his own secretary, and employing as well a notary public, John ap Rice, who recorded the interrogatory and replies in the most solemn form.[2] When he had before him a man of no significance, the interrogation, though clearly still thorough, was a good deal more casual, as when he reported to the King concerning one Leynham who had talked too much:[3]

Of a long season he hath been a mad prophet; assuredly, as far as any man may judge, the man is but a peevish fool, and no part of the spirit of true prophecy can be found in him. Many such fools have been in time, and (as I think) the field of the world will never be without such noyful weeds amongst the good corn.

Good corn is right.

[1] SP 1/103, fo. 76 (*LP* x. 614).
[2] SP 1/92, fo. 34 (*LP* viii. 565 [1]): 'Acta sunt hec omnia et singula prout superior describuntur et recitantur vicesimo die Aprilis Anno Domini 1535 et regni dicti invictissimi domini nostri Regis Henrici octaui anno 26°, coram memorato honorabile viro Magistro Thome Crumwell, ipsius regis maiestatis Secretario primario, in domo solite habitationis eiusdem honorandi viri vulgo nuncupata the Rolles...Me etiam Joanne Rheso Notario publico premissa vidente et audiente qui ea omnia mea ipsius manu scripsi et eisdem subscripsi...iussus ad id specialiter per dictum honorabilem virum Magistrum T.C. et legitime requisitus.'
[3] Merriman, ii. 214–15. Leynham continued his prophetical career until 1546 at least (Thomas, *Religion and the Decline of Magic*, 401).

Scores of men had the experience of being questioned by Thomas Cromwell but few have left us any knowledge of their feelings. As one might expect, his reputation was grim. It badly affected one William Wetheral who tried to run away while Bishop Tunstall was bringing him up to London from Kent. He fled after breakfasting with the bishop but was caught again near Gravesend. All he would say by way of excuse was that he feared to face Cromwell, though when Tunstall called this no reasonable excuse he went so far as to admit that 'the devil was in him and made him afeared without cause'.[1] However, this is the only explicit reference extant to sheer dread of facing Cromwell, and others have left less horrified testimony. Gabriel Pecock, warden of the Observant Franciscans at Southampton, arrested by Cromwell's orders after some delay and brought before him in March 1534, could later write of the secretary's 'noble and rare (among such of your authority) virtue of facility and readiness to hear all manner of men's reasonable matters with a most natural and gentle entertainment'.[2] Another cleric, Richard Master, attainted with the Nun of Kent, appealed to Cromwell and in the course of his petition recalled 'those amiable words which your mastership of your free mind and great goodness did speak in my behalf in presence of that most noble and most honourable Council, fathers of high and singular prudence, of our most noble and most merciful prince'. As it happened, Master was pardoned.[3] Cromwell's gentle behaviour during his early examinations of Sir Thomas More is well known from the victim's own description of it to his daughter.[4]

At any rate, investigating directly or supervising the investigations of others, Cromwell was responsible for such system of internal security as there was. It is not surprising to find that he held clear views about the manner in which the work was to be done. He expected local authorities to go into every case of suspicion that came to their notice; if they thought the charge proven they were to keep the accused in prison until the King's further pleasure was known, and if the accusers could not convince them they were to bind both parties in sureties to appear when called for and let them go free. Those were his instructions in the

---

[1] SP 1/105, fo. 20 (*LP* xi. 58).
[2] SP 1/85, fos. 63–4 (*LP* vii. 982). For Pecock's case see above, pp. 14–15.
[3] SP 1/82, fos. 83–4; C 82/685 (*LP* vii. 71, 1026 [10]).
[4] See below, pp. 419–20.

case of Richard Smith, a Pembrokeshire priest accused of words 'sounding to treason'.[1] When Lord Sandys enquired for general guidance, Cromwell was even more particular:

I should commit them to ward or else take surety for their forthcoming when they should be called to answer for their offences...and then to advertise his lordship with the depositions, which should be seen and answer made for the order of such persons, being indeed or thought offenders.[2]

In this way Cromwell hoped to get at the truth. If a man was condemned locally, the government would still be able to decide whether the case was genuine or malicious; if he was let go, they still had the means to investigate and apprehend him further in case he had been freed improperly. The only authority which regularly proceeded against traitors without referring first to the King and Cromwell was the Council of the North, equipped with the necessary powers and encouraged to use them because of the disturbed state of their region in 1536–1538. It is not always clear whether every indictment was preceded by a study of the papers at the centre, but the majority seem to have been. In general, Cromwell practised control in these matters rather than let the locality have its way as it pleased. As the charges in his own attainder were to show, the King held him responsible; and responsibility demanded both universal knowledge and the claim to make all final decisions. His chief problems, therefore, were to make sure that all instances of treason, real or suspected, were brought to the notice of his local contacts – that is, mainly the justices of the peace and others in the service of the Crown – and that these contacts did their duty by reporting all cases to him rather than use their discretion about passing on information. Both these problems were beset by difficulties that limited the efficiency of this primitive police system, but up to a point they could be overcome.

Since the government expected to hear about treasonable offences from private persons in close contact with the offender, and since it made no attempt to stimulate informing either by offering rewards or by organising a spy system, the task of collecting material was seriously troubled in two respects. Men might decide not to tell even when they knew of treasons: 'concealment' was the bane of the government's

---

[1] Merriman, ii. 249–50.
[2] SP 1/133, fo. 1 (LP xiii. I. 1141).

police work. Or men might decide to tell of treasons never committed: the part played by private hatred and malice had to be assessed. The evidence shows that it was so assessed and that the task of separating the genuine from the pretended came to loom rather large. In many cases, of course, information reached the right quarters quite readily. The bulk of the several hundred delations shows a simple progression from local informer through local worthy to Cromwell and Council. Sometimes the intermediary allowed his reluctance to appear, as when Sir Giles Strangeways notified Cromwell in April 1534 of a Dorset priest accused of words against the King and Queen. The accused was 'but a simple person of no great wit ne understanding', and Strangeways had not arrested him but taken sureties. 'However, I suppose I can do no less of my duty than to inform you as one of the King's most honourable Council of this accusation.'[1] In September 1533, John Salcot, abbot of Hyde and bishop-elect of Bangor, wrote about one Thomas Merwell who had 'lewdly used' himself in conversation by speaking ill of Hyde Abbey, but said he brought the matter up only because Cromwell's servant Thomas Wriothesley had told him to do so and because (though he would not wish to be an accuser) it was necessary for the public weal that such lewdness be punished.[2] It is assuredly of some significance that one finds no such expressions of reluctance later in the decade, even from people who expressly cast doubt upon the charges they were passing on; clearly Cromwell succeeded in instilling in the rulers of the countryside a full understanding of what he required of them.

Concealment in the first instance was another matter, and we shall never know how much dissatisfaction and discontent failed altogether to come to the ears of the authorities. Cromwell's servant Anthony Rous had cause to send the rector of Dennington in Suffolk, one Richard Croukar S.T.D., to his master: Croukar had preached 'that the priest is bound to conceal treason revealed to him in confession' and on leaving for London repeated this honourable and strictly accurate opinion, which was thoroughly inconvenient for the government, with an assertion that all the clergy of the realm who 'have not utterly in contempt the cure of man's soul' would agree with him.[3] Even if charges were ultimately laid, temporary concealment caused serious

---

[1] SP 1/83, fo. 91 (*LP* vii. 480).   [2] SP 1/79, fo. 7 (*LP* vi. 1067).

[3] SP 1/130, fo. 215 (*LP* xiii. I. 633). This was as late as March 1538; nothing further is known about the case or the rector's fate.

trouble because delay made the investigation much more difficult. In September 1538 a number of the villagers of Herestoft in Derbyshire accused one of their number, William Roland, of saying about the time that the King 'was made supreme head of the Church of England' that he could not think him to be so 'for that consideration that he could not give a man that thing he should have when he came into the world nor when he went forth out of the world'. Sir Godfrey Foljambe J.P., confronted with a story four years old, bound accused and accuser to appear before King and Council, or the justices of oyer and terminer, but also enquired what he was to do about such accusers that so long concealed their knowledge. There is no sign that Roland was troubled further; yet if the charge was true he had drastically denied the supremacy, and the matter assuredly needed looking into.[1] The difficulties come out more clearly still in the case of a priest, Ralph Wendon, accused rather belatedly by a fellow priest, Thomas Gebons, of having said in April 1533 that Anne Boleyn 'was a whore and a harlot and maintained such heretics as he [Gebons] was...There was a prophecy that a queen should be burned at Smithfield, and that he trusted it should be the end of Queen Anne.'[2] The matter was examined by Thomas Bedyll. Wendon denied the charge, and Gebons admitted that the only other witness was now dead. However, he claimed to have informed the bishop of Exeter, John Veysey, though again he admitted that no one was present when he did so. The bishop, 'laying his hand upon his breast and looking upon the holy gospels, speaking in word of a bishop and taking it upon his faith that he oweth to God and the King', denied that he had ever received such information. The investigation revealed that Gebons was a young clerk of unsatisfactory behaviour – the bishop had in the hearing of others referred to his 'manifold misdemeanours...both at Oxford and Cambridge and in his native country' – who had been disappointed of a chaplaincy at Exeter; witnesses were produced by him who testified against him; his own relatives let him down. No doubt his charge was baseless, and so far as the evidence goes that is what Bedyll reported. But the investigation of an alleged offence even eighteen months old posed every sort of problem.

[1] SP 1/137, fo. 131 (*LP* xiii. II. 553).

[2] SP 6/7, arts. 6–10 (*LP* vi. 733). The examination probably took place in late 1534: there is a reference to June 22nd last being a Monday which in the relevant period fits only 1534.

The concealing of a treason was not always the fault of the first accuser. When William Cobbe, in November 1536, announced his doubts concerning the abolition of the pope's authority, the informant at once made a note of these words and told a Dover magistrate who claimed that he passed the bill to a justice of the peace and had heard no more about it. All this matter was at least six months old when the informer took fresh steps and got Cobbe imprisoned in Canterbury gaol.[1] Again, no more is known, but in this case one suspects a drastic end to the story; at any rate, the negligent intermediaries were asked to explain themselves. Once information was received, delay was certainly treated as culpable, as Archbishop Lee hinted in 1535 when he told some gentlemen to convey their knowledge of a priest's treasonable utterance at once to King and Council: 'In my next letters, I will write of him to Mr Secretary, but I advise you to make speed because you have heard him and spoken with him.'[2] William Fyldyng, reporting a delation to Cromwell in the same year, somewhat spoiled the effect of his avowal that as King's servant he was bound to inform the Council of all treasons by adding that what moved him to act was his 'duty of misprision' – his fear of the consequences if he did not.[3]

Asked to explain long delays, people were not usually so honest as that William Williams who (as we have seen) explained that he would not accuse his uncle while he had hopes of benefits from him.[4] William Draper of Radley (Berks.) accused his curate John Davy of treason. John Wellesbourne, sending him up, added that 'doubtless he hath kept it too long, whatsoever the cause hath been: he cannot tell, he saith, to whom he should show it'. Many of the poor of the parish now admitted hearing the words alleged; they had concealed them from fear of their priest.[5] It is worth remembering that the small world could easily bear more heavily on men than the great; the task of a government ruling right down to village level was far from easy. Of course, these excuses do not always ring true. William Bodnam charged his master, the much troubled Dr Robert Holdsworth, vicar of Halifax, with a finely calculated set of remarks. Holdsworth allegedly complained that he had lost 'by the King's act of Parliament' some eighty marks a year in mortuary fees, and went on: 'By my troth, William, if the King reign any space

---

[1] Cf. above, p. 19.
[2] *LP* viii. 990.
[3] SP 1/92, fo. 133 (*LP* viii. 643).   Above, p. 340.
[5] SP 1/138, fo. 30 (*LP* xiii. II. 699).

he will take all from us of the Church that ever we have, and therefore I pray God send him a short reign; and, William, I may tell thee in counsel here, upon Harry all England may weary.' Bodnam claimed never to have realised that he was bound to report this sort of thing to those in authority, until some friends, to whom he happened to tell of the vicar's sayings, advised him to safeguard himself by informing Sir Richard Tempest.[1]

In the circumstances, the only thing the government could do was to look savagely upon all concealers of treason. Even the faithful Rowland Lee could get a flea in his ear if Cromwell had reason to think him slow in action, as when three men were accused before him of seditious talk but the informer thought to move things on faster by repeating the charge also to the lord privy seal direct. Lee claimed that Cromwell's rebuke was the first he had heard of the matter.[2] In the middle of 1534 there was trouble at Windsor where Christopher Plummer, one of the canons, had used words against the King; the charge was first mentioned by a fellow canon, Miles Willen. But he failed to pass it on effectively, which was done by two other men, John Griffiths and Nicholas Wyddon. When Griffiths asked Willen, 'Why have ye so long kept secret this matter and not declared it according to your duty?', the canon replied that he had asked advice of another colleague, Dr Tate, 'who said, Mr Plummer is but a railing person and this is but a trifling matter – never speak further of it'. When Willen heard that the King was to be informed he tried to stop Griffiths from acting, but Griffiths, who had already written his letter, snubbed him. The canon lamented that 'ye have undone me', to which he got the unfeeling reply: 'Choose you, I care not, the matter touches my master so near that I will set it forward with speed.' But Plummer and Willen went to the Tower where they still were a year later.[3] Both, in fact, were attainted in the next session of Parliament, being included in Bishop Fisher's Act of Attainder, and both suffered for misprision of treason under the Act of

---

[1] E 36/120, fo. 104 (*LP* ix. 404). Holdsworth survived all his troubles and most of his accusers, dying in 1556 (R. B. Smith, *Land and Politics in the England of Henry VIII* [1970], 93).

[2] SP 1/158, fo. 170; 159, fo. 80; E 36/120, fo. 105 (*LP* xv. 447, 510; xiii. I. 808). The last document shows that the accuser deposed before the Council in the Marches in April 1537; the charge touched the sort of rumours of coming confiscations which had caused so much trouble in the north the year before. The other letters from Lee to Cromwell, placed by *LP* in 1540, also belong to 1537.

[3] SP 1/84, fo. 197; 94, fo. 3 (*LP* vii. 828; viii. 1001).

Succession. This suggests that something more meaningful and serious than we know of lay behind those letters concerning concealment. Willen promptly lost his various preferments, but in 1536 both he and Plummer were pardoned of all their treasons and set free.[1]

Some men were tried for concealment, though known cases are few. In the big process against the monks and others of Lenton priory, who were indicted at Nottingham Assizes partly for treason but mainly for concealing Dan Ralph Swenson's treason, the prior, seven monks and one secular priest were put on trial; of them, three were executed and six monks were either convicted of misprision or altogether acquitted.[2] The case shows what could happen – though it seems to have happened rarely – under the statute of 1534 to those who committed this negative form of misprision of treason. When John Henmarshe of Postington (Beds.) told his parishioners in November 1536, 'Take ye heed what ye do, for the Lincolnshire men are up, and they come for a common wealth and a good intent, and their opinion is good and yours is nought', they did not report him; but the matter leaked out much later and in Lent 1539 five of them were tried with him at a gaol delivery at Bedford. Henmarshe was sentenced to death for treason, the others to life imprisonment for concealment.[3]

It has already become clear that the question of concealment was quite closely linked to the alternative problem of malice: how was one to tell whether a man had remembered his duty or decided to get at an enemy, when necessarily the alleged matter lay well in the past and witnesses would be very hard to come by? The easiest thing of all, of course, would have been to accept all informations at face value, but the record shows clearly enough how careful investigators were of the good faith of their sources. Naturally, men accused claimed regularly to be the victims of malice, and it is hard to know at times what value to put on such protestations. But Francis Brown, of Stamford, seems to have been truly unfortunate. His son Anthony wrote to Cromwell early in 1537 to complain that his father had been put in ward upon a charge 'levied of old rancour and malice' to the effect that he had spoken

---

[1] 26 Henry VIII, c. 22 (*SR* iii. 527–8); *LP* viii. 149 (27, 28, 30); x. 597 (36); xii. I. 1104 (9).

[2] KB 9/542/8, 11. F. A. Gasquet, *Henry VIII and the English Monasteries* (ed. 1910), 283, confuses the issue by adding to the tally five laymen from quite different trials (KB 29/171, rot. 31) who had nothing to do with Lenton.

[3] KB 9/541/93.

contrary to his allegiance during the late rebellion. An enquiry ordered by Cromwell had omitted to give Brown his chance to answer, and Anthony now asked for him to be either released if innocent or dealt with at Cromwell's pleasure if guilty. Francis Brown re-appeared in the Lincolnshire commission of the peace in November 1537 and stayed there.[1]

Sometimes both sides accused each other of malice, as did the abbot of Wigmore and John Lee, one of his canons, in 1538. Lee claimed that he tried to get to see Cromwell in order to disclose matter about the abbot (John Smart) who thereupon counter-accused him and tried to get John Brydges (him who married the Lady Belknap) to arrest him at Wigmore Castle where he was acting as chaplain to the deputy constable, Thomas Crofte. As Crofte told the story, he could not allow Lee to be arrested because he lacked the authority required, but had suggested that Brydges should lay his charge before Crofte's father, a magistrate, next day. This Brydges agreed to do, but neither he nor anyone else turned up when the time came. According to the abbot and his friends, a search of Lee's chamber for a stolen vestment discovered a letter from John Cragge, parson of Ludlow, which contained treason; but Brydges, trying to arrest the suspect, was prevented by Crofte who threatened to break his head and lay him by the heels. They therefore turned to the arrest of Cragge whose house they searched and inventoried; he seems to have been acting as a local deposit bank, and they took £20 out of a bag containing £71 to cover the cost of the search, arrest and despatch of Cragge to London.[2] No more is heard of the alleged treasons of Smart and Lee who two months later in peaceful accord appended their signatures to the surrender of the house;[3] Cragge also disappears from the record.

Some denunciations are so clearly preposterous that no one in his senses would take notice of them: and no one did. When John Catheran, a labourer of Shereford in Norfolk, wished to annoy the local miller, he accused him of marvelling aloud at the King's exactions from both the

[1] SP 1/122, fo. 186 (*LP* xii. II. 196); *LP* xii. II. 1150 (16); xv. 282 (19).
[2] SP 1/136, fos. 135, 139 (*LP* xiii. II. 329, 333). £20 was a generous assessment of costs. Lee's articles against the abbot, which contain only one small hint of possibly political matter in a welter of moral charges, presumably belong to this dispute rather than to Bishop Foxe's attempt to discipline Smart in 1537 where *LP* xii. I. 742, with reservations, put them. Cf. also Knowles, iii. 345–6.
[3] *Deputy Keeper's Reports*, viii, App. ii, 49.

laity and the clergy: 'the King's grace intendeth to make a general hand with money, and then to avoid this realm and let your subjects shift as they could'. But he spoiled the story by revealing the way in which he had come to think of it: the miller, William Joly, had also threatened to drive Catheran from the country, so that he dared not visit his own house and 'poor wife, having a young child'.[1] The quarrel, already described, between two Oxfordshire women also revealed old malice. Sir Walter Stonor had them both to the constable's ward to cool off and reported to Cromwell; it is possible that they were punished locally, but most unlikely that anything further was done about their supposed treasons.[2]

How very carefully Cromwell sorted information is well illustrated by the troubles of Dr John London, warden of New College, Oxford, and something of a conservative in religion. In July 1536 the warden had reason to fear for his favour at court and even his place in the world, if not for his life, because his nephew Edward had made a dangerous deposition before the King's Council.[3] Edward was himself in trouble because he had allowed his anti-popish views to lead him into innovation in religion; he had used subversive discourse and written a pamphlet in favour of what his uncle allegedly regarded as heresy. One day, Dr London called for his erring kinsman at five in the morning and for five hours walked him about his garden. The speech put in his mouth by Edward has the right avuncular air:

Edward, he said, you be my nephew, and although I have not at all times outwardly declared it, yet nevertheless I have loved you with all my heart. Wherefore I have now sent for you only to give you counsel: that if God hath endowed you with any grace to that you may return to grace again. Sir, he said, it is so that I am informed you have written a declamation against the bishop of Rome full of many detestable heresies...which thing, he said, makes me so pensive that I cannot imagine what either to say either do, partly for your own shame, partly for mine, and thirdly for your poor mother. For, he said, if you prefix steadfastly to abide in this your opinion, you shall not only make all your friends sorry for you, but all the world also will cry out upon you. Again, he said, my lord of Winchester [Bishop Gardiner] at his

---

[1] SP 1/89, fo. 122 (*LP* viii. 146). The will of one William Joly of Shereford, bachelor, was proved in 1586 (*Norfolk Record Soc.* vol. 21, p. 99); he may just possibly have been the same person.

[2] Above, p. 279.

[3] SP 6/6, art. 6 (*LP* vii. 146: but it probably belongs into 1536).

visitation and my last being with him did wholly glory and rejoice that this our University was so clear from all this new fashions and heresies; but now he shall not only hear say that it is corrupted of one of his own College to his great discomfort but also of my kinsman; which will turn to my great shame. Thirdly, your mother, after that she shall hear what an abominable heretic she hath to her son, I am well certain (he said) that she will never eat more bread that shall do her good. Alas, he said, remember that hitherto there never was heretic of all our kin. Remember that our forefathers, ancient well-learned and holy men, could not have erred these many hundred years. Remember how often in times past these ways hath been attempted and what end the authors thereof hath come unto. Remember that this world will not continue long. For (he said) although the King hath now conceived a little malice against the bishop of Rome because he would not agree to this marriage, yet I trust the blessed King will wear harness on his own back to fight against such heretics as thou art...If thou wilt not make revocation, thou shalt be expelled thy College and utterly undone.

If such things – that is, the last few sentences, which may well be the only piece of invention in this speech – were being reported of him, it is no wonder that Dr London should hear a rumour that Cromwell, who so recently had employed him in the visitation of the monasteries, had turned against him. He wrote post-haste to his friend Thomas Bedyll, one of the King's lesser councillors. Edward's story was a lie: he was being egged on by one who wanted a piece of the doctor's property at Hornchurch. It was right enough that Cromwell should in the King's affairs be 'a straight examiner', but London did 'not mistrust his wisdom'. As one who had consistently written in defence of the second marriage and was the second man in Oxford to take the oath of succession, would he be so unwise as 'to say to this young man any words sounding contrary to mine own pen and corporal oath?' A second letter went to Cromwell himself in which the warden defended himself against charges of favouring popish practices and not doing his duty as a visitor to the monasteries. Again he charged his accusers, unlearned men whom he had had to reprove before this, with evil intent. Bedyll supported his pleas.[1] London continued in office, favour and authority, though he certainly inclined to the old ways and

---

[1] SP 1/77, fos. 122–3 (*LP* vi. 739: probably 1536); 105, fos. 70, 76 (*LP* xi. 96, 118). *LP* suggest that there were two occasions on which London roused suspicion, and this may have been so; but Bedyll's letter definitely belongs to 1536 and contains what seems a clear reference to London's letter to Bedyll; this in turn makes mention of Edward's denunciation.

later became a notorious persecutor under the Act of Six Articles. Yet if he said anything resembling the words cited by his nephew, Cromwell and the Council were being criminally negligent in letting him be; it is plain that they considered the information and rejected it.

Sometimes the private motives behind a denunciation are disarmingly plain. If a man could be attacked with reason, the minister would no doubt not care why the matter was brought up. No less a person than Sir John Porte, the judge, suggested to Cromwell's agent, Thomas Legh, who had great difficulty in getting the master of the hospital of Burton Lazars to resign his office, that things would be greatly eased if Cromwell were informed 'what a papist he is'.[1] The 'continual malice' between Nicholas Staunton, parson of Woodborough (Wilts.), and his neighbours, which the investigators discovered, did not alter the fact that he had talked unwisely, though the additional circumstance that he was drunk at the time ('as he will be often times, as knoweth our Lord') would probably, if other cases are anything to go by, count in his favour. The trouble had arisen over the low wages he offered to a curate – a mere eight marks a year. A witness, standing by, said, 'Mr Parson, it is too little wages'. Staunton protested that he was 'beggared – I can give him no more.' Asked why not, he burst out: 'My trees be cut down, and I have been indicted, and the King is my patron, and I am his beadman, and if he will not be good to me in my right I pray to God, little while may he reign among us.' Others also heard these words, but one man, a better friend who had not heard the outburst, intervened when the witnesses took Staunton up on his words to urge that the parson was drunk and should be left alone to sleep it off. His fate is unknown.[2]

More suspect is the information laid before Star Chamber by William Obyns of South Witham (Lincs.) who charged his parish priest Robert Winter with calling the King and Queen Lollards and heretics 'and wishes his knife in their bellies'. He claimed that two men present said

---

[1] SP 1/127, fo. 224 (*LP* xii. II, App. 14). Legh wanted the mastership for himself; he acquired the reversion on 10 March 1537 (*LP* xii. II. 795 [17]). The very next day, the duke of Norfolk protested to Cromwell that Legh was a married man and therefore disqualified by the rules from occupying the place; the duke also made plain how much he disliked Legh – 'such a vicious man' – and that he regarded his own interest as involved. Legh was still trying in August 1537 (*LP* xii. II. 502), but by early 1539, when a muster roll annotated the Burton Lazars contingent as 'servants of Dr Legh' (*LP* xiv. I, p. 275), he seems to have been successful.

[2] SP 1/128, fos. 106, 108–9 (*LP* xiii. I. 194).

they would attach Winter for treason but he bought them off with all he had. This led to trouble for Obyns who had paid Winter £6 for three cows, sixteen sheep, three sows and a boar, and now could not get his livestock because the blackmailers would not surrender what they had acquired. When Obyns went to a justice of the peace, the blackmailers got him and his wife attached for felony, and he spent thirty-three weeks in Lincoln Castle. He claimed to be now only concerned to reveal concealment of treason, but one wonders what tale the other side would have told.[1] Star Chamber was also approached by Peter Otley, parson of Wanstead (Essex), with a complicated tale of local persecution. He had brought a suit in the Court of the Arches against two of his parishioners 'to reform certain spiritual wrongs by them against your said orator committed', a phrase which seems likely to hide the collection of a fee. They in turn charged him with treason, and one of them carried him off to the Tower in the rudest possible fashion, scarcely allowing him once to drink by the way though he was then 'right faint, wet and weary'. The lieutenant of the Tower took a kinder view: after taking a bond from him, he let him go. Otley's enemies then tackled him in other ways, bringing actions in the London Hustings, getting him gaoled at Colchester, and telling all the Wanstead victuallers to boycott him. In consequence he neither dared come to his own house nor could afford to pursue the action in the Arches.[2] The prevalence of treason was certainly a useful weapon in private quarrels.

That many dubious and purely malicious charges were made is certain enough; on occasion, forwarding magistrates warned the minister of an informer's unreliability and cast doubt upon his tale. In 1535, a Yorkshire priest was accused by a fellow cleric of refusing to pray for the King; Sir George Lawson, passing this on as in duty bound, remarked that the accuser was well known as 'a naughty fellow, and the other priest of a good conversation'.[3] In the same year, Dr Robert Oking, the bishop of Bangor's commissary, faced an accusation of popery, but Sir Richard Bulkeley wrote from Beaumaris that the informer had been put up to it by Oking's predecessor in office who wanted his old job back; five years later, Oking was still commissary.[4] In Worcestershire, parson Gilbert Rouse was troubled by men of the

---

[1] St Ch 2/33/75.   [2] Ibid. 32/9.
[3] SP 1/92, fo. 126 (*LP* viii. 620).
[4] SP 1/92, fos. 134–5 (*LP* viii. 644); *LP* xv. 1013.

parish who claimed that he had called King and Council Lollards and praised the Carthusians as true martyrs and saints in heaven. Rouse had to admit that he had got into conversations which his enemies had been able to twist. When he was told that an order had gone out that no tithe corn was to be paid until 'the tiller had sown his ground again, found his house and paid his debts', with other restrictions, he had replied: 'If we be so dealt with, we be worse dealt with than Turks and Jews and as evil as we were heretics and Lollards.' On another occasion, asked about the monks executed in London, he had called them 'unfortunate and unwise' for opposing the King, but had added that 'if their opinion had been for the faith of God then they had been martyrs'. This was to sail very close to the wind, and Sir John Russell, the magistrate who had refused to do anything about the delation, acted less zealously than Cromwell expected. However, when challenged he relied against the accusing witnesses on a general testimonial from the parish which called Rouse 'a good churchman' and 'a true man in word and deed to the King our sovereign lord'. Knowing that there was old malice between the parties, and on the advice of a fellow magistrate, he decided to let the matter rest until he should hear more. Some of this went back to August 1533; it was not until 1535 that the government heard about it and ordered an enquiry; and yet, despite Rouse's near-admissions, the parson does not seem to have been troubled further.[1] Writing from Gloucestershire, Roger Morton J.P. reported a charge of treasonable words, adding that the accuser 'is a light person and of no reputation' while the accused 'is a soft man of spirit and outward very innocent'; the accuser had in fact once admitted that the charge was false and procured by a personal enemy of the accused, though later he changed his tale again.[2] And in 1537, real confusion was created at Walsingham by a mix-up in the plot to accuse a priest, Henry Manser, of saying that if Norfolk and Suffolk had risen when the north was up 'they had been able to have gone through the realm'. The charge was laid by Robert Sutton, but one of the witnesses first deposed that Sutton had so spoken to Manser, only to come back an hour later to say that he now could not remember who had said what to whom. The constables

---

[1] SP 1/95, fos. 78–83 (*LP* ix. 84). The part that Russell heard in 1533 touched only the tithe story; the second charge, which was serious but became so only after 1534, was added in 1535.

[2] SP 1/103, fos. 141, 144 (*LP* x. 693).

of Walsingham had the lowest opinion of Sutton, 'a sore and diseased person asking his alms daily' at the chapel door who had ignored several requests from Manser to keep away from the door itself where he was annoying the pilgrims. Since he would only reply in 'forward and naughty words' they finally had him to the stocks, and it was both on the way there and while in the stocks that he came up with his accusation against Manser. They clearly did not believe a word of it.[1]

Even clearer are the cases where an actual investigation established that an accusation was false and malicious, and the accused went free. Sometimes an informal enquiry in the locality would clear a man. In 1534, for instance, this method ended their troubles for a Kentish priest pursued by the malice of enemies, and for one Mrs Hey pursued by the malice of her husband.[2] These last had quarrelled and, 'as she had divers times before', she had left him. He tried to bring her back by calling her a 'traitrix' in public who 'had railed against the Queen's grace'. In a letter full of things so 'lewd and evil' that Cromwell's correspondent could not bring himself to quote them, he had warned the relatives with whom she had taken refuge that he would get her indicted unless they returned her to him. A group of justices looked into the matter, decided the charges were lies, and put Hey to bail while Cromwell determined whether his letter constituted grounds for an accusation against him instead. In 1537, when one John Newman allegedly spoke treason in Northamptonshire – even ignoring a warning to take care, for 'a little word is treason' – two investigating justices discovered from a witness who recanted his testimony that the matter had been got up by Margaret Perc, 'intending thereby to put him to trouble and business'.[3] Things were more clear-cut still in the case of William Jurdon who, just before he was himself executed for treason at Exeter in 1538, scattered broadcast charges of sedition against various people, including one of the witnesses against himself; again the justices though it necessary to investigate but could report mere malice.[4] Sir William Parr reported a boy who denounced his master for praying that the northern rebels should defeat the King; the truth, as he discovered, was that the man had failed to pay his accuser's wages.[5]

In all these cases the person denounced was at most bound to appear

[1] SP 1/121, fo. 31 (LP xii. II. 21).   [2] SP 1/87, fos. 38, 90 (LP vii. 1440, 1510).
[3] SP 1/126, fo. 136 (LP xii. II. 1068).   [4] SP 1/129, fo. 230 (LP xiii. I. 453).
[5] SP 1/126, fo. 177v (LP xii. II. 1102).

before Cromwell if the minister should decide to doubt the local man's decision, but we know of no single instance in which the justices were overruled. On other occasions, the fact of malice was established only at the trial when a jury acquitted on those grounds; the defendant had then suffered longer uncertainty but was even more securely rid of his troubles in the end. In a sense every acquittal probably reflected the jury's conviction that the accused had been persecuted by false witness, but explicit mention of malice is in fact rare. William Thwaytes (already mentioned) was in 1535 alleged to have complained of the King's policy. 'All realms christened have forsaken us but only the Lutherans', and the money exacted by the King would be used to bribe them into serving the King's 'false purpose'. There was an interdict on the land which 'lay at Calais and other ports without the realm, and if it were conveyed in we should have no more Christian burial than dogs; howbeit, the King will not obey it'. The King should be destroyed 'by the most vile people in the world...and should be glad to take a boat for safeguard of his life and flee into the sea...and masters, there hangs a cloud over us, what as yet it means I know not'. This is extensive and circumstantial stuff; there were three witnesses to it all and two more to testify to lesser instances of insubordination, and Cromwell had apparently sifted the charges and remitted Thwaytes for trial; but at the York Assizes in March 1536 the grand jury threw the bill out 'for it was said that all was spoken of malice'. Thwaytes was probably lucky to have faced his accusers before the Pilgrimage of Grace.[1] William Bowerman, a Somerset parson, went through a more complicated series of trials and was more certainly innocent. He had been accused by John Delton of treason and heresy, before the Council in the West: the supposed heresy was a charge of perjury, and the alleged treason an attempt to exact peter's pence despite the statute. As Bowerman said, not only were the facts untrue, but neither would support the charge preferred; and so the Council in the West decided. Delton got another man to renew the attack with a bill in Star Chamber, but there Bowerman simply pleaded the earlier dismissal and the pardon obtained, disdaining to plead to the facts because he did not wish 'to contend with his most gracious sovereign lord in the matter, albeit it was untrue'. There then ensued an exchange of actions from both sides which extended into 1544 when Delton once more petitioned the Star Chamber; that last investi-

[1] Cf. above, pp. 58, 314.

gation revealed an ancient animosity between the parties which had started with the cutting down of a box tree and a yew tree in Corscombe churchyard.[1]

In an age as disturbed as that of the early Reformation was, one would no doubt expect to encounter many purely malicious and false informations; but would one also expect such evidence that the authorities troubled to make sure whether a charge was true or not? It is abundantly clear that men were very far from being at the mercy of any informer: the government, local and central, was bound by the assumption that it would act only against men who really seemed to be guilty. Nor did informers meet with that invariable favour which the theory of a 'reign of terror' would require; their lot could be quite unhappy. One such unfortunate was John Parkins who, accusing two abbots of treason in 1537, instead found himself treated as the guilty party by the King's commissioners.[2] He did not stand alone. Another who found it a mistake to become involved in attacking an abbot was Richard Alford, monk of Burton, who in June 1536 landed in the Fleet, suspected of forging a licence and of conspiring to accuse his superior of treason. He denied everything, though he tried to implicate others. The investigation left the abbot in the clear; Alford survived his experience to enjoy his pension in due course.[3] Less happy in their issue were the internal troubles of Lenton priory. In 1538 the prior, Nicholas Heath, and one of his people were executed for treasons committed by words,[4] but Heath had been subject to suspicion since early in 1535 when he first drew Cromwell's attention to the low quality of his accuser, Dan Hamlet Pencrick, who for a full year had been informing against his superior. Dan Hamlet, suborned by the prior's personal enemies in Nottingham, 'is now run forth of his religion, as he hath done two times before'; on the last occasion some of the goods of the house went with him.[5] Heath's words seem to have left an impression in govern-

---

[1] St Ch 2/12/180.   [2] Cf. above, p. 93.

[3] SP 1/104, fos. 171–3 (LP x. 1126); LP xv. p. 543.

[4] Above, p. 350 and cf. Knowles, iii. 372–3. The prior's treason, of which Knowles could not discover the facts, is given in KB 9/542/10, the record of his indictment at Nottingham on 13 April 1538. He was alleged to have said: 'Brethren, I hear say the King is now married and to one of the same generation as evil as the other Queen was before. The devil is in him, for he is past grace; he will never amend in this world. I warrant him [to] have as shameful a death as ever king had in England. A vengeance on him!'

[5] SP 1/69, fo. 248 (LP x. 655).

ment circles: by mid-1537 Pencrick was in the Fleet by Audley's order and appealing to Cromwell with offers of further information.[1] It was probably at this time that he reported the dangerous conversations of Dan Ralph Swenson which were in the end to bring the priory low, but for the present his charges were not listened to, at least in part because Cromwell once more received a very adverse report on the informer, this time from a local gentleman, steward of the priory.[2] What caused the matter to be reopened in April 1538 is not known; Cromwell may have been biding his time, or (as the evidence accumulating here suggests) a careful sorting of the charges could not be done in a day, especially if the informer was so clearly suspect. Though it is not known what happened to Pencrick in the end, it is worth noting that his informing activities, in which, as it turned out, he spoke some truth, earned him a spell in the Fleet.

Perhaps one feels little surprise to find that a man who muttered of knowledge dangerous to, among others, Cromwell's old friend Thomas Rush in Suffolk should end up in ward (put there by Rush!) when he would not become explicit.[3] The story of William Wood's denunciation of Robert Kirkby and Robert Lyon, the priest and parish clerk of Kirkby Moorside in Yorkshire, is more revealing just because it is the run-of-the-mill sort of case in which one would not expect that sufficient trouble would be taken to sort truth from falsehood or establish the reliability of the informer. The tale told by Wood was this.[4] In June 1538, while praying in church, he overheard a conversation between Kirkby, Lyon and one John Thomson. Lyon told the others that the magic of Mabel Brigge had worked and the King was dead.[5] Kirkby was content: 'Vengeance must needs light upon him because he hath put so many men wrongfully to death.' Lyon added that 'if Cromwell were dead also it were not a halfpenny loss'; and Kirkby agreed that all would have been well 'if any of the great men had had a switch at the King's neck a twelvemonth since, before this

---

[1] SP 1/120, fo. 270 (*LP* xii. I. 1327).
[2] The anonymous information against Swenson (SP 1/118, fo. 112 [*LP* xii. I. 892]) contains the charge later included in Swenson's indictment (KB 9/542/11); the words were said in Pencrick's presence, and that the informer was not the subprior (as Knowles, iii. 373 supposes) is clear from the fact that the subprior is mentioned in the third person. The steward's letter is SP 1/118, fo. 136 (*LP* xii. I. 912).
[3] SP 1/113, fo. 27 (*LP* xi. 1357).   [4] SP 1/183, fo. 241 (*LP* xiii. I. 1282).
[5] Above, p. 57.

business began'. Wood challenged them for their traitorous sayings and declared that he would report them 'for mine own discharge'. To this Kirkby said: 'If I may know that thou go out of this dale to show anything that we have said either to knight or justice, I shall have of thee either a leg or an arm, or thou comest at them.' Kirkby also told Wood's uncle Robert that 'better it were that such a vagabond lately comen from London should have a mischief than he for to trouble any neighbours for such words as we have spoken'. All this went to the Council of the North, but so far from it being death to Kirkby it merely led to a thorough investigation into William Wood, quickly warded at York.

On inspection, Wood turned out to be a very odd character of whom his uncle said that as a child he had been caught stealing so often that the family had thought of putting him to sea in a cobble.[1] He was three times interrogated at great length in York Castle and told a story of his life which makes his mere nineteen years barely credible.[2] Ever since he was seven or eight years old he had been on the move. First in service with a husbandman near Guisborough, from whom he ran away, he had become a jobbing tailor who in about six years had worked for masters in London (where he claimed to have spent four years with a tailor in Fleet Street but could remember no neighbour's name or even his mistress's), Windsor, Maidenhead, by stages back to Yorkshire, then south again through Beverley, Hull, Lincoln and home again, off once more to London and neighbourhood, and then home again to his mother's. The itineraries and details do not quite fit: clearly the interrogators kept pecking away for a more detailed report of his movements, with dates and lengths of stay, which it is not surprising that he could not give exactly. But he sounded thoroughly suspicious, truly a vagabond, and his reputation at home was low. This came out in the enquiry when a reason for his enmity to Lyon was laid bare. He had quarrelled with the family. It all started when, walking one day with two friends, he watched Robert Lyon's daughter Bess ride pillion with a young man: apparently she cut a ludicrous figure. One of the young men said, 'away with her'; the other, 'she will be down, [I] believe'; the first, 'nay, he hath hold on her'. The chaff does not seem to have troubled Bess, but walking on alone Wood caught up with her,

[1] *LP* xiii. I. 1326.
[2] SP 1/134, fos. 104–6; E 36/120, fos. 152–4 (*LP* xiii. I. 1326 [2]).

now on foot and accompanied by some children. He asked her, 'Will the young man let you ride no further?' She snubbed him – 'What if his way lay no further?' Wood told her he would not have ridden so far 'for the mock that ye had'. At this she bridled: 'What is that for thee?', and Wood mumbled it was nothing for him. She then sat down on the grass, clearly determined to be rid of his attentions, and when he suggested walking on she called him a knave and a thief – 'thou hast broken a shop in London and such apparel as thou hast thou didst steal there and darest not go thither again'. This started a brawl which may have got as far as blows; at least Bess claimed that William struck her 'that she swooned', a point confirmed by the two little boys watching. The scene was interrupted by John Thomson coming by with his son who told them to hold their peace 'for shame...Folks will say ye be all drunken if they hear of this.' However, thereafter Robert Lyon would not be civil to Wood (he told him 'to keep thy good morrows to thyself'); the Lyons spread it around that Wood was a thief and had robbed a place in London, and Kirkby, acting the parish priest, tried to set him down too.

None of this can have helped to make his accusation more credible; in addition, John Thomson, Wood's supposed witness, denied hearing the treasonable conversation. He had no support; he looked to be a suspect man and a liar; and it is no wonder that the matter was allowed to drop. Yet, for what it is worth, it may be said that his story had quite a powerful air of truth: would he, for instance, have been able to dream up the reference to the prophetess executed at York? If Kirkby Moorside decided to keep the dale's affairs private, it may well have made a good job of it, and in the process it demonstrated that there could be disadvantages attached to doing one's bounden duty to the King.

Those informers had been troubled, but they had not suffered. The 'lewd fellow' who in 1538 accused one of the duke of Suffolk's servants of treason and found his four witnesses depose against him ended up in the pillory.[1] Worse befell John Drury, though unofficially only, as it were. He tangled with a martial priest of Detling in Kent, and the encounter left him, according to himself, 'utterly maimed and undone for ever...in my prince's quarrel'.[2] While the northern rebellion was on he journeyed towards London with this priest, one Sir Davy, and

[1] SP 1/137, fo. 128 (*LP* xiii. II. 554).
[2] SP 1/125, fos. 207–8 (*LP* xii. II. 908).

when Drury said that he would take his prince's side in this civil war the other man exploded:

The prince, said he, no, a tyrant more cruel than Nero; for Nero destroyed but a part of Rome, but this tyrant destroyed his whole realm. And as Egeas did pursue the apostles of Christ, much more doth this tiger persecute Holy Church, and not only the Church and the goods of the same but also he destroyeth the ministers of the same.

'Marry, fie on thee, traitor priest,' said loyal Drury, 'thou shalt not escape these words.' This threat he endeavoured to make good by fleeing to the kitchen 'where mine host and hostess was, he grinding of malt and she dressing her child by the fire'. Davy caught him up and thrust his 'long pragc' through his two doublets and shirts and 'a little perished my flesh, not to me knowing till mine hostess spied'. Drury tried to defend himself with his half-broken dagger but was thrown on the ground and, despite the host's attempt to intervene, was struck in the face so that he cried out that he was slain. This sobered his attacker who took off, not stopping till he got to Headcorn, some five miles away, where he told the curate that he had killed a man. He was allegedly saved by Mr Hughes, the commissary of Maidstone, who provided him with clothing and money and got him out of the country. Hughes offered to make peace by looking after Drury in his trouble, paying for 'both boarding and leechcraft'; this was refused, but, destitute and badly injured, Drury had to rely on friends. Now he was being pursued, in some obscure way, by the priest's friends and appealed for aid to Cromwell. The truth of the tale was vouched for by a Kentish knight, Sir John Fogge, in whose service both contestants had at one time been and who in the end came to Drury's assistance;[1] but Davy was gone, and the informer had nothing to show for his pains but scars.

It was only to be expected that informers might meet obloquy and menaces, like one Henry Wolward, threatened at Cambridge by John Ridley, the proctor's servant, for being the cause of a young man's imprisonment.[2] The violent changes of the decade could trick men into curious positions. In 1536, Robert Colyns, the conservative vicar of Tenby, thought he saw a chance of avenging an old injury done to him

---

[1] SP 1/125, fo. 264 (*LP* xii. II. 959).
[2] SP 1/83, fo. 261 (*LP* vii. 629). For Ridley see my *Star Chamber Stories*, 63, 73–4.

by John Barlow, dean of Westbury and a close ally of Cromwell's: Barlow had for long been among the inner group of the Boleyn faction. So when the Queen's fall coincided with Barlow's sudden arrival in Wales, Colyns, pretending a great air of patriotism and concern, went about marvelling and warning:

If I were an officer of the country or able to give them counsel...they should be sure of him here till our prince's pleasure might be known, lest he, as one privy to such treason, might haply start away from Milford Haven by water.

But Barlow proved far from down; he worked up a charge of misprision of treason against Colyns on the grounds that in some of the books of his church the word *papa* was insufficiently blotted out; and Colyns had to write for help from prison.[1] Some informers divided the locality, like that Hugh Rawlyngs of Gloucester whose story has already been told.[2] On that occasion Cromwell rescued a man both from his accusers and from those who resented his turning informer himself. The men who tried to bring trouble to the priory of Worcester in 1535 ran into difficulties with Prior More's local acquaintance. One of the restive monks, John Musard, was imprisoned by the prior at the instigation of a justice of the peace; a friend of his, though eager to serve Cromwell, warned that after this it would be hard to collect evidence. A third, especially instructed by Cromwell to take charge of the house's property, suffered public humiliation.[3] It does not seem in this instance that people quaked because the secretary had his eye on them.

All these activities – finding out about offences, preventing concealment, sorting true from false, and protecting informers – were only the beginning, though perhaps also the main part, of the police work required of the government. When a man had been delated and there seemed cause to take the charge seriously, the case was not done with, and at all further stages the technical short-comings of sixteenth-century administration, and especially the ability of local men to frustrate the will of the centre, cut across simplicity. At the very least, a good deal was being asked of everybody involved, including money. The sending up of an arrested man involved expenses: the journey would normally

[1] SP 1/104, fos. 207–8 (*LP* x. 1182). [2] Above, pp. 121–3.
[3] For Worcester priory cf. above, pp. 124–8; for the present details see SP 1/96, fo. 8; 97, fo. 91; 102. fos. 43–4 (*LP* ix. 204, 497; x. 311).

take days, and there would be food and lodging required during it for two or three men and their horses. Evidence on this point is very slight; one must presume that ordinarily local magistrates and gentlemen who despatched their servants with a suspect expected to cover the cost themselves. Very exceptionally, people tried to recover their outlay, like that abbot of Wigmore who took £20 of an arrested man's savings for the purpose.[1] William Jackson, innkeeper at Hougham in Lincolnshire, in 1537 arrested and, with the help of a yeoman of the village, brought to London a Yorkshireman, William Moke, who on his journey home had put up at Jackson's inn and had talked too largely about politics and executions, promising to warn the people about his country not to obey any summons and wishing that Cromwell 'were beyond Doncaster bridge'. Jackson's dutiful action seems to have appeared entirely natural to him: he made nothing of the fact that, on the word of a justice, he and his friend had carried the suspect all the way to London. But he did ask that Cromwell might 'have respect' to his expenses in the matter.[2] Probably he got nothing, for there are very few signs that people could expect repayment; the only cases to come to notice are those of the people who brought one James Prestwich all the way from York and received £6 13s 4d for the double journey, and of Sir Thomas Denys's two servants who had £4 when they brought up a suspect Breton priest from Devon.[3] The costs were particularly severe when the suspect was sent from Calais, with a Channel crossing to add to the burden, and it is no wonder that the deputy there, Lord Lisle, sought relief. In reply, Cranmer (who normally received Calais suspects for further despatch) snubbed him with an explanation of what indeed would seem to have been the normal practice:

And as for that you require of me to know how such charges should be borne when men are thus sent for: my lord, as far as I have experience I know not the contrary but that in such matters as touch the King's highness every subject is bound to bear his expenses, or else such of the King's officers as make deliverance of any such person, as I myself must bear his charges to the court from where I abide.

---

[1] Above, p. 351.   [2] SP 1/120, fo. 154 (*LP* xii. I. 1319).

[3] *LP* xiii. II. 1280, fos. 31b, 35. Prestwich several times, in writing and speech, affirmed his belief that the King could not be supreme head of the Church; he was caught trying to escape abroad and told a tale of looking for his girl friend beyond Durham (SP 1/134, fos. 190–2, 216–17 [*LP* xiii. I. 1402–3, 1428]). In the end he was attainted by the Parliament of 1539, though from his place in the list it is not clear whether he was

Nevertheless, in the kindness of his heart he sent Lisle ten shillings towards his expenses on this occasion.[1]

The keeping of a suspect set a further problem, and it is quite surprising that in most cases – as in that of William Moke – messengers arrived safely with the alleged traitor firmly in tow. There were exceptions. John Clerke, accused of words 'meet to have been unspoken', was being carried up from no further than Maidstone when through his guard's negligence he escaped: he could not be found.[2] John Davy of Exeter fled as soon as he heard that information was being laid against him, until rumour said that he had got to Westminster and was living in a house in King Street. The locality thankfully remitted the search to the centre.[3] There were many weak spots in the chain of police control. When Cromwell, in 1537, instructed the earl of Worcester to arrest and send up one Friar Gawen, his letter was handed by mistake to the friar's servant for delivery to the earl, and it was the sheerest accident that the suspect did not learn what was in store and make himself scarce.[4] On two occasions, in 1535 and 1537, Lord Cobham reported trouble from Gravesend and urged Cromwell to make better arrangements for that convenient bolthole. The first time, a gentleman arrived claiming to come from Cromwell and that a ship was waiting for him; as soon as he got past the customs officers and on board 'he spoke opprobrious words' against the King and Queen and sailed away. This was alleged to be a favourite escape route for enemies of the government.[5] On the other occasion, Cobham took steps against one who had attacked royal taxation because he thought that sort of talk especially dangerous in 'such a town of resort and wild people'; he felt that stricter instructions should go to the chief men of the town.[6]

already executed (31 Henry VIII, c. 15). I have been unable to find any further trace of him, and he may have been among those who suffered during the 1541 clearing of the Tower.

[1] SP 1/115, fo. 92 (*LP* xii. I. 258).   [2] SP 1/128, fo. 46 (*LP* xiii. I. 37).
[3] SP 1/129, fo. 201 (*LP* xiii. I. 416).
[4] SP 1/121, fo. 181 (*LP* xii. II. 158). Gawen seems to have been guilty of something well short of treason, for a little time later Latimer interceded on his behalf, asking that after condign punishment he might be charitably dealt with and let go (SP 1/126, fo. 108 [*LP* xii. II. 1044]). He may have been that Friar Gawen, warden of the grey friars of Plymouth, who in 1533 was examined upon an accusation by two of his convent (SP 1/80, fo. 193 [*LP* vi. 1503]); the depositions, now missing, were among Cromwell's papers by early 1534 (E 36/139, fo. 74).
[5] SP 1/98, fo. 81 (*LP* ix. 691).   [6] SP 1/120, fo. 150 (*LP* xii. I. 1245).

The uncertainties of sixteenth-century gaols further complicated the work, nor was this a problem peculiar to the age of Cromwell. A man indicted of treason in 1528 had managed to break gaol at Shrewsbury; recaptured, he was indicted for the second offence (the first indictment seemingly forgotten), but process was stayed by *mandamus* out of the King's Bench when the sheriff responsible was in his turn indicted for allowing the escape.[1] One in Wales who 'spoke railing words' against Cromwell was rescued from strict ward by some of the earl of Worcester's servants and in his appreciative gratitude put on the earl's service and livery. Despite this, Bishop Lee arrested both him and his rescuer (one Llewellyn ap Morris ap Rees ap Atha); this second man had been locally convicted of the gaol-break, but Lee respited him because he wished to try the railer for treason and the aider as an accessory, for a more formidable example. However, the principal offender died in Shrewsbury gaol awaiting trial.[2] A big prison break occurred at Hexham in 1538; among those who got away was Richard More, a priest of Chichester who was somehow busy conspiring in the north. He escaped to Scotland but daringly took boat south again and was recaptured when storms drove the vessel into Shields harbour. With him there were two Irish priests, and all three carried seditious correspondence linking them with the activities of Cardinal Pole; to add to his offence, More tried to persuade his guard on the way to York that the King and his subjects were heretics while the bishop of Rome was the true head of the Church.[3] The Council of the North had clearly uncovered a genuine infiltration of agents from abroad.

These technical difficulties could, up to a point, be got over by energy and vigilance; more intractable was the problem posed by the feelings of the locality where a suspect might have better or more useful friends than his accuser. Prior More of Worcester and Robert Winter, the Lincolnshire parson, owed their immunity to the good offices, respectively, of a soundly conservative lady and of a couple of blackmailers who saw advantages for themselves in another man's treason which they did not propose to share with the Crown.[4] John Raven, who admitted calling Henry and Cromwell fools, found the constable, Robert

---

[1] KB 9/514/62.

[2] SP 1/125, fo. 197; 127, fo. 34; 130, fo. 196 (*LP* xii. II. 896, 1183; xiii. I. 624 [3]).

[3] SP 1/140, fo. 196 (*LP* xiii. II. 1146); *StP* v. 151–2; Merriman, ii. 193–4. All three appear in the general Act of Attainder of 1539 (31 Henry VIII, c. 15) and were undoubtedly executed.　　　　[4] Above, pp. 127, 355.

Hornyngold, on his side. Hornyngold told him that he had spoken words against the King, 'I warn thee, deny them'; otherwise 'thou wilt sure to be hanged unless thy neighbours be good to thee, and if thou still deny them thou mayest happen scape'. But someone denounced him, and so he tried to wriggle out by retorting the charges upon his accusers.[1] Lawrence Taylor, of Havant (Hants.), enjoyed the benefit of having once been servant to a justice of the peace when he came under suspicion of having spread seditious rumours in 1538. The justice, John Gunter, arrested him but let him go, a fact discovered by the earl of Southampton when a poor man petitioned him on behalf of his wife whom Gunter was holding in custody as the alleged author of the rumours. Gunter explained that he had not known what to do with Taylor and had let him go, thinking he had gone to a wedding. This 'unwise answer' was too much for the earl; 'somewhat moved', he took Gunter apart, 'learned and expert' though he might be. The justice went pale and 'with tears and sobbing pitifully' begged for mercy; he would do his duty now. His men soon found Taylor, and the subsequent investigation showed him to have been behind the rumour, though he tried to put the blame on two silly women who had spread it further. He also found another man, already in prison in London, on whom to father the authorship of the tale. Southampton left it there till he heard further.[2] In the case of Peter Grisling of Plymouth, delated to Cromwell, it is not clear whether the ensuing difficulties arose from the activities of his friends in intimidating witnesses (as the town magistrates claimed) or from the supposed witnesses' opinion that there had been no treason spoken but only the sort of raging malice that they were familiar with in Grisling, 'and namely upon drink'. Either way, he enjoyed the protection of the locality.[3]

Of course, local prejudice could work another way, as in the dark case of parson Thomas Hemyngton of Sudborough (Northants.) who accused Sir William Parr of using his office of sheriff in 1538 to black-mail him by means of a trumped-up treason charge. Rather than risk things further, Hemyngton agreed to pay the sheriff £40. The matter came into the open because he could not raise the money, had to hand

---

[1] Cf. above, p. 9.

[2] SP 1/136, fos. 200-5 (*LP* xiii. II. 392-3).

[3] SP 1/101, fo. 44 (*LP* x. 42). The only words mentioned did not touch the King, but Cromwell's servant Richard Pollard, who often kept an eye for him on Devon matters, seems to have thought that there was substance to investigate.

over produce, and for several years allowed Parr to take the tithe; but he still owed a debt at the end of it all which Parr tried to recover at law. Hemyngton petitioned Star Chamber, claiming that the original bond was extorted.[1] Many men also did their duty, unasked, as the prior of Norwich found to his cost when the municipality instituted a spontaneous search for him after he had preached his highly offensive sermon.[2] Naturally, the evidence overwhelmingly suggests cooperation; it is only occasionally that failure to act as in duty bound would become known. The government's task was to render this unlikely, to apply pressure locally and to supervise what went on, but from all that has been said it is plain enough how difficult that would be if real reluctance and resistance developed.

These difficulties explain Cromwell's devotion to regular and frequent exhortations – his policy of circulars and letters which has already been discussed. One justice, who took the royal letter personally, resented being told in 1537 that his majesty marvelled at any failure to carry out the various instructions received over the years, so that the laws, statutes and virtuous admonitions 'by his highness made and set forth upon his tender zeal and loving mind to the common weal of his realm' were not being enforced. This was not so. He had never ceased to seek out 'the fautors of the venomous papistical faction of Rome with the corrupt members and adherents of the same'. Any that he discovered he had put in prison 'until the Sessions or Assizes' on which occasions he had taken care to see them punished, as a warning to others. 'Some such odible persons I have presented to your lordship.' As for 'tellers of seditious news and spreaders abroad of factious bruits', he had himself at the last Sessions urged that they were to be presented, 'for they are sowers of much unthriftiness, bringers up of new ills, and maintainers of mischief'. He also felt quite content with his handling of vagabonds and private disputes.[3] No doubt his virtue shone, and no doubt there were others as virtuous. But the constant worrying away at the gentry was not a sign of mere fussiness, and the sheriff of Hampshire had reason to tell Cromwell of the splendid address delivered to Quarter Sessions by Thomas Wriothesley, the minister's secretary but also a

[1] St Ch 2/32/16. That at least was Hemyngton's story: the patchy evidence leaves matters in doubt. Parr claimed to have lost the bond arbitrators believed had been entered into without any blackmail, as part of an ordinary loan transaction.
[2] Above, p. 17.
[3] SP 1/241, fo. 110 (LP Add. 1241), in reply to the circular of April 1537.

local worthy, in April 1539. Wriothesley reminded the assembly of the gratitude they owed to the King for setting forth God's Word and regretted that his majesty's desire for indifferent justice should be hampered by two faults 'due to us commissioners and gentlemen, not excepting himself', namely bad religious instruction and attacks on good preachers on the one hand, and on the other the practice of abusing the commission of the peace for personal ends. He ended with a solemn and severe adjuration to do justice.[1] Policy depended on the readiness of the gentlemen of the shires not so much to enforce it against any known to have offended as to cooperate in the universal vigilance against possible dissidents and enemies.

It also depended, of course, on the readiness of all sorts of people to speak up and give evidence, a readiness which had to overcome local ties and such fears as those of Mary Brusher of Bognor who hesitated to testify against William Hamlyn (accused of having cursed the King for his taxes) because he was her landlord: 'she and her husband hath six children, and she knew well Hamlyn would put her out of the door if she told the truth'. One way to overcome this natural reluctance was that finally chosen by Mrs Brusher: pressed to tell, she struck a pose to the effect that rather than conceal slanders against the King and his Council she would 'beg her bread with all her children'.[2] It would be quite pointlessly cynical to doubt that such feelings were often entirely genuine; far too many people spoke against their neighbours without the stimulus of either private malice or public fear to allow one to overlook the very real devotion to King and realm and authority which manifestly existed. Still, no government can simply sit back and rely on such sentiments appearing when needed: hence the repeated earnestness with which people were reminded of their duty, of all they owed to the King, and of the heinousness involved in failure to act. It might be thought that, however little of a proper spy system there may have been, the exhortations and threats employed created a real feeling of terror in the country which helped to supply the Crown with a massive contingent of volunteers, unorganised but cowed into telling any tale they heard. It is difficult to disprove such notions entirely; sixteenth-century evidence rarely permits the safe establishment of a negative. That they are impossible to demonstrate as well would not deter those who hold them; in the nature of the case, one cannot expect detailed

[1] LP xiv. I. 775.   [2] SP 1/132, fos. 79–82 (LP xiii. I. 966).

proof that men, professing to act from high motives, were really only driven by fear.

Against the idea of a universal pall of terror one may adduce the plentiful evidence of free talking and rash action, as well as the clear signs that malice often failed of its purpose and that the government could do little without effective local support. There are occasional remarks to show that people were not without fear, but explicit mention is exceedingly rare. Lisle's London agent John Hussey excused his empty letters during the critical days of December 1536 by pointing out that he could not risk his life, 'for there is divers here that hath been punished for reading and copying with publishing abroad of news'. Some were in the Tower and 'like to suffer therefor'.[1] But that was at the time when the north seethed with armed rebels and the whole Tudor monarchy seemed poised on an edge. That particular situation also accounts for the duke of Norfolk's hopes, in April 1537, to have lots of delations brought in by the people of the north parts who 'be in such fear, God be thanked, and also be desirous to deserve thanks in part of recompense of their offences' that they would hasten to denounce all and sundry.[2] There are no statements of this sort in more ordinary times, despite the supposed general reaction at Cromwell's fall. What seemingly shocked people was not the pillorying or executing of little men for talking too freely without meaning much by it, but the attacks on the great, the merciless pursuit of the Poles and Montagues and their like. Lord Darcy's well known attack on Cromwell for wishing all noblemen a head shorter, or the earl of Surrey's rejoicing at the death of the foul churl 'so ambitious of others' blood', reflect the general aristocratic hatred of the upstart and the fear of what, with the King behind him, he might do. This prevalent feeling that the great were most in danger was also brought out in the conversation which Thomas Neville allegedly had in 1537 with the widow Towler, housekeeper to the parson of Aldham in Essex, at that time in custody with the earl of Oxford. She asked him: 'Alas, Mr Neville, shall my master be put to death upon a false wretch's saying?' but got the reassuring

[1] SP 1/240, fos. 200v–201 (*LP Add.* 1148). This referred to Sir William Essex, 'in the Tower...for writing and publishing of news' (SP 1/240, fo. 203 [*LP Add.* 1151]); for the details cf. SP 1/113, fos. 68–73 (*LP* xi. 1406). He did not, in fact, suffer but was fully restored to favour; thus e.g. in 1540 he attended Anne of Cleves's arrival as a King's councillor at large (*LP* xv, p. 5).
[2] SP 1/117, fo. 262 (*LP* xii. I. 825).

reply: 'No, Margaret, he shall not be put to death, for he hath no lands or goods to lose; but if he were either a knight or a lord...then he should lose his life.' Her master would be kept in prison for three or six months, 'his benefice given away to another good fellow, and then he shall be turned out of prison again'. She said that surely 'the King's grace will put no man to death neither for goods nor lands', but Neville replied sadly, 'Yes, by God, Margaret, but he would'.[1] This sort of feeling may have been widespread, but it is well short of a general state of terror and would hardly account for the stream of denunciations against men of no importance.

However, as has been seen, the government depended on its ability to buttress natural loyalties and eagerness to serve the King with a useful impression that someone was keeping watch; and though after forty years of Tudor government there was nothing new about this in 1530, it does look as though Cromwell's energy sharpened the effect. The fact may account for the appearance, now and again, of impostors endeavouring to exploit a mysterious air of somehow being in with Cromwell. Curiously enough, all the known cases occurred early in the decade. In March 1534, two men claiming to be Cromwell's servants were throwing their weight about at London and at Gillingham in Kent, threatening people with *praemunire* in an attempt to extort hush-money. A draper of Ludgate fell into their trap. Before they could be apprehended, one of them wangled his way into Queen Anne's service and assisted the other into Cranmer's.[2] In July that year, Gabriel Pecock at Southampton nearly fell for a bogus visitor allegedly sent by the King's authority. The man, dressed as a black friar, assembled the convent by ringing the chapter bell and read them a document under the King's seal which claimed to recite a patent granted to the provincials of the Austin and Dominican friars to carry out a visitation. From his robe they took him to be the latter, namely Dr John Hilsey, nor did he deny it when asked directly by Pecock. However, one of the prior's servants happened to know Hilsey and explained that the visitor must be somebody else. So Pecock, sure that King and Council would not be trying tricks, asked him for his authority since what he had read out did not include him. He displayed an illegible scribble and refused to hand

[1] SP 1/124, fo. 193 (*LP* xii. II. 655). It was these words which Audley reckoned could not be proved treason because there was but the one witness (above, p. 309).
[2] SP 1/82, fo. 288 (*LP* vii. 330).

over the patent he had read aloud. Pecock offered to accept a letter from Cromwell as sufficient authority; 'howbeit, in vain was all our labour to him', and he left, breathing threats which left the convent very uneasy. But they never heard more of the matter, and their refusal to be deceived is as impressive as the imposition itself.[1]

The most extraordinary tale of an impostor occurred earlier still, on 21 September 1532, when one Harry Enesham, with an assistant, waylaid a priest, John Bentley, near Updotery in Somerset, explaining that he had orders from Cromwell to take Bentley before the King's Council.[2] After showing him briefly to a local justice (who insisted that the old priest's feet be unbound beneath his horse's belly) they took him fifteen miles to Enesham's house where they kept him locked up from Saturday to Monday morning. On Monday they started for London, Bentley now on one of Enesham's nags and once more tied up. When they reached Lamport, Enesham told his prisoner that since he had friends here he could borrow some money for the journey – 'ye cannot stick for £20 in this town; and if ye do go up without money, ye are but cast away, for there ye shall surely lie in irons'. The reason for this solicitude became plain later. Bentley in fact could find no one to lend him money, but he did manage to make contact with his servant who, it was agreed, should fetch the priest's own mare from Enesham's house. Next morning, as they started off again, Enesham made to tie Bentley up, but the 'honest men' of Lamport interceded for him; however, Enesham would not give way until one of the bystanders offered to go surety for the priest. It was soon after this display of professional police zeal that Enesham uncovered his real purpose. As they were slowly riding on to Maiden Bradley, fourteen miles further off, he suddenly told Bentley that if he were 'content to fashion him like an honest man' he should go free. Bentley shrewdly asked how this could be, seeing he claimed to have a warrant for his arrest, but Enesham simply repeated his first remark. Aged, weary and frightened as he was, the priest asked what was meant by fashion, but when this turned out to involve the surrender of a pension worth £8 by the year he firmly said no. So Enesham asked for ' £20, £10, and so lower and lower', without moving his victim. They rode on.

That night at Maiden Bradley, across the shire border into Wiltshire,

---

[1] SP 1/132, fos. 63–4 (*LP* vii. 982). For Pecock cf. above, pp. 14–15.

[2] E 36/120, fo. 121 (*LP* vi. 87).

Enesham tried again: 'if he did not know how sore that Mr Cromwell was against priests and how grievously he did handle them, he would liefer spend all the goods he hath than to come before him; for he is a man without conscience against priests'. Still Bentley held out, but in the morning Enesham at last found a successful argument. 'I am very sorry for you,' he told his captive, 'for now the King's grace is gone over [to France – which was true], and Mr Cromwell was gone before to provide for him, so that now there is no remedy but I must needs put you in prison till he cometh home again.' At this Bentley, afraid of prison and afraid of what he had been told of Cromwell, gave way and offered 40s. Enesham would seem to have been but an inefficient crook, after all. He accepted the offer and carried the old man back to his own house. But when there he asked for his money, Bentley raised the question of his mare, left behind at Enesham's house and not yet returned, and oddly enough valued at precisely £2. They agreed that the priest's servant should go with Enesham and exchange the mare for the cash. However, when they got to Enesham's place he pretended that he could not find the animal and forced the servant by threats to hand over the money. So Bentley was done out of his mare: which is the only reason that we know of these events at all. For when he got a contemptuous message from Harry Enesham – 'that so he might use himself that he should have her again, and so he might use himself that he should never have her' – he promptly went off to Sir Nicholas Wadham and laid an information for the recovery of his property. He told his tale only to explain how he came to have lost his mare, not to complain of the kidnapping, and there is no sign that action was taken against the impostor. His enterprise suggests that Cromwell's name may have caused some terror as early as this, though in fact Bentley talked as though the first he heard about Cromwell's ill will against priests came from Enesham's broad hints. Certainly Bentley's subsequent action shows no fear of Cromwell's government; but then it was early days, before the Treason Act, before the Succession Act, even before the fate of the Nun of Kent.

Whether all this amounts to evidence of a 'reign of terror' may have to remain debatable. Some men clearly dreaded the lord privy seal and saw themselves pursued by his ever watchful – and imagined – hordes. Others as clearly ignored and frustrated him. If there was terror it existed in the mind only, and the evidence for this is thin and circumstantial.

Cromwell's terror did not mean the indiscriminate extermination of those against whom accusations were brought; it did not mean the organised supervision of people's thoughts, words and deeds; it did not mean the use of *agents provocateurs* or necessarily even that all England became a happy hunting ground for informers. His control involved the enforcement of the law as it stood, by the age's lawful methods of trial and investigation; such success as it obtained it owed not to the creation of new machinery or the introduction of new principles, but to the energy with which the normal interaction of local event and central authority was exploited, and to the vigorous encouragement, by exhortation as much as by threats, of the loyal cooperation of all sorts of Englishmen on which Tudor government depended at all times. If this necessarily resulted in encouragement for private malice and grudges, it is also plain that great care was taken to establish the truth before the power of the law was brought into action. In short, Cromwell's methods of policing the state against opponents and subverters amounted to an example of normal Tudor methods of government at work in a situation so special that they appeared more stark and more formidable, a heightening but not a replacement of the ordinary.

Few stories so well illustrate the realities involved in enforcing the law as that of the fortunes of Edward Large, parson of Hampton Episcopi in Warwickshire and a person of no importance. For some reason, the parson had made enemies in Stratford who were organised against him by one William Clapton, gent. On the other hand, he had the friendship of a Warwickshire J.P., William Lucy, who on the whole commanded the support of two of his colleagues, John Greville and John Coombs. Large was one of the new learning ('as they commonly', commented Lucy, 'call all them that preach the pure and sincere Word of God, and also all them that favour them that preach the same'), a fact which no doubt accounted for some at least of the local hostility, as it certainly explained Latimer's prejudice in favour of the priest.[1] In fact, when Large first got into trouble, Lucy, on his behalf, wrote anxiously and angrily to the bishop of Worcester.[2] This was on 21 July 1537. Soon after he wrote on the same business to Cromwell – a twenty-three page letter in his own hand in which he carefully unravelled the whole story as he saw it.[3]

[1] *Latimer's Works*, ii. 381–3, 399. [2] SP 1/123, fos. 42–5 (*LP* xii. II. 302).
[3] SP 1/123, fos. 46–57 (*LP* xii. II. 303).

On 10 April 1537 Large was indicted of heresy at Warwick Assizes. The charge was that in a sermon preached on Easter Monday (April 2nd) he had said, 'All who use our Lady's psalter shall be damned', and also 'that there was a bishop of Rome that kept a paramour which was called Imber, and she desired of the bishop that she might have every quarter in the year three fasting days, where the said bishop for her sake caused the fasting days to be had which now are called ember days'. Though it is hard to see that any of this was serious heresy, he was committed to ward until bailed upon Cromwell's intervention on his behalf. In fact, his friends had rallied round, so much so that at the Sessions of May 29th his case was put off till the next Assizes 'at which the judges would be there, and they to have the hearing of the matter'. Meanwhile his allies had secured from Cromwell a commission of investigation directed to Lucy, Greville and Coombs. The commissioners sat on July 2nd and examined the foreman of the indicting jury who at length admitted that the jury had had no evidence before them but had proceeded upon mere rumour. The rumour was brought home to one Richard Coton whom the commissioners then took to pieces, although Clapton, Coton's impressario, was present and tried to interfere. Coton asked for mercy, and Lucy promised to do for him 'as I would for mine own brother if he were in like case'. They persuaded him that he had done very ill to slander the priest and speak rudely to him in the pulpit after the sermon, and he showed himself very remorseful, also explaining that unless he could have a chance to practise his craft in custody his wife and family would perish. All this the commissioners conceded. A little later, however, they discovered that Clapton's party had that day composed a new written information against Large which added fresh charges but left out the joke about the ember days. This bill was signed by two men of Stratford who were next examined and proved to be very vague about the alleged occasion of Large's indiscreet remarks. Clapton, seeing his witnesses rattled, intervened to say that there were many others in Stratford who would support the charge; Lucy retorted that none of Hampton would. No, said Clapton, for they were too frightened of Lucy to do otherwise. Against this imputation Lucy defended himself at length to Cromwell.

The commissioners, still trying to get at the truth, now asked the two signatories of the bill to swear to it. They answered, revealingly, that 'they would be loath to be sworn upon a book, for as hitherto in all their life they had never sworn upon a book for no such matter'. They asked the commissioners to be good to them and got the very proper reply 'that they must be good unto themselves, for we sat there as the King's grace's commissioners and must certify again to his grace's Council all such things as should be there presented to us'. The discussion went on for a long time, but in the end the men of Stratford gave in and themselves asked for the bill to be torn up. But Lucy was not yet done with Coton and his patron Clapton. Though unwilling to be hard on the man, he did expect him to make public confession of his slander since he had spread his accusation far and wide. Clapton chose to treat this as an intolerable humiliation, said that he would rather Coton lay in gaol 'till his feet rotted' than that he should be put to such open shame (which, we may note, would reflect on his protector), and that if this was what Lucy intended 'it would not be best for the priest'. In Lucy's friends' presence he marvelled at Lucy's notion of fraternal behaviour and swore that if he, Clapton, were his brother, 'he would thrust his dagger in me'.

Next day there was a good deal of toing and froing, much talk and dining among all the parties, at Fulke Greville's house (brother to John), but what mattered was that Clapton put his threat into operation. This he did by mobilising Stratford opinion once more. It was now July 4th, market day there, and he used the occasion to collect signatures to yet another bill of information against Large which he meant to send to London. Among others, he sent for Richard Lightfoot, the baker of the town, to sign the bill: 'forasmuch as you are my tenant I trust you will do as your neighbours do.' Lightfoot, unable to read, asked to hear the bill read, and when that was done he said he could not sign it because he had never heard Large speak the words alleged. Clapton accused him of currying favour with John Coombs who had allegedly promised to make him master of the gild, but honest Lightfoot only replied, 'I will never belie no man falsely' and went off.[1] The new charges, to which some of Stratford later deposed,[2] were a good deal more serious than the first, for Clapton was a man of his word. Large was now alleged to have said two things, one pure heresy and the other probable treason: 'Christ did not die ne suffer death for them that be now alive but for them that died before his Incarnation', and 'Who put Christ to death

[1] All this Lightfoot confirmed in his own deposition: E 36/120, fo. 1 (LP xii. II. 215).
[2] E 36/120, fos. 165–6 (not in LP).

but the peers of the realm in those days that were high learned men both temporal and spiritual? And if Christ were now alive again, he should die a cruel death, as ye see how their heads goeth off nowadays.' The manner in which more serious 'sayings' were brought up when the first attack had failed throws much light not only on this particular situation but on the whole business of denunciations and informations.

Thoroughly alarmed, Lucy went into action in his turn, travelling to London to intercede with Cromwell. However, he first consulted Latimer, then in town, who uncharacteristically counselled caution: 'peradventure yet Mr Clapton would not be hasty in opening this matter as he pretended'. Lucy respectfully suggested that he would but agreed to do nothing further for the present if Latimer would remember that the matter had been fully put before him. On his return, he and his friends obeyed a ruling of Cromwell's and discharged Coton upon a private admission of his ill-doing, without any public humiliation. Then Lucy got Greville and Coombs to collect depositions from the parishioners of Hampton in Large's favour, which was done.[1] All seemed now at peace, but when, a few days later, the Assize opened, Lucy found Large's new indictment still before the jury; he also found that Clapton's Stratford party had been successful in influencing the judge, Sir Anthony Fitzherbert, a man of eminence but only a year off death and strongly inclined to the old ways.[2] Indeed, Lucy nearly got into very bad trouble when he tried to intercept Fitzherbert on his way to court in Warwick Hall with a plea for Large, waving the parish's attestation in the judge's face; he was told that if he meddled any further his lordship would himself put him up as an accessory. The words were heard by Lucy's enemies, standing by, which made them no sweeter. Greville, who was included in the Assize commission, once more tried to interest Fitzherbert in the bill, but the judge rounded on

[1] E 36/120, fos. 2–3 (LP xii. II. 496), on 10 August 1537. Twenty-three deponents exonerated their priest, saying that 'God's Word and his word were all one'.

[2] See above, p. 32. Fitzherbert in fact endeavoured to conduct a one-man campaign against suspected radicals. In the spring of 1536 he committed an allegedly heretical husbandman of Staffordshire to the chancellor of Coventry and Lichfield (SP 1/128, fos. 197–8 [LP xiii. I. 188]), while in March 1538 he insisted on holding in prison a man against whom an indictment for treason had been found at Nottingham but who had been 'not undeserved' reprieved at the oyer and terminer over which the judge had presided. In this latter case, however, the accused may have benefited from improper favour, and the sheriff asked Cromwell to allow the trial to proceed. This was done, and the man was acquitted (SP 1/130, fos. 131, 154 [LP xiii. I. 595, 788]; KB 9/542/3).

him too, asking 'if he would give evidence there against the King, and that treason was laid to the priest's charge'. It was clear who had been at him: he had been thoroughly primed against the Lucy faction. Large was then promptly indicted of both heresy and treason, though the indictment called him Edmund instead of Edward, a slip which (if it had become necessary) could easily have saved him.

That is where the matter stood when Lucy wrote his long account to Cromwell. He explained at some length about the sermon on Easter Monday and produced impeccable witnesses to testify that it had been entirely proper and had not included any of the statements alleged. He himself, being sick, had for once not attended, but his wife had been there, two of her brothers, Mr Coombs, and many others. Lucy himself could testify that such sayings were altogether out of character for Large; as to the heretical denial of Christ's sacrifice for those born after the Incarnation, he had often heard him preach the exact opposite. It must be said that the defence carries full conviction. Lucy could even adduce a servant of Clapton's who had recently admitted that 'if nothing had been done to Coton, all this business had not been'. Cromwell seems to have read Lucy's twenty-three pages and he certainly consulted Latimer; he judged the matter in precisely the way one might expect from a metropolitan statesman looking upon these rural antics when he told Latimer that he reckoned 'malice to be in the one part and simplicity in the other'.[1] There is no reason to dissent from his verdict. But it is worth remembering, in all this welter of pettifogging persecution, that a man stood in real danger of burning or quartering.

Cromwell in some manner rescued Large; the Assize trial came to nothing. However, he thought it necessary to put a stop to the sort of unrest that had been going on around Hampton and Stratford and therefore ordered Large to preach an exculpatory sermon, a copy of which was deposited among the minister's papers.[2] The preacher demonstrated an unexpected touch of sly humour: obeying the lord privy seal's command to explain to the parish that he had never been a traitor or heretic, he chose to preach on the text 'Render unto Caesar'. He specifically addressed himself to the two charges of the second indictment and ignored the first, denying that he had ever said anything about Christ's sacrifice benefiting only those who had died before it,

[1] *Latimer's Works*, ii. 384.
[2] SP 1/141, fos. 195–207 (*LP* xiii. II. 1279: misdated).

and repeating that when he had alluded to Christ's probable fate if he were to return now he had said nothing about peers of the realm or sympathy for rebels. He quoted his original words: 'Think you not, if Christ had been alive within these four years, that he should not have been put to death as cruelly as he was? Yes, I do not doubt, for it is not unknown how Christ's Word hath been burned, and surely Christ and his Word is all one.' It is no wonder that he made enemies among his conservative hearers. This gospelling strain was further backed up with some near-Lutheran remarks on faith and works, though he took pains to add at some length that works were to be performed because commanded by God and beneficial to society. As for rebellion, he recalled remarks he had made during the rising, namely that if his father were alive and had joined the rebels he 'would as soon in my prince's quarrel kill him'. Large showed neither contrition nor abatement of his position; the main burden of his sermon was to castigate the audience for not listening carefully enough and then spreading false stories, and he ended by once more exhorting them to pay better attention another time.

Thus Large went unscathed and soon after secured promotion to the rectory of Cherington, but he was a man born to enemies and trouble. Two years later he was once more indicted, of heresy and felony, for saying on 19 October 1539 that no one in his parish or elsewhere should 'set tapers there before the rood, for it is but cost to the parish there and naught else'.[1] He clearly had plenty of foes still: not only was this harmless statement well in accord with the tenor of Cromwell's 1538 Injunctions, but it is a marvel that any jury could be found to call this *vera billa*. This time he was quicker in his rescue operations: within three weeks of being found, the indictment was called up into King's Bench, and that was the end of it.

However, the story of Edward Large demonstrates in some detail the sort of problems that arose in the course of an investigation, the part played by personal enmity, the importance of local cross-currents – all the weaknesses of a police system dependent on the voluntary and unrewarded activity of the locality. One might have thought that these deficiencies would promote thoughts of drastic reform, but in an age filled with programmes and schemes devices for tightening the police organisation and control over traitors are conspicuously non-existent.

[1] KB 9/545/75.

True, early in 1534, early in his career as the King's chief commissioner of police, Cromwell made some notes which showed that he was not without ideas on the subject.[1] He contemplated swearing 'the most assured and substantial' gentlemen in all shires of the King's Council; they and the substantial men of all the towns were to make systematic search for any that preached, taught or spoke in favour of the pope's authority, and to arrest any that they found. But whereas other notes in the same paper, forecasting propaganda devices, were soon carried into action, nothing came of this plan to systematise the normal activities of the local authorities. Nor were two larger proposals touching law-enforcement, which in this decade emerged from the Cromwell circle, any more concerned with the problem of security against traitors. The well-known scheme for a Court of Conservators of the Commonweal, to sit at Westminster and command the services of a national police force, confined itself entirely to the enforcement of statutes penal and popular, that is acts for the control of manners and the economy which tried to attract prosecutions by offering rewards to informers. These did not include the treason acts.[2] Points of slightly more relevance are included in another draft proposal, probably of 1539 and more probably still in the hand of Ralph Sadler, one of Cromwell's two chief secretaries.[3] This is in the main concerned with reforming the 'manrede' or military organisation of the realm; it is a proposal for a militia and for enforcing the laws governing the military training of the nation. It fits other schemes of the times because it concentrates on providing machinery – a chain of command from chief commissioners through 'head-men' to all the existing local officers of humble station, both royal and private – and it faintly echoes Cromwell's notes of 1534 by providing that all substantial gentlemen should be sworn to the King's service, 'to serve his grace and none other person at all times when it shall please his grace to command'. But its possible concern with ordinary internal security is minimal. The head-men were to be sworn to resist and reveal anything they might hear 'prejudicial or contrary to the King's honour or surety of his royal person... by unsitting words or otherwise', and each

---

[1] BM, Tit. B. i, fo. 466 (*LP* vii. 420).

[2] T. F. T. Plucknett, 'Some Proposed Legislation of Henry VIII,' *TRHS* (1936), 119 ff.; the draft is printed ibid. 135 ff. For the view that it was properly speaking not a government proposal see Elton in *Bull. Inst. Hist. Research*, xxv (1952), 123 f.; and for statutes penal see e.g. Elton, *Star Chamber Stories*, 78 ff.

[3] SP 1/144, fos. 205–14 (*LP* xiv. I. 643).

commissioner was to bind himself to 'do as much as in him is for the preservation and surety of the King's highness and his succession' as well as 'for the good advancement of justice and maintenance of the common weal of the realm'. Pious phrases of this sort would hardly have made this 'manrede' into an effective police organisation for the enforcement of the treason laws, even if the proposal had ever got beyond the drafting stage.

It must therefore be concluded that Thomas Cromwell's administration, faced with the big task of steering the realm through a revolution which called forth much hostility and a fair amount of resistance, rested content with the existing and traditional police machinery of the realm, a phrase which somewhat overstates the means at its disposal. The Crown relied on the activities of private individuals both for the initial discovery of offences, the passing of information to the centre, and executive action against suspects and offenders. No attempt was made to organise these methods, themselves a direct reflection of the social hierarchy of the day, into anything resembling a network of spies; no rewards or inducements were offered; no plans existed for reforming or replacing these essentially informal arrangements. Cromwell may well have thought that he learned as much in this way and kept as close a watch on the realm as he might have done with the aid of a central organisation which in any case would have been well beyond the resources of Henry's government. Of necessity, however, he was thus compelled not only to use the locality but, up to a point, to defer to the locality; however much he wrestled with the possibility of concealment or malice, he depended in the last resort on the willingness, prejudices and private ends of men over whom he had no hold except what general adjurations and general warnings could add to general loyalty and the desire to stand well with the fountain of patronage. All his actions plainly demonstrate his recognition that everything turned on the gentry. He could not hope to mobilise, influence or control by direct action the minds and doings of men lower down the scale; but he could work away at their betters. He demanded reports and he sent instructions. Cromwell's ultimate weapon in the fight against disaffection was his correspondence.

9

VICTIMS AND VICTORS

I

THE LAW, especially that of treason, was severe, reached far, and could punish even casual utterances with savagery. Its administration, though governed by comprehensive rules which imposed limits on the exercise of mere power, was intensive and precise. Police activity, in discovering and communicating suspects, was energetic and continuous. All this, one would suppose, should lend support to the notion that the 1530's produced a large tally of victims, of men and women almost innocently caught in the toils of the law and brought to the frightful end which execution for treason meant in the sixteenth century. That familiar assumption constituted the starting point of this enquiry. Yet, as has been seen throughout, the story is a good deal more complex and less easily judged in terms of black and white. We have had occasion to note quite a few instances in which the investigators ignored the denunciations brought to them, as well as several acquittals by juries and similar happy outcomes to prosecutions. Yet isolated cases may not prove anything. The difficulties of the evidence raise obvious problems, and historians have therefore commonly taken it for granted that the famous cases – Fisher, More, Reynolds, Houghton, and so forth – were typical, and that the obscurer cases must have ended in the same way. Can one be more precise about the weight of the government's enforcement and its effect upon those who opposed the King's policy? One would like to have statistics, and up to a point they can be got.

In practice, the attempt to supply precision must confine itself to such facts and figures as can be discovered about people accused of treasonable behaviour. Sedition or disaffection short of treason, and the sort of resistance manifested in failure to erase the pope's name from books, certainly occurred and appear often enough in the record, but unfortunately our knowledge is bound to remain entirely unsystematic. Sometimes local magistrates reported cases of this kind and evidence survives in Cromwell's correspondence, but pressure to do so was much less than in cases of suspected treason, nor was the aid of the government and its major courts required for dealing with these lesser offenders. They usually received attention on the spot, and justice seems commonly to have been summary, at the pleasure of the magistrate. In the early days there was some uncertainty. Thus one Roger Dycker allegedly expressed, in June 1532, his conviction that the King would never desert 'so noble a lady so high born and so gracious' as Queen Catherine for Sir Thomas Boleyn's daughter, implying at the same time that he knew all about Mistress Anne; he found himself a prisoner in the Marshalsea, claiming to have been the victim of other people's malice.[1] He was already sixty-nine years of age, 'sore brushed in the King's wars': most likely he was sent home, especially as his words would never have been treason by any statute, though he had been less than polite.

By the end of 1533 Cromwell had evidently decided that this sort of misbehaviour was best handled at home, and a Cornwall justice of the peace was using the pillory and stocks 'in market places and days' to punish people, 'according to the contents of your former letters to me directed'.[2] He gave neither names nor numbers, and other men no doubt did not even report the doing of it. What was reported shows that the same method lasted through the 1530's. 'A light person...in Northampton' had his ears nailed to the pillory in August 1537.[3] Robert Dalyvell, of Royston (Herts.), lost his there in 1538 for saying that 'a horse of ten shillings shall bear all the lords within England within three years', though he had first been suspected of larger matters and had been interrogated by Cromwell himself who remitted him to the locality for his lesser punishment.[4] Thomas Croft, a Kentishman, on the other hand, could thank Cromwell for the preservation of his ears which a local magistrate had wanted to cut off before Cromwell wrote to say that an hour in the pillory would be enough.[5] These offences were not felonious, so that the authorities acted without the processes of the

[1] SP 1/68, fo. 123 (LP v. 628). [2] SP 1/80, fo. 193 (LP vii. 1503).
[3] SP 1/124, fo. 9v (LP xii. II. 489).
[4] SP 1/121, fos. 92–3; BM, Calig. B. i, fos. 130–1; SP 1/140, fo. 125 (LP xii. II. 74 [2, 3]; xiii. II. 1090). Poor Dalyvell (cf. above, pp. 58–9) had been to Scotland and on his return claimed to have had a vision according to which he was to warn Henry against the Scots. This got him into hot water. Evidently he was thought to be a spy, and Cromwell went after him, drawing up the interrogatory with his own hand and having him racked in the Tower for better information. In the end, Dalyvell was sent home, and although he was punished for his seditious words he could in manner think himself lucky. [5] SP 1/157, fo. 23 (LP xv. 318).

criminal law; only in Wales and its marches, under the rule of Rowland Lee, does it seem to have been thought necessary to use the machinery of indictment and trial. In February 1538, when John Payne was executed for high treason at Gloucester, two companions, found guilty of seditious words only, escaped with the pillory and nailed ears.[1] A curious problem arose at Pembroke in December 1537 when a Portuguese sea-captain was convicted by a jury of seditious words against King Henry; but Lee, doubtful about a foreign subject's position, prevented judgment from being given until he knew the King's pleasure, of which we unfortunately remain ignorant.[2]

In short, sedition short of treason occurred, was punished, and often unquestionably failed to get into the record. But this matters the less from the point of view of our question because its punishment was rarely in the hands of the King's government, and because the question of a reign of terror must first and foremost depend on what happened in capital cases. Even here, since there are no systematic police records and since – thanks to the decentralised administration of the criminal law – the rolls of the central courts also provide no complete list of cases, we cannot suppose that any list we may compile can be complete.[3] But three things help. In the first place, traitors were dealt with by the formal processes of the law, by judge and jury, with the exception of people convicted by Act of Attainder whose fate then stands on the statute book. Secondly, treason could not be tried in any of the local courts or even at Quarter Sessions, so that the enormous deficiencies of those records and the difficulty of surveying all there is do not affect the tally.[4] And lastly, Cromwell's insistence from first to last that all suspicion of treason, however trivial, be reported to him makes his extant correspondence an exceptionally satisfactory register of persons denounced, though not necessarily of persons convicted. We have very few records of the proceedings of those commissions of oyer and terminer which dealt with most treasons, and the records of the King's

---

[1] SP 1/129, fo. 161 (*LP* xiii. I. 371).   [2] SP 1/127, fo. 34 (*LP* xii. II. 1183).

[3] The massive collection of writs and process returned into King's Bench remains at present inaccessible at the PRO. It is possible that it might add some information.

[4] I have made no systematic search through municipal archives, and virtually no Sessions material exists for this period. But what is in print confirms that the rule against trying treason in such courts was observed, and this reliable indication is further confirmed by the work done in many local archives by Dr D. J. Guth. Looking for enforcement of the King's laws there he has found many cases but none of treason.

Bench, for technical reasons already stated, are more likely to contain acquittals and quashings than convictions. However, people also quite often wrote to Cromwell to report the outcome of a trial. Additional evidence has been gleaned from all available casual materials, especially from Wriothesley's *Chronicle* which faithfully records all executions in London and some elsewhere. Gathering all this information together, I have endeavoured to produce a catalogue of people denounced or investigated for treason, or in any way brought within the dangers of the treason laws, in the years 1532–1540, and I have tried to discover what I could about the end of each man's troubles. I do not, of course, claim that the list is perfect even within the limitations already explained. There is, for instance, the problem of identifying individuals which sometimes ties Gordian knots to be resolved only in the traditional but dubious manner. Some reports touch men whose names are not given and who might be identical with the subjects of other reports, treated in ignorance as separate. The complexities are considerable, and I cannot help thinking that I must on occasion have been guilty of plain error, too. But not, I believe, to an extent which calls conclusions in doubt.

The important point is that the problem of what happened to people yields much more often to investigation than Merriman, for instance, supposed.[1] In many cases it can certainly be solved: when we find evidence of execution or evidence of unquestionable survival at liberty some time after the first investigation, we know where we are. What, however, are we to do with people of whom we know that they were convicted and sentenced without having explicit record of their deaths? Like everybody else, I used to suppose that when the formal record of a trial ended in condemnation, with the ominous letters 'T & S' (drawn and hanged) in the lower margin, the man was executed – until I found such a complete record in the King's Bench with the convicted man's pardon attached.[2] 'T & S', it seems, hides the gerund and not the past participle: 'to be drawn and hanged': and more could happen thereafter. Nevertheless, we should regard this sort of event as so exceptional that recorded convictions can be treated as equal to executions unless there is positive evidence to the contrary. As for people whose cases

[1] Above, p. 3.
[2] KB 29/172, Rex, rot. 6d, Trinity term 1541. The case of Richard Sharpe, for which see above, p. 136.

were dismissed by the investigation (as a rule because there was no case), the fact can very often be established, and at other times it can, for a variety of reasons, be presumed with almost perfect certainty. Thus, for instance, I have found no single person condemned to death whose first denunciation included the local magistrate's comment that in his opinion there was nothing, or only malice, in the story. Certainly, a number of cases call for the use of one's personal judgment, and I can only say that I have tried to be both careful and cautious.

TABLE A. *Cases of treason, 1532–1540*

	1		2	3	4	5	6	7	8	9	10	11	12
	Words	(Before the act)	Writing	Conspiracy	March treason	Unknown treason	Attainder	Total 1–6	Boleyns	Poles, etc.	Lincs.	Pilgrimage of Grace	Total 7–11
Executed	52		1	38	0	10	9	110	6	14	46	132	308
Probably executed	11		0	1	0	5	0	17	0	4	1	0	21
Acquitted	11		0	2	2	1	1	17	0	0	1	14	32
Probably acquitted	3		0	0	0	2	0	5	0	0	0	0	5
Quashed	7	(1)	0	0	0	0	0	7	0	0	0	0	7
Probably quashed	6		0	0	0	0	0	6	0	0	0	0	6
Pardoned	9	(3)	1	23	0	5	0	38	0	2	55	1	96
Probably pardoned	3		0	0	0	0	0	3	0	0	9	0	12
Not indicted	16		0	9	0	4	0	29	0	0	0	8	37
Reprieved	9		0	1	0	0	0	10	0	1	0	3	14
Probably reprieved	0		0	0	0	1	0	1	0	1	0	0	2
Fled	6		0	2	0	3	0	11	0	4	8	6	29
Died in prison	19		0	2	0	0	0	12	0	0	0	3	15
Probably died	0		0	1	0	0	0	1	0	0	0	0	1
Dropped	89	(22)	2	9	0	13	0	113	0	1	0	0	114
Probably dropped	95	(18)	5	7	0	2	0	109	0	0	0	0	109
Unknown	68	(5)	1	2	0	2	0	73	0	1	0	0	74
Total	394	(47)	10	98	2	48	10	562	6	28	120	167	883

The results of all these compilations are presented in Table A. I have there divided cases into those certainly, and those probably, executed or acquitted or dismissed, and so on, and I must stress that I have included no case in a 'probably' category unless the probability is overwhelming. Thus for practical purposes and reasonable analysis, the certain and probable figures can safely be counted together. Also I have thought it right to weight the calculations as far as possible against the government, partly because deficiencies in the evidence could have worked the other way, and partly because any possibility of correcting received views depends on one's not overstating the revisionary argument. I have therefore included in the count a number of people not actually executed by Cromwell's regime, that is to say such persons as were sentenced to death in his time but not put to death until after his fall (for instance, the countess of Salisbury, Giles Heron, the three Catholic victims of Cromwell's fall – Thomas Abell, Edward Powell, Richard Featherstone). It could be held that their temporary survival argues something favourable for his administration; here they are added to the people destroyed by it. Because it concludes the story as here considered, Thomas Cromwell's own death also appears in the statistics, as though he had caused it himself (as in a way he had).

Figures of the kind put forward here must always retain an element of the problematical. It is not always easy to establish whether a report (even a report of executions) touches treason or some non-political felony, there are always pitfalls in the identification of survivors, our evidence of pardons and reprieves is incomplete. I do not doubt that another scholar working over this same ground again might well alter this or that total. I myself have been quite unable to make the number of victims in the northern risings come up to the 216 given by the Misses Dodds, even though I have used the same materials.[1] All I can say is that I have been as careful as I could be, have always tried to lean to the worse outcome rather than the better, and believe such errors or variations as might be discovered to be no more than marginal. They do not affect the positive conclusions to be derived from the statistics.

2

In the years 1532–1540, 883 people in England, Wales and Calais came within the compass of the treason law, and 308 of them, or some 38%, suffered death in consequence. This is a figure to make one pause, for it

---

[1] Dodds, 226. I suspect that they included a good many cases after the rebellion which were loosely linked to it; these, in order to test the Cromwell regime as severely as possible, I have included in column 1. Columns 10 and 11 include only people punished for immediate participation in the rebellions. It is also possible that the Dodds figures reckon as dead the thirty-six Lincolnshire rebels who in my opinion were almost certainly pardoned, but even by adding those I can arrive at only 214 altogether. And I have no doubt myself that it would be wrong to add them.

gives support to those who would condemn the Cromwell regime in the tradition-hallowed manner: but it is also unreal. That 883 conceals a variety of things. 287 of them were people involved in open and manifest rebellion, having raised war against the King, and whatever one may think of arrests and executions for such a cause it is certain that at that time (and others) no regime in Europe would or could escape the need for vengeful retribution against full-scale rebels. As it was, the Lincolnshire rising and the Pilgrimage of Grace – though fifty-six people were pardoned after conviction – cost the lives of 178 men and women.[1] Of this total, seventy-four were the victims of Norfolk's proceedings at Carlisle where, with banners displayed, he used martial law to destroy a belated and isolated uprising during the panic that endured beyond the suppression of the main rebellion. A further thirty-four people involved in treason, of whom twenty died, belong to another special category: the victims of high dynastic and court politics, caught in the destruction of the Boleyn, Pole and Courtenay interests. Those were savage enough events, in all conscience, but they have very little to do with the enforcement problems of the new order, religious disaffection proving at best a subsidiary cause of those victims' fate. What happened to them needs to be judged in the context of the struggles among noble factions and against rival claimants to the crown which had been a political commonplace since the reign of Henry VI. There were complications which made the Henrician phase of this endemic business exceptionally brutal – the King's matrimonial involvements as well as his ferocious personality, the treasonable intrigues with foreign powers which followed upon the repudiation of Catherine of

[1] These figures are worth setting against some others. We do not know exactly how many men took part in the risings, but the Lincs. rebels' numbers certainly ran into five figures and about 30,000 northerners assembled at Doncaster in the great pilgrims' camp (J. D. Mackie, *The Earlier Tudors* [1952], 388–9). The German peasants' war of 1525, in which much larger numbers were involved, cost the lives of tens of thousands. In Monmouth's rebellion (1685) in which perhaps 5000 people took part, some 150 were executed and four times as many transported into slavery (G. N. Clark, *The Later Stuarts* [1934], 114–15). The Jacobite rising of 1715 produced 26 executions, and the government has been called 'comparatively merciful' for dealing with only a twentieth part of the rebel forces – 700 men transported (B. Williams, *The Whig Supremacy* [1939], 156). In Henry VIII's northern rebellions only about one man in 2000 was even troubled and one in 3500 executed; the far less dangerous rising of 1569 brought death to three times more men than suffered in 1536–7, partly at least because Elizabeth's government freely used martial law where Henry's preferred the common law (J. B. Blackie, *The Reign of Elizabeth* [1936], 111–12).

Aragon and the pope – but essentially the downfall of the Poles is no different from that of Buckingham in 1521 or Warwick in 1499. Unlike, for instance, Sir Thomas More or the Carthusians, those executed in the collapse of the second marriage or the struggles of 1538 died through involvement in politics. In any judgment on the reign of Henry VIII they must not be forgotten, but in an investigation of enforcement policy they stand apart.

The figures, therefore, which concern us in assessing the nature of the regime which pushed through the Reformation and encountered opposition in doing so, are those in columns 1–7. Here we are dealing with 562 people, still a very considerable figure. Of them 22% were executed, 4·5% acquitted, 2·5% had their convictions quashed, in 5% of the cases the grand jury threw out the indictment, 7·5% received a pardon, 2·5% died in prison, and 2% fled before the law could get hold of them. But against the 110 who died we must set the 212 (40·5%) whose cases were dropped after investigation. And even these figures do not tell the heart of the story. The 98 people who engaged in treasonable conspiracies (and who produced a high rate of executions: 38%) – as for instance the Walsingham men or the Taunton rebels[1] – are really in a different category from the rest. Guilty of offences not newly added to the law in 1534, they would have been executed by any government because theirs was a fundamental form of treason at any time before the nineteenth century. On the other side stand the victims of condemnation by attainder only (one of whom is marked acquitted because he survived without formal pardon) who must be regarded as having been treated with exceptional harshness; they include the Nun of Kent and her accomplices as well as a few later instances in which the case seemed clear to the government but would not have stood up in court.[2] They also, of course, include Cromwell himself. The special savagery of this treatment was remarked at the time, and some people rejoiced to see Cromwell disposed of by a method he had allegedly invented, but in fact condemnation by attainder without judicial trial was, as we have seen, established by 1459.[3] This does not make the method any less

[1] Above, pp. 108 ff., 144 ff.
[2] For the Nun of Kent cf. above, p. 274; attainder only was used against Giles Heron because but one witness could be found (above, p. 308); no one has ever discovered why the countess of Salisbury was included without trial in an Act of Attainder mainly concerned with persons condemned by law, but probably Henry's dynastic fears must take the blame. [3] Above, p. 275, n. 3.

disagreeable, legal though it was. Even so it is worth remarking that the number of people so dealt with remained very small, and that of the victims of this form of conviction only the five involved in Elizabeth Barton's treason actually died while Cromwell had charge of affairs.

Thus the facts crucial for our purpose are recorded in column 1. This lists the people whose denunciations in the Cromwell correspondence have been largely responsible for giving the regime the general air of a reign of terror, the people charged with treason by words – those whose 'comparatively slight misdemeanours' were, according to Merriman, 'not seldom rewarded with death'. (Of course, 'comparatively slight' and 'not seldom' are exceptionally flexible terms.) Here also we find the well known martyrs for the papal supremacy. The total of that column comes to 394 persons, a large enough figure. Since in only sixty-eight cases (17%) we really neither know nor can safely conjecture the outcome, we do, I think, have a reasonably secure basis for assessing the realities. Sixty-three people died a traitor's death for words against the supremacy, which is quite enough for a period of five and a half years;[1] but accusation was obviously in no sense equal to condemnation. In sixteen cases, the Crown could not obtain an indictment from the grand jury, and in fourteen the trial jury refused to convict: in view of the broad scope of the law and the care taken to prepare charges, this does not look like tame submission to a tyrannical government. Twelve men obtained pardons and nine a reprieve after conviction, actions which represent Crown initiative and may show no more than that some people saved themselves by turning informer against their fellows. But at any rate, those twenty-one escaped death. The processes of the law saved seven more who could prove technical errors in their trials. Above all, as the figure of 184 shows, a person denounced stood approximately three times as good a chance of being dismissed without any consequences as of being brought to his death. Not far short of half the cases investigated – more than half if, say, half the

---

[1] The ten who died in prison include the nine London Carthusians whom, it is commonly supposed, the government preferred to starve to death rather than risk putting on public trial (e.g. Knowles, iii. 235–6). There are difficulties in the story which rests entirely on partisan accounts and does not fit with the usual policy of the government. Imprisonment was intended to reduce the victim to submission, not simply to kill him, and the chronology of the Carthusians' deaths suggests that disease rather than deliberate starvation may have been the final cause. The government behaved abominably, but in strict accuracy these men did not suffer on account of the treason laws.

'unknowns' are added to the same category – were dropped because a party's innocence became apparent.

Even this analysis does not fully describe the behaviour of the enforcing agencies in this time of revolution. In the first place, it is worth emphasising once again that the law was nearly always observed with precise rigour. Thus forty-seven people were denounced for the sort of offence which the act of 1534 made treason but before the act came into effect. Not one of these is known to have suffered. Nearly all of them, in fact, were never proceeded against at all, though one was indicted (an indictment that was quashed) and three played safe by getting pardons without having been tried. So far as dangerous speech went, the date of 1 February 1535 proved to be precisely the watershed which in law it should have been.

And secondly, the sixty-three victims need another closer look. Of them, twenty-three were executed by the Council of the North in the years 1537–1540, after the Pilgrimage of Grace was over. It is quite plain, nor in the least surprising, that the rebellion completely changed attitudes and reactions in the north. Before the Pilgrimage, eighteen men had been accused of treason in the northern Council's area of operation; of these, only one was executed while twelve went free.[1] After the middle of 1537, forty-one denunciations were received of which more than half ended in disaster. In the north the rebellion evidently produced a state of vigilance bordering on panic, the more so as the central government was inclined to blame the Council of the North for the whole outbreak. When it is remembered that of all subordinate authorities only that Council ever acted in treason cases without reference to Cromwell or the Privy Council, these twenty-three deaths stand forth as highly special and hardly to be placed to the government's general debit account. They do indeed rest upon the conscience of the revolution, but they exemplify the special fears and troubles of a regime lately so utterly disturbed that relatively slight threats of fresh trouble were bound to provoke severe retaliation. If Cromwell's behaviour as an enforcer of the treason laws is to be assessed as fairly as possible, those forty-one cases and twenty-three executions should also be subtracted. We then find that in his years of power he investigated approximately 350 cases of treason by words and that forty

[1] The march treasons of Lord Dacre and Sir Christopher Dacre, both acquitted by the jury, also came within the Council's purview but belong to a different category of treason.

people suffered death in consequence – about one case in nine. This is not to forget that 329 people died altogether in the troubles of that revolutionary era, but it is to put his police activities into a much more correct (and, let it be said, a much better) light than usually falls upon them.

Unless, therefore, a man committed his treason in open rebellion or unquestioned conspiracy to rebel, or got caught up in the high politics of a violent age, he was very far from being the automatic victim of every denunciation offered to a suspicious and tyrannical regime. Indeed, these figures almost suggest the opposite conclusion. If care was taken to distinguish truth from falsehood, and if of those brought to the government's attention in the settled part of the realm only a ninth died for treason, we should have to suppose that false denunciations exceeded legally sound ones by more than eight to one, a very unlikely supposition. Many of the cases dismissed have throughout this book provided convincing evidence of what people were saying, and it is really certain that by no means everybody who escaped had been innocent of what was alleged against him. What the facts and figures indicate is not so much an overwhelming flood of false accusations, but rather that some acquittals or quashings, and some decisions not to proceed, represent legal scruple in the face of not quite sufficient evidence or good luck on the part of people who in strict law could well have joined the ranks of the victims. As we shall see, the charges raised against Cromwell at his fall offer surprising support to this possibility.

The distribution of victims in time, place and personal status – those denounced as well as those executed – requires analysis. The process of enforcement quite evidently did not proceed at one steady level throughout those eight years.[1] Though denunciations came in small numbers from 1532 onwards, there were no executions at all before 1534, and in that year, when forty-four reports were received, only the five victims of the Nun of Kent case died. The passage of the Treason Act and the energetic police action initiated by the circular of 16 April 1535 produced an immediate increase which rose to a peak in 1537. However, the years 1536 and 1537 are slightly distorted by special cases. In the former year, the treasonable riot at Taunton added twenty-eight to those denounced and twelve to those put to death; in the latter the Norfolk conspiracies similarly added thirty-one and fifteen respectively. If these exceptional events are subtracted, the years still reach a high

---

[1] See Table B and Graph, which take account only of columns 1–6 in Table A.

TABLE B. *Delations and executions*

	Delations	Executions
1532	4	0
1533	14	0
1534	44	5
1535	79	15
1536	110	22
1537	128	34
1538	89	24
1539	33	13
1540 (to Aug.)	30	10

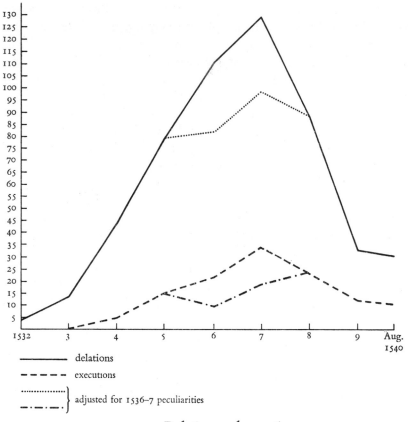

—————— delations

- - - - - executions

················· } adjusted for 1536-7 peculiarities
-·-·-·-·

GRAPH. *Delations and executions*

394

point of informations, but executions actually drop from 1535 to 1536. More important, they very definitely drop after 1537; in 1539 fewer people were denounced than in 1534, and there is a further slight drop in Cromwell's last months of power, even though the thirty denounced and ten executed include himself and the three Catholics put to death in July 1540. It thus looks either as though after 1538 the country refused to cooperate effectively with the policy of suppression, or as though that policy had done its work to the point where resistance, and even casual opposition, had been largely overcome. Since nothing else in the record – contemporary comment, the pressure of central action, a relaxation of vigilance – supports the first alternative, the second, in itself the more probable, should be preferred. Perhaps the most striking point shown in the graph is the changing gap between the lines for denunciations and executions. The very much steeper rise and fall of the first suggests that when policy was first made plain a good many people decided to use the opportunity to work off private grudges, but that this activity declined as it was realised that false accusations stood little chance of success.

These conclusions are also supported by what happened after Cromwell's fall. In the absence of his correspondence, our knowledge of enforcement matters is severely reduced and no very conclusive comparison between the 1530's and Henry VIII's last six and a half years is really possible. The survival of Privy Council registers offers some help, but they do not supply anything like the information on people under suspicion and being investigated that can be got from Cromwell's letters. Still, for what they are worth the figures obtainable indicate that the trend of 1538–1540 continued. Between Cromwell's death and Henry's, a total of ninety-six persons are known to have come within the operation of the treason law.[1] They include fourteen, all executed, involved in the rather mysterious Yorkshire conspiracy of 1541. Rather more of the total belong to the earlier years than the later. That this marked decline – an average of roughly fifteen cases a year compared with about seventy in Cromwell's day – probably represents not only our inferior information but also something like reality is suggested by the number of executions, information on which is likely to be better. These also dropped to fourteen, or twenty-eight if the Yorkshire rebels

[1] Excluding the people concerned in Catherine Howard's treason, the only group comparable to the totals accumulated in Table A, columns 8–11.

are included, for the whole period. Fourteen out of eighty-two (one in six) represents a higher proportion of successful prosecutions than we found for Cromwell's years, but this difference could well be accounted for by our ignorance of further discarded denunciations: these, in the second period, make up about 32% of the total as against close to 50% under Cromwell. Thus it does look as though the downward curve of 1538–1540 continued for the rest of the reign, while at the same time the post-Cromwellian regime seems to have been neither more nor less severe than Cromwell had been. Above all, there are here very strong indications that Cromwell's work as chief of police proved successful. From 1534 to 1537 he battled against mounting opposition and growing disaffection – and this quite apart from the great risings which, of course, testify to the same effect but form a special case. It was in the settled parts of the country that the difficulties were increasing. His energetic, but always discriminating and law-controlled, enforcement of the treason law combined with the defeat of the rebellions to bring about a quite rapid collapse in resistance – or a more willing acceptance of the new order – which lasted so long as the throne remained in the hands of Henry VIII. What happened in the reign of his infant son is another matter, but also a special case.

The geographical distribution of information was no more equal than that in time. It is true that not a single English county is missing from the tally. Even Cumberland produced four names, Westmorland and Northumberland two each, and Durham (where Tunstall may have been less energetic than his duty required) one. But the numbers per county vary a good deal and not exactly with the likely variation in population. Not only the north but also the north-west reported few traitors: three each in Cheshire and Lancashire. Devon and Cornwall raised fifteen between them, fewer than Essex with seventeen or Oxfordshire with eighteen. The Midlands did quite evenly: fourteen in Berkshire, fourteen in Northamptonshire, six in Leicestershire, seven in Warwickshire, sixteen in Nottinghamshire, though only three as one moves north into Derbyshire. Several counties outdid the rest. The fifty-six cases tentatively assignable to London include sixteen Carthusians properly belonging there as well as a good many people tried in the capital though guilty of treason elsewhere. On the other hand, the fifty-two alleged traitors from Yorkshire say something about the size of the county, the amount of disaffection, and the vigilance of the

Council of the North after 1537. Norfolk's fifty-three (compared with Suffolk's mere eight) are swollen by the 1537 conspiracies, but even without these the county forwarded twenty-two names, a high total. Similarly, Somerset contrasts with all its neighbours by contributing forty-one, but of these twenty-eight are the Taunton rebels. No such special circumstances, however, produced the forty-one men from Kent denounced for treason. The county, highly populous, had a long tradition of resistance to government; in the diocese of Canterbury, Cranmer bore down hard in the interests of reform, while in that of Rochester Fisher's fate impinged more directly than elsewhere; and the county was much visited by disturbing travellers both through Dover and through the ports of the estuary. Yet Surrey, as close to London as Essex and Kent, yielded only three, and similar unsystematic variations are found at every point. Only two people were denounced in Shropshire and two in Herefordshire, as against seventeen in Gloucestershire and twenty-one in Worcestershire: does this prove nothing, or are we to see special significance in Latimer's episcopal supervision of the latter two counties? Figures vary so much and are individually so small that no useful argument can be constructed from them. No doubt the fact that so little was heard from the remoter north may be ascribed to unwillingness to inform rather than humble obedience to the new order; beyond that, it looks as though there simply happened to be more offenders – or more personal enemies preferring false charges – in one place than in another. Except for the few conspiracies, disaffection was sporadically individual rather than defined territorially.

What one really wants to know is whether our knowledge, which is the government's knowledge, was anything like complete. Was there a good deal of loose and treasonable talk that never got reported at all? Naturally, since the government's knowledge depended not only on the willingness of gentry and aristocracy to report what they heard – a willingness which the evidence suggests was obtained – but also on the readiness of neighbours, friends, enemies and acquaintances to denounce the supposed traitors, we may take it for granted that not everything reached Cromwell's ears. For the many who spoke unwisely, in rage or in their cups, and were brought to the attention of the authorities, there must at least have been some who got away with like sayings because they had chosen their company better. Yet three points already established strongly indicate that the stream of information ran powerfully rather than sluggishly, and that we have no very good reason for supposing that disaffection and resistance were markedly more wide-spread than the government knew. We have noted the evident appre-hension aroused around the country by the often proclaimed dangers of what was summed up as misprision – failure to report. We have noted the very large number of cases investigated and dropped: much more than was real got reported. And we have noted that in spite of con-tinued pressure from the centre denunciations declined after 1537. For all these reasons it is my guess – and more one cannot offer – that the government got to hear of an exceptionally high proportion of the dangerous talk and behaviour that were to be found in the country, at least everywhere except in the north-west and the real north. All the signs are that the realm was well policed.

The people denounced came in all types, too; though one might have supposed that the clergy would overwhelmingly dominate the ranks of alleged traitors, this was not in fact so. Of the 562 persons dealt with in the ordinary way of enforcement (leaving out politics and major rebellion) 254 were laymen (including 16 women, of whom 5 died) and 308 clergy. The former divide into 25 gentlemen and 229 com-moners; the latter into 187 secular priests and 121 regular – monks and friars. Since the total of the clergy was probably no more than 5% of the whole adult population,[1] they obviously supplied a dispropor-tionately high percentage of the people in trouble, but in absolute figures the laity preserved a balance. Such a disproportion was indeed likely since government policy was bound to find most opposition among those it attacked, and it was the clergy who were being attacked. Nevertheless, the figures suggest a not inconsiderable support for clerical grievances among the laity. On the other hand, figures for executions surprisingly show a likelihood that a priest might form a readier target for mere malice than a layman. One would hardly expect the clergy to attract more pity and mercy from Cromwell and his men, yet the executed percentage of people denounced does not suggest the special animus against priests which he is supposed to have had. In this respect the worst sufferers were the gentry, with 40% of those reported put to death, but since in this case 40% means only 10 people, and since

[1] On the assumption of a population of rather less than 2½ millions and something over 50,000 beneficed, unbeneficed and enclosed clergy. These are at best highly approxi-mate figures.

obviously the upper classes were less liable to casual denunciation, this signifies little. Of the 229 commoners, 26% died, a figure once again affected by the events at Taunton and in Norfolk without which we arrive at 20% of about 170. Even this is still markedly higher than the rate of death among secular priests – all those parsons who cut loose in pulpit and alehouse – of whom only 24 (13%) suffered. But it is topped by the most vulnerable sector of all, the members of the orders, who produced 32 deaths (27%). This proportion testifies in particular to the heroic stand of a few houses and some exceptional men, but it also reflects the fact of the Dissolution which encountered some of the most determined resistance. Possibly it also indicates at least some exasperation, perhaps some positive hatred, directed against the form of life which the reformed order of society could least tolerate, though it should be noted that even amongst monks and friars seven supposed traitors went free for every three that died. It needs to be remembered that those regulars who suffered death for sticking to their convictions had in fact become guilty in law: in a very real sense, those who would call them martyrs justify their executions.

In sum then, the available figures of investigations and executions for treason show that the campaign of enforcement succeeded in getting a remarkable amount of information and went a long way towards exacting the obedience so often enjoined. In so far as there was a police system it worked very well, for sixteenth-century conditions. The application of penalties, moreover, remained well within the confines of the law. A few exceptional cases apart where politics or personal feelings played a major role, there was neither ruthless persecution nor any savage lashing out at alleged opponents. The instruments of enforcement were used rigorously and stringently: no one would attempt to suggest that this government was of a gentle, merciful or tolerant disposition. But it worked to the facts which it made every effort to establish; it did not choose the easy solution of disposing of all, or even most, of the people denounced. Its ingrained legalism – a rigid regard for the forms of trial and conviction at common law – in itself prevented any such policy, but the evidence of investigations and of discrimination demonstrates that there was never any intention to do more than punish real guilt as defined by law. Treason was abhorred and to be rooted out, but treason also had to be properly proved in every case. There was a real revolution, but a revolution under the law, and while the first fact produced a severe law and energetic enforcement, the second ensured that there should be neither holocaust nor reign of terror.

3

Such a verdict will not readily meet universal acceptance, however precise one attempts to be in analysing all the evidence. In particular it will be resisted by those who are less concerned with the fate of many small and unimportant people than with the destruction by Henry and Cromwell of a few outstanding men. In those outstanding cases, policy, law and politics intermingled beyond the ordinary, but while one might understand the government's occasional dilemma it remains possible to wonder whether it did not allow the last of those three at times to over-shadow the rest to a point where its action became entirely improper and wrong. How badly, in fact, did the government behave in those notorious cases which have ever since blighted the reputation of King and minister alike? By way of a test, I propose to reconsider the most famous story of all, the tribulations and death of Sir Thomas More. It is the severest test to which the government can be submitted, for of all the major victims of those years More was the only one who in law appeared to have avoided committing any offence at all and who seemed totally apart from the political involvements which struck down some other men. Yet he, too, ended on the scaffold. Was he, then, pure victim – innocent in every sense of the word and wantonly destroyed? Is it true that he was hounded to death by a wicked King and his slavish tools, all determined to have his head and from first to last willing to rig law and procedure against him? The existing accounts of More's life from the time of his arrest onwards all in effect assume this; they argue not only his total innocence of the charge preferred but also that he had so fully withdrawn from the world that the persecution to which he was subjected was peculiarly superfluous. No one, today, can do anything but deplore his end and wish that things had turned out differently; no one will deny the horror of doing More to death or the futile folly of it. But what actually happened? Despite the many accounts of these events several points still remain unclear, and the behaviour of various actors in the story needs reconsidering.[1]

[1] The standard views are well represented by the two most popular biographies of More, by R. W. Chambers (1935) and E. E. Reynolds (1953). Far and away the best treat-

After his resignation in May 1532, Sir Thomas More, who until then had played his part in resisting the development of the King's anti-papal and anticlerical policy,[1] withdrew entirely from public life. However, the presence in the realm of so eminent a critic, however silent, was a serious embarrassment to the government who could hardly avoid remembering him when the occasion arose. After all, the rest of the world, especially abroad, always did. His first serious trouble occurred in connection with the Nun of Kent. The King wanted to include him in the Act of Attainder as a misprisioner of the Nun's treason, as Bishop Fisher was included; but representations from the Council persuaded him to change his mind. Yet, as More knew, he was by this time firmly set against his ex-chancellor, and the oath of succession gave him his chance. More was the only layman summoned to take the oath at Lambeth Palace on 13 May 1535, and for his refusal he was sent to the Tower on the 17th. The four days' delay, spent in the abbot of Westminster's custody, was apparently caused by uncertainty. Under the act, refusal to take the oath was misprision of treason, punishable by perpetual imprisonment and loss of all property, but, of course, the application of these penalties depended on a conviction in court. More was not tried for this offence, and since he had not been attainted with the Nun he stood in a different case from Fisher who was already in the Tower as a man condemned for misprision of treason. He was being held rather than punished. The same treatment was applied to Nicholas Wilson who also refused the oath and also went to the Tower where persuasion and the pressure of circumstances made him waver till he obtained his pardon and release on 29 May 1537.[2] That is to say, he was imprisoned in the hope that he could be brought to see things in a different light, and that, as the hesitation of mid-May indicates, was also the intention with respect to More.

Thus originally More's imprisonment was neither the first move in a campaign to destroy him altogether nor necessarily intended to be permanent. His goods were deliberately not attached,[3] and he was given

ment of the trial is J. D. M. Derrett, 'The Trial of Sir Thomas More,' *Eng. Hist. Rev.* lxxix (1964), 450–77, which for the first time brought a lawyer's understanding of trial procedure to bear on this subject. E. E. Reynolds, *The Trial of St Thomas More* (1964), on the other hand, adds nothing to the traditional story.

[1] Cf. G. R. Elton, 'Sir Thomas More and the Opposition to Henry VIII,' *Bull. Inst. Hist. Research* lxi (1968), 19–34.   [2] *LP* viii. 1001; xii. I. 1330 (64).

[3] Alice More's petition of December 1534 (Rogers, 547–9) states that by his refusal of the oath More had forfeited his property but that the King had graciously permitted the family to keep it.

(with some carefully spaced interruptions) the usual freedoms of state prisoners against whom no definite action was yet planned. If the purpose was to get him to change his mind it was desirable to put him under pressure, and, as his letters show, the pressure relied on was that of his family and friends.[1] More bore their appeals with a mixture of patience and occasional exasperation, and by the autumn of 1534 he seems to have persuaded them that he would never take the oath. Till this point, it seems that only he thought of his imprisonment as permanent. In a way the most interesting letter he wrote at this time was not one of those to his daughter Margaret, whom he soon convinced of the resolution which his conscience had forced upon him, but the one in which he responded to Wilson's appeal for help and advice.[2] As always, More took great care to avoid saying anything that could give the government a chance to charge him with influencing others, and Wilson in fact got no advice. But he was bound to see that in More's view only one attitude was reckoned acceptable, for More stated his own position plainly enough. He had resolved to give no further thought to the whole business of the Divorce, had disposed of all the papers on it which he had possessed or borrowed, therefore neither could nor would discuss it again, and equally neither would nor could reveal his reasons for refusing the oath. 'They be secret in my conscience.' He looked for no release except death because he knew that release depended on the one impossible thing – surrender.

When Parliament met again in November 1534, the fact that imprisonment had failed to change his mind was manifest, and it was therefore decided to regularise the position by getting More attainted.[3] The attainder was necessary to conclude one stage in the treatment of More; it would have been superfluous only if the government had, like More, from the first regarded his incarceration in the Tower as permanent. More was now condemned for refusing the oath since May 1st, there being a suggestion that he had been offered it more than once. That Henry himself promoted this attainder is indicated by its terms: the act spoke of More's offence in that 'he hath unkindly and ingrately served our sovereign lord by divers and sundry ways'. No such phrase occurs in the parallel attainder of Fisher, Wilson and four others for refusing the oath;[4] it alone necessitated a separate act for More and

[1] Rogers, esp. nos. 202–3, 206.   [2] Ibid. no. 208.
[3] 26 Henry VIII, c. 23 (SR iii. 528).   [4] 26 Henry VIII, c. 22 (SR iii. 527–8).

must, therefore, be read as significant and not mere verbiage. The attainder served in lieu of a conviction in court. From now on, More's imprisonment was indeed perpetual, and he and his family were reduced to penury, a fact reflected in his wife's appeal to the King for a pardon which was put up soon after the session ended.[1] The earlier leniency, calculated in its way, was now at an end; as a policy it had failed of its purpose. Dame Alice's petition went unanswered, and More's imprisonment was now much straiter. The full punishment for misprision was being exacted.

But was any more in the King's mind at this point? He always made it plain that he wanted More's explicit support for his policies, and the ex-chancellor's refusal had evidently become a cause of real resentment, even hatred. The hint in the Act of Attainder sufficiently shows how Henry felt about a man whom he had so much favoured and who now, when loyalty was required, instead constituted himself the hostile conscience of Christendom. In such circumstances, the King's self-righteous and vindictive temperament did not need the urging of Queen Anne to which (without proof) More's family were in due course to ascribe Sir Thomas's troubles. However, More was now a prisoner for the rest of his days, out of sight and – for people in general – out of mind. It would have been wisdom to leave things thus, and at first that would appear to have been the general idea. Though the Act of Supremacy passed in November 1534, no one troubled More about it till the following May. Even if one supposes that the government preferred to wait until the Treason Act became effective in early February, they took so long to resume their attack on More that one cannot readily agree with those to whom the whole sequence of events from the attainder to the execution represents a single sustained assault always intended to end on the scaffold. It looks very much as though for the present Henry (and Cromwell) preferred to leave More where he was, either to rot (and the Tower was likely to kill a man of his years and health before very long) or possibly in the end to give way and obtain his pardon, a possibility for which his wife pleaded and which Wilson's later experience showed always existed. More was not treated very badly, though not nearly so well as he had been in 1534.

Yet in May 1535, the government suddenly decided to secure the consent of both More and Fisher to the supremacy. Why? The reason

[1] Rogers, no. 212.

usually advanced is that they had now resolved to make an end of both, but a closer look at the first interrogation may suggest another answer. It took place on May 7th, not on April 30th, as More himself thought, and we have his personal and careful account of it.[1] He was examined by a group of professionals with the secretary himself in charge – the attorney- and solicitor-general (Christopher Hales and Richard Riche), and two civilians (Thomas Bedyll and John Tregonwell). Cromwell did all the talking. He asked if More had seen the acts of the last session and especially the Act of Supremacy. More had. Cromwell explained that the King now wanted More's opinion about his new title. More expressed his surprise and regret: he had quite resolved never to argue these matters any more and had thought he might be left in peace. From the first he took his stand upon a refusal to speak to the issue. Cromwell may have realised at once that More had found the perfect defence, for the Treason Act did not punish silence, only an express denial of the supremacy. He tried, however, to get More to see sense (as it would have appeared to him) by persuasion. The King would not like this evasion and 'would exact a full answer'; and More might like to remember that the King would show mercy to a man who, whatever he had done in the past, now proved himself penitent. This, of course, failed to move More who replied with the words used in his later indictment:

I had fully determined with myself neither to study nor meddle with any matter of this world, but that my whole study should be upon the passion of Christ and mine own passage out of this world.

The commissioners sent him out of the room while they considered what to do. Recalled, he was reminded that his being a perpetual prisoner did not absolve him from obedience to the King and his

[1] Rogers, no. 214. There is a conflict of evidence between More's indictment (Harpsfield, 270) which dates this occasion to May 7th, and More's letter (Rogers, 551) in which he mentions 'Friday the last day of April'. There was only one such meeting, not two: both accounts list the same interrogators, and the words cited in the indictment were, according to More himself, spoken on that occasion (ibid. 552). I incline to preferring the date of the indictment. So elementary an error in it, which could have been used to defeat it but was not raised at the trial by More when he was exploiting every legal device, is highly improbable. It seems more likely that a close prisoner in the Tower, much exercised by the trial of the Carthusians (as he says) which took place on April 26th, could have been out of reckoning by a week. It should be noted that Fisher was also interrogated on May 7th by the same committee who asked him the same questions (*LP* viii, p. 326: in 1535, Ascension Day was May 6th).

demands, a point which More did not deny. Cromwell then went on to threaten: obedience would bring mercy, but obstinacy would cause the King 'to follow the course of his laws'. More's behaviour was encouraging others to stand stiff in this matter. To this the prisoner replied that he had never advised anyone and was in no way responsible for other people's actions. He spoke at this point in some passion:

I do nobody harm, I say none harm, I think none harm, but wish everybody good. And if this be not enough to keep a man alive, in good faith I long not to live. And I am dying already and have, since I came here, been divers times in the case that I thought to die within one hour; and I thank the Lord, I was never sorry for it but rather sorry when I saw the pang passed. And therefore my poor body is at the King's pleasure; would God my death might do him good.

Cromwell was evidently impressed: he spoke 'full gently' and said that 'none advantage should be taken' of anything More had said, though More could not remember whether he added that in fact there was none to be taken. He would report to the King and discover 'his gracious pleasure'.

There is nothing in this exchange to support the view that Cromwell was trying to hang More. He sought consent to the supremacy, and it was More who, aware of his total inability to agree and resolved in consequence to say nothing, introduced the theme of death into the conversation. Indeed, he here came as near as ever he did to wishing himself safely dead. One of More's problems throughout was that if he did speak his mind he was in effect committing suicide, and he seems to have thought it against the law of God to die on the scaffold for an offence which by silence could be avoided.[1] Cromwell's purpose in hinting at the prospect of possible consequences was to move More to compliance, not to contemplate a certainty for which preparations were being made. We know that More would never give in, and More knew it; but there is no reason to think that Cromwell, or Henry, was equally convinced that he could not be budged. And it is only such knowledge that justifies one in supposing that the government were by this time resolved on More's death; his account of the interrogation does not. Cromwell's parting words really leave no doubt: he had no instructions what to do if More should prove obdurate.

[1] Rogers, 559.

And Cromwell had also explained the reason why now, after months of delay, More was asked to speak out about the supremacy: the effect which reports of his stand had upon others and upon the whole complex of resistance. The policy of leaving More forgotten in the Tower had failed. It was all very well for More to say that he was influencing nobody; in the strict, and the law-court, sense he was speaking the truth. But, as his earlier letter to Wilson showed, it was impossible for him to do as he did – whether or not he ever explained what he was doing and why – without in effect issuing a powerful proclamation of where in his view the truth lay, and the government were perfectly correct in supposing that his example was widely noted. It had played its unquestionable part in the resolute behaviour of Father Reynolds and Prior Houghton, and it was the recent discovery of this fact which must account for the belated attempt to bring More round. Alive or dead, silent or vocal, Thomas More was a total embarrassment to the King and a boulder of resistance to Thomas Cromwell's enforcement policy; King and Cromwell really had no choice but at least to try for More's support. What was needed was his surrender which would have been a major propaganda triumph, not his death which was to be a major propaganda defeat.

However, More's tactics of silence had baffled the government; once again, hesitation supervened and for nearly a whole month he was left alone. The next interrogation took place on June 3rd and was altogether different from the first.[1] On this occasion the committee consisted of Audley, Suffolk, Wiltshire and Cromwell, leading councillors all and a much more formidable body to face. Cromwell began by very fairly rehearsing the previous interview: More was grateful that no attempt was made to put words in his mouth. But, as expected, the King had indeed been 'nothing content and satisfied with mine answer'. Once more Cromwell emphasised that in Henry's view More 'had been occasion of much grudge and harm in the realm'; the King now thought him an enemy and insisted on a plain answer, yes or no, to the question of the supremacy. The rest of the meeting was taken up with unavailing attempts to extract such an answer. More came as near as ever he did to committing himself when he said that it would be a hard thing to make him 'say either precisely with [the statute] against my conscience to the loss of my soul or precisely against it to the destruction of my body',

[1] Ibid. no. 216.

but he once again displayed his ingenuity by setting the remark in a purely hypothetical context: 'if it so were that my conscience gave me against the statute (which how my mind giveth me I make no declaration).' The councillors could get nothing more from him. On parting Cromwell said he liked More 'much worse' than on the previous occasion; then he had pitied him, but now he thought he meant ill.

The whole atmosphere and purpose of this second examination were different from the first. True, More saw no difference: 'for as far as I can see, the whole purpose is either to drive me to say precisely the one way, or else precisely the other'. But then More alone knew that there could never be any question of giving up, and he alone therefore thought consistently in terms of the penalties of the law. On May 7th only the one way had really been intended; on June 3rd, the two alternatives were starkly present. Audley had a form of the oath of supremacy in his pocket which he wanted More to swear. The commissioners' temper was markedly less tolerant and more severe. It was evident that they had plain instructions to force a surrender or else a positively treasonable utterance from More, instructions as evidently absent on the earlier occasion. When were these instructions given? Surely not at once, in early May, when Cromwell first reported More's non-answer to the King, for why then wait over three weeks before doing something about it? The long interval suggests that Henry had not at once decided to increase the pressure on More – indeed, that he had not made up his mind till about the end of the month. Something had happened which suddenly decided him to go all out.

We know quite well what that something was, for Chapuys explained it all to Charles V. About the end of May Henry had learned that Paul III had created Fisher a cardinal, and he promptly exploded in typical anger. If his enemies abroad thought they could demonstrate their affection for the traitors in his realm, he would show them who was king. The explosion, with its dire consequences in the short and the long term, was highly characteristic of the King at his most dangerous and least statesmanlike. Cromwell later confirmed to the ambassador that that news had indeed been the reason why Fisher and More had died.[1] And the evidence of the examinations in the Tower bears this out. It was only at this point that the King finally decided to be rid of them both, and immediately after he heard the news from Rome he sent the

[1] *LP* viii, pp. 345, 372–3.

councillors into action. We have seen that Cromwell showed himself sufficiently aware of the King's fury to give More none of the comfortable words that he had thought suitable in early May. But even though the King's mind was now probably set on death, this by no means solved the problem. Since Parliament stood prorogued, More could not be dealt with by attainder; in any case, this was one treason that Henry meant to demonstrate in open court.[1] But if More was to be tried, where was the evidence? Fisher posed no problem. Apart from his very dubious dealings some years before in which he came into near-treasonable contact with the imperial ambassador, he had made sufficient statements close to treason to prove that he possessed neither More's acumen nor his severe discretion; unlike More's, his servants were interrogated and matter enough was found. According to his indictment he categorically denied the supremacy during the interrogation on May 7th, and though this seems unlikely it is probable that he said enough, for he was always inclined to say too much.[2]

As everybody knows, the case against More proved very much harder to construct, but from about June 10th Cromwell was evidently engaged upon the task. On the 12th occurred Riche's fateful visit to the Tower, to collect More's books, an action which in itself demonstrates that the drastic decision had now been taken. Riche claimed to have had a conversation with More about the supremacy, and in the end More's trial turned essentially on what was said on that occasion, a point to which we shall recur in the proper place. Riche made an immediate record in his own hand which survives, unfortunately damaged in a crucial line.[3] On the 14th, More was again interrogated, but in quite a different manner. This time there appeared no leading councillors; instead, a body of professional examiners (led by Bedyll) came to the Tower with two formal interrogatories, two witnesses, and a notary.[4]

---

[1] Note the emphasis placed on strictly legal methods in the draft propaganda tract of 1539 (above, p. 198).

[2] LP viii. 886 (iii). William Rastell (Harpsfield, 232–4) preserved a story that Fisher had been tricked by someone (soon, for no known reason, conjectured to have been Riche) into an outright denial of the supremacy when he thought that nothing he said at the time would be used against him. Unless Fisher was a total innocent, the tale rings far from true; the detailed speeches recorded by Rastell must in any case be artifice rather than report. Nor were Fisher's remarks 'used to arraign and condemn him'; they are not in the indictment.

[3] SP 2/R, fos. 24–5 (LP viii. 814 [ii]). Printed with several errors in Reynolds, *Trial of More*, 166–7. [4] StP i. 432–6.

This was the proper procedure in pre-trial investigations, intended to discover the precise charges to be brought against a person accused. The two interrogatories dealt, respectively, with More's exchange of letters with Fisher in the Tower, and with the consent to the supremacy. To the first he made long and careful answers, while to the second he refused to reply.

Thus, about the middle of the month, the government set about drawing up the indictment. But even now it looks as though no absolutely irrevocable decision had been taken. We have seen that the circular of June 9th (drafted, of course, at least a few days earlier) made no reference to the treasons of Fisher and More, whereas that of June 25th did.[1] And Cromwell's notes show that he had no final instructions for More even after Fisher had been condemned and was waiting for execution.[2] We can only guess at the reason for this renewed dithering. Since in the end More was tried and executed, we may safely suppose that Henry wanted his death, but it looks as though Cromwell had his doubts as late as the third week of June or thereabouts. He had been trying to draw an indictment and must have been aware how hard it would be to prove treason against More: his hesitation may have arisen from nothing else. On the other hand, he had throughout shown more sympathy for the fallen lord chancellor and may also have better appreciated the likely effect an execution would have on opinion. At any rate, so far from More being relentlessly hounded to the scaffold, the question of what to do with him remained unsettled even after the necessary steps preliminary to a trial had been taken.

In the end the King insisted, and More faced the court on July 1st, in one of the famous trial scenes of history. Famous indeed, but only recently correctly interpreted. Mr Derrett's reconstruction has produced as accurate an account as we are ever likely to have, and the detail of events is best read in his paper.[3] He has shown how More's behaviour and the conduct of the trial become comprehensible only in the light of the normal and proper procedure in criminal trials, and also that More carried himself with immense ability, using both law and procedure to the fullest extent possible. In particular, it is now clear that his famous speech after the verdict was not a final defiance in which silence was at

---

[1] Above, p. 241.
[2] *LP* viii. 892: 'When Master Fisher shall go to execution...What shall be done further touching Master More.'   [3] *Eng. Hist. Rev.* lxxix. 450 ff.

last broken, but a motion in arrest of judgment which brilliantly used the only argument still open to the prisoner: an attack on the validity of the indictment on the grounds that it rested on an insufficient act. But the same legal competence and brilliant advocacy were apparent throughout: More fought for his life to the last. The indictment effectively comprehended four counts.[1] The first three ran as follows: (1) By his silence on May 7th More had denied the supremacy; his words about no longer meddling in such matters were used to suggest a positive act. (2) He had been actively engaged in a conspiratorial correspondence with Fisher, a known traitor (by this time convicted in the law) and had abetted him; their exchange of letters formed the substance of this charge. (3) He had repeated his offence of silence on June 3rd and had on that occasion displayed his malicious mind by calling the Act of Supremacy 'a two-edged sword' by which a man was bound to put either his soul or his body in jeopardy. These are the three points omitted in Roper's *Life* but contained in the other early accounts which, in turn, omit the last. This was (4) that on June 12th he had specifically spoken treason in his conversation with Riche.

As Mr Derrett has demonstrated, More argued that the first three counts did not contain any offence under the statute and the court upheld these submissions. He pleaded not guilty to the fourth count when the court would not accept a similar submission, and this was the issue tried. The treason of which he was convicted was that allegedly spoken to Riche. According to Roper, More accused Riche of inventing or distorting his testimony, and when an attempt was made to offer the solicitor-general the support of two further witnesses, Sir Richard Southwell and one Palmer, both said that they had been too busy parcelling up More's books to hear what was being said. Unfortunately, for all this we have only Roper's account, written some twenty years after the event and by one who, though he had information from lawyer friends who had attended the trial, had not himself been there. It is certainly odd that the accounts circulated immediately after the event said nothing of the only dramatic moments in court that day. Still, More was unquestionably convicted on that fourth count, and it would be unduly sceptical to disregard Roper altogether. But the silence of the other evidence does raise the question whether he did not embellish the story too well. In particular, it would be very unwise to

---

[1] For the indictment see Harpsfield, 269–76.

put much reliance on the speeches put in More's mouth, or at least on the precise words of them; altogether, when Roper uses *oratio recta* we must remember the conventions which governed such writing in that century.

We have three versions of what passed between More and Riche on June 12th. The official one in the indictment is a straight Latin translation of Riche's own English memorandum, so far as that can be read.[1] Roper gives a paraphrase, though in direct speech, which includes two additions or variations, one of them crucial. According to Riche himself, he felt 'charitably moved' to urge More once more to submit, but More only said, 'your conscience shall save you and my conscience shall save me'. Riche persisted: though for him to offer advice to a man of such 'experience, learning and wisdom' would be like pouring water into the Thames, and though he had no commission to discuss the matter, he wished to say more. He put the question: 'if it were enacted by Parliament that I should be king and whoever said nay, it should be treason', would it be an offence then to assert that Riche was king? More agreed: it would not. But, he went on, Riche had put a small case – let him try a higher one: 'Sir, I put case it were enacted by Parliament that God were not God and if any repugned at the same act it should be treason', would Riche then be acting properly if he denied that God was God? That, Riche replied (quite fairly), was not a proper case since Parliament could in no way affect the existence of the deity; how about a case in the middle – the statute declaring the King to be supreme head? To this More replied – traitorously, according to the indictment – that the cases were not compatible: 'A king may be made by Parliament and a king deprived by Parliament', and to such an act a subject 'being of the Parliament' may give his consent; but with respect to the supremacy, 'a subject cannot be bound because he cannot give his consent [of himself to the] Parliament'.[2] Besides, though the King were accepted in England, 'yet most utter [outward] parts do not affirm the same'. According to Roper's report, supposedly based on the testimony given at the trial, the conversation had included a question about Parliament making Riche pope and had ended with More saying, to Riche's reply that Parliament can make no law to declare that God

---

[1] I use my own transcript rather than Reynolds's, completed from the Latin text in the indictment.

[2] At this crucial point the English document is very badly damaged; the Latin reads 'quia consensum suum ab eo ad parliamentum prebere non potest', which does not make much better sense.

be not God: 'No more could the Parliament make the King supreme head.'[1] The first addition may be disregarded, except that it helps to indicate the inaccuracy of Roper's information, but if Riche swore to the final statement he was proving More guilty of a straightforward denial of the supremacy of which there is no trace in his memorandum or in the indictment.

If Roper is to be trusted, More countered this testimony with great vigour. He gave the court his version of the conversation which unfortunately is not preserved, and he violently attacked the witness's credit. Was it credible, he asked, that he who had so steadfastly refused to speak his conscience on the supremacy should have revealed all to this man whom he had always regarded as a disreputable person? But, lawyer-fashion, he went on to argue that even if the conversation took place as alleged it was in private and 'only in putting of cases', so that it could not prove the existence of malice which the statute demanded to make the words treasonable. Possibly he continued along this tangential line, passing from Riche's testimony to the argument that he had never entertained malice towards the King and that the fourth count collapsed over this, a point he elaborated at some length.[2] I am inclined to believe that these were indeed the arguments that More used against Riche, but I have some difficulty in accepting all the detail as authentic. If More really said that, if Riche's oath were true, he (More) hoped never to see God in the face, 'which I would not say, were it otherwise, to win the whole world', he must be believed without question. But why then did he add to this total and convincing denial the further point that, supposing the conversation to have taken place as reported, it failed to prove his treason on grounds based on the terms of the statute? Would he not have been taking away from the effect of the one genuine *cri du coeur* that is reported of him throughout the trial? Those words read suspiciously like what a future saint *ought* to have said to prove his truth, and they as well as some of the picturesque detail of More's abuse of Riche do not to me have the ring of authenticity.

[1] Roper, 244–5.
[2] Derrett argues that here Roper's account transposes the proper sequence (*Eng. Hist. Rev.* lxxix. 465). He may be right, but he seems at this juncture to rely too much on his view of what More was trying to do. The point about malice follows naturally from More's attack on Riche and could well have been produced in the manner described by Roper. In that case, More's speech on count four rather ominously swerved away from the facts alleged into matters liable to confuse the issue.

The question is what More was denying: that there had been a conversation about the Act of Supremacy, or that he had spoken the particular words alleged? Roper clearly wants him to say the first (witness the point about the improbability that More would speak to Riche, of all people, about the act) but does not help his case by omitting More's version of what happened on June 12th. Still, are we to suppose that the whole story was Riche's invention? The memorandum on which the count in the indictment was based certainly looks to have been written immediately after the conversation, and there is one sentence in it which lends it credence. According to himself, Riche had not recognised anything new in what More had said. On the contrary, he left with these words:

Well, sir, God comfort you, for I see your mind will not change, which, I fear, will be very dangerous to you; for I suppose your concealment to the question that hath been asked of you is as high offence as other that hath denied [it], and for this Jesu send you better grace.

Riche had been at the first interrogation when More's tactic of silence ('concealment') first appeared, and he plainly thought that this was still the problem. It was More's old silence, not some new express denial, that he detected in the conversation; the peril he prophesied was to be embodied in the first count of the indictment, not the fourth. And this agrees with More's protest that there had been but a putting of cases, a conjectural argument of the kind that More had engaged in before. Indeed, it could be held that this part of More's answer at the trial really removes the possibility that the conversation, in some form, had never taken place. It would therefore seem that only afterwards, perhaps when Cromwell or the King saw the report, the inherent possibilities were recognised and the fourth count constructed. Very possibly, the government fell back on Riche's memorandum when the formal interrogation on June 14th produced only a refusal to say a single word to questions about the supremacy. If that is so, the charge of perjury would presumably rest upon some twisting of words only, either in the indictment (and memorandum) or in the testimony given at the trial. The first may be ruled out since we have seen that Riche wrote down his account without meaning to suggest that fatal words had been spoken; the second is certainly supported by what Roper says Riche testified to in court.

However, even the indictment and memorandum have More say more about the obligation to agree with the statute than he had ever said to his interrogators. This, though Riche failed to see it at the time, is what made the conversation useful to Cromwell. And More had a good point when he spoke of the unlikelihood that he should have given himself away in those circumstances. Thus there may be something in both indictment and testimony that went beyond what More recalled had been said, and the possibility that a revising hand had been at work is, of course, supported by Southwell's and Palmer's refusal to testify. Admittedly, if the Crown had really invented some damning statement and then produced two witnesses who denied hearing it, the prosecution's incompetence passes the limits of the probable. Can we trust the story of those defaulting witnesses? There are some difficulties. Their collapse seems to have impressed nobody, not even the original reporters who quite failed to mention it, and certainly not the jury. More oddly still, those broken reeds came to no harm at all. Nothing much is known of Palmer, except that he was a servant of Cromwell's, but Richard Southwell, a careerist client of his, continued serenely on his successful way to wealth and a little power. Is it to be believed that a man who had jeopardised the outcome of a state trial upon which his master's credit with King Henry hung could only three weeks later have written to Cromwell to remind him of a favour lately promised?[1] Largely because we have only Roper's account of the argument around count four, the story of this crux of the trial remains full of improbabilities that cannot be well sorted out. I believe myself that the report of More's speech is reasonably accurate, but I have great difficulty in swallowing the tale of the conscience-stricken witnesses.

One other point is very odd about this fatal count in the indictment. It was customary for indictments, themselves in Latin, to introduce allegations of treasonable words with the phrase *in verbis anglicanis* or simply *anglice*, and the earlier quotations in More's indictment cite such words in English. The fourth count translates an available English version into Latin. A reason can only be conjectured. Perhaps it was thought that the relatively harmless truth could in that way be presented to look different. But we know the translation to be faithful, though the

---

[1] *LP* viii. 1087. Southwell survived Cromwell's fall to be knighted in 1542, become a councillor under Edward VI, and remain in office under Mary. None of this is readily reconciled with his alleged part in More's trial.

crucial sentence at the end is too much damaged in the memorandum to enable one to understand the precise import, and too oddly worded in the indictment to be readily re-translated into English. Yet if this is where the drafter of the indictment put in his twist, the twister could as easily have supplied a truly explicit phrase to pretend treason. Perhaps Riche's memorandum was translated because the conversation took place without witnesses (*pace* Southwell and Palmer who were certainly present), so that the usual practice of tying a man to his *ipsissima verba* did not seem possible. In that case, the obscurity of the last phrase may represent More's well attested skill at wrapping up his opinion, and Riche may have improved the situation in his verbal testimony. The whole notion that the government invented either the whole conversation or at least some useful phrase in it is hampered by the inadequacy of count four to make its point. Anyone wanting to make More speak treason on that occasion and unscrupulous enough to resort to invention could have done very much better.

In a great matter so complex and so ill-documented some uncertainty is bound to remain. But I would suggest that More and Riche did indeed have a conversation about acts of Parliament in the course of which More, perhaps beguiled by memories of 'putting cases' with other lawyers, said something concerning the Act of Supremacy that was less careful than was his habit, though it fell well short of an outright denial of the act's validity. That denial he reserved for his great speech after the verdict, his motion in arrest of judgment.[1] I think that More did slip in that conversation, and I am encouraged in that opinion because he had always regarded putting his view hypothetically to be a perfect safeguard. It is simply not true that More had consistently offered only silence to questions about the supremacy. He did so at the formal interrogation, in the presence of a notary and for the record, on June 14th; but before the two groups of councillors he had argued at length and now and again spoken more definitely than seems to be generally realised. When Cromwell first put the act to him, More did not remain silent but gave an answer later thought insufficient:

I had well trusted [he reports himself as saying] that the King's highness would never have commanded any such question to be demanded of me, considering that I ever from the beginning well and truly from time to time declared my

---

[1] Derrett, *Eng. Hist. Rev.* lxxix. 469–73. He is quite right to see in this speech a most important discussion of the nature of statute and fundamental law.

mind unto his highness, and since that time I had, I said, unto your master-ship, Master Secretary, also, both by mouth and by writing. And now I have in good faith discharged my mind of all such matters, and neither will dispute kings' titles nor popes', but the King's true faithful subject I am and will be, and daily I pray for him and for all his, and for you all that are of his honour-able Council, and for all the realm, and otherwise than thus I never intend to meddle.[1]

That is to say (setting aside the mixture of impatience and offhand courtesy at the end): the King and Council both know well that I can never accept the supremacy, but I will certainly not say so now and fall foul of the statute. Safe enough, indeed, but also not really ambiguous or silent.

On June 3rd, as we have seen, More went farther, indeed so far ('putting a case') as to speak of the impropriety of forcing him to choose between the death of his body and that of his soul, a statement which makes sense only on the assumption that acceptance of the act is equal to eternal damnation. It must be believed that on that occasion, too, he called the act a two-edged sword because, to quote the indictment, 'if I should answer one way I should offend my conscience, and if I should answer the other way I put my life in jeopardy'.[2] It is the same point as before. More did not mention the phrase in his own report, but he did not deny it at the trial and explained Fisher's use of the same words as mere coincidence.[3] There was never any doubt that More's so-called silence meant total disapproval, and in these statements he stopped short on the very threshold of a condemnation of the act. One more tiny step and he would have spoken treason, which he never did, either before the councillors or (almost certainly) to Riche. The remarkable thing is that no one attempted to use his hypothetic statements as legal proof of treason. It is perfectly true that in law they were no such thing, but this only underlines a fundamental fact: the law was observed, even in the case of Sir Thomas More whose head King Henry desired. It seems not unlikely, in the circumstances, that in his conversation with

[1] Rogers, 552.   [2] Harpsfield, 273.

[3] The exchange of letters with Fisher raises dark questions. More claimed to have advised Fisher to avoid all suspicion of collusion (=conspiracy) and himself to have done nothing to concert their efforts at defence. But why were all the letters burned, if so harmless? The answers offered by Fisher's servants need satisfy us no better than they evidently satisfied the interrogators. And why did Fisher and his servants agree to deny the exchange altogether, unless put on oath (*LP* viii, p. 239)?

Riche More for once took the hypothetical manner of argument just that little bit too far, saying something that made it possible to persuade the jury that treason had in fact been spoken.

Sir Thomas More died for conscience' sake, but not for freedom of conscience, freedom of thought, or tolerance in religion. The conscience he had in mind did occasionally come rather close to the practice of that individual judgment which he objected to in Protestants, as when he told Riche that their respective consciences must save each one of them. But that was not his usual meaning. By conscience he meant a recognition of an established truth, and he argued that the truth was established by a greater consensus than was available in one realm alone. The one time that Cromwell really got under his guard was at the second interrogation when he reminded More that in his days as chancellor he, or the bishops with his approval, had forced heretics to say yes or no to questions on the pope's supremacy: 'and why should not then the King, since it is a law made here that his grace is head of the Church here, compel men to answer precisely to the law here as they did then concerning the pope?' More replied that there was a difference in compelling men to affirm what the whole body of Christendom had recognised (namely the pope's authority) and what was law in but one realm and not elsewhere. To this Cromwell, rather characteristically, retorted 'that they were as well burned for the denying of that as they be beheaded for denying of this, and therefore as good reason to compel them to make precise answer to the one as to the other'.[1]

But in fact Cromwell's grim jest disguised their fundamental difference as well as a fundamental weakness in More's position as he stated it at this point. In identifying 'the whole corps of Christendom' with that part of it which had accepted the papal supremacy, More begged rather a large question. Here his argument was really rather shaky, as though his conviction regarding the papal primacy rested on a majority vote and no more. At his trial (if, once again, we may trust Roper) he certainly used a more principled argument when he alleged that the Act of Supremacy was 'directly repugnant to the laws of God and his Holy Church' and that the pope's rule of that Church derived directly from Christ's grant to Peter. More's considered position therefore combined two elements: the truth of the papal claim to divinely instituted primacy, and the proof of that claim in the universal (as he

---

[1] Rogers, 557–8.

saw it) acceptance of it by Christians past and present. At the last he made it perfectly plain that by conscience he did not mean his right to judge for himself, but his duty to accept a vision granted to the great body of Christians: 'And therefore,' he told Audley, 'I am not bound to conform my conscience to the council of one realm against the general council of Christendom.'[1] To this conscience Cromwell opposed the conscience of the subject, the member of the community of England who owed a duty to obey the law made for that community by the King-in-Parliament, a duty which he could not agree conflicted with the divine law because the pope's primacy rested on no such scriptural authority. Cromwell's vision was in many ways the clearer of the two and certainly the simpler; in practice, too, it promised to benefit the nation rather more than adherence to the primacy of a man like Paul III might do. But the point that matters is that in these two persons there clashed two fundamental principles neither of which had anything to do with those intellectual or spiritual freedoms which we may call the liberal virtues. Cromwell was quite right: a man might be as well burned for denying the pope as beheaded for opposing the King. The end would be all one: principle needed power to assert it, and only the law could control power. Therefore the statute must rule. More earned his sainthood at the hands of the papacy; Cromwell might have been amused at the thought that the modern national state might find some way of canonising him.

The whole story of More's final persecution must now look rather different from the usual version. Certainly, Henry wanted his conformity and, failing that, meant to punish him, at last with death. But that last decision was a long time coming; from May 1534 to early June 1535, the real purpose was to win a surrender. Even after there had clearly ceased to be any hope of that, it still took the fury aroused by the pope's tactless bestowal of the cardinal's hat on Fisher to get the government to abandon their earlier intention to let More die quietly in prison, in the ordinary course of nature – a fate he himself foresaw several times. His true opinion was known throughout, but no attempt was made to use against him statements which came close to treason: his care to avoid undoubted treason was allowed to work. When Henry finally demanded his death, the difficult task of drawing an indictment was discharged with limited success, though the indictment would

[1] Roper, 250–1.

probably have flattened a less able and less self-possessed defendant, and though it took no force or threats in this case to get the jury to convict. All through the forms of the law were scrupulously observed, even if those forms included an Act of Attainder without trial, not a serious matter in More's case since, had he been tried, he could not have avoided conviction for refusing the oath, the offence for which he was attainted. The final trial was exceptionally careful of legal forms and legal rights, and the accused, still one of the foremost lawyers of his day, took very full advantage of it all. More's trial is the only Tudor state trial in which the only personal abuse seems to have come from the defendant. Certainly, More's fate was a tragedy, and not only Henry's and Cromwell's reputations but the whole of early-Tudor history would have benefited if it had never occurred. However, More held to an opinion which encapsuled legal treason. Down to April 1532 he had actively opposed the King's policy. Thereafter, whether he liked it or not, he became a symbol of resistance. Though in law he almost certainly never committed treason, he constituted a threat to the revolution. The King's outburst of ungovernable fury closed the road of wisdom and compassion, and though More may have died for the papacy he died because of Henry VIII.

4

Though the King throughout displayed his animus against a man who, as he saw it, had betrayed both trust and friendship, the behaviour of a government forced by political circumstances into a thoroughly unhappy and bad decision was scrupulous rather than tyrannical. Cromwell, for one, does not seem to have wanted More's death at all. During their encounters he not only preserved the courtesies but did all he could to show himself well disposed. Only the prejudice which supposes Cromwell incapable of decent or genuine feelings can deny this. He went out of his way to demonstrate his pleasure when More was put out of the Nun's attainder, taking the trouble to inform Roper at the first opportunity and asking him to pass the good news to his father-in-law.[1] In May 1534, when More refused the oath and explained that he would stand against Parliament because he had the greater part of Christendom on his side, Cromwell, 'as one that tenderly favoureth me', swore a great oath and said 'that he had liefer that his only son...

[1] Roper, 237.

had lost his head' than that More should thus have made sure of the King's determined hostility.[1] It was Cromwell who warned More that his notion of a special royal licence permitting him to speak without fear of any statute would not work, since no king's letters could protect a man against the effects of an act of Parliament. 'In this good warning,' added More, 'he showed himself my special tender friend.'[2] We have noted More's appreciation of the secretary's compassionate behaviour on May 7th, and if on June 3rd he showed a darker face, the combination of the prisoner's skilful resistance and the King's newly kindled fury sufficiently accounts for that. Cromwell, it would seem, continued to have his doubts about killing More till very near the end. Of course, he neither approved of the stand More took nor wished to save him once the King had decided. But such evidence as we have – including in effect the failure of More's early biographers to treat Cromwell with hatred or abuse – suggests that he respected another great man and regretted the necessity of the conflict. Cromwell and More were sufficiently well acquainted – Londoners both – with at least one close common friend in the merchant Antony Bonvisi, fellow-councillors to King Henry for nearly two years. Bonvisi thought them very different men, as indeed they were,[3] but such differences do not exclude some mutual regard, however deep the political gulf between them. Cromwell did what he thought he had to do; the hatred and vindictiveness belonged to the King.

And that is a conclusion which applies beyond the case of Sir Thomas More. Cromwell, to be sure, carried most of the practical responsibility for the actions required by the enforcement of policy. Occasionally one finds the King taking an active part,[4] but in general he left

[1] Rogers, 506.

[2] Ibid. 541. Roper, 242, asserts that some time in May 1535 Cromwell paid More another visit, pretending friendship and holding out hopes of the King's willingness to leave More's conscience alone, but this otherwise unsupported story probably stems from the confusion over the date of Cromwell's official visit of May 7th.

[3] Harpsfield, 138. The worthy archdeacon remarks that he had heard many 'notable and as yet commonly unknown things' about both men from Bonvisi, 'whereof there is now no place to talk'. One sees why the middle ages raised the question *an archidiaconus salvari potest*.

[4] In 1537 e.g. he made some marginal notes on part of the record of John Hallam's examination. Against the name of a friar from Knaresborough he wrote: 'This knave to be taken and, well examined, to suffer'; against the names of three Beverley men there stand the words, 'it were meet that these suffered if they already have not' (SP 1/115, fo. 220 [*LP* xii. I. 370]).

those things to his lord privy seal. In September 1539, Henry required Cromwell to examine certain prisoners in the Tower and 'to travail therein after your accustomed fashion'; he did not doubt that 'ye will do in the same as much as man's wit can comprehend'. Three days later, having apparently heard from Cromwell that he could not find the time just then, Henry relented: Cromwell was not to trouble his head with those matters 'but to set men thereto, for their examination, as ye think most convenient, and when these great matters be past then ye may examine them at leisure'. All this was communicated through the earl of Southampton who in a postscript added that the King in his kindness had said: 'I would for no good that his mind should be so troubled that it should cast him into any disease.'[1] In this business of treason, Henry till very near the end trusted Cromwell without question, and he was right to do so. As Cranmer expressed it in 1535 when informing the minister of an alleged offence: 'which treason I pray you to detect unto the King's highness, which I am most sure you would do although I required you to the contrary.'[2]

All this makes a strange background to the charge in Cromwell's attainder that he had 'taken upon him to set at liberty divers persons being convicted and attainted of misprision of treason, and divers other being apprehended and in prison for suspicion of high treason' without the King's command or agreement.[3] This is hardly an accusation one expects to hear levelled against the Cromwell of tradition, though in the circumstances it was no doubt a useful sort of thing to insinuate into the King's mind. The charge elicited a comment from one of the smuggest beneficiaries of Cromwell's alleged negligence, Richard Pate, then on embassy in the Netherlands. 'Methought', he wrote, 'that he that of long time hath had the examination of all transgressions, the knowledge and weighing of so many and sundry treasons against your highness intended and pretended, should have been more circumspect.'[4] He should indeed, for six months later Pate deserted and joined Cardinal Pole at Rome. As we have seen throughout this study, Cromwell regarded it as his duty to seek out genuine treasons and punish them without mercy, but he did not suppose that he was to crush all men denounced regardless of the truth. The attainder mentions no particular instances of his alleged interference, and it is on the face of it hard to see

[1] *StP* i. 617–19.   [2] *Cranmer's Works*, 309–10.
[3] Burnet, iv. 416.   [4] *StP* viii. 364.

421

how he should come to release convicted misprisioners on his own authority,[1] but it was certainly the case that there could be differences between his understanding of an accusation and Henry's. Again and again the King insisted on further investigation and expressed his conviction that treason had been committed when in fact the examination had pointed the other way.[2] All Henry's servants knew that the sure way to encounter suspicion was to appear slack in police vigilance, a knowledge which shines through the embarrassed letter in which seven leading councillors explained, on 1 December 1538, that they had not felt able to order Lord de la Warr to the Tower.[3] There just had not been enough evidence, and they thought that if they had committed the man unfairly his reputation would never have recovered from the slur. But this very proper – and rather surprising – sentiment they had to dress up with a good deal of humble apology and painful hope that his highness might not be offended.

It was against the background of that looming and menacing figure, forever suspicious, increasingly unwilling to trust, and incidentally apprehensive of treason in the most unlikely places, that Thomas Cromwell discharged the often dreadful duty of keeping King and realm safe in a revolution. He certainly neither hesitated nor, we may be sure, had any regrets for the men whom he, and the law, sent to their deaths. He could be savage, as in the flaming rebuke he sent to the Council of Calais whom he suspected, in mid-1537, of tolerating papists, though even on that occasion he cited the King's instructions in such a way as to suggest that he was really only passing on another man's fury. The King thought his councillors there very much remiss and threatened a clean sweep: he would find men to serve him better.

It is thought against all reason that the prayers of women and their fond flickerings should move any of you to do that thing that should in any wise displeasure your prince and sovereign lord or offend his just laws. And if you think any extremity in this writing you must thank yourselves that have procured it.[4]

For himself, Cromwell could now and again remember the prayers of women. As the northern rebellion receded, he contemplating asking

[1] The attainder, which makes much play with Cromwell's willingness to take bribes, does not say that he did these things for money.

[2] Above, pp. 112, 125, 333 ff.   [3] Ellis, i. II. 124–5.

[4] Merriman, ii. 65.

the King for a general pardon, though it was not until early 1539 that the thought bore fruit in the last proclamation concerning Anabaptists. He also reminded himself to compile a list 'of the wives and poor children of such as have suffered, to the intent his grace may extend his mercy to them for their livings'.[1] He had been involved in getting pardons for prisoners in the Tower in late 1533,[2] but on this later occasion he does not seem to have succeeded in getting the King to make some provision for the desolate dependants of the men hanged for their rebellion. He was no more successful in saving the cowed remnant of the London Carthusians from dispersal, though for their sake he risked some very serious displeasure from Henry.[3]

The administration of the law, and especially the law of treason, demanded qualities which no sensible or sensitive mind can admire, and Cromwell possessed them to the full. But without such activities society collapses, and it was probably fortunate for England that at that sad time of violence and revolution the man charged with the security of the realm remembered to distinguish between the true and the false, the real traitor and the victim of malice and error. More than that no one could really expect of him, and with a king like Henry VIII to serve, who so often acted in outbursts of rage, a cool and discriminating chief of police was something of a blessing – except, as it turned out, to himself. Moreover, Cromwell served a purpose beyond the protection of King Henry. The revolution which he guided had major constructive ends in view: the consolidation of the realm behind the legislative authority of the King-in-Parliament and the executive authority of the King-in-

[1] BM, Tit. B. i, fo. 459 (LP xii. I. 1315).   [2] BM, Tit. B. i, fo. 449 (LP vii. 48 [4]).

[3] StP 1. 459, a letter from Ralph Sadler reporting Henry's annoyance at the fact that a long standing order to Cromwell to get the house cleared had not been carried out. 'And now,' the King went on, 'he wrote to you that they be reconciled, but seeing that they have been so long obstinate I will not now admit their obedience; and so write to my lord privy seal.' This letter, dated Sept. 27th and placed in 1536, raises complications. The Carthusian remnant swore the oath of supremacy on 18 May 1537 and surrendered their house on June 10th that year (LP xii. I. 1232; II. 64). One would suppose that the first event represents the reconciliation which Cromwell reported and the second the putting out of their house which Henry demanded, but Sadler's letter does not fit the time-sequence, even supposing it were redated into 1537. The only reconstruction which makes some sort of sense is that the Carthusians had signified their willingness to surrender in September 1536 only to find that this did not avert the King's vengeance; apparently Cromwell held off their fate by another eight months before the King had his way and the monks took the oath and left the house within less than four weeks.

Council, and the promotion of reform. As Starkey told him in 1536, he meant 'to bring men to a sincerity and that they may be so taken and reputed of our master and sovereign lord, wherein assuredly your lordship shall do both to God and to our prince the highest service that any man may do, in such a suspicious time as we be now in'.[1] Cromwell wanted, not to kill men, but to bring them to a better condition, and his undoubted ruthlessness against genuine opposition owed more to the pressure of his positive convictions than to lust for power or subservience to the King. It was because he had a vision of an England reformed in body and soul that he proceeded as he did. 'Who cannot', wrote Richard Taverner in dedicating to Cromwell his translation of the Augsburg Confession which Cromwell had ordered him to undertake,

Who cannot, unless he be mortally infected with the pestiferous poison of envy, most highly commend, magnify and extol your right honourable lordship's most circumspect godliness and most godly circumspection in the cause and matter of our Christian religion [who] to the uttermost of your power do promote and further the cause of Christ, and not only that but also do animate and encourage others to do the same.[2]

Taverner knew what he was talking about. He was twice more instructed by Cromwell to produce translations of works which contributed nothing to political problems or the propaganda of the day: the *Loci Communes* of Erasmus Sarcerius, an eminent Lutheran divine of moderate temper, and a purely devotional work – *The Epitome of the Psalms* – written by Wolfgang Capito, the outstanding reformer of Strassburg.[3] Contrary to all appearance and recent tradition, Thomas Cromwell really was a genuine sort of Protestant, and within the limits set by his own cool temperament and the hesitations of his monarch he promoted the reform in Church and state for as long as he was able.

In that larger purpose, the circumstances and necessities of law-enforcement take their proper place. It was through those labours of persuasion and punishment that Cromwell settled in the realm the first – and extensive – measures designed to advance the great transformation

[1] SP 1/105, fo. 48 (misdated into 1535 by *LP* xi. 73).
[2] Richard Taverner, *The Confession of the Faith of the Germans* (n.d. [1536]: *STC* 909), prefatory letter.
[3] *STC* 21753, 23710. Cf. John K. Yost, 'Taverner's Use of Erasmus and the Protestantization of English Humanism,' *Renaissance Quarterly*, xxiii (1970), 266–76, esp. 268 n. 6.

he sought after. Eight years are a short time in the life of a nation, but those eight years of Cromwell's ascendancy – rarely total, always liable to be undermined – achieved remarkable and remarkably enduring things. The work done was so well founded that all the later upheavals could not seriously disturb it, and the labours of a century, required to make certain and complete it, also could do nothing but develop and enlarge it. In this creative enterprise Cromwell had of necessity also to practise much destruction; where he infused life, he also, and without qualms, bestowed much death. When his own fate reached him he died, as he knew, too soon; but he could also know that of all those that died he alone was both victim and victor.

INDEX

Only main entries are given for Henry VIII and Thomas Cromwell; references to modern writers are confined to those involving some discussion in text or footnotes; references to counties do not include particular placenames which are separately indexed.

INDEX